Ca

MW00604660

THE URBAN MINISTRY INSTITUTE
a ministry of WORLD IMPACT, INC.

Rev. Dr. Don L. Davis

with contributions by

Rev. Terry Cornett *and* **Rev. Don Allsman**

Picturing Theology

An A-Z Collection of TUMI's Key Diagrams, Charts, Graphics, and Articles

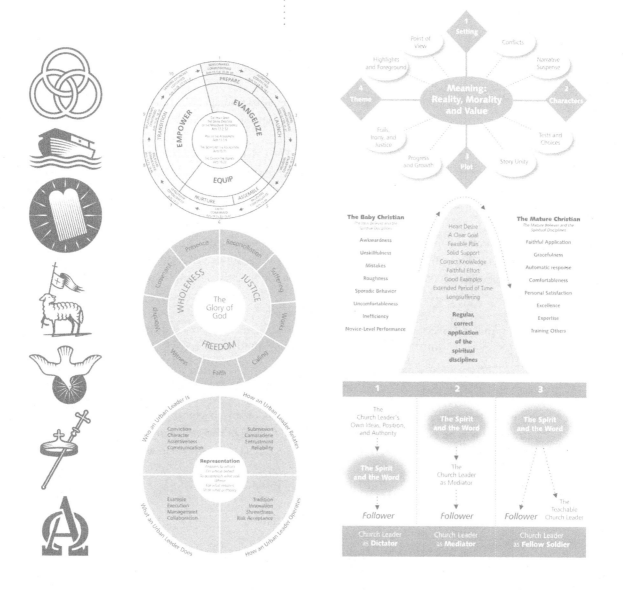

TUMI Press | 3701 East Thirteenth Street North | Wichita, Kansas 67208

Picturing Theology
An A-Z Collecton of TUMI's Key Diagrams, Charts, Graphics, and Articles

This publication contains the collected appendices from TUMI's 16-module
seminary-level resource called The Capstone Curriculum.

The contents of this book first appeared in The Capstone Curriculum with this history:
© 2005, 2011, 2013, 2015, 2019 The Urban Ministry Institute. All Rights Reserved.
First edition 2005, Second edition 2011, Third edition 2013, Fourth edition 2015.

Picturing Theology
An A-Z Collecton of TUMI's Key Diagrams, Charts, Graphics, and Articles
© 2019 The Urban Ministry Institute. All Rights Reserved.

ISBN: 978-1-62932-017-5

The Urban Ministry Institute,
3701 E. 13th Street,
Wichita, KS 67208

The Urban Ministry Institute is a ministry of World Impact, Inc.

Table of Contents

Introduction

It is hard to argue against the value of graphics, symbols, diagrams, and charts to simplify the presentation of difficult theological themes. Who doesn't like pictures and graphics when given to explain thorny ethical and theological issues? In many ways, we are image-making creatures, addicted to both symbol and metaphor as we communicate with others in the course of our everyday lives. The old adage, "A picture is worth a thousand words," proves true in daily conversation as well as in poetry, science, or any other intellectual work.

More often than not, I find it difficult to finally comprehend the significance of an idea until I have illustrated, graphed, or symbolized the concept in some fashion or other. Good graphs and metaphors are ready tools to represent and summarize the key concepts and categories of any serious subject or field of study. The use of diagrams and picture graphs can greatly aid us as we seek to comprehend the deeper meanings of complex or hard-to-understand theological notions or spiritual concepts.

Of course, all such effort in schematizing ideas and concepts via graphs and charts is more than a little over simplifying the truth, to say the least. Still, depicting complex ideas visually in graphs and diagrams is an essential and helpful aid to helping us look into and understand something that is extremely complex and difficult to understand. Although a graphic may sometimes be offered as a poor substitute for clear reasoning about an idea or concept, good metaphors, diagrams, or symbols can often be just the tool to help us grasp some mystery with better comprehension.

The prophets and apostles often used visual pictures and metaphors to help God's people understand God's analysis of a situation, or lean into the meaning of some mystery or concept God was communicating with them. For example, the apostles used pictures of ordinary and familiar things to help us better comprehend the mysteries of God. Think of the metaphors related to the Church: it is the *family* of God, the *body* of Christ, and *temple* of the Holy Spirit. In order to know truly what the church is, you must delve into the meaning what a family is, how a body functions, and what a temple's purpose consists of. Actually, without those pictures, you will never come to understand or fully appreciate what the Church really is, and what she should be doing in the world.

I offer to you, the reader, these graphs, tables, and diagrams with humility and with some reserve. They were drawn to help my students wrestle with the meaning of the Bible's deep truths and mysteries. From the positive feedback from my students, I can say that they did prove helpful to many. I pray that with the independent release of these pictures and graphs that they will also prove beneficial in your study and reflections. I am convinced that with some meditation the graphics in this collection will boost your confidence and willingness to engage the truth of the Scriptures for the sake of maximum impact in your life. Truly, if a picture is worth a thousand words, this collection has much to say about the wonder and depth of the truths of God's Word.

Rev. Dr. Don L. Davis
Wichita, Kansas

Advancing the Kingdom in the City
Multiplying Congregations with a Common Identity
Rev. Dr. Don L. Davis

Acts 2:41-47 (ESV) - So those who received his word were baptized, and there were added that day about three thousand souls. [42] And they devoted themselves to the apostles' teaching and fellowship, to the breaking of bread and the prayers. [43] And awe came upon every soul, and many wonders and signs were being done through the apostles. [44] And all who believed were together and had all things in common. [45] And they were selling their possessions and belongings and distributing the proceeds to all, as any had need. [46] And day by day, attending the temple together and breaking bread in their homes, they received their food with glad and generous hearts, [47] praising God and having favor with all the people. And the Lord added to their number day by day those who were being saved.

koinonia (pronunciation: [koy-nohn-ee'-ah])

Trinitarian Principle: Unity • Diversity • Equality

World Impact seeks to plant churches that are kingdom-oriented communities where Christ is exalted as Lord and the Kingdom of God is advanced in every facet of community life, and, we seek to do this in a way that respects and acknowledges the validity and significance of incarnating this community life in the receiving culture. In order to ensure the viability, protection, and flourishing of these congregations, we ought to explore forming close-knit associations between congregations where a common identity, confession, and faith are practiced, under a common oversight and governance, that connects in a fundamental way the resources and visions of each church without lording over them.

Following is a chart that sketches what might be the elements of such a common coalition of churches which would link their lives in a strategic way for the well-being and enrichment of the entire fellowship of churches. (Cf. *Imagining a Unified, Connected C1 Church Planting Movement* [see *www.tumi.org/Capstone* under the header *Appendices*] which in a comprehensive way suggests what may be included along ecclesial and missional, liturgical, and catechetical lines in such a fellowship).

Advancing the Kingdom in the City (continued)

Sharing a Common Identity, Purpose, and Mission	
A Common Name and Association	Understanding the churches as fundamentally linked in history, identity, legacy, and destiny
A Common Confession of Faith	Developing a common theological and doctrinal vision
A Common Celebration and Worship	Practicing a common liturgy with shared worship approaches
A Common Discipleship and Catechism	Sharing a common curriculum and process for welcoming, incorporating, and discipling new believers into our fellowship
A Common Governance and Oversight	Answering to a common accountability for leadership and care
A Common Service and Missionary Outreach	Developing integrated processes and programs of justice, good works, outreach, evangelism, and missions, both at home and throughout the world
A Common Stewardship and Partnership	Combining resources through consistent mutual contribution to maximize impact for the entire association

Benefits of a Common Movement

1. Sense of belonging through a shared faith and identity
2. Efficiency and economy of effort
3. Ability to plant multiple plants in many different venues and populations
4. Cultivating genuine unity and diversity, with a spirit of mutuality and equality among the congregations
5. Increased productivity and viability within our missions efforts and churches
6. Interchangability and cross pollination
7. Ongoing support and encouragement of our leaders
8. Provide leverage for new projects and new initiatives
9. Standardized processes and procedures for incorporation and training
10. Greater opportunities for convocation and exposure to other like-minded believers

Analytical vs. Christocentric Approach to Old Testament Study

Rev. Dr. Don L. Davis

An Analytical Approach	A Christocentric Approach
Focuses on individual verses, chapters, books, and sections in and of themselves	Focuses on how the content of book points to and gives witness to Messiah Jesus
Breaks Old Testament into many pieces for analysis and exegesis	Looks at Old Testament as single whole which gives single witness to Jesus
Concentrates on studying each book as its own self-contained unit	Concentrates on studying each book as it provides contribution to Christ's coming
Demands linguistic and socio-cultural expertise	Demands spiritual wisdom and discernment
Can only be legitimately done by experts	Can be done by all the saints of God
Difficult to give overview of Old Testament	Uses Christ as key to the interpretation of the Old Testament overview
Focuses on knowledge of content	Focuses on developing relationship to Christ
Hard to disciple others in knowledge of Old Testament and its contents	Designed to help teachers ground believers in the knowledge of Christ through the Old Testament
Can be remarkably boring and dry	Stirs the heart in longing and love for Jesus

The Apostles' Creed

I believe in God, the Father Almighty, Maker of heaven and earth; and in Jesus Christ his only Son, our Lord; who was conceived by the Holy Spirit, born of the Virgin Mary, suffered under Pontius Pilate, was crucified, dead, and buried; he descended into hell; the third day he arose again from the dead; he ascended into heaven and sits on the right hand of God the Father Almighty; from thence he shall come to judge the quick and the dead.

I believe in the Holy Spirit, the holy catholic church, the communion of saints, the forgiveness of sins, the resurrection of the body, and the life everlasting. Amen.

Apostolic Band
Cultivating Outreach for Dynamic Harvest
Rev. Dr. Don L. Davis

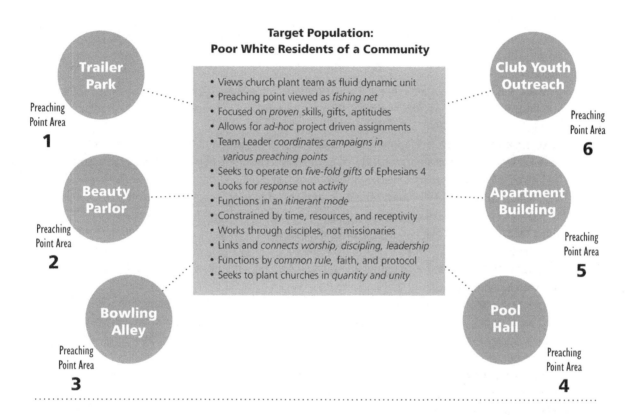

Target Population:
Poor White Residents of a Community

- Views church plant team as fluid dynamic unit
- Preaching point viewed as *fishing net*
- Focused on *proven* skills, gifts, aptitudes
- Allows for *ad-hoc* project driven assignments
- Team Leader *coordinates campaigns in various preaching points*
- Seeks to operate on *five-fold gifts* of Ephesians 4
- Looks for *response* not *activity*
- Functions in an *itinerant mode*
- Constrained by time, resources, and receptivity
- Works through disciples, not missionaries
- Links and *connects worship, discipling, leadership*
- Functions by *common rule*, faith, and protocol
- Seeks to plant churches in *quantity and unity*

Trailer Park
Preaching Point Area **1**

Beauty Parlor
Preaching Point Area **2**

Bowling Alley
Preaching Point Area **3**

Club Youth Outreach
Preaching Point Area **6**

Apartment Building
Preaching Point Area **5**

Pool Hall
Preaching Point Area **4**

Principle Concepts

1. Itinerancy- an apostolic band functions <u>in multiple-contexts simultaneously</u> organized around a common target population
2. Commonality- an apostolic band uses <u>similar forms, methods, and protocols</u> to win and build converts
3. Authority- an apostolic band functions under a <u>common authority structure</u> and <u>leadership core</u>
4. Identity- an apostolic band plants <u>churches of a kind</u> with shared doctrine, practice, structures and traditions
5. Gifting- an apostolic band is organized around <u>the proven gifts of the band,</u> not availability and assignment alone
6. Fluidity- an apostolic band invests in <u>contacts who respond in preaching points,</u> giving <u>the receptive</u> their critical attention
7. Coordination- an apostolic band will <u>draft and employ select individuals for contribution</u> at critical times for particular projects
8. Consolidation- an apostolic band <u>consolidates the fruit in an area</u> with an eye toward movement and growth, not permanence
9. Discipline- an apostolic band functions according to an <u>order and structure</u>, equipping disciples in the disciplines of the faith
10. Germinal- an apostolic band seeks to <u>inaugurate and initiate spiritual birth and formation</u>, entrusting the lion's share of the congregation's growth and maturity to pastoral oversight

DEFINITION OF TERMS:

Apostolic Band–a fluid team of gifted, available, and committed workers assigned to play particular roles or accomplish specific tasks contributing to the <u>outreach to a population</u>

Preaching Point–a distinct area, venue, or place where people of the <u>target population live or gather</u>

Team Charter–a fluid agreement based on the prospective time and resources necessary to <u>present the Gospel credibly to a target population</u> in a given venue

Project Management–putting together a temporary group of people, strategies, and resources to <u>complete a particular task, outreach, or event</u>

Apostolicity
The Unique Place of the Apostles in Christian Faith and Practice
Rev. Dr. Don L. Davis

Gal. 1.8-9 (ESV) - But even if we or an angel from heaven should preach to you a gospel contrary to the one we preached to you, let him be accursed. **[9]** As we have said before, so now I say again: If anyone is preaching to you a gospel contrary to the one you received, let him be accursed.

2 Thess. 3.6 (ESV) - Now we command you, brothers, in the name of our Lord Jesus Christ, that you keep away from any brother who is walking in idleness and not in accord with the tradition that you received from us.

Luke 1.1-4 (ESV) - Inasmuch as many have undertaken to compile a narrative of the things that have been accomplished among us, **[2]** just as those who from the beginning were eyewitnesses and ministers of the word have delivered them to us, **[3]** it seemed good to me also, having followed all things closely for some time past, to write an orderly account for you, most excellent Theophilus, [4] that you may have certainty concerning the things you have been taught.

John 15.27 (ESV) - And you also will bear witness, because you have been with me from the beginning.

Acts 1.3 (ESV) - To them he presented himself alive after his suffering by many proofs, appearing to them during forty days and speaking about the kingdom of God.

Acts 1.21-22 (ESV) - So one of the men who have accompanied us during all the time that the Lord Jesus went in and out among us, **[22]** beginning from the baptism of John until the day when he was taken up from us—one of these men must become with us a witness to his resurrection.

1 John 1.1-3 (ESV) - That which was from the beginning, which we have heard, which we have seen with our eyes, which we looked upon and have touched with our hands, concerning the word of life— **[2]** the life was made manifest, and we have seen it, and testify to it and proclaim to you the eternal life, which was with the Father and was made manifest to us— **[3]** that which we have seen and heard we proclaim also to you, so that you too may have fellowship with us; and indeed our fellowship is with the Father and with his Son Jesus Christ.

"Apostolicity"

**Focused on
Messiah Jesus**

**Infallible
(Authoritative)**

**Universally
acknowledged
among
the churches**

**Clear standard
for credentialing
ordained leaders**

**Standard for
NT canon**

Appearances of the Resurrected Messiah

Dr. Don L. Davis

	Appearance	Scripture
1	Appearance to Mary Magdalene	John 20.11-17; Mark 16.9-11
2	Appearance to the women	Matt. 28.9-10
3	Appearance to Peter	Luke 24.34; 1 Cor. 15.5
4	Appearance to the disciples on the road to Emmaus	Mark 16.12-13; Luke 24.13-35
5	Appearance to the ten disciples, referred to as the "Eleven" (with Thomas absent)	Mark 16.14; Luke 24.36-43; John 20.19-24
6	Appearance to the Eleven with Thomas present one week later	John 20.26-29
7	Appearance to seven disciples by the Sea of Galilee	John 21.1-23
8	Appearance to five hundred	1 Cor. 15.6
9	Appearance to James, the Lord's brother	1 Cor. 15.7
10	Appearance to the eleven disciples on the mountain in Galilee*	Matt. 28.16-20
11	Appearance to his disciples at his ascension on the Mount of Olives*	Luke 24.44-53; Acts 1.3-9
12	Appearance to Stephen prior to his death as the Church's first martyr (witness)	Acts 7.55-56
13	Appearance to Paul on the road to Damascus	Acts 9.3-6; cf. 22.6-11; 26.13-18; 1 Cor. 15.8
14	Appearance to Paul in Arabia	Acts 20.24; 26.17; Gal. 1.12,17
15	Appearance to Paul in the Temple	Acts 22.17-21; cf. 9.26-30; Gal. 1.18
16	Appearance to Paul in prison in Caesarea	Acts 23.11
17	Appearance to John during his exile in Patmos	Rev. 1.12-20

* Items 10 and 11 describe the events commonly referred to as "The Great Commission" and "The Ascension," respectively.

Areas of Disagreement among Christians Concerning Spiritual Gifts

Rev. Terry G. Cornett

I.   What Is the Relationship between "Natural Talents or Capacities" and "Spiritual Gifts"?

A.   View #1 - Spiritual gifts are what the natural talents and abilities latent in every human being look like when they are energized, empowered, broadened, and redirected by the Spirit of God regenerating a person.

This view is concerned to safeguard the fact that:

1.   There is no discontinuity between the activity of the Spirit who creates and who recreates. (Salvation is restorative in nature making us the full human beings we were originally created to be.)

2.   That God has chosen to work his gifts through human beings which includes using their minds, bodies, and personalities. He includes us in his work so that even though his power will enable us to do far more than mere human accomplishments, it is still at work in, with, and through us as we actually are.

3.   God foreknew us and was at work prior to our salvation (cf. Jer. 1.5)

a.   Jer. 1.5 (ESV) - Before I formed you in the womb I knew you, and before you were born I consecrated you; I appointed you a prophet to the nations.

b.   Eph. 2.10 (ESV) - For we are his workmanship, created in Christ Jesus for good works, which God prepared beforehand, that we should walk in them.

Areas of Disagreement among Christians Concerning Spiritual Gifts (continued)

4. That even those who are unsaved and in rebellion against God rely on his creation and gifts of grace (suppressed, corrupted, or misdirected as they may be) for their very being and productivity.

    a. 1 Cor. 4.7 (ESV) - For who sees anything different in you? What do you have that you did not receive? If then you received it, why do you boast as if you did not receive it? (Cf. Ps. 104.)

    b. Matt. 5.45 (ESV) - . . . so that you may be sons of your Father who is in heaven. For he makes his sun rise on the evil and on the good, and sends rain on the just and on the unjust.

    c. "The same God is God of creation and of new creation, working out both through his perfect will. . . . God's gracious purpose for each of us is eternal. It was formed and even "given" to us in Christ "before eternal time" (2 Tim. 1.9, literally); God chose us to be holy and destined us to be his sons through Jesus Christ "before the foundation of the world" (Eph. 1.4,5); and the good works for which were re-created in Christ are precisely those "which God prepared beforehand." This fundamental truth that God planned the end from the beginning should warn us against . . . [too easily separating] . . . between nature and grace, between our pre-conversion and our post-conversion life" (John R. W. Stott, *Baptism and Fullness: The Work of the Holy Spirit Today*).

B. View #2 - Spiritual gifts are new supernatural abilities given to Christians which are only available to us through God's power and are able to accomplish things far beyond the reach of human ability.

This view is concerned to safeguard the fact that:

1. Salvation is transformative as well as restorative.

2.   God is able to supply whatever is needed in a situation regardless of the resources we seem to have available. We are dependent upon God's Spirit, not our own resources.

3.   Supernatural powers exceeding anything possible in the natural order are available to the body of Christ.

4.   We all are commanded to seek certain spiritual gifts that are of benefit to the body (1 Cor. 12.31 & 14.12). The gifts are always spoken of in relation to how they build up Christ's body. There is no scriptural reference to spiritual gifts apart from their use in and by the Church.

   a.   1 Cor. 1.26-29 (ESV) - For consider your calling, brothers: not many of you were wise according to worldly standards, not many were powerful, not many were of noble birth. [27] But God chose what is foolish in the world to shame the wise; God chose what is weak in the world to shame the strong; [28] God chose what is low and despised in the world, even things that are not, to bring to nothing things that are, [29] so that no human being might boast in the presence of God.

   b.   Non-Christians have talents through common grace. . . but these are talents, not gifts. No unbeliever has a spiritual gift. Only believers are gifted spiritually. . . .Talents depend on natural power, gifts on spiritual endowment (Leslie B. Flynn, *19 Gifts of the Spirit*).

C.   View #3 - A Middle Way which suggests that spiritual gifts can be either the energizing of God-given natural talents or the creation of entirely new talents.

1. Note that logically, at least, it is not necessary for these two views to be mutually exclusive. It is at least possible that both types of spiritual gifts exist, some that are latent and some that are new.

2. Perhaps a more useful way to think about this would be to remember that gifts are the "manifestation" of the Spirit for the common good.

3. The Spirit being manifested is the emphasis not the means by which it happens. It is always a "gracious gift" when this happens. It always happens solely because of the Spirit's decision and because of the Spirit's power. Thus, whether the Spirit chooses to empower a natural capacity or create an entirely new one, each is a "charisma" — a gift of grace. A God given ability to teach exercised by a non-believer is a gracious gift (given by the Spirit in creation) but it is not a "manifestation of the Spirit" until that person submits themselves to the Holy Spirit and uses that gift under his direction and for his purposes.

II. Are All the Gifts Listed in the New Testament Available Today?

A. Some traditions answer "No."

1. Some traditions argue for the ceasing of certain gifts: usually apostleship, prophecy, tongues and interpretation (sometimes miracles).

2. There are at least two theological reasons why this is believed.

a. First, there is a concern for safeguarding God's revelation in Scripture.

If apostles, prophets, and tongues continue to function as a means of ongoing revelation, the integrity of Scripture is potentially put at risk. Again and again in the history of the Church, people have come along that claimed a new, prophetic revelation which contradicted or went beyond the claims of Scripture. The scriptural testimony to Jesus as God's final Word cannot be compromised and these theological traditions do not see a way to reconcile the possibility of new revelations with that fact.

b. Second, the role of the apostles as the "foundation" of the Church seems to imply a unique place in Church history.

The Gospels and the Book of Acts are seen as a pivot point of history during which God works uniquely and unrepeatably to change his revelation from the Old Covenant to the New Covenant. This is accomplished by the granting of new revelations (which form the New Testament Scriptures) and signs and wonders which confirm and establish this testimony as authentic. The Church now is to exist by the testimony of that Word, guarding the deposit of faith but not adding to it or subtracting from it.

(1) Jude 1.3 (ESV) - Beloved, although I was very eager to write to you about our common salvation, I found it necessary to write appealing to you to contend for the faith that was once for all delivered to the saints.

(2) Heb. 1.1-3 (ESV) - Long ago, at many times and in many ways, God spoke to our fathers by the prophets, [2] but in these last days he has spoken to us by his Son, whom he appointed the heir of all things, through whom also he created the world. [3] He is the radiance of the glory of God and the exact imprint of his nature, and he upholds the universe by the word of his power. After making purification for sins, he sat down at the right hand of the Majesty on high.

(3) Gal. 1.8-9 (ESV) - But even if we or an angel from heaven should preach to you a gospel contrary to the one we preached to you, let him be accursed. [9] As we have said before, so now I say again: If anyone is preaching to you a gospel contrary to the one you received, let him be accursed.

B. Some traditions answer "Yes."

"All may agree that there appears no new revelation to be expected concerning God in Christ. But there appears to be no good reason why the living God, who both speaks and acts (in contrast to dead idols), cannot use the gift of prophecy to give particular local guidance to a church, nation or individual, or to warn or encourage by way of prediction as well as by reminders, in full accord with the written word of Scripture, by which all such utterances must be tested. Certainly the NT does not see it as the job of the prophet to be a doctrinal innovator, but to deliver the word the Spirit gives him in line with the truth once for all delivered to the saints (Jude 3), to challenge and encourage our faith" (J. P. Baker, "Prophecy," *New Bible Dictionary*, 2nd Edition, J. D. Douglas and others, eds.).

1. The ministry of Jesus and the example of the Apostles and the New Testament Church is our inspired model for ministry and all of them used miraculous gifts in ministry.

2. The only time that Scripture speaks to the question of when gifts will cease it refers to the return of Christ (1 Cor. 13.8-12).

3. The Holy Spirit is free and sovereign. He can give (or withhold) any gift at any time for whatever purpose he chooses (1 Cor. 12.11 – gives as he determines).

4. The Craig S. Keener reading (*Gift and Giver*—pp. 89-112) makes the basic arguments for the view that all are available.

Arrangement of the Twelve Tribes around the Tabernacle

Vern S. Poythress, The Shadow of Christ in the Law of Moses.

Tribes Encamped

Manasseh		Dan		Issachar
	Asher		Naphtali	
Ephraim		**TABERNACLE**		Judah
	Simeon		Gad	
Benjamin		Reuben		Zebulon

Tribes Marching

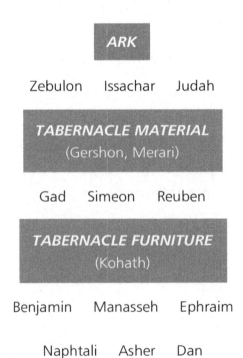

ARK

Zebulon   Issachar   Judah

TABERNACLE MATERIAL
(Gershon, Merari)

Gad   Simeon   Reuben

TABERNACLE FURNITURE
(Kohath)

Benjamin   Manasseh   Ephraim

Naphtali   Asher   Dan

Authentic Freedom in Jesus Christ

Rev. Dr. Don L. Davis

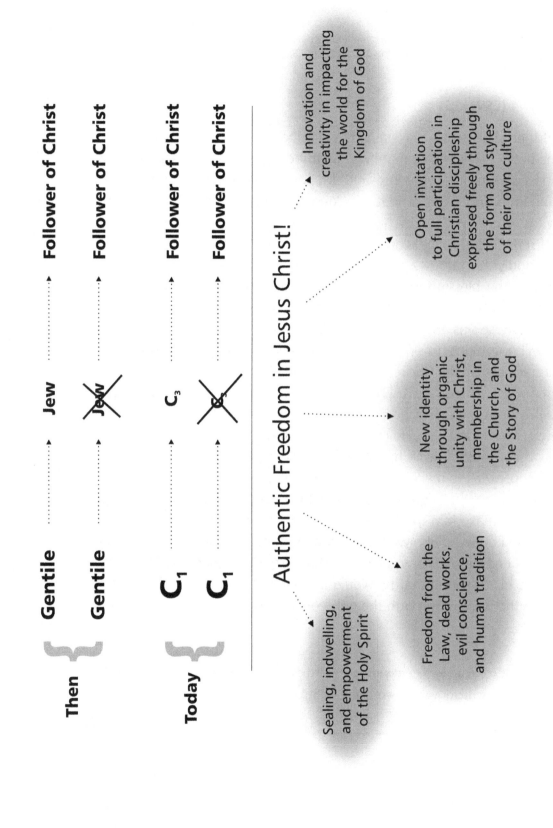

Bible Study Tools Worksheet

Read through the following Scripture passage and then answer the questions that follow using a Strong's Concordance, Vine's Expository Dictionary of Old and New Testament Words, and the New Bible Dictionary.

Romans 4 (ESV)

What then shall we say was gained by Abraham, our forefather according to the flesh? [2] For if Abraham was **justified** by works, he has something to boast about, but not before God. [3] For what does the Scripture say? "Abraham believed God, and it was counted to him as righteousness." [4] Now to the one who works, his wages are not counted as a gift but as his due. [5] And to the one who does not work but trusts him who justifies the ungodly, his faith is counted as righteousness, [6] just as David also speaks of the blessing of the one to whom God counts righteousness apart from works: [7] "Blessed are those whose lawless deeds are forgiven, and whose sins are covered; [8] blessed is the man against whom the Lord will not count his sin." [9] Is this blessing then only for the circumcised, or also for the uncircumcised? We say that faith was counted to Abraham as righteousness. [10] How then was it counted to him? Was it before or after he had been circumcised? It was not after, but before he was circumcised. [11] He received the sign of circumcision as a seal of the righteousness that he had by faith while he was still uncircumcised. The purpose was to make him the father of all who believe without being circumcised, so that righteousness would be counted to them as well, [12] and to make him the father of the circumcised who are not merely circumcised but who also walk in the footsteps of the faith that our father Abraham had before he was circumcised. [13] For the promise to Abraham and his offspring that he would be heir of the world did not come through the law but through the righteousness of faith.

1. Use your concordance to identify the word that is translated "justified" in verse 2 and then write down the word and its Strong's number in the space below:

   Greek word _____ Strong's number _____

2. Look up this word in your *Vine's Expository Dictionary* and read the entry for this word. What does this information add to your understanding of the word and the passage?

_____

_____

_____

3. Use your concordance to identify the word that is translated "walk" in verse 12 and then write down the word and its Strong's number in the space below.

Greek word _____ Strong's number _____

4. Look up this word in *Vine's Expository Dictionary* and read the entry.

Why do you think the Apostle Paul chose this word rather than one of the other Greek words for walking? What does knowing the definition of this word for "walk" add to your understanding of this passage?

_____

_____

_____

_____

5. Using the *New Bible Dictionary*, look up and read the article on "Abraham." In what way does this deepen your understanding of the Scripture passage?

_____

_____

_____

_____

Biblical Justification for the Resurrection of Messiah Jesus

Dr. Don L. Davis

	Reasons for His Resurrection	Scriptural Text
1	To fulfill the prophecy of Holy Scripture	Ps. 16.9-10; 22.22; 118.22-24
2	To demonstrate his true identity	Acts 2.24; Rom. 1.1-4
3	To realize the promise of the Davidic covenant	2 Sam. 7.12-16; Ps. 89.20-37; Isa. 9.6-7; Luke 1.31-33; Acts 2.25-31
4	To become the source of eternal life for all who believe in him	John 10.10-11; 11.25-26; Eph. 2.6; Col. 3.1-4; 1 John 5.11-12
5	To become the source of resurrection power to others	Matt. 28.18; Eph. 1.19-21; Phil. 4.13
6	To be exalted as head over the Church	Eph. 1.20-23
7	To demonstrate that God's imputation of our righteousness has been made complete	Rom. 4.25
8	To reign until all enemies have been placed under his feet	1 Cor. 15.20-28
9	To become the first fruits of the future resurrection	1 Cor. 15.20-23
10	To assert the authority given to him by God to take his life back again	John 10.18

A Bibliography for Biblical Hermeneutics

Archer, Gleason L. *Encyclopedia of Bible Difficulties*. Grand Rapids: Zondervan, 1982.

Black, David Alan. *Linguistics for Students of New Testament Greek: A Survey of Basic Concepts and Applications*. Grand Rapids: Baker, 1988.

------. *Using New Testament Greek in Ministry: A Practical Guide for Students and Pastors*. Grand Rapids: Baker Books, 1993.

Blomberg, Craig L. *Interpreting the Parables*. Leicester: Apollos, 1990.

Bowman, Robert M., Jr. *Understanding Jehovah's Witnesses: Why They Read the Bible the Way They Do*. Grand Rapids: Baker, 1991.

Bray, Gerald. *Biblical Interpretation Past and Present*. Downers Grove/Leicester: IVP, 2000.

Bullinger, E. W. *Figures of Speech Used in the Bible*. Grand Rapids: Baker Book House, 1968.

Caird, G. B. *Language and Biblical Imagery*. Gerald Duckworth & Co. Ltd, 1981.

Carson, D. A. *Exegetical Fallacies*. 2nd ed. Grand Rapids/Carlisle: Baker Books/ Paternoster Press, 1996.

Carson, D. A. and John D. Woodbridge, eds. *Hermeneutics, Authority and Canon*. Leicester: IVP, 1986.

------. *Scripture and Truth*. Leicester: IVP, 1983.

Castelli, Elizabeth A. et al, eds. *The Postmodern Bible*. Yale University Press, 1997.

Coggins, R. J. and J. L. Houlden, eds. *A Dictionary of Biblical Interpretation*. London: SCM Press Ltd., 1990.

Cotterall, Peter, and Max Turner. *Linguistics and Biblical Interpretation*. Downers Grove: InterVarsity Press, 1989.

A Bibliography for Biblical Hermeneutics (continued)

Erickson, Millard J. *Evangelical Interpretation: Perspectives on Hermeneutical Issues.* Grand Rapids: Baker Books, 1993.

Evans, Craig A. *Noncanonical Writings and New Testament Interpretation.* Peabody, MA: Hendrickson Publishers, 1992.

Fee, Gordon D. *New Testament Exegesis: A Handbook for Students and Pastors.* Philadelphia: Westminster Press, 1983.

Fee, Gordon D. and Douglas Stewart. *How to Read the Bible for All its Worth: A Guide to Understanding the Bible.* 2nd ed. Grand Rapids: Zondervan, 1993.

Goldingay, John. *Approaches to Old Testament Interpretation.* Updated ed. Leicester: Apollos, 1990.

Greidanus, Sidney. *The Modern Preacher and the Ancient Text: Interpreting and Preaching Biblical Literature.* Grand Rapids: Eerdmans, 1988.

Hendrickson, Walter. *A Layman's Guide to Interpreting the Bible.* Grand Rapids: Zondervan, 1978.

Johnson, Elliott E. *Expository Hermeneutics: An Introduction.* Grand Rapids: Zondervan, 1990.

Kaiser, Walter C., Jr. *Toward an Exegetical Theology: Biblical Exegesis for Preaching and Teaching.* Grand Rapids: Baker, 1981.

Kaiser, Walter C., Jr. Peter H. Davids, F. F. Bruce, and Manfred T. Brauch. *Hard Sayings of the Bible.* Downers Grove: InterVarsity Press, 1996.

Kaiser, Walter C., Jr. and Moises Silva. *An Introduction to Biblical Hermeneutics: The Search for Meaning.* Grand Rapids: Zondervan, 1994.

Klein, William W., Craig L. Blomberg, and Robert L. Hubbard. *Introduction to Biblical Interpretation.* Dallas: Word Publishing, 1993.

Kurht, Wilfred. *Interpreting the Bible: A Handbook of Biblical Interpretation.* Welwyn: Evangelical Press, 1983.

Long, V. Philips. *The Art of Biblical Interpretation. Foundations of Contemporary Interpretation.* Vol. 5. Leicester: InterVarsity Press, 1994.

Longman, Tremper, III. *How to Read the Psalms.* Downers Grove: InterVaristy Press, 1988.

A Bibliography for Biblical Hermeneutics (continued)

------. *Literary Approaches to Biblical Interpretation. Foundations of Contemporary Interpretation.* Vol. 3. Leicester: InterVarsity Press, 1987.

------. *Reading the Bible with Heart and Mind.* Navpress Publishing Group, 1996.

Longenecker, Richard N. *Biblical Exegesis in the Apostolic Period.* Carlisle: Paternoster Press, 1995.

Lundin, Roger. *Disciplining Hermeneutics: Interpretation in Christian Perspective.* Grand Rapids: Eerdmans, 1997.

McKnight, Scot, ed. *Introduction to New Testament Interpretation.* Grand Rapids: Baker Books, 1989.

Marshall, I. H., ed. *New Testament Interpretation: Essays on Principles and Methods.* Rev. 1979. Carlisle: Paternoster Press, 1992.

Neill, Stephen. *The Interpretation of the New Testament 1861-1961.* Oxford: Oxford University Press, 1964.

Osborne, Grant R. *The Hermeneutical Spiral: A Comprehensive Introduction to Biblical Interpretation.* Downers Grove: InterVarsity Press, 1991.

Poythress, Vern Sheridan. *Symphonic Theology: The Validity of Multiple Perspectives in Theology.* Grand Rapids: Zondervan, 1987.

Pratt, Richard L., Jr. *He Gave Us Stories: The Bible Student's Guide to Interpreting Old Testament Narratives.* Phillipsburg, NJ: Presbyterian and Reformed, 1993.

Scalise, Charles J. From *Scripture to Theology: A Canonical Journey into Hermeneutics.* Downers Grove: IVP, 1996.

Silva, Moises. *Biblical Words and Their Meaning: An Introduction to Lexical Semantics.* Revised and expanded ed. Grand Rapids: Zondervan, 1994.

------. *God, Language and Scripture. Foundations of Contemporary Interpretation.* Vol. 4. Grand Rapids: Zondervan, 1990.

------. *Has the Church Misread the Bible? The History of Interpretation in the Light of Current Issues. Foundations of Contemporary Interpretation.* Vol 1. Grand Rapids: Zondervan, 1987.

A Bibliography for Biblical Hermeneutics (continued)

Sire, James W. *Scripture Twisting: 20 Ways the Cults Misread the Bible.* Leicester: InterVarsity Press, 1980.

Stein, Robert H. *A Basic Guide to Interpreting the Bible: Playing by the Rules.* Grand Rapids: Baker, 1994.

Stenger, Werner. *Introduction to New Testament Exegesis.* Grand Rapids: Eerdmans, 1987.

Stuart, Douglas. *Old Testament Exegesis: A Primer for Students and Pastors.* 2nd ed. Revised and expanded. Philadelphia: The Westminster Press, 1984.

Tate, Randolph W. *Biblical Interpretation: An Integrated Approach.* Peabody, MA: Hendrickson Publishers, 1997.

Thistleton, Anthony C. *New Horizons in Hermeneutics: The Theory and Practice of Transforming Biblical Reading.* Grand Rapids: Zondervan, 1992.

------. *Promise of Hermeneutics.* Carlisle: Paternoster Press, 1999

------. *The Two Horizons: New Testament Hermeneutics and Philosophical Description with Special Reference to Heideggar, Bultmann, Gadamer, and Wittgenstein.* Carlisle: Paternoster Press, 1980.

Capturing God's Vision for His People
The "Enduring Solidarity" of Our Search for the Land of Promise

Heb. 11.13-16 (ESV) - These all died in faith, not having received the things promised, but having seen them and greeted them from afar, and having acknowledged that they were strangers and exiles on the earth. [14] For people who speak thus make it clear that they are seeking a homeland. [15] If they had been thinking of that land from which they had gone out, they would have had opportunity to return. [16] But as it is, they desire a better country, that is, a heavenly one. Therefore God is not ashamed to be called their God, for he has prepared for them a city.

A whole galaxy of auxiliary images oscillate around the analogy of "the people of God" for Christians and the Christian church. These include in the Pauline letters the following: "God's elect" (Rom. 8.33; Eph. 1.4; Col. 3.12), "Abraham's descendants" (Rom. 4.16; Gal. 3.29; 4.26-28), "the true circumcision" (Phil. 3.3; Col. 2.11), and even "Israel of God" (Gal. 6.16). All of these images assert, in some manner, an enduring solidarity of the people of the church with the people of Israel, whose history provides the church with an authoritative account of the principles and actions of God's past redemptive working. It is the task of exegesis and theology to spell out the nature of this relationship.

~ Richard Longenecker, ed.
Community Formation in the Early Church and in the Church Today.
Peabody, MA: Hendrickson Publishers, 2002. p. 75.

The Center and Circumference: Christianity Is Jesus Christ

Don L. Davis

Introduction: The world that we live in is not the one which appears to be the real one, but typically is the one that we or another has composed for us to live in.

Callin' Something Somethin'

Three umpires at an umpires convention boasting to each other about their prowess as major league umps:

I.   Umpire One: Some call 'em balls and others call 'em strikes, but *I call 'em how I see 'em!*

II. Umpire Two: Some call 'em balls and others call 'em strikes, but *I call 'em what they truly is!*

III. Umpire Three: Some call 'em balls and others call 'em strikes, but *they ain't nothin' till I call 'em somethin'!*

What is the essence of the Christian faith journey, the nature of Christian theology and doctrine, the heart of Christian ethics, the core of Christian hope?

It is the person of Jesus Christ. He is the center and the circumference of the Christian's faith and practice.

All that we are, all that we believe, and all that we understand God is doing in the world is related to this unique and yet humble person:

- Of whom we know little regarding his appearance and personage

- Who didn't travel 200 miles from his place of birth

- Of whom we have only a few birth narratives and a story regarding his adolescence

- Whose years of life from twelve to thirty are silent, even from those who adored him the most

- Who ministered only three years, and was rejected by his peers, countrymen, and the religious establishment

- Who died in shame, was executed publicly between two thieves, and placed in a borrowed tomb

Yet all of the persons, books, philosophies, systems, governments, artists, educators, religious leaders, military conquerors, persons of influence and power put together have not had the impact of this one itinerant Jewish preacher has had on the structure and fate of the world.

Christianity is Jesus Christ. The story is about his person and influence and calling and vision and work and future. To understand all that God wants us to know and be and do, all one must do is master the life and person of Christ, which his followers confess to be alive today.

The Text for Today

Col. 1.15-20 (ESV) - He is the image of the invisible God, the firstborn of all creation. [16] For by him all things were created, in heaven and on earth, visible and invisible, whether thrones or dominions or rulers or authorities—all things were created through him and for him. [17] And he is before all things, and in him all things hold together. [18] And he is the head of the body, the church. He is the beginning, the firstborn from the dead, that in everything he might be preeminent.[19] For in him all the fullness of God was pleased to dwell, [20] and through him to reconcile to himself all things, whether on earth or in heaven, making peace by the blood of his cross.

I. **Jesus the Final and Full Revelation of God. In Order to Understand the Father, We Must Come to Know the Person of Jesus Christ, Who Is Both the Means and End of Creation Itself.**

A. Jesus is the express image of God's person through whom God made the entire created spheres. Col. 1.15-16 (ESV) - He is the image of the invisible God, the firstborn of all creation. [16] For by him all things were created, in heaven and on earth, visible and invisible, whether

The Center and Circumference: Christianity Is Jesus Christ (continued)

thrones or dominions or rulers or authorities—all things were created through him and for him.

B.   Jesus is the exact representation (exact imprint of his nature) of God in human form, Heb. 1.1-4 (ESV) - Long ago, at many times and in many ways, God spoke to our fathers by the prophets, [2] but in these last days he has spoken to us by his Son, whom he appointed the heir of all things, through whom also he created the world. [3] He is the radiance of the glory of God and the exact imprint of his nature, and he upholds the universe by the word of his power. After making purification for sins, he sat down at the right hand of the Majesty on high, [4] having become as much superior to angels as the name he has inherited is more excellent than theirs.

C.   Jesus is the Word made flesh, the revelator of the splendor and beauty of God.

John 1.14 (ESV) - And the Word became flesh and dwelt among us, and we have seen his glory, glory as of the only Son from the Father, full of grace and truth.

John 1.18 (ESV) - No one has ever seen God; the only God, who is at the Father's side, he has made him known.

D.   The person of Jesus is the full and unadulterated picture of the character and beauty of the Father God whom we love and worship. We know God through him.

Many are content to possess a shallow and familiar knowledge of the person of Jesus, neither recognizing nor reveling in the mystery of the meaning of "Christ in you, the hope of Glory."

During the children's sermon the Assistant Pastor asked the kids, "What is gray, has a bushy tail and gathers nuts in the fall?" One five year old raised his hand. "I know the answer should be Jesus," he began, "but it sounds like a squirrel to me" (*Reader's Digest*).

The Center and Circumference: Christianity Is Jesus Christ (continued)

- For Christians, there exists no saving knowledge of God that is not mediated through the person of Jesus Christ, John 14.6.

- For us who believe, the very glory of God shines in the face of Jesus, 2 Cor. 4.6.

- The fullness of the Godhead, the glorious beauty of God is seen most clearly in the person and work of Jesus Christ, Col. 2.9 (ESV) - For in him the whole fullness of deity dwells bodily.

E. Christianity is the person of Christ, relating to God in the person of Jesus Christ, who we believe lived, died, and rose again in order to bring us into a right relationship with God

- It is not ethics and do-gooding (we live right after we meet Christ)

- It is not merely family life (we become what God wants us to become after we come to know Christ)

- It is not religious studies and liturgies (other religions have fine ethics, great worship programs, devoted teaching, and many holy books)

Jesus Is the Only Way to God

A traveler engaged a guide to take him across a desert area. When the two men arrived at the edge of the desert, the traveler, looking ahead, saw before him trackless sands without a single footprint, path, or marker of any kind. Turning to his guide, he asked in a tone of surprise, "Where is the road?" With a reproving glance, the guide replied, "I am the road."

The Scriptures Point to Christ

Five times in the NT the Scriptures refer to Jesus as the express purpose of the writing of the Holy Scriptures. He is the reason for the story, divided into two unequal halves (Gen. 1.1-3.15, and Gen. 3.16 - Rev. 21). If you look at any part of the Bible, you will see him there. There is a bronze copy of the Declaration of Independence carved right into a bronze slate, done in meticulous accuracy

The Center and Circumference: Christianity Is Jesus Christ (continued)

and splendid detail. If you back away from the rendering of the Declaration, however, you can see the image of George Washington emerge from the writing. It was done with the proper shading and sculpting to reveal the person of Mr. Washington from the rendering of the Declaration. In my mind, the Bible has a single dominating purpose–to reveal the glory of the person of Jesus Christ, so that, through faith in him, we might become one of the Father's children!

All that we do at TUMI is to find ways to declare the majesty and might of the Person and Work of Christ, and how it relates to being an urban disciple and doing urban ministry through urban churches among the poor.

Hundreds of names, types, images, and metaphors refer to Christ in Scripture:

- He is the *Bread of life* - the One of total nourishment and strength

- He is the *Second Adam* - the head of an entire new race of humanity

- He is the *Resurrection and the Life* - the One whose name alone can conquer death and corruption

- He is the *Lord of all* - the chosen ruler of God to restore God's reign

- He is *Prince of Peace* - the One whose power alone will restore peace to our troubled world

Jesus is the key to understanding the person and work of Almighty God.

II. Next, We See that this Text Reveals that Jesus Is the Finished Redemption of God. Jesus Alone Is God's Anointed Prophet and Priest to Bring Us Back into Relationship to God.

A. Jesus is the only way to be reconciled with God; no other person or name exists that can bring us into new and redeemed relation with God. Look again at Colossians 1.17-20 (ESV) - And he is before all things, and in him all things hold together. [18] And he is the head of the body, the church. He is the beginning, the firstborn from the dead, that in everything he might be preeminent. [19] For in him all the fullness of God was pleased to dwell, [20] and through him to reconcile to himself all things, whether on earth or in heaven, making peace by the blood of his cross.

B.   According to the Scriptures, God was in the person of Jesus Christ reconciling the world unto himself. 2 Cor. 5.18-21 (ESV) - All this is from God, who through Christ reconciled us to himself and gave us the ministry of reconciliation; [19] that is, in Christ God was reconciling the world to himself, not counting their trespasses against them, and entrusting to us the message of reconciliation. [20] Therefore, we are ambassadors for Christ, God making his appeal through us. We implore you on behalf of Christ, be reconciled to God. [21] For our sake he made him to be sin who knew no sin, so that in him we might become the righteousness of God.

C.   Jesus alone is the sole deliverer, redeemer, and reconciler of humankind back to God.

  •   He is the just One who died for us unjust ones, in order to bring us to God, 1 Pet.3.18.

  •   His is the only name under heaven given to us in order that we must be saved, Acts 4.12 (ESV) - And there is salvation in no one else, for there is no other name under heaven given among men by which we must be saved."

  •   He alone is the One who became God's *Christus Victum* in order to raise and become our *Christus Victor*, Col. 2.13-15 (ESV) - And you, who were dead in your trespasses and the uncircumcision of your flesh, God made alive together with him, having forgiven us all our trespasses,[14] by canceling the record of debt that stood against us with its legal demands. This he set aside, nailing it to the cross. [15] He disarmed the rulers and authorities and put them to open shame, by triumphing over them in him.

The Center and Circumference: Christianity Is Jesus Christ (continued)

The Father sacrificed his very own Son in order to redeem the world, to reconcile the breach between us on account of our disobedience to God, and give us new birth as adopted children into God's family.

> A man had the duty to raise a drawbridge to allow the steamers to pass on the river below and to lower it again for trains to cross over on land. One day, this man's son visited him, desiring to watch his father at work. Quite curious, as most boys are, he peeked into a trap door that was always left open so his father could keep an eye on the great machinery which raised and lowered the bridge. Suddenly, the boy lost his footing and tumbled into the gears. As the father tried to reach down and pull him out, he heard the whistle of an approaching train. He knew the cars would be full of people and that it would be impossible to stop the fast-moving locomotive, therefore, the bridge must be lowered! A terrible dilemma confronted him; for if he saved the people, his son would be crushed in the cogs. Frantically, he tried to free the boy, but to no avail. Finally, the father put his hand to the lever that would start the machinery. He paused and then, with tears he pulled it. The giant gears began to work and the bridge clamped down just in time to save the train. The passengers, not knowing what the father had done, were laughing and making merry; yet the bridge keeper had chosen to save their lives at the cost of his son's.

No one and nothing can detail the expense of the price the Father provided in order to bring us back to himself to Christ. This reveals the awesome majesty of the love of God for each of us, that he would give his only Son up for our redemption.

III. Finally, Not Only Is Jesus God's Full Revelation and Finished Redemption, He Is Also the Final Rule and Standard of True Humanity.

A. Jesus is God's pattern, his ruler, his final standard for all that we are and soon will become. Look again at Colossians 1.18-19 (ESV) - And he is the head of the body, the church. He is the beginning, the firstborn from the dead, that in everything he might be preeminent. [19] For in him all the fullness of God was pleased to dwell.

B. God's design is that Jesus be the first, the head, the center, the heart of all that he communicates and does. To know God is to know Christ, to please God is to become like Christ, to obey God is to follow Christ's example: he is our example.

John 13.13-16 (ESV) - You call me Teacher and Lord, and you are right, for so I am. [14] If I then, your Lord and Teacher, have washed your feet, you also ought to wash one another's feet. [15] For I have given you an example, that you also should do just as I have done to you. [16] Truly, truly, I say to you, a servant is not greater than his master, nor is a messenger greater than the one who sent him.

C. A number of texts in the NT clearly reveal that God's purpose is to conform us to the very image of Jesus Christ, to join us to him, and then to make us like him. God intends to make Jesus the head of a new human family which will be conformed to his person and his destiny.

*   Rom. 8.28-29 (ESV) - And we know that for those who love God all things work together for good, for those who are called according to his purpose.[29] For those whom he foreknew he also predestined to be conformed to the image of his Son, in order that he might be the firstborn among many brothers.

*   1 Cor. 15.49 (ESV) - Just as we have borne the image of the man of dust, we shall also bear the image of the man of heaven.

*   2 Cor. 3.18 (ESV) - And we all, with unveiled face, beholding the glory of the Lord, are being transformed into the same image from one degree of glory to another. For this comes from the Lord who is the Spirit.

*   Paul commands in Philippians 2.5 (ESV) "Have this mind among yourselves, which is yours in Christ Jesus."

*   In Philippians 3.20, Paul says that our citizenship is in the heavens where we look for the person of our Lord, Christ Jesus who, according to Philippians 3.21 (ESV) "will transform our lowly body to be like his glorious body, by the power that enables him even to subject all things to himself."

The Center and Circumference: Christianity Is Jesus Christ (continued)

- Peter says in his second epistle in 2 Peter 3.18 (ESV) that we are to "grow in the grace and knowledge of our Lord and Savior Jesus Christ. To him be the glory both now and to the day of eternity. Amen."

- His is the only name under heaven given to us in order that we must be saved, Acts 4.12 (ESV) - And there is salvation in no one else, for there is no other name under heaven given among men by which we must be saved.

- John the Apostle says in his first epistle 1 John 3.1-3 (ESV) - See what kind of love the Father has given to us, that we should be called children of God; and so we are. The reason why the world does not know us is that it did not know him. [2] Beloved, we are God's children now, and what we will be has not yet appeared; but we know that when he appears we will be like him, because we shall see him as he is. [3] And everyone who thus hopes in him purifies himself as he is pure.

D. According to God's will, we have been baptized (placed into and surrounded by) Christ himself, who is our hope of glory, we are now said to be "in Christ." We who believe have been identified with Christ Jesus, and made a part of the Church of God, which is the "Mystery" revealed: the open secret of God

- Romans 16.25-27, the "revelation of the mystery"

- Ephesians 3.7-10, God's wisdom displayed through the Church

- Colossians 1.25-27, Christ in us, the hope of glory

E. Jesus is God's ruler, God's pattern, God's principle of intimacy and identification for the redeemed. God's intention is to conform each of us who believe to the very life and perfection of Christ himself. Listen to what the NT teaches about our connection to our Lord.

- We are "made one in Christ," 1 Cor. 6.15-17.

- We were baptized into him, 1 Cor. 12.13.

- We died with him, Rom. 6.3-4.

The Center and Circumference: Christianity Is Jesus Christ (continued)

- We were buried with him, Rom. 6.3-4.

- We were raised with him, Eph. 2.4-7.

- We are ascended with him, Eph. 2.6.

- We sit in the heavenly places with him, Eph. 2.6.

- In this world, we take his yoke upon us and carry the burden and cross that he has assigned to us, Matt. 11.28-30.

- In this world, we are called to suffer with him, Rom. 8.17-18; Phil. 1.29-30.

- Whether we live or die, we belong completely to the Lord Jesus, Rom. 14.7-9 (ESV) - For none of us lives to himself, and none of us dies to himself. [8] If we live, we live to the Lord, and if we die, we die to the Lord. So then, whether we live or whether we die, we are the Lord's. [9] For to this end Christ died and lived again, that he might be Lord both of the dead and of the living.

- We will be glorified with him, Rom. 8.17.

- We will be resurrected in him, 1 Cor. 15.48-49.

- We will be made like him, 1 John 3.2.

- We are joint-heirs with him, Rom. 8.17.

- We will reign forever with him, Rev. 3.

The Center and Circumference: Christianity Is Jesus Christ (continued)

Hast thou no scar?

No hidden scar on foot, or side, or hand?

I hear thee sung as mighty in the land.

I hear them hail thy bright ascendant star.

Has thou no scar?

Hast thou no wound?

Yet I was wounded by the archers, spent,

Leaned Me against a tree to die; and rent

By ravening beasts that compassed Me, I swooned;

Has thou no wound?

No wound, no scar?

Yet, as the Master shall the servant be,

And, pierced are the feet that follow Me;

But thine are whole; can he have followed far

Who has no wound or scar?

~ Amy Carmichael

I.   Jesus the Final and Full Revelation of God: In order to understand the Father, we must come to know the person of Jesus Christ.

II. Jesus the Finished Redemption of God: Jesus alone is God's anointed prophet and priest to bring us back into relationship to God.

III. Finally, not only is Jesus God's Full Revelation and finished Redemption, he is also the Final Rule and standard of true humanity.

Chart of Biblical Studies

Rev. Dr. Don L. Davis

Type of Criticism	The Task in Bible Study	What is Studied	View of the Bible	Proof Level	Strengths	Weaknesses	Level of Criticism
Form Criticism	Trace the oral traditions and earliest stories associated with the texts	Oral traditions of the people of God, along with the early Church	Product of human tradition	Low	Evolving sense of the Bible's origin	Too speculative	Higher
Source Criticism	Discover the written sources used in the creation of the books	Comparing texts in various books to see similarities and contrasts	Product of human ingenuity	Low	Ability to identify key sources	No way to prove its claims	Higher
Linguistic Criticism	Study the ancient languages, words and grammar	Study of the ancient Hebrew, koine Greek, and Aramaic	Product of human culture	Mid	In-depth meaning of ancient language	Too far removed from the language	Lower
Textual Criticism	Compare the variant manuscripts to find the best reading	Focus on different manuscripts and their families of texts	Product of textual research	High	Multitude of reliable manuscripts available	Far too extensive number	Lower
Literary Criticism	Determine the author, style, recipient, and genre	Different types of literature, background study on the books	Product of literary genius	High	Discovering what types of literature mean	We tend to read too much into it	Higher

Chart of Biblical Studies (continued)

Type of Criticism	The Task in Bible Study	What is Studied	View of the Bible	Proof Level	Strengths	Weaknesses	Level of Criticism
Canonical Criticism	Analyze the Church's acceptance, view and use of the text	History of the Bible in ancient Israel and the early Church (councils, conventions)	Product of religious community	High	Taking the community's view of the Bible seriously	Tends to make the Bible merely a group book	Higher
Redaction Criticism	Focus on the theology of the person who wrote it	Intense study of individual books to understand the meaning of the author's theme and views	Product of creative personality	Mid	Deep analysis of an author's entire collection of writings	Does not correlate the Bible with other books	Higher
Historical Criticism	Investigate the historical setting, culture, and background	Research of the ancient cultures, their customs, and their history	Product of historical forces	Mid	Firmer grasp of historical issues of the text	Too far removed from the history	Higher
Translation Studies	Provide a clear, readable translation based on the best manuscripts	Understanding of the receiving culture's language along with the meanings of the text for the best translation	Product of dynamic interpretation	Mid	Pursuing a version of the Bible in one's own tongue and thought world	Reflects our own opinions about the text's meaning	Lower

Checklist of Narrative Elements

Adapted from Leland Ryken. How to Read the Bible as Literature.

I.   What Is the *Setting* of the Story?

A. Physical surroundings

B. Historical environment

C. Cultural situation

D. Interpersonal relationships and situation

II. Who Are the *Characters* in the Story?

A. Who are the main/supporting players in the story?

B. Who is the "protagonist?" Who is the "antagonist?"

C. How does the author describe the character's development?

D. What is the final outcome of the character's life and choices?

III. What Plot *Conflicts* Exist within the Story?

A. What are the central conflicts with God?

B. What are the central conflicts with others?

C. What are the central conflicts within the characters themselves?

D. What are the central conflicts between the character and their situation?

IV. What Are the Aspects of *Narrative Suspense* Revealed in the Story?

A. What influences make us sympathize with the characters?

B. What produces disgust and aversion between us and the characters?

C. How are we made to approve of what the characters did?

D. What events or happenings cause us to disapprove of the characters?

Checklist of Narrative Elements (continued)

V. What Insight Do the Characters Give Us as a "Commentary on Living"?

   A. Reality: What is the view of reality portrayed in the story and the character?

   B. Morality: What constitutes good and bad in the context of this story?

   C. Value: What is of ultimate concern and value in the story?

VI. How Does the Story *Unify* Itself in its Various Parts?

   A. How does the organization of the story contribute to its unity?

   B. What is the sequence of events in this story? (Beginning, Middle, and End)

   C. In what way does the story's end resolve the questions raised at the beginning?

VII. How Are the Characters *Tested*, and What *Choices* Do They Make?

   A. What is the dilemma/problem/conflict the protagonist is seeking to overcome?

   B. What character quality is tested in the protagonist ?

   C. What alternative life choices are open to the characters in the story?

   D. Which decisions do the characters make, and what is the result of their decisions?

VIII. How Do the Characters *Progress and Grow* (or Decline and Fall) in the Story?

   A. Where do the characters begin in the story?

   B. How do the experiences of the character affect their development?

   C. Where do the individual characters eventually wind up as a result of their experiences, and the choices they made within them?

IX. What *Foils, Dramatic Irony, and Poetic Justice* Are Used in the Story?

A. Foils: what characters are set against each other as foes in the story?

B. Dramatic irony: When is the reader informed of situations and realities that the characters themselves are unaware of?

X. What Items Are *Repeated, Highlighted, and Foregrounded* in the Story?

A. Repetition: what phrases, items, themes, issues, or actions are repeated?

B. Highlighting: what things in the characters and events are emphasized above other things?

C. Foregrounding: what things are made to stand out "center stage" in the flow of the story?

XI. What Is the *Point of View* of the Author of the Story?

A. What comments does the author give us about the characters and events in the story?

B. What feelings do you believe the story is intending to generate?

C. How are the materials and details arranged to communicate the author's viewpoint clearly?

Christ's View of the Bible

Paul P. Enns. The Moody Handbook of Theology (electronic ed.). Chicago: Moody Press, 1997.

In determining the nature of biblical inspiration, nothing could be more significant than determining the view Christ held regarding the Scriptures. Certainly no one ought to hold a lower view of Scripture than He held; His view of the Scriptures ought to be the determinant and the norm for other persons' views. That is the foundational argument of R. Laird Harris. In defending the inspiration of the Scriptures he does not use 2 Timothy 3.16 or 2 Peter 1.21 as the primary argument (although he recognizes their validity); he instead argues from the standpoint of Christ's view of the Scriptures.

(1) Inspiration of the whole. In His use of the Old Testament Christ gave credence to the inspiration of the entire Old Testament. In Matthew 5.17–18 Christ affirmed that not the smallest letter or stroke would pass from the law until it would be fulfilled. In v. 17 He referred to the law or the prophets, a common phrase designating the entire Old Testament. In this rather strong statement, Jesus affirmed the inviolability of the entire Old Testament and thereby affirmed the inspiration of the entire Old Testament.

In Luke 24.44 Jesus reminded the disciples that all the things written about Him in the law of Moses, the prophets, and the Psalms must be fulfilled. The disciples had failed to understand the teachings concerning the death and resurrection of Christ in the Old Testament, but because of the inspiration of the Old Testament, those prophesied events had to take place. By His threefold designation of the Old Testament, Christ was affirming the inspiration and authority of the entire Old Testament.

When Jesus debated with the unbelieving Jews concerning His right to be called the Son of God He referred them to Psalm 82.6 and reminded them "the Scripture cannot be broken" (John 10.35). "It means that Scripture cannot be emptied of its force by being shown to be erroneous." It is noteworthy that Jesus referred to a rather insignificant passage from the Old Testament and indicated that the Scripture could not be set aside or annulled.

(2) Inspiration of the parts. Christ quoted from the Old Testament profusely and frequently. His arguments hinged on the integrity of the Old Testament passage He was quoting. By this method of argumentation, Christ was affirming the inspiration of the individual texts or books of the Old Testament. A few examples will suffice. In Jesus' encounter with Satan at the time of His

temptation, He refuted the arguments of Satan by a reference to Deuteronomy. In Matthew 4.4, 7, 10 Jesus quoted from Deuteronomy 8.3; 6.13, 16, indicating Satan was wrong and emphasizing that these words written in Deuteronomy had to be fulfilled. In Matthew 21.42 Jesus quoted from Psalm 118.22, which teaches that the Messiah would be rejected. In Matthew 12.18–21 Jesus quoted from Isaiah 42.1–4, showing that His peaceable, gentle disposition and His inclusion of the Gentiles had all been foretold in the prophetic writings. These are only selected examples, revealing that Christ quoted from various parts of the Old Testament, affirming their inspiration and authority.

(3) Inspiration of the words. In defending the doctrine of the resurrection to the Sadducees, Jesus quoted from Exodus 3.6 (significant because the Sadducees held only to the Pentateuch), "I am the God of Abraham." In this response Jesus' entire argument hinged on the words "I am." Jesus was apparently supplying the verb which the Hebrew text only implies. Thus He supported the Septuagint (Greek) version which includes the verb. That version was so highly regarded by many of the Lord's contemporaries that it was practically equated with the original Scriptures.

In affirming the resurrection Jesus reminded the Sadducees that Exodus 3.6 said "I am." He elaborated: "God is not the God of the dead but of the living." If the words of the Old Testament were not inspired, His argument was useless; but if the very words of the Old Testament were actually inspired, then His argument carried enormous weight. In fact, Jesus' argument hinges on the present tense of the statement. Because it was written in Exodus 3.6, "I am....", the doctrine of the resurrection could be affirmed; God is the God of the living patriarchs.

A similar example is found in Matthew 22.44 where Jesus, in debating the Pharisees, explained that their concept of Messiah was wrong. The Pharisees thought of Messiah as a political redeemer but Jesus shows them in His quotation from Psalm 110.1 that David, Israel's greatest king, saw Messiah as greater than himself, calling Him Lord. The entire argument of Christ rests on the phrase "my Lord." In quoting Psalm 110.1, Jesus rested His argument on the inspiration of the precise words "my Lord." If Psalm 110.1 did not read exactly "my Lord" then Christ's argument was in vain. An additional example is Christ's use of Psalm 82.6 in John 10.34 where His entire argument rests on the word "gods."

(4) Inspiration of the letters. In a number of His statements Christ reveals that He believed the letters of Scripture were inspired. In Matthew 5.18 Jesus declared, "not the smallest letter or stroke shall pass away from the Law, until all is accomplished." The term "smallest letter" refers to the Hebrew letter yodh, which looks like an apostrophe ('). The "stroke" refers to the minute distinction between two Hebrew letters. An equivalent would be the distinction between an O and a Q. Only the little "tail" distinguishes the Q from the O. Jesus emphasized that all the details of the Old Testament writings would be fulfilled down to the very letter.

(5) Inspiration of the New Testament. In the Upper Room discourse Christ made a significant statement that seems to point to the ultimate, accurate recording of the New Testament writings. In John 14.26 Jesus indicated that the Holy Spirit would provide accurate recall for the apostles as they penned the words of Scripture, thus guaranteeing their accuracy (cf. John 16.12–15). This may explain how an old man such as John, when penning the life of Christ, could accurately describe the details of the events that occurred years earlier. The Holy Spirit gave John and the other writers accurate recall of the events. Hence, Jesus affirmed not only the inspiration of the Old Testament but also the New Testament.

An obvious conclusion is that Jesus Christ held a very high view of Scripture, affirming its inspiration in the entire Old Testament–the various books of the Old Testament, the precise words, the actual letters–and He pointed to the inspiration of the New Testament. Surely those who hold to only conceptual inspiration or other variants need to reconsider the attitude of Jesus to the Scriptures. Ought His view of the Bible not to be the standard? Is it legitimate to hold a lower view of Scripture than He held?

Christus Victor
An Integrated Vision for the Christian Life

Rev. Dr. Don L. Davis

For the Church

- The Church is the primary extension of Jesus in the world
- Ransomed treasure of the victorious, risen Christ
- Laos: The people of God
- God's new creation: presence of the future
- Locus and agent of the Already/Not Yet Kingdom

For Gifts

- God's gracious endowments and benefits from *Christus Victor*
- Pastoral offices to the Church
- The Holy Spirit's sovereign dispensing of the gifts
- Stewardship: divine, diverse gifts for the common good

For Theology and Doctrine

- The authoritative Word of Christ's victory: the Apostolic Tradition: the Holy Scriptures
- Theology as commentary on the grand narrative of God
- *Christus Victor* as the core theological framework for meaning in the world
- The Nicene Creed: the Story of God's triumphant grace

For Spirituality

- The Holy Spirit's presence and power in the midst of God's people
- Sharing in the disciplines of the Spirit
- Gatherings, lectionary, liturgy, and our observances in the Church Year
- Living the life of the risen Christ in the rhythm of our ordinary lives

For Worship

- People of the Resurrection: unending celebration of the people of God
- Remembering, participating in the Christ event in our worship
- Listen and respond to the Word
- Transformed at the Table, the Lord's Supper
- The presence of the Father through the Son in the Spirit

Christus Victor

*Destroyer of Evil and Death
Restorer of Creation
Victor o'er Hades and Sin
Crusher of Satan*

For Evangelism and Mission

- Evangelism as unashamed declaration and demonstration of *Christus Victor* to the world
- The Gospel as Good News of kingdom pledge
- We proclaim God's Kingdom come in the person of Jesus of Nazareth
- The Great Commission: go to all people groups making disciples of Christ and his Kingdom
- Proclaiming Christ as Lord and Messiah

For Justice and Compassion

- The gracious and generous expressions of Jesus through the Church
- The Church displays the very life of the Kingdom
- The Church demonstrates the very life of the Kingdom of heaven right here and now
- Having freely received, we freely give (no sense of merit or pride)
- Justice as tangible evidence of the Kingdom come

Chronological Table of the New Testament

Rev. Dr. Don L. Davis, adapted from Robert Yarbrough

Date	Christian History	NT	Roman History
c. 28-30	Public ministry of Jesus	Gospels	14-37, Tiberious, emperor
c. 33	Conversion of Paul	Acts 9.1-13	—
c. 35	Paul's first post-conversion Jerusalem visit	Gal. 1.18	—
c. 35-46	Paul in Cilicia and Syria	Gal. 1.21	—
—	—	—	c. 37-41, Gaius, emperor c. 41-54, Claudius, emperor
c. 46	Paul's second Jerusalem visit	Gal. 2.1; Acts 11.27-50	—
c. 47-48	Paul and Barnabas in Cyprus and Galatia (1st Journey)	Acts 13-14	—
c. 48?	Letter to the Galatians	—	—
c. 49	Council of Jerusalem	Acts 15	—
c. 49-50	Paul and Silas from Syrian Antioch through Asia Minor to Macedonia and Achaia (2nd Journey)	Acts 15.36-18.21	—
c. 50	Letters to the Thessalonians	—	—
c. 50-52	Paul in Corinth	—	c. 51-52, Gallio, proconsul of Achaia
Summer 52	Paul's third Jerusalem visit	—	c. 52-59, Felix, procurator of Judea
c. 52-55	Paul in Ephesus	—	c. 54-68, Nero, emperor
c. 55-56	Letters to the Corinthians	—	—
c. 55-57	Paul in Macedonia, Illyricum, and Achaia (3rd Journey)	Acts 18.22-21.15	—
Early 57	Letter to the Romans	—	—
May 57	Paul's fourth (and last) Jerusalem visit	Acts 21.17	—
c. 57-59	Paul's imprisonment in Caesarea	Acts 23.23	c. 59, Festus succeeds Felix as procurator of Judea
Sept. 59	Paul's voyage to Rome begins	Acts 27-28	—
Feb. 60	Paul's arrival in Rome	—	—
c. 60-62	Paul's house arrest in Rome	—	—
c. 60-62?	Captivity Letters (Ephesians, Philippians, Colossians, Philemon)	—	c. 62, death of Festus; Albinus procurator of Judea
c. 65?	Paul visits Spain (4th Journey?)	—	c. 64, Fire of Rome
c. ??	Pastoral Letters (1 and 2 Timothy, Titus)	—	—
c. 65?	Death of Paul	—	—

The Church Leadership Paradigm
The Case for Biblical Leadership
Rev. Dr. Don L. Davis

1. The ***Kingdom of God*** has come in the person of ***Jesus of Nazareth***, and is now manifest through the Spirit in the Church.

2. The cities of the world, as strongholds of the devil, desperately need the ***presence*** and ***witness*** of the Church.

3. The Church cannot thrive and provide witness without ***leadership***.

4. Authentic leadership in the Church must be ***called by God, represent Jesus Christ, be gifted by the Spirit, and confirmed by others*** in the body.

5. Called, endowed, and confirmed leaders must be given ***authority, resources, and opportunity*** in order to facilitate maturity and equip the saints for ministry.

The Church Plant Team
Forming an Apostolic Band
World Impact, Inc.

Multiple Team Leader

Volunteers

Team Leader

Support Team
Members

Core Team
Members

Support Team
Members

Volunteers

Volunteers

Adopting a New Ministry Lifestyle
Resourcing and Oversight
Team Charter
Building and Sustaining
Christian Community

Church Planting Models

Rev. Dr. Don L. Davis

The following questions are designed to help us explore the various options available to the cross-cultural urban church planter in establishing congregations among the poor. Our dialogue today hopefully will isolate some of the critical issues necessary for a church plant team to think through in order to make its selection as to what particular kind of church they ought to plant, given the culture, population, and other factors encountered in its particular mission field.

1.   What is the definition of the phrase "church planting models"? Why might it be important to consider various options in planting a church among the poor in the city?

2.   How would you characterize the various models (or other) which are available to an urban church plant team? What would you consider to be its strengths and/or weaknesses in regard to planting churches among the poor in the city?

   a.   Founding pastor model - a leader moves into a community with a commitment to lead and shepherd the church that is planted.

   b.   Church split model?! - a new church is formed due to fundamental disagreement over some issue of morality, Bible interpretation, or schism.

   c.   Colonization model - a central assembly commissions an entire group (usually with leadership and members already organized) into an unreached community as a kind of ready-made nucleus of the church which is to be formed.

   d.   Beachhead or Mother Church model - a strong, central congregation determines to become a kind of sending center and nurturing headquarters for new churches planted through its oversight and auspices, in the immediate area and/or beyond.

   e.   Cell Church model - once centralized assembly which considers the heart of its life and ministry to occur in the cells which are connected structurally and pastorally to the central congregation; their participation together constitutes the church.

Church Planting Models (continued)

f.   Home Church model - a church, which although similar to a cell church model, is intentionally planted with greater attention given to the authority and autonomy of the gathering of Christians who meet regularly in their respective homes.

g.   Missionary model - a church where a cross-cultural church planter seeks to plant a church among an unreached people with an intent from the beginning to help the church to be self-propagating, self-governing, and self-supporting.

3.   What are the critical issues (e.g., culture, the tradition of the church planters, and contextualization) which ought to be factored most into selecting the appropriate model for in planting a church cross-culturally in the city?

4.   Of all the things which a church planter may be aware of, what do you believe is the central element he or she must understand in order to choose the "right" option for them?

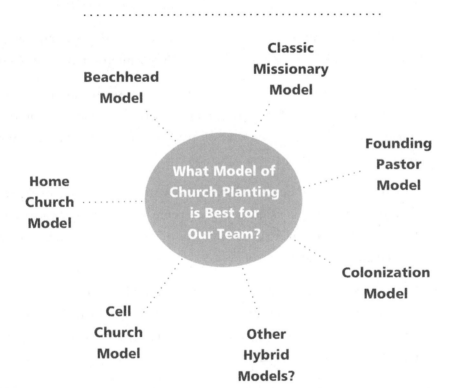

The Church Year (Western Church)

The Urban Ministry Institute

The purpose of the liturgical calendar is to relive the major events in Jesus' life in real time.

Date	Event	Purpose
Begins late Nov. or early Dec.	Advent	A season of anticipation and repentance which focuses on **the First and Second Comings of Christ**. The dual focus means that Advent both begins and ends the Christian year (Isa. 9.1-7, 11.1-16; Mark 1.1-8).
Dec. 25	Christmas	Celebrates **the Birth of Christ** (Luke 2.1-20).
Jan. 6	Epiphany	The Feast of Epiphany on January 6 commemorates the coming of the Magi which reveals Christ's mission to the world. The entire season of Epiphany then emphasizes **the way in which Christ revealed himself to the world as the Son of God** (Luke 2.32; Matt. 17.1-6; John 12.32).
The seventh Wednesday before Easter	Ash Wednesday	A day of fasting and repentance that reminds us that we are disciples about to begin **the journey with Jesus that ends in the cross** (Luke 9.51). Ash Wednesday begins the observance of Lent.
40 days before Easter (excluding Sundays)	Lent	A time for reflection on **the suffering and death of Jesus**. Lent also emphasizes "death to self" so that, like Jesus, we prepare ourselves to obey God no matter what sacrifice it involves. Lenten observance calls for people to fast as a way of affirming this attitude of obedience (Luke 5.35; 1 Cor. 9.27; 2 Tim. 2.4; Heb. 11.1-3).
Moveable depending on the date of Easter Sunday which occurs in March or April	Holy Week	*Palm Sunday* The Sunday before Easter which commemorates **the Triumphal Entry of Christ** (John 12.12-18). *Maundy* Thursday* The Thursday before Easter which commemorates the giving of **the New Commandment and the Lord's Supper** prior to Christ's Death (Mark 14.12-26; John 13). (* From the Latin mandatum novarum - "new commandment.") *Good Friday* The Friday before Easter which commemorates **the crucifixion of Christ** (John 18-19). *Easter Sunday* The Sunday which celebrates **the resurrection of Christ** (John 20).
40 days after Easter	Ascension Day	Celebrates **the Ascension of Christ** to heaven at which time God "seated him at his right hand in the heavenly realms, far above all rule and authority, power and dominion, and every title that can be given, not only in the present age but also in the one to come" (Eph. 1.20b-21; 1 Pet. 3.22; Luke 24.17-53).
7th Sunday after Easter	Pentecost	The day which commemorates the coming of the Holy Spirit to the Church. **Jesus is now present with all his people** (John 16; Acts 2).
Nov. 1st	All Saints Day	A time to remember those heroes of the faith who have come before us (especially those who died for the Gospel). **The living Christ is now seen in the world through the words and deeds of his people** (John 14.12; Heb. 11; Rev. 17.6).

The Church Year (continued)

The Church Year Follows the Ordering of the Gospels and Acts

- It begins with the birth of Christ (Advent to Epiphany).

- It then focuses on the revelation of his mission to the world (Epiphany).

- It reminds us that Jesus set his face toward Jerusalem and the cross (Ash Wednesday and Lent).

- It chronicles his final week, his crucifixion and his resurrection (Holy Week).

- It affirms his Ascension to the Father's right hand in glory (Ascension Day).

- It celebrates the birth of his Church through the ministry of his Spirit (Pentecost).

- It remembers the history of his Church throughout the ages (All Saints Day).

- Advent both ends the cycle and begins it again. It looks forward to his Second Coming as the conclusion of the Church year but also prepares to remember again his first coming and thus starts the Church year afresh.

Birth
⇩
Ministry
⇩
Passion
⇩
Ascension
⇩
Descent of the Spirit
⇩
The Church through the Ages
⇩
Second Coming

Colors Associated With the Church Year

Christmas Season (Christmas Day through start of Epiphany) - *White and Gold*

Epiphany Season – *Green*

Ash Wednesday and Lent – **Purple**

Holy Week

  Palm Sunday - *Purple*

  Maundy Thursday - *Purple*

  Good Friday - *Black*

  Easter Sunday - *White and Gold*

Ascension Day - *White and Gold*

Pentecost – *Red*

All Saints Day – *Red*

Advent Season (Fourth Sunday before Christmas through Christmas Eve) - *Purple*

The Meaning of the Colors

Black
Mourning, Death

Gold
Majesty, Glory

Green
Hope, Life

Purple
Royalty, Repentance

Red
Holy Spirit (flame)
Martyrdom (blood)

White
Innocence, Holiness, Joy

Circle of Jewish Calendar

Robert Webber, The Biblical Foundations of Christian Worship. Peabody: Hendrickson, 1993. p. 191.

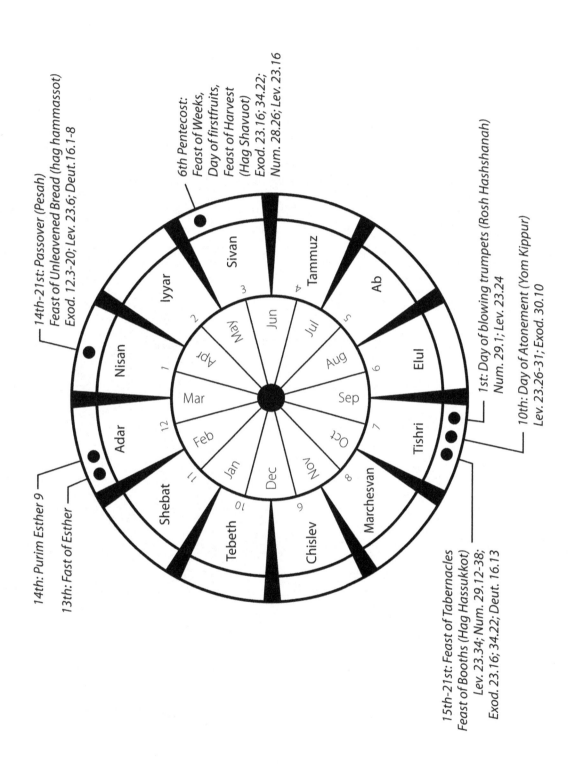

14th-21st: Passover (Pesah)
Feast of Unleavened Bread (hag hammassot)
Exod. 12.3-20; Lev. 23.6; Deut.16.1-8

6th Pentecost:
Feast of Weeks,
Day of firstfruits,
Feast of Harvest
(Hag Shavuot)
Exod. 23.16; 34.22;
Num. 28.26; Lev. 23.16

1st: Day of blowing trumpets (Rosh Hashshanah)
Num. 29.1; Lev. 23.24

10th: Day of Atonement (Yom Kippur)
Lev. 23.26-31; Exod. 30.10

14th: Purim Esther 9

13th: Fast of Esther

15th-21st: Feast of Tabernacles
Feast of Booths (Hag Hassukkot)
Lev. 23.34; Num. 29.12-38;
Exod. 23.16; 34.22; Deut. 16.13

The Communal Context of Authentic Christian Leadership

Rev. Dr. Don L. Davis

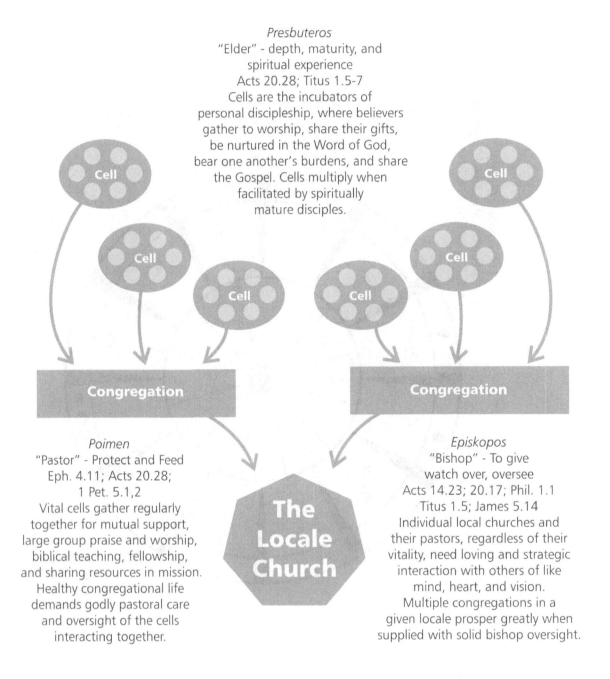

Presbuteros
"Elder" - depth, maturity, and spiritual experience
Acts 20.28; Titus 1.5-7
Cells are the incubators of personal discipleship, where believers gather to worship, share their gifts, be nurtured in the Word of God, bear one another's burdens, and share the Gospel. Cells multiply when facilitated by spiritually mature disciples.

Cell

Cell

Cell

Cell

Cell

Cell

Congregation

Congregation

Poimen
"Pastor" - Protect and Feed
Eph. 4.11; Acts 20.28;
1 Pet. 5.1,2
Vital cells gather regularly together for mutual support, large group praise and worship, biblical teaching, fellowship, and sharing resources in mission. Healthy congregational life demands godly pastoral care and oversight of the cells interacting together.

The Locale Church

Episkopos
"Bishop" - To give watch over, oversee
Acts 14.23; 20.17; Phil. 1.1
Titus 1.5; James 5.14
Individual local churches and their pastors, regardless of their vitality, need loving and strategic interaction with others of like mind, heart, and vision. Multiple congregations in a given locale prosper greatly when supplied with solid bishop oversight.

Presbuteros, "an elder" is another term for the same person as bishop or overseer . . . . The term "elder" indicates the mature spiritual experience and understanding of those so described; the term "bishop" or "overseer," indicates the character of the work undertaken. According to the divine will and appointment, as in the NT, there were to be bishops in every local church, Acts 14.23; 20.17; Phil. 1.1; Titus 1.5; James 5.14." - *Vines Complete Expository Dictionary*. Nashville: Thomas Nelson Publishers, 1996. p. 195

Communicating Messiah: The Relationship of the Gospels

Adapted from N. R. Ericson and L. M. Perry. John: A New Look at the Fourth Gospel

	Matthew	Mark	Luke	John
Date	c. 65	c. 59	c 61	c. 90
Chapters	28	16	24	21
Verses	1,071	666	1.151	879
Period	36 years	4 years	37 years	4 years
Audience	The Jews	The Romans	The Greeks	The World
Christ As	The King	The Servant	The Man	The Son of God
Emphasis	Sovereignty	Humility	Humanity	Deity
Sign	The Lion	The Ox	The Man	The Eagle
Ending	Resurrection	Empty Tomb	Promise of the Spirit	Promise of his Second Comin
Written In	Antioch?	Rome	Rome	Ephesus
Key Verse	27.37	10.45	19.10	20.30-31
Key Word	Kingdom	Service	Salvation	Believe
Purpose	Presentation of Jesus Christ		Interpretation of Jesus the Messiah	
Time to Read	2 hours	1 ¼ hours	2 ¼ hours	1 ½ hours

A Comparison of Translation Philosophies
Common English Versions of the Bible
Rev. Dr. Don L. Davis

Most Literally Word-for-Word ◄ ·········   ·········► *Least Literally Word-for-Word*

Formal Equivalence   **Dynamic Equivalence**   **Paraphrase**

New American Standard Bible (NASB)

New King James Version (NKJV)

New Revised Standard Version (NRSV)

English Standard Version (ESV)

International Version(NIV)

New Jerusalem Bible (NJB)

Revised English Bible (REB)

Today's English Version (TEV)

Contemporary English Version (CEV)

New Living Translation (NLT)

JB Phillips Version (Phillips)

The Living Bible (LB)

The Message

Cotton Patch Gospels

The Compass of Narrative Elements

Charting a Course toward a Story's Meaning

Rev. Dr. Don L. Davis

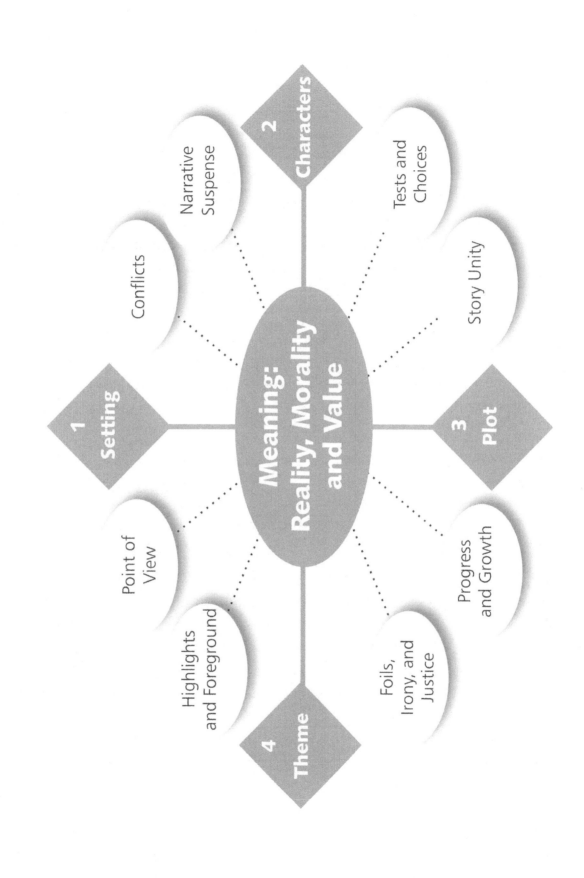

The Complexity of Difference: Race, Culture, Class

Don L. Davis and Terry Cornett

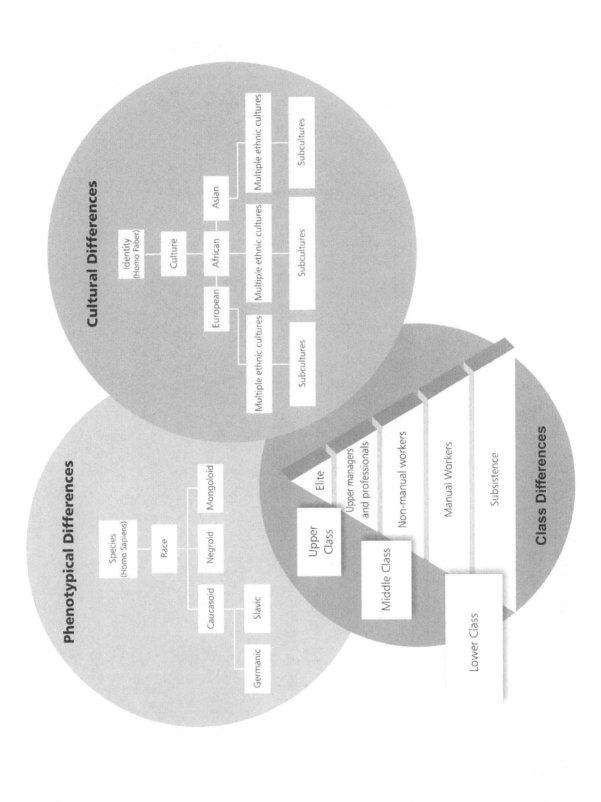

Cultural Differences

Identity (Homo Faber)

Culture

European · African · Asian

Multiple ethnic cultures — Multiple ethnic cultures — Multiple ethnic cultures

Subcultures — Subcultures — Subcultures

Phenotypical Differences

Species (Homo Sapiens)

Race

Caucasoid · Negroid · Mongoloid

Germanic · Slavic

Class Differences

Upper Class — Elite

Middle Class — Upper managers and professionals

Non-manual workers

Manual Workers

Lower Class — Subsistence

Contextualization Among Muslims, Hindus, and Buddhists: A Focus on "Insider Movements"

John and Anna Travis

This article was taken from Mission Frontiers: The Bulletin of the US Center for World Mission, Vol. 27, No. 5; September-October 2005; ISSN 0889-9436.

John and Anna Travis, along with their two children, have lived in a tight-knit Asian Muslim neighborhood for nearly 20 years. They are involved in contextualized sharing of the good news, Bible translation and the ministry of prayer for inner healing. They have also helped train field workers in a number of Asian, Middle Eastern and North African countries. Both are pursuing graduate degrees, with John a Ph.D. candidate.

*The following is excerpted by permission of the authors. A larger version of this article is found in chapter 23 of **Appropriate Christianity** (William Carey Library Publishers, 2005).*

Much has been written over the past 25 years on the application of contextualization in ministry among Muslims. In 1998 I (John) wrote an article for the *Evangelical Missions Quarterly* in which I presented a model for comparing six different types of ekklesia or congregations (which I refer to as "Christ-centered communities") found in the Muslim world today (Travis 1998). These six types of Christ-centered communities are differentiated in terms of three factors: language, cultural forms, and religious identity. This model, referred to as the C1-C6 spectrum (or continuum), has generated much discussion, especially around the issue of fellowships of "Muslim followers of Jesus" (the C5 position on the scale).

Parshall (1998), an advocate of contextualization, feels that C5 crosses the line and falls into dangerous syncretism. In subsequent writings many of Parshall's concerns have been addressed (see Massey 2000, Gilliland 1998, Winter 1999, Travis 1998 and 2000). *Yet in spite of concerns that some may have on this issue, the fact remains that in a number of countries today, there are groups of Muslims who have genuinely come to faith in Jesus Christ, yet have remained legally and socio-religiously within the local Muslim community. . . .*

We will not be contending that C5 is the best or only thing God is doing in the Muslim world today; indeed God is bringing Muslims to Himself in a great diversity of ways, some of which we may only understand in eternity. What we will argue, however, is that one way God is moving at this point in salvation history, is by sovereignly drawing Muslims to Himself, revolutionizing them spiritually, yet calling them to remain as salt and light in the religious community of their birth. . . .

In recent years we have had the privilege of meeting a number of C5 Muslims, and although our religious backgrounds and forms of worship are quite different, we have experienced sweet fellowship in Isa the Messiah. There is no question in our minds that these C5 Muslims are born-again members of the Kingdom of God, called to live out the Gospel inside the religious borders of their birth. As we have continued to see the limits of C4 in our context, and as our burden for lost Muslims only grows heavier, we have become convinced that a C5 expression of faith could actually be viable for our precious Muslim neighbors and probably large blocs of the Muslim world. We ourselves, being "Christian-background-believers," maintain a C4 lifestyle, but we believe God has called us to help "birth a C5 movement" in our context . . . .

We have attended many Muslim funerals. We grieve every time we see another Muslim friend buried, having passed into eternity without salvation in Christ. As we have seen the resistance toward changing religions and the huge gap between the Muslim and Christian communities, we feel that fighting the religion-changing battle is the wrong battle. We have little hope in our lifetime to believe for a major enough cultural, political and religious change to occur in our context such that Muslims would become open to entering Christianity on a wide scale.

But we do have great hope, as great as the promises of God, to believe that an "insider movement" could get off the ground – that vast numbers could discover that salvation in Isa the Messiah is waiting for every Muslim who will believe. We sense the desire of Jesus Himself to take the "yeast" of His Gospel to the inner chambers of Muslim communities, calling men, women and children to walk with Him as Lord and Savior, remaining vital members of their families and Muslim communities.

Theoretical and Theological Issues Regarding C5 Movements

. . . Our intent is not to prove if C5 *can* happen, as case studies already indicate that it *is* happening. Rather, we hope to help build a framework from which to understand this phenomenon and to answer some of the questions which have arisen such as: From a biblical perspective, can a person be truly saved and continue to be a Muslim? Doesn't a follower of Christ need to identify himself as a Christian and officially join the Christian faith? Can a Muslim follower of Christ retain all Muslim practices, in particular praying in the mosque toward Mecca and continuing to repeat the Muslim creed? This section will be framed around ten premises [elaborated in the full version of this article].

- *Premise 1*: For Muslims, culture, politics and religion are nearly inseparable, making changing religions a total break with society.

- *Premise 2*: Salvation is by grace alone through relationship / allegiance to Jesus Christ. Changing religions is not a prerequisite for nor a guarantee of salvation.

- *Premise 3*: Jesus' primary concern was the establishment of the Kingdom of God, not the founding of a new religion.

- *Premise 4*: The very term "Christian" is often misleading – not all called Christian are in Christ and not all in Christ are called Christian.

- *Premise 5*: Often gaps exist between what people actually believe and what their religion or group officially teaches.

- *Premise 6*: Some Islamic beliefs and practices are in keeping with the Word of God; some are not.

- *Premise 7*: Salvation involves a process. Often the exact point of transfer from the kingdom of darkness to the Kingdom of light is not known.

- *Premise 8*: A follower of Christ needs to be set free by Jesus from spiritual bondages in order to thrive in his/her life with Him.

- *Premise 9*: Due to the lack of Church structure and organization, C5 movements must have an exceptionally high reliance on the Spirit and the Word as their primary source of instruction.

- *Premise 10*: A contextual theology can only properly be developed through a dynamic interaction of actual ministry experience, the specific leading of the Spirit and the study of the Word of God.

A Look Beyond the Islamic Milieu

. . . An amazing book has just been republished by William Carey Library – *Churchless Christianity* (Hoefer 2001). The author, while formerly teaching at a seminary in India, began hearing stories of Hindus who in fact were worshipping and following Jesus in the privacy of their own homes. Knowing that there are many Hindus who have high regard for Jesus as a teacher, he set out to determine

"The Church Emerges from the Inside"
A missionary couple working in Asia report, "In 1990 we were sent out into the field as church planters. But over the last year we have observed that when the gospel is sown on fertile soil within already established social groupings – like a circle of close neighbor friends, or the multi-generations an extended household – the church emerges from the inside. It is not so much that we are planting a church but that we are planting the gospel, and as the gospel seed grows, the church or churches form to the shape of existing networks."

Contextualization Among Muslims, Hindus, and Buddhists (continued)

if indeed they had accepted Him as Lord and Savior or only as an enlightened guru. His quest became the basis of a doctoral dissertation in which he interviewed 80 such Hindu and Muslim families in the area of Madras, India.

Hoefer found that that a large number of these families, which have never been baptized or joined churches, indeed have a true relationship with Christ and pray and study His Word fervently. Hoefer says that most want baptism, but have never seen a baptism which is not one in the same with becoming an official member of a particular church. His conclusion after a very extensive process of interviews and statistical analysis is that in Madras there are 200,000 Hindus and Muslims who worship Jesus – an amount equal to the total number of Christians in that city!

It is instructive to note that 200 years ago, William Carey referred to Hindu followers of Jesus as "Christian Hindoos." Apparently this was due to the strong linkage in the minds of the Indians (and presumably William Carey) between being Hindu and being Indian (etymologically the word India comes from Hindia, the land of the Hindus). Rather than Hinduism being close to monotheistic faiths, it is just the opposite: adherents can worship any number of gods and goddesses. It appears that this openness allows room to exclusively worship the God of the Bible as the one true God (note the words of Joshua in Joshua 24:14-15).

In the early 1900s, Indian evangelist Sadhu Sundar Singh ran into hidden groups of Jesus followers among Hindus. As he preached the Gospel in Benares, his listeners told him of a Hindu holy man who had been preaching the same message. Singh spent the night at the man's home and heard his claim that his Hindu order had been founded long ago by the apostle Thomas, and now had up to 40,000 members. Singh later observed their services (including worship, prayer, baptism and communion) which were held in places which looked exactly like Hindu shrines and temples, minus the idols. "When Sundar tried to persuade them that they should openly declare themselves as Christians, they assured him that they were doing a more effective work as secret disciples, accepted as ordinary sadhus, but drawing men's minds toward the true faith in readiness for the day when open discipleship became possible" (Davey 1950:80) [*sic*].

Recently, we met a man doing outreach among Buddhists, among whom there is an extremely high fusion of culture and religion. To my surprise he had taken the C1-C6 continuum and adapted it to a Buddhist context. Though it appears impossible for the Gospel to thrive inside Buddhism, might there not be millions of Buddhists who are nominal believers and who are only Buddhist due to birth and nationality? As Kraft has stated (1996:212-213), once this principle of true spiritual allegiance versus formal religion is grasped, "we begin to discover exciting possibilities for working within, say, Jewish or Islamic or Hindu or Buddhist or animistic cultures to reach people who will be culturally Jewish or Muslim or Hindu or animist to the end of their days but Christian in their faith allegiance". (Note: in his book Kraft defines Christian with a capital "C" as follower of Christ verses *christian* with a small "c" referring to the religious institution).

What is all of this leading to? Is there not blatant idolatry in traditional Hinduism? Yes, but not among those Hindu followers of Christ described by Hoefer and Davey. Is there not a denial by most Muslims that Jesus died on the cross? Yes, but not by those Muslims we have known who have put their faith in Christ. Is it not true that Jews teach the Messiah is yet to come? Yes, but thousands of Jews go to Messianic synagogues and believe, as did thousands of Jews in the first century, that Yeshua is indeed the long awaited Son of David.

We are tentatively coming to the conviction that God is doing a new thing to reach these remaining nations (*ta ethne*) dominated by mega-faiths. If Bosch had it right that faith in Christ wasn't meant to be a religion, could it be that we are witnessing some of the first fruits of vast movements where Jesus is causing the Gospel to break out of "Christianity"? Where those who know Jesus remain as a sweet fragrance inside the religion of their birth, and eventually the number of born-again adherents grows so large that a reform movement from inside that religion is birthed?

The process may be theologically messy, but we see no alternative. If we view both culture and religion as a person's own skin, we can look beyond it to the millions of human hearts longing for God yet longing to remain in community with their own people. This is in no way universalism (the belief that in the end all will be saved). Rather, this is a call to take much more seriously Christ's final words to go into all the world – Hindu, Buddhist, Muslim, Christian – and make disciples of all nations.

References

Bosch, David J. 1991 *Transforming Mission*. Maryknoll, NY: Orbis Books.

Davey, Cyril J. 1980 *Sadhu Sundar Singh*. Kent, UK: STL Books.

Contextualization Among Muslims, Hindus, and Buddhists (continued)

Gilliland, Dean S. 1998 "Context is Critical in Islampur Case." *Evangelical Missions Quarterly* 34(4): 415-417.

Hoefer, Herbert E. 2001 *Churchless Christianity*. Pasadena, CA: William Carey Library.

Kraft, Charles H. 1996 *Anthropology for Christian Witness*. Maryknoll, NY: Orbis Books.

Massey, Joshua. 2000 "God's Amazing Diversity in Drawing Muslims to Christ." *International Journal of Frontier Missions* 17 (1): 5-14.

Parshall, Phil. 1998 "Danger! New Directions in Contextualization." *Evangelical Missions Quarterly*. 43(4): 404-406, 409-410.

Travis, John. 1998 "Must all Muslims Leave Islam to Follow Jesus?" *Evangelical Missions Quarterly* 34(4): 411-415.

------. 2000 "Messianic Muslim Followers of Isa: A Closer Look at C5 Believers and Congregations." *International Journal of Frontier Missions* 17 (1): 53-59.

Winter, Ralph. 1999 "Going Far Enough? Taking Some Tips from the Historical Record." In *Perspectives on the World Christian Movement*. Ralph Winter and Steven Hawthorne, eds. Pp. 666-617. Pasadena, CA: William Carey Library.

Creating Coherent Urban Church Planting Movements

Discerning the Elements of Authentic Urban Christian Community

Rev. Dr. Don L. Davis

Core Evangelical Convictions

This circle represents *its most fundamental convictions and commitments*, its Affirmation of Faith, its commitment to the Gospel and those truths contained in the early Christian creeds (i.e., The Nicene Creed). These convictions are anchored in its confidence in the Word of God, and represent our unequivocal commitment to historic orthodoxy.

As members of the one, holy, apostolic, and catholic (universal) body of Christ, movements must be **ready and willing to die for their core evangelical convictions**. These convictions serve as the connection of the movements to the historic Christian faith, and as such, can never be compromised or altered.

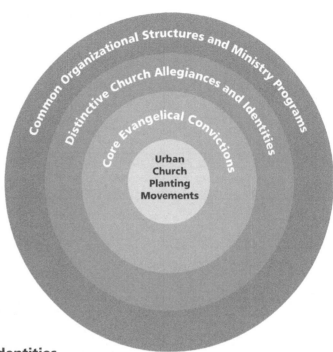

Distinctive Church Allegiances and Identities

This circle represents their distinctive *church allegiances and identities.* Urban church plant movements will coalesce around their own distinctive traditions, overseen by leaders who provide those movements with vision, instruction, and direction as they move forward together to represent Christ and his Kingdom in the inner city.

Specific traditions seek to express and live out this faithfulness to the Authoritative and Great Traditions through their worship, teaching, and service. They seek to make the Gospel clear within new cultures or sub-cultures, speaking and modeling the hope of Christ into new situations shaped by their own set of questions posed in light of their own unique circumstances. These movements, therefore, seek to contextualize the Authoritative Tradition in a way that faithfully and effectively leads new groups of people to faith in Jesus Christ, and incorporates those who believe into the community of faith that obeys his teachings and gives witness of him to others.

Urban church plant movements must be **ready and willing to articulate and defend their unique distinctives** as God's kingdom community in the city.

Common Organizational Structure and Ministry Programs

This circle represents the ways in which coherent urban church plant movements express their convictions and identity *through their own distinct organizational structures and ministry programs*. These structures and programs are designed and executed through their own specific strategies, policies, decisions, and procedures. The structures and programs represent their self-chosen methods of fleshing out their understanding of the faith as it pertains to their community purpose and mission. These are subject to change under their own legitimate processes as they apply accumulated wisdom in *how best* to accomplish their purposes in the city.

As a communities of faith in Christ, urban church movements must be encouraged to **dialogue about their structures and ministry programs** in order to discover the best possible means to contextualize the Gospel and advance the Kingdom of God among their neighbors.

Culture, Not Color: Interaction of Class, Culture, and Race

World Impact Inc.

Asian

Hispanic

African-American

White

C_1 C_2 C_3

Dominant Class and Mainstream Culture

Other Indicators of Culture:

1. Kinship and friendships
2. Upbringing
3. Values and norms
4. Language habits
5. Socio-economic background
6. Education
7. Customs

Major Cultural Indicators:

Where they live
Where they work
Where educated

Dealing With Old Ways

Adapted from Paul Hiebert

Old Beliefs, Rituals, Stories, Songs, Customs, Art, Music, Etc.

Total Denial of the Old (No Contextualization)	**Critically Dealing with the Old** (Critical Contextualization)	**Uncritically Accepting the Old** (Uncritical Contextualization)
Gospel Is Foreign - Gospel Rejected	**1) Gather Info on the Old**	**Syncretism**
Old Goes Under - Syncretism	**2) Study Biblical Teachings**	
	3) Evaluate Old in Light of Theology	
	4) New Contextualized Christian Practice	

Defining the Leaders and Members of a Church Plant Team

Rev. Dr. Don L. Davis

CD - City Director   TL - Team Leader   MTL - Multiple Team Leader

	Team Member	Team Leader	Multiple Team Leader
Definition	Member of cross-cultural church planting team	Leader of cross-cultural church plant team	Facilitator and coordinator of multiple teams
Relationship to World Impact	May be a staff member or volunteer	May be a staff member or volunteer	May be a World Impact staff member or experienced planter
Responsibility	To employ gifts to enhance the ministry of the team as it plants a viable church	To facilitate the effective operation of the team	To provide counsel, resources, and support to all teams in a given area
Training	Initial training and ongoing team input	Specialized training curriculum, personal mentoring and TUMI	TUMI course work, mentoring and regional training, and specialized input
Accountable to Whom?	Team Leader	City Director (support from MTL)	Regional VP and City Director
Time Commitments	Associated with team to plant for specified period of time as core or support member	Throughout the duration of the church plant	Regular review and substantive ministry assessment at end of CPT time
Resources	Team members and leaders, CPT "kit" (initial resource allotment)	Team members, ministry budget, access to MTL and CD	Access to sites of CPTs, access to team leaders for training and support ministries
Authority	To pursue those steps necessary to evangelize, disciple, and plant - reports to the team leader	To lead the team in its operations as it seeks to plant a church - reports to the CD and MTL	To support the team during its charter period, and decide at the end if the plant warrants further time and effort
Assignment	By CD and TL for particular time and role	By CD for duration of the church plant	By Regional VP and CD as they determine necessary
Composition	Primary members, support members, and/or volunteers	Individual or co-leaders (interns)	Individual selected by Regional VP and CD

Degrees of Authority Given to Fruit of Christocentric Use of the Old Testament

Rev. Dr. Don L. Davis

The Old Testament correlates with the New Testament, and through the aid of the Holy Spirit and the test of Scripture we may explore these connections between the people, events, and happenings of the Old Testament so as to understand how they testify of and foreshadow the Messiah, Jesus of Nazareth.

Unbiblical	Plausible	Persuasive	Binding

Denial of Scripture

Heresy

Denial of historic orthodoxy

Errors to avoid:

1. Assuming that no correlations are present

2. Assuming that something is there, but we can't see it

3. Assuming that something is there, I can see it, but I need not prove my associations

What is biblically provable

What is held by Christians

Everywhere

At all times

In all places

Heb. 5.11-14; 1 Thess. 5.21; John 7.24; Isa. 8.19-20

Delegation and Authority in Christian Leadership
Rev. Dr. Don L. Davis

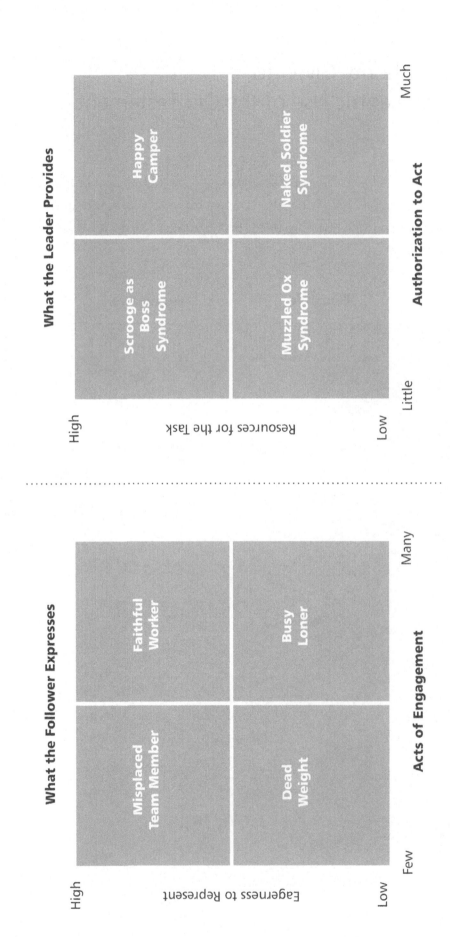

What the Leader Provides

Scrooge as Boss Syndrome

Happy Camper

Muzzled Ox Syndrome

Naked Soldier Syndrome

Resources for the Task — High / Low

Authorization to Act — Little / Much

What the Follower Expresses

Misplaced Team Member

Faithful Worker

Dead Weight

Busy Loner

Eagerness to Represent — High / Low

Acts of Engagement — Few / Many

Denominational Statements on "Sanctification"

Church of the Lutheran Brethren

http://www.clba.org/aboutus.phtml

Sanctification

Sanctification is God's gracious, continual work of spiritual renewal and growth in the life of every justified person. Through the means of grace, the Holy Spirit works to reproduce the character of Christ within the lives of all believers, instructing and urging them to live out their new nature. The Holy Spirit enables believers more and more to resist the devil, to overcome the world, and to count themselves dead to sin but alive to God in Christ Jesus. The Holy Spirit produces spiritual fruit in and bestows spiritual gifts upon all believers. He calls, empowers and equips them to serve God in the home, in the community, and as part of the Church Universal. The process of sanctification will be complete only when the believer reaches glory.

Presbyterian Church in America

http://www.pcanet.org/general/cof_chapxi-xv.htm#chapxiii

The Westminster Confession of Faith

CHAP. XIII. - Of Sanctification.

1. They, who are once effectually called, and regenerated, having a new heart, and a new spirit created in them, are further sanctified, really and personally, through the virtue of Christ's death and resurrection, by His Word and Spirit dwelling in them, the dominion of the whole body of sin is destroyed, and the several lusts thereof are more and more weakened and mortified; and they more and more quickened and strengthened in all saving graces, to the practice of true holiness, without which no man shall see the Lord.

2. This sanctification is throughout, in the whole man; yet imperfect in this life, there abiding still some remnants of corruption in every part; whence ariseth a continual and irreconcilable war, the flesh lusting against the Spirit, and the Spirit against the flesh.

3. In which war, although the remaining corruption, for a time, may much prevail; yet, through the continual supply of strength from the sanctifying Spirit of Christ, the regenerate part doth overcome; and so, the saints grow in grace, perfecting holiness in the fear of God.

Southern Baptist Convention

http://www.sbc.net/bfm/bfm2000.asp#iv

Salvation involves the redemption of the whole man, and is offered freely to all who accept Jesus Christ as Lord and Saviour, who by His own blood obtained eternal redemption for the believer. In its broadest sense salvation includes regeneration, justification, sanctification, and glorification. There is no salvation apart from personal faith in Jesus Christ as Lord.

1. Regeneration, or the new birth, is a work of God's grace whereby believers become new creatures in Christ Jesus. It is a change of heart wrought by the Holy Spirit through conviction of sin, to which the sinner responds in repentance toward God and faith in the Lord Jesus Christ. Repentance and faith are inseparable experiences of grace.

   Repentance is a genuine turning from sin toward God. Faith is the acceptance of Jesus Christ and commitment of the entire personality to Him as Lord and Saviour.

2. Justification is God's gracious and full acquittal upon principles of His righteousness of all sinners who repent and believe in Christ. Justification brings the believer unto a relationship of peace and favor with God.

3. Sanctification is the experience, beginning in regeneration, by which the believer is set apart to God's purposes, and is enabled to progress toward moral and spiritual maturity through the presence and power of the Holy Spirit dwelling in him. Growth in grace should continue throughout the regenerate person's life.

4. Glorification is the culmination of salvation and is the final blessed and abiding state of the redeemed.

   Gen. 3.15; Exod. 3.14-17; 6.2-8; Matt. 1.21; 4.17; 16.21-26; 27.22-28.6; Luke 1.68-69; 2.28-32; John 1.11-14,29; 3.3-21,36; 5.24; 10.9,28-29; 15.1-16; 17.17;

Acts 2.21; 4.12; 15.11; 16.30-31; 17.30-31; 20.32; Rom. 1.16-18; 2.4; 3.23-25; 4.3ff.; 5.8-10; 6.1-23; 8.1-18,29-39; 10.9-10,13; 13.11-14; 1 Cor. 1.18,30; 6.19-20; 15.10; 2 Cor. 5.17-20; Gal. 2.20; 3.13; 5.22-25; 6.15; Eph. 1.7; 2.8-22; 4.11-16; Phil. 2.12-13; Col. 1.9-22; 3.1ff.; 1 Thess. 5.23-24; 2 Tim. 1.12; Titus 2.11-14; Heb. 2.1-3; 5.8-9; 9.24-28; 11.1-12.8,14; James 2.14-26; 1 Pet. 1.2-23; 1 John 1.6-2.11; Rev. 3.20; 21.1-22.5.

Statements from Holiness Denominations

Church of the Nazarene

www.nazarene.org/gensec/we_believe.html

Articles of Faith

We believe that entire sanctification is that act of God, subsequent to regeneration, by which believers are made free from original sin, or depravity, and brought into a state of entire devotement to God, and the holy obedience of love made perfect. It is wrought by the baptism with the Holy Spirit, and comprehends in one experience the cleansing of the heart from sin and the abiding, indwelling presence of the Holy Spirit, empowering the believer for life and service. Entire sanctification is provided by the blood of Jesus, is wrought instantaneously by faith, preceded by entire consecration; and to this work and state of grace the Holy Spirit bears witness. This experience is also known by various terms representing its different phases, such as "Christian perfection," "perfect love," "heart purity," "the baptism with the Holy Spirit," "the fullness of the blessing," and "Christian holiness."

We believe that there is a marked distinction between a pure heart and a mature character. The former is obtained in an instant, the result of entire sanctification; the latter is the result of growth in grace. We believe that the grace of entire sanctification includes the impulse to grow in grace. However, this impulse must be consciously nurtured, and careful attention given to the requisites and processes of spiritual development and improvement in Christlikeness of character and personality. Without such purposeful endeavor one's witness may be impaired and the grace itself frustrated and ultimately lost.

(Jer. 31.31-34; Ezek. 36.25-27; Mal. 3.2-3; Matt. 3.11-12; Luke 3.16-17; John 7.37-39; 14.15-23; 17.6-20; Acts 1.5; 2.1-4; 15.8-9; Rom. 6.11-13, 19; 8.1-4, 8-14; 12.1-2; 2 Cor. 6.14-7.1; Gal. 2.20; 5.16-25; Eph. 3.14-21; 5.17-18, 25-27; Phil. 3.10-15; Col. 3.1-17; 1 Thess. 5.23-24; Heb. 4.9-11; 10.10-17; 12.1-2; 13.12; 1 John 1.7, 9) ("Christian perfection," "perfect love": Deut. 30.6; Matt. 5.43-48; 22.37-40; Rom.

12.9-21; 13.8-10; 1 Cor. 13; Phil. 3.10-15; Heb. 6.1; 1 John 4.17-18 "Heart purity": Matt. 5.8; Acts 15.8-9; 1 Pet. 1.22; 1 John 3.3 "Baptism with the Holy Spirit": Jer. 31.31-34; Ezek. 36.25-27; Mal. 3.2-3; Matt. 3.11-12; Luke 3.16-17; Acts 1.5; 2.1-4; 15.8-9 "Fullness of the blessing": Rom. 15.29 "Christian holiness": Matt. 5.1-7.29; John 15.1-11; Rom. 12.1-15.3; 2 Cor. 7.1; Eph. 4.17-5.20; Phil. 1.9-11; 3.12-15; Col. 2.20-3.17; 1 Thess. 3.13;.7-8;5.23; 2 Tim. 2.19-22; Heb. 10.19-25; 12.14; 13.20-21; 1 Pet. 1.15-16; 2 Pet. 1.1-11; 3.18; Jude 20-21)

Free Methodist Church

www.fmc-canada.org/articles.htm

Articles of Religion

Entire sanctification is that work of the Holy Spirit, subsequent to regeneration, by which the fully consecrated believer, upon exercise of faith in the atoning blood of Christ, is cleansed in that moment from all inward sin and empowered for service. The resulting relationship is attested by the witness of the Holy Spirit and is maintained by faith and obedience. Entire sanctification enables the believer to love God with all his heart, soul, strength, and mind, and his neighbor as himself, and it prepares him for greater growth in grace. (Lev. 20.7-8; John 14.16-17; 17.19; Acts 1.8; 2.4; 15.8-9; Rom. 5.3-5; 8.12-17; 12.1-2; 1 Cor 6.11; 12.4-11; Gal. 5.22-25; Eph. 4.22-24; 1 Thess 4.7; 5.23-24; 2 Thess 2.13; Heb. 10.14)

Wesleyan Church

www.wesleyan.org/doctrine.htm

The Articles of Religion

We believe that sanctification is that work of the Holy Spirit by which the child of God is separated from sin unto God and is enabled to love God with all the heart and to walk in all His holy commandments blameless. Sanctification is initiated at the moment of justification and regeneration. From that moment there is a gradual or progressive sanctification as the believer walks with God and daily grows in grace and in a more perfect obedience to God. This prepares for the crisis of entire sanctification which is wrought instantaneously when believers present themselves as living sacrifices, holy and acceptable to God, through faith in Jesus Christ, being effected by the baptism with the Holy Spirit who cleanses the heart from all inbred sin. The crisis of entire sanctification perfects the believer in love and empowers that person for effective service. It is followed by lifelong growth in grace and the knowledge of our Lord and Savior Jesus Christ. The life of holiness continues through faith in the sanctifying blood of Christ and evidences itself by loving obedience to God's revealed will.

Gen. 17.1; Deut. 30.6; Ps. 130.8; Isa. 6.1-6; Ezek. 36.25-29; Matt. 5.8, 48; Luke 1.74-75; 3.16-17; 24.49; John 17.1-26; Acts 1.4-5, 8; 2.1-4; 15.8-9; 26.18; Rom. 8.3-4; 1 Cor. 1.2; 6.11; 2 Cor. 7.1; Eph. 4.13, 24; 5.25-27; 1 Thess. 3.10, 12-13; 4.3, 7-8; 5.23-24; 2 Thess. 2.13; Titus 2.11-14; Heb. 10.14; 12.14; 13.12; James 3.17-18; 4.8; 1 Peter 1.2; 2 Peter 1.4; 1 John 1.7, 9; 3.8-9; 4.17-18; Jude 24.

Developing Ears that Hear
Responding to the Spirit and the Word
Rev. Dr. Don L. Davis

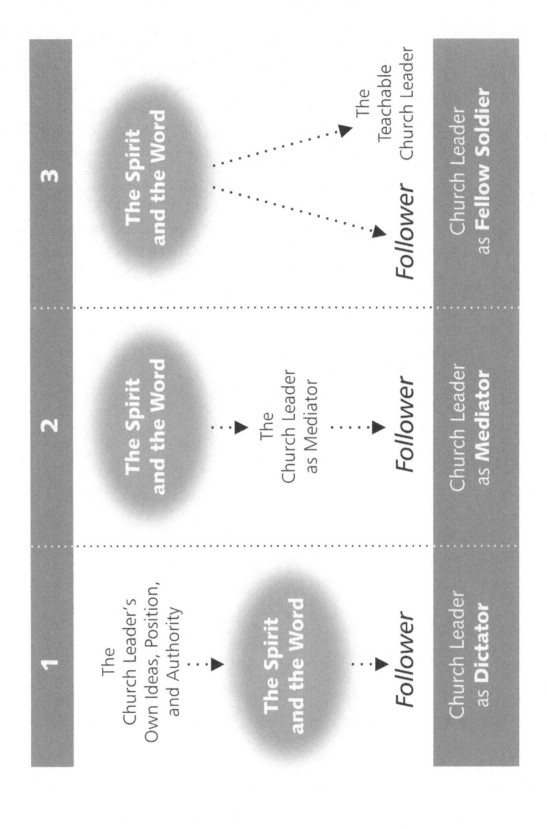

1

The Church Leader's Own Ideas, Position, and Authority

⋯▶ **The Spirit and the Word**

⋯▶ *Follower*

Church Leader as **Dictator**

2

The Spirit and the Word

⋯▶ The Church Leader as Mediator

⋯▶ *Follower*

Church Leader as **Mediator**

3

The Spirit and the Word

⋯▶ The Teachable Church Leader

⋯▶ *Follower* Church Leader

Church Leader as **Fellow Soldier**

Different Traditions of African-American Response

Interpreting a Legacy, Shaping an Identity, and Pursuing a Destiny as a Minority Culture Person

Adapted from and informed by Cornell West's Prophecy Deliverance

I. Exceptionalism — Afro-centrism and Superiority - "Above"

A. Definition: tendency to respond in terms of exalted, superior, and even romanticized view of one's own cultural and racial roots

B. Example: Louis Farrakhan, W.E.B. DuBois

C. Issues

1. Pendulum swing: same bigotry as oppressive group, only inverted ("Same shoe, different foot")

2. Isolationist and separatistic; have no desire to be in relationship with people of majority culture and/or race

3. See separation and segregation as an essential step on the road to a full personhood as a minority group

4. To gain one's own identity is the prime goal, not relating to people of another culture

II. Assimilationism: Adopting the Predominant Culture as One's Primary (and in some cases) Only Culture - "Behind"

A. Definition: the tendency to ignore or bypass one's particular cultural roots in order to identify with a more general, broad, and accepted majority culture identity

B. Example: Shelby Steele, Alan Keyes

C. Issues

1. Advocate a full blown adoption of the predominant cultural identity (e.g., "I am not Black, but American")

2. Tends to ignore the specialness of difference

3. Need not be committed to obliterating culture, only ignoring difference in order that we may all meld into one common pot

4. Perpetually defers to the cultural mores and habits of the dominant culture

III. Marginalism: Inferiority, Shame and Hatred, Denial - "Outside"

A. Definition: tendency to deny, overlook, or even reject one's own cultural legacy as pathological, insignificant, and even detrimental to one's own growth and prosperity

B. Example: Joseph Washington, E. Franklin Frazier

C. Issues

1. Breeds contempt for oneself; self-deprecation is not viewed as a negative in reference to the overall badness of the culture

2. Ignores God's role in shaping culture

3. Oversimplifies one's own cultural legacy as either insignificant or immoral

IV. Integrationism: Modern-day Multi-culturalism - "Among"

A. Definition: tendency to strive for a multi-cultural integration of peoples within society that guarantees the rights and privileges of citizenry, equality, and justice

B. Example: Jesse Jackson, Thurgood Marshall, traditional civil rights vision

C. Issues

1. Focus on attaining distributive justice in society among all the people groups within it ("equal treatment under the law", and "cut the societal pie correctly")

2. Seeks limited goods within the society of equality and fairness under the law, and does not focus (usually) on friendship but equal treatment

3. Appeals mainly to issues related to economic issues, distribution of wealth, and the overall benefits of society

4. May focus on establishing coalitions of people of different culture in order to sway the hand of government and society for equal and just treatment

5. Legislates its agenda, does not emphasize relationship

V. Celebrationism: Acknowledgment, Delight, Critique and Relationship "Alongside"

A. Definition: tendency to see all cultures as significant and unique, and intentionally celebrates the differences between cultures while 1) critiquing its immoral elements according to a biblical vision and, 2) arguing against exclusion and bigotry on the basis of the differences.

B. Example: Martin Luther King, Jr.

C. Issues

1. Grounded in a Christian vision of God's creation

2. Ethic of a Christian community, and its prophetic message

3. Affirms culture as a distinctly human phenomenon

4. Attaches no pejorative connotation to cultural identity or preference

Discerning the Call: The Profile of a Cross-Cultural Urban Church Planter

Rev. Dr. Don L. Davis

	Commission	Character	Community	Competence
Definition	Recognizes the call of God and replies with prompt obedience to his lordship and leading	Reflects the character of Christ in their personal convictions, conduct, and lifestyle	Regards multiplying disciples in the body of Christ as the primary role of ministry	Responds in the power of the Spirit with excellence in carrying out their appointed tasks and ministry
Key Scripture	2 Tim. 1.6-14; 1 Tim. 4.14; Acts 1.8; Matt. 28.18-20	John 15.4-5; 2 Tim. 2.2; 1 Cor. 4.2; Gal. 5.16-23	Eph. 4.9-15; 1 Cor. 12.1-27	2 Tim. 2.15; 3.16-17; Rom. 15.14; 1 Cor. 12
Critical Concept	The Authority of God: God's leader acts on God's recognized call and authority, acknowledged by the saints and God's leaders	The Humility of Christ: God's leader demonstrates the mind and lifestyle of Christ in his or her actions and relationships	The Growth of the Church: God's leader uses all of his or her resources to equip and empower the body of Christ for his/her goal and task	The Power of the Spirit: God's leader operates in the gifting and anointing of the Holy Spirit
Central Elements	A clear call from God Authentic testimony before God and others Deep sense of personal conviction based on Scripture Personal burden for a particular task or people Confirmation by leaders and the body	Passion for Christlikeness Radical life style for the Kingdom Serious pursuit of holiness Discipline in the personal life Fulfills role-relationships as bondslave of Jesus Christ Provides an attractive model for others in their conduct, speech, and lifestyle (the fruit of the Spirit)	Genuine love for and desire to serve God's people Disciples faithful individuals Facilitates growth in small groups Pastors and equips believers in the congregation Nurtures associations and networks among Christians and churches Advances new movements among God's people locally	Endowments and gifts from the Spirit Sound discipling from an able mentor Skill in the spiritual disciplines Ability in the Word Able to evangelize, follow up, and disciple new converts Strategic in the use of resources and people to accomplish God's task
Satanic Strategy to Abort	Operates on the basis of personality or position rather than on God's appointed call and ongoing authority	Substitutes ministry activity and/or hard work and industry for godliness and Christlikeness	Exalts tasks and activities above equipping the saints and developing Christian community	Functions on natural gifting and personal ingenuity rather than on the Spirit's leading and gifting
Key Steps	Identify God's call Discover your burden Be confirmed by leaders	Abide in Christ Discipline for godliness Pursue holiness in all	Embrace God's Church Learn leadership's contexts Equip concentrically	Discover the Spirit's gifts Receive excellent training Hone your performance
Results	Deep confidence in God arising from God's call	Powerful Christlike example provided for others to follow	Multiplying disciples in the Church	Dynamic working of the Holy Spirit

Discipleship Diagram

Rev. Dr. Don L. Davis

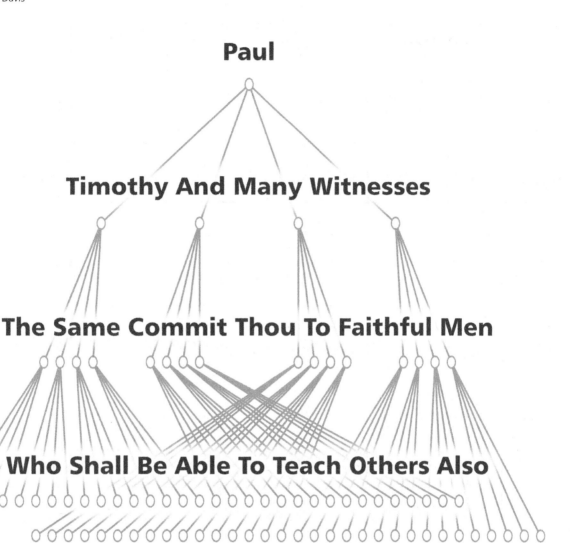

Paul

Timothy And Many Witnesses

The Same Commit Thou To Faithful Men

Who Shall Be Able To Teach Others Also

2 Tim. 2.2 (ESV) - And what you have heard from me in the presence of many witnesses entrust to faithful men who will be able to teach others also.

Discipling the Faithful: Establishing Leaders for the Urban Church

Crowns of Beauty Conference. Don Davis. February 1998.

	Commission	Character	Competence	Community
Definition	Recognizes the call of God and replies with prompt obedience to his lordship and leading	Reflects the character of Christ in their personal convictions, conduct, and lifestyle	Responds in the power of the Spirit with excellence in carrying out their appointed tasks and ministry	Regards multiplying disciples in the body of Christ as the primary role of ministry
Key Scripture	2 Tim. 1.6-14; 1 Tim. 4.14; Acts 1.8; Matt. 28.18-20	John 15.4-5; 2 Tim. 2.2; 1 Cor. 4.2; Gal. 5.16-23	2 Tim. 2.15; 3.16-17; Rom. 15.14; 1 Cor. 12	Eph. 4.9-15; 1 Cor. 12.1-27
Critical Concept	The Authority of God: God's leader acts on God's recognized call and authority, acknowledged by the saints and God's leaders	The Humility of Christ: God's leader demonstrates the mind and lifestyle of Christ in his or her actions and relationships	The Power of the Spirit: God's leader operates in the gifting and anointing of the Holy Spirit	The Growth of the Church: God's leader uses all of his or her resources to equip and empower the body of Christ for his/her goal and task
Central Elements	A clear call from God Authentic testimony before God and others Deep sense of personal conviction based on Scripture Personal burden for a particular task or people Confirmation by leaders and the body	Passion for Christlikeness Radical lifestyle for the Kingdom Serious pursuit of holiness Discipline in the personal life Fulfills role-relationships as bondslave of Jesus Christ Provides an attractive model for others in their conduct, speech, and lifestyle (the fruit of the Spirit)	Endowments and gifts from the Spirit Sound discipling from an able mentor Skill in the spiritual disciplines Ability in the Word Able to evangelize, follow up, and disciple new converts Strategic in the use of resources and people to accomplish God's task	Genuine love for and desire to serve God's people Disciples faithful individuals Facilitates growth in small groups Pastors and equips believers in the congregation Nurtures associations and networks among Christians and churches Advances new movements among God's people locally
Satanic Strategy to Abort	Operates on the basis of personality or position rather than on God's appointed call and ongoing authority	Substitutes ministry activity and/or hard work and industry for godliness and Christlikeness	Functions on natural gifting and personal ingenuity rather than on the Spirit's leading and gifting	Exalts tasks and activities above equipping the saints and developing Christian community
Key Steps	Identify God's call Discover your burden Be confirmed by leaders	Abide in Christ Discipline for godliness Pursue holiness in all	Discover the Spirit's gifts Receive excellent training Hone your performance	Embrace God's Church Learn leadership's contexts Equip concentrically
Results	Deep confidence in God arising from God's call	Powerful Christlike example provided for others to follow	Dynamic working of the Holy Spirit	Multiplying disciples in the Church

Documenting Your Work
A Guide to Help You Give Credit Where Credit Is Due
The Urban Ministry Institute

Avoiding Plagiarism

Plagiarism is using another person's ideas as if they belonged to you without giving them proper credit. In academic work it is just as wrong to steal a person's ideas as it is to steal a person's property. These ideas may come from the author of a book, an article you have read, or from a fellow student. The way to avoid plagiarism is to carefully use "notes" (textnotes, footnotes, endnotes, etc.) and a "Works Cited" section to help people who read your work know when an idea is one you thought of, and when you are borrowing an idea from another person.

Using Citation References

A citation reference is required in a paper whenever you use ideas or information that came from another person's work.

All citation references involve two parts:

- Notes in the body of your paper placed next to each quotation which came from an outside source.

- A "Works Cited" page at the end of your paper or project which gives information about the sources you have used

Using Notes in Your Paper

There are three basic kinds of notes: parenthetical notes, footnotes, and endnotes. At The Urban Ministry Institute, we recommend that students use parenthetical notes. These notes give the author's last name(s), the date the book was published, and the page number(s) on which you found the information. Example:

> In trying to understand the meaning of Genesis 14.1-24, it is important to recognize that in biblical stories "the place where dialogue is first introduced will be an important moment in revealing the character of the speaker . . ." (Kaiser and Silva 1994, 73). This is certainly true of the character of Melchizedek who speaks words of blessing. This identification of Melchizedek as a positive spiritual influence is reinforced by the fact that he is the King of Salem, since Salem means "safe, at peace" (Wiseman 1996, 1045).

Documenting Your Work (continued)

A "Works Cited" page should be placed at the end of your paper. This page:

**Creating a Works
Cited Page**

- lists every source you quoted in your paper

- is in alphabetical order by author's last name

- includes the date of publication and information about the publisher

The following formatting rules should be followed:

1. Title

The title "Works Cited" should be used and centered on the first line of the page following the top margin.

2. Content

Each reference should list:

- the author's full name (last name first)

- the date of publication

- the title and any special information (Revised edition, 2nd edition, reprint) taken from the cover or title page should be noted

- the city where the publisher is headquartered followed by a colon and the name of the publisher

3. Basic form

- Each piece of information should be separated by a period.

- The second line of a reference (and all following lines) should be indented.

- Book titles should be underlined (or italicized).

- Article titles should be placed in quotes.

Example:

Fee, Gordon D. 1991. *Gospel and Spirit: Issues in New Testament Hermeneutics.* Peabody, MA: Hendrickson Publishers.

Documenting Your Work (continued)

4. Special Forms

A book with multiple authors:

> Kaiser, Walter C., and Moisés Silva. 1994. *An Introduction to Biblical Hermeneutics: The Search for Meaning.* Grand Rapids: Zondervan Publishing House.

An edited book:

> Greenway, Roger S., ed. 1992. *Discipling the City: A Comprehensive Approach to Urban Mission.* 2nd ed. Grand Rapids: Baker Book House.

A book that is part of a series:

> Morris, Leon. 1971. *The Gospel According to John.* Grand Rapids: Wm. B. Eerdmans Publishing Co. The New International Commentary on the New Testament. Gen. ed. F. F. Bruce.

An article in a reference book:

> Wiseman, D. J. "Salem." 1982. In *New Bible Dictionary.* Leicester, England - Downers Grove, IL: InterVarsity Press. Eds. I. H. Marshall and others.

(An example of a "Works Cited" page is located on the next page.)

For Further Research

Standard guides to documenting academic work in the areas of philosophy, religion, theology, and ethics include:

> Atchert, Walter S., and Joseph Gibaldi. 1985. *The MLA Style Manual.* New York: Modern Language Association.

> *The Chicago Manual of Style.* 1993. 14th ed. Chicago: The University of Chicago Press.

> Turabian, Kate L. 1987. *A Manual for Writers of Term Papers, Theses, and Dissertations.* 5th edition. Bonnie Bertwistle Honigsblum, ed. Chicago: The University of Chicago Press.

Works Cited

Fee, Gordon D. 1991. *Gospel and Spirit: Issues in New Testament Hermeneutics.* Peabody, MA: Hendrickson Publishers.

Greenway, Roger S., ed. 1992. *Discipling the City: A Comprehensive Approach to Urban Mission.* 2nd ed. Grand Rapids: Baker Book House.

Kaiser, Walter C., and Moisés Silva. 1994. *An Introduction to Biblical Hermeneutics: The Search for Meaning.* Grand Rapids: Zondervan Publishing House.

Morris, Leon. 1971. *The Gospel According to John.* Grand Rapids: Wm. B. Eerdmans Publishing Co. *The New International Commentary on the New Testament.* Gen. ed. F. F. Bruce.

Wiseman, D. J. "Salem." 1982. In *New Bible Dictionary.* Leicester, England-Downers Grove, IL: InterVarsity Press. Eds. I. H. Marshall and others.

Dynamics of Credible Spiritual Vision

Rev. Dr. Don L. Davis

Vision originates in calling

Vision presumes gifting

Vision assures confirmation

Vision inspires commitment

Vision identifies opportunity

Vision demands strategy

Vision requires resources

Calling

+

Gifting

+

Confirmation

+

Commitment

+

Opportunity

+

Strategy

+

Resources

=

Results for God

Editorial

Ralph D. Winter

This article was taken from Mission Frontiers: The Bulletin of the US Center for World Mission, Vol. 27, No. 5; September-October 2005; ISSN 0889-9436.
Copyright 2005 by the U.S. Center for World Mission. Used by permission. All Rights Reserved.

Dear Reader,

This time you must learn a new phrase: Insider Movements.

This idea as a mission strategy was so shockingly new in Paul's day that almost no one (either then or now) gets the point. That's why we are devoting this entire issue to "Insider Movements." That's why the 2005 annual meeting of the International Society for Frontier Missiology is devoted to the same subject. (See *www.ijfm.org/ isfm.*)

First of all, be warned: many mission donors and prayer warriors, and even some missionaries, heartily disagree with the idea.

One outstanding missionary found that even his mission board director could not agree. He was finally asked to find another mission agency to work under. Why? His director was a fine former pastor who had never lived among a totally strange people. After a couple of years of increasingly serious correspondence between the director and the missionary family, the relationship had to come to an end.

Okay, so this is serious business. Why is *Insider Movements* such a troubling concept?

Well, everywhere Paul went "Judaizers" followed him and tried to destroy the Insider Movement he had established.

Some of those Judaizers were earnest followers of Christ who simply could not imagine how a Greek – still a Greek in dress, language and culture – could become a believer in Jesus Christ without casting off a huge amount of his Greek culture, get circumcised, follow the "kosher" dietary rules and the "new moons and Sabbaths", etc.

The flagrant language of Paul's letter to the Galatians is one result. The very serious text of his letter to the Romans is another. Years ago the scales fell off my eyes when I read that "Israel, who pursued a law of righteousness, has not attained it ... Why not? Because they pursued it not by faith but as if it were by works" (Rom. 9:32 NIV).

*Ralph D. Winter is the Editor of **Mission Frontiers** and the General Director of the Frontier Mission Fellowship.*

Paul was not saying the Jewish religious culture was defective or that the Greek culture was superior. He was emphasizing that heart faith is the key element in any culture—that *forms* were not the key thing but the *faith*. Greeks who yielded in heart faith to the Gospel did not need to become Jews culturally and follow Jewish forms.

Paul said, in effect, "I am very, very proud of a Gospel that is the power of God to save people who obey God in faith, no matter whether they follow Jewish or Greek customs" (Rom. 1:16).

But the real trick is not simply for people of faith in every culture to stay and stagnate in their own cultural cul-de-sac, but both to retain their own culture and at the same time recognize the validity of versions of the faith within other cultures and the universality of the Body of Christ.

Different sources of European Christianity flowed over into the United States, producing some 200 different "flavors" of Christianity—some born here (Mormons, Jehovah's Witnesses), some quite biblical, some not so biblical, some very strange.

The same thing happens on the mission field: a lot of different movements emerge. The ideal is for the Gospel to become effectively expressed within the language and culture of a people and not just be a transplant from the missionary's culture.

H. Richard Niebhur's famous book, *Social Sources of Denominationalism*, is known for pointing out that different denominations did not just have doctrinal differences (often very minor) but usually reflected, at least for a time, social differences that were the real difference. Note, however, the Christian faith was in many cases an "Insider Movement" and was expressed within different social streams, taking on characteristics of those different streams.

But, back to missions. The Jewish/Greek thing is far more and far "worse" than the differences between Methodists who pray that their trespasses be forgiven and Presbyterians who pray that their debts be forgiven!

No, in Paul's day circumcision was undoubtedly a major barrier to adult Greek men becoming culturally Jewish followers of Christ. Another sensitive point was the question of eating meat that had been offered to idols, and so on.

Ralph D. Winter Editorial (continued)

Later in history, the Jewish/Greek tension was paralleled by a Latin/German tension. This time, we see a profound difference in attitudes toward clerical marriage vs. celibacy and the use of Latin in church services.

For centuries Latin was *the language* of Europe, enabling ministers, attorneys, medical doctors, and public officials to read the books of their trade in a single language. That lasted a long time! For centuries a unifying reading language did a lot of good. But the Bible did not come into its own until it was translated into the heart languages of Europe.

The deep rumbling that modernized Europe was the unleashed Bible.

It is an exciting and maybe disturbing thing—the idea that biblical faith can be clothed in any language and culture. Witness the awesome reality in the so-called mission lands today. Whether Africa, India or China, it may well be that the largest number of genuine believers in Jesus Christ do not show up in what we usually call Christian churches!

Can you believe it? They may still consider themselves Muslims or Hindus (in a cultural sense).

Alas, today Christianity itself is identified with the cultural vehicle of the civilization of the West. People in mission lands who do not wish to be "westernized" feel they need to stay clear of the Christian Church, which in their own country is often a church highly Western in its culture, theology, interpretation of the Bible, etc.

For example, in Japan there are "churches" that are so Western that in the last forty years they have not grown by a single member. Many astute observers have concluded that there is not yet "a Japanese form of Christianity." When one emerges, it may not want to associate with the Western Christian tradition except in a fraternal way.

In India we now know that there are actually millions of Hindus who have chosen to follow Christ, reading the Bible daily and worshipping at the household level, but not often frequenting the West-related Christian churches of that land.

In some places thousands of people who consider themselves Muslims are nevertheless heart-and-soul followers of Jesus Christ who carry the New Testament with them into the mosques.

In Africa there are more than 50 million believers (of a sort) within a vast sphere called "the African Initiated Churches." The people in the more formally "Christian church" may not regard these others as Christians at all. Indeed, some of them are a whole lot further from pure biblical faith than Mormons. But, if they revere and study the Bible, we need to let the Bible do its work. These groups range from the wildly heretical to the seriously biblical within over ten thousand "denominations" which are not related to any overt Christian body.

Thus, not all "insider" movements are ideal. Our own Christianity is not very successfully [*sic*] "inside" our culture, since many "Christians" are Christian in name only. Even mission "church planting" activities may or may not be "insider" at all, and even if they are they may not be ideal.

Around the world some of these movements do not baptize. In other cases they do. I have been asked, "Are you promoting the idea of non-baptized believers?" No, in reporting the existence of these millions of people, we are reporting on the incredible power of the Bible. We are not promoting all the ideas they reflect or the practices they follow. The Bible is like an underground fire burning out of control! In one sense we can be very happy.

Empowering People for Freedom, Wholeness, and Justice

Theological and Ethical Foundations for World Impact's Development Ministries

Don Davis and Terry Cornett

A Theology of Development

Love of God and love of neighbor have been pivotal themes of both Old and New Testament theology from their inception. From the time of the early Church forward, there has been a concern to demonstrate God's love and character to the world in word and deed, through faith and works, by both evangelistic proclamation and acts of justice and mercy.

Starting with its forerunners in Puritan, Pietistic, Moravian, and Wesleyan reform and revival movements, and extending into the modern Protestant missions movement, evangelical missionaries have combined a strong emphasis on evangelism and the establishment of churches with a serious attempt to engage in action that would foster justice and righteousness, especially on behalf of the poor and oppressed.

Evangelical reformers and missionaries have started schools and hospitals aimed at being accessible to the least advantaged segments of society, formed orphanages and worked for the reform of child labor laws, established businesses and cooperative ventures among the poor, supported legislation to abolish slavery and to ensure the protection of human rights, worked to upgrade the status of women in society, and mediated conflicts between warring groups and nations.[1]

Although Christians generally agree that evangelism and social action are important responsibilities of the Church, there is considerable variation in both the terms that are used to designate these responsibilities, and the way in which they are defined and placed in relation to one another. As a missions agency which is engaged in both of these activities, it is important to establish our definition of terms and a statement of the theological relationship which exists between these two tasks.

Prologue

1 See Paul E. Pierson' article, "Missions and Community Development: A Historical Perspective," (Elliston 1989, 1-22) for an introduction to the history of development work in evangelical missions and Donald W. Dayton's book "Discovering an Evangelical Heritage" (Dayton, 1988) for a helpful look at evangelical reform movements.

Empowering People for Freedom, Wholeness, and Justice (continued)

1. The Kingdom of God as the Basis of Evangelism, Church Planting and Development

2 See George Eldon Ladd (1974, 45-134), for an introduction to a biblical theology of the Kingdom.

1.1 The Kingdom of God as the Basis for Mission

"Missiology is more and more coming to see the Kingdom of God as the hub around which all of mission work revolves" (Verkuyl 1978, 203). Evangelism, church-planting and development work are not based on a few isolated "proof-texts," but are an abiding response to the theme of the Kingdom which is woven throughout the scriptural record. The Kingdom of God embodies the essence of what God's mission (*Missio Dei*) in the world is and provides a basis for seeing how our own activities are intended to fit into God's overall plan.[2]

1.2 The Kingdom as Restoration

The Scriptures assert what human experience everywhere reveals; something has gone dramatically wrong with the world. The Bible teaches that the basis of this problem is humanity's rejection of God's rulership. The Genesis account of the Fall shows humanity repudiating God's right to give direction and boundaries to their decisions. From that time forward, evil filled the void left by the absence of God's loving rule. The world ceased to function correctly; death replaced life; disease replaced health; enmity replaced friendship; domination replaced cooperation; and scarcity replaced abundance. All human relationships with God and with each other were poisoned by the inner desire of each individual and social group to replace God's authority with their own rule.

In a response of grace to this situation, God decided not to reject and destroy the world, but to redeem it. He set in motion a plan to liberate the world from its bondage to evil powers, and to restore all things to perfection under his Kingly rule. Throughout the Scriptures this plan of reclamation is described as the "*Kingdom of God*," and insight into its nature and means of coming are progressively revealed.

Johannes Verkuyl summarizes the message of the Kingdom in this fashion:

3 That is, the One who in his own person fully embodies the rule of God.

> *The heart of the message of the Old and New Testament is that God . . . is actively engaged in the reestablishment of His liberating dominion over the cosmos and all of humankind. In seeking out Israel, He sought all of us and our entire world, and in Jesus Christ He laid the foundation of the Kingdom. Jesus Christ the Messiah "promised to the fathers," is the auto basileia[3]: in Him the Kingdom has both come, and is coming in an absolutely unique way and with exceptional clarity. In His preaching Jesus divulges the riches, the thesaurus of that Kingdom: reconciliation, the forgiveness of sins, victory*

over demonic powers. Standing within the tradition of the Mosaic law, He expounds the core message of . . . the prophets; He accomplishes the reconciliation of the world to God; He opens the way to the present and future Kingdom which demands decisions of us in all aspects of life (Verkuyl 1993, 72).

1.3 Responsibilities for Those Who Seek God's Kingdom

The implications of the Kingdom of God for mission can be delineated in three central truths. A kingdom-centered theology and missiology will be concerned for:

- Evangelizing so that people are converted to Christ as Lord.

- Creating churches where people are discipled and bear fruit.

- Helping the Church live out its commitment to bring freedom, wholeness, and justice in the world.

Thus:

A truly Kingdom-centered theology . . . can never neglect the call for the conversion of persons among all peoples and religious communities. To everyone of whatever religious persuasion the message must be repeated: "The Kingdom of God is at hand; repent, and believe in the Gospel.". . . Kingdom-centered theology entails a call to recognition of the lordship of the King and new orientation to the constitution of His Kingdom. In the absence of this aspect, proclamation of the good news of the Gospel is impossible. A theology and missiology informed by the biblical notion of the rule of Christ will never fail to identify personal conversion as one of the inclusive goals of God's Kingdom . . .

The Church . . . is raised up by God among all nations to share in the salvation and suffering service of the Kingdom . . . The Church constitutes the firstling, the early harvest of the Kingdom. Thus, although not limited to the Church, the Kingdom is unthinkable without the Church. Conversely, growth and expansion of the Church should not be viewed as ends but rather as means to be used in the service of the Kingdom. . . . The keys of the Kingdom have been given to the Church. It does not fulfill its mandate by relinquishing those keys but rather by using them to open up the avenues of approach to the Kingdom for all peoples and all population groups at every level of human society . . .

> *Finally, the gospel of the Kingdom addresses itself to all immediate human need, both physical and mental. It aims to right what is wrong on earth. It enjoins engagement in the struggle for racial, social, cultural, economic, and political justice. . . . The good news of the Kingdom has to do with all of these things. For this reason missiology must bend its efforts to the erection of a multiplicity of visible signs of God's Kingdom throughout the length and breadth of this planet (Verkuyl 1993, 72-73).*

Evangelism, church planting and development spring from a common theological base: a desire to live out the implications of the Kingdom of God which has broken into this present age in the person of Jesus Christ, the King of kings. This Kingdom is both *already* and *not yet*. It is currently *forcefully advancing and spreading like yeast through dough*, but also awaiting the return of Christ *when every knee will bow* and there will be a *new heaven and a new earth*. Our evangelism and our development work acknowledge God's kingly rule, now, during a time when the world, as a whole, does not. We announce the good news of the in-breaking Kingdom of peace and justice, call people to repentance and salvation through faith in its King, hope in its inevitable complete triumph, and live out obedience to its commands and values in the present moment.

2. Kingdom Work

Since evangelism/church planting and development work are intimately related, those who engage in them often find that their roles and projects overlap. While this is both normal and good, a clear beginning definition of each role may help to minimize the confusion which can sometimes result from this process.

2.1 Missionaries

Missionaries are called to pioneer new outreaches that focus on the evangelization of peoples in unreached (or under-reached) areas, social classes, or cultural groups.

Therefore, we assert that:

> *Missionaries cross class and cultural barriers to evangelize and disciple unreached groups so that reproducing churches are formed among them and placed at the service of God's kingdom rule.*

Empowering People for Freedom, Wholeness, and Justice (continued)

2.2 Development Workers

Development workers are called to confront conditions and structures in the world that do not submit themselves to the rule of God.

Therefore, we assert that:

> *Development workers enable individuals, churches and communities to experience movement toward the freedom, wholeness, and justice of the Kingdom of God.*

2.3 The Common Link

Both missionaries and Christian development workers are united in their common commitment to further God's kingdom rule in all areas of life.

Missionary activity is centered around the proclamation of "good news" that calls people into the Kingdom of God through an experience of salvation and regeneration. It focuses on bringing unreached peoples, cultures, and subcultures into the community of the redeemed (i.e., "bringing the world into the Church"). All of this is done with an eye toward creating churches which can disciple their members to acknowledge God's rulership and live out the values of his Kingdom in their individual and corporate life.

Missionary activity also encompasses development that seeks to call every area of life into conformity with God's kingdom rule. It evaluates every concrete life-situation in light of the Lord's Prayer ("thy Kingdom come, thy will be done, on earth as it is in heaven") and engages in deeds of compassion, love, and justice that demonstrate the nature of God's divine plan for all peoples. It focuses on bringing God's rule to bear on every human relationship and structure (i.e., "bringing the Church into the world").

3.1 A Partnership Relationship

Missionary evangelism and church-planting and Christian development work are partners in the process of proclaiming, demonstrating, and extending the rule of the King. Both are responses to the fact that God has announced his desire to reconcile the world to himself through the gift of his Son. Although each is a legitimate response to God's plan for the world, neither is a sufficient response

3. Theological Relationship between Evangelism and Development

in and of itself. Both word and deed are necessary components of the Church's announcement of, and faithfulness to, the Kingdom of God.

3.2 Interdependence and Interconnectedness

The relationship between Missions and Development is not a simple one. Their interconnectedness has many facets.

- *They are connected by a common goal.*

  Neither missionaries nor development workers are satisfied until God's reconciliation with man and man's reconciliation with man is completely realized. We believe that this makes both missions and development work Christocentric in orientation, since it is "in Christ" that God is reconciling the world to himself. Christ is the King. It is his sacrificial, reconciling death that provides the objective basis for reconciliation between humanity and God, and within human relationships and structures. It is his kingly authority and presence that allows the Kingdom to break into this present age destroying the works of darkness and creating authentic communities gathered under God's rule.

- *They retain a degree of independence from each other.*

  Evangelism and church-planting can sometimes be done without any immediate focus on development work. Conversely, development work can be sometimes be done without accompanying church-planting activity. Because both are authentic responses to God's activity in the world, they can, when appropriate, operate independently from each other. While each is a legitimate activity in its own right, it will obviously be healthier and more normal to find them occurring together.

- *They need each other for lasting effectiveness.*

  Without evangelism, there are no changed lives, no reconcilers who understand God's plan for man and society, and who undertake change in the power of the Spirit. Without development, the churches established by mission become withdrawn, and do not function as "salt and light" within their local and national communities. Missionary efforts are undermined when the existing church does not make visible in its life the effects of

Empowering People for Freedom, Wholeness, and Justice (continued)

God's kingdom rule. The integration of the two is aptly expressed in Ephesians 2:8-10 which states, "For by grace you have been saved through faith. And this is not your own doing; it is the gift of God, [9] not a result of works, so that no one may boast. [10] For we are his workmanship, created in Christ Jesus for good works, which God prepared beforehand, that we should walk in them."

These facets may be summarized as "a threefold relationship between evangelism and social activity. First, Christian social activity [development] is a *consequence* of evangelism, since it is the evangelized who engage in it. Second it is a *bridge* to evangelism, since it expresses God's love and so both overcomes prejudice and opens closed doors. Third, it is a *partner* of evangelism, so that they are 'like two blades of a pair of scissors or the two wings of a bird'" (Stott 1995, 52).

3.3 The Need for Specialization

Modern missions have seen the rise of both mission and development agencies. This occurs as organizations specialize in one component of the overall task God has given. This recognition of the need for specialization arose early on in the life of the Church.

J. Chongham Cho comments:

> *In Acts 6 . . . a distinction between evangelism and social action was made. This was not a division in essence but for the sake of practical efficacy of the church's mission and as the solution to a problem which arose in the church. This is a necessary deduction from the nature of the church as Christ's body. Although we should resist polarization between evangelism and social action, we should not resist specialization (Cho 1985, 229).*

As a missions agency, our primary focus is evangelism and discipleship which results in the planting of indigenous churches. The fact that evangelism, church-planting and development are interconnected means that missions agencies, especially those who focus on the poor and oppressed, will engage in some form of development work. However, the mission agency must be careful to structure its development work so that it encourages the central task of evangelism and church-planting rather than detracts from it.[4] We should engage in development work which fosters the formation, health, growth, and reproducibility of indigenous churches among the poor.

4 See Appendix A for a variety of perspectives on how improperly implemented development work can adversely affect missionary work.

Empowering People for Freedom, Wholeness, and Justice (continued)

Specialization allows organizations to maximize the training and resources that can be committed to a specific part of the overall task of mission. The development agency may engage in many good and necessary projects that have no immediate connection to evangelism and the planting and nurturing of emerging churches. The missions agency appreciates the many development agencies that engage in this type of work. Although the mission agency will want to network with them (and pray that God will vastly increase their number and effectiveness), the mission agency itself will focus on development projects that assist the task of evangelism, discipleship, and the establishment of indigenous churches. Without this commitment to specialization, the mission agency will lose its ability to accomplish its part of the larger task.

4. Development Work within Our Mission Agency

4.1 *Statement of Purpose*

While we recognize the legitimacy of engaging in development work for its own sake as a direct godly response to human need, we believe that we are called to specialize in development work that specifically supports and contributes to the task of evangelism, discipleship and church-planting. In light of this, we affirm the following statement.

The aim of World Impact's development ministries is to support the evangelism, discipleship, and church-planting goals of World Impact by:

- *Demonstrating the Love of Christ*

   Many oppressed people have little basis for understanding God's love for them and the essential justice and compassion of his character. Development work can provide a living witness to the love of Christ and his concern for justice and peace in urban neighborhoods. Holistic ministry can come alongside the verbal proclamation of the Gospel, verifying its credibility and enriching the depth of understanding among its hearers. Development work can function pre-evangelistically to prepare people to genuinely listen to the claims of Christ and his message of salvation.

- *Empowering Emerging Churches*

   Emerging urban churches often have few physical resources with which to face the enormous needs of the city. Development work can partner with the pastors of planted-churches, giving access to resources and

Empowering People for Freedom, Wholeness, and Justice (continued)

programs that can meet immediate needs within their congregation, encourage leadership development, and help their congregations engage in effective holistic outreach to their community.

• *Modeling the Implications of the Gospel*

We cannot hope to reproduce churches committed to engage in a task they have never seen lived out in practice. We engage in development work because we expect newly planted churches to do likewise. We want to provide a living example that the Gospel will necessarily move from belief to action, from word to deed.

4.2 An Important Reminder

One cautionary note is in order. We cannot, through our own efforts, bring the Kingdom of God. As Paul Hiebert reminds us, "Our paradigms are flawed if we begin missions with human activity. Mission is not primarily what we do. It is what God does" (Hiebert 1993, 158). Evangelism, church-planting and development work all function, first and foremost, at the disposal of the Spirit of God. Knowing what should be done, and how we should do it, is never primarily determined through strategic diagrams or well-thought-out organizational approaches. Our first duty is to be faithful to the King, to listen to his instructions, and to respond to his initiatives.

An Ethic of Development

We have stated that:

> *Development workers enable individuals, churches and communities to experience movement toward the freedom, wholeness, and justice of the Kingdom of God.*

The process by which we move toward this goal, and the decisions we make to achieve these ends must be guided by an ethic which is consistent with God's standard for human relationships.

Ethics has to do with human conduct and character. It is the systematic study of the principles and methods for distinguishing right from wrong and good from bad. A Christian ethic of development helps us make decisions about development issues

5. Introduction

in light of biblical revelation and theology. It enables us to think and act clearly so that we can discern what is right to do and how it should be done.

Ethics is concerned that our theology be applied to our behaviors and attitudes. It is not content to simply understand the truth. Instead, it continually seeks to help us discover how to apply the truth (and attempts to motivate us to do so). True ethical behavior means that ethical principles are understood, internalized, and applied to the situation through the development of specific strategies and practices. In an organization, true ethical behavior also requires that strategies and practices undergo regular testing, evaluation and refinement. This ensures that the organization is accomplishing in practice what it affirms in principle.

Finally, it should be noted that our experiences always confront us with paradoxes, anomalies and competing priorities. An ethic of development does not attempt to condense life into a neatly packaged system. Rather, it provides principles that will help us to clarify what is most important in the particular situation that are facing. Each ethical decision must involve discussion about how the various principles outlined below interrelate and about which are the most significant values for a given decision. Only in dialogue and in prayer can the correct decision be discerned.

The ethical principles of the Kingdom of God can be expressed in the values of freedom, wholeness, and justice. These values are the root and the fruit of doing development from a kingdom perspective.

6. World Impact's Development Work is Committed to Freedom

Freedom is the ability to exercise our God-given capacity to make choices that express love. Therefore, development should engender freedom by helping individuals:

- Gain dignity and respect.

- Be empowered to make wise choices.

- Take responsibility for themselves and others.

This process involves helping individuals *understand* and *achieve* what they need to live freely in community as biblically responsible, self-directing, maturing servants of God's Kingdom. It implies the development of relationships characterized neither by dependence nor independence, but by loving *interdependence* that results in partnership, mutuality, and increased freedom.

Empowering People for Freedom, Wholeness, and Justice (continued)

6.1 *Development affirms human beings as precious and unique in the sight of God, and believes that they have been granted unique capacities and potentials by God.*

Explanation

As beings made in the image of God, every person regardless of station or place, is worthy of dignity and respect. People are to be cherished, nurtured, and provided for according to their intrinsic value and preciousness to God. Biblically based development will never exploit people for the sake of economic purposes or treat people as instruments, but instead will value them as ends-in-themselves, to be loved and respected for their worth before God.

Implications

- *People are to be given priority in every dimension of development.*

  Development should contribute to the potential for self-sufficiency, should enhance the quality of life, and should encourage good stewardship among those participating in the programs.

- *Mutual respect is foundational to authentic development.*

  For the poor, life in the urban community is full of inconvenience, difficulty, and shame. The needy daily experience the indignities of being poor in an affluent society. Oftentimes they are accused of moral laxity, subjected to stifling bureaucracies, and pre-judged as causing their own poverty through incompetence or lack of motivation. Development is sensitive to these messages which are given to the needy in our society. It recognizes that the poor are the objects of God's compassion and good news, chosen to be rich in faith and heirs to the Kingdom of God (James 2.5). Development seeks to demonstrate God's righteous cherishing of the poor through its specific actions and relationships.

  Aid not founded on genuine respect can easily humiliate the poor. Therefore, assistance offered to those in need must affirm their dignity and self-respect. Anything that diminishes the worth and significance of the poor in the development process is sinful and injurious to the well-being of all, both those offering the aid and those receiving it.

- *The workplace should operate as a caring community.*

   While an impersonal atmosphere characterizes many business environments, Christian development strives to create a relational framework for trainees and employees. Development workers and those participating in the development project must develop habit patterns of caring for each other beyond the constraints of the project at hand.

6.2 Development should empower people to take full responsibility for their own lives and to care for the needs of others.

Explanation

Development emerges from the conviction that all work is honorable. God has mandated that human beings earn their living with integrity and excellence. This mandate for individual work is grounded in God's initial command given to humankind at creation, and continues on and is reaffirmed in the teachings of the apostles. While God demands that his people be generous and hospitable to the needy and the stranger (2 Cor. 9), God likewise commands all to work honestly with their own hands (1 Thess. 4), and further charges that those who refuse to work ought to correspondingly be denied benevolent aid, that is, "if anyone will not work, neither let him eat," (cf. 2 Thess. 3.10).

Development rejects the notion that the creation of wealth is intrinsically evil. Such a view is simplistic and fails to grapple with the biblical notion of Christian stewardship. Development aims to create abundance, but never for the sake of selfish gain or lustful greed. Rather, development takes seriously the biblical requirement that we work, not merely to meet our own needs, but so that from the abundance God has provided we may use our goods and resources to meet the needs of others, especially those who are our brothers and sisters in the body of Christ (cf. Eph. 4; 2 Cor. 8; Gal. 6). The biblical standard is that those who stole before they entered the Kingdom are to steal no more, but to work honorably in quietness and integrity, in order that they may have sufficient resources to meet their own needs, and have sufficient wealth to care for others. Development not only seeks to honor the needy by ensuring they can participate in the basic human right to work, it also challenges them to trust God to supply their needs through honorable labor that allows them to be providers for themselves and others.

Empowering People for Freedom, Wholeness, and Justice (continued)

Implications

- *Nothing can excuse a worker, leader, or professional from the perils and potentials of personal responsibility.*

  Christian workers are not exempt from the vices of laziness, slothfulness, mismanagement, and greed, and they will not be spared from the consequences of such habits and conduct.

- *It is a primary aim of development to increase the maturity of everyone involved in the process.*

  It is assumed that the maturing individual will be increasingly characterized by vision (establishing and owning life-long purposes, aspirations and priorities), responsibility (acting on those purposes, aspirations and priorities with motivation, perseverance and integrity), and wisdom (increasing in skill, understanding and the ability to discern and do what is right for themselves and others).

  Maturing individuals should move from dependence toward autonomy, from passivity toward activity, from small abilities to large abilities, from narrow interests to broad interests, from egocentricity to altruism, from ignorance toward enlightenment, from self-rejection toward self-acceptance, from compartmentability toward integration, from imitation toward originality and from a need for rigidity toward a tolerance for ambiguity (Klopfenstein 1993, 95-96).

- *Decisions are best handled at the closest point to those affected.*

  National policies and procedures exist to:

  » Provide a framework for effective decision making.

  » Express the values and purposes that are corporately shared.

  » Ensure equity between peoples and projects at many different sites.

  » Provide accountability which safeguards integrity.

  Responsible decision making within a community assumes that there are mature individuals with a commitment to these common purposes and that open communication exists between the people involved. When these elements are present, most decision making should be done by the people

Empowering People for Freedom, Wholeness, and Justice (continued)

who are responsible to implement the decisions. All decisions must take into consideration the local context and the unique people, relationships, and project conditions that are present.

- *Wages should be fair.*

  When development work involves employment, the employee should be compensated equitably in relation to their contribution toward the success or profitability of the project.

- *Training programs should include teaching on the importance of stewardship and giving.*

  The need for people to give to God, to others and to their community should be made explicit in the development process. Each person's self-identity as a contributor should be reinforced and the intrinsic connection between receiving and giving (Luke 6.38) should be established.

6.3 Development work must discourage the inclination toward dependency.

<u>Explanation</u>

Development emphasizes that each person should be trained and equipped to achieve their potential to be self-sustaining and self-directing. Creating or nurturing dependency undercuts the deep human need to be a co-creator with God in using our gifts to honor him, and finding our significance and place in the world. Dependency can occur from either end of the people-helping relationship; the developer can create a sense of his or her own indispensability which leads to dependency, or the trainee can easily refuse to progress and grow on to interdependence and depth. Dependency pollutes the process of authentic development by creating unhealthy relationships which damage the trainee's initiative and self-motivation.

<u>Implications</u>

- *Trainees must be required to demonstrated initiative.*

  The basic rule of thumb is "Don't do for people what they can do for themselves-even if it means that the project (or training) will go slowly" (Hoke and Voorhies 1989, 224). When too much is done for the people

Empowering People for Freedom, Wholeness, and Justice (continued)

who are being assisted, the developer has taken from the trainees the opportunity to learn from their mistakes. Dependency, even when resulting from a spirit of benevolence and sympathy, inevitably stunts the growth of those who are so affected.

- *Development should avoid the extremes of authoritarian paternalism, on the one hand, and non-directive laissez-faire(ism) on the other.*

Developers, by definition, are leaders, and cannot avoid their responsibility to mentor, train, teach, and provide direction to those they serve. Maintaining complete decision-making control, however, does not foster interdependent relationships. While close accountability is essential in the earliest stages of training, development workers must recognize the need to modify strategies and involvement based on the competency and ongoing progress of the learners.[5]

- *Projects should help trainees gain control of their own destiny.*

Projects must be regularly evaluated to insure that they are not keeping people dependent on long-term employment by WIS. Projects which equip people to gain employment with existing businesses or start businesses of their own are the goal.

5 For a discussion of the Hersey-Blanchard training model that tailors leadership style to the competencies and attitudes of the trainee see **Leadership Research** *(Klopfenstein, 1995)*

Wholeness (*Shalom*) is the personal and communal experience of peace, abundance, goodness, soundness, well-being, and belonging. Wholeness is founded on *righteousness* (right relationships with God and man), *truth* (right beliefs about God and man), and *holiness* (right actions before God and man). Shalom is a gift of God and a sign of his Kingdom's presence.

7. World Impact's Development Work Is Committed to Wholeness

7.1 Development should create an environment where cooperative relationships can flourish.

Explanation

Development that leads to wholeness acknowledges that human activity takes place in community. The web of relationships that occurs in the work environment (e.g. trainer to trainee, co-worker to co-worker, etc.), must reflect our values of Christian community.

Implications

- *People are not means to an end.*

  Development seeks, first of all, to develop people. This will necessarily involve equipping them (and holding them accountable to) accomplishing tasks. However, it is the maturing of the person, not the completion of the task that is always the primary end of development work.

- *All people in the development process should work for each other as if they are working for Christ himself.*

  Colossians 3.23-24 reminds us that our work is ultimately directed toward and rewarded by Christ. Development projects must operationalize this principle. This suggests that our work must be done with excellence, integrity, diligence, meekness, love and whatever other virtues are necessary for proper service to God.

- *Relational dynamics must be taken seriously.*

  A development project which produces an excellent product and equips people with marketable skills, but which is characterized by disharmony or disunity among its employees has not achieved its goal. The developer must seek to develop genuine community within the workplace.

7.2 *Development activities should demonstrate the truth of the Gospel.*

Explanation

1 John 3:18 exhorts us to love not merely with words or tongue, "but with actions and in truth." The love of Christ is given not to "souls" but to whole persons. Development activities should minister unashamedly to the whole person and should serve as evangelism by example. Development work functions as a sign of the Kingdom by enabling people, families, and\or communities to experience the love and care of Christ. This suggests that development workers must know Christ intimately and be able to communicate his love to others.

Implications

- *Development projects may emphasize mental, physical, social, or economic development.*

Empowering People for Freedom, Wholeness, and Justice (continued)

All aspects of human need are of concern to the development worker. As the development worker's love for people takes shape in concrete actions, it should be their intent that people "may see your good deeds and praise your Father in heaven." (Matt. 5.16).

• *Development workers should be maturing disciples of Christ who are actively engaged in ongoing spiritual growth.*

Who we are is more important than what we do. Only as development workers are actively seeking to live in Christ's love and listen to his Spirit, will they effectively communicate his love to those they work with.

• *Development workers must receive care for their own physical, mental, emotional, and spiritual health and development.*

Development workers face unique pressures in dealing with human need. They often feel particular stress from standing in between, and identifying with, both the interests of the particular people they serve and the organization they represent (See Hiebert 1989, 83). Physical, emotional or spiritual burn-out is an ever present possibility. Therefore, it is important that development workers give adequate time and attention to maintaining their own health so that they can continue to effectively minister to the needs of others.

• *Development workers need to be specifically equipped in evangelism and an understanding of missions.*

Christian development workers usually understand that development and evangelism should work in partnership, but are often undertrained in evangelism (See Hoke and Voorhies 1989). Development workers also need to receive general training in missions and management in addition to being trained for their specific task of development (See Pickett and Hawthorne 1992, D218-19) since many of their daily tasks require an understanding of these disciplines.

7.3 *Development activities should be above reproach.*

<u>Explanation</u>

Wholeness and holiness are inseparable concepts. The way in which development work is conducted will have a profound impact on its ability to effect transformation. For development work to contribute to the wholeness, soundness, and well-being of people it must take special care to sustain integrity in word and deed.

<u>Implications</u>

* *Development projects should maintain high ethical standards.*

    Lack of adequate funds or personnel and the pressures of immediate human need can tempt us to "cut corners" in the way we develop and administrate projects. This temptation must be resisted. Our product cannot be artificially separated from our process. Development projects must serve as a witness to the government, society at large, and the people they train through adherence to high ethical standards of business conduct.

* *Development projects must work within the framework of our 501(c)(3) non-profit status.*

    State and Federal laws limit the ability of non-profits to create situations where individuals directly receive wealth and resources from the corporation. (This prevents individuals inside and outside of the organization from abusing the non-profit status for personal gain). As programs are created to empower people and share resources, the development workers must make sure that they are structured in such a way that they fall within the legal guidelines.

* *Appeals to donors must not motivate by guilt, overstate the need, promise unrealistic results, or demean the dignity of aid recipients.*

    Compressing the complexity of human need and relationships into an appeal to donors is a difficult and complicated task. It is, however, necessary and important work. Development workers in the field should take personal responsibility for relaying needs and vision in an accurate manner to those involved in publishing printed materials about a project.

Empowering People for Freedom, Wholeness, and Justice (continued)

Justice results from a recognition that all things belong to God and should be shared in accordance with his liberality and impartiality. Biblical justice is concerned both with equitable treatment and with the restoration of right relationship. It abhors oppression, prejudice and inequality because it understands that these separate people from each other and from God. Development which is based on justice is an important step toward repairing damaged relationships between individuals, classes and cultures which may harbor suspicion and ill-will toward one another. Development work seeks to engender right actions which lead to right relationships.

8. World Impact's Development Work Is Committed to Justice

8.1 Development is rooted in a biblical understanding of God as Creator and Ruler of the universe which demands that all things be reconciled in him.

Explanation

God has delegated to humanity the responsibility to be stewards of his world. This understanding manifests itself in concern for three broad categories of relationship: relations with God, relations with others, and relations with the environment (See Elliston 1989, *Transformation*, 176). Although these relationships were broken by the entrance of sin in the world, God's kingdom rule now demands their restoration.

Development recognizes that until the fullness of the Kingdom of Christ is manifested, there will inevitably be poverty, exploitation, and misery caused by sin's perversion of these three areas of relationship. This realization, neither paralyzes nor discourages authentic Christian development. While understanding the nature of moral evil in the world, authentic development seeks to demonstrate models of justice and reconciliation which reflect the justice of Christ's Kingdom.

Implications

* *Development intends to move people toward right relationship with God.*

    Authentic reconciliation between people is based on their mutual reconciliation with God. Although "common grace" and the "image of God" provide a ground for some degree of reconciliation between all people, it is ultimately in right relationship with God through Christ that the most profound and lasting form of reconciliation can occur.

Empowering People for Freedom, Wholeness, and Justice (continued)

Therefore, development work is eager to assist in preparing people for hearing the Gospel by witnessing to its truth and living out its implications.

• *Reconciliation between individuals, classes, and cultures is a key value.*

Development will inevitably involve new ways of power-sharing, using resources, making decisions, enforcing policy, and relating to others. There is a need to innovate rather than simply imitate existing models. It is extremely important that the viewpoints of peoples from different classes and cultures be represented in the planning of any development project.

• *Development projects must not be wasteful of resources or harmful to the physical environment.*

God's command to humankind is to recognize his ownership, and neither exploit nor destroy his earth, but to tend and care for it. Stewardship involves using the earth's resources to glorify him and meet the needs of our neighbors while keeping in mind our responsibility to future generations. Development must be sustainable, i.e., it must not simply consume resources but cultivate them as well.

8.2 Development recognizes the systemic and institutional foundations of producing wealth and experiencing poverty.

Explanation

The Bible delineates various moral vices that can lead to poverty in the lives of individuals (e.g., laziness, sloth, neglect of responsibility, cf. Prov. 6; Prov. 24, etc.), However, it is also clear that poverty can be caused by large scale societal and economic factors that create conditions of need, oppression, and want (cf. Isa. 1; Isa. 54, Amos 4, 5, etc.). Even a cursory reading of Scripture reveals that throughout biblical history the prophets condemned certain practices of business, politics, law, industry, and even religion that contributed to the imbalances among various groups within society, and led to the oppression of the poor. Development seeks to be prophetic by affirming that God is committed to the poor and the needy, and will not tolerate their oppression indefinitely. Development is not naive. It does not attribute all poverty in society to individual moral vice. On the contrary, struggling against injustice demands that people recognize the ever-present possibility of demonic influence in human structures (1 John 5.19).

Empowering People for Freedom, Wholeness, and Justice (continued)

Implications

- *Spiritual warfare is a key component of the development process.*

  Ephesians 6.12 reminds us that "we do not wrestle against flesh and blood, but against the rulers, against the authorities, against the cosmic powers over this present darkness, against the spiritual forces of evil in the heavenly places." Development work that does not intentionally and regularly set aside time for prayer and other spiritual disciplines is unlikely to effect lasting change. Development workers should have a plan for spiritual warfare that is as significant a focus as the plan for the development work itself.

  Development workers should also realize that their projects will experience spiritual attack. The accumulation of money or power within a project can be entry points for the perversion of that project despite its best intentions. Relationships between development project leaders, or between development workers and those they are training, can be twisted through the stress of conflict, jealousy, miscommunication, and cultural differences. Both personal relationships and institutional programs need to be protected from spiritual forces that would corrupt or destroy them. This requires an ongoing commitment to spiritual warfare, and to personal and corporate holiness.[6]

- *Development work should challenge unjust practices.*

  Development workers must prepare people to speak out against unjust practices in ways which demonstrate both the love and justice of God. While the non-profit organization is not itself a forum for political advocacy, it is responsible to train people to value justice and to make decisions in a moral context. In the marketplace, workers will be confronted by individual and systemic injustices and should be trained to respond to them in a manner which honors Christ and the values of his Kingdom.

- *The role of the Church in development must not be neglected.*

  Ephesians 2.14 records that it is "Christ himself" who is our peace and who has "destroyed the barrier, the dividing wall of hostility" between Jew and Gentiles. Reconciliation is rooted in the person and work of

*6 See Thomas McAlpine, **Facing the Powers** (McAlpine, 1991) for a helpful discussion of ways in which Reformed, Anabaptist, Charismatic, and Social Science perspectives share both differing perspectives and common ground in understanding and confronting spiritual powers.*

Empowering People for Freedom, Wholeness, and Justice (continued)

Christ and thus the importance of Christ's body, the Church, cannot be overlooked. Missionary development projects should both flow out of and result in dynamic churches.

8.3 Development does not seek to guarantee equality of outcome, but equality of opportunity.

Explanation

Development concentrates on providing an environment in which people can learn the importance and disciplines of work, gain skills which enhance the value of their work, and apply the disciplines and skills they acquire. However, no human endeavor is exempt from the moral force of our ability to choose, i.e., to decide whether or not to fully use the gifts, opportunities, and potentials we have been given. Because of variations of motivation, effort and preparation, differences in incomes are inevitable, and ought to be expected. Development programs should both teach and reward initiative.

Implications

- *Each trainee plays a critical role in their own success.*

    While the developers can offer a vast amount of expertise and aid in creating wealth for the trainees, many of the most important attributes necessary for prolonged success are controlled by the trainees. Without the requisite vision, energy, and commitment to do the work for long enough time so profits can be seen, success will not occur. These qualities arise from the drive and conviction of the trainees, not merely from the availability of the developers. Because of this, development cannot guarantee the success of all those involved in the project.

- *Faithful stewardship should lead to increased responsibility.*

    All development projects should have a plan for rewarding faithfulness, skill development, and diligence. Justice demands that increased effort lead to increased reward.

Empowering People for Freedom, Wholeness, and Justice (continued)

8.4 Development workers should respect cultural differences and strive to create a training style that is culturally conducive to those being empowered.

Explanation

Every human culture is "a blueprint that gives the individuals of a society a way of explaining and coping with life. It teaches people how to think, act and respond appropriately in any given situation. It allows people to work together based on a common understanding of reality. It organizes ways of thinking and acting into forms that can be passed on to others" (Cornett 1991, 2). Culture shapes every form of human activity from the observable behaviors (language, dress, food, etc.) to the internal thoughts and attitudes (thinking styles, definitions of beauty and worth, etc.). Understanding how a culture perceives reality, what it values, and how it functions is fundamental information for the development worker.

Although all human cultures are affected by sinful perspectives, attitudes and behaviors which must be confronted by the Gospel, human cultures themselves are celebrated by the Scriptures. The apostles confirmed that becoming a Christian did not entail having to change one's original culture (Acts 15). The vision of God's Kingdom from Old Testament (Micah 4) to New (Rev. 7.9) involves people from every nation, language and ethnicity. Missionaries from Paul onward have contextualized the Gospel, putting eternal truth in forms that could be understood and practiced by people of diverse cultures (See Cornett 1991, 6-9). Development workers, likewise, must respect cultural differences and seek to contextualize their instruction and resources (See Elliston, Hoke and Voorhies 1989).

Development workers have a unique interest in empowering groups that have been marginalized, oppressed or neglected by the larger society. This will frequently involve working with groups or individuals that are distinct from the dominant culture. Development work will effectively empower immigrants, unassimilated people groups, or people who have been victimized by race or class discrimination, only if it understands and respects the cultural distinctives of these groups.

Finally, development workers must prepare people to live and work in a pluralistic society. Learning how to successfully relate to customers and co-workers from other cultures has become a key component of job training. Although development work must start with the cultural context of those being assisted, it must also enable those workers to respect other cultures and to successfully work in the larger society.

Implications

7 Basic resources for gaining an understanding of culture include **The Missionary and Culture** *(Cornett 1991),* **Beyond Culture** *(Hall 1976),* Christianity Confronts Culture *(Mayers 1974),* **Ministering Cross-Culturally** *(Lingenfelter and Mayers 1986) and* **Cross-Cultural Conflicts: Building Relationships for Effective Ministry** *(Elmer 1993).*

- *Development workers should understand the culture(s) and sub-culture(s) of the people they work with.*

   Development workers should, first of all, gain a basic understanding of the nature of human culture and of strategies for developing effective cross-cultural training relationships.[7] They should gain the fundamental skills necessary for working in the cross-cultural environment (language acquisition, etc.). It is highly desirable for the development worker to have a mentor either from the culture or who is an experienced observer of the culture to assist in the training process.

- *The work environment should be functionally appropriate and aesthetically pleasing when viewed from the perspective of the culture(s) that work or do business there.*

   All human cultures desire environments that combine functionality with beauty. There is significant variation, however, in how beauty and functionality are defined, prioritized and applied from one culture to another. The physical environment in which the development project occurs should take cultural concerns into account.

- *Development workers should be sensitive to how conflict is handled by the culture of the people they work among.*

   Conflict is an inevitable part of working together. It can be a healthy opportunity for growth if handled correctly. Cultural differences, however, can sabotage the process of conflict management. The development worker must take cultural attitudes toward directness/indirectness, shame/guilt, individualism/collectivism, etc. seriously and adapt their conflict management style to reflect those concerns. They must also take seriously their responsibility to prepare people from sub-cultures to work within the dominant culture.

- *Development workers should be sensitive to roles or work that is considered degrading by the culture.*

   Although all honest work carries dignity before God, cultural perceptions of role and status have tremendous power to shape attitudes. Whenever possible, work should be chosen that is not repugnant to the culture.

Empowering People for Freedom, Wholeness, and Justice (continued)

If this is not possible, careful preparation and training should be done to ensure that each person understands the necessity and dignity of the work involved. In some cases it may be necessary to challenge the cultural value system (see Miller, 1989) but this should be done sensitively and with adequate preparation and involvement of the trainees.

- *Developers should prepare trainees for situations that they are likely to encounter in the workplace.*

People from event-oriented cultures, for example, need to understand the time-oriented culture that defines American business practices. Helping workers learn skills and disciplines for success in the larger society is an important part of the training process.

8.5 *The goal of development is to glorify God through excellence and service, not merely to make a profit.*

Explanation

In the ethics of the corporate world, the highest indicator of success is usually the profitability of the business. However, development work that is informed by kingdom values involves a broader vision. Development seeks to emphasize the importance of people-nurturing and training and the production of a quality product that meets human need.

Since producing quality Christian and professional leadership models is a high aim of our development efforts, we must unashamedly emphasize both external profits as well as internal gains. On the one hand, a business, if it is to survive, must be profitable and able to stand on its on. On the other hand, we must strive to produce men and women who are spiritually mature as well as professionally oriented and technically competent. The creation of wealth is not an end in itself; it is a by-product of engaging in business with an eye toward excellence, in the name of Christ.

Empowering People for Freedom, Wholeness, and Justice (continued)

Implications

- *No skill will be taught or product produced simply because it is valued by society or likely to produce a profit.*

  All skills and products must be consistent with the aims of justice, peace and wholeness that characterize the kingdom rule of Christ. Skills and modes of production that degrade human dignity and products that promote injustice, inequity, or human misery are not to be considered fitting for development regardless of their acceptance by the society at large.

- *The aim of development work must not only be to help people obtain and generate resources but also to help them commit to using those resources on behalf of the Kingdom of God.*

  Helping people to obtain education, skills or wealth is ultimately unproductive if these things are not placed at God's service and the service of others. Good development projects will offer people the opportunity to serve God not only with the profits from their labor but through the work itself. Developers must teach and model that work is an opportunity for service to God (Col. 3.23-24).

9. The Need for Application

Each of the points listed above has a section titled "Explanation" and a section titled "Implications." However, for the paper to be complete one more step is necessary. Every implication must be accompanied by a series of *applications*. These applications should be created by development workers in the field, and structured for the unique needs of the local situation.

In creating these applications, the following guidelines should be followed:

- Each local ministry should thoroughly review the "Implications" sections and decide on specific steps which will enable them to apply these principles to their particular development project.

- These steps should be developed in a way that involves the people most affected by each development project.

- Once finalized, the application steps should be committed to writing.

- These applications should be regularly taught and reviewed.

Empowering People for Freedom, Wholeness, and Justice (continued)

- These applications should be included in each regularly scheduled evaluation done by the project.

- Following each scheduled evaluation, there should be a revising and updating of these applications based on what has been learned in experience.

Appendix A

Selected Quotes on the Role of Development Work within the Mission Agency

Christian social transformation differs from secular relief and development in that it serves in an integrated, symbiotic relationship with other ministries of the Church, including evangelism and church planting (Elliston 1989, 172).

My experience with scores of ministries among the poor has taught me that economic projects, when used as entrees into communities, do not facilitate church planting or growth. . . . the two goals—relief and church planting—are different. They are both Christian, and at times compatible. But many times they do not support each other well at all. . . . It appears that where workers enter a community with a priority to proclaim, many deeds of mercy, acts of justice and signs of power will occur. From these the church will be established. But when workers enter with a priority of dealing with economic need, they may assist the people economically very well, but they rarely establish as church. There is a time for both, and there are life callings to do both, but they must be distinguished (Grigg 1992, 163-64).

Avoid institutions if possible at the beachhead stage (community development programs unrelated to church planting, schools, clinics, etc.); they will come later. In Honduras we developed community development work but it grew out of the churches, not vice versa. We taught obedience to the great commandment of loving our neighbor in a practical way. A poverty program can aid church planting if the two are integrated by the Holy Spirit. But churches dependent on charitable institutions are almost always dominated by the foreign missionary and seldom reproduce (Patterson 1992, D-80).

Empowering People for Freedom, Wholeness, and Justice (continued)

All too often native pastors and churches have become preoccupied with ministries that attract Western dollars (such as orphan work) while neglecting more basic pastoral care and evangelism. Even development work, if not wisely administered, can hinder church growth (Ott 1993, 289).

There is a very real danger of recruiting missionary-evangelists primarily on the basis of their abilities and expertise. "Whatever your special interest is, we can use it in our mission"— this is an all-too-common approach to recruitment. As a result, many workers become frustrated when their special ability is not fully utilized; they react by simply "doing their thing" and contributing only indirectly to the task of planting growing churches. Consequently, the so-called secondary or supporting ministries have a way of becoming primary and actually eclipsing the central task! (Hesselgrave 1980, 112).

It is unfortunate that Christian service and witness often seem to be competing concerns in Christian outreach when, in fact, both are biblical and complementary. . . . One reason for this tension is that service enterprises such as hospitals and educational institutions have a way of preempting finances and energies so that evangelism and witness tend to get crowded out (Hesselgrave 1980 p. 328).

Since we believe in the unity of the Bible, we must say that 'The Great Commission is not an isolated command, (but) a natural outflow of the character of God. . . The missionary purpose and thrust of God. . .' Thus, we should not take the Great Commandment and the Great Commission as though they are mutually exclusive. We should take the Great Commandment—to love others—and the Great Commission—to preach—together, integrated in the mission of Jesus Christ, for it is the same Lord, who commanded and commissioned the same disciples and his followers. Therefore, as Di Gangi says, 'to communicate the gospel effectively we must obey the great commandment as well as the great commission' (Cho 1985, 229).

Empowering People for Freedom, Wholeness, and Justice (continued)

Works Cited

Cho, J. Chongham. "The Mission of the Church." See Nicholls, 1985.

Cornett, Terry G., ed. "The Missionary and Culture." *World Impact Ministry Resources*. Los Angeles: World Impact Mission Studies Training Paper, 1991.

Dayton, Donald W. *Discovering an Evangelical Heritage*. 1976. Peabody, MA: Hendrickson, 1988.

Elliston, Edgar J., ed. *Christian Relief and Development: Developing Workers for Effective Ministry*. Dallas: Word Publishing, 1989.

------. "Christian Social Transformation Distinctives." See Elliston, 1989.

Elliston, Edgar J., Stephen J. Hoke, and Samuel Voorhies. "Issues in Contextualizing Christian Leadership." See Elliston, 1989.

Grigg, Viv. "Church of the Poor." *Discipling the City*. 2nd ed. Ed. Roger S. Greenway. Grand Rapids: Baker Book House, 1992.

Hall, Edward T. *Beyond Culture*. Garden City, NY: Anchor Books, 1976.

Hesselgrave, David. *Planting Churches Cross-Culturally: A Guide for Home and Foreign Missions*. Grand Rapids: Baker Book House, 1980.

Hiebert, Paul G. "Evangelism, Church, and Kingdom." See Van Engen, et. al., 1993.

------. "Anthropological Insights for Whole Ministries." See Elliston, 1989.

Hoke, Stephen J. and Samuel J. Voorhies. "Training Relief and Development Workers in the Two-Thirds World." See Elliston, 1989.

Klopfenstein, David E. and Dorothy A. Klopfenstein. "Leadership Research." CityGates. 1 (1995): 21-26.

Klopfenstein, David, Dotty Klopfenstein and Bud Williams. *Come Yourselves Apart: Christian Leadership in the Temporary Community*. Azusa, CA: Holysm Publishing, 1993.

Ladd, George Eldon. *A Theology of the New Testament*. Grand Rapids: Wm. B. Eerdmans, 1974.

Empowering People for Freedom, Wholeness, and Justice (continued)

McAlpine, Thomas H. *Facing the Powers: What are the Options?* Monrovia, CA: MARC-World Vision, 1991.

Miller, Darrow L. "The Development Ethic: Hope for a Culture of Poverty." See Elliston, 1989.

Nicholls, Bruce J., ed. *In Word and Deed: Evangelism and Social Responsibility.* Grand Rapids: Wm. B. Eerdmans, 1985.

Ott, Craig. "Let the Buyer Beware." *Evangelical Missions Quarterly,* 29 (1993): 286-291.

Patterson, George. "The Spontaneous Multiplication of Churches." See Winter and Hawthorne, 1992.

Pickett, Robert C. and Steven C. Hawthorne. "Helping Others Help Themselves: Christian Community Development." See Winter and Hawthorne, 1992.

Stott, John. "Twenty Years After Lausanne: Some Personal Reflections." *International Bulletin of Missionary Research.* 19 (1995): 50-55.

Van Engen, Charles, et. al., eds. *The Good News of the Kingdom: Mission Theology for the Third Millennium.* Maryknoll: Orbis Books, 1993.

Verkuyl, Johannes. *Contemporary Missiology: An Introduction.* Grand Rapids: Wm. B. Eerdmans, 1978.

------. "The Biblical Notion of Kingdom: Test of Validity for Theology of Religion." See Van Engen, et. al., 1993.

Winter, Ralph D. and Steven C. Hawthorne, eds. *Perspectives on the World Christian Movement: A Reader.* Rev. ed. Pasadena: William Carey Library, 1992.

Equipping the Church Plant Team Member
Developing Workable Training Strategies
Rev. Dr. Don L. Davis

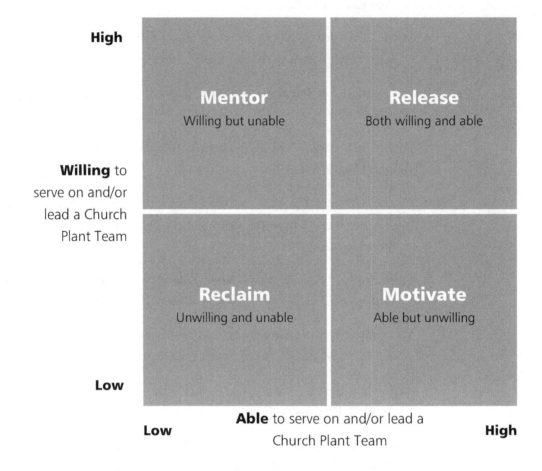

High

Mentor
Willing but unable

Release
Both willing and able

Willing to
serve on and/or
lead a Church
Plant Team

Reclaim
Unwilling and unable

Motivate
Able but unwilling

Low

Low

Able to serve on and/or lead a
Church Plant Team

High

Ethics of the New Testament: Living in the Upside-Down Kingdom of God
True Myth and Biblical Fairy Tale
Dr. Don L. Davis

The Principle of Reversal

The Principle Expressed	Scripture
The poor shall become rich, and the rich shall become poor	Luke 6.20-26
The law breaker and the undeserving are saved	Matt. 21.31-32
Those who humble themselves shall be exalted	1 Pet. 5.5-6
Those who exalt themselves shall be brought low	Luke 18.14
The blind shall be given sight	John 9.39
Those claiming to see shall be made blind	John 9.40-41
We become free by being Christ's slave	Rom. 12.1-2
God has chosen what is foolish in the world to shame the wise	1 Cor. 1.27
God has chosen what is weak in the world to shame the strong	1 Cor. 1.27
God has chosen the low and despised to bring to nothing things that are	1 Cor. 1.28
We gain the next world by losing this one	1 Tim. 6.7
Love this life and you'll lose it; hate this life, and you'll keep the next	John 12.25
You become the greatest by being the servant of all	Matt. 10.42-45
Store up treasures here, you forfeit heaven's reward	Matt. 6.19
Store up treasures above, you gain heaven's wealth	Matt. 6.20
Accept your own death to yourself in order to live fully	John 12.24
Release all earthly reputation to gain heaven's favor	Phil. 3.3-7
The first shall be last, and the last shall become first	Mark 9.35
The grace of Jesus is perfected in your weakness, not your strength	2 Cor. 12.9
God's highest sacrifice is contrition and brokenness	Ps. 51.17
It is better to give to others than to receive from them	Acts 20.35
Give away all you have in order to receive God's best	Luke 6.38

An Example of the Practice of Textual Criticism

Adapted from R. C. Briggs, **Interpreting the New Testament Today**.

Mark 1.1 The beginning of the Gospel of Jesus Christ *(the Son of God)*

According to the critical apparatus, the following manuscripts (or group of manuscripts) read

Ιησοῦ Χριστοῦ υἱού θεοῦ

A (*Codex Alexandrinus*). Fifth century. Byzantine text (in the Gospels).

B (*Codex Vaticanus*). Fourth century. Alexandrian text (in the Gospels and Acts).

D (*Codex Bezae*). Fifth or sixth century. Western text.

W (*Washington Codex*). Fifth century. Western text (in Mark 1.1-5.30).

Ω (*koine*). Group of late uncial and minuscule manuscripts dating from the seventh century. Western text.

λ (*Family 1, Lake Group*). Twelfth century and later. Akin to fourth- and fifth-century Caesarean text.

φ (*Family 13, Ferrar Group*). Twelfth century and later. Akin to Caesarean text.

it (*Itala or Old Latin*). Eleventh century and later. Text is early Western (prior to date of Vulgate).

vg (*Vulgate*). Authorized Latin translation, completed by Jerome in A. D. 405 (Gospels A. D. 385). Western text.

sy[P] (*Peshitta*). Authorized fifth-century Syriac translation. Akin to the Byzantine text (in the Gospels).

sa (*Sahidic*). Fourth-century Coptic (Egyptian) translation. Alexandrian text, with Western influence.

bo (*Bohairic*). Coptic translation, later than Sahidic. Western text. The critical apparatus also lists two significant manuscripts which preserve the shorter reading.

S also designated ~ (*Codex Sinaiticus*). Fourth century. Like B, a primary representative of the Alexandrian text.

Θ (*Codex Koridethi*). Ninth century. Text akin to third- and fourth-century Alexandrian text.

Examples of Denominational Statements on "Baptism in the Holy Spirit" Which Illustrate the Differing Views

Single Stage View

Evangelical Presbyterian Church

Excerpted from Position Paper on the Holy Spirit, www.epc.org/about-epc/position-papers/holy-spirit.html

As a denomination in the Reformed tradition, we subscribe to the ancient affirmation of orthodox Christian faith and believe in "one Lord, one faith, one baptism" (Ephesians 4:5). This baptism, while visibly expressed in the covenant sacrament that bears its name is invisibly the work of the Spirit that takes place at the time of the new birth. Paul expresses this truth in I Corinthians 12:13, when he tells the Corinthians "…we were all baptized by one Spirit into one body…"

Thus, we hold to the concept of the baptism in or with the Holy Spirit as the act of the Spirit that takes an unregenerate individual and, through the new birth, adopts him into the family of God. All the works of the Spirit that follow, then, are because of this initial baptism rather than separate from it.

Since Christians are called to "…be filled with the Spirit…" (Ephesians 5:18) all believers in Christ having been baptized into His body by the Holy Spirit should seek to experience the fulfillment of this command. We believe that Christians are called upon to proclaim a grace that reaches out to forgive, to redeem and to give new spiritual power to life through Jesus Christ and the infilling of the Holy Spirit." (*Book of Worship*, 1-3).

Multiple Stage View: Holiness

Church of the Nazarene

Excerpted from Articles of Faith, www.nazarene.org/gensec/we_believe.html

We believe that entire sanctification is that act of God, subsequent to regeneration, by which believers are made free from original sin, or depravity, and brought into a state of entire devotement to God, and the holy obedience of love made perfect.

It is wrought by the baptism with the Holy Spirit, and comprehends in one experience the cleansing of the heart from sin and the abiding, indwelling presence of the Holy Spirit, empowering the believer for life and service.

Examples of Denominational Statements on "Baptism in the Holy Spirit" (continued)

Entire sanctification is provided by the blood of Jesus, is wrought instantaneously by faith, preceded by entire consecration; and to this work and state of grace the Holy Spirit bears witness.

This experience is also known by various terms representing its different phases, such as "Christian perfection," "perfect love," "heart purity," "the baptism with the Holy Spirit," "the fullness of the blessing," and "Christian holiness."

We believe that there is a marked distinction between a pure heart and a mature character. The former is obtained in an instant, the result of entire sanctification; the latter is the result of growth in grace.

We believe that the grace of entire sanctification includes the impulse to grow in grace. However, this impulse must be consciously nurtured, and careful attention given to the requisites and processes of spiritual development and improvement in Christlikeness of character and personality. Without such purposeful endeavor one's witness may be impaired and the grace itself frustrated and ultimately lost.

Assemblies of God

Excerpted from The Initial Physical Evidence of the Baptism in the Holy Spirit, http://ag.org/top/position_papers/0000_index.cfm

Multiple Stage View: Pentecostal

The term baptism in the Holy Spirit is taken from Scripture. John the Baptist was the first to use it shortly before Jesus began His public ministry. He said, "He [Jesus] shall baptize you with the Holy Ghost" (Matthew 3:11). At the conclusion of His earthly ministry, Jesus referred to John's statement (Acts 1:5); and Peter, in reporting on the events in the home of Cornelius, also repeated the statement (Acts 11:16).

The baptism in the Spirit (also referred to herein as the Baptism) is subsequent to and distinct from the new birth. Scripture makes it clear there is an experience in which the Holy Spirit baptizes believers into the body of Christ (1 Corinthians 12:13), and there is the experience in which Christ baptizes believers in the Holy Spirit (Matthew 3:11). These cannot refer to the same experience since the agent who does the baptizing and the element into which the candidate is baptized are different in each case.

The distinctiveness of the experiences is illustrated in several places. The case of the Ephesian disciples is an example. After they stated they had experienced only

Examples of Denominational Statements on "Baptism in the Holy Spirit" (continued)

John's baptism (Acts 19:3), Paul explained they were to believe on Christ Jesus. Then these disciples were baptized in water, after which Paul laid hands on them and the Holy Spirit came on them. The lapse of time was brief between these disciples' believing on Christ and the Holy Spirit's coming upon them, but it was long enough for them to be baptized in water. The baptism in the Spirit was distinct from and subsequent to salvation.

The baptism in the Spirit is not an end in itself, but a means to an end. The scriptural ideal for the believer is to be continually filled with the Spirit. The Baptism is the crisis experience which introduces the believer to the process experience of living a Spirit-filled life.

The expression initial physical evidence of the Baptism refers to the first outward sign that the Holy Spirit has come in filling power. A study of Scripture indicates there was a physical sign by which observers knew that believers had been baptized in the Holy Spirit. The evidence always occurred at the very time the believers were baptized in the Spirit and not on some future occasion.

In the home of Cornelius there was convincing evidence of the Holy Spirit being poured out on the Gentiles (Acts 10:44-48). Later, when Peter was called upon to explain to the leaders of the church in Jerusalem his ministry in the home of Cornelius, he referred to observable evidence of the believers being baptized in the Holy Spirit. He cited this as the reason why he arranged for the believers to be baptized in water (Acts 11:15-17).

While speaking in tongues has initial evidential value, it is designed by God to be much more than evidence of a past experience. It also continues to bring enrichment to the individual believer in personal devotions, and to the congregation when accompanied by the interpretation of tongues.

**Combination View:
Pentecostal-Holiness**

Church of God in Christ

Excerpted from The Doctrines of the Church of God in Christ, http://www.cogic.org/doctrnes.htm

We believe that the Baptism of the Holy Ghost is an experience subsequent to conversion and sanctification and that tongue-speaking is the consequence of the baptism in the Holy Ghost with the manifestations of the fruit of the spirit (Galatians 5:22-23; Acts 10:46, 19:1-6). We believe that we are not baptized with the Holy Ghost in order to be saved (Acts 19:1-6; John 3:5). When one receives

Examples of Denominational Statements on "Baptism in the Holy Spirit" (continued)

a baptismal Holy Ghost experience, we believe one will speak with a tongue unknown to oneself according to the sovereign will of Christ. To be filled with the Spirit means to be Spirit controlled as expressed by Paul in Ephesians 5:18-19. Since the charismatic demonstrations were necessary to help the early church to be successful in implementing the command of Christ, we therefore, believe that a Holy Ghost experience is mandatory for all men today.

Association of Vineyard Churches

*Excerpted from **Vineyard Statement of Faith**,
www.vineyardusa.org/about/beliefs/beliefs_index/faith/paragraph_07.htm*

WE BELIEVE that the Holy Spirit was poured out on the Church at Pentecost in power, baptizing believers into the Body of Christ and releasing the gifts of the Spirit to them. The Spirit brings the permanent indwelling presence of God to us for spiritual worship, personal sanctification, building up the Church, gifting us for ministry, and driving back the kingdom of Satan by the evangelization of the world through proclaiming the word of Jesus and doing the works of Jesus.

WE BELIEVE that the Holy Spirit indwells every believer in Jesus Christ and that He is our abiding Helper, Teacher, and Guide. We believe in the filling or empowering of the Holy Spirit, often a conscious experience, for ministry today. We believe in the present ministry of the Spirit and in the exercise of all of the biblical gifts of the Spirit. We practice the laying on of hands for the empowering of the Spirit, for healing, and for recognition and empowering of those whom God has ordained to lead and serve the Church.

**Combination View:
Charismatic**

Faithfully Re-Presenting Jesus of Nazareth

Don L. Davis

Eph. 4.20-23 (ESV) - But that is not the way you learned Christ! - [21] assuming that you have heard about him and were taught in him, as the truth is in Jesus, [22] to put off your old self, which belongs to your former manner of life and is corrupt through deceitful desires, [23] and to be renewed in the spirit of your minds.

Rediscover the OT prophetic roots of the Messianic kingdom hope (return)

Faithfully Re-present Jesus of Nazareth

with fidelity to Holy Scripture in sync with apostolic tradition contextualizing biblical language without cultural distortion

Recognize the present cultural captivity of much evangelical Christian identity and practice (exile)

Re-experience and embrace the power of the NT apostolic vision and drama [myth] (possession)

Eph. 4.17-19 (ESV) - Now this I say and testify in the Lord, that you must no longer walk as the Gentiles do, in the futility of their minds. [18] They are darkened in their understanding, alienated from the life of God because of the ignorance that is in them, due to their hardness of heart. [19] They have become callous and have given themselves up to sensuality, greedy to practice every kind of impurity.

Eph. 4.24-25 (ESV) - and to put on the new self, created after the likeness of God in true righteousness and holiness. [25] Therefore, having put away falsehood, let each one of you speak the truth with his neighbor, for we are members one of another.

The Father, Son, and Holy Ghost
Share the Same Divine Attributes and Works
Supporting Scriptures

Adapted from Edward Henry Bickersteth, **The Trinity**. *Grand Rapids: Kregel Publications, 1957. Rpt. 1980.*

Attribute of God	God the Father	God the Son	God the Holy Spirit
God Is Eternal (Deut. 33.27)	Isa. 44.6; Rom. 16.26	John 8.58; Rev. 1.17-18	Heb. 9.14
God Created All Things (Rev. 4.11) and Is the Source of Life (Deut. 30.20)	Pss. 36.9; 100.3; 1 Cor. 8.6	John 1.3, 4; Col. 1.16	Gen. 1.2; Pss. 33.6; 104.30; Job 33.4; John 7.38-39; Rom. 8.11
God Is Incomprehensible (1 Tim. 6.16) and Omniscient (Jer. 16.17)	Isa. 46.9-10; Matt. 11.27; Heb. 4.13	Matt. 11.27; John 21.17	Isa. 40.13-14; 1 Cor. 2.10; John 16.15
God Is Omnipresent (Jer. 23.24)	Acts 17.27-28	Matt. 18.20; 28.20	Ps. 139.7-10
God Is Omnipotent (2 Chron. 20.6) and Sovereignly Acts as He Chooses (Job 42.2)	Luke 1.37; Eph. 1.11	John 14.14; Matt. 11.27	Zech. 4.6; Rom. 15.19; 1 Cor. 12.11
God Is True, Holy, Righteous, and Good (Ps. 119)	Ps. 34.8; John 7.28; 17.11, 25	John 14.6; 10.11; Acts 3.14	1 John 5.6; John 14.26; Ps. 143.10
God is the Source of Strength for His People (Exod. 15.2)	Ps. 18.32	Phil. 4.13	Eph. 3.16
God Alone Forgives and Cleanses from Sin (Pss. 51.7; 130.3-4)	Exod. 34.6-7	Mark 2.7-11	1 Cor. 6.11; Heb. 9.14

The Father, Son, and Holy Ghost Share the Same Divine Attributes and Works (continued)

Attribute of God	God the Father	God the Son	God the Holy Spirit
God Gave Humanity the Divine Law Which Revealed His Character and Will (2 Tim. 3.16)	Ezek. 2.4; Isa. 40.8; Deut. 9.10	Matt. 24.35; John 5.39; Heb. 1.1-2	2 Sam. 23.2; 2 Pet. 1.21; Rom. 8.2
God Dwells in and among the People Who Believe in Him (Isa. 57.15)	2 Cor. 6.16; 1 Cor. 14.25	Eph. 3.17; Matt. 18.20	John 14.17; 1 Cor. 6.19; Eph. 2.22
God Is the Supreme, Highest Being Who Has No Equal, Who Reigns as Lord and King over All Creation, and Who Alone Is to Be Worshiped and Glorified	Isa. 42.8; Ps. 47.2; 1 Tim. 6.15; Matt. 4.10; Rev. 22.8-9	John 20.28-29; Rev. 17.14; Heb. 1.3, 6-8	Matt. 12.31; Luke 1.35; 2 Cor. 3.18; 1 Pet. 4.14; John 4.24

Figures of Speech

Bob Smith. Basics of Bible Interpretation. Waco: Word Publishers, 1978. pp. 113-120.

One of the most enlightening aspects of language is the study of figurative expressions. Milton Terry introduces us to this subject with keen insight:

The natural operations of the human mind prompt men to trace analogies and make comparisons. Pleasing emotions are excited and the imagination is gratified by the use of metaphors and similes. Were we to suppose a language sufficiently copious in words to express all possible conceptions, the human mind would still require us to compare and contrast our concepts, and such a procedure would soon necessitate a variety of figures of speech. So much of our knowledge is acquired through the senses, that all our abstract ideas and our spiritual language have a material base. "It is not too much to say," observes Max Muller, "that the whole dictionary of ancient religion is made up of metaphors. With us these metaphors are all forgotten. We speak of *spirit* without thinking of *breath*, of *heaven* without thinking of *sky*, of *pardon* without thinking of a *release*, of *revelation* without thinking of a *veil*. But in ancient language every one of these words, nay, every word that does not refer to sensuous objects, is still in a chrysalis stage, half material and half spiritual, and rising and falling in its character according to the capacities of its speakers and hearers."[1]

What potent possibilities, then, lie in concepts conveyed by figurative language! So, moving to specifics, let's explore the various figures of speech. I'll list some of them, along with illustrations of their use on the following pages.

[1] *Milton S. Terry. **Biblical Hermeneutics**. Grand Rapids: Zondervan Publishing House, n.d. p. 244.*

Figures of Speech

SIMILE (*similis* = like)	A formal comparison using "*as . . . so*" or "like" to express resemblance. "*Even so*, husbands should love their own wives as their own bodies . . ." (Eph. 5.28).
METAPHOR (*Meta+phero* = a carrying over)	An implied comparison, a word applied to something it is not, to suggest a resemblance. "Benjamin is a ravenous wolf . . ." (Gen. 49.27).

Figures of Speech (continued)

IRONY (*Eiron* = a dissembling speaker)	The speaker or writer says the very opposite of what he intends to convey. "*. . . you are the people and wisdom will die with you*" (Job 12.1).
METONYMY (*Meta+onoma* = a change of name)	One word is used in place of another to portray some actual relationship between the things signified. "*Kill the passover . . .*" (Exod. 12.21 KJV) where the paschal lamb is meant.
HYPERBOLE (*Huper+bole*) = a throwing beyond	Intentional exaggeration for the purpose of emphasis, or magnifying beyond reality. "*If your right eye causes you to sin, pluck it out and throw it away . . .*" (Matt. 5.29).
PERSONIFICATION (to make like a person)	Inanimate objects are spoken of as persons, as if they had life. "*The sea looked and fled . . .*" (Ps. 114.3).
APOSTROPHE (*apo+strepho* = to turn from)	Turning from the immediate hearers to address an absent or imaginary person or thing. "*Ah, sword of the Lord! How long till you are quiet?*" (Jer. 47.6).
SYNECDOCHE (*sun+ekdechomai* = to receive from and associate with)	Where the whole is put for a part, or a part for the whole, an individual for a class and vice-versa. "*And we were in all 276 souls . . .*" in Acts 27.37, where soul is used for the whole person.

Simile

First, let's compare simile and metaphor. Ephesians 5:22-27 is a simile, making a formal comparison between Christ and the church on the one hand, and husbands and wives on the other. The words "as . . . so" or "even so" make this very clear. And this figure heightens our interest and dignifies the marriage relationship, especially if we see it in outline form, like this:

Figures of Speech (continued)

AS with CHRIST AND THE CHURCH	SO with HUSBANDS AND WIVES
CHRIST LOVED THE CHURCH and gave himself up for her (Eph. 5.25)	*HUSBANDS, LOVE your WIVES as CHRIST LOVED the CHURCH* (Eph. 5.25)
"THAT he might sanctify her" (Eph. 5.26) i.e. that we might be put to the intended use for which he created us: a) as an expression of his own *LIFE* and *CHARACTER* b) to fulfill our calling, enjoy our God-given ministries c) and much more (you add the rest)	THAT the husband might sanctify his wife. i.e. that she might SHARE HIS LIFE, be his helper, etc. a) expressing her own personality and life in Christ b) employing her gifts in a spiritual ministry. c) be the *ruler* of the *home*, in all that means to her husband and children
"THAT he might present the church to himself in splendor" (Eph. 5.27) i.e. that he might enjoy the benefits stemming from his unselfish love - in enjoying his Bride. And lead us on to the fulfillment of our manhood and womanhood by his love.	THAT the husband might seek his wife's fulfillment, and enjoy her, i.e. that he may enjoy the beauty and glory of her fulfilled womanhood, as he undertakes the responsibility of his headship leading her with the leadership of love to ultimate fulfillment
"THAT she might be holy and without blemish" (Eph. 5.27). i.e. that his work in us may go on to completion, that we may be wholly his.	THAT the husband be faithful, hanging in there, i.e. that his commitment may be steadfast and permanent, in spite of problems.
"Having cleansed her by the washing of water with the word" (Eph. 5.26) Based on *COMMUNICATION* which his loving heart initiates - to keep us close, mutually enjoying our love relationship.	Husbands are to keep communication channels open, remembering that *LOVE finds a way to COMMUNICATE, and it's his initiative* if he is going to love as CHRIST LOVED.

Metaphor

By contrast, a metaphor is not so straightforward. It communicates an impression more by implication. In the expressions, "You *are the salt of the earth* . . ." (Matt. 5:13) and "*You are the light of the world*" (Matt. 5:14), our Lord Jesus is multiplying metaphors to communicate graphic truth about the determinative role Christians are to play in affecting the world. In those early days, salt was the major means of arresting corruption in meat or fish, so the figure is not lost on those who listened to Jesus. Light, in any age, enables us to function with any degree of confidence. It dispels darkness. When we can't see, we're in trouble! The words "salt" and "light" are used as implied comparison. These metaphors speak with penetrating force, even though they are implicit in nature.

Irony

The use of irony as a figure of speech, though it has a bite to it, often has its humorous side. Our Lord was using both effects when he said, ". . . how can you say to your brother, 'Brother, let me take out the speck that is in your eye,' when you yourself do not see the log that is in your own eye?" (Luke 6:42).

In 1 Corinthians 4:8 the apostle Paul uses irony with great force, "Already you are filled! Already you have become rich! Without us you have become kings! And would that you did reign, so that we might share the rule with you." As we read on, Paul proceeds to contrast the state of the apostles as being the last—not the first, as spectacles to the world, as fools. Then he uses irony again, "We are fools for Christ's sake, but you are wise in Christ. We are weak, but you are strong. You are held in honor, but we in disrepute" (1 Cor. 4:10). Can you imagine how the Corinthian Christians must have felt the shame of their misplaced value systems, how this pointed word of sarcasm must have punctured their swollen pride in men? Would that we should review *our* value systems, today, and discover the only ground of boasting—the Lord Jesus and his life in us.

Metonymy

Then there's metonymy (a change of name). Speaking to the Pharisees concerning Herod, Christ says "Go and tell that fox . . ." (*Luke* 13:32) and with one word he characterized that politically crafty king. And, "The way of the fool is right in his own eyes . . ." (Prov. 12:15) where *eyes* represents the way he sees things, or his mental perspective. And, ". . . *the tongue* of the wise brings healing" (Prov. 12:18) in which *tongue* stands for what the wise one says, his words of wisdom.

In the New Testament, "Then went out to him Jerusalem and all Judea and all the region about the Jordan . . ." (Matt. 3:5) in which it is obvious that *people*, not places, are meant in the mention of these various regions. Then, we look at "You cannot drink the cup of the Lord and the cup of demons. You cannot partake of the table of the Lord and the table of demons" (1 Cor. 10:21). Here *cup* and *table* are used for what they contain and what they offer. Again, in Romans 3:30 *the circumcision is* used to represent the Jewish people, while *uncircumcision* refers to the Gentiles.

I'm sure from these examples you can see how commonly metonymy is used in the Bible. We use the same figure today when we call a person "a tiger" or "a kitten."

Hyperbole

Painting a picture larger than life by intentional exaggeration beyond reality is a common feature of our own speech, so hyperbole (a *throwing beyond*) should be thoroughly familiar to us.

In the anguish of his torment Job indulges in this kind of language. More graphically than any other form of speech it expresses the awfulness of his feeling of affliction.

> And now my soul is poured out within me; days of affliction
>   have taken hold of me.
>
> The night racks my bones, and the pain that gnaws me takes
>   no rest.
>
> With violence it seizes my garment; it binds me about like
>   the collar of my tunic.
>
> God has cast me into the mire, and I have become like dust
>   and ashes.
>
> I cry to thee and thou dost not answer me; I stand, and thou
>   dost not heed me.

> Thou hast turned cruel to me; with the might of thy
> hand thou dost persecute me.
>
> Thou liftest me up on the wind, thou makest me ride
> on it, and thou tossest me about in the roar of
> the storm.
>
> Yea, I know that thou wilt bring me to death, and to
> the house appointed for all living
>
> ~ Job 30.16-23

Certainly we get the keen sense of his utter despair from this highly expressive, but extravagant, language.

The apostle John in the New Testament uses hyperbolic language in this statement: "But there are also many other things which Jesus did; were every one of them to be written, I suppose that the world itself could not contain the books that would be written" (John 21:25). If we considered Christ's eternal existence, perhaps this statement could betaken literally, but if we limit it to the deeds of the Lord Jesus in his humanity (which I believe is what John has in mind) then it is clearly a use of hyperbole.

Personification

Referring to inanimate objects as if they possessed life and personality is especially evident in the language of imagination and feeling. In Numbers 16:32,". . . the earth opened its mouth and swallowed them up . . ." speaks of Korah and his men. Here the earth is personified as having a mouth to devour these men.

The Lord Jesus uses personification in, "O Jerusalem, Jerusalem, killing the prophets and stoning those who are sent to you! How often would I have gathered your children together as a hen gathers her brood under her wings, and you would not!" (Matt. 23:37). The city of Jerusalem is here personified. Our Lord's concern was for its people, yet he addresses the city as if it were they.

Again, our Lord personifies *tomorrow* in these words: "Therefore do not be anxious about tomorrow, for tomorrow will be anxious for itself" (Matt. 6:34). Here *tomorrow* is invested with characteristics of human personality, as being beset with anxious cares.

Figures of Speech (continued)

Apostrophe

This is a strange but graphic figure which sounds as if the speaker were talking to himself in a sort of externalized soliloquy. For instance, David says to his dead son, "O my son Absalom, my son, my son Absalom! Would I had died instead of you, O Absalom, my son, my son!" (2 Sam. 18:33). What a moving expression of David's grief this is; no other mode of expression could be quite so expressive in this instance.

Then there is the use of this figure in which the kings of earth address a fallen city, "Alas! alas! thou great city, thou mighty city, Babylon! In one hour has thy judgment come!" (Rev. 18:10).

This figure of speech seems best adapted to the expression of deep emotion. As such, it readily grabs our attention and draws out our interest.

Synechdoche

Here's one most of us never heard of, but which we frequently use in everyday speech. We say, "This is his hour" when we don't really mean an hour just sixty minutes long. We mean this is his time of glory, or suffering, or whatever we associate with his current experience. We have substituted a part for the whole. In Scripture it occurs in such passages as this: in Judges 12:7 we are told Jephthah was buried "in the cities of Gilead" (Hebrew) though actually only one of those cities is meant; in Luke 2:1 "all the world" is used to mean the world of the Roman Empire; in Deuteronomy 32:41 "if I whet the lightning of my sword" the word *lightning is* used for the flashing edge of the gleaming blade.

Perhaps now we have seen enough of the prevalence and expressive value of figures of speech to help us appreciate the color and realism they lend to the language of the Bible. Also, interpretively, our review should take some of the mystery out of our encounters with these forms, in studying the Bible.

Fit to Represent
Multiplying Disciples of the Kingdom of God

Rev. Dr. Don L. Davis • Luke 10.16 (ESV) - The one who hears you hears me, and the one who rejects you rejects me, and the one who rejects me rejects him who sent me

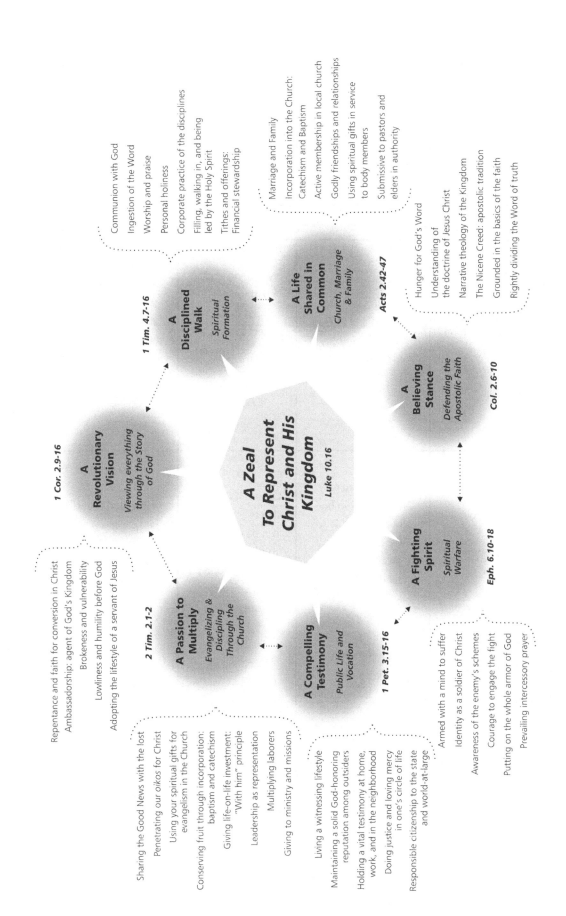

A Zeal
To Represent
Christ and His
Kingdom
Luke 10.16

A Disciplined Walk
Spiritual Formation
1 Tim. 4.7-16

- Communion with God
- Ingestion of the Word
- Worship and praise
- Personal holiness
- Corporate practice of the disciplines
- Filling, walking in, and being led by the Holy Spirit
- Tithes and offerings: Financial stewardship

A Life Shared in Common
Church, Marriage & Family
Acts 2.42-47

- Marriage and Family
- Incorporation into the Church: Catechism and Baptism
- Active membership in local church
- Godly friendships and relationships
- Using spiritual gifts in service to body members
- Submissive to pastors and elders in authority

A Believing Stance
Defending the Apostolic Faith
Col. 2.6-10

- Hunger for God's Word
- Understanding of the doctrine of Jesus Christ
- Narrative theology of the Kingdom
- The Nicene Creed: apostolic tradition
- Grounded in the basics of the faith
- Rightly dividing the Word of truth

A Revolutionary Vision
Viewing everything through the Story of God
1 Cor. 2.9-16

- Repentance and faith for conversion in Christ
- Ambassadorship: agent of God's Kingdom
- Brokeness and vulnerability
- Lowliness and humility before God
- Adopting the lifestyle of a servant of Jesus

A Passion to Multiply
Evangelizing & Discipling Through the Church
2 Tim. 2.1-2

- Sharing the Good News with the lost
- Penetrating our *oikos* for Christ
- Using your spiritual gifts for evangelism in the Church
- Conserving fruit through incorporation: baptism and catechism
- Giving life-on-life investment: "With him" principle
- Leadership as representation
- Multiplying laborers
- Giving to ministry and missions

A Compelling Testimony
Public Life and Vocation
1 Pet. 3.15-16

- Living a witnessing lifestyle
- Maintaining a solid God-honoring reputation among outsiders
- Holding a vital testimony at home, work, and in the neighborhood
- Doing justice and loving mercy in one's circle of life
- Responsible citizenship to the state and world-at-large

A Fighting Spirit
Spiritual Warfare
Eph. 6.10-18

- Armed with a mind to suffer
- Identity as a soldier of Christ
- Awareness of the enemy's schemes
- Courage to engage the fight
- Putting on the whole armor of God
- Prevailing intercessory prayer

Five Views of the Relationship between Christ and Culture

*Based on **Christ and Culture** by H. Richard Niebuhr, New York: Harper and Row, 1951*

Christ against Culture	Christ and Culture in Paradox	Christ the Transformer of Culture	Christ above Culture	The Christ of Culture
Opposition	*Tension*	*Conversion*	*Cooperation*	*Acceptance*
Therefore come out from them and be separate, says the Lord. Touch no unclean thing, and I will receive you. - 2 Cor. 6.17 (cf. 1 John 2.15)	Give to Caesar what is Caesar's, and to God what is God's. - Matt. 22.21 (cf. 1 Pet. 2.13-17)	In putting everything under him, God left nothing that is not subject to him. Yet at present we do not see everything subject to him. - Heb. 2.8 (cf. Col. 1.16-18)	Indeed, when Gentiles, who do not have the law, do by nature things required by the law, they are a law for themselves. - Rom 2.14 (cf. Rom. 13.1, 5-6)	Every good and perfect gift is from above, coming down from the Father of the heavenly lights, who does no change like shifting shadows. - James 1.17 (cf. Phil. 4.8)
Culture is radically affected by sin and constantly opposes the will of God. Separation and opposition are the natural responses of the Christian community which is itself an alternative culture.	Culture is radically affected by sin but does have a role to play. It is necessary to delineate between spheres: Culture as law (restrains wickedness), Christianity as grace (gives righteousness). Both are an important part of life but the two cannot be confused or merged.	Culture is radically affected by sin but can be redeemed to play a positive role in restoring righteousness. Christians should work to have their culture acknowledge Christ's lordship and be changed by it.	Culture is a product of human reason and is part of a God-given way to discover truth. Although culture can discern real truth, sin limits its capacities which must be aided by revelation. Seeks to use culture as a first step toward the understanding of God and his revelation.	Culture is God's gift to help man overcome his bondage to nature and fear and advance in knowledge and goodness. Human culture is what allows us to conserve the truth humanity has learned. Jesus' moral teaching moves human culture upward to a new level.
Tertullian, Menno Simons Anabaptists	Martin Luther Lutherans	St. Augustine, John Calvin Reformed	Thomas Aquinas Roman Catholic	Peter Abelard Immanual Kant Liberal Protestant

Following the Life of Christ throughout Each Year
Rev. Dr. Don L. Davis

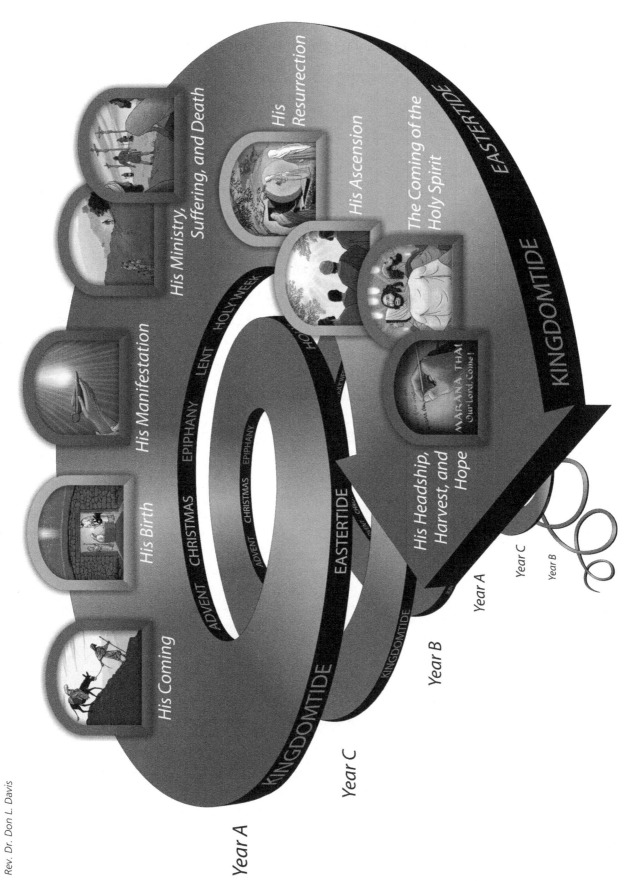

Four Contexts of Urban Christian Leadership Development

Rev. Dr. Don L. Davis

1. Personal Friendships, Mentoring, and Discipleship

2. Small Group Nurture and Cell Groups

3. Congregational Life and Governance

4. Inter-congregational Cooperation and Collaboration

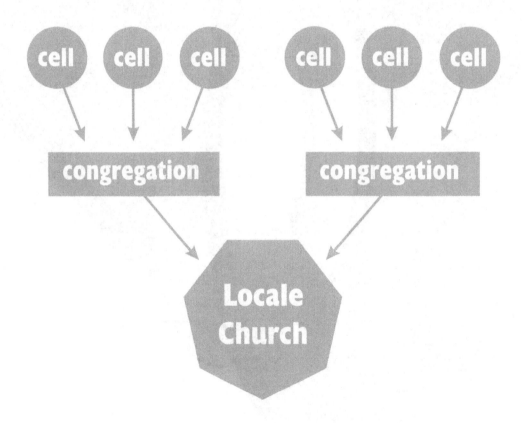

From Before to Beyond Time
The Plan of God and Human History

Adapted from Suzanne de Dietrich. **God's Unfolding Purpose.** *Philadelphia: Westminster Press, 1976.*

I.   Before Time (Eternity Past) 1 Cor. 2.7
   A. The Eternal Triune God
   B. God's Eternal Purpose
   C. The Mystery of Iniquity
   D. The Principalities and Powers

II. Beginning of Time (Creation and Fall) Gen. 1.1
   A. Creative Word
   B. Humanity
   C. Fall
   D. Reign of Death and First Signs of Grace

III. Unfolding of Time (God's Plan Revealed Through Israel) Gal. 3.8
   A. Promise (Patriarchs)
   B. Exodus and Covenant at Sinai
   C. Promised Land
   D. The City, the Temple, and the Throne (Prophet, Priest, and King)
   E. Exile
   F. Remnant

IV. Fullness of Time (Incarnation of the Messiah) Gal. 4.4-5
   A. The King Comes to His Kingdom
   B. The Present Reality of His Reign
   C. The Secret of the Kingdom: the Already and the Not Yet
   D. The Crucified King
   E. The Risen Lord

V.   The Last Times (The Descent of the Holy Spirit) Acts 2.16-18
   A. Between the Times: the Church as Foretaste of the Kingdom
   B. The Church as Agent of the Kingdom
   C. The Conflict Between the Kingdoms of Darkness and Light

VI. The Fulfillment of Time (The Second Coming) Matt. 13.40-43
   A. The Return of Christ
   B. Judgment
   C. The Consummation of His Kingdom

VII. Beyond Time (Eternity Future) 1 Cor. 15.24-28
   A. Kingdom Handed Over to God the Father
   B. God as All in All

From Before to Beyond Time
Scriptures for Major Outlines Points

I. Before Time (Eternity Past)

1 Cor. 2.7 (ESV) - But we impart a secret and hidden wisdom of God, *which God decreed before the ages* for our glory (cf. Titus 1.2).

II. Beginning of Time (Creation and Fall)

Gen. 1.1 (ESV) - *In the beginning*, God created the heavens and the earth.

III. Unfolding of Time (God's Plan Revealed Through Israel)

Gal. 3.8 (ESV) - And the Scripture, foreseeing that God would justify the Gentiles by faith, *preached the Gospel beforehand to Abraham*, saying, "In you shall all the nations be blessed" (cf. Rom. 9.4-5).

IV. Fullness of Time (The Incarnation of the Messiah)

Gal. 4.4-5 (ESV) - *But when the fullness of time had come*, God sent forth his Son, born of woman, born under the law, to redeem those who were under the law, so that we might receive adoption as sons.

V. The Last Times (The Descent of the Holy Spirit)

Acts 2.16-18 (ESV) - But this is what was uttered through the prophet Joel: "'*And in the last days it shall be*,' God declares, 'that I will pour out my Spirit on all flesh, and your sons and your daughters shall prophesy, and your young men shall see visions, and your old men shall dream dreams; even on my male servants and female servants in those days I will pour out my Spirit, and they shall prophesy.'"

VI. The Fulfillment of Time (The Second Coming)

Matt. 13.40-43 (ESV) - Just as the weeds are gathered and burned with fire, *so will it be at the close of the age*. The Son of Man will send his angels, and they will gather out of his Kingdom all causes of sin and all lawbreakers, and throw them into the fiery furnace. In that place there will be weeping and gnashing of teeth. Then the righteous will shine like the sun in the Kingdom of their Father. He who has ears, let him hear.

VII. Beyond Time (Eternity Future)

1 Cor. 15.24-28 (ESV) - Then comes the end, when he delivers the Kingdom to God the Father after destroying every rule and every authority and power. For he must reign until he has put all his enemies under his feet. The last enemy to be destroyed is death. For "God has put all things in subjection under his feet." But when it says, "all things are put in subjection," it is plain that he is excepted who put all things in subjection under him. When all things are subjected to him, then the Son himself will also be subjected to him who put all things in subjection under him, that God may be all in all.

From Deep Ignorance to Credible Witness

Rev. Dr. Don L. Davis

Witness - Ability to give witness and teach

2 Tim. 2.2
Matt. 28.18-20
1 John 1.1-4
Prov. 20.6
2 Cor. 5.18-21

And the things you have heard me say in the presence of many witnesses entrust to reliable men who will also be qualified to teach others. ~ 2 Tim. 2.2

8

Lifestyle - Consistent appropriation and habitual practice based on beliefs

Heb. 5.11-6.2
Eph. 4.11-16
2 Pet. 3.18
1 Tim. 4.7-10

And Jesus increased in wisdom and in stature, and in favor with God and man. ~ Luke 2.52

7

Demonstration - Expressing conviction in corresponding conduct, speech, and behavior

James 2.14-26
2 Cor. 4.13
2 Pet. 1.5-9
1 Thess. 1.3-10

Nevertheless, at your word I will let down the net. ~ Luke 5.5

6

Conviction - Committing oneself to think, speak, and act in light of information

Heb. 2.3-4
Heb. 11.1, 6
Heb. 3.15-19
Heb. 4.2-6

Do you believe this? ~ John 11.26

5

Discernment - Understanding the meaning and implications of information

John 16.13
Eph. 1.15-18
Col. 1.9-10
Isa. 6.10; 29.10

Do you understand what you are reading? ~ Acts 8.30

4

Knowledge - Ability to recall and recite information

2 Tim. 3.16-17
1 Cor. 2.9-16
1 John 2.20-27
John 14.26

For what does the Scripture say? ~ Rom. 4.3

3

Interest - Responding to ideas or information with both curiosity and openness

Ps. 42.1-2
Acts 9.4-5
John 12.21
1 Sam. 3.4-10

We will hear you again on this matter. ~ Acts 17.32

2

Awareness - General exposure to ideas and information

Mark 7.6-8
Acts 19.1-7
John 5.39-40
Matt. 7.21-23

At that time, Herod the tetrarch heard about the fame of Jesus. ~ Matt. 14.1

1

Ignorance - Unfamiliarity with information due to naivete, indifference, or hardness

Eph. 4.17-19
Ps. 2.1-3
Rom. 1.21; 2.19
1 John 2.11

Who is the Lord that I should heed his voice? ~ Exod. 5.2

0

General Facts Concerning the New Testament

A Comparative Chart of the Four Gospels

Robert H. Gundry. ***A Survey of the New Testament****. Grand Rapids: Zondervan, 1981.*

	Probable Date of Writing	Probable Place of Writing	First Intended Audience	Theme and Focus
Mark	50's	Rome	Gentiles in Rome	Jesus' redemptive activity
Matthew	50's or 60's	Antioch in Syria	Jews in Palestine	Jesus the Jewish Messiah, and the disciples as the new people of God
Luke	60's	Rome	Interested Gentile seekers	The historical certainty of the Gospel account
John	80's or 90's	Ephesus	General Population in Asia Minor	Believing in Jesus as the Messiah for eternal life

Old Testament Apocrypha

Walter A. Elwell and Robert W. Yarbrough. ***Encountering the New Testament****. Grand Rapids: Baker Books, 1998.*

Roman Catholics and some Eastern Orthodox churches recognize the writings listed below as Scripture. Protestants acknowledge their literary value and historical significance but do not view them as possessing spiritual authority		
Additions to Esther Baruch Bel and the Dragon Ecclesiasticus (Wisdom of Jesus Son of Sirach) 1 Esdras 2 Esdras	Judith Letter of Jeremiah 1 Maccabees 2 Maccabees 3 Maccabees 4 Maccabees Prayer of Azariah	Prayer of Mannasseh Psalm 151 Song of the Three Jews Susanna Tobit Wisdom of Solomon

General Facts about the New Testament

1. The NT is the testament of God's saving work in more recent times and announces the Savior that the OT awaits.

2. The NT contains 27 books, four dealing with Jesus' life and ministry called *Gospels*, one dealing with history of the Church, Acts, and 21 *Epistles* or letters, and one book of *prophecy*.

3. The collection of books in the NT comprise the *canon*, an authorized collection that came together over 3 centuries.

4. NT manuscripts were first written on papyrus (a paper made from reeds, and then on leather). Nearly 300 others are written on *uncials*, in capital letters, usually on leather. *Minuscules* represent the largest group and display a kind of cursive writing that developed in *Byzantium* around the ninth century. *Lectionaries*, books used in Church worship, include portions of Scripture as well.

5. The NT is reliable because of 1) the extensive evidence supporting it; 2) the authors wrote them within the first generation or two of Christian history, and 3) ancient versions were widely distributed.

6. The personal tone of the NT is seen in the fact that of the 27 books, 24 are personal letters, and 3 are personalized accounts of the life and work of Christ.

7. The Apocrypha includes 14 *non-canonical* books written between 200 B.C. and A.D. 100.

8. Jesus was seen as a threat by the Jews because he made controversial claims about himself and took liberties with Jewish customs.

9. Jesus appeared at a time when the traditions of Judaism dictated much of Jewish life and practice. A knowledge of these customs can greatly aid our understanding of the NT.

Getting a Firm Grasp of Scripture

From Leroy Eims, The Lost Art of Disciple Making, p. 81

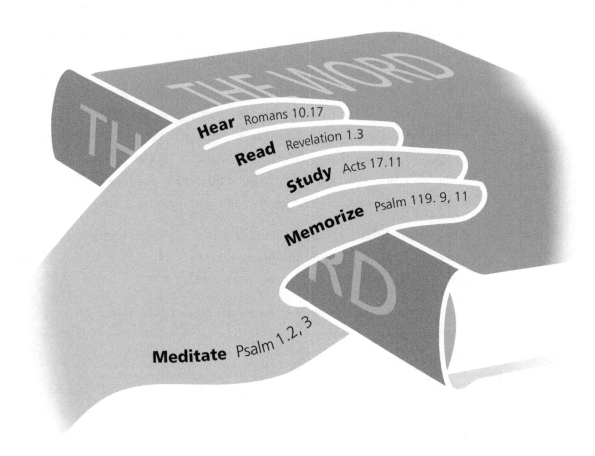

Hear Romans 10.17

Read Revelation 1.3

Study Acts 17.11

Memorize Psalm 119. 9, 11

Meditate Psalm 1.2, 3

Giving Glory to God

Rev. Dr. Don L. Davis

John 17.3-4 (ESV) - And this is eternal life, that they know you the only true God, and Jesus Christ whom you have sent. [4] I glorified you on earth, having accomplished the work that you gave me to do.

It is amazing how we can misunderstand things. We think we know what something is all about, and we act on our wrong assumptions, and then we are amazed at how bad things are going, or are surprised when we learn that we were off in our thinking.

> *One evening, a little girl was saying bedtime prayers with her mother. "Dear Harold, please bless Mother and Daddy and all my friends," she prayed. "Wait a minute", interrupted her mother, "who's Harold?" "That's God's name," was the answer. "Who told you that was God's name?" asked the mother. "I learned it in Sunday school, Mommy. 'Our Father, Who art in heaven, Harold be Thy name.'"*
>
> ~ Bruce Larson

I believe that for many Christians today, the Christian life is primarily misconceived and misconstrued. While they believe they have a proper understanding of things, they are wrong, and like the little child, they continue to go on with their error, not knowing they have misconceived the purpose of the entire Christian vision.

This morning we are going to speak about the final purpose of all things, and the high aim of the Christian religion, all church life, and our *raison d'etre* (our reason for being). We exist for the glory of God!

I.   What is the Definition of Glorifying God?

A.   *To glorify God* means that we give him what he is worthy of; worship is "worth-ship," giving to God what he is due by virtue of his person and work.

   B.   *Glorifying God* means acknowledging him as our source, our significance, and our security in all that we are and do.

II. All Heaven and Earth Were Created in Order to Bring God Glory.

All things that have life and exist, whether they are aware of it or not, were created by the hand of God in order to give him glory. He will get it from us, whether by life, or death, whether through honor or through tragedy.

   A.   Scriptures

       1.   Ps. 103.22

       2.   Ps. 145.10

       3.   Ps. 148.7-13

       4.   Prov. 16.4

       5.   Rom. 11.36

       6.   Phil. 2.9-11

       7.   Rev. 4.11

   B.   Illustrations and Principles

       1.   The key to effective living is living for the purpose that the Lord made you, understanding who you are, and why God put you here.

       2.   The Psalmist declares that everything that has breath ought to praise the Lord, Ps. 150.6.

       3.   In the not-too-distant future, God declares that all human beings everywhere will in fact acknowledge God as source, and give him the glory that he deserves, Rev. 5.12-14.

III. The Redeemed of the Lord Were Selected by God in Order to Bring Glory to Him, 1 Pet. 4.11, 14

While God intends for all things to praise him, he has especially brought his people to him in order that they might praise him in a higher mode. God saved you, cleansed you, brought you back from a life of sin and disgrace in order that you might now be a light, a trophy, a shining example of his grace and power. He saved you in order that you might glorify his name.

A. Scriptures

     1. Isa. 43.7, 21

     2. 1 Pet. 2.9-10

     3. 1 Cor. 10.31

     4. Eph. 1.5, 6, 12

     5. Col. 3.16-17

     6. John 15.8

     7. Eph. 5.19-20

B. Illustrations

     1. What is the glory of a thing? To do well what it was made for!

         a. A chain saw

         b. A surgeon's scalpel

         c. A guitar

         d. We are his people, and the sheep of his hand, Ps. 95.6-7.

     2. In letting our light shine, God receives more glory, Matt. 5.14-16.

     3. We glorify God in proportion to our recognition of the good things that he has done for us.

         a. Isa. 63.7

         b. Ps. 9.13-14

Giving Glory to God (continued)

4. We are called to glorify God for his doings.

    a. We praise him for *what he has done*: Calvary.

    b. We praise him for *what he is doing*: Redemption.

    c. We praise him for *what he is going to do*: the Second Coming.

C. God's glory must be supreme in our minds.

    1. More than our *safety*, Acts 20.24

    2. More than our *convenience*, Heb. 12.2-3

    3. More than *our very lives*, Phil 1.20

God wants to be glorified in us no matter what, when we are poor or rich, when we are happy or miserable, whether we are healthy or sick. Yes, God can even be glorified in our illness! The following is a wonderful prayer by a beloved Christian from Norway, Ole Hallesby, which captures the Christian's attitude regarding illness: "Lord, if it will be to Your glory, heal suddenly. If it will glorify You more, heal gradually; if it will glorify You even more, may your servant remain sick awhile; and if it will glorify Your name still more, take him to Yourself in heaven."

IV. The Essence of Sin Is to Fail to Give God His Due; Sin Is Robbing God of the Glory that is Rightfully Due to Him (Rom. 3.23).

We Can Rob God of Glory in at Least Four Respects.

A. First, we can *take for ourselves the glory* that is reserved for God alone.

    1. *Satan*, Isa. 14.13-20

    2. *Herod*, Acts 12.20-23

    3. Illustrations and Principles

        a. One of the hardest things in life is for us to know that God does things for his own sake, and not for our sake, Isa. 48.11.

        b. The credit for all things belongs to God and not to us, Ps. 115.1.

c. The tendency to take the credit usually occurs when we segment God off to a little part of our lives, rather than seeing everything we do as capable of honoring or dishonoring God—everything!

The well-known Christian author, Keith Miller, makes this point well: "It has never ceased to amaze me that we Christians have developed a kind of selective vision which allows us to be deeply and sincerely involved in worship and church activities and yet almost totally pagan [oblivious to God] in the day-in, day-out guts of our business lives and never realize it."

B. Second, we can rob God of *the praise and adoration he deserves by ascribing the glory we owe to him alone to someone or something else*, Isa. 42.8.

The threefold power grid of sin and substitute for God: money, sex, and power (greed, lust, and pride), 1 John 2.15-17; Exod. 20.2-3.

It is possible to practice unconscious idolatry, even as a Christian, that is, to temporarily worship something else by giving it our love and allegiance.

1. You may worship the god of pleasure.

2. Many people today worship at the altar of greed and possession. (We live in a culture that glorifies acquisition, buying, selling, getting, as the most significant thing in our lives.)

    Between 1983 and 1988, Americans bought 62 million microwave ovens, 88 million cars and light trucks, 105 million color television sets, 63 million VCR's, 31 million cordless phones, and 30 million telephone answering machines.

    ~ Newsweek

3. Do not worship the god of sport.

4. Offer no sacrifices to the god of marriage and family.

5. Do not seek to glorify the god of ethnicity and country.

Giving Glory to God (continued)

    6.   You many not worship the god of work.

    7.   Do not bow down to the god of possessions

    8.   The god of Religion

    9.   Illustrations

        a.   We as a society are more psyched over *Michael Jordan and Michael Jackson* than the Lord Jesus.

        b.   The four C's: people are more committed to *country, color, culture, and clan* than Christ.

        c.   *What John Lennon said about the Beatles*

C. Third, we can rob God of the glory that is due him by *being indifferent to his praise*—not really caring about it one way or another.

    1.   We can be *unconcerned and even nonchalant about what we give to God,* Mal. 1.7.

    2.   We can *find giving glory to God contemptible* (this is a fault and a problem of many young people who feel forced to believe in God because of their parent's faith), Mal. 1.7.

What do you suppose is the central task of one of the devil's tempters of human beings, what do they seek to do most?

C.S. Lewis, the author of The Screwtape Letters, suggests that it is to keep you indifferent to the things of God. In this book the devil counsels his nephew, Wormwood, on the subtleties and techniques of tempting people. The goal, he counsels, is not wickedness but indifference. Satan cautions his nephew to keep us, his prospect and patient, comfortable at all costs. If he should become concerned about anything of importance, encourage him to think about other little plans; not to worry, it could induce indigestion. Then the devil counsels his nephew to this eery job description: "I, the devil, will always see to it that there are bad people. Your job, my dear Wormwood, is to provide me with the people who do not care."

See Philippians 2.21 in the New King James Version and The Living Bible.

Giving Glory to God (continued)

D. Fourth, we can *rob God of the glory that is due him by giving God less than he deserves*, Mal. 1.6-8, 12-14.

   1. We can be *stingy our offerings to God, giving him the crumbs of our harvest and of our hearts*, Mal. 3.8-10.

   2. We can *give God sacrifices that are imperfect and filled with blemishes*, Mal. 1.8, 13.

   3. We can *give to God offerings that are polluted, stained by the unconfessed sin and wrong in our lives, (it is possible to come to church when things are a total mess in the rest of our lives)*, Mal. 1.7.

   4. Illustrations

      a. "Any old thing will do" syndrome

      b. God doesn't mind

      c. There are three kinds of people who live for the Lord.

There are three kinds of Christians who live for the Lord — the *flint*, the *sponge* and the *honeycomb*. To get anything out of a flint you must hammer it. *Flint Christians* give God a little, and only after a lot of hammering. And then you get only chips and sparks. To get water out of a sponge you must squeeze it, and the more you use pressure, the more you will get. *Sponge Christians* give God his due, but you have to constantly squeeze them in order to get them to participate. But the honeycomb just overflows with its own sweetness. A *honeycomb Christian* is full of God's heart and simply gives out of her abundant love and commitment to him. Which kind of Christian lifestyle do you lead right now?

V. The High Calling of Every Christian Is to Glorify God in All that We Are, All We Say, and All We Do, 1 Cor. 10.31.

A. We are to glorify God *in our bodies*, 1 Cor. 3.16,17; 6.19-20.

   1. Sexual Purity

   2. Physical health

Giving Glory to God (continued)

B. We are to glorify God *in our thoughts*, Rom. 8.5-8; 2 Cor. 10.3-5.

   1. More than 19,000 thoughts per day, think four to five times as fast as a person can talk.

   2. The last battleground of your life is your thought life; be careful what you think about.

   3. Prov. 23.7

C. We are to glorify God *in the words of our conversation*, 1 Cor. 10.31; Eph. 4.29, James 3.2.

   1. Attitude makes all the difference; more Christians dishonor God in their attitudes probably more than in any other single way.

   2. Attitudes are contagious and infectious, whether good or bad.

   3. Your tongue is connected to your heart.

   4. Not just profanity and cussing

   5. Negativism and sarcasm

   6. Complaining and murmuring

   7. Backbiting and gossip

D. We are to glorify God *in our conduct and our character*, Matt. 5.16; Eph. 2.8-10.

   1. God can receive glory from the kind of things you do, just your everyday actions.

   2. Your character, your reputation is stitched to the reputation of Christ.

   3. No matter what you say, you can never go beyond the kind of conduct and life you are living.

E. We are to glorify God *in all of our relationships*, 1 Pet. 2.11-12.

   1. In our marriages

   2. In our parenting

   3. In our extended family

4. With our brothers and sisters in the body of Christ

5. In our friendships

6. In our work relationships

7. In our neighborhood relationships

2 Thess. 1.11-12 (ESV) - To this end we always pray for you, that our God may make you worthy of his calling and may fulfill every resolve for good and every work of faith by his power, [12] so that the name of our Lord Jesus may be glorified in you, and you in him, according to the grace of our God and the Lord Jesus Christ.

God's Sovereignty and Universal Revelation
Conflicting Theories of God and the Universe
Rev. Dr. Don L. Davis

I am not trying, Lord, to penetrate your sublimity, for my understanding is not up to that. But I long in some measure to understand your truth, which my heart believes and loves. For I am not seeking to understand in order to believe, but I believe in order that I may understand. For this too I believe: that unless I believe, I shall not understand.

~ Anselm. Proslogion 1.
Anselm of Canterbury, Volume 1:
Monologion, Proslogion, Debate with Gaunilo, and a Meditation on Human Redemption.
Edited and translated by Jasper Hopkins and Herbert W. Richardson.
New York: The Edwin Mellen Press, 1975. p. 93.

The correct order is to believe the deep things of the Christian faith before undertaking to discuss them by reason. But we are negligent if, having come to a firm faith, we do not seek to understand what we believe. By God's prevenient grace, I consider myself to hold the faith of our redemption, so that even were I totally unable to understand it, nothing could shake the constancy of my belief. Please show me what, as you know, many others as well all seek to know: Why should God, who is omnipotent, have assumed the smallness and frailty of human nature in order to renew it?

Anselm. Cur Deus Homo (Boso to Anselm) 1:2.
Why God Became Man and The Virgin Conception and Original Sin,
by Anselm of Canterbury. Albany, NY: Magi Books, 1969. p. 65.

Questions to Ponder

- According to Anselm, what is the relationship between believing and understanding the truths of the Christian faith?

- Why does Anselm believe it to be wrong not to engage the truths of our Christian belief at the deepest levels of reason and argument?

- What is more critical for theological understanding: our reflection on the truth we understand or our commitment to understand the truth we do not? Explain your answer.

*All references to Erickson in this outline refer to: Millard J. Erickson, **Introducing Christian Doctrine**. Grand Rapids: Baker Books, 1992.*

I. **God's Sovereignty and Revelation**

A. The definition of revelation (Erickson, p. 33)

    1. God cannot be known unless he reveals himself to us, John 6.44.

        a. We are finite, whereas God is infinite.

        b. We are sinful, whereas God is holy.

        c. We are human, whereas God is divine.

    2. General revelation

    3. Special revelation

B. What are the "*modes*" (i.e., *the means by which*) God makes himself known to humankind in general revelation? (Erickson, p. 34)

    1. The created physical order (cf. Erickson, pp. 38-39)

        a. Ps. 19

        b. Rom. 1-2

        c. Acts 14.15-17

        d. Acts 17.22-31

    2. History

        a. Acts 2.22-24

        b. Historical preservation of Israel

    3. Human beings (capacities and qualities) *Imago Dei*

        a. Personhood: personality

        b. Intellect: reason

        c. Morality: conscience

        d. Spirituality: religious natures

God's Sovereignty and Universal Revelation (continued)

C. Questions concerning general revelation

1. Is it accessible to everyone?

2. Can we all understand the implications of it?

3. Does its content actually reveal God's purposes to us?

4. Can we respond to it in saving faith?

II. The Reality and Efficacy of General Revelation: Is it Legitimate and Effective?

A. "Natural Theology"

1. Basic assumption #1: God has made himself known in nature.

    a. It is objectively verifiable.

    b. It is basically intact.

2. Basic assumption #2: The effects of the fall or the natural human limitations of human beings prevent them from perceiving this revelation.

3. Basic assumption #3: The order of the human mind corresponds to the order of the universe.

    a. Congruity of the mind and the world

    b. The sufficiency of the laws of logic

    c. The basic adequacy of reason alone

B. *Thomas Aquinas*: Natural Theology's theologian par excellence (Erickson, p. 35)

1. *Cosmological* argument (Erickson, p. 35)

2. *Teleological* argument (Erickson, p. 35)

3. *Anthropological* argument, (Immanuel Kant) (Erickson, p. 36)

4. *Ontological* argument, (Anselm) (Erickson, p. 36)

C. Problems with Natural Theology

1. The proofs *may work against us*: they have leaks and cracks (Erickson, p. 37).

2. The assumptions they contain may be *unprovable* (Erickson, p. 37).

3. Some contain *logical flaws*: can you argue effectively from the observable to that which cannot be (or has not been) experienced? (Erickson, p. 37)

4. Other alternative explanations deal with the same evidence in a different way: teleology versus mutation (Erickson, p. 38).

5. Do the proofs demonstrate what kind of God that God is? (What about the existence of evil, "theodicy"?) (Erickson, p. 38)

D. John Calvin: General Revelation without Natural Theology (Erickson, p. 39)

1. The revelation of God in nature is *objective and valid*.

2. Due to human sin and limitations due to that sin, *humankind cannot adequately perceive God* in that general revelation (Erickson, p. 39).

3. *Human fallibility*, therefore, restricts the efficacy (i.e., adequateness, effectiveness) of general revelation for unregenerated humanity (Erickson, p. 40).

4. We require the "*spectacles of faith*" (Erickson, p. 40).

E. Can general revelation provide enough content for someone to be saved?

1. The case against

    a. What of personal faith in Jesus Christ?

    b. What of the Romans 10 necessity?

    c. What of the impulse to "go into all the world?" (Cf. Matt 28.18-20)

Basically, this is the view that God has given us an objective, valid, rational revelation of himself in nature, history, and human personality. It is there for anyone who wants to observe it. General revelation is not something read into nature by those who know God on other grounds; it is already present by the creation and continuing providence of God.
~ Erickson, p. 39.

God's Sovereignty and Universal Revelation (continued)

    2.   The case in favor

        a.   Throwing ourselves on the mercy of God

        b.   The analogy with Old Testament believers

        c.   Must you be conscious of the provision that has been made for your salvation to be saved?

        d.   The single ground of salvation for Old Testament and the New: Christ's deliverance from the Law (Galatians 3-4)

III. The Implications of General Revelation

A.   Because of God's general revelation, all human beings share access to God's revelation of himself.

    1.   We share common capacities.

    2.   We share God's glorious creation.

B.   Truth about God is accessible outside of special revelation (Erickson, p. 41).

    1.   This truth is objective.

    2.   This truth is supplemental to special revelation from God, not a substitute for it.

C.   General revelation eliminates the claim of innocence for anyone who refuses to seek God.

    1.   God's power and Godhead is known to all.

    2.   Our suppression of that truth makes us all susceptible to condemnation.

D.   The reality of religion in human experience arises from general revelation.

    1.   Every human community has a knowledge of God.

    2.   The religious impulse is an attempt to make sense of our suppressed, unclear knowledge of God in general revelation.

E. Biblical truth and the created order are both revelations of God, and correspond and reinforce one another (Erickson, p. 42).

    1.   God is the source for both kinds of revelation.

    2.   As sources of truth about God, they complement and supplement each other.

F. Human knowledge and human morality, to the extent that they are truth, all arise from God (Erickson, p. 42).

    1.   All truth everywhere in every domain is God's truth.

    2.   All right in every sphere mirrors God's own righteousness.

    3.   Human knowledge and ethical right is a "spark" from the flame of the Almighty.

God's Three-In-Oneness: The Trinity

Rev. Dr. Don L. Davis

The Church has not hesitated to teach the doctrine of the Trinity. Without pretending to understand, she has given her witness, she has repeated what the Holy Scriptures teach. Some deny that the Scriptures teach the Trinity of the Godhead on the ground that the whole idea of trinity in unity is a contradiction in terms; but since we cannot understand the fall of a leaf by the roadside or the hatching of a robin's egg in the nest yonder, why should the Trinity be a problem to us? "We think more loftily of God," says Michael de Molinos, "by knowing that He is incomprehensible, and above our understanding, than by conceiving Him under any image, and creature beauty, according to our rude understanding."

~ A. W. Tozer. **The Knowledge of the Holy**.
New York: Harper Collins, 1961. pp. 18-19.

"Glory be to the Father," sings the church, "and to the Son, and to the Holy Ghost." What is this? we ask—praise to three gods? No; praise to one God in three persons. As the hymn puts it, "Jehovah! Father, Spirit, Son! Mysterious Godhead! Three in One! This is the God whom Christians worship — the triune Jehovah. The heart of Christian faith in God is the revealed mystery of the Trinity. Trinitas is a Latin word meaning threeness. Christianity rests on the doctrine of the trinitas, the threeness, the tripersonality, of God.

~ J. I. Packer. **Knowing God**.
Downers Grove: InterVarsity Press, 1993. p. 65.

Questions to Ponder

- What is the relationship between understanding something and giving witness to something?

- Why do you suppose the Church's best testimony of the Trinity is captured in its hymns and worship as well as its doctrines and teachings?

- In what ways is a keen understanding of the nature of mystery so important in studying the doctrine of the Trinity?

- Why is understanding God as Trinity so important for both our own spiritual growth as well as our ministry to others?

Some Initial Difficulties in Pondering God as Trinity

* Beyond our ability to understand

* No earthly analogies exist

* Modernity, post-modernity, and the dominance of science: the character of our age

* Biblical illiteracy, theological novices, and no sermons

The Need for Wonder

* God is utterly incomprehensible as he is in himself.

* We must take off our sandals in the presence of such a being.

* Worship, not calculation, is the end of such reflection.

The Need for Submission

* The Scriptures are infallible as our rule of faith and practice.

* The Church's teaching must guide us true.

* Our wills, not our intellects must finally overcome our human inability to grasp that which cannot be fully grasped.

The doctrine of the Trinity is truth for the heart. The spirit of man alone can enter through the veil and penetrate into that Holy of Holies. "Let me seek Thee in longing," pleaded Anselm, "let me long for Thee in seeking; let me find Thee in love, and love Thee in finding." Love and faith are at home in the mystery of the Godhead. Let reason kneel in reverence outside.

A. W. Tozer. **The Knowledge of the Holy.** p. 20.

God's Three-In-Oneness: The Trinity (continued)

I. The Biblical Basis for the Trinity (Erickson, p. 97)

A. God is ONE.

All references to Erickson in this outline refer to: Millard J. Erickson, Introducing Christian Doctrine. Grand Rapids: Baker Books, 1992.

1. The unity of God is witnessed to in the Decalogue (i.e., the Ten Commandments), Exod. 20.2-4.

   a. The first commandment, Exod. 20.2-3.

   b. The second commandment, Exod. 20.4.

2. The unity of God is testified in the *Shema* of Deuteronomy 6, (the Great Commandment of Jesus), Deut. 6.4.

3. The OT witness

   a. Neh. 9.6

   b. Isa. 42.8

   c. Isa. 43.10

   d. Isa. 44.6,8

   e. Isa. 45.6,21-22

   f. Isa. 46.9

   g. Zech. 14.9

4. The NT Witness

   a. James 2.19

   b. Mark 12.29-32

   c. John 5.44

   d. John 17.3

   e. 1 Cor. 8.4,6

   f. Eph. 4.5-6

   g. 1 Tim. 2.5

God's Three-In-Oneness: The Trinity (continued)

B. The Deity of Three is asserted (Erickson, p. 98).

Each person of the Godhead, (Father, Son, and Holy Spirit) is described as possessing the attributes which are affirmed of God alone.

1. The Father is God (universally asserted).

2. The Son is God (Phil. 2.5-11; John 1.1-18; Heb. 1.1-12; John 8.58, etc.).

3. The Holy Spirit is God (Acts 5.3-4; John 16.8-11; 1 Cor. 12.4-11; 3.16-17; Matt. 28.19; 2 Cor. 13.14).

4. All three of these biblical personages share the same attributes together.

    a. Eternal, Rom. 16.26 with Rev. 22.13; Heb. 9.14

    b. Holy, Rev. 4.8, 15.4, Acts 3.14, 1 John 9.14

    c. True, John 7.28, John 17.3, Rev. 3.7

    d. Omnipresent, Jer. 23.24, Eph. 1.23; Ps. 139.7

    e. Omnipotent, Gen. 17.1 with Rev. 1.8; Rom.15.19; Jer. 32.17

    f. Omniscient, Acts 15.18; John 21.17; 1 Cor. 2.10-11

    g. Creator, Gen. 1.1 with Col. 1.16; Job 33.4; Ps. 148.5 with John 1.3, and Job 26.13

    h. Source of eternal life, Rom. 6.23; John 10.28; Gal. 6.8

    i. Raising Christ from the dead, 1 Cor. 6.14 with John 2.19 and 1 Pet. 3.18

C. God as THREE?: logical inference or biblical teaching (Erickson, p. 99)

1. Textual clues: the problem of 1 John 5.7

2. The plural form of the noun for God: Elohim, Gen. 1.26, Isa. 6.8

3. The Imago Dei in humankind, Gen. 1.27 with 2.24

4. Equal naming: unity and plurality, Matt. 3.16-17; 28.19; 2 Cor. 13.14

5. John the Apostle's threefold formula

    a. John 1.33-34

God's Three-In-Oneness: The Trinity (continued)

      b. John 14.16,26

      c. John 16.13-15

      d. John 20.21-22

  6. The assertion of Jesus' oneness with the Father

      a. John 1.1-18

      b. John 10.30

      c. John 14.9

      d. John 17.21

II. Historical Models and Arguments for the Trinity (Erickson, p. 101)

A. The "Economic" View of the Trinity (Hippolytus and Tertullian)

  1. No attempt to explore the eternal relations among the three members of the Trinity

  2. Focus on creation and redemption: Son and Spirit are not the Father, but are inseparably with him in his eternal being

  3. Analogy: the mental functions of a human being

B. Dynamic Monarchianism (Late 2nd and 3rd centuries)

Monarchianism = "sole sovereignty" (stress both the uniqueness and unity of God); both views of monarchianism are seeking to preserve the idea of God's oneness and unity

  1. Originator: Theodotus

  2. God was present *in* the life of the man, Jesus of Nazareth.

  3. A working force *upon, in, or through Jesus,* but no real presence of God *within* Jesus

  4. Before his baptism, Jesus was simply an ordinary (albeit virtuous) man, cf. Matt. 3.16-17.

5. At the baptism, the Spirit descended on Jesus and God's power flowed through him.

6. This view never became popular.

C. Modalistic Monarchianism

   1. There is one Godhead which may be designated as Father, Son, or Spirit.

   2. These terms do not stand for real distinctions of different personalities or members, but names appropriate for God's one working at different times.

   3. Father, Son, and Spirit are the identical, ongoing revelations of the same, single person.

   4. One person with three different names, activities, or roles

   5. This view insufficient to take full biblical data seriously

D. The Orthodox Formulation (Erickson, pp.102-103)

   1. The Council of Constantinople (381) and the view of Athanasius (293-373) and the "Cappadocian fathers" (Basil, Gregory of Nazianzus, and Gregory of Nyssa)

   2. One *ousia* [substance] in three *hypostases* [persons] (a common substance but multiple, separate persons)

      a. The Godhead exists of only one essence

      b. The Godhead exists at one and the same time in three modes or beings or *hypostases* (persons)

   3. The Cappadocian focus

      a. Individual *hypostases* is the *ousia* of Godhead.

      b. Each of the persons are distinguished by the characteristics or properties unique to him (like individual humans are to universal humanity).

God's Three-In-Oneness: The Trinity (continued)

4. Not tri-theism: belief in three gods. Why?

a. "If we can find a single activity of the Father, Son, and Holy Spirit which is in no way different in any of the three persons, we must conclude that there is but one identical substance involved" (Erickson, p.102).

b. The persons of the Trinity may be distinguished numerically as persons, but cannot be distinguished in their essence or substance (different in persons, one in being).

III. Essential Elements, Analogies, and Implications of the Trinity (Erickson, 103)

A. Essential elements

1. God is one, not several.

2. The Father, Son, and Holy Spirit are each one divine. (Each possesses the attributes and qualities of the one true God.)

3. God's oneness and God's threeness are not, in reality, contradictory.

4. The Trinity is eternal.

5. Subordination among the persons does not suggest inferiority in their essence.

a. The Son is subject to the Father.

b. The Spirit is subject to the Father.

c. The Spirit is subject to the Son as well as to the Father.

d. This subordination is functional only; the subjection never speaks of inferiority.

6. The Trinity is incomprehensible.

B. The search for analogies of the Trinity

    1. Analogies from physical nature

        a. The egg: yolk, white, and shell

        b. Water: solid, liquid, and vaporous form

        c. Suggestive not persuasive

    2. Analogies from human personality: Augustine and *De trinitate*

        a. The analogy of the individual human self-conscious personality: self-referential thinking

        b. The analogy of interpersonal human relations: twins

C. Implications of the Doctrine of the Trinity

    1. Know God: Father, Son, and Holy Spirit

    2. Worship God: Father, Son, and Holy Spirit

    3. Pray to God: Father, Son, and Holy Spirit

    4. Obey God: Father, Son, and Holy Spirit

    5. Imitate God: Live in love, affection, and community

Going Forward by Looking Back
Toward an Evangelical Retrieval of the Great Tradition
Rev. Dr. Don L. Davis

Rediscovering the "Great Tradition"

In a wonderful little book, Ola Tjorhom,[1] describes the Great Tradition of the Church (sometimes called the "classical Christian tradition") as "living, organic, and dynamic."[2] The Great Tradition represents that evangelical, apostolic, and catholic core of Christian faith and practice which came largely to fruition from 100-500 AD.[3] Its rich legacy and treasures represent the Church's confession of what the Church has always believed, the worship that the ancient, undivided Church celebrated and embodied, and the mission that it embraced and undertook.

While the Great Tradition neither can substitute for the Apostolic Tradition (i.e., the authoritative source of all Christian faith, the Scriptures), nor should it overshadow the living presence of Christ in the Church through the Holy Spirit, it is still authoritative and revitalizing for the people of God. It has and still can provide God's people through time with the substance of its confession and faith. The Great Tradition has been embraced and affirmed as authoritative by Catholic, Orthodox, Anglican, and Protestant theologians, those ancient and modern, as it has produced the seminal documents, doctrines, confessions, and practices of the Church (e.g., the canon of Scriptures, the doctrines of the Trinity, the deity of Christ, etc.).

---

[1] Ola Tjorhom, *Visible Church–Visible Unity: Ecumenical Ecclesiology and "The Great Tradition of the Church."* Collegeville, Minnesota: Liturgical Press, 2004. Robert Webber defined the Great Tradition in this way: "[It is] the broad outline of Christian belief and practice developed from the Scriptures between the time of Christ and the middle of the fifth century." Robert E. Webber, *The Majestic Tapestry*. Nashville: Thomas Nelson Publishers, 1986, p. 10.

[2] *Ibid.*, p. 35.

[3] The core of the Great Tradition concentrates on the formulations, confessions, and practices of the Church's first five centuries of life and work. Thomas Oden, in my judgment, rightly asserts that ". . . . most of what is enduringly valuable in contemporary biblical exegesis was discovered by the fifth century" (cf. Thomas C. Oden, *The Word of Life.* San Francisco: HarperSanFrancisco, 1989, p. xi.).

Many evangelical scholars today believe that the way forward for dynamic faith and spiritual renewal will entail looking back, not with sentimental longings for the "good old days" of a pristine, problem-free early church, or a naive and even futile attempt to ape their heroic journey of faith. Rather, with a critical eye to history, a devout spirit of respect for the ancient Church, and a deep commitment to Scripture, we ought to rediscover through the Great Tradition the seeds of a new, authentic, and empowered faith. We can be transformed as we retrieve and are informed by the core beliefs and practices of the Church before the horrible divisions and fragmentations of Church history.

Well, if we do believe we ought to at least look again at the early Church and its life, or better yet, are convinced even to retrieve the Great Tradition for the sake of renewal in the Church—what exactly are we hoping to get back? Are we to uncritically accept everything the ancient Church said and did as "gospel," to be truthful simply because it is closer to the amazing events of Jesus of Nazareth in the world? Is old "hip," in and of itself?

No. We neither accept all things uncritically, nor do we believe that old, in and of itself, is truly good. Truth for us is more than ideas or ancient claims; for us, truth was incarnated in the person of Jesus of Nazareth, and the Scriptures give authoritative and final claim to the meaning of his revelation and salvation in history. We cannot accept things simply because they are reported to have been done in the past, or begun in the past. Amazingly, the Great Tradition itself argued for us to be critical, to contend for the faith once delivered to the saints (Jude 3), to embrace and celebrate the tradition received from the Apostles, rooted and interpreted by the Holy Scriptures themselves, and expressed in Christian confession and practice.

Core Dimensions of the Great Tradition

While Tjorhom offers his own list of ten elements of the theological content of the Great Tradition that he believes is worthy of reinterpretation and regard,[4] I believe there are seven dimensions that, from a biblical and spiritual vantage point, can enable us to understand what the early Church believed, how they worshiped and lived, and the ways they defended their living faith in Jesus Christ. Through their allegiance to the documents, confessions, and practices of this period, the ancient Church bore witness to God's salvation promise in the midst

[4] *Ibid.*, pp. 27-29. Tjorhom's ten elements are argued in the context of his work where he also argues for the structural elements and the ecumenical implications of retrieving the Great Tradition. I wholeheartedly agree with the general thrust of his argument, which, like my own belief, makes the claim that an interest in and study of the Great Tradition can renew and enrich the contemporary Church in its worship, service, and mission.

of a pagan and crooked generation. The core of our current faith and practice was developed in this era, and deserves a second (and twenty-second) look.

Adapting, redacting, and extending Tjorhom's notions of the Great Tradition, I list here what I take to be, as a start, a simple listing of the critical dimensions that deserve our undivided attention and wholehearted retrieval.

1. ***The Apostolic Tradition.*** The Great Tradition is rooted in the Apostolic Tradition, i.e., the apostles' eyewitness testimony and firsthand experience of Jesus of Nazareth, their authoritative witness to his life and work recounted in the Holy Scriptures, the canon of our Bible today. The Church is apostolic, built on the foundation of the prophets and the apostles, with Christ himself being the Cornerstone. The Scriptures themselves represent the source of our interpretation about the Kingdom of God, that story of God's redemptive love embodied in the promise to Abraham and the patriarchs, in the covenants and experience of Israel, and which culminates in the revelation of God in Christ Jesus, as predicted in the prophets and explicated in the apostolic testimony.

2. ***The Ecumenical Councils and Creeds, Especially the Nicene Creed.*** The Great Tradition declares the truth and sets the bounds of the historic orthodox faith as defined and asserted in the ecumenical creeds of the ancient and undivided Church, with special focus on the Nicene Creed. Their declarations were taken to be an accurate interpretation and commentary on the teachings of the apostles set in Scripture. While not the source of the Faith itself, the confession of the ecumenical councils and creeds represents the *substance of its teachings*,[5] especially those before the fifth century (where virtually all of the elemental doctrines concerning God, Christ, and salvation were articulated and embraced).[6]

[5] I am indebted to the late Dr. Robert E. Webber for this helpful distinction between the source and the substance of Christian faith and interpretation.

[6] While the seven ecumenical Councils (along with others) are affirmed by both Catholic and Orthodox communions as binding, it is the first four Councils that are to be considered the critical, most essential confessions of the ancient, undivided Church. I and others argue for this largely because the first four articulate and settle once and for all what is to be considered our orthodox faith on the doctrines of the Trinity and the Incarnation (cf. Philip Schaff, *The Creeds of Christendom*, v. 1. Grand Rapids: Baker Book House, 1996, p. 44). Similarly, even the magisterial Reformers embraced the teaching of the Great Tradition, and held its most significant confessions as authoritative. Correspondingly, Calvin could argue in his own theological interpretations that "Thus

3. *The Ancient Rule of Faith.* The Great Tradition embraced the substance of this core Christian faith in a rule, i.e., an ancient standard rule of faith, that was considered to be the yardstick by which claims and propositions regarding the interpretation of the biblical faith were to be assessed. This rule, when applied reverently and rigorously, can clearly allow us to define the core Christian confession of the ancient and undivided Church expressed clearly in that instruction and adage of Vincent of Lerins: "that which has always been believed, everywhere, and by all."[7]

4. *The Christus Victor Worldview.* The Great Tradition celebrates and affirms Jesus of Nazareth as the Christ, the promised Messiah of the Hebrew Scriptures, the risen and exalted Lord, and Head of the Church. In Jesus of Nazareth alone, God has reasserted his reign over the universe, having destroyed death in his dying, conquering God's enemies through his incarnation, death, resurrection, and ascension, and ransoming humanity from its penalty due to its transgression of the Law. Now resurrected from the dead, ascended and exalted at the right hand of God, he has sent the Holy Spirit into the world to empower the Church in its life and witness. The Church is to be considered the people of the victory of Christ. At his return, he will consummate his work as Lord. This worldview was expressed in the ancient Church's confession, preaching, worship, and witness. Today, through its liturgy and practice of the Church Year, the Church acknowledges,

. . . .

councils would come to have the majesty that is their due; yet in the meantime Scripture would stand out in the higher place, with everything subject to its standard. In this way, we willingly embrace and reverence as holy the early councils, such as those of Nicea, Constantinople, the first of Ephesus I, Chalcedon, and the like, which were concerned with refuting errors–in so far as they relate to the teachings of faith. For they contain nothing but the pure and genuine exposition of Scripture, which the holy Fathers applied with spiritual prudence to crush the enemies of religion who had then arisen" (cf. John Calvin, *Institutes of the Christian Religion*, IV, ix. 8. John T. McNeill, ed. Ford Lewis Battles, trans. Philadelphia: Westminster Press, 1960, pp. 1171-72).

[7] This rule, which has won well-deserved favor down through the years as a sound theological yardstick for authentic Christian truth, weaves three cords of critical assessment to determine what may be counted as orthodox or not in the Church's teaching. St. Vincent of Lerins, a theological commentator who died before 450 AD, authored what has come to be called the "Vincentian canon, a three-fold test of catholicity: *quod ubique, quod semper, quod ab omnibus creditum est* (what has been believed everywhere, always and by all). By this three-fold test of ecumenicity, antiquity, and consent, the church may discern between true and false traditions." (cf. Thomas C. Oden, *Classical Pastoral Care*, vol. 4. Grand Rapids: Baker Books, 1987, p. 243).

celebrates, embodies, and proclaims this victory of Christ: the destruction of sin and evil and the restoration of all creation.

5. ***The Centrality of the Church.*** The Great Tradition confidently confessed the Church as the people of God. The faithful assembly of believers, under the authority of the Shepherd Christ Jesus, is now the locus and agent of the Kingdom of God on earth. In its worship, fellowship, teaching, service, and witness, Christ continues to live and move. The Great Tradition insists that the Church, under the authority of its undershepherds and the entirety of the priesthood of believers, is visibly the dwelling of God in the Spirit in the world today. With Christ himself being the Chief Cornerstone, the Church is the temple of God, the body of Christ, and the temple of the Holy Spirit. All believers, living, dead, and yet unborn–make up the one, holy, catholic (universal), and apostolic community. Gathering together regularly in believing assembly, members of the Church meet locally to worship God through Word and sacrament, and to bear witness in its good works and proclamation of the Gospel. Incorporating new believers into the Church through baptism, the Church embodies the life of the Kingdom in its fellowship, and demonstrates in word and deed the reality of the Kingdom of God through its life together and service to the world.

6. ***The Unity of the Faith.*** The Great Tradition affirms unequivocally the catholicity of the Church of Jesus Christ, in that it is concerned with keeping communion and continuity with the worship and theology of the Church throughout the ages (Church universal). Since there has been and can only be one hope, calling, and faith, the Great Tradition fought and strove for oneness in word, in doctrine, in worship, in charity.

7. ***The Evangelical Mandate of the Risen Christ.*** The Great Tradition affirms the apostolic mandate to make known to the nations the victory of God in Jesus Christ, proclaiming salvation by grace through faith in his name, and inviting all peoples to repentance and faith to enter into the Kingdom of God. Through acts of justice and righteousness, the Church displays the life of the Kingdom in the world today, and through its preaching and life together provides a witness and sign of the Kingdom present in and for the world (*sacramentum mundi*), and as the pillar and ground of the truth. As evidence of the Kingdom of God and custodians of the Word of God, the Church is charged to define clearly and defend the faith once for all delivered to the Church by the apostles.

Conclusion: Finding Our Future by Looking Back

In a time where so many are confused by the noisy chaos of so many claiming to speak for God, it is high time for us to rediscover the roots of our faith, to go back to the beginning of Christian confession and practice, and see, if in fact, we can recover our identity in the stream of Christ worship and discipleship that changed the world. In my judgment, this can be done through a critical, evangelical appropriation of the Great Tradition, that core belief and practice which is the source of all our traditions, whether Catholic, Orthodox, Anglican, or Protestant.

Of course, specific traditions will continue to seek to express and live out their commitment to the Authoritative Tradition (i.e., the Scriptures) and Great Tradition through their worship, teaching, and service. Our diverse Christian traditions (little "t"), when they are rooted in and expressive of the teaching of Scripture and led by the Holy Spirit, will continue to make the Gospel clear within new cultures or sub-cultures, speaking and modeling the hope of Christ into new situations shaped by their own set of questions posed in light of their own unique circumstances. Our traditions are essentially movements of contextualization, that is they are attempts to make plain within people groups the Authoritative Tradition in a way that faithfully and effectively leads them to faith in Jesus Christ.

We ought, therefore, to find ways to enrich our contemporary traditions by reconnecting and integrating our contemporary confessions and practices with the Great Tradition. Let us never forget that Christianity, at its core, is a faithful witness to God's saving acts in history. As such, we will always be a people who seek to find our futures by looking back through time at those moments of revelation and action where the Rule of God was made plain through the incarnation, passion, resurrection, ascension, and soon-coming of Christ. Let us then remember, celebrate, reenact, learn afresh, and passionately proclaim what believers have confessed since the morning of the empty tomb–the saving story of God's promise in Jesus of Nazareth to redeem and save a people for his own.

A Guide to Determining Your Worship Profile

Taken from Robert Webber, Planning Blended Worship, Nashville: Abingdon Press, 1998

1. Which of the following categories best describes your church?

    _____ Affected by Catholic and mainline worship renewal

    _____ Affected by the Pentecostal, charismatic, or praise and worship renewal

    _____ Affected by the movement to blend traditional and contemporary worship

    _____ Not affected by any of the worship renewal movements

2. Identify the age make-up of the people in your church

    ____% of people in our church are boosters (born before 1945)

    ____% of people in our church are boomers (born between 1945 and 1961)

    ____% of people in our church are from generation X (born after 1961)

3. Of the 8 common elements of worship renewal, which ones have made an impact on the worship of your church? Evaluate each of the areas on a scale of 1 (least impact) to 10 (most impact). Then take time to discuss those areas that are weakest.

    a. Our church draws from a biblical understanding of worship.   1 2 3 4 5 6 7 8 9 10

    b. The worship of our church draws from the past, especially the early Church. 1 2 3 4 5 6 7 8 9 10

    c. Our church has experienced a new focus on Sunday worship.   1 2 3 4 5 6 7 8 9 10

    d. Our church draws from the music of the whole Church.   1 2 3 4 5 6 7 8 9 10

    e. Our church has restored the use of the arts.   1 2 3 4 5 6 7 8 9 10

    f. Our church follows the calendar of the Christian year effectively.   1 2 3 4 5 6 7 8 9 10

    g. Our church has experienced the restoration of life in the sacred actions of worship. 1 2 3 4 5 6 7 8 9 10

    h. The worship of our church empowers its outreach ministries.   1 2 3 4 5 6 7 8 9 10

4. Evaluate the content, structure, and style of your worship. Again, use a scale of 1 ("That does not describe our church at all.") to 10 ("Yes, that is our church!"). Discuss areas of greatest weakness.

   a. The content of our worship is the full story of Scripture.   1   2   3   4   5   6   7   8   9   10

   b. The structure of our worship is the universally accepted
      fourfold pattern.   1   2   3   4   5   6   7   8   9   10

   c. The style of our worship is appropriate to our
      congregation and to the people we attract.   1   2   3   4   5   6   7   8   9   10

5. Answer the following:

   a. The approach to worship in our church is based upon: Conceptual language/Symbolic language

   b. The communication style of our church will relate best to: Boosters/Boomers/Generation X

                                                   All of the above

6. I would describe our church as: An old paradigm church/A new paradigm church

7. Draw from each of the previous questions to create a worship profile of the church. Do so by completing each of the following sentences:

   a. Our church has been affected by (which stream of worship renewal)

   b. Our age group is primarily

   c. Of the eight aspects of worship renewal, we draw on

   d. The content of our worship is

   e. The structure of our worship is

   f. The style of our worship is

   g. Our approach to communication is

8. To complete this study, comment on the kinds of changes you would like to see occur in the worship of your church.

A Harmony of the Ministry of Jesus

Adapted from Walter M. Dunnett, Exploring the New Testament, p. 14.

Gospel	The Period of Preparation	The Period of Public Ministry		The Period of Suffering	The Period of Triumph
		Opening	Closing		
Matthew	1.1-4.16	4.17-16.20	16.21-26.2	26.3-27.66	28.1-20
Mark	1.1-1.13	1.14-8.30	8.31-13.37	14.1-15.47	16.1-20
Luke	1.1-4.13	4.14-9.21	9.22-21.38	22.1-23.56	24.1-53
John	1.1-34	1.35-6.71	7.1-12.50	13.1-19.42	20.1-21.25

Hindrances to Christlike Servanthood

Don L. Davis

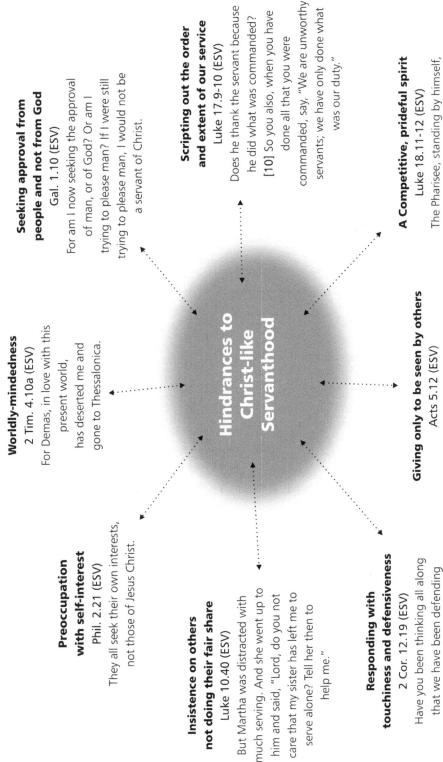

Hindrances to Christ-like Servanthood

Seeking approval from people and not from God
Gal. 1.10 (ESV)
For am I now seeking the approval of man, or of God? Or am I trying to please man? If I were still trying to please man, I would not be a servant of Christ.

Scripting out the order and extent of our service
Luke 17.9-10 (ESV)
Does he thank the servant because he did what was commanded? [10] So you also, when you have done all that you were commanded, say, "We are unworthy servants; we have only done what was our duty."

A Competitive, prideful spirit
Luke 18.11-12 (ESV)
The Pharisee, standing by himself, prayed thus: "God I thank you that I am not like other men, extortioners, unjust, adulterers, or even like this tax collector. [12] I fast twice a week; I give tithes of all that I get."

Worldly-mindedness
2 Tim. 4.10a (ESV)
For Demas, in love with this present world, has deserted me and gone to Thessalonica.

Giving only to be seen by others
Acts 5.12 (ESV)
But a man named Ananias, with his wife Sapphira, sold a piece of property, [2] and with his wife's knowledge he kept back for himself some of the proceeds and brought only a part of it and laid it at the apostles' feet.

Preoccupation with self-interest
Phil. 2.21 (ESV)
They all seek their own interests, not those of Jesus Christ.

Insistence on others not doing their fair share
Luke 10.40 (ESV)
But Martha was distracted with much serving. And she went up to him and said, "Lord, do you not care that my sister has left me to serve alone? Tell her then to help me."

Responding with touchiness and defensiveness
2 Cor. 12.19 (ESV)
Have you been thinking all along that we have been defending ourselves to you? It is in the sight of God that we have been speaking in Christ, and all for your upbuilding, beloved.

How to Interpret a Narrative (Story)
Don L. Davis

All stories have a particular shape and possess a number of elements that make it possible to experience the truth of the story, whether historical or imaginative, in a way that is powerful, challenging, and entertaining.

The Elements of Narrative Study

I. **Note with Special Care the SETTING of the Story.**

    A. Place: where geographically is the story taking place?

    B. Physical surroundings: what are the details physically?

    C. Temporal (time) setting: what are the time elements of the story?

    D. Cultural-historical surroundings: what details of culture or history are present?

II. **Identify the CHARACTERS of the Story.**

    A. Who are the prime characters in the story? The "hero" and "villain"?

    B. Note the precise order and details of the actions, conversation, and events of the characters.

    C. How are the characters shown to us?

        1. Direct descriptions

        2. Indirect characterization

            a. Appearance

            b. Words and conversation

            c. Thoughts and attitudes

            d. Influence and effects

            e. Actions and character

    D. How are the characters tested, and what choices do they make?

    E. How do the characters grow or decline (rise or fall) in the story?

III. Watch for the Author's POINT-OF-VIEW and VOICE.

    A. Note the author's comments about the characters and events.

        1. Attitude (positive, negative, or neutral)

        2. Judgment (negative or affirmative)

        3. Conclusion (summarizing, absent, closure?)

How to Interpret a Narrative (continued)

    B.   Consider what voice the story is being written in:

        1.   The Omniscient narrator (the Holy Spirit)

        2.   The First-person testimonial

        3.   The Third-person narrator

IV. Detect the PLOT DEVELOPMENT within the Story.

    A. Note the exact order and details of the events and actions.

    B. Note also how the story begins, develops, and ends.

    C. Ask and answer questions about the actual plot.

        1.   Why did the events happen as they did?

        2.   Why did the characters respond as they did?

        3.   Could they have done things in a different manner?

    D. Use John Legget's elements of story.

        1.   Doormat — the intro of the story

2. Complications — Conflicts, problems, issues, threats

3. Climax — Peak and turning point of the action

4. Denouement — How the story resolves itself

5. End — Finis!

V. Note the THEME of the Story

A. What key principles and truths can be drawn out of this story?

B. What is the "commentary on living" portrayed in this story?

1. What is the story's view of "reality" (what is the world like, and what is our role in it?)

2. What is the story's view of "morality (i.e., what constitutes good and bad in the story?)

3. What is the story's view of "value and meaning" (i.e., what is of ultimate concern and importance in the story?)

C. How do the truths of the story intersect with the challenges, opportunities, threats, and issues of our lives?

How to PLANT a Church

Don L. Davis

Mark 16.15-18 (ESV) - And he said to them, "Go into all the world and proclaim the gospel to the whole creation. [16] Whoever believes and is baptized will be saved, but whoever does not believe will be condemned. [17] And these signs will accompany those who believe: in my name they will cast out demons; they will speak in new tongues; [18] they will pick up serpents with their hands; and if they drink any deadly poison, it will not hurt them; they will lay their hands on the sick, and they will recover."

Evangelize

I. Prepare

Luke 24.46-49 (ESV) - and he said to them, "Thus it is written, that the Christ should suffer and on the third day rise from the dead, [47] and that repentance and forgiveness of sins should be proclaimed in his name to all nations, beginning from Jerusalem. [48] You are witnesses of these things. [49] And behold, I am sending the promise of my Father upon you. But stay in the city until you are clothed with power from on high."

A. Form a church-plant team.

B. Pray.

C. Select a target area and population.

D. Do demographic and ethnographic studies.

II. Launch

Gal. 2.7-10 (ESV) - On the contrary, when they saw that I had been entrusted with the gospel to the uncircumcised, just as Peter had been entrusted with the gospel to the circumcised [8] (for he who worked through Peter for his apostolic ministry to the circumcised worked also through me for mine to the Gentiles), [9] and when James and Cephas and John, who seemed to be pillars, perceived the grace that was given to me, they gave the right hand of fellowship to Barnabas and me, that we should go to the Gentiles and they to the circumcised. [10] Only, they asked us to remember the poor, the very thing I was eager to do.

A. Recruit and train volunteers.

B. Conduct evangelistic events and door-to-door evangelism.

Equip

Eph. 4.11-16 (ESV) - And he gave the apostles, the prophets, the evangelists, the pastors and teachers, [12] to equip the saints for the work of ministry, for building up the body of Christ, [13] until we all attain to the unity of the faith and of the knowledge of the Son of God, to mature manhood, to the measure of the stature of the fullness of Christ, [14] so that we may no longer be children, tossed to and fro by the waves and carried about by every wind of doctrine, by human cunning, by craftiness in deceitful schemes. [15] Rather, speaking the truth in love, we are to grow up in every way into him who is the head, into Christ, [16] from whom the whole body, joined and held together by every joint with which it is equipped, when each part is working properly, makes the body grow so that it builds itself up in love.

III. Assemble

Acts 2.41-47 (ESV) - So those who received his word were baptized, and there were added that day about three thousand souls. [42] And they devoted themselves to the apostles' teaching and fellowship, to the breaking of bread and the prayers. [43] And awe came upon every soul, and many wonders and signs were being done through the apostles. [44] And all who believed were together and had all things in common. [45] And they were selling their possessions and belongings and distributing the proceeds to all, as any had need. [46] And day by day, attending the temple together and breaking bread in their homes, they received their food with glad and generous hearts, [47] praising God and having favor with all the people. And the Lord added to their number day by day those who were being saved.

A. Form cell groups, Bible studies, etc. to follow up new believers, to continue evangelism, and to identify and train emerging leaders.

B. Announce the birth of a new church to the neighborhood and meet regularly for public worship, instruction and fellowship.

How to PLANT a Church (continued)

IV. Nurture

1 Thess. 2.5-9 (ESV) - For we never came with words of flattery, as you know, nor with a pretext for greed— God is witness. [6] Nor did we seek glory from people, whether from you or from others, though we could have made demands as apostles of Christ. [7] But we were gentle among you, like a nursing mother taking care of her own children. [8] So, being affectionately desirous of you, we were ready to share with you not only the gospel of God but also our own selves, because you had become very dear to us. [9] For you remember, brothers, our labor and toil: we worked night and day, that we might not be a burden to any of you, while we proclaimed to you the gospel of God.

A. Develop individual and group discipleship.

B. Fill key roles in the church: identify and use spiritual gifts.

Acts 20.28 (ESV) - Pay careful attention to yourselves and to all the flock, in which the Holy Spirit has made you overseers, to care for the church of God, which he obtained with his own blood.

Empower

Acts 20.32(ESV) - And now I commend you to God and to the word of his grace, which is able to build you up and to give you the inheritance among all those who are sanctified.

V. Transition

Titus 1.4-5 (ESV) - To Titus, my true child in a common faith: Grace and peace from God the Father and Christ Jesus our Savior. [5] This is why I left you in Crete, so that you might put what remained into order, and appoint elders in every town as I directed you—

A. Transfer leadership to indigenous leaders so they become self-governing, self-supporting and self-reproducing (appoint elders and pastors).

B. Finalize decisions about denominational or other affiliations.

C. Commission the church.

D. Foster association with World Impact and other urban churches for fellowship, support, and mission ministry.

How to PLANT a Church

Evangelize

PREPARE

- Form a church-plant team.

- Pray.

- Select a target area and population.

- Do demographic and ethnographic studies.

LAUNCH

- Recruit and train volunteers

- Conduct evangelistic events and door-to-door evangelism

Equip

ASSEMBLE

- Form cell groups, Bible studies, etc. to follow up new believers, to continue evangelism, and to identify and train emerging leaders.

- Announce the birth of a new church to the neighborhood and meet regularly for public worship, instruction and fellowship.

NURTURE

- Develop individual and group discipleship.

- Fill key roles in the church; identify and use spiritual gifts.

Empower

TRANSITION

- Transfer leadership to indigenous leaders so they become self-governing, self-supporting and self-reproducing (appoint elders and pastors).

- Finalize decisions about denominational or other affiliations.

- Commission the church.

- Foster association with World Impact and other urban churches for fellowship, support and mission ministry.

How to PLANT a Church (continued)

Pauline Precedents From Acts: The Pauline Cycle

1. Missionaries Commissioned: Acts 13.1-4; 15.39-40. Ga. 1.15-16.

2. Audience Contacted: Acts 13.14-16; 14.1; 16.13-15; 17.16-19.

3. Gospel Communicated: Acts 13.17-41; 16.31; Rom. 10.9-14; 2 Tim. 2.8.

4. Hearers Converted: Acts. 13.48; 16.14-15; 20.21; 26.20; 1 Thess. 1.9-10.

5. Believers Congregated: Acts 13.43; 19.9; Rom 16.4-5; 1 Cor. 14.26.

6. Faith Confirmed: Acts 14.21-22; 15.41; Rom 16.17; Col. 1.28; 2 Thess. 2.15; 1 Tim. 1.3.

7. Leadership Consecrated; Acts 14.23; 2 Tim. 2.2; Titus 1.5.

8. Believers Commended; Acts 14.23; 16.40; 21.32 (2 Tim. 4.9 and Titus 3.12 by implication).

9. Relationships Continued: Acts 15.36; 18.23; 1 Cor. 16.5; Eph. 6.21-22; Col. 4.7-8.

10. Sending Churches Convened: Acts 14.26-27; 15.1-4.

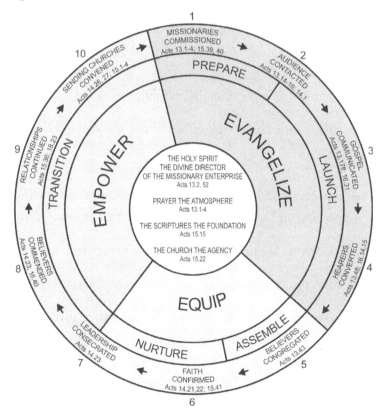

The "Pauline Cycle" terminology, stages, and diagram are taken from **David J. Hesselgrave,** *Planting Churches Cross-Culturally,* 2nd ed. Grand Rapids: Baker Book House, 2000.

"Evangelize, Equip, and Empower" and "P.L.A.N.T." schemas for church planting taken from **Crowns of Beauty: Planting Urban Churches Conference Binder** Los Angeles: World Impact Press, 1999.

Ten Principles of Church Planting

1. **Jesus is Lord.** (Matt. 9.37-38) All church plant activity is made effective and fruitful under the watch care and power of the Lord Jesus, who himself is the Lord of the harvest.

2. **Evangelize, Equip, and Empower unreached people to reach people.** (1 Thess. 1.6-8) Our goal in reaching others for Christ is not only for solid conversion but also for dynamic multiplication; those who are reached must be trained to reach others as well.

3. **Be inclusive: whosoever will may come.** (Rom. 10.12) No strategy should forbid any person or group from entering into the Kingdom through Jesus Christ by faith.

4. **Be culturally neutral: Come just as you are.** (Col. 3.11) The Gospel places no demands on any seeker to change their culture as a prerequisite for coming to Jesus; they may come just as they are.

5. **Avoid a fortress mentality.** (Acts 1.8) The goal of missions is not to create an impregnable castle in the midst of an unsaved community, but a dynamic outpost of the Kingdom which launches a witness for Jesus within and unto the very borders of their world.

6. **Continue to evangelize to avoid stagnation.** (Rom. 1.16-17) Keep looking to the horizons with the vision of the Great Commission in mind; foster an environment of aggressive witness for Christ.

7. **Cross racial, class, gender, and language barriers.** (1 Cor. 9.19-22) Use your freedom in Christ to find new, credible ways to communicate the kingdom message to those farthest from the cultural spectrum of the traditional church.

8. **Respect the dominance of the receiving culture.** (Acts 15.23-29) Allow the Holy Spirit to incarnate the vision and the ethics of the Kingdom of God in the words, language, customs, styles, and experience of those who have embraced Jesus as their Lord.

9. **Avoid dependence.** (Eph. 4.11-16) Neither patronize nor be overly stingy towards the growing congregation; do not underestimate the power of the Spirit in the midst of even the smallest Christian community to accomplish God's work in their community.

How to PLANT a Church (continued)

10. **Think reproducibility.** (2 Tim. 2.2; Phil. 1.18) In every activity and project you initiate, think in terms of equipping others to do the same by maintaining an open mind regarding the means and ends of your missionary endeavors.

Resources for Further Study

Cornett, Terry G. and James D. Parker. *"Developing Urban Congregations: A Framework for World Impact Church Planters."* World Impact Ministry Resources. Los Angeles: World Impact Press, 1991.

Davis, Don L. and Terry G. Cornett. *"An Outline for a Theology of the Church."* Crowns of Beauty: Planting Urban Churches (Training Manual). Los Angeles: World Impact Press, 1999.

Hesselgrave, David J. *Planting Churches Cross Culturally: A Biblical Guide.* Grand Rapids: Baker Book House, 2000.

Hodges, Melvin L. *The Indigenous Church: A Handbook on How to Grow Young Churches.* Springfield, MO: Gospel Publishing House, 1976.

Shenk, David W. And Ervin R. Stutzman. *Creating Communities of the Kingdom: New Testament Models of Church Planting.* Scottsdale, PA: Herald Press, 1988.

How to Start Reading the Bible

Rev. Don Allsman and Rev. Dr. Don L. Davis

1. Read individual passage, texts, and even books in light of the context of the whole Story of the Bible. How does it fit in God's redemptive plan to win all that was lost at the Fall?

2. Observe the situation. Put yourself in the setting, noticing the surroundings, the sights, the smells. Imagine what it must have been like.

3. Pay attention to commands, warnings, instructions, and inspiration that shape how you live and think so you can seek his Kingdom first.

Ways to Read through the Bible

Bible Reading Plan #1: From Genesis to Revelation

1. Start by reading through the book of John. This will give you an overview of Jesus' life and help you get some background as you read the rest of the Bible.

2. Go back to Genesis 1 and read straight through the Bible.

3. Do not get stuck on details, but read through the whole Bible to enjoy its richness and variety. Write down questions you have about words you don't understand or things that are confusing so you can ask someone or look them up later.

Bible Reading Plan #2: Chronological Reading Guide

(www.tumistore.org)

You also can read through the Bible each year, reading the various books in the order that Christian scholars believe it was written.

Many believers read through the Scriptures together every year "chronologically"(through time), seeking to gain greater insight on the entire Story of God *as it occurred in historical order of events.*

You may acquire a guide of this outline from *www.tumistore.org*. This simple listing of the books of Scripture will allow you to read through the Story of the Bible in the order the events happened. This will give you an overall sense of the Bible as one unfolding drama, and not as independent books disconnected from one another. It also helps we who read through the Bible each year stay on point regarding the true subject matter and theme of the Scriptures: the salvation of God in the person of Jesus of Nazareth, the Christ.

This guide will provide rich insight into the events of Scripture, and help you better comprehend the meaning of the whole story of God's wondrous salvation and grace, which climaxes in the Christ event, his death, burial, resurrection, ascension, and return.

The Hump

Rev. Dr. Don L. Davis • *1 Tim. 4.9-16; Heb. 5.11-14*

The Mature Christian
The Mature Believer and the Spiritual Disciplines

Faithful Application

Gracefulness

Automatic response

Comfortableness

Personal Satisfaction

Excellence

Expertise

Training Others

Heart Desire
A Clear Goal
Feasible Plan
Solid Support
Correct Knowledge
Faithful Effort
Good Examples
Extended Period of Time
Longsuffering

Regular, correct application of the spiritual disciplines

The Baby Christian
The New Believer and the Spiritual Disciplines

Awkwardness

Unskillfulness

Mistakes

Roughness

Sporadic Behavior

Uncomfortableness

Inefficiency

Novice-Level Performance

I Find My Lord in the Book

Author unknown

I find my Lord in the Bible, wherever I chance to look,

He is the theme of the Bible, the center and heart of the Book;

He is the Rose of Sharon, He is the Lily fair,

Where ever I open my Bible, the Lord of the Book is there.

He, at the Book's beginning, gave to the earth its form,

He is the Ark of shelter, bearing the brunt of the storm

The Burning Bush of the desert, the budding of Aaron's Rod,

Where ever I look in the Bible, I see the Son of God.

The Ram upon Mount Moriah, the Ladder from earth to sky,

The Scarlet Cord in the window, and the Serpent lifted high,

The smitten Rock in the desert, the Shepherd with staff and crook,

The face of the Lord I discover, where ever I open the Book.

He is the Seed of the Woman, the Savior Virgin-born

He is the Son of David, whom men rejected with scorn,

His garments of grace and of beauty the stately Aaron deck,

Yet He is a priest forever, for He is Melchizedek.

Lord of eternal glory Whom John, the Apostle, saw;

Light of the golden city, Lamb without spot or flaw,

Bridegroom coming at midnight, for whom the Virgins look.

Where ever I open my Bible, I find my Lord in the Book.

In Christ

Rev. Dr. Don L. Davis

"In Christ"

The Mystery of Our
Total Identification
with Christ
John 15.4-5

We were **baptized into him**,
1 Cor. 12.13

We were **crucified with him**,
Gal. 2.20

We **died with him**,
Rom. 6.3-4; Col. 3.3

We were **buried with him**,
Rom. 6.3-4

We were **raised with him**,
Eph. 2.4-7; Col. 3.1

We **ascended with him**,
Eph. 2.6

We **sit with him** in
heavenly places,
Eph. 2.6

We are "**made one in Christ**,"
1 Cor. 6.15-17

We will **reign forever with him**,
Rev. 3.21

We will be **joint-heirs with him**,
Rom. 8.17

We will be **made like him**,
1 John 3.2

We will be **glorified with him**,
Rom. 8.17

We will be **resurrected in him**,
1 Cor. 15.48-49

We **suffer with him**,
Rom. 8.17-18

We will be
caught up together with him,
1 Thess. 4.13-18

Investment, Empowerment, and Assessment

How Leadership as Representation Provides Freedom to Innovate

Rev. Dr. Don L. Davis

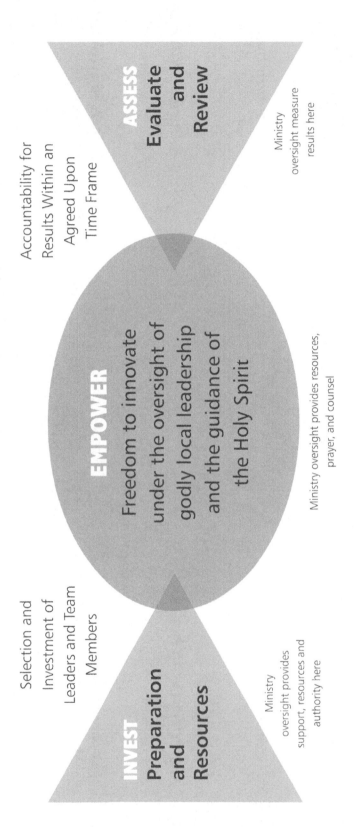

ASSESS

Evaluate and Review

Ministry oversight measure results here

Accountability for Results Within an Agreed Upon Time Frame

EMPOWER

Freedom to innovate under the oversight of godly local leadership and the guidance of the Holy Spirit

Ministry oversight provides resources, prayer, and counsel

Evaluation by sending authority
Review of results in light of task
Faithfulness and loyalty assessed
Overall evaluation of plan and strategy
Critical evaluation of leadership performance
Formal determination of operation's "success"
Reassignment in light of evaluation

Selection and Investment of Leaders and Team Members

INVEST

Preparation and Resources

Ministry oversight provides support, resources and authority here

Formal leadership selection
Acknowledgment of personal call
Determination of task and assignment
Training in spiritual warfare
Authorization to act defined and given
Necessary resources given and logistics planned
Commissioning: deputization formally recognized

Jesus and the Poor
Don L. Davis

Thesis: The heart of Jesus' ministry of the Kingdom was the transformation and renewal of the those on the underside of life, the poor. He demonstrated his personal heart vision in how he inaugurated his ministry, authenticated his ministry, defined the heart and soul of ministry, identifying himself directly with the poor.

I. Jesus Inaugurated His Ministry with an Outreach to the Poor.

A. The inaugural sermon at Nazareth, Luke 4.16-21

Luke 4.16-21 (ESV) - And he came to Nazareth, where he had been brought up. And as was his custom, he went to the synagogue on the Sabbath day, and he stood up to read. [17] And the scroll of the prophet Isaiah was given to him. He unrolled the scroll and found the place where it was written, [18] "The Spirit of the Lord is upon me, because he has anointed me to proclaim good news to the poor. He has sent me to proclaim liberty to the captives and recovering of sight to the blind, to set at liberty those who are oppressed, [19] to proclaim the year of the Lord's favor." [20] And he rolled up the scroll and gave it back to the attendant and sat down. And the eyes of all in the synagogue were fixed on him. [21] And he began to say to them, "Today this Scripture has been fulfilled in your hearing."

B. The meaning of this inauguration

1. The object of his attention: his choice of texts

2. The object of his calling: his Spirit anointing

Jesus and the Poor (continued)

   3.   The objects of his love:

       a.   Good news to the poor

       b.   Release to the captives

       c.   Recovery of sight to the blind

       d.   Letting the oppressed go free

   4.   The object of his ministry: the Year of the Lord's favor

C. *Ministry to the poor as the cornerstone of his inaugural ministry*

II. Jesus Authenticated His Ministry by His Actions toward the Poor.

A. John's query regarding Jesus' authenticity, Luke 7.18-23

Luke 7.18-23 (ESV) - The disciples of John reported all these things to him. And John, [19] calling two of his disciples to him, sent them to the Lord, saying, "Are you the one who is to come, or shall we look for another?" [20] And when the men had come to him, they said, "John the Baptist has sent us to you, saying, 'Are you the one who is to come, or shall we look for another?'" [21] In that hour he healed many people of diseases and plagues and evil spirits, and on many who were blind he bestowed sight. [22] And he answered them, "Go and tell John what you have seen and heard: the BLIND RECEIVE THEIR SIGHT, the lame walk, lepers are cleansed, and the deaf hear, the dead are raised up, the POOR HAVE GOOD NEWS PREACHED TO THEM. [23] And blessed is the one who is not offended by me."

B. Will the real Messiah please stand up?

   1.   The question of John, 19-20

   2.   The actions of Jesus, 21 (the show-side of "show-and-tell")

3.   The explanation of his identity, 22-23

   a.   Go and tell John what you have seen and heard.

   b.   Blind seeing, lame walking, lepers cleansed, deaf hearing, dead being raising, the poor hearing the Gospel

C.   *Ministry to the poor is undeniable proof of the Messiah's identity.*

III.   Jesus Verified Salvation in Relation to One's Treatment of the Poor.

A.   The story of Zaccheus, Luke 19.1-9

Luke 19.1-9 (ESV) - He entered Jericho and was passing through. [2] And there was a man named Zacchaeus. He was a chief tax collector and was rich. [3] And he was seeking to see who Jesus was, but on account of the crowd he could not, because he was small of stature. [4] So he ran on ahead and climbed up into a sycamore tree to see him, for he was about to pass that way. [5] And when Jesus came to the place, he looked up and said to him, "Zacchaeus, hurry and come down, for I must stay at your house today." [6] So he hurried and came down and received him joyfully. [7] And when they saw it, they all grumbled, "He has gone in to be the guest of a man who is a sinner." [8] And Zacchaeus stood and said to the Lord, "Behold, Lord, the half of my goods I give to the poor. And if I have defrauded anyone of anything, I restore it fourfold." [9] And Jesus said to him, "Today salvation has come to this house, since he also is a son of Abraham."

1.   The palpitations of Zaccheus

2.   The salutation of Zaccheus (to Jesus)

3.   The declaration of Zaccheus

   a.   Half of all I own I give to the poor.

   b.   I restore those wrongly treated by me four-fold.

Jesus and the Poor (continued)

      4.   The salvation of Zaccheus, vv.9-10

   B. Plucking Grain on the Sabbath, Matt.12.1-8

Matt. 12.1-8 (ESV) - At that time Jesus went through the grainfields on the Sabbath. His disciples were hungry, and they began to pluck heads of grain and to eat. [2] But when the Pharisees saw it, they said to him, "Look, your disciples are doing what is not lawful to do on the Sabbath." [3] He said to them, "Have you not read what David did when he was hungry, and those who were with him: [4] how he entered the house of God and ate the bread of the Presence, which it was not lawful for him to eat nor for those who were with him, but only for the priests? [5] Or have you not read in the Law how on the Sabbath the priests in the temple profane the Sabbath and are guiltless? [6] I tell you, something greater than the temple is here. [7] And if you had known what this means, 'I DESIRE MERCY, AND NOT SACRIFICE,' you would not have condemned the guiltless. [8] For the Son of Man is lord of the Sabbath."

      1.   Disciples snacking on corn on the Sabbath

      2.   The Pharisees disputation: "Look, your disciples are doing what is not lawful to do on the sabbath."

      3.   Jesus' retort: "I desire mercy and not sacrifice."

         a.   Mercy to the poor and broken, not ritual faithfulness

         b.   Compassion for the broken, not religious discipline

   C. *Ministry to the poor is the litmus test of authentic salvation.*

IV. Jesus Identifies Himself Unreservedly with the Poor.

   A. Those who cannot repay you, Luke 14.11-15

Luke 14.11-14 (ESV) - "For everyone who exalts himself will be humbled, and he who humbles himself will be exalted." [12] He said also to the man who had invited him, "When you give a dinner or a banquet, do not invite your friends or your brothers or your relatives or rich neighbors, lest they also invite you in return and you be repaid. [13] But when you give a feast, invite the poor, the crippled, the lame, the blind, [14] and you will be blessed, because they cannot repay you. You will be repaid at the resurrection of the just."

B. The Judgment Seat of the King, Matt. 25.31-45

Matt. 25.34-40 (ESV) - Then the King will say to those on his right, "Come, you who are blessed by my Father, inherit the kingdom prepared for you from the foundation of the world. [35] For I was hungry and you gave me food, I was thirsty and you gave me drink, I was a stranger and you welcomed me, [36] I was naked and you clothed me, I was sick and you visited me, I was in prison and you came to me." [37] Then the righteous will answer him, saying, "Lord, when did we see you hungry and feed you, or thirsty and give you drink? [38] And when did we see you a stranger and welcome you, or naked and clothe you? [39] And when did we see you sick or in prison and visit you?" [40] And the King will answer them, "Truly, I say to you, as you did it to one of the least of these my brothers, you did it to me."

1. Two sets of people: sheep and goats

2. Two responses: one blessed and embraced, one judged and rejected

3. Two destinies: the sheep in the Kingdom inherited, prepared from the foundation of the world, the goats in the eternal fire prepared for the devil and his angels

4. Two reactions: one was hospitable, charitable, generous; the other apathetic, heartless, negligent

Jesus and the Poor (continued)

    5.   The same group of people: the hungry, the thirsty, the stranger, the naked, the sick, the prisoner

    6.   *The same standard: in the way you treated or mistreated these people, those on the underside of life, so you responded to me.*

  C.   Jesus made it appear as those who were least deserving but repentant would become heirs of the Kingdom.

Matt. 21.31 (ESV) - "Which of the two did the will of his father?" They said, "The first." Jesus said to them, "Truly, I say to you, the tax collectors and the prostitutes go into the kingdom of God before you."

Mark 2.15-17 (ESV) - And as he reclined at table in his house, many tax collectors and sinners were reclining with Jesus and his disciples, for there were many who followed him. [16] And the scribes of the Pharisees, when they saw that he was eating with sinners and tax collectors, said to his disciples, "Why does he eat with tax collectors and sinners?" [17] And when Jesus heard it, he said to them, "Those who are well have no need of a physician, but those who are sick. I came not to call the righteous, but sinners."

  D.   Ministry to the poor is ministry to the Lord Jesus - his identification with them is complete.

Conclusion: The heart and soul of Jesus' ministry was directed toward the transformation and liberation of those who were most vulnerable, most forgotten, most neglected. As disciples, may we demonstrate the same.

Jesus Christ, the Subject and Theme of the Bible

Rev. Dr. Don L. Davis

Adapted from Norman Geisler, *A Popular Survey of the Old Testament*. Grand Rapids, MI: Baker Books, 1977, pp. 11ff

Jesus Christ, the Subject and Theme of the Bible — Luke 24.27, 44; Heb. 10.7; Matt. 5.17; John 5.39

Two-fold Structure of the Bible	Four-fold Structure of the Bible	Eight-fold Structure of the Bible
Old Testament: *Anticipation* Concealed Contained The precept In shadow In ritual In picture As foretold In prophecy In Pre-incarnations	**The Law** *Foundation for Christ*	***The Law:*** Foundation for Christ (Genesis-Deuteronomy)
		History: Preparation for Christ (Joshua-Esther)
	The Prophets *Expectation of Christ*	***Poetry:*** Aspiration for Christ (Job-Song of Solomon)
		Prophets: Expectation of Christ (Isaiah-Malachi)
New Testament: *Realization* Revealed Explained Its perfection In substance In reality In person As fulfilled In history In the Incarnation	**The Gospels** *Manifestation of Christ*	***Gospels:*** Manifestation of Christ (Matthew-John)
		Acts: Propagation of Christ (The Acts of the Apostles)
	The Epistles *Interpretation of Christ*	***Epistles:*** Interpretation of Christ (Romans-Jude)
		Revelation: Consummation in Christ (The Revelation of John)

Jesus of Nazareth: The Presence of the Future

Rev. Dr. Don L. Davis

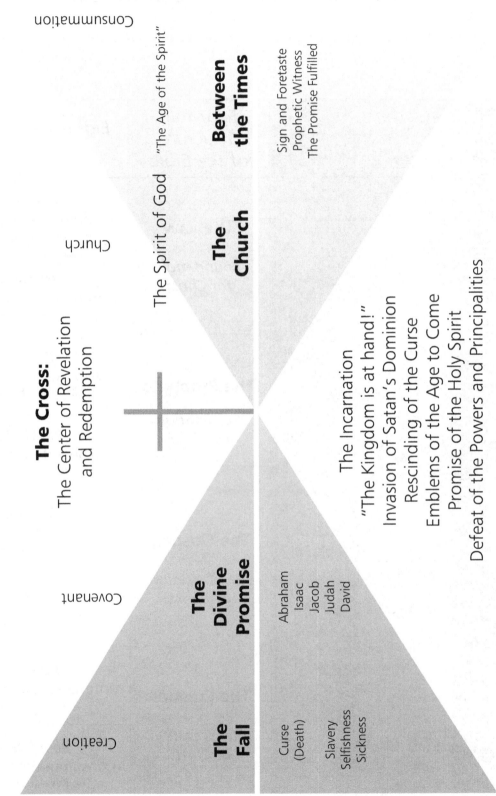

Glorification: New Heavens and New Earth

Consummation

Between the Times

"The Age of the Spirit"

The Spirit of God

Sign and Foretaste
Prophetic Witness
The Promise Fulfilled

The Church

Church

The Cross:
The Center of Revelation and Redemption

The Incarnation
"The Kingdom is at hand!"
Invasion of Satan's Dominion
Rescinding of the Curse
Emblems of the Age to Come
Promise of the Holy Spirit
Defeat of the Powers and Principalities

The Divine Promise

Covenant

Abraham
Isaac
Jacob
Judah
David

The Fall

Creation

Curse
(Death)

Slavery
Selfishness
Sickness

Creation: The Reign of Almighty God

The Key Passages on Spiritual Gifts in the New Testament

Romans 12.3-12 (ESV)

For by the grace given to me I say to everyone among you not to think of himself more highly than he ought to think, but to think with sober judgment, each according to the measure of faith that God has assigned. [4] For as in one body we have many members, and the members do not all have the same function, [5] so we, though many, are one body in Christ, and individually members one of another. [6] Having gifts that differ according to the grace given to us, let us use them: if prophecy, in proportion to our faith; [7] if service, in our serving; the one who teaches, in his teaching; [8] the one who exhorts, in his exhortation; the one who contributes, in generosity; the one who leads, with zeal; the one who does acts of mercy, with cheerfulness. [9] Let love be genuine. Abhor what is evil; hold fast to what is good. [10] Love one another with brotherly affection. Outdo one another in showing honor. [11] Do not be slothful in zeal, be fervent in spirit, serve the Lord. [12] Rejoice in hope, be patient in tribulation, be constant in prayer.

1 Corinthians 12.1-31a (ESV)

Now concerning spiritual gifts, brothers, I do not want you to be uninformed. [2] You know that when you were pagans you were led astray to mute idols, however you were led. [3] Therefore I want you to understand that no one speaking in the Spirit of God ever says "Jesus is accursed!" and no one can say "Jesus is Lord" except in the Holy Spirit. [4] Now there are varieties of gifts, but the same Spirit; [5] and there are varieties of service, but the same Lord; [6] and there are varieties of activities, but it is the same God who empowers them all in everyone. [7] To each is given the manifestation of the Spirit for the common good. [8] To one is given through the Spirit the utterance of wisdom, and to another the utterance of knowledge according to the same Spirit, [9] to another faith by the same Spirit, to another gifts of healing by the one Spirit, [10] to another the working of miracles, to another prophecy, to another the ability to distinguish between spirits, to another various kinds of tongues, to another the interpretation of tongues. [11] All these are empowered by one and the same Spirit, who apportions to each one individually as he wills. [12] For just as the body is one and has many members, and all the members of the body, though many, are one body, so it is with Christ. [13] For in one Spirit we

The Key Passages on Spiritual Gifts in the New Testament (continued)

were all baptized into one body— Jews or Greeks, slaves or free—and all were made to drink of one Spirit. [14] For the body does not consist of one member but of many. [15] If the foot should say, "Because I am not a hand, I do not belong to the body," that would not make it any less a part of the body. [16] And if the ear should say, "Because I am not an eye, I do not belong to the body," that would not make it any less a part of the body. [17] If the whole body were an eye, where would be the sense of hearing? If the whole body were an ear, where would be the sense of smell? [18] But as it is, God arranged the members in the body, each one of them, as he chose. [19] If all were a single member, where would the body be? [20] As it is, there are many parts, yet one body. [21] The eye cannot say to the hand, "I have no need of you," nor again the head to the feet, "I have no need of you." [22] On the contrary, the parts of the body that seem to be weaker are indispensable, [23] and on those parts of the body that we think less honorable we bestow the greater honor, and our unpresentable parts are treated with greater modesty, [24] which our more presentable parts do not require. But God has so composed the body, giving greater honor to the part that lacked it, [25] that there may be no division in the body, but that the members may have the same care for one another. [26] If one member suffers, all suffer together; if one member is honored, all rejoice together. [27] Now you are the body of Christ and individually members of it. [28] And God has appointed in the church first apostles, second prophets, third teachers, then miracles, then gifts of healing, helping, administrating, and various kinds of tongues. [29] Are all apostles? Are all prophets? Are all teachers? Do all work miracles? [30] Do all possess gifts of healing? Do all speak with tongues? Do all interpret? [31] But earnestly desire the higher gifts (cf. 1 Cor. 14.1-40).

Ephesians 4.7-16 (ESV)

But grace was given to each one of us according to the measure of Christ's gift. [8] Therefore it says, "When he ascended on high he led a host of captives, and he gave gifts to men." [9] (In saying, "He ascended," what does it mean but that he had also descended into the lower parts of the earth? [10] He who descended is the one who also ascended far above all the heavens, that he might fill all things.) [11] And he gave the apostles, the prophets, the evangelists, the pastors and teachers, [12] to equip the saints for the work of ministry, for building up the body of Christ, [13] until we all attain to the unity of the faith and of the knowledge of the Son of God, to mature manhood, to the measure of the stature of the fullness of Christ, [14] so that we may no longer be children, tossed to and fro by the waves and carried about by every wind of doctrine, by human cunning, by craftiness in deceitful schemes. [15] Rather, speaking the truth in love, we are to grow up in every way into him who is the head, into Christ, [16] from whom the whole body, joined and held together by every joint with which it is equipped, when each part is working properly, makes the body grow so that it builds itself up in love.

1 Peter 4.7-11 (ESV)

The end of all things is at hand; therefore be self-controlled and sober-minded for the sake of your prayers. [8] Above all, keep loving one another earnestly, since love covers a multitude of sins. [9] Show hospitality to one another without grumbling. [10] As each has received a gift, use it to serve one another, as good stewards of God's varied grace: [11] whoever speaks, as one who speaks oracles of God; whoever serves, as one who serves by the strength that God supplies—in order that in everything God may be glorified through Jesus Christ. To him belong glory and dominion forever and ever. Amen.

Keys to Bible Interpretation
Some Keys to Interpreting the Scriptures Accurately
Terry G. Cornett and Don L. Davis. Revised ed.

Key Principles

To gain an accurate understanding of a book or passage from the Bible, the interpreter must:

1. Believe that the Scriptures are inspired, infallible and the authoritative rule for life and doctrine.

    Presuppositions

2. Realize that it is not possible to fully understand and apply the Scriptures without:

    *   having been "born from above" by faith in Christ

    *   being filled with God's Holy Spirit

    *   being diligent to pursue its meaning through regular study

    *   being willing to obey its message, once revealed

3. Allow the process of interpretation to engage the "whole person." The study of Scripture should captivate your emotions and your will as well as your mind. "We aim to be objective but not disinterested readers."

4. Understand that all Scripture is in some way a testimony to Christ. Christ is the Bible's subject; all of its doctrine, teaching and ethics point to him.

5. Take into account both the divine and the human side of Scripture.

Keys to Bible Interpretation (continued)

6. Seek to "extract" or take out the meaning that is in the text (exegesis), not read into the text his or her own beliefs or ideas (eisegesis).

7. Seek to explain:

   • the "unclear" passages by the clearer statements

   • the symbolic portions by the stated teachings of Scripture

   • the Old Testament by the New Testament

8. Take into account the whole context of the book and the passage where any particular text is found.

Understanding the Original Situation

9. Identify the human author and the intended audience. Start by attempting to discover what the author was trying to say to the original audience. "A passage cannot mean what it never meant."

10. Use information about the manuscripts, languages, grammar, literary forms, history, and culture to help discover the author's intended meaning.

11. Take seriously the genre and types of language used by the author, then interpret the Scriptures literally, meaning that we take the plain sense of the language as it is normally used in that genre.

Finding General Principles

12. Look for the ideas, values, and truths that a story, command, or prophecy is trying to communicate. Seek to state those principles in a way that is true and useful for all people, at all times, and in all situations.

13. Use Scripture to interpret Scripture. In order to understand any individual part of Scripture, compare that portion to the message of the whole Bible.

Keys to Bible Interpretation (continued)

Once this understanding has been reached, one must also reinterpret his/her understanding of the whole of Scripture (theology and doctrine) in light of the new information gained from the passage (The Hermeneutical Circle).

14. Understand that reason, tradition, and experience are significant factors in the process of interpreting Scripture. Principles must be clear, logical and defensible; they must be compatible with the way Christians have interpreted the Scriptures throughout history; and they must help to make sense out of human experience.

15. Carefully move from what Scripture "meant" to its original audience to what it "means" for the current reader.

Applying General sPrinciples Today

16. Apply the general truths to specific situations faced by people today.

    • Remember that the Holy Spirit is the primary guide in the application of truth. Ask him for guidance about the meaning for today and then prayerfully meditate on the meaning of the passage.

    • Seek the Spirit's guidance by seeing how he has led other Christians (both inside and outside your own denominational tradition) to interpret the meaning and application of the passage for today.

17. Put the principles and the applications in language that makes sense to modern readers.

18. Keep the proper "end goals" in view. The intent of all Bible study is to mature the reader in the life and love of Jesus Christ, to the glory of God. Not knowledge alone, but life transformation is the goal of Bible interpretation.

Key Perspective

Discovering the Word and Works of God in the Lives of the People of Scripture

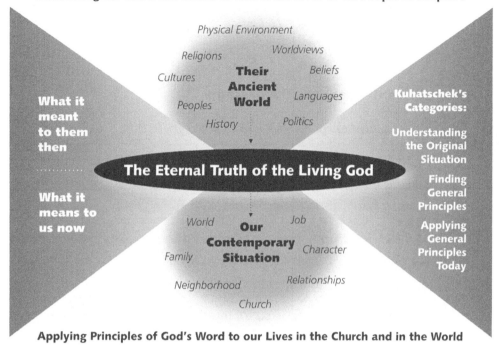

Applying Principles of God's Word to our Lives in the Church and in the World

*Note: In this diagram, Kuhatschek's categories refer to the three steps of Biblical interpretation outlined by Jack Kuhatschek in **Applying the Bible** Downer's Grove: IVP, 1990.*

Key Steps to Interpretation

Step One: Understanding the Original Situation

The focus of this step is on understanding the *world of the Bible, the author, and God's message to a particular group of people at a particular time and place.*

A. Ask God to open your eyes to truth through the ministry of the Holy Spirit as you read his Word.

Tell God that you want to be changed as well as informed by your reading of the Scriptures. Ask him to reveal specific actions and attitudes in your own life which need to be changed or disciplined. Ask God to use the Word to reveal Jesus and to make you more like his Son. Thank God for the gifts of his Spirit, his Son, and the Scriptures. Many believers began their study of God's Word by simply praying the words of Psalms 119.18.

Heavenly Father, open my eyes to see wonderful things in your word. Amen.

Keys to Bible Interpretation (continued)

B. Identify the author of the book, the approximate date it was written, why it was written, and to whom it was written.

Key Tools: Bible Dictionary, Bible Handbook, or Bible Commentary

C. Read the context around the passage.

Key Tool: A standard translation (not a paraphrase) of the Bible

- Look to see where natural "breaks" are in and around the passage and make sure that you are looking at the entire passage during the process of interpretation.

- Read the material around the passage. It is a good rule of thumb to read *at least* one chapter before and one chapter following the passage you are studying.

- The shorter the passage selected for interpretation, the greater the danger becomes in ignoring context. The old proverb is correct: "A text without a *con*text is a *pre*text."

D. Observe the passage carefully.

- Identify who is speaking and who is being spoken to.

- Observe the main ideas and the details.

  - Make a simple outline of the passage.

  - Identify the main ideas.

  - Look for repeated words or images.

  - Find "cause-and-effect" relationships.

  - Look for comparisons, contrasts, and connections.

E. Read the passage in another translation of Scripture.

Key Tool: A translation or paraphrase of the Scriptures that uses a different translation philosophy than the version of Scripture you regularly use

- Write down any questions that this new translation raises in your mind and stay alert for answers as you do further study.

F. Read any parallel accounts or passages from other parts of Scripture.

Key Tool: A concordance and/or a Bible which includes cross-references

- Note what details are added to the passage you are studying from the other accounts in Scripture.

- Why did the author choose to omit some details and emphasize others? What significance does this have for understanding the author's intent.

G. Study the words and the grammatical structures.

Key Tools: Hebrew and Greek Lexicons and Expository Dictionaries help deepen our understanding of word meanings and usage. Exegetical Commentaries help explain grammatical constructions and how they affect the meaning of the text.

- Make a note of words that are being used in a unique way by the writer and of special grammatical forms like imperatives, verbs that show continuous action, etc.

H. Identify the genre (type of literature) and consider any special rules that apply to it.

Key Tool: Bible Dictionary and Bible Commentaries

- Each type of literature has to be taken seriously for what it is. We must not interpret poetry in the same way we interpret prophecy, or narratives in the way we interpret commands.

Keys to Bible Interpretation (continued)

I. Look for literary structures that might influence the way the text is understood.

Key Tool: Exegetical Commentaries

   •   Literary structures include figures of speech, metaphors, typologies, symbols, poetic structures, chiasmic structures, etc.

J. Identify the historical events and the cultural issues which might effect the people or influence the ideas described in the passage.

Key Tools: Bible Dictionaries and Bible Commentaries

   •   Constantly ask, "What was happening in history and society that would affect the way the audience heard the message in this text?"

K. Summarize what you believe the author was trying to say and why it was important for the original audience.

   •   Your goal in this step is to write the key truths of the passage in such a way that the original author and the original listeners would agree with them if they heard them.

The focus of this step is identifying *the central message, commands, and principles in a portion of Scripture* which teach God's purposes for all people.

Step Two: Finding General Principles

A. List in sentence form what you believe are the general principles in the passage which apply to all people, at all times, in all cultures.

B. Check these statements against other parts of Scripture for clarity and accuracy.

Key Tools: Concordance, Topical Bible

Ask yourself:

   •   Are the principles I listed supported by other passages in the Bible?

- Which of these principles might be difficult or impossible to explain when compared with other passages of Scripture?

- Must any of these principles be ruled out in light of other passages of Scripture?

- What new information about God and his will does this passage add to my overall knowledge of Scripture and doctrine?

C. Adjust or modify your statements of God's principles in light of the discoveries you made above.

- Rewrite your key principles to reflect the insight gained from other portions of Scripture.

D. Read commentaries to discover some of the key principles and doctrines that others in the Church have drawn from this passage.

- Compare and contrast the information from the commentaries with your own reading. Be willing to abandon, change, or defend your views as necessary as you come across new information.

E. Again adjust or modify your statements of God's principles in light of the discoveries you made above.

Step Three: Applying General Principles Today

The focus of this step is on moving *from what Scripture "meant" to what it "means."* What does obedience to God's commands and purposes look like today in our culture, with our families and friends, and with the problems and opportunities that we face in our lives?

A. Ask God to speak to you and reveal the meaning of this passage for your life.

Keys to Bible Interpretation (continued)

- Meditate on the passage and the things you have learned from your study so far while asking the Holy Spirit to point out the specific applications of the truths discovered for yourself and those around you.

B. How is this passage "Good News" to me and others?

- How does it reveal more about Jesus and his coming Kingdom?

- How does it relate to God's overall plan of salvation?

C. How should knowing the truth from this passage:

Affect my relationship with God?

- Try to determine how the principles and examples from these Scriptures might help you to love and obey God more perfectly.

Affect my relationships with others?

- This includes my church family, my physical family, my co-workers, my friends, my neighbors, my enemies, strangers, and the poor or oppressed.

Challenge beliefs, attitudes, and actions that my culture views as normal?

- How must my thinking and acting be different from those in the world around me?

D. Attempt to answer the questions "What am I to believe?" and "What am I to do?" now that I have studied this passage.

- Do I need to repent from old ways of thinking and acting?

- How can I act on this truth so that I become a wise person?

E. How can I share what I have learned with others in a way that draws attention to Christ and builds them up?

Kingdom of God Timeline

Rev. Dr. Don L. Davis

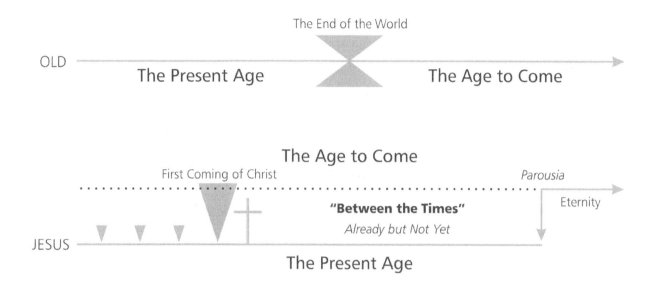

The **"*malkuth*" of Yahweh, the "*basileia tou Theou.*"** First century Palestinian Jews saw God as King, of his people Israel and all the earth. Yet, due to the rebellion of humankind and Satan and his angels, God's reign in the earth is **yet future**. It shall be: 1) nationalistic--the salvation and sovereignty of Israel over her enemies, 2) universal knowledge and reign of God, 3) *tsidkenu* (righteousness, justice) and *shalom* (peace), 4) obedience to the Law of God, 5) the final battle with the Gentile nations - Armageddon, 6) occur by a supernatural cataclysm realized at the end of time, 7) transformation of the heavens and earth to pre-Edenic splendor, 8) rule by the son of David-son of Man, 9) rescinding the effects of the curse, 10) the resurrection of the dead, 11) and judgment and destruction of all of God's enemies - sin, death, evil, the "world," the devil and his angels, and 12) eternal life.

Jesus' proclamation: **The Kingdom of God has now appeared in the life, person, and ministry of Messiah Jesus.** In Jesus' words (*kerygma*), his deeds of compassion (*diakinia*), his miracles, his exorcisms of demons, his passion, death, and resurrection, and the sending of the Spirit, **the promised-for Kingdom has come.** The Kingdom is **both** present and future; he announces **the presence of the future.** Present kingdom blessings include 1) the Church as sign and foretaste, 2) the pledge of the Holy Spirit, 3) the forgiveness of sin, 4) the proclamation of the Kingdom worldwide, 5) reconciliation and peace with God, 6) the binding of Satan, with authority given to Christ's disciples.

Kingdom Texts in the New Testament

Matt. 3.2 (ESV) - Repent, for the kingdom of heaven is at hand.

Matt. 4.17 (ESV) - From that time Jesus began to preach saying, "Repent, for the kingdom of heaven is at hand."

Matt. 4.23 (ESV) - And he went throughout all Galilee, teaching in their synagogues and proclaiming the gospel of the kingdom and healing every disease and every affliction among the people.

Matt. 5.3 (ESV) - Blessed are the poor in spirit, for theirs is the kingdom of heaven.

Matt. 5.10 (ESV) - Blessed are those who are persecuted for righteousness' sake, for theirs is the kingdom of heaven.

Matt. 5.19-20 (ESV) - Therefore whoever relaxes one of the least of these commandments and teaches others to do the same will be called least in the kingdom of heaven, but whoever does them and teaches them will be called great in the kingdom of heaven. [20] For I tell you, unless your righteousness exceeds that of the scribes and Pharisees, you will never enter the kingdom of heaven..

Matt. 6.10 (ESV) - Your kingdom come, your will be done, on earth as it is in heaven.

Matt. 6.33 (ESV) - But seek first the kingdom of God and his righteousness, and all these things will be added to you.

Matt. 7.21 (ESV) - Not everyone who says to me, "Lord, Lord," will enter the kingdom of heaven, but the one who does the will of my Father who is in heaven.

Matt. 8.11-12 (ESV) - I tell you, many will come from east and west and recline at table with Abraham, Isaac, and Jacob in the kingdom of heaven, [12] while the sons of the kingdom will be thrown into the outer darkness. In that place there will be weeping and gnashing of teeth.

Matt. 9.35 (ESV) - And Jesus went throughout all the cities and villages, teaching in their synagogues and proclaiming the gospel of the kingdom and healing every disease and every affliction.

Matt. 10.7 (ESV) - And proclaim as you go, saying, "The kingdom of heaven is at hand."

Matt. 11.11-12 (ESV) - Truly, I say to you, among those born of women there has arisen no one greater than John the Baptist. Yet the one who is least in the kingdom of heaven is greater than he. [12] From the days of John the Baptist until now the kingdom of heaven has suffered violence, and the violent take it by force.

Matt. 12.25-26 (ESV) - Knowing their thoughts, he said to them, "Every kingdom divided against itself is laid waste, and no city or house divided against itself will stand. [26] And if Satan casts out Satan, he is divided against himself. How then will his kingdom stand?"

Matt. 12.28 (ESV) - But if it is by the Spirit of God that I cast out demons, then the kingdom of God has come upon you.

Matt. 13.11 (ESV) - And he answered them, "To you it has been given to know the secrets of the kingdom of heaven, but to them it has not been given."

Matt. 13.19 (ESV) - When anyone hears the word of the kingdom, and does not understand it, the evil one comes and snatches away what has been sown in his heart. This is what was sown along the path.

Matt. 13.24 (ESV) - He put another parable before them, saying, "The kingdom of heaven may be compared to a man who sowed good seed in his field."

Matt. 13.31 (ESV) - He put another parable before them, saying, "The kingdom of heaven is like a grain of mustard seed that a man took and sowed in his field."

Matt. 13.33 (ESV) - He told them another parable. "The kingdom of heaven is like leaven, that a woman took and hid in three measures of flour, till it was all leavened."

Matt. 13.38 (ESV) - The field is the world, and the good seed is the children of the kingdom. The weeds are the sons of the evil one.

Matt. 13.41 (ESV) - The Son of Man will send his angels, and they will gather out of his kingdom all causes of sin and all law-breakers.

Kingdom Texts in the New Testament (continued)

Matt. 13.43-45 (ESV) - Then the righteous will shine like the sun in the kingdom of their Father. He who has ears, let him hear. The kingdom of heaven is like treasure hidden in a field, which a man found and covered up. Then in his joy he goes and sells all that he has and buys that field. Again, the kingdom of heaven is like a merchant in search of fine pearls.

Matt. 13.47 (ESV) - Again, the kingdom of heaven is like a net that was thrown into the sea and gathered fish of every kind.

Matt. 13.52 (ESV) - And he said to them, "Therefore every scribe who has been trained for the kingdom of heaven is like a master of a house, who brings out of his treasure what is new and what is old."

Matt. 16.19 (ESV) - I will give you the keys of the kingdom of heaven, and whatever you bind on earth shall be bound in heaven, and whatever you loose on earth shall be loosed in heaven.

Matt. 16.28 (ESV) - Truly I say to you, there are some standing here who will not taste death until they see the Son of Man coming in his kingdom.

Matt. 18.1, 3-4 (ESV) - At that time the disciples came to Jesus, saying, "Who is greatest in the kingdom of heaven?" . . . "Truly, I say to you, unless you turn and become like children, you will never enter the kingdom of heaven. Whoever humbles himself like this child is the greatest in the kingdom of heaven."

Matt. 18.23 (ESV) - Therefore the kingdom of heaven may be compared to a king who wished to settle accounts with his servants.

Matt. 19.12 (ESV) - For there are eunuchs who have been so from birth, and there are eunuchs who have been made eunuchs by men, and there are eunuchs who have made themselves eunuchs for the sake of the kingdom of heaven. Let the one who is able to receive this receive it.

Matt. 19.14 (ESV) - . . . but Jesus said, "Let the little children come to me and do not hinder them, for to such belongs the kingdom of heaven."

Matt. 19.23-24 (ESV) - And Jesus said to his disciples, "Truly, I say to you, only with difficulty will a rich person enter the kingdom of heaven. Again I tell you, it is easier for a camel to go through the eye of a needle than for a rich person to enter the kingdom of God."

Matt. 20.1 (ESV) - For the kingdom of heaven is like a master of a house who went out early in the morning to hire laborers for his vineyard.

Matt. 20.21 (ESV) - And he said to her, "What do you want?" She said to him, "Say that these two sons of mine are to sit, one at your right hand and one at your left, in your kingdom."

Matt. 21.31 (ESV) - "Which of the two did the will of his father?" They said, "The first." Jesus said to them, "Truly, I say to you, the tax collectors and the prostitutes go into the kingdom of God before you."

Matt. 21.43 (ESV) - Therefore I tell you, the kingdom of God will be taken away from you and given to a people producing its fruits.

Matt. 22.2 (ESV) - The kingdom of heaven may be compared to a king who gave a wedding feast for his son.

Matt. 23.13 (ESV) - But woe to you, scribes and Pharisees, hypocrites! For you shut the kingdom of heaven in people's faces. For you neither enter yourselves nor allow those who would enter to go in.

Matt. 24.7 (ESV) - For nation will rise against nation, and kingdom against kingdom, and there will be famines and earthquakes in various places.

Matt. 24.14 (ESV) - And this gospel of the kingdom will be proclaimed throughout the whole world as a testimony to all nations, and then the end will come.

Matt. 25.1 (ESV) - Then the kingdom of heaven will be like ten virgins who took their lamps and went to meet the bridegroom.

Matt. 25.34 (ESV) - Then the King will say to those on his right, "Come, you who are blessed by my Father, inherit the kingdom prepared for you from the foundation of the world."

Matt. 26.29 (ESV) - I tell you, I will not drink again of this fruit of the vine until that day when I drink it new with you in my Father's kingdom.

Mark 1.15 (ESV) - . . . and saying, "The time is fulfilled, and the kingdom of God is at hand; repent and believe in the gospel."

Mark 3.24 (ESV) - And if a kingdom is divided against itself, that kingdom cannot stand.

Kingdom Texts in the New Testament (continued)

Mark 4.11 (ESV) - And he said to them, "To you has been given the secret of the kingdom of God, but for those outside everything is in parables."

Mark 4.26 (ESV) - And he said, "The kingdom of God is as if a man should scatter seed on the ground."

Mark 4.30 (ESV) - And he said, "With what can we compare the kingdom of God, or what parable shall we use for it?"

Mark 6.23 (ESV) - And he vowed to her, "Whatever you ask of me, I will give you, up to half of my kingdom."

Mark 9.1 (ESV) - And he said to them, "Truly, I say to you, there are some standing here who will not taste death until they see the kingdom of God after it has come with power."

Mark 9.47 (ESV) - And if your eye causes you to sin, tear it out; it is better for you to enter the kingdom of God with one eye than with two eyes to be thrown into hell.

Mark 10.14-15 (ESV) - But when Jesus saw it, he was indignant and said to them, "Let the children to come to me; do not hinder them, for to such belongs kingdom of God. Truly, I say to you, whoever does not receive the kingdom of God like a child shall not enter it."

Mark 10.23-25 (ESV) - And Jesus looked around and said to his disciples, "How difficult it will be for those who have wealth to enter the kingdom of God!" And the disciples were amazed at his words. But Jesus said to them again, "Children, how difficult it is to enter the Kingdom of God! It is easier for a camel to go through the eye of a needle than for a rich person to enter the kingdom of God."

Mark 11.10 (ESV) - Blessed is the coming kingdom of our father David! Hosanna in the highest!

Mark 12.34 (ESV) - And when Jesus saw that he answered wisely, he said to him, "You are not far from the kingdom of God." And after that, no one dared to ask him any more questions.

Mark 13.8 (ESV) - For nation will arise against nation, and kingdom against kingdom. There will be earthquakes in various places; there will be famines. These are but the beginning of the birth pains.

Mark 14.25 (ESV) - Truly, I say to you, I will not drink again of the fruit of the vine until that day when I drink it new in the kingdom of God.

Mark 15.43 (ESV) - Joseph of Arimathea, a respected member of the Council, who was also himself looking for the kingdom of God, took courage and went to Pilate and asked for the body of Jesus.

Luke 1.33 (ESV) - . . . and he will reign over the house of Jacob forever, and of his kingdom there will be no end.

Luke 4.43 (ESV) - . . . but he said to them, "I must preach the good news of the kingdom of God to the other towns as well; for I was sent for this purpose."

Luke 6.20 (ESV) - And he lifted up his eyes on his disciples, and said, "Blessed are you who are poor, for yours is the kingdom of God."

Luke 7.28 (ESV) - I tell you, among those born of women none is greater than John. Yet the one who is least in the kingdom of God is greater than he.

Luke 8.1 (ESV) - Soon afterwards he went on through cities and villages, proclaiming and bringing the good news of the kingdom of God. And the twelve were with him.

Luke 8.10 (ESV) - . . . he said, "To you it has been given to know the secrets of the kingdom of God, but for others they are in parables, so that 'Seeing they may not see, and hearing they may not understand.'"

Luke 9.2 (ESV) - . . . and he sent them out to proclaim the kingdom of God and to heal.

Luke 9.11 (ESV) - When the crowds learned it, they followed him; and he welcomed them and spoke to them of the kingdom of God and cured those who had need of healing.

Luke 9.27 (ESV) - But I tell you truly, there are some standing here who will not taste death until they see the kingdom of God.

Luke 9.60 (ESV) - And Jesus said to him, "Leave the dead to bury their own dead; but as for you, go and proclaim everywhere the kingdom of God."

Luke 9.62 (ESV) - Jesus said to him, "No one who puts his hand to the plow and looks back is fit for the kingdom of God."

Kingdom Texts in the New Testament (continued)

Luke 10.9 (ESV) - Heal the sick in it and say to them, "The kingdom of God has come near to you."

Luke 10.11 (ESV) - Even the dust of your town that clings to our feet we wipe off against you. Nonetheless know this, that the kingdom of God has come near.

Luke 11.2 (ESV) - And he said to them, "When you pray, say: 'Father, hallowed be your name. Your kingdom come.'"

Luke 11.17-18 (ESV) - But he, knowing their thoughts, said to them, "Every kingdom divided against itself is laid waste, and a divided household falls. And if Satan also is divided against himself, how will his kingdom stand? For you say that I cast out demons by Beelzebul."

Luke 11.20 (ESV) - But if it is by the finger of God that I cast out demons, then the kingdom of God has come upon you.

Luke 12.31-32 (ESV) - Instead, seek his kingdom, and these things will be added to you. Fear not, little flock, for it is your Father's good pleasure to give you the kingdom.

Luke 13.18 (ESV) - He said therefore, "What is the kingdom of God like? And to what shall I compare it?"

Luke 13.20 (ESV) - And again he said, "To what shall I compare the kingdom of God?"

Luke 13.28-29 (ESV) - In that place there will be weeping and gnashing of teeth, when you see Abraham and Isaac and Jacob and all the prophets in the kingdom of God but you yourselves cast out. And people will come from east and west, and from north and south, and will recline at table in the kingdom of God.

Luke 14.15 (ESV) - When one of those who reclined at table with him heard these things, he said to him, "Blessed is everyone who will eat bread in the kingdom of God!"

Luke 16.16 (ESV) - The Law and the Prophets were until John; since then the good news of the kingdom of God is preached, and everyone forces his way into it.

Luke 17.20-21 (ESV) - Being asked by the Pharisees when the kingdom of God would come, he answered them, "The kingdom of God is not coming with signs to be observed, nor will they say, 'Look, here it is!' or 'There!' for behold, the kingdom of God is in the midst of you."

Luke 18.16-17 (ESV) - But Jesus called them to him, saying, "Let the children come to me, and do not hinder them, for to such belongs the kingdom of God. Truly, I say to you, whoever does not receive the kingdom of God like a child shall not enter it."

Luke 18.24-25 (ESV) - Jesus, looking at him with sadness, said, "How difficult it is for those who have wealth to enter the kingdom of God! For it is easier for a camel to go through the eye of a needle than for a rich person to enter the kingdom of God."

Luke 18.29 (ESV) - And he said to them, "Truly I say to you, there is no one who has left house or wife or brothers or parents or children, for the sake of the kingdom of God . . ."

Luke 19.11-12 (ESV) - As they heard these things, he proceeded to tell a parable, because he was near to Jerusalem, and because they supposed that the kingdom of God was to appear immediately. He said therefore, "A nobleman went into a far country to receive for himself a kingdom for himself and then return."

Luke 19.15 (ESV) - When he returned, having received the kingdom, he ordered these servants to whom he had given the money to be called to him, that he might know what they had gained by doing business.

Luke 21.10 (ESV) - Then he said to them, "Nation will rise against nation, and kingdom against kingdom."

Luke 21.31 (ESV) - So also, when you see these things taking place, you know that the kingdom of God is near.

Luke 22.16 (ESV) - For I tell you, I will not eat it until it is fulfilled in the kingdom of God.

Luke 22.18 (ESV) - For I tell you that from now on I will not drink of the fruit of the vine until the kingdom of God comes.

Kingdom Texts in the New Testament (continued)

Luke 22.29-30 (ESV) - . . . and I assign to you, as my Father assigned to me, a kingdom, that you may eat and drink at my table in my kingdom, and sit on thrones judging the twelve tribes of Israel.

Luke 23.42 (ESV) - And he said, "Jesus, remember me when you come into your kingdom."

Luke 23.51 (ESV) - . . . who had not consented to their decision and action; and he was looking for the kingdom of God.

John 3.3 (ESV) - Jesus answered him, "Truly, truly, I say to you, unless one is born again, he cannot see the kingdom of God."

John 3.5 (ESV) - Jesus answered, "Truly, truly, I say to you, unless one is born of water and the Spirit, he cannot enter the kingdom of God."

John 18.36 (ESV) - Jesus answered, "My kingdom is not of this world. If my kingdom were of this world, my servants would have been fighting, that I might not be delivered over to the Jews. But my kingdom is not from the world."

Acts 1.3 (ESV) - To them he presented himself alive after his suffering by many proofs, appearing to them during forty days and speaking about the kingdom of God.

Acts 1.6 (ESV) - So when they had come together, they asked him, "Lord, will you at this time restore the kingdom to Israel?"

Acts 8.12 (ESV) - But when they believed Philip as he preached good news about the kingdom of God and the name of Jesus Christ, they were baptized, both men and women.

Acts 14.22 (ESV) - . . . strengthening the souls of the disciples, encouraging them to continue in the faith, and saying that through many tribulations we must enter the kingdom of God.

Acts 20.25 (ESV) - And now, behold, I know that none of you among whom I have gone about proclaiming the kingdom will see my face again.

Acts 28.23 (ESV) - When they had appointed a day for him, they came to him at his lodging in greater numbers. From morning till evening he expounded to them, testifying to the kingdom of God and trying to convince them about Jesus both from the Law of Moses and from the Prophets.

Acts 28.31 (ESV) - . . . proclaiming the kingdom of God and teaching about the Lord Jesus Christ with all openness and without hindrance.

Rom. 14.17 (ESV) - . . . for the kingdom of God is not eating and drinking, but righteousness and peace and joy in the Holy Spirit.

1 Cor. 4.20 (ESV) - For the kingdom of God does not consist in words, but in power.

1 Cor. 6.9-10 (ESV) - Do you not know that the unrighteous will not inherit the kingdom of God? Do not be deceived: neither the sexually immoral, nor idolaters, nor adulterers, nor men who practice homosexuality, [10] nor thieves, nor the greedy, nor drunkards, nor revilers, nor swindlers will inherit the kingdom of God.

1 Cor. 15.24 (ESV) - Then comes the end, when he delivers the kingdom to God the Father after destroying every rule and every authority and power.

1 Cor. 15.50 (ESV) - I tell you this, brothers: flesh and blood cannot inherit the kingdom of God, nor does the perishable inherit the imperishable.

Gal. 5.21 (ESV) - . . . envy, drunkenness, orgies, and things like these. I warn you, as I warned you before, that those who do such things will not inherit the kingdom of God.

Eph. 5.5 (ESV) - For you may be sure of this, that everyone who is sexually immoral or impure, or who is covetous (that is, an idolater), has no inheritance in the kingdom of Christ and God.

Col. 1.13 (ESV) - He has delivered us from the domain of darkness and transferred us to the kingdom of his beloved Son.

Col. 4.11 (ESV) - . . . and Jesus who is called Justus. These are the only men of the circumcision among my fellow workers for the kingdom of God, and they have been a comfort to me.

1 Thess. 2.12 (ESV) - . . . we exhorted each one of you and encouraged you and charged you to walk in a manner worthy of God, who calls you into his own kingdom and glory.

2 Thess. 1.5 (ESV) - This is evidence of the righteous judgment of God, that you may be considered worthy of the kingdom of God, for which you are also suffering.

Kingdom Texts in the New Testament (continued)

2 Tim. 4.1 (ESV) - I charge you in the presence of God and of Christ Jesus, who is to judge the living and the dead, and by his appearing and his kingdom.

2 Tim. 4.18 (ESV) - The Lord will rescue me from every evil deed and bring me safely into his heavenly kingdom. To him be the glory forever and ever. Amen.

Heb. 1.8 (ESV) - But of the Son he says, "Your throne, O God, is forever and ever, the scepter of uprightness is the scepter of your kingdom.

Heb. 12.28 (ESV) - Therefore let us be grateful for receiving a kingdom that cannot be shaken, and thus let us offer to God acceptable worship, with reverence and awe.

James 2.5 (ESV) - Listen, my beloved brothers, has not God chosen those who are poor in the world to be rich in faith and heirs of the kingdom, which he has promised to those who love him?

2 Pet. 1.11 (ESV) - For in this way there will be richly provided for you an entrance into the eternal kingdom of our Lord and Savior Jesus Christ.

Rev. 1.6 (ESV) - . . . and made us a kingdom, priests to his God and Father, to him be glory and dominion forever and ever. Amen.

Rev. 1.9 (ESV) - I, John, your brother and partner in the tribulation and the kingdom and the patient endurance that are in Jesus, was on the island called Patmos on account of the word of God and the testimony of Jesus.

Rev. 5.10 (ESV) - . . . and you have made them a kingdom and priests to our God, and they shall reign on the earth.

Rev. 11.15 (ESV) - Then the seventh angel blew his trumpet, and there were loud voices in heaven, saying, "The kingdom of the world has become the kingdom of our Lord and of his Christ, and he shall reign forever and ever."

Rev. 12.10 (ESV) - And I heard a loud voice in heaven, saying, "Now the salvation and the power and the kingdom of our God and the authority of his Christ have come, for the accuser of our brothers has been thrown down, who accuses them day and night before our God.

Rev. 16.10 (ESV) - The fifth angel poured out his bowl on the throne of the beast, and its kingdom was plunged into darkness. People gnawed their tongues in anguish.

Rev. 17.12 (ESV) - And the ten horns that you saw are ten kings who have not yet received royal power, but they are to receive authority as kings for one hour, together with the beast.

Rev. 17.17 (ESV) - . . . for God has put it into their hearts to carry out his purpose by being of one mind and handing over their royal power to the beast, until the words of God are fulfilled.

Kingdom Texts in the Old Testament

Exod. 19.3-6 (ESV) - . . . while Moses went up to God. The LORD called to him out of the mountain, saying, "Thus you shall say to the house of Jacob, and tell the people of Israel: [4] You yourselves have seen what I did to the Egyptians, and how I bore you on eagles' wings and brought you to myself. [5] Now therefore, if you will indeed obey my voice and keep my covenant, you shall be my treasured possession among all peoples, for all the earth is mine; [6] and you shall be to me a kingdom of priests and a holy nation. These are the words that you shall speak to the people of Israel."

2 Sam. 7.12-16 (ESV) - When your days are fulfilled and you lie down with your fathers, I will raise up your offspring after you, who shall come from your body, and I will establish his kingdom. [13] He shall build a house for my name, and I will establish the throne of his kingdom forever. [14] I will be to him a father, and he shall be to me a son. When he commits iniquity, I will discipline him with the rod of men, with the stripes of the sons of men, [15] but my steadfast love will not depart from him, as I took it from Saul, whom I put away from before you. [16] And your house and your kingdom shall be made sure forever before me. Your throne shall be established forever.'"

1 Chron. 14.2 (ESV) - And David knew that the LORD had established him as king over Israel, and that his kingdom was highly exalted for the sake of his people Israel.

1 Chron. 16.20 (ESV) - . . . wandering from nation to nation, from one kingdom to another people . . .

1 Chron. 17.11-14 (ESV) - When your days are fulfilled to walk with your fathers, I will raise up your offspring after you, one of your own sons, and I will establish his kingdom. [12] He shall build a house for me, and I will establish his throne forever. [13] I will be to him a father, and he shall be to me a son. I will not take my steadfast love from him, as I took it from him who was before you, [14] but I will confirm him in my house and in my kingdom forever, and his throne shall be established forever.

1 Chron. 22.10 (ESV) - He shall build a house for my name. He shall be my son, and I will be his father, and I will establish his royal throne in Israel forever.

1 Chron. 28.7 (ESV) - I will establish his kingdom forever if he continues strong in keeping my commandments and my rules, as he is today.

1 Chron. 29.10-12 (ESV) - Therefore David blessed the LORD in the presence of all the assembly. And David said: "Blessed are you, O LORD, the God of Israel our father, forever and ever. [11] Yours, O LORD, is the greatness and the power and the glory and the victory and the majesty, for all that is in the heavens and in the earth is yours. Yours is the kingdom, O LORD, and you are exalted as head above all. [12] Both riches and honor come from you, and you rule over all. In your hand are power and might, and in your hand it is to make great and to give strength to all."

2 Chron. 32.15 (ESV) - Now, therefore, do not let Hezekiah deceive you or mislead you in this fashion, and do not believe him, for no god of any nation or kingdom has been able to deliver his people from my hand or from the hand of my fathers. How much less will your God deliver you out of my hand!

2 Chron. 33.13 (ESV) - He prayed to him, and God was moved by his entreaty and heard his plea and brought him again to Jerusalem into his kingdom. Then Manasseh knew that the LORD was God.

Neh. 9.32-35 (ESV) - Now, therefore, our God, the great, the mighty, and the awesome God, who keeps covenant and steadfast love, let not all the hardship seem little to you that has come upon us, upon our kings, our princes, our priests, our prophets, our fathers, and all your people, since the time of the kings of Assyria until this day. [33] Yet you have been righteous in all that has come upon us, for you have dealt faithfully and we have acted wickedly. [34] Our kings, our princes, our priests, and our fathers have not kept your law or paid attention to your commandments and your warnings that you gave them. [35] Even in their own kingdom, enjoying your great goodness that you gave them, and in the large and rich land that you set before them, they did not serve you or turn from their wicked works.

Ps. 9.7-8 (ESV) - But the Lord sits enthroned forever; he has established his throne for justice, [8] and he judges the world with righteousness; he judges the peoples with uprightness.

Kingdom Texts in the Old Testament (continued)

Ps. 22.27-28 (ESV) - All the ends of the earth shall remember and turn to the LORD, and all the families of the nations shall worship before you. [28] For kingship belongs to the LORD, and he rules over the nations.

Ps. 45.6 (ESV) - Your throne, O God, is forever and ever. The scepter of your kingdom is a scepter of uprightness.

Ps. 47.7-8 (ESV) - For God is the King of all the earth; sing praises with a psalm! [8] God reigns over the nations; God sits on his holy throne.

Ps. 103.17-19 (ESV) - But the steadfast love of the LORD is from everlasting to everlasting on those who fear him, and his righteousness to children's children, [18] to those who keep his covenant and remember to do his commandments. [19] The LORD has established his throne in the heavens, and his kingdom rules over all.

Ps. 105.13 (ESV) - . . . wandering from nation to nation, from one kingdom to another people.

Ps. 145.9-13 (ESV) - The LORD is good to all, and his mercy is over all that he has made. [10] All your works shall give thanks to you, O LORD, and all your saints shall bless you! [11] They shall speak of the glory of your kingdom and tell of your power, [12] to make known to the children of man your [2] mighty deeds, and the glorious splendor of your kingdom. [13] Your kingdom is an everlasting kingdom, and your dominion endures throughout all generations.

Isa. 2.2-5 (ESV) - It shall come to pass in the latter days that the mountain of the house of the LORD shall be established as the highest of the mountains, and shall be lifted up above the hills; and all the nations shall flow to it, [3] and many peoples shall come, and say: "Come, let us go up to the mountain of the LORD, to the house of the God of Jacob, that he may teach us his ways and that we may walk in his paths." For out of Zion shall go the law, and the word of the LORD from Jerusalem. [4] He shall judge between the nations, and shall decide disputes for many peoples; and they shall beat their swords into plowshares, and their spears into pruning hooks; nation shall not lift up sword against nation, neither shall they learn war anymore. [5] O house of Jacob, come, let us walk in the light of the LORD.

Isa. 9.6-7 (ESV) - For to us a child is born, to us a son is given; and the government shall be upon his shoulder, and his name shall be called Wonderful Counselor, Mighty God, Everlasting Father, Prince of Peace. [7] Of the increase of his government and of peace there will be no end, on the throne of David and over his kingdom, to establish it and to uphold it with justice and with righteousness from this time forth and forevermore. The zeal of the LORD of hosts will do this.

Isa. 11.1-12.6 (ESV) - There shall come forth a shoot from the stump of Jesse, and a branch from his roots shall bear fruit. [2] And the Spirit of the LORD shall rest upon him, the Spirit of wisdom and understanding, the Spirit of counsel and might, the Spirit of knowledge and the fear of the LORD. [3] And his delight shall be in the fear of the LORD. He shall not judge by what his eyes see, or decide disputes by what his ears hear, [4] but with righteousness he shall judge the poor, and decide with equity for the meek of the earth; and he shall strike the earth with the rod of his mouth, and with the breath of his lips he shall kill the wicked. [5] Righteousness shall be the belt of his waist, and faithfulness the belt of his loins. [6] The wolf shall dwell with the lamb, and the leopard shall lie down with the young goat, and the calf and the lion and the fattened calf together; and a little child shall lead them. [7] The cow and the bear shall graze; their young shall lie down together; and the lion shall eat straw like the ox. [8] The nursing child shall play over the hole of the cobra, and the weaned child shall put his hand on the adder's den. [9] They shall not hurt or destroy in all my holy mountain; for the earth shall be full of the knowledge of the LORD as the waters cover the sea. [10] In that day the root of Jesse, who shall stand as a signal for the peoples—of him shall the nations inquire, and his resting place shall be glorious. [11] In that day the Lord will extend his hand yet a second time to recover the remnant that remains of his people, from Assyria, from Egypt, from Pathros, from Cush, [1] from Elam, from Shinar, from Hamath, and from the coastlands of the sea. [12] He will raise a signal for the nations and will assemble the banished of Israel, and gather the dispersed of Judah from the four corners of the earth. [13] The jealousy of Ephraim shall depart, and those who harass Judah shall be cut off; Ephraim shall not be jealous of Judah, and Judah shall not harass Ephraim. [14] But they shall swoop down on the shoulder of the Philistines in the west, and together they shall plunder the people of the east. They shall put out their hand against Edom and Moab, and the Ammonites shall obey them. [15] And the LORD will utterly destroy the tongue of the Sea

Kingdom Texts in the Old Testament (continued)

of Egypt, and will wave his hand over the River with his scorching breath, and strike it into seven channels, and he will lead people across in sandals. [16] And there will be a highway from Assyria for the remnant that remains of his people, as there was for Israel when they came up from the land of Egypt.

[XII.] You will say in that day: "I will give thanks to you, O LORD, for though you were angry with me, your anger turned away, that you might comfort me. [2] "Behold, God is my salvation; I will trust, and will not be afraid; for the LORD GOD [2] is my strength and my song, and he has become my salvation." [3] With joy you will draw water from the wells of salvation. [4] And you will say in that day: "Give thanks to the LORD, call upon his name, make known his deeds among the peoples, proclaim that his name is exalted. [5] "Sing praises to the LORD, for he has done gloriously; let this be made known in all the earth. [6] Shout, and sing for joy, O inhabitant of Zion, for great in your midst is the Holy One of Israel."

Isa. 19.2 (ESV) - And I will stir up Egyptians against Egyptians, and they will fight, each against another and each against his neighbor, city against city, kingdom against kingdom.

Isa. 51.4-5 (ESV) - Give attention to me, my people, and give ear to me, my nation; for a law will go out from me, and I will set my justice for a light to the peoples. [5] My righteousness draws near, my salvation has gone out, and my arms will judge the peoples; the coastlands hope for me, and for my arm they wait.

Isa. 60.9-13 (ESV) - For the coastlands shall hope for me, the ships of Tarshish first, to bring your children from afar, their silver and gold with them, for the name of the LORD your God, and for the Holy One of Israel, because he has made you beautiful. [10] Foreigners shall build up your walls, and their kings shall minister to you; for in my wrath I struck you, but in my favor I have had mercy on you. [11] Your gates shall be open continually; day and night they shall not be shut, that people may bring to you the wealth of the nations, with their kings led in procession. [12] For the nation and kingdom that will not serve you shall perish; those nations shall be utterly laid waste. [13] The glory of Lebanon shall come to you, the cypress, the plane, and the pine, to beautify the place of my sanctuary, and I will make the place of my feet glorious.

Isa. 61.1-4 (ESV) - The Spirit of the Lord GOD is upon me, because the LORD has anointed me to bring good news to the poor; he has sent me to bind up the brokenhearted, to proclaim liberty to the captives, and the opening of the prison to those who are bound; [2] to proclaim the year of the LORD's favor, and the day of vengeance of our God; to comfort all who mourn; [3] to grant to those who mourn in Zion—to give them a beautiful headdress instead of ashes, the oil of gladness instead of mourning, the garment of praise instead of a faint spirit; that they may be called oaks of righteousness, the planting of the LORD, that he may be glorified. [4] They shall build up the ancient ruins; they shall raise up the former devastations; they shall repair the ruined cities, the devastations of many generations.

Jer. 23.5-6 (ESV) - Behold, the days are coming, declares the LORD, when I will raise up for David a righteous Branch, and he shall reign as king and deal wisely, and shall execute justice and righteousness in the land. [6] In his days Judah will be saved, and Israel will dwell securely. And this is the name by which he will be called: "The LORD is our righteousness."

Lam. 2.2 (ESV) - The Lord has swallowed up without mercy all the habitations of Jacob; in his wrath he has broken down the strongholds of the daughter of Judah; he has brought down to the ground in dishonor the kingdom and its rulers.

Dan. 2.37 (ESV) - You, O king, the king of kings, to whom the God of heaven has given the kingdom, the power, and the might, and the glory.

Dan. 2.44 (ESV) - And in the days of those kings the God of heaven will set up a kingdom that shall never be destroyed, nor shall the kingdom be left to another people. It shall break in pieces all these kingdoms and bring them to an end, and it shall stand forever.

Dan. 4.34-36 (ESV) - At the end of the days I, Nebuchadnezzar, lifted my eyes to heaven, and my reason returned to me, and I blessed the Most High, and praised and honored him who lives forever, for his dominion is an everlasting dominion, and his kingdom endures from generation to generation; [35] all the inhabitants of the earth are accounted as nothing, and he does according to his will among the host of heaven and among the inhabitants of the earth; and none can stay his hand or say to him, "What have you done?" [36] At the same

Kingdom Texts in the Old Testament (continued)

time my reason returned to me, and for the glory of my kingdom, my majesty and splendor returned to me. My counselors and my lords sought me, and I was established in my kingdom, and still more greatness was added to me.

Dan. 5.26-28 (ESV) - This is the interpretation of the matter: MENE, God has numbered the days of your kingdom and brought it to an end; [27] TEKEL, you have been weighed in the balances and found wanting; [28] PERES, your kingdom is divided and given to the Medes and Persians.

Dan. 6.25-27 (ESV) - Then King Darius wrote to all the peoples, nations, and languages that dwell in all the earth: "Peace be multiplied to you. [26] I make a decree, that in all my royal dominion people are to tremble and fear before the God of Daniel, for he is the living God, enduring forever; his kingdom shall never be destroyed, and his dominion shall be to the end. [27] He delivers and rescues; he works signs and wonders in heaven and on earth, he who has saved Daniel from the power of the lions."

Dan. 7.13-14 (ESV) - I saw in the night visions, and behold, with the clouds of heaven there came one like a son of man, and he came to the Ancient of Days and was presented before him. [14] And to him was given dominion and glory and a kingdom, that all peoples, nations, and languages should serve him; his dominion is an everlasting dominion, which shall not pass away, and his kingdom one that shall not be destroyed.

Dan. 7.18 (ESV) - But the saints of the Most High shall receive the kingdom and possess the kingdom forever, forever and ever.

Dan. 7.22 (ESV) - . . . until the Ancient of Days came, and judgment was given for the saints of the Most High, and the time came when the saints possessed the kingdom.

Dan. 7.27 (ESV) - And the kingdom and the dominion and the greatness of the kingdoms under the whole heaven shall be given to the people of the saints of the Most High; their kingdom shall be an everlasting kingdom, and all dominions shall serve and obey them.

Mic. 4.1-3 (ESV) - It shall come to pass in the latter days that the mountain of the house of the LORD shall be established as the highest of the mountains, and it shall be lifted up above the hills; and peoples shall flow to it, [2] and many nations shall come, and say: "Come, let us go up to the mountain of the LORD, to the house of the God of Jacob, that he may teach us his ways and that we may walk in his paths." For out of Zion shall go forth the law, and the word of the LORD from Jerusalem. [3] He shall judge between many peoples, and shall decide for strong nations afar off; and they shall beat their swords into plowshares, and their spears into pruning hooks; nation shall not lift up sword against nation, neither shall they learn war anymore.

Mic. 5.4-5 (ESV) - And he shall stand and shepherd his flock in the strength of the LORD, in the majesty of the name of the LORD his God. And they shall dwell secure, for now he shall be great to the ends of the earth. [5] And he shall be their peace. When the Assyrian comes into our land and treads in our palaces, then we will raise against him seven shepherds and eight princes of men.

Hos. 1.4 (ESV) - And the LORD said to him, "Call his name Jezreel, for in just a little while I will punish the house of Jehu for the blood of Jezreel, and I will put an end to the kingdom of the house of Israel.

Amos 9.8 (ESV) - "Behold, the eyes of the Lord God are upon the sinful kingdom, and I will destroy it from the surface of the ground, except that I will not utterly destroy the house of Jacob," declares the LORD.

Obad. 1.21 (ESV) - Saviors shall go up to Mount Zion to rule Mount Esau, and the kingdom shall be the LORD's.

Joel 2.26-32 (ESV) - You shall eat in plenty and be satisfied, and praise the name of the LORD your God, who has dealt wondrously with you. And my people shall never again be put to shame. [27] You shall know that I am in the midst of Israel, and that I am the LORD your God and there is none else. And my people shall never again be put to shame. [28] And it shall come to pass afterward, that I will pour out my Spirit on all flesh; your sons and your daughters shall prophesy, your old men shall dream dreams, and your young men shall see visions. [29] Even on the male and female servants in those days I will pour out my Spirit. [30] And I will show wonders in the heavens and on the earth, blood and fire and columns of smoke. [31] The sun shall be turned to darkness, and the moon to blood, before the great and awesome day of the LORD comes. [32] And it shall come to pass that everyone who calls on the name of the LORD shall be saved. For in Mount Zion and in Jerusalem there shall be those who escape, as the LORD has said, and among the survivors shall be those whom the LORD calls.

Kingdom Texts in the Old Testament (continued)

Zech. 8.22 (ESV) - Many peoples and strong nations shall come to seek the LORD of hosts in Jerusalem and to entreat the favor of the LORD.

Zech. 14.9 (ESV) - And the LORD will be king over all the earth. On that day the Lord will be one and his name one.

Learning to Be a Theo-smith
Adopting a Hebraic Approach to Truth
Rev. Dr. Don L. Davis

**Understanding and seeking truth, not from a scientific rationalistic base,
but a mythopoetic foundation**

S tories and the Story of God

M ystery, dialectic, the unknowable, and the "really real"

I magery, symbol, and metaphor

T ypes, analogies, connections, and inspired associations

H olism, global thinking, concreteness, sacred place, and enactment

S alvific passion for the Kingdom of God

Let God Arise!

A Sober Call to Prevailing Prayer for a Dynamic Spiritual Awakening and the Aggressive Advancement of the Kingdom in America's Inner Cities
Rev. Dr. Don L. Davis, January 1, 2003

> *Written in honor of all those who for these long years have in faith and sacrifice refused to let go of the Lord until he blessed them on behalf of the poor in the city*

What a long title for a short essay! This is my tribute to the wonderful piece penned by the churchman and intellectual Jonathan Edwards, leader in the Awakenings in the northeast in the 18th century regarding the need for intercession to spawn new movements for God. His original title was long as well: "A Humble Attempt to Promote Explicit Agreement and Visible Union of God's People, in Extraordinary Prayer, for the Revival of Religion and the Advancement of Christ's Kingdom on Earth." Edwards wrote his little tract in 1746 after experiencing two remarkable movements of the Spirit of God, in 1734-35 and 1740-42 respectively.

Edwards's tract displayed his deep conviction that when God's people pray fervently, intensely, and powerfully for revival, he would release the power of his Spirit in society. This remarkable visitation would then result in many people repenting and believing in Christ as Lord, and would trigger a worldwide "revival of religion" and an "advancement of the Kingdom on earth." All committed Christians, according to Edwards, have a positive duty to pray for this. Having argued his points primarily from careful reasoning and his exegesis of Zechariah 8.18-23 (among other texts), Edwards sought to support his "humble plea" for a more dedicated and organized movement of prayer pleading to him for his visitation. He was neither the first nor the only Christian leader of the time that was calling for "extraordinary prayer." As a matter of fact, a "Memorial" was written by certain Scottish ministers who circulated their ideas at the time of his tract-writing. This memorial had been circulated throughout many English-speaking churches, but especially in England. It called for a new emphasis of "extraordinary prayer" at certain times, a schedule which Edwards himself endorsed, specifically on "Saturday evenings, Sunday mornings and the first Tuesday of each quarter, for an initial period of seven years."

While history does not record another widespread period of renewal in the English-speaking world until the 1770's (followed by another in the 1790's), Edwards's little tract has been consulted and studied by many a disciple and congregation longing to see a fresh and powerful visitation from God on the Church and in the world.

As I write this morning, I realize that we are presently a long way and time from the 18th century English and Scottish societies wherein Edwards wrote his essay on "revival of religion." As I pen my musings on this subject from my home here in urban America, I am aware that with the turn of a new millennium and the beginning of a new year, we have inherited a world decidedly more dangerous, complex, and frightening than that of Edwards and his contemporaries in Scotland and England. More than six billion people inhabit a planet reeling from pollution and overpopulation. We stand on the brink of war, with reports of terrorist threats and ethnic conflicts shrieking through our airwaves. Millions live with malnourishment and squalor, and vast numbers live in despair and hopelessness in a world that is fundamentally unjust and ungodly. If there ever were a time to renew a humble and sober call for "extraordinary prayer" on behalf of a people, a time, and an hour, it is now.

Of all the hardest and most difficult to reach fields on earth today, America's inner cities are arguably one of the toughest. The levels of poverty, violence, despair, and hopelessness make ordinary efforts fall short and seem completely futile. I am convinced that only if God visits, if the Lord arises and scatters his enemies, as spoken in Psalms 68, will freedom, wholeness, and justice prevail, both within God's people of the city and through them to those who are in desperate need for God's grace and provision.

This tract, like that of Edwards, represents another humble attempt to mobilize believers to cry out day and night to God on behalf of a slumbering Church and those suffering and dying without Christ. The heart cry here, however, is focused on the inner cities of America. This represents an earnest plea to call out a nucleus, an army of godly and available intercessors who will pledge themselves to lay hold of God in prevailing prayer for a breakthrough of God's divine power, for spiritual awakening for his people and advancement of his Kingdom in the city.

Let God Arise! (continued)

A Sober Call to Prevailing Prayer

When Edwards wrote his call to the churches of England and Scotland to pray for revival, he focused on Zechariah 8.18-23 which reads:

> Zech. 8.18-23 (ESV) - And the word of the Lord of hosts came to me, saying, [19] "Thus says the Lord of hosts: The fast of the fourth month and the fast of the fifth and the fast of the seventh and the fast of the tenth shall be to the house of Judah seasons of joy and gladness and cheerful feasts. Therefore love truth and peace. [20] Thus says the Lord of hosts: Peoples shall yet come, even the inhabitants of many cities. [21] The inhabitants of one city shall go to another, saying, 'Let us go at once to entreat the favor of the Lord and to seek the Lord of hosts; I myself am going.' [22] Many peoples and strong nations shall come to seek the Lord of hosts in Jerusalem and to entreat the favor of the Lord. [23] Thus says the Lord of hosts: In those days ten men from the nations of every tongue shall take hold of the robe of a Jew, saying, 'Let us go with you, for we have heard that God is with you.'"

Edwards related this text to prophecies of the very end of time where God would bring dramatic and glorious renewal to the entire earth through the focused intercession of God's people. I do not believe that Edwards was incorrect. Furthermore, I am convinced that God's promise to move in regard to extraordinary prayer by his holy people is a given throughout Scripture, sustained with many examples, both in biblical history and in contemporary life. God Almighty answers prayer.

We make therefore a sober call to all believers who love the Lord Jesus and the cities of America to join us in forming new movements of prayer for the city, for all those who live in them, especially God's people. We are making a call to prevailing prayer in the name of Jesus Christ for God's glory. We are asking that God might send to us his very own Holy Spirit, to break through the darkness, evil, and despair of the city and bring refreshment and revolutionary change among the poorest of America's urban poor.

This is not a call to repeat the "good old days" of the past (i.e., a nostalgic return to the glory days of the great awakening revival meetings, or any other revivals of history). Nor is this a call for the sleepy-headed to simply spend a few more hours in prayer over the unimportant. Nor do we make any pleas here for simply a little more effort in prayer, a kind of seasonal emphasis in prayer for the cities that could be done leisurely and conveniently "every other quarter" or so. Rather, what we advocate here is an entirely new vision of ourselves and the city as powerless without the Lord's intervention. We are asking here for a radical reorientation of our lives toward prayer to God based on a rediscovery and reaffirmation that only God can change the inner cities of America.

Frankly speaking, my deepest conviction continues to be that America's inner cities are simply unwinnable without a new and fresh visitation from God. Nearly sixty million people live in our poorest urban communities, with more than 90% of these residents claiming no knowledge of or relationship to God in Jesus Christ. These tortured communities have been deeply scarred and marred by violence, are severely neglected and exploited economically, and suffer from horrific and severe health-related problems. Our American inner cities are hazardous on a number of different points, and yet they continue to swell from immigrant populations and mind-numbing ethnic and racial diversity. Perhaps the greatest liability of all, America's inner cities suffer from discouragement and nihilistic despair; everyone seems to live in fear and dread, with a keen sense of hopelessness.

Tragically, you can even find Scripture-quoting Christians prophesying alongside the chorus of liberal and conservative nay-sayers who lament the tragedy and demise of the city. Some missiologists suggest that America is already won, and that ethnic and urban churches can finish the job in America's inner cities. Others even doubt whether the city is worth winning, giving a kind of grotesque judgment that those who suffer there are merely reaping what they deliberately have sown. In the face of such physical poverty, broken families, sub-par schools, inferior social services, and general spiritual darkness, most expect little from the city. Their words and demeanor give their deepest beliefs away: they truly wonder if anything good can *really* come out of our inner cities, arguably our 21st century Nazareths.

Despite such low levels of belief, I am convinced that the biblical record is correct when it asserts that nothing is impossible with God (Luke 1.37). Nothing is too hard for God (Jer. 32.26), and he through his power can touch and transform the inhabitants of the city! We stand ever ready and hopeful that God will visit his people in the city, and that through outpourings of his Spirit we can see explosive movements of spiritual awakening and cross-cultural disciple making among the urban poor. These movements will not occur due to human ingenuity and effort, but through times of refreshing that come from the Lord (Acts 3.19). We are convinced that only a breakthrough of God's divine power in remarkable ways and levels will suffice for the winning of America's inner cities. Only God visiting his people through the presence and power of his Holy Spirit will guarantee a new and fruitful kind of effective urban outreach that can result in the changing of thousands of lives through Christ's power.

As believers and fellow soldiers in kingdom witness, we call for believers everywhere touched by the need of America's inner cities to join us in the *Let God Arise!* movement. We call all who love those who dwell in the city to a new way of living–under the supreme lordship of Jesus Christ. We call all who love the Church in the city to a new way of seeking God–with fervency and passion, who will cry out both day and night to the Lord. Filled with a spirit of longing and humility, we must earnestly seek the Lord's face in intercession, and do so strategically, in an organized and effective manner.

Hear me well, fellow warrior in Christ! The *Let God Arise!* movement, in the same spirit as brother Edwards did in England, is another humble attempt to implore every disciple concerned about the poor in urban America to join us in constant prayer for God to arise and scatter his enemies. We are seeking to facilitate and challenge individuals, small groups, entire congregations in different locales to meet regularly in their homes, in churches, in businesses, in schools–wherever the Lord leads them to pray–to petition God's visitation upon the city.

A Blueprint for Seeking God and Entreating His Favor

Our highest priority in intercession, as the Zechariah text suggests, is that our primary aim would be to "seek the Lord" above all other requests. We must not substitute his blessings or benefits for seeking him first. *Let God Arise!* is primarily a call for disciples of Jesus to recommit to a new level of spirituality, openness, and brokenness before God that will lead to God's special visitation of his people in the city. This sober call to prevailing prayer is anchored in a sense of our impotency without the Lord. This call is not meant as some kind of work where we could claim to earn God's favor, nor are we attempting to bribe God with a manageable and abbreviated season of humbleness before him. On the contrary, our desire is to be transformed by God entirely. We desire that God visit the city, but only if he visits us as well! We desire the transformation of the city, but we desire even more that this awakening begin with the transformation of our very lives under the lordship of Jesus Christ! We are hungry for more of him–more love, more power, more of the Lord. We desire first and foremost to prevail in prayer soberly, openly, humbly, seeking the Lord himself, coming to know him intimately and glorifying him in our very lives–by who we are. Above all else, *Let God Arise!* desires that urban believers seek the person of the Lord first, to know him, to see him, and to experience in new ways his power and blessing in our lives as his disciples.

This means that as a movement, *Let God Arise!* understands the legitimacy of the priorities spelled out throughout Scripture, and especially in the Zechariah chapter 8 text. Verse 22 makes this plain: "Many peoples and strong nations shall come to seek the Lord of hosts in Jerusalem and to entreat the favor of the Lord." We come boldly to the throne of God's grace, not at the earthly Jerusalem, but to the Mount Zion above, where our gracious God dwells. Hebrews chapter 12.22-24 (ESV) underscores this: "But you have come to Mount Zion and to the city of the living God, the heavenly Jerusalem, and to innumerable angels in festal gathering, [23] and to the assembly of the firstborn who are enrolled in heaven, and to God, the judge of all, and to the spirits of the righteous made perfect, [24] and to Jesus, the mediator of a new covenant, and to the sprinkled blood that speaks a better word than the blood of Abel."

Indeed, our first priority, above all else, is to seek the face of the Lord with all our hearts, to know him, and to make him alone our aim and goal in prayer.

Adoration, Admission, and Availability

The following descriptions of the various elements of a *Let God Arise!* prayer session represent a quick summary of the kind of praying and approach to God we seek to have. We are not seeking to be formulaic or wooden in our suggestions, but offer the following merely as a kind of skeleton, a blueprint or road map to guide us along together as we seek God's face and manifestation. Hopefully these elements can give us practical direction as we gather in our homes and churches for prevailing prayer to the Lord.

To begin with, we start our prayer sessions therefore with worship of the Lord, the *Adoration* phase of our prayer concerts. All of our *Let God Arise!* gatherings encourage those present to begin your concert and session of prevailing prayer with a time of adoration and praise, with singing and exaltation, where we delight and enjoy the Lord with clapping, shouts of joy, and heartfelt praise. We must thank

Let God Arise! (continued)

God for his gracious work for us in Christ, and be grateful for the opportunity to come before his presence through the blood of Christ. Above all else (all needs, petitions, and desires), our God is worthy in himself to be worshiped and adored!

Next, we move to the *Admission* portion of our prayer time. After acknowledging the glory and majesty of the God and Father of our Lord Jesus, we then spend ample time admitting our faults and neediness before his mighty hand. Let us learn to bow before the Lord in humble confession of our sin, and the admission that we are powerless, helpless, and defenseless without his oversight, provision, and grace. Let us not hide our sin but readily confess it. Let us not protest our innocence nor boast in our spiritual accomplishment (Luke 18.9-14), but honestly humble ourselves in the sight of the Lord in order that he might lift us up (1 Pet. 5.6). God does in fact resist those who are proud (i.e., those pretending to be sufficient and adequate in their own wisdom, strength, and power) and gives his grace to the humble (i.e., those willing to admit their powerlessness and desperation before the Lord, James 4.6).

Finally, the "*Availability*" portion of our concert focuses on our joyful dedication of our lives to the Lord for his glory and purposes. During this time we dedicate ourselves afresh to the Lord, affirming our death with Christ and our resurrection in him to new life for God's glory and praise (Rom. 6.1-4). We surrender all we are and everything we own to Jesus Christ in order that he might separate us to his causes and interests, and that he might be pleased as a result of all that we are becoming, doing, and achieving in our lives. Paul makes this point when he says to the Corinthians in 2 Cor. 5.9-10 (ESV) "So whether we are at home or away, we make it our aim to please him. [10] For we must all appear before the judgment seat of Christ, so that each one may receive what is due for what he has done in the body, whether good or evil." Our intent and explicit aim is to please the Lord!

In prayer, therefore, let us place no confidence in our own fleshly wisdom or strength. Further, let us abandon all reliance on worldly wisdom, and fully consecrate ourselves in dedication to be and do whatever the Lord Jesus demands, however taxing, difficult, or costly. In humble prayer, may we in the thousands bow our knees to the Lord in authentic surrender, allowing his Spirit the right and privilege to lead us wherever he determines, by whatever path and for whatever purpose he may so ably direct (John 3.8). Only this kind of radical, unconditional availability to God will allow him to use us when he pours his Holy Spirit out upon the inner cities of America!

For a Dynamic Spiritual Awakening

Regardless of the terms used in scholarly literature on God's visitation in revival or awakenings (e.g., revival, renewal, refreshing, revelation, etc.), the reality spoken of within these materials all refer to the same truth. What is this truth? These materials all point toward the need, above all else, of God's presence as the critical factor in all renewal and witness for the Kingdom. America's inner cities today especially demand a fresh visitation from the Lord. God must arise in the city; he must come down and scatter his enemies, and shed abroad his goodness and provision. The Holy Spirit must be outpoured upon the city if it is to be won for Christ.

Nothing short of God's own presence in the city will suffice. No other solutions hold the promise of lasting or comprehensive change occurring in the lives of the millions who languish in the city. None of the typical answers can touch the lives of so many; no solutions of government, social philanthropy, political or jurisprudential reform, or the hiring more policemen and crime fighters or eliminating various kinds of "immoral elements" in impoverished neighborhoods will overcome the spiritual powers and principalities which plague our inner city communities. Spiritual needs must be met with spiritual resources.

Neither will an anemic, sluggish, and worldly-minded church accomplish this task of setting the captives free. We are called as believers to be strong in the Lord and in the power of his might (Eph. 6.10-12). Jesus is the warrior of God who will consummate God's victory on earth at his Second Coming (cf. Revelation 19.8ff). Only when Christ reveals himself, he who alone is able to bind "the strong man of the devil" and set his captives free (cf. Matt. 12.25-30), can we expect the freedom, wholeness, and justice of the Kingdom to liberate the lost in the city.

Entreat the Favor of the Lord for Global and Local Concerns

Because we wholeheartedly believe that God loves all peoples everywhere, we concentrate our prayer efforts with an emphasis on both *global* and *local* concerns.

"Global" concerns mean that every time we gather we do not merely pray for the needs of America's inner cities alone, but for the needs of the entire globe, in cities, nations, and among people groups where the Church of Jesus Christ is bearing witness, as well as for all those who have not yet heard of the saving Gospel of the Lord.

Let God Arise! (continued)

We believe in the Nicene Creed, that there is only one, holy, catholic (universal), and apostolic Church, and that what concerns Christians anywhere ought to concern Christians everywhere. We also believe in the Great Commission of Jesus, that the Church has been called for these last two millennia to bear witness to the Kingdom of God in Jesus Christ among every people group on earth. We therefore pray for the *Awakening* of the Church of Jesus Christ everywhere, pleading to God to act for congregations of believers wherever they gather, in other nations and continents, all with an intent that God will glorify himself among his people wherever they meet.

"Local" concerns must equally capture our attention and petition. By *local* we mean the particular church which we belong to, the churches in our denomination and immediate neighboring community, and the church in our locale or region. Each region of the church has its own peculiar and unique issues, challenges, and concerns, and our intercession recognizes these specific concerns for our church community. We entreat the favor of the Lord on behalf of our local church assembly, and the assemblies in our city, locale, and region.

We therefore begin our intercession with special entreaties, supplications, and prayers offered on behalf of God's people for a dynamic spiritual *Awakening*. Let us pray for the Church in the world (and in different parts of the world) that believers would be refreshed by repeated and powerful outpourings and manifestations of the Holy Spirit's presence among his people. Let us pray that God will associate these outpourings with signs and wonders which direct attention to his glory and reign, and that the spiritual character of the churches would be renewed to obey the Great Commandment with full energy. Let us pray that the churches globally and locally will love God with all their hearts, and their neighbors as themselves. Let us pray for reconciliation, unity, and restored relationships among believers all over the earth, and ask God to create a new spirit of unity and agreement around the advancement of God's Kingdom in our churches.

In this regard, let us pray for a revolutionary rediscovery of the lordship of Jesus Christ in our churches, with refreshing manifestations of humility, confession, brokenness, and love among members, all for the glory of God. Let us pray these and like-minded prayers on behalf of God's people, as fervently and intelligently as possible, praying specific prayers of petitions to God for the revival and renewal of his people globally, and specifically in the cities of America.

With an open heart full of faith, then, let us pray for the churches in the inner cities of America. Let us pray for their protection from the violence and corruption all around them. Let us pray for boldness and frankness as they give witness to the risen Christ in their works of justice, love, and evangelism. Let us pray for a new sense of joy and power in the Holy Spirit, a greater revelation from the Word of God, a new experience of the cleansing power of the blood of Christ, and an enriched walk with God. Let us pray for a spirit of tranquility and peace, the binding of the enemy, in order that the Gospel can go forth.

Also, let us pray for a new spirit of praise, worship, and rejoicing in the urban churches, and for new creativity, delight, and pleasure in the presence of God. Let us pray for a new level of openness and unity among the believers, and a deeper, richer love and awe of God in the churches. Let us pray for new levels of reverence and fear among God's people, and new aggressive movements of worship, prayer, and celebration in the communities.

Let us not stop here. Let us pray that God will break the stranglehold of the enemy on the minds and hearts of those who dwell in America's inner cities (2 Cor. 4.4). Let us pray that the Holy Spirit will thwart the devil's programs of deception and despair, and that new doors will be opened for the display and proclamation of the Word of God at all levels. Pray that the Church will boldly give witness in word and deed to the reign of God in Jesus Christ, that individual believers, young, middle-aged, and senior, will demonstrate in their lives new levels of the Lord's love and power among their families, friends, and relationship networks.

Pray for new levels of interest, curiosity, and awareness of spiritual things among all who live in the city, but especially new levels of reality and power among believers in the inner city. Pray that the devil will not be able to stop the openings of God to Christ in all levels of the communities, societies, and neighborhoods. Pray for an outpouring of God upon the city, that entire cities of America can be awakened to their need for God in Jesus Christ!

For the Advancement of the Kingdom

As we humble ourselves in prayer for a dynamic spiritual *Awakening* among the people of God, we must equally petition God to move on behalf of the lost, those people and regions which have not yet come to know the mercy of God in the person of the Lord Jesus Christ. Every time we gather in concerts of prayer, we ought to cry out to God to move in the inner cities, in order that there might be a sustained and aggressive *Advancement of the Kingdom* within them. One of the central features of the entire **Let God Arise!** movement is to see God move in this twofold sense: awakening the urban communities to his glory and power in a renewed and revitalized Church, and seeing his reign advance among those who live in the city and yet who have neither heard nor responded to God's love in Christ.

Let us therefore pray during our *Advancement* portion of the concert for the breakthrough of spiritual power over the enemy, both globally around the world, in specific contexts which we know about, and locally, in the specific areas in our locale and region. Let us pray that the Holy Spirit will pour his power upon God's servants, teams, organizations, and churches which are winning souls, making disciples, and planting churches around the world. In places that do not allow for Christian witness, let us pray that God will move on the hearts of government and religious officials, permitting believers to enter their societies and communities to speak freely of the Gospel of the Kingdom.

Pray too that the Holy Spirit will give extraordinary revelations of God and Christ to the lost, that he would give them dreams and visions, as he did in the case of the Macedonians (cf. Acts 16.9ff.). These manifestations could lay a spiritual foundation for the presentation of the Word of God concerning Christ in difficult and recalcitrant fields. Pray that revitalized churches, denominations, and mission agencies will form new strategic alliances which will lead to vital evangelistic thrusts and movements among the hardest, most difficult, and most unreached pioneer fields overseas and here at home.

Furthermore, pray that the awakening of the Church both globally and locally will lead to wholesale effective efforts to mobilize members of the Church for a new advance in mission. Let us pray that God will stir individuals, pastors, Christian workers, and ordinary believers from every congregation to pray for their unsaved family and friends, to be trained to share their faith effectively, and to commit to redouble their giving and contribution to fulfilling the Great Commission. Pray that many singles and couples will volunteer to do mission, not merely on a short term basis, but for some as a total life calling. Pray that some who respond will be sent by the Lord of the harvest to the harvest fields of America's untouched inner city communities.

Moreover, let us pray fervently that inner city churches will combine their efforts, funds, initiatives, and projects to make their own unique and powerful contribution to global and local mission. Pray that God would move on the hearts of those in charge of many mission agencies, that they will no longer ignore the rich resources of the urban churches, but will make it feasible for urban disciples to be deployed to evangelize, disciple, and plant churches, especially among the dozens and dozens of communities where no evangelical presence exists.

Above all, let us cry out to God day and night for a new level of rigor and discipline among his people. Pray for a tough minded but tender hearted faith to embrace the small congregations and store fronts in the city. Let us pray for them, that God will provide them with a kingdom warfare consciousness, the rigorous kind of mentality that will allow urban disciples to adopt the necessary mindset to endure hardness and suffer in spiritual warfare for their communities. Let us pray for new levels of boldness and power, for new aggressive outreaches, for more dedicated and prevailing prayer movements among urban churches, and new networks of leadership and support that will link urban disciples of good will to mobilize their resources for maximum impact on the city.

Intercede passionately to God to provide the resources for urban churches to initiate new outreaches of compassion, justice, and peace on behalf of the homeless, oppressed, fatherless, the mentally challenged, those plagued with HIV and other communicable diseases, for the elderly, those sick and in prison and neglected. Pray for an outpouring of love from the Church that amazes and creates new hunger for Jesus in the lost, a kind of love that serves as a foundation to express and authenticate the Gospel of Christ. Pray that God will use the efforts of justice and righteousness as a gateway for hundreds of thousands to be converted to the Lord.

Do not neglect to pray for your own particular locality, and its need to see the signs of the Kingdom manifested within it in word and deed. Pray for your church, your pastor, your community, civic and city leaders, your neighbors, principals, law officers, and all others in leadership in your midst. Pray for the release of new levels of boldness and clarity in preaching, and more authentic signs of the Kingdom in your community so God can reveal to the lost there the majesty and wonder of the Lord Jesus. Pray for yourself and family for a new availability to see the Kingdom advanced at your work, your school, your neighborhood, your family, in your life. God will answer us if we only will ask him in faith and authentic surrender to his will (Matt. 6.6; John 15.16).

Let God Arise! (continued)

In America's Inner Cities

The entire *Let God Arise!* idea began with a deep conviction that the American inner city cannot be won without the direct intervention and provision of the Lord. The hardness of this field makes plain and clear the truth of the psalmist's argument in Psalms 127.1 (ESV), "Unless the Lord builds the house, those who build it labor in vain. Unless the Lord watches over the city, the watchman stays awake in vain." This movement believes that all efforts at winning the unreached millions in America's inner cities will be futile unless God visits the city. We further hold that this visitation will only occur if godly men and women lay hold of God in intercession on the city's behalf. Only a breakthrough of God's power will transform our cities.

While the city is arguably the greatest single creation of humankind in civilization, it has nothing to glory of, in and of itself. The modern megapolis represents the bastion of injustice, ungodliness, and immorality. Truly, it is not possible to think of America without its greatest and most influential cities–New York, Washington D.C., Los Angeles, Philadelphia, Chicago, Houston, Miami, San Francisco, Boston, Portland, Atlanta, Denver, St. Louis, Dallas, Seattle, San Antonio, and on and on and on. These great centers represent the highest in culture, education, art, medicine, law, jurisprudence, government, politics, business, commerce, industry, entertainment, and power. Yet they also represent some of the most desperate places on earth; our cities bulge with teeming millions whose lives are filled with empty pleasures, great injustices, and horrible experiences.

Undoubtedly, the levels of darkness, poverty, and discouragement in America's inner cities are at an all-time high. Tragically, many evangelical congregations and Christian denominations have abandoned the city, escaping to calmer winds in the suburbs, taking along with them their Bible Colleges, seminaries, Christian publishing houses, and para-church organizations. Believers have left the cities in record numbers, and abandoned those who do not know Christ to their own devices and oppression.

Content to reduce Christianity to their own kind of parochial religion, many evangelicals have narrowed the scope of our Cosmic Drama; they have whittled down the majestic call of saving faith in Christ to nuclear family ethics, strong patriotic fervor and political conservatism. With no sense of a stained or disturbed conscience, many Christians have turned their backs to the cries of the dying in the city. For a Church called to be like our Master, this is totally unacceptable!

Affirmation and Acknowledgment

The final two dimensions of a ***Let God Arise!*** prayer concert, *Affirmation* and *Acknowledgment* respectively, allow for the giving of testimonies and final prayers which affirm God's truth about himself and his intention to win the city.

While we affirm the cruel oppression and persistent evil of the city, we likewise affirm the hope of the city's salvation, as in the case with Nineveh of the book of Jonah, Assyria's dark capital of violence, which God pardoned. In his forgiveness of their transgression and his relenting of judgment of that dark city, we see God's deep love for lost and rebellious humankind, and his willingness to relent from judgment of even the most wicked city if its inhabitants merely humble themselves before him. If God would deliver the thousands-filled Nineveh of biblical time, surely we can affirm that the same God can deliver the tens of millions-filled New York, or the dozens of millons-filled Mexico City! The analogy is biblical and persuasive; God Almighty responds to the cries of the broken, the contrite, and the penitent (Ps. 34.18).

During the *Affirmation* session, we affirm to God in prayer and to each other in testimony what the Lord has spoken to us during our time of seeking and entreating the Lord. We affirm the eternal love of a God who sent his only Son for our redemption (John 3.16), and we remind one another of God's historical action to respond when his people, called by his name, humble themselves, pray, seek his face, and repent from their wicked way of self-preoccupation, self-indulgence, and self-reliance (2 Chron. 7.14). God works in response to his people crying out to him in their affliction, brokenness, and neediness before him (Deut. 26.5-10).

We leave our session of *Affirmation* with a finale of prayers where we *Acknowledge* the veracity (truthfulness) and sovereignty of God. We covenant together to wait on the Lord, to look for his coming, to him who alone can strengthen our hearts (Ps. 27.14). Though we may grow weary in our praying, we are assured that we will prevail with God, for we are praying according to his will and to his heart (Isa. 40.28-31). We will not doubt or give up or lose heart (James 1.5; Gal. 6.9). If we start to intercede, we may be tempted to falter but, like the widow who pestered the judge until he responded on her behalf, we remind each other that we must beg God for action until he responds (Luke 18.1-8).

Our hearts are fixed, and we are determined, like the patriarch Jacob, to wrestle with God, to implore him, to lay hold of him and not let him go until he blesses

Let God Arise! (continued)

us (Gen. 32.24-32). Like Jehoshaphat, we have no strength against the rulers of this present darkness and spiritual forces gathered to destroy America's inner cities, nor do we know what to do, but our eyes are on the Lord (2 Chron. 20.12).

We are convinced that one day God will give the cities of this world to his Son (including America's inner cities!), which are merely one significant part of the inheritance the Father has been pleased to give to the Risen Lord (Ps. 2.8). Knowing that our Lord Jesus must reign until all of his enemies are placed under his feet (1 Cor. 15.24-28), we will neither doubt his intentions nor be impatient in the timing of his answers. God will respond to us, in his own time and in his own way. As we leave our gathering to scatter again in our particular circles of influence and relationship, we acknowledge our dependence on him whether our prayer session has been a half-hour, an entire morning, or full days and weeks of fasting and prayer, we know that the promise of the Lord is sure:

> Isa. 55.6-11 (ESV) - "Seek the Lord while he may be found; call upon him while he is near; [7] let the wicked forsake his way, and the unrighteous man his thoughts; let him return to the Lord, that he may have compassion on him, and to our God, for he will abundantly pardon. [8] For my thoughts are not your thoughts, neither are your ways my ways, declares the Lord. [9] For as the heavens are higher than the earth, so are my ways higher than your ways and my thoughts than your thoughts. [10] "For as the rain and the snow come down from heaven and do not return there but water the earth, making it bring forth and sprout, giving seed to the sower and bread to the eater, [11] so shall my word be that goes out from my mouth; it shall not return to me empty, but it shall accomplish that which I purpose, and shall succeed in the thing for which I sent it."

Truly, the Word of the Lord cannot return back to him either fruitless or empty. The purposes of our God, this great God, shall stand (Isa.40.8)!

Conclusion:
Respond in Humility to the
Sober Call to Prevailing Prayer for the Inner City

Dear friend, let me ask you a question: What do you take to be the critical need of the hour for the inner cities of America?

In my mind, it is not merely the infusion of more business and money, nor simply a new influx of better politicians, better urban crime-stopping initiatives, family planning seminars, nor food programs. The *critical* need for the city is for the Lord to make his presence known within it. The decisive factor that will lead to a transformation of America's inner cities is God's visitation, repeated outpourings of the Holy Spirit in the midst of his people in the city. Such visitations of the presence and power of God would revolutionize these communities; God's visitation would create such a variety of healing, compassion, and justice that no one, not even the most politically liberal-minded hopeful or stubborn atheist could explain it. Psalm 68 is a testament to what can occur when the Lord comes down, rather, arises and scatters his enemies, and leaves in his wake the blessings of his great heart love for humankind:

[1] God shall arise, his enemies shall be scattered; and those who hate him shall flee before him!

[2] As smoke is driven away, so you shall drive them away; as wax melts before fire, so the wicked shall perish before God!

[3] But the righteous shall be glad; they shall exult before God; they shall be jubilant with joy!

[4] Sing to God, sing praises to his name; lift up a song to him who rides through the deserts; his name is the LORD; exult before him!

[5] Father of the fatherless and protector of widows is God in his holy habitation.

[6] God settles the solitary in a home; he leads out the prisoners to prosperity, but the rebellious dwell in a parched land.

Let God Arise! (continued)

[7] O God, when you went out before your people, when you marched through the wilderness, Selah

[8] the earth quaked, the heavens poured down rain, before God, the One of Sinai, before God, the God of Israel.

[9] Rain in abundance, O God, you shed abroad; you restored your inheritance as it languished;

[10] your flock found a dwelling in it; in your goodness, O God, you provided for the needy.

~ Psalm 68.1-10 (ESV)

Let God Arise! in the midst of his people!

Let God Arise! in the midst of the urban squalor and decay!

Let God Arise! in the seats of power and influence!

Let God Arise! in the neighborhoods plagued by violence and fear!

Let God Arise! in the sanctuaries and congregations intimidated and under siege!

Let God Arise! with an outpouring of his Holy Spirit that will result in the spiritual awakening and dramatic advance of the Kingdom among the poorest of the poor in America's inner cities.

We issue to you the *call* to prevailing prayer: will you not join us in crying out to God day and night on behalf of the city and its inhabitants, from New York to Los Angeles, and all those who need to hear of God's saving love in Christ?

We issue to you the *sober* call to prevailing prayer: do you catch the sense of how significant your contribution can be if you only devote yourself to unbroken, unwavering, faith-filled entreaty to God on behalf of one of the greatest and most difficult mission fields in the world?

We issue to you the sober call to *prevailing prayer*: will you allow God, the Holy Spirit to train you to become a warrior in the spiritual realm, laying hold of God in intercession on behalf of a Church that is slumbering and needs to be awakened, and a world that is dying and needs to hear of God's life-giving and in-breaking reign won for us through Jesus Christ and his death on the cross?

Only God Can Renew His People. Only God Can Save the City.

Let us meet in holy agreement, whether two or three (Matt. 18.20) or an entire gallery of petitioners (2 Chron. 20) to seek the Lord and entreat the favor of the Lord on behalf of the city. Let us do so in our individual prayer closets, our cell groups and small group studies, in our congregations and church services, in our prayer meetings and convocations, in our concerts of prayer–in vigils, retreats, homes, schools–wherever the Lord lays on our hearts to petition him for a visitation for the cities, and for our city.

Let us commit to laying hold of God until he visits us. If we do, the cities of America (and perhaps, of the entire world) will never be the same.

Let God Arise!

The Seven "A's" of Seeking the Lord and Entreating His Favor

Rev. Dr. Don L. Davis

#		THEME	SCRIPTURE	AWARENESS		CONCERT OF PRAYER
1	Adoration	• Delight and Enjoyment in God • Overwhelming Gratefulness • Acknowledging God in his Person and Works	Ps. 29.1-2 Rev. 4-11 Rom. 11.33-36 Ps. 27.4-8	Of God's Majestic Glory		Gather to Worship and Pray
2	Admission	• Powerlessness • Helplessness • Awareness of One's Desperate Need for God	Ps. 34.18-19 Prov. 28.13 Dan. 4.34-35 Isa. 30.1-5	Of Our Brokenness before God	God's Face	Confess Your Powerlessness
3	Availability	• Dying to preoccupation with self and love of the world • No confidence in fleshly wisdom, resources, or method • Consecrating ourselves as living sacrifices to God	Rom. 12.1-5 John 12.24 Phil. 3.3-8 Gal. 6.14	Of Our Yieldedness to God		Surrender Your All to Christ
4	Awakening *Global and Local*	• Refreshment: outpouring of the Holy Spirit on God's people • Renewal: Obedience to the Great Commandment - Loving God and neighbor • Revolution: Radical new orientation to Christ as Lord	Hos. 6.1-3 Eph. 3.15-21 Matt. 22.37-40 John 14.15	Asking for the Spirit's Filling	Fullness	
5	Advancement *Global and Local*	• Movements: outreaches to unreached, pioneer regions • Mobilization: of every assembly to fulfill the Great Commission • Military mindset: Adopting a warfare mentality to suffer and endure hardness in spiritual warfare	Acts 1.8 Mark 16.15-16 Matt. 28.18-20 Matt. 11.12 Luke 19.41-42 2 Tim. 2.1-4	Asking for the Spirit's Moving	Fulfillment	Fervently Intercede on Behalf of Others
6	Affirmation	• Giving Testimony over what the Lord has done • Challenging one another by speaking the truth in Love	Ps. 107.1-2 Heb. 3.13 2 Cor. 4.13 Mal. 3.16-18	The Redeemed Saying So	The Faith	Encourage One Another in Truth and Testimony
7	Acknowledgment	• Waiting patiently on God to act by his timing and methods • Living confidently as though God is answering our petitions • Acting as if God will do precisely what he says he will do	Ps. 27.14 2 Chron. 20.12 Prov. 3.5-6 Isa. 55.8-11 Ps. 2.8	Keeping Our Eyes on the Lord	The Fight	Scatter to Work and Wait

"Seek the Lord" — Zechariah 8.18-23 • Isaiah 55.6 (rows 1–3)

"Entreat the Favor of the Lord" — Zechariah 8.18-23 • Jeremiah 33.3 (rows 4–7)

The Life of Christ according to Seasons and Years

Adapted from Ray E. Baughman, The Life of Christ Visualized

Key Events - Spring

Key Events - Spring	M	M	L	J
- Birth at Bethlehem, shepherds, angels			2.1-20	1.14
- Adoration of Simeon, Anna, wise men	2.1-12		2.21-38	
- Bethlehem babies killed	2.16-18			
- Into Egypt (Flight of Joseph, Mary, and Jesus)	2.13-15			
- Egyptian exile ended, settled in Nazareth	2.19-23		2.39-40	
- Search for Jesus (12 years old, visit to Jerusalem)			2.41-52	
- Belligerent rejection (1st), at Nazareth			4.23-30	
- Large catch of fish, call of disciples (Galilee)	4.18-22	1.16-20	5.1-11	
- Demoniac healed (Capernaum)		1.21-28	4.31-37	
- Peter's mother-in-law healed (Capernaum)	8.14-17	1.29-34	4.38-41	
- Galilean Tour (2nd) with four disciples	4.23-25	1.35-39	4.42-44	
- Leper healed (sent to Jerusalem)	8.2-4	1.40-45	5.12-16	
- Roof opened for sick man (Capernaum)	9.1-8	2.1-12	5.17-26	
- Call of Matthew, his party (Capernaum)	9.9-17	2.13-22	5.27-39	

Key Events - Summer

Key Events - Summer	M	M	L	J
- Cana, changing water into wine (first miracle)				2.1-11
- Capernaum (first sojourn at future home)				2.12
- First Passover during ministry (Jerusalem)				2.13
- First cleansing of the Temple (Jerusalem)				2.14-25
- Nicodemus' interview (Jerusalem)				3.1-21
- Judean ministry of John and Jesus				3.22-36
- Jesus leaves Judea as John is imprisoned (Machaerus)	4.12-17	1.14	3.19-20	4.1-4
- Impotent man at the pool (Jerusalem)				5.1-47
- Disciples pluck grain (Galilee)	12.1-8	2.23-28	6.1-5	
- Man with withered hand (Capernaum)	12.9-21	3.1-12	6.6-11	
- Jesus chooses twelve apostles (Galilee)		3.13-19	6.12-16	
- Sermon on the Mount (horns of Hattin)	5.1-8.1		6.17-49	
- Centurion's servant healed (Capernaum)	8.5-13		7.1-10	
- Widow's son raised (Nain)			7.11-17	
- John's disciples inquire of Jesus (Galilee)	11.2-30		7.18-35	
- First anointing of Jesus' feet (Capernaum)			7.36-50	
- Galilean tour (3rd) with disciples			8.1-3	
- Demon possessed, blind-dumb man healed (Capernaum?)	12.22-23			
- Beelzebub charged against Jesus	12.24-45	3.22-30		
- Friends and family believe he is insane	12.46-50	3.20-21, 31-35	8.19-21	

Key Events - Fall

Key Events - Fall	M	M	L	J
- Baptism of Jesus (Jordan River)	3.1-17	1.9-11	3.1-18, 21-37	
- Temptation (Wilderness of Judea)	4.1-11	1.12-13	4.1-13	
- Testimony of John the Baptist (Jordan)				1.15-34
- Jesus' first five disciples (Jordan)				1.35-51
- Woman at the well (Sychar)				4.5-42
- Noble man's son made well (Jesus at Cana and son at Capernaum)				4.43-54
- Jesus preaches in synagogues of Galilee, is well received (first Galilean tour)		1.14-15	4.14-22	
- Kingdom of heaven parables by the sea (Capernaum)	13.1-53	4.1-34	8.4-18	
- Stilling the sea and the wind	8.18-27	4.35-41	8.22-25	
- Demoniac in graveyard, swine into the sea (Gadarenes)	8.28-34	5.1-20	8.26-39	
- Crossing back over the sea to Capernaum and four miracles: Jairus' daughter raised, woman touches Messiah's garment	9.18-26	5.21-43	8.40-56	
- Two blind men and dumb demoniac healed	9.27-34			

(Watermark year markers appear across the table: B.C. – A.D. 26, 27, 28.)

The Life of Christ according to Seasons and Years (continued)

Key Events - Spring

Key Events - Spring	M	M	L	J
Second rejection at Nazareth	13.54-58	6.1-6		
Twelve sent forth (4th Galilean Tour)	9.35-11.1	6.6-13	9.1-6	
John the Baptist's death (Machearus)	14.1-12	6.14-29	9.7-9	
Teaching in Perea, warned about Herod			13.22-35	10.40-42
Healing of man on Sabbath			14.1-6	
Parables on humility, rewards, excuses, discipleship			14.7-35	
Lost sheep, coin, son			15.1-32	
Rich man and Lazarus			16.1-10 / 17.10	
Raising of Lazarus (Bethany)				11.1-44
Conspiring to kill Jesus				11.45-57
Ten lepers healed (Samaria)			17.11-37	
Answered prayer, divorce, little children, rich young ruler	19.1-20.16	10.1-31	18.1-30	
Foretold death and resurrection	20.17-28	10.32-45	18.31-34	
Blind men of Jericho	20.29-34	10.46-52	18.35-43	
Zacchaeus's transformation			19.1-27	
Last stop, 2nd anointing	26.6-13	14.3-9		12.1-11

Key Events - Summer

Key Events - Summer	M	M	L	J
Feeding of the 5,000 (Sea of Galilee)	14.13-21	6.30-44	9.10-17	6.1-15
Walking on water, Bread of Life discourse	14.22-36	6.45-56		6.16-71
Eating with unwashed hands (Capernaum)	15.1-20	7.1-23		
Daughter of Syrophoenician healed (Phonecia)	15.21-28	7.24-30		
Deaf and dumb man healed	15.29-31	7.31-37		
Feeding of the 4,000 (Decapolis)	15.32-38	8.1-9		
Pharisees and Sadducees seek a sign	15.39 - 16.4	8.10-12		
Warning against false teaching	16.5-12	8.13-21		
Blind man healed at Bethsaida		8.22-26		
Peter's good confession (Caesarea Philippi)	16.13-20	8.27-30	9.18-21	
Foretelling death, resurrection, second coming	16.21-28	8.31 - 9.1	9.22-27	
Transfiguration (Mount Hermon)	17.1-13	9.2-13	9.28-36	
Demon possessed boy healed	17.14-21	9.14-29	9.37-42	
Foretells death and resurrection (to Galilee)	17.22-23	9.30-32	9.43-44	
Coin in fish's mouth (Capernaum)	17.24-27			
Instructions to disciples	18.1-35	9.33-50	9.46-62	
Sunday - Triumphal Entry	21.1-11	11.1-11	19.28-44	12.12-19
Monday - Second cleansing of the Temple	21.12-22	11.12-26	19.45-48	12.20-50
Tuesday - Jesus challenged, Olivet Discourse	21.23-26.5; 26.14-16	11.27 - 14.2, 10-11	20.1-22.6	
Wednesday				
Thursday - Passover supper, Upper Room Discourse, Gethsemane, Arrest	26.17-56	14.12-52	22.7-53	13.1 - 18.11
Friday - Trial, crucifixion, burial	26.57-27.66	14.53-15.47	22.54-23.56	18.12-19.42
Saturday - in the tomb				

Key Events - Fall

Key Events - Fall	M	M	L	J
Tabernacle Feast (Jerusalem)				7.1-8.1
Adulterous woman				8.2-11
Light of the world				8.12-59
Man born blind healed				9.1-41
Good shepherd discourse				10.1-21
Seventy sent out (Judea)			10.1-24	
Good Samaritan			10.25-37	
Supper at Mary and Martha's (Bethany)			10.38-42	
Disciples taught to pray			11.1-13	
Accused of tie with Beelzebub, demoniac healed			11.14-36	
Eating with Pharisee			11.37-54	
Hypocrisy denounced (Judea)			12.1-21	
Parables on service			12.22 -13.9	
Healing of a crippled woman			13.10-21	
Feast of Dedication (Jerusalem)				10.22-39
Earthquake as angel rolls away the stone	28.1-4			
Women visit tomb	28.5-8	16.1-8	24.1-10	20.1-2
Peter and John visit tomb			24.11-12	20.3-10
Jesus appears to Mary Magdalene (Jerusalem)		16.9-11		20.11-18
Jesus appears to other women	28.9-10			
Guards report to rulers	28.11-15			
Jesus appears to disciples on road to Emmaus (& Simon)		16.12-13	24.13-35	
Jesus appears to 10 disciples			24.36-43	20.19-25
Jesus appears to all, w/Thomas		16.14		20.26-31
Jesus appears to 7 disciples by the sea of Galilee (second miracle of the fish)				21.1-25
Jesus appears to 500 disciples (cf. 1 Cor. 15.5-7)	28.16-20	16.15-18	24.44-53	
The Ascension (Acts 1.9-12)		16.19-20		

Living in the Already and the Not Yet Kingdom

Rev. Dr. Don L. Davis

The Spirit: The pledge of the inheritance **(arrabon)**
The Church: The foretaste **(aparche)** of the Kingdom
"In Christ": The rich life **(en Christos)** we share as citizens of the Kingdom

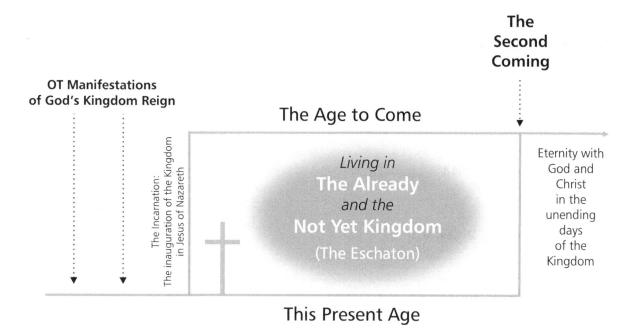

Internal enemy: The flesh (*sarx*) and the sin nature
External enemy: The world (*kosmos*) the systems of greed, lust, and pride
Infernal enemy: The devil (*kakos*) the animating spirit of falsehood and fear

Jewish View of Time

This Present Age   The Age to Come

The Coming of Messiah
The restoration of Israel
The end of Gentile oppression
The return of the earth to Edenic glory
Universal knowledge of the Lord

Living the Disciplines

Rev. Dr. Don L. Davis

1. **Understand Why, Matt. 22.29**

2. **Study How, Ezra 7.10**

3. **Commit it to God, Ps. 5.1-3**

4. **Get Proper Guidance, Acts 8.30-31**

5. **Start Small, Luke 18.9-14**

6. **Begin Immediately, 2 Cor. 6.1**

7. **Set Realistic Goals, Ps. 119.64**

8. **Recruit Partners, Ps. 34.1-4**

9. **Be Consistent, Dan. 6.5-10**

10. **Take Steps to Improve, 2 Pet. 3.18**

11. **Help Others Grow, Heb. 5.11-14**

12. **Keep it All in Focus, Phil. 1.20-21**

Lording Over vs. Serving Among
Differing Styles and Models of Leadership
*Adapted from George Mallone, **Furnace of Renewal**.*

Secular Authority	Servant Authority
Functions on the basis of power	Functions on basis of love and obedience
Primarily rules by giving orders	Serves as one who is under orders of another
Unwilling to fail: blame-shifts for leverage	Unafraid to receive responsibility for failure
Sees itself as absolutely necessary	Willing to be used and expended for the body
Drives others (cow-punching mentality)	Leads others (shepherding mentality)
Subjects others to threat of loss and pain	Builds others by encouragement and challenge
Consolidates power for maximum impact	Stewards authority for greatest good
Has gold, makes rules	Follows the Golden Rule
Uses position for personal advancement	Exercises authority to please the Master
Expects benefits from service	Expects to expend oneself in service to others
Strength, not character, is decisive	Character, not strength, carries most weight

The Lord's Supper: Four Views

Rev. Terry G. Cornett

	Transubstantiation	Consubstantiation	Reformed	Memorialist
Groups	Roman Catholic	Lutheran	Presbyterian and other Reformed Churches, Episcopalians	Baptists, Mennonites, Pentecostals
Key Person	Thomas Aquinas	Martin Luther	John Calvin	Ulrich Zwingli
Presence of Christ	After being consecrated by the priest, the bread changes into Christ's body and the wine changes into Christ's blood so that Christ is present in the elements themselves	The elements do not change but Christ is actually present in, with, and under the elements of bread and wine	Christ is not literally present in the elements since Christ's body is in heaven.

Christ is spiritually present and at work in the partaking of the elements through the Holy Spirit when received in faith. | Christ is not present in the elements either literally or spiritually. |
| What Takes Place | Spiritual food is given to the soul which strengthens the participant spiritually and cleanses them from venial sins.

Christ's sacrifice on the cross is made present anew at each mass. | Sins are forgiven and the new covenant promises are reconfirmed. Unless the elements are received in faith, the sacrament has no benefit. | As the elements are received in faith, the partaker receives spiritual nourishment which strengthens the soul, is brought close to the presence of Christ and has a renewed experience of God's grace. | Christ's command is obeyed and Christ's death is commemorated so that the partaker is reminded of the benefits of salvation accomplished by his sacrificial death. Love for God is renewed through the remembering of his love for us. |
Key Verses	John 6.53-58 Matt. 26.26 1 Cor. 10.16	Matt. 26.26 1 Cor. 10.16	John 6.63; 16.7 Col. 3.1	Luke 22.19 1 Cor. 11.24-25
Term Used	Sacrament	Sacrament	Sacrament	Ordinance
Who Presides	Priest	Ordained Minister	Church Leaders (Clergy or Laity)	Church Leaders (Clergy or Laity)

Messiah Jesus: Fulfillment of the Old Testament Types

Adapted from Norman Geisler, To Understand the Bible, Look for Jesus, pp. 38-41.

Messiah Jesus Fulfills the Tabernacle Types

Tabernacle Types	Jesus of Nazareth as the Antitype
The One Door	I am the Door John 10.9
The Brazen Altar	Gives his life as a ransom for many Mark 10.45
The Laver	If I do not wash you, you have no part with me John 13.8, 10; 1 John 1.7
The Lampstand	I am the Light of the Word John 8.12
The Shewbread	I am the Bread of Life John 6.48
The Altar of Incense	I am praying for them John 17.9
The Veil	This is my body Matt. 26.26
The Mercy Seat	I lay down my life for the sheep John 10.15

Messiah Jesus: Fulfillment of the Old Testament Types (continued)

Contrast Between Aaron's and Melchizedek's Priesthood

Nature of the Order	The Order of Aaron's Levitical Priesthood	The Order of Messiah Jesus' Priesthood (Melchizedek's Priesthood)
Consecration	Temporal and fading	Eternal priesthood Heb. 7.21-23
Priest	Fallible, vulnerable to sin	Sinless and perfect Heb. 7.26
Priesthood	Changeable	Unchangeable priesthood Heb. 7.24
Ministry	Continual offering of sacrifice	Secured an eternal redemption once for all Heb. 9.12, 26
Mediation	Imperfect representation	Perfect representation between God and humankind Heb. 2.14-18
Sacrifice	Unable and insufficient to take the sin of the offenders away	Offered a single sacrifice for sin for all time Heb. 10.11-12
Intercession	Was interrupted by weakness and death	Always lives to make intercession for us Heb. 7.25

Messiah Jesus Fulfills the Levitical Sacrifices and Offerings

The Levitical Offering	How Offering is Fulfilled in Jesus of Nazareth
The Burnt Offering	The perfection of his life Heb. 9.14
The Meal Offering	The dedication and presentation of his life Heb. 5.7; John 4.34
The Peace Offering	He is the peace of our relationships and souls Heb. 4.1-2; Eph. 2.14
The Sin Offering	He bore the penalty for our offense Heb. 10.12; 1 John 2.2
The Trespass Offering	Provision for the offender Heb. 10.20-21; 1 John 1.7

Messiah Jesus: Fulfillment of the Old Testament Types (continued)

Messiah Jesus Fulfills the Levitical Feasts and Festivals

Levitical Feast (Lev. 23)	The Fulfillment in Jesus of Nazareth
The Passover (April)	The death of Jesus Christ 2 Cor. 5.17
Unleavened Bread (April)	Holy and humble walk for Jesus 1 Cor. 5.8
First Fruits (April)	The resurrection of Messiah Jesus 1 Cor. 15.23
The Feast of Pentecost (June)	Outpouring of the Spirit by the Father and the Son Acts 1.5; 2.4
Trumpets (September)	Messiah Jesus' regathering of the Nation Israel Matt. 24.31
The Day of Atonement (September)	Propitiation and cleansing through Jesus Rom. 11.26
Tabernacles (September)	Rest and reunion with Messiah Jesus Zech. 14.16-18

Messiah Yeshua in Every Book of the Bible

Adapted from Norman L. Geisler, A Popular Survey of the Old Testament

Christ in the Books of the Old Testament

1. The Seed of the Woman (Gen. 3.15)

2. The Passover Lamb (Exod. 12.3-4)

3. The Atoning Sacrifice (Lev. 17.11)

4. The Smitten Rock (Num. 20.8, 11)

5. The Faithful Prophet (Deut. 18.18)

6. The Captain of the Lord's Host (Josh. 5.15)

7. The Divine Deliverer (Judg. 2.18)

8. The Kinsman Redeemer (Ruth 3.12)

9. The Anointed One (1 Sam. 2.10)

10. The Son of David (2 Sam. 7.14)

11. The Coming King (1 Kings)

12. The Coming King (2 Kings)

13. The Builder of the Temple (1 Chron. 28.20)

14. The Builder of the Temple (2 Chron.)

15. The Restorer of the Temple (Ezra 6.14, 15)

16. The Restorer of the Nation (Neh. 6.15)

17. The Preserver of the Nation (Esther 4.14)

18. The Living Redeemer (Job 19.25)

19. The Praise of Israel (Ps. 150.6)

20. The Wisdom of God (Prov. 8.22, 23)

21. The Great Teacher (Eccles. 12.11)

22. The Fairest of Ten Thousand (Song of Sol. 5.10)

23. The Suffering Servant (Isa. 53.11)

24. The Maker of the New Covenant (Jer. 31.31)

25. The Man of Sorrows (Lam. 3.28-30)

26. The Glory of God (Ezek. 43.2)

27. The Coming Messiah (Dan. 9.25)

28. The Lover of the Unfaithful (Hos. 3.1)

29. The Hope of Israel (Joel 3.16)

30. The Husbandman (Amos 9.13)

31. The Savior (Obad. 21)

32. The Resurrected One (Jon. 2.10)

33. The Ruler in Israel (Mic. 5.2)

34. The Avenger (Nah. 2.1)

35. The Holy God (Hab. 1.13)

36. The King of Israel (Zeph. 3.15)

37. The Desire of Nations (Hag. 2.7)

38. The Righteous Branch (Zech. 3.8)

39. The Sun of Righteousness (Mal. 4.2))

Messiah Yeshua in Every Book of the Bible (continued)

Christ in the Books of the New Testament

1. The King of the Jews (Matt. 2.2)

2. The Servant of the Lord (Mark 10.45)

3. The Son of Man (Luke 19.10)

4. The Son of God (John 1.1)

5. The Ascended Lord (Acts 1.10)

6. The Believer's Righteousness (Rom. 1.17)

7. Our Sanctification (1 Cor. 1.30)

8. Our Sufficiency (2 Cor. 12.9)

9. Our Liberty (Gal. 2.4)

10. The Exalted Head of the Church (Eph. 1.22)

11. The Christian's Joy (Phil. 1.26)

12. The Fullness of Deity (Col. 2.9)

13. The Believer's Comfort (1 Thess. 4.16, 17)

14. The Believer's Glory (2 Thess. 1.12)

15. The Christian's Preserver (1 Tim. 4.10)

16. The Christian's Rewarder (2 Tim. 4.8)

17. The Blessed Hope (Titus 2.13)

18. Our Substitute (Philem. 17)

19. The Great High Priest (Heb. 4.15)

20. The Giver of Wisdom (James 1.5)

21. The Rock (1 Pet. 2.6)

22. The Precious Promise (2 Pet. 1.4)

23. The Life (1 John)

24. The Truth (2 John)

25. The Way (3 John)

26. The Advocate (Jude)

27. The King of kings and Lord of lords (Rev. 19.16)

Messianic Prophecies Cited in the New Testament

Rev. Dr. Don L. Davis

	NT Citation	OT Reference	Indication of the Fulfillment of the Messianic Prophecy
1	Matt. 1.23	Isa. 7.14	The virgin birth of Jesus of Nazareth
2	Matt. 2.6	Mic. 5.2	The birth of Messiah in Bethlehem
3	Matt. 2.15	Hos. 11.1	That Yahweh would call Messiah out of Egypt, the second Israel
4	Matt. 2.18	Jer. 31.15	Rachel weeping over infants slain by Herod seeking to destroy Messianic seed
5	Matt. 3.3	Isa. 40.3	John the Baptist's preaching fulfills the Messianic forerunner of Isaiah
6	Matt. 4.15-16	Isa. 9.1-2	Galilean ministry of Jesus fulfills Isaiah's prophecy of Messiah's light to the Gentiles
7	Matt. 8.17	Isa. 53.4	Healing ministry of Jesus fulfills Isaiah prophecy regarding Messiah's power to exorcize and heal
8	Matt. 11.14-15	Isa. 35.5-6; 61.1	Jesus' healing ministry confirms his identity as Yahweh's anointed Messiah
9	Matt. 11.10	Mal. 3.1	Jesus confirms John the Baptist's identity as the messenger of Yahweh in Malachi
10	Matt. 12.18-21	Isa. 42.1-4	Jesus' healing ministry fulfills Isaiah's prophecy of Messiah's compassion for the weak
11	Matt. 12.40	Jon. 1.17	As Jonah was three days and nights in the belly of the sea monster, so Jesus would be in the earth
12	Matt. 13.14-15	Isa. 6.9-10	The spiritual dullness of Jesus' audience
13	Matt. 13.35	Ps. 78.2	Messiah would teach in parables to the people
14	Matt. 15.8-9	Isa. 29.13	Hypocritical nature of the audience of Jesus
15	Matt. 21.5	Zech. 9.9	Triumphal entry of Messiah the King into Jerusalem upon the foal of a donkey
16	Matt. 21.9	Ps. 118.26-27	Hosannas to the King of Jerusalem
17	Matt. 21.16	Ps. 8.2	Out of the mouth of babes Yahweh declares salvation
18	Matt. 21.42	Ps. 118.22	The Stone which the builders rejected has become the Capstone
19	Matt. 23.39	Ps. 110.1	The enthronement of Yahweh's Lord

Messianic Prophecies Cited in the New Testament (continued)

	NT Citation	OT Reference	Indication of the Fulfillment of the Messianic Prophecy
20	Matt. 24.30	Dan. 7.13	The Son of Man to come, of Daniel's prophecy, is none other than Jesus of Nazareth
21	Matt. 26.31	Zech. 13.7	The Shepherd smitten by Yahweh and the sheep scattered
22	Matt. 26.64	Ps. 110.1	Jesus of Nazareth is the fulfillment of Daniel's Messianic Son of Man
23	Matt. 26.64	Dan. 7.3	Jesus will come in the clouds of heaven as Daniel's exalted ruler
24	Matt. 27.9-10	Zech. 11.12-13	Messiah is betrayed for thirty pieces of silver
25	Matt. 27.34-35	Ps. 69.21	God's anointed is given wine mingled with gall
26	Matt. 27.35	Ps. 22.18	The soldiers cast lots for the garments of the Messiah
27	Matt. 27.43	Ps. 22.8	Messiah receives mockery and derision upon the cross
28	Matt. 27.46	Ps. 22.1	Messiah forsaken by God for the sake of others
29	Mark 1.2	Mal. 3.1	John the Baptist is the fulfillment of the prophecy regarding the Lord's messenger
30	Mark 1.3	Isa. 40.3	John the Baptist is the voice calling in the wilderness to prepare the Lord's way
31	Mark 4.12	Isa. 6.9	The spiritual dullness of the audience in regards to Messiah's message
32	Mark 7.6	Isa. 29.13	Hypocrisy of the audience in their response to Messiah
33	Mark 11.9	Ps. 118.25	Hosanna's given to Messiah's entry as King into Jerusalem
34	Mark 12.10-11	Ps. 118.25	The stone which the builders rejected has become the chief cornerstone
35	Mark 12.36	Ps. 110.1	The Lord enthrones the Lord of David upon his throne in Zion
36	Mark 13.26	Dan. 7.13	Jesus is the prophesied Son of Man who will return in glory in the clouds
37	Mark 14.27	Zech 13.7	Jesus will be forsaken by his own, for the shepherd will be smitten and the sheep scattered
38	Mark 14.62	Dan. 7.13	Jesus is the Messiah, the Son of Man of Daniel's vision
39	Mark 14.62	Ps. 110.1	The Son of Man, who is Jesus, will come from the right hand of Yahweh
40	Mark 15.24	Ps. 22.18	Lots are cast for the garments of Messiah during his passion
41	Mark 15.34	Ps. 22.1	Messiah is forsaken by God for the redemption of the world

Messianic Prophecies Cited in the New Testament (continued)

	NT Citation	OT Reference	Indication of the Fulfillment of the Messianic Prophecy
42	Luke 1.17	Mal. 4.6	John the Baptist will come in the power and the spirit of Elijah
43	Luke 1.76	Mal. 3.1	John goes before the Lord to prepare the way
44	Luke 1.79	Isa. 9.1-2	Messiah will give light to those who dwell in darkness
45	Luke 2.32	Isa. 42.6; 49.6	Messiah will be a light to the Gentiles
46	Luke 3.4-5	Isa. 40.3	John is Isaiah's voice that cries in the wilderness to prepare the Lord's way
47	Luke 4.18-19	Isa. 61.1-2	Jesus is Yahweh's servant, anointed by his Spirit to bring the good news of the Kingdom
48	Luke 7.27	Mal. 3.1	Jesus confirms John's identity as the preparer of the Lord's way
49	Luke 8.10	Isa. 6.9	The dullness of the audience to Messiah Jesus
50	Luke 19.38	Ps. 118.26	Jesus fulfills in his entry into Jerusalem the Messianic prophecy of the King of Israel
51	Luke 20.17	Ps. 118.26	Jesus is Yahweh's stone which the builders rejected, which has become the Capstone
52	Luke 20.42-43	Ps. 110.1	David calls his lord the Messiah and Lord, who is enthroned in Zion by Yahweh
53	Luke 22.37	Isa. 53.12	Messiah is classed among criminals
54	Luke 22.69	Ps. 110.1	Jesus will return from the right hand of God, from where he has been enthroned
55	Luke 23.34	Ps. 22.18	Lots are cast for the garments of Messiah
56	John 1.23	Isa. 40.3	John's preaching is the fulfillment of Isaiah's prophecy about the forerunner of the Messiah
57	John 2.17	Ps. 69.17	Zeal for the house of the Lord will consume the Messiah
58	John 6.45	Isa. 54.13	All those whom God teaches will come to Messiah
59	John 7.42	Ps. 89.4; Mic. 5.2	Messiah, the seed of David, will be from Bethlehem
60	John 12.13	Ps. 118.25-26	Hosannas are given to Israel's triumphant Messiah King
61	John 12.15	Zech. 9.9	The King of Israel enters Jerusalem upon the foal of a donkey
62	John 12.38	Isa. 53.1	As Isaiah prophesied, few believed the report of Yahweh about his anointed one
63	John 12.40	Isa. 6.10	Isaiah saw the glory of Messiah and spoke of the dullness of his audience to him

Messianic Prophecies Cited in the New Testament (continued)

	NT Citation	OT Reference	Indication of the Fulfillment of the Messianic Prophecy
64	John 13.18; cf. 17.12	Ps. 41.9	Betrayal of Messiah by one of his intimate followers
65	John 15.25	Pss. 35.19; 69.4	Messiah will be hated without cause
66	John 19.24	Ps. 22.18	The garments of Messiah will be divided
67	John 19.28	Ps. 69.21	Messiah will be offered wine upon the cross
68	John 19.36	Exod. 12.46; Num. 9.12; Ps. 34.20	Not one bone of the Messiah will be broken
69	John 19.37	Zech. 12.10	The repentant nation of Israel will look upon him whom they have pierced
70	Acts 1.20	Pss. 69.25; 109.8	Judas is to be replaced with another
71	Acts 2.16-21	Joel 2.28-32	The Spirit is to be poured out in the last days upon all flesh
72	Acts 2.25-28	Ps. 16.8-11	Messiah could not undergo decay or corruption in Sheol
73	Acts 2.34-35	Ps. 110.1	Messiah is enthroned at Yahweh's right hand until his enemies are defeated
74	Acts 3.22-23	Deut. 18.15, 19	God would raise up for the people a prophet like Moses
75	Acts 3.25	Gen. 22.18	All nations of the earth would be blessed in the seed of Abraham
76	Acts 4.11	Ps. 118.22	Messiah Jesus is the rejected stone whom God has made the cornerstone
77	Acts 4.25	Ps. 2.1	Yahweh will laugh at the opposition given by the nations to him and his anointed
78	Acts 7.37	Deut. 18.15	Yahweh will give to Israel a prophet like Moses
79	Acts 8.32-33	Isa. 53.7-9	Messiah Jesus is the Suffering Servant of Yahweh
80	Acts 13.33	Ps. 2.7	God has fulfilled the promise to Israel in Jesus by raising him from the dead
81	Acts 13.34	Isa. 53.3	Messiah Jesus is the fulfillment of the sure mercies of David
82	Acts 13.35	Ps. 16.10	Messiah would not undergo corruption in the grave
83	Acts 13.47	Isa. 49.6	Through Paul, the message of Messiah becomes a light to the nations
84	Acts 15.16-18	Amos 9.11-12	The dynasty of David is restored in Jesus, and Gentiles are welcomed into the Kingdom
85	Rom. 9.25-26	Hos. 2.23; 1.10	Gentiles are to become the people of God

Messianic Prophecies Cited in the New Testament (continued)

	NT Citation	OT Reference	Indication of the Fulfillment of the Messianic Prophecy
86	Rom. 9.33; 10.11	Isa. 28.16	Messiah becomes a stone of stumbling to those who reject God's salvation
87	Rom. 10.13	Joel 2.32	Anyone calling on the name of the Lord will be saved
88	Rom. 11.8	Isa. 29.10	Israel through unbelief has been hardened to Messiah
89	Rom. 11.9-10	Ps. 69.22-23	Judgment has hardened upon Israel
90	Rom. 11.26	Isa. 59.20-21	A deliverer will come from Zion
91	Rom. 11.27	Isa. 27.9	Forgiveness of sins will be given through a new covenant
92	Rom. 14.11	Isa. 45.23	All will be finally judged by Yahweh
93	Rom. 15.9	Ps. 18.49	Gentiles praise God through faith in Messiah
94	Rom. 15.10	Deut. 32.43	God receives praise from the nations
95	Rom. 15.11	Ps. 117.1	The peoples of the earth give God glory
96	Rom. 15.12	Isa. 11.10	Gentiles will hope in the root of Jesse
97	Rom. 15.21	Isa. 52.15	The Good News will be preached to those without understanding
98	1 Cor. 15.27	Ps. 8.7	All things are under the feet of God's representative head
99	1 Cor. 15.54	Isa. 25.8	Death will be swallowed up in victory
100	1 Cor. 15.55	Hos. 13.14	Death will one day lose its sting altogether
101	2 Cor. 6.2	Isa. 49.8	Now is the day of salvation through faith in Messiah Jesus
102	2 Cor. 6.16	Ezek. 37.27	God will dwell with his people
103	2 Cor. 6.18	Hos. 1.10; Isa 43.6	Believers in Messiah Jesus are the sons and daughters of God
104	Gal. 3.8, 16	Gen. 12.3; 13.15; 17.8	The Scriptures, foreseeing Gentile justification by faith, preached the Gospel beforehand through the promise to Abraham, that all nations would be blessed in his seed
105	Gal. 4.27	Isa. 54.1	Jerusalem is the mother of us all
106	Eph. 2.17	Isa. 57.19	Peace of Messiah Jesus is preached both to the Jew and the Gentile
107	Eph. 4.8	Ps. 68.18	Messiah in his ascension has conquered and given gifts to us all by his grace
108	Eph. 5.14	Isa. 26.19; 51.17; 52.1; 60.1	The regeneration of the Lord has occurred; his light has shined on us

Messianic Prophecies Cited in the New Testament (continued)

	NT Citation	OT Reference	Indication of the Fulfillment of the Messianic Prophecy
109	Heb. 1.5	Ps. 2.7	Messiah is God's Son
110	Heb. 1.5	2 Sam. 7.14	Messiah Jesus is the anointed Son of God
111	Heb. 1.6	Deut. 32.43	Angels worshiped Messiah when he entered the world
112	Heb. 1.8-9	Ps. 45.6-7	Messiah Jesus is referred to as God by Yahweh in direct address
113	Heb. 1.10-12	Ps. 102.25-27	The Son is the agent of God's creation and is eternal
114	Heb. 1.13	Ps. 110.1	Messiah Jesus is enthroned at the Father's right hand
115	Heb. 2.6-8	Ps. 8.4-6	All things have been made subject to the Son's authority
116	Heb. 2.12	Ps. 22.22	Messiah Jesus is a brother to all of the redeemed
117	Heb. 2.13	Isa. 8.17-18	Messiah puts his trust in Yahweh God
118	Heb. 5.5	Ps. 2.7	Messiah is God's Son
119	Heb. 5.6	Ps. 110.4	Messiah is an eternal priest after the order of Melchizedek
120	Heb. 7.17, 21	Ps. 110.4	Messiah Jesus is an eternal High Priest
121	Heb. 8.8-12	Jer. 31.31-34	A new covenant has been made in the blood of Jesus
122	Heb. 10.5-9	Ps. 40.6	The death of Messiah Jesus replaces the atoning system of Temple sacrifice
123	Heb. 10.13	Ps. 110.1	Yahweh has enthroned Messiah Jesus as Lord
124	Heb. 10.16-17	Jer. 31.33-34	The Holy Spirit bears witness of the sufficiency of the New Covenant
125	Heb. 10.37-38	Hab. 2.3-4	He who will come will do so, in a little while
126	Heb. 12.26	Hag. 2.6	All heaven and earth will be shaken
127	1 Pet. 2.6	Isa. 28.16	God lays a cornerstone in Zion
128	1 Pet. 2.7	Ps. 118.22	The stone which the builders rejected, God has made the Capstone
129	1 Pet. 2.8	Isa. 8.14	Messiah is a stone of stumbling to those who do not believe
130	1 Pet. 2.10	Hos. 1.10; 2.23	Gentiles through Messiah are now invited to become the people of God
131	1 Pet. 2.22	Isa. 53.9	The sinless Messiah Jesus was sacrificed for us

The Method of the Master
Faithful Servants Representin'

[Jesus'] concern was not with programs to reach the multitudes, but with men whom the multitudes would follow. Remarkable as it may seem, Jesus started to gather those men before he ever organized an evangelistic campaign or even preached a sermon in public. Men were to be his method of winning the world to God. . . . Jesus devoted most of his remaining life on earth to these few disciples. He literally staked his whole ministry on them. The world could be indifferent toward him and still not defeat his strategy. It even caused him no great concern when his followers on the fringes of things gave up their allegiance when confronted with the true meaning of the Kingdom (John 6.66). But he could not bear to have his close disciples miss his purpose. They had to understand the truth and be sanctified by it (John 17.17), else all would be lost. Thus he prayed "not for the world," but for the few God gave him "out of the world (John 17.6, 9). Everything depended on their faithfulness if the world would believe in him "through their word" (John 17.20).

~ Robert Coleman, **The Master Plan of Evangelism.** pp. 27, 31.

The Ministry of Praise and Worship

Rev. Dr. Don L. Davis

The Special Call to the Ministry of Praise and Worship

The praise which overcomes is not merely occasional or spasmodic praise, praise that fluctuates with moods and circumstances. It is continuous praise, praise that is a vocation, a way of life. "I will bless [praise] the Lord at all times; his praise shall continually be in my mouth" (Psalms 34.1). Blessed are they that dwell in thy house; they will be still [always] praising thee" (Psalms 84.4). It has been pointed out that in heaven praise is so important that it constitutes the total occupation of a certain order of beings (Revelation 4.8). God gave to King David such a revelation of the importance and power of praise upon earth that, following the heavenly pattern, he set aside and dedicated an army of four thousand Levites whose sole occupation was to praise the Lord! (1 Chronicles 23.5). They did nothing else. One of the last official acts of King David before his death was the organization of a formal program of praise. Each morning and each evening a contingent of these four thousand Levites engaged in this service. "And to stand every morning to thank and praise the Lord, and likewise at evening," (1 Chronicles 23.30, New Scofield). To the shame and defeat of the Church, the significance of the massive praise content of the Word has been largely overlooked. To be most effective, then, praise must be massive, continuous, a fixed habit, a full-time occupation, a diligently pursued vocation, a total way of life. This principle is emphasized in Psalm 57.7: "My hearted is fixed, O God, my heart is fixed; I will sing and give praise." This suggests a premeditated and predetermined habit of praise. "My heart is FIXED." This kind of praise depends on something more than temporary euphoria.

~ Paul Billheimer, **Destined for the Throne**, pp. 121-22.

I. Exalted God-centered Purpose, Ps. 150.5; Rev. 4.11; Ps. 29.1-2

A. "That's why we praise him, that's why we sing!"

1. To express our joy in God in the Holy Spirit

2. To acknowledge the grace of God in the person of Jesus Christ

3. To experience the presence of God

4. To see the beauty of God in the midst of his people

B. Worship is not

1. Good music alone

2. Professionally performed liturgies

3. Outstanding gear and equipment

C. Worship represents the expression of the saved heart who approaches the Father through the Son in the power of the Holy Spirit for his praise and glory alone! (John 4.24)

D. Worship leading is imitating a GE light bulb

1. When it is most effective, you never notice it, only the effects of its working

2. When it is not working is the only time you give attention to it!

II. The Goal: to Acknowledge and Extol the Excellence of God in Every Dimension of Our Lives, Our Praises of God, 1 Pet. 2.8-9

Principles of Effective Worship Leading

I. To Be an Effective Worship Leader One Must Understand the Nature, Design, and Importance of Worship

A. Worship as spiritual inquiry (*darash*), Ezra 4.2, 6.21

B. Worship as reverent obedience (*yare*), Exod.14.31; Deut.31.12-13

C. Worship as loyal service (*abad*), Exod. 5.18; Num. 8.25

D. Worship as personal ministry (*sharat*), Deut. 10.8, 18.5-7

E. Worship as genuine humility (*shaha*), most common Isa. 49.7; Gen.47.31; Exod. 34.8 cf. Isa. 66.2

The Ministry of Praise and Worship (continued)

    F. Worship as prostration in prayer (*segid*), Dan.3.5-7, 10-12, 14-18, 28

    G. Worship as nearness to God (*nagash*), Ps. 69.18; Isa. 58.2

II. To Be an Effective Worship Leader One Must above All Else Become an Effective Worshiper

    A. Modeling: the cardinal principle of Christian discipleship

        1. Luke 6.40

        2. 1 Tim. 4.6-16

        3. 1 Cor. 11.1

        4. 1 Cor. 15.1-4

        5. Phil. 3.12-15

        6. Phil. 4.6-9

        7. 1 Pet. 5.1-4

    B. God desires that we worship him in spirit and in truth (John 4.34)

    C. With wholehearted passion: the big three

        1. Moses, Exod. 33-34

        2. David, Ps. 27.1ff; 34.1-3; 104

        3. Paul, Phil.1.18-21

III. To Be an Effective Worship Leader One Must Understand the Principles and Practice of Worship as They Have Displayed Themselves in the History of the Saints

    A. Liturgical Theology

        1. Liturgical theology does not focus primarily on the data of the Bible

2. It concentrates on the history of the Church, that is, what the Church has done in its historical practice to bring glory and honor to God

3. Use of reason and sociology

B. Tendencies toward shallowness: the problem of ignoring historical worship practice of the Church

1. Create the rut of ignoring everything that has gone on before, concentrate on what we like and have done

2. Ignore the power of the Spirit to work in the past

3. Deny the anointing that God has given to his people throughout every era

4. Short-change those you lead by isolating them from their brothers and sisters of long ago

C. Views regarding Liturgical Theology

1. *Anabaptist view*: reproduce NT practice unchanged

2. *Lutheran, Anglican, Reformed view*: biblical principles and changing conditions

3. *Jewish synagogue practice*: innovation (things included in the Jewish synagogue practice which were not contained in the OT)

4. *Historic Christian practice*: cultural, fluid, in line with Scripture

D. Doxological Theology (cf. Robert Webber)

1. How Jewish and Christian worship can inform theology

2. Explaining precisely what is the tie between theology and worship, Phil. 2.5-11

3. Historical outline of theology through detailed study of worship

The Ministry of Praise and Worship (continued)

E. Key subject of liturgical theology: the liturgical calendar (the story of God in the service of the Church)

   1. Judaism

      a. Elaborate calendar of holy days in Judaism (similar in some respects to the Catholic calendar)

      b. One weekly (Sabbath), one monthly (the new moon)

      c. Leviticus 23 as biblical description of some of the key festivals and feasts

      d. All days of festival included feasts except the Day of Atonement (a fast)

      e. Feast of Purim added later, along with Dedication (cf. John 10.22)

      f. Worship as ritual drama (remembrance and re-enactment)

   2. Gentile Christianity (after the first century)

      a. Exempted from literal law obedience (the council of Jerusalem, Acts 15)

      b. Destruction of the Temple in AD 70, prominence of Gentile form

      c. Christian calendar consisted of Christian holy-days shortly thereafter

      d. The Lord's Day, Sunday

      e. Fasts on Wednesday and Friday (opposed to Jewish on Monday and Thursday)

      f. Borrowed from Judaism – Easter (*Pascha*, i.e., the Passover)

      g. Ascension Day, Epiphany, and Christmas

      h. Trinity Sunday (10th c., western)

F. Summary of Liturgical Theology: celebrates the course of the Revelation story culminating in the life, death, exaltation, and return of Christ

IV. To Be an Effective Worship Leader One Must Comprehend Specifically and Biblically the Power and Significance of Music

A. The power of music

1. As a spiritual force

2. As a cultural phenomenon

3. As an emotional response

4. As a form of communication

5. As a artistic expression

B. Love music as an expression of your heart to the Lord: Psalm 150 (worship is to be unbroken, undiluted, high-energy, wholehearted, and uncompromising)

C. Learning to be a member of a band: the power of contribution

1. Band vs. individual

2. Contribution's elements

a. Developing an ear for "our sound:" playing a role on a team

b. Dashes and pinches: the "Lazy Susan" approach to contribution

c. Learning to downshift: providing sound only when it contributes

d. Your goal: "I intend to play on my instrument all that and no more which each song requires to give the overall sense and impression that we together intend to make."

D. Master and employ to the full the *Basic Building Blocks* of music.

1. Rhythm - Beat

2. Tempo

The Ministry of Praise and Worship (continued)

    3.   Melody

    4.   Harmony

    5.   Lyrics

    6.   Dynamics

  E. The importance of regular practice

    1.   Alone

    2.   Together

  F. Familiarity: becoming best friends with your instrument

V. To Be an Effective Worship Leader One Must Concentrate on Developing Mastery in Musicianship and Identify Gifts and Passions in Worship

  A. Mastery comes with discipline: 1 Tim. 4.7-8

  B. Identify what your best gifts are (under the scrutiny of loving critique!)

    1.   Is it my voice?

    2.   Is it my instrumentation?

    3.   Is it both? Is it neither? Is it something else altogether?

  C. Design your worship themes, sets of music, and approaches to the service

    1.   In conjunction with the theme: forming links, connections, and associations

        a.   Invocation and opening praise: beckoning the saints to worship ("Come, Now is the Time to Worship")

b. Joyous celebration in the presence of the Lord ("We Bring the Sacrifice of Praise")

c. Adoration and worship ("We Declare Your Majesty")

d. Commitment and benediction ("Lift Up Your Hearts")

2. In conjunction with the proclaimed Word of the Lord

3. In conjunction with the styles

4. In conjunction with your time constraints

D. Shaping each song within your music set

1. A song as a story: introductions, middles, transitions, and ends

2. The art of transposition, changed tempo, voices dropping out, etc.

3. From trickle to stream to rapids to ocean

4. Avoiding the "wall of sound" problem associated with young musicians

E. Learning to help every worship team member make their unique contribution to the worship experience through who they are and what they do

1. Don't simply play or sing; listen to yourself and contribute

2. The cycle of unending noise

a. We're playing loud; I cannot hear myself

b. I turn myself up; others can't hear themselves, they turn themselves up

c. We're all playing even louder now; I cannot hear myself

d. Etc.

F. Note the difference between merely playing well vs. enhancing the body's worship

   1. Between performing a concert and leading worship

   2. Between highlighting your play and contributing to the feeling and mood of the song

   3. Between beautifying our song together and playing your instrument

G. Obtain and use the Appropriate Gear

   1. Make the financial and emotional investment

      a. From the church: becoming a part of the church's budget

      b. From the musician: investing wisely in the right materials

   2. Quality

      a. Avoid the cheapest gear

      b. Don't go broke on the high end

      c. Middle-of-the-road is not bad today: modest investments can produce CD quality return

   3. Tastiness: the art of tweaking

   4. "Less is more:" If in doubt, dumb down for greatest impact

VI. To Be an Effective Worship Leader One Must Know How to Build and Sustain a Focused Worship Team

A. The many voices, contributions, and gifts in coordination = greatest worship experience for the congregation

B. The importance of worship as a *community event*

C. The Trinitarian Principle applied to worship: unity, diversity, and equality

1. The symphony as model for worship in the Church of Jesus Christ

2. European styles dominate in American churches

3. The Nicene Creed: the Church is one, holy, apostolic, and catholic

    a. Hundreds of styles of praise

    b. Offered to God in scores of languages

    c. Ethno-musicology - the science of human music and learning

    d. No form is superior; all forms are acceptable if done in conjunction with the biblical edicts

4. Dangerous to ignore this principle: hegemony of European styles and power

D. Have clear standards and policies for everyone involved

E. Be careful not to become too professional; emphasize quality but allow for full participation by the body

F. Offer clear and encouraging leadership at all times

G. Recruit from a broad base of people

H. Organize for maximum success and effectiveness

The Ministry of Praise and Worship (continued)

VII. To Be an Effective Worship Leader One Must Creatively Use Resources to Blend the Old and New (the Ancient and the Modern) in Worship and Praise

A. The broadness of expression in the Church of Jesus Christ

    1. The biblical plethora: Revelation 5 (from every tribe, language, kindred, and nation)

    2. Within these many different styles are reflected, expressed, and enjoyed

        a. Differences according to time: traditional styles versus contemporary styles

        b. Differences according to culture: southern gospel to hip-hop

        c. Differences according to volume

        d. Differences according to meanings of music

    3. The "fight" is real and meaningful

    4. Not "either/or" but "both/and"

B. Why is a blended worship approach so important?

    1. Variety is truly the spice of life, and the nature of God's person and working

    2. To hear the Lord's voice afresh: the case for contemporary

    3. To remember the Lord's work in our past: the case for traditional

C. One person's garbage is another person's wealth: the tyranny and phases of ethnocentrism (see Acts 10: Peter and the Jewish band's reaction to Cornelius)

    1. Phase one: ours is *preferred* over theirs

    2. Phase two: ours is *better* than theirs

    3. Phase three: ours is *right*, theirs is somewhat iffy

4.   Phase four: mine is God-ordained and *superior*, and everyone else's is odd and wrong

D.   Blending: an affirmation of the importance of difference of expression and the holding of tradition in our worship experience in God. How do you blend?

1.   In the songs you select

2.   In the styles you play

3.   In the instrumentation you select

4.   In the vocal arrangements you choose

E.   Respecting difference while allowing for preferences and self-expression: the constant challenge of the worship leader

1.   Integrate the service with genuine appreciation of styles

2.   Tease out meaning by playing the same music in differing styles

Eph. 2.19-22 (ESV)
So then you are no longer strangers and aliens, but you are fellow citizens with the saints and members of the household of God, [20] built on the foundation of the apostles and prophets, Christ Jesus himself being the cornerstone, [21] in whom the whole structure, being joined together, grows into a holy temple in the Lord. [22] In him you also are being built together into a dwelling place for God by the Spirit.

VIII. The Summary of Worship: Glorifying God in God-Pleasing Harmony

A.   Members of the household of God: worship as the expression of saved spirits

B.   Built on the foundation of the apostles and prophets, with Jesus Christ as the Chief and Precious Cornerstone: worship as the response to God's historical self-revelation through his Word

C.   Joined together as a holy temple in the Lord: worship as the people of God becoming a holy sanctuary where his praises dwell

D.   Built together into a dwelling place for God by the Spirit: we ourselves are the place where God's praises originate and where he dwells

E.   All that we are and do can harmonize together as leaders, congregation, and worship team into a praise offering sweet and pure enough for our God to dwell!

The Miracles of Jesus

adapted from The Bible Made Easy. Peabody: Hendrickson Publishers, 1997.

1	Water changed to wine	John 2.1-11
2	Nobleman's son healed	John 4.46-54
3	Lame man by the Bethesda pool	John 5.1-9
4	Man born blind	John 9.1-41
5	Lazarus raised from the dead	John 11.1-44
6	153 fish captured	John 21.1-11
7	Jesus walks on water	John 6.19-21
8	5,000 people fed	John 6.5-13
9	Demon-possessed man loosed	Luke 4.33-35
10	Peter's mother-in-law healed	Luke 4.38-39
11	Large catch of fish	Luke 5.1-11
12	Leper cleansed	Luke 5.12-13
13	Paralyzed man restored	Luke 5.18-25
14	Shriveled hand made whole	Luke 5.5-10
15	Centurion's steward healed	Luke 7.1-10
16	Widow's dead son raised	Luke 7.11-15
17	The storm calmed	Luke 8.22-25
18	The man with Legion exorcized	Luke 27-35

19	Jairus' daughter raised	Luke 8.41-56
20	Woman with hemorrhage healed	Luke 8.43-48
21	Demon-possessed boy delivered	Luke 8.43-48
22	Mute, demon-possessed man healed	Luke 9.38-43
23	Crippled woman straightened	Luke 13.11-13
24	Ten lepers cleansed	Luke 17.11-19
25	Blind Bartimeus made well	Luke 18.35-43
26	Malchus' ear restored	Luke 22.50-51
27	Two blind men healed	Matt. 9.27-31
28	Demon-possessed mute healed	Matt. 9.32-33
29	Coin in the fish's mouth	Matt. 17.24-27
30	Woman's daughter made whole	Matt. 15.21-28
31	4,000 people fed	Matt. 15.32-38
32	Fig tree cursed	Matt. 21.18-22
33	Deaf and mute man healed	Mark 7.31-37
34	Blind man restored	Mark 8.22-26
35	Man with dropsy healed	Luke 14.1-4

Missions in the 21st Century
Working with Social Entrepreneurs?
Rebecca Lewis

This article was taken from Mission Frontiers: The Bulletin of the US Center for World Mission, Vol. 27, No. 5; September-October 2005; ISSN 0889-9436.

Rebecca Lewis spent eight years in Morocco on a church planting team and currently creates curricula to help young people see how they can live their lives for God's purposes.

The challenge is this: how to catalyze an "insider movement" to Christ in a society closed to traditional mission work? For this to happen, the gospel needs to spread through pre-existing social networks, which become the "church." People should not be drawn out of their families or communities into new social structures in order to become believers. God seems to be opening a new avenue of opportunity into closed societies through working with community agents of change – entrepreneurs working for social reform.

Historically, the most successful model for achieving lasting social change has been neither government nor business but the voluntary society (also known as the "citizen sector" or "civil society"). The idea of citizens banding together to reform society took a great step forward during the Evangelical Awakening, initiated by John Wesley in the 18th century. Out of this revival, and the Second Great Awakening in the early 19th century, came hundreds of voluntary, cross-denominational associations or "societies." Founded by visionary social entrepreneurs, each society attacked a certain issue, everything from abolishing slavery to creating special "Sunday schools" to teach reading to children who worked all week. Why not harness this successful model as a vehicle for advancing God's purposes among today's least-reached people groups?

Today the door is wide open in most countries to people who would catalyze grass-roots initiatives to address social problems. During the 1990s the number of international non-profit organizations jumped from 6000 to 26,000, a growth rate of over 400%. Likewise, hundreds of thousands of national NGOs (non-government organizations) have been formed in non-Western countries. Why the sudden growth? First, since the fall of the Soviet Union, many governments have been releasing control of the economy and nurturing the private sector. Second, social entrepreneurs and the civil society sector are now widely recognized for their success in solving formerly intractable problems.

Missions in the 21st Century: Working with Social Entrepreneurs? (continued)

Third, governments are increasingly embarrassed if they try to block non-profit initiatives, because a global value for "empathy" has been established by the rapidly-spreading evangelical movement and the incorporation of Christian values in secular education worldwide. Fourth, there is a new openness to change in general. As people in remote places have become exposed to the rest of the world through mass media, they are reconsidering their behavior patterns and traditional beliefs. People everywhere are putting their hope in education and valuing progress as never before. As a result, local communities, as well as national governments, are getting behind citizen organizations seeking to implement solutions to systemic problems.

If the goal is to produce insider movements to Christ, why work with social entrepreneurs? Christian workers can build extensive relationships with leaders and families within a community by assisting social entrepreneurs (whether they are believers or not) with their vision to attack a problem. These types of broad relational networks – proactively bringing change to the community – form an excellent basis for the spread of the gospel in a way that leads to insider movements. Through helping the civil sector, workers have a role that is understandable and beneficial both in the eyes of the local people and the government. Also, like Jesus, they can announce the Kingdom in the context of bringing healing to the community.

To those who would like to learn more about finding and assisting social entrepreneurs, I recommend David Bornstein's fascinating book, *How to Change the World: Social Entrepreneurs and the Power of New Ideas* (Oxford University Press, 2003).

Models of the Kingdom
Howard A Snyder, March 2002.

1. The Kingdom as Future Hope - the Future Kingdom

This has been a dominant model in the history of the Church. The emphasis is strongly on the future: a final culmination and reconciliation of all things which is more than merely the eternal existence of the soul. The model draws heavily on NT material. While some of the following models also represent future hope, here the note of futurity is determinative.

2. The Kingdom as Inner Spiritual Experience - the Interior Kingdom

A "spiritual kingdom" to be experienced in the heart or soul; "beatific vision." Highly mystical, therefore individualistic; an experience that can't really be shared with others. Examples: Julian of Norwich, other mystics; also some contemporary Protestant examples.

3. The Kingdom as Mystical Communion - the Heavenly Kingdom

The "communion of saints"; the Kingdom as essentially identified with heaven. Less individualistic. Often centers especially in worship and liturgy. Examples: John of Damascus, John Tauler; in somewhat different ways, Wesley and 19th and 20th-century revivalistic and Evangelical Protestantism. Kingdom is primarily other-worldly and future.

4. The Kingdom as Institutional Church - the Ecclesiastical Kingdom

The dominant view of medieval Christianity; dominant in Roman Catholicism until Vatican II. Pope as Vicar of Christ rules on earth in Christ's stead. The tension between the Church and the Kingdom largely dissolves. Traces to Augustine's City of God, but was developed differently from what Augustine believed. Protestant variations appear whenever the Church and Kingdom are too closely identified. Modern "Church Growth" thinking has been criticized at this point.

Models of the Kingdom (continued)

5. The Kingdom as Counter-System - the Subversive Kingdom

May be a protest to #4; sees the Kingdom as a reality which prophetically judges the sociopolitical order as well as the Church. One of the best examples: Francis of Assisi; also 16th century Radical Reformers; "Radical Christians" today; Sojourners magazine. Sees Church as counter-culture embodying the new order of the Kingdom.

6. The Kingdom as Political State - the Theocratic Kingdom

Kingdom may be seen as a political theocracy; Church and society not necessarily to be organized democratically. Tends to work from O.T. models, especially the Davidic Kingdom. Constantinian model; Byzantine Christianity a good example. Calvin's Geneva, perhaps, in a somewhat different sense. Problem of Luther's "two kingdoms" view.

7. The Kingdom as Christianized Society - the Transforming Kingdom

Here also the Kingdom provides a model for society, but more in terms of values & principles to be worked out in society. Kingdom in its fullness would be society completely leavened by Christian values. Post-millennialism; many mid-19th-century Evangelicals; early 20th-century Social Gospel. Kingdom manifested progressively in society, in contrast to premillennialism.

8. The Kingdom as Earthly Utopia - the Earthly Kingdom

May be seen as #7 taken to extreme. This view of the Kingdom is literally utopian. Tends to deny or downplay sin, or see evil as purely environmental. The view of many utopian communities (Cohn, *Pursuit of the Millennium*) including 19th-century U.S. and British examples. In a different way, the view of many of America's Founding Fathers. Most influential 20th-century example: Marxism. Liberation theology, to some degree. In a starkly different way: U.S. Fundamentalist premillennialism, combining this model with #1, #2 and/or #3 -Kingdom has no contemporary relevance, but will be literal utopia in the future. Thus similarities between Marxism and Fundamentalism.

The Names of Almighty God
Rev. Dr. Don L. Davis

I. The Names of God

A. *Elohim*

1. *Elohim* is a Hebrew plural form used more than 2000 times in the Old Testament, usually termed a "plural of majesty" of the general name for God.

2. Derived from El, whose root meaning is "to be strong" (cf. Gen. 17.1; 28.3; 35.11; Josh. 3.10) or "to be preeminent."(cf. Frank M. Cross, "El," in *Theological Dictionary of the Old Testament*, 6 vols., revised, edited by G. Johannes Botterweck and Helmer Ringgren (Grand Rapids: Eerdmans, 1977, 1:244.)

3. *Elohim* is usually translated "God" in English translations.

4. This name *emphasizes God's transcendence* (cf. that God is above all others who are called God). *Elohim* is the plural form of El; the terms seem to be interchangeable (cf. Exod. 34.14; Ps. 18.31; Deut. 32.17, 21).

5. *El* may signify in some texts (such as Isa. 31.3) the "power and strength of God and the defenselessness of human enemies" (cf. Hos. 11.9). (Cf. 34. Helmer Ringgren, "*Elohim*," in *Theological Dictionary of the Old Testament*, 1:273–74.)

B. *Adonai*

1. The term *Adonai* (Heb. *Adhon* or *Adhonay*) in its root means "lord" or "master" and is usually translated "Lord" in English Bibles.

2. It occurs 449 times in the Old Testament and 315 times with Yahweh. *Adhon* emphasizes the servant-master relationship (cf. Gen. 24.9) and suggests God's authority as Master, i.e., the One rules with absolute authority (cf. Ps. 8.1; Hos. 12.14).

The Names of Almighty God (continued)

3. *Adonai* can be understood to mean "*Lord of all*" or "*Lord par excellence*" (cf. Deut. 10.17; Josh. 3.11). (Cf. Merrill F. Unger and William White, Jr., eds., *Nelson's Expository Dictionary of the Old Testament* [Nashville: Nelson, 1980], pp. 228–29; and Otto Eissfeldt, "*Adhon*," in *Theological Dictionary of the Old Testament*, 1:59–72.)

C. *Yahweh* (Jehovah)

1. The name *Yahweh* translates the Hebrew *tetragrammaton* (four lettered expression) YHWH. Since the original name contained no vowels, it is uncertain how it should be pronounced. (For instance, the ASV translates it "Jehovah," whereas most modern translations simply render it "LORD" [to distinguish it from *Adonai*, "Lord"]).

2. Jewish scholars generally pronounce it as "*Adonai*" rather than voicing YHWH, out of respect for its sacredness.

3. It is used as a common designation (used 6,828 times in the Old Testament), and some suggest it may be related to the verb "to be." (Cf. Exod. 3.14–15 the Lord declares, "I AM WHO I AM...The Lord . . . has sent me to you. This is my name forever.)

4. *Yahweh* as the I AM connects to the "I AM" claims of Messiah Jesus (cf. John 6.35; 8.12; 10.9, 11; 11.25; 14.6; 15.1), who claimed equality with Yahweh.

5. *Yahweh*, the name of covenant relationship

   a. The name of the Abrahamic Covenant (Gen. 12.8)

   b. The name of the Exodus (Exod. 6.6; 20.2)

   c. *A unique relationship*: although the terms *Elohim* and *Adonai* were terms known to other peoples, Yahweh was unique to Israel.

II. Compound Names: the Name of God Involving the Names El (or Elohim) and Yahweh

A. *El Shaddai*

1. Translated "God Almighty"

2. Probably relates to the word *mountain*, suggesting the power or strength of God

3. The name of God as a covenant-keeping God (Gen. 17.1; cf. vv. 1–8)

B. *El Elyon*

1. Translated "God Most High"

2. This terms refers to *the supremacy of God*

3. *Yahweh* God is a god above all so-called gods (cf. Gen. 14.18–22). Melchizedek recognized him as "God Most High" inasmuch as he is possessor of heaven and earth (v. 19).

C. *El Olam*

1. Translated the "Everlasting God"

2. Emphasizes *the unchanging character of God* (Gen. 21.33; Isa. 40.28)

D. *Yahweh* compound names

1. Adonai-Yahweh, "*The Lord our Sovereign*," Gen. 15.2, 8

2. Yahweh-Jireh, "*The Lord will provide*," Gen. 22.14

3. Yahweh Elohim, "*The Lord God*," Gen. 2.4-25

4. Yahweh-Nissi , "*The Lord our banner*," Exod. 17.15

5. Yahweh-Rapha, "*The Lord our healer*," Exod. 15.26

6. Yahweh-Rohi, "*The Lord our shepherd*," Ps. 23.1

The Names of Almighty God (continued)

7. Yahweh-Shammah, *"The Lord is there,"* Ezek. 48.35

8. Yahweh-Hoseenu, *"The Lord our Maker,"* Ps. 95.6

9. Yahweh-Shalom, *"The Lord our peace,"* Judg. 6.24

10. Yahweh-Sabbaoth, *"The Lord of armies,"* 1 Sam. 1.3

11. Yahweh-Mekaddishkem, *"The Lord your sanctifier,"* Exod. 31.13

12. Yahweh-Tsidkenu, *"The Lord our righteousness,"* Jer. 23.6

New Testament Readings

The Problem: Who Precisely Was Jesus of Nazareth?

➤ C. S. Lewis, *Mere Christianity*. New York: Touchstone by Simon and Schuster, (1943) 1996. p. 52

A man who was merely a man and said the sort of things Jesus said wouldn't be a great moral teacher. He would either be a lunatic–on a level with a man who says he is a poached egg–or else he'd be the devil of hell. You must make your choice. Either this man was, and is, the Son of God, or else a madman or something worse.

Tell Us Plainly: Are You the Messiah, or Not?

➤ Archibald M. Hunter, *The Work and Words of Jesus*. Philadelphia: The Westminster Press, (1950) 1973. p. 134

Always at the center of the Jews' concern is the question of questions, "Can this Galilean possibly be the Messiah?" On his part, Jesus does not give them the unequivocal answer which they desire, but in a simple parable "drawn from ancient Palestinian tradition," John 10.1-5, he does make a veiled Messianic claim. "I am no interloper," he says in effect, "but the rightful shepherd of God's flock. I need no signs to prove my authority which is self-authenticating: it lies in the fact that my sheep follow my leadership because they recognize in me the accents and actions of Israel's true shepherd" (see Ezekiel 34).

Why Didn't Jesus Embrace More Publicly His Identity as Messiah, and Therefore Silence His Adversaries?

➤ Archibald M. Hunter, *The Work and Words of Jesus*. p. 103

Jesus knew himself to be the Messiah, albeit in his own terms, during his ministry. What does this mean? That he was the person through whom God's rule was being realized and the ancient prophecies fulfilled. Yet when Peter or Caiaphas sought to apply the title to him, Jesus seemed to shy away from it and talk instead of the Son of Man. Why?

The only convincing answer is that Jesus conceived his Messiahship in spiritual and eschatological terms, not in nationalist and political ones. One indication of what it means to him comes in his reply to John the Baptist's questions. "I am," he replies in effect, "the fulfiller of the great Isaianic prophecies (Isa. 29.18-19; 35.5-6; and 61.1), and come to bring healing, life, and good news to God's needy children." Another clue he gives in his mode of entry into the holy city recalls Zechariah's prince of peace (Zech. 9.9-10). Not the Psalms of Solomon but Servant Songs of Isaiah and the Psalms of the Righteous Sufferer (22, 69, etc.) shaped his thought of the Messiah."

The Nicene Creed

We believe in one God, the Father Almighty, maker of heaven and earth and of all things visible and invisible.

We believe in one Lord Jesus Christ, the only begotten Son of God, begotten of the Father before all ages, God from God, Light from Light, True God from True God, begotten not created, of the same essence as the Father, through whom all things were made.

Who for us men and for our salvation came down from heaven and was incarnate by the Holy Spirit and the virgin Mary and became human. Who for us too, was crucified under Pontius Pilate, suffered and was buried. The third day he rose again according to the Scriptures, ascended into heaven and is seated at the right hand of the Father. He will come again in glory to judge the living and the dead, and his Kingdom will have no end.

We believe in the Holy Spirit, the Lord and life-giver, who proceeds from the Father and the Son. Who together with the Father and Son is worshiped and glorified. Who spoke by the prophets.

We believe in one holy, catholic, and apostolic church.

We acknowledge one baptism for the forgiveness of sin, and we look for the resurrection of the dead and the life of the age to come. Amen.

Nicene Creed with Biblical Support

We believe in one God, (*Deut. 6.4-5; Mark 12.29; 1 Cor. 8.6*)
　　the Father Almighty, (*Gen. 17.1; Dan. 4.35; Matt. 6.9; Eph. 4.6; Rev. 1.8*)
　　Maker of heaven and earth (*Gen 1.1; Isa. 40.28; Rev. 10.6*)
　　and of all things visible and invisible. (*Ps. 148; Rom. 11.36; Rev. 4.11*)

We believe in one Lord Jesus Christ, the only Begotten Son of God,
　　begotten of the Father before all ages,
　　God from God, Light from Light, True God from True God,
　　begotten not created,
　　of the same essence as the Father, (*John 1.1-2; 3.18; 8.58; 14.9-10; 20.28; Col. 1.15, 17; Heb. 1.3-6*)
　　through whom all things were made. (*John 1.3; Col. 1.16*)

Who for us men and for our salvation came down from heaven
　　and was incarnate by the Holy Spirit and the virgin Mary
　　and became human. (*Matt. 1.20-23; John 1.14; 6.38; Luke 19.10*)
　　Who for us too, was crucified under Pontius Pilate,
　　suffered, and was buried. (*Matt. 27.1-2; Mark 15.24-39, 43-47; Acts 13.29; Rom. 5.8; Heb. 2.10; 13.12*)
　　The third day he rose again
　　according to the Scriptures, (*Mark 16.5-7; Luke 24.6-8; Acts 1.3; Rom. 6.9; 10.9; 2 Tim. 2.8*)
　　ascended into heaven,
　　and is seated at the right hand of the Father. (*Mark 16.19; Eph. 1.19-20*)
　　He will come again in glory
　　to judge the living and the dead,
　　and his Kingdom will have no end.
　　　　(*Isa. 9.7; Matt. 24.30; John 5.22; Acts 1.11; 17.31; Rom. 14.9; 2 Cor. 5.10; 2 Tim. 4.1*)

We believe in the Holy Spirit, the Lord and life-giver,
　　　　(*Gen. 1.1-2; Job 33.4; Ps. 104.30; 139.7-8; Luke 4.18-19; John 3.5-6; Acts 1.1-2; 1 Cor. 2.11; Rev. 3.22*)
　　who proceeds from the Father and the Son, (*John 14.16-18, 26; 15.26; 20.22*)
　　who together with the Father and Son
　　is worshiped and glorified, (*Isa. 6.3; Matt. 28.19; 2 Cor. 13.14; Rev. 4.8*)
　　who spoke by the prophets. (*Num. 11.29; Mic. 3.8; Acts 2.17-18; 2 Pet. 1.21*)

We believe in one holy, catholic, and apostolic Church.
　　　　(*Matt. 16.18; Eph. 5.25-28; 1 Cor. 1.2; 10.17; 1 Tim. 3.15; Rev. 7.9*)

We acknowledge one baptism for the forgiveness of sin, (*Acts 22.16; 1 Pet. 3.21; Eph. 4.4-5*)
　　And we look for the resurrection of the dead
　　　　And the life of the age to come. (*Isa. 11.6-10; Mic. 4.1-7; Luke 18.29-30; Rev. 21.1-5; 21.22-22.5*)

Amen.

Nurturing Authentic Christian Leadership

Rev. Dr. Don L. Davis

Cliff On-One-Side	Cliff On-the-Other-Side
Laying on hands too quickly	Always postponing delegation to the indigenous
Ignoring culture in leadership training	Elevating culture above truth
Demoting doctrine and theology	Supposing doctrine and theology as only criteria
Highlighting skills and gifts above availability and character	Substituting availability and character for genuine giftedness
Emphasizing administrative abilities above spiritual dynamism	Ignoring administration's role in spiritual vitality and power
Equating readiness with Christian perfection	Ignoring the importance of biblical standards
Limiting candidacy for leadership based on gender and ethnicity	Setting quotas of leadership based on gender and ethnicity
Seeing everyone as a leader	Seeing virtually no one as worthy to lead

The Obedient Christian in Action

The Navigators

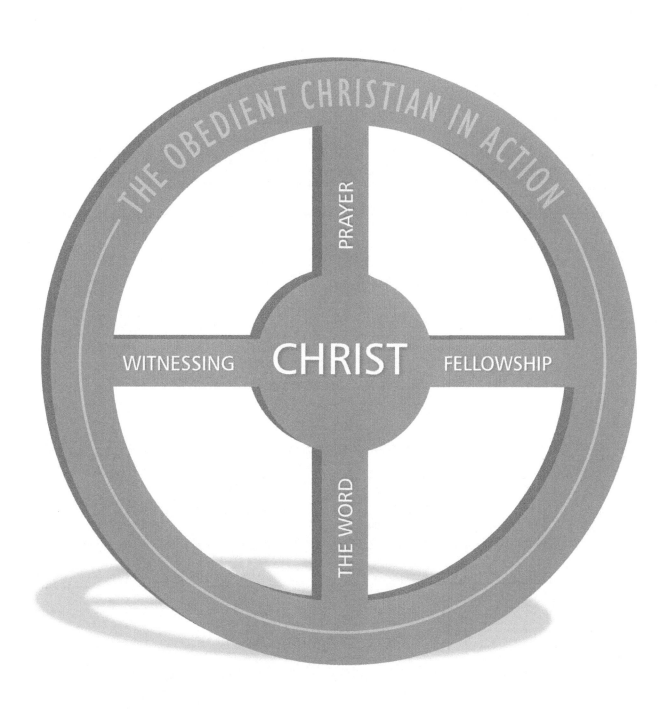

The *Oikos* Factor
Spheres of Relationship and Influence
Rev. Dr. Don L. Davis

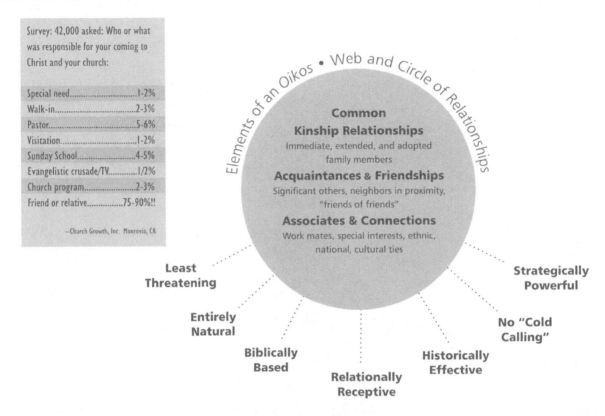

Survey: 42,000 asked: Who or what was responsible for your coming to Christ and your church:

Special need	1-2%
Walk-in	2-3%
Pastor	5-6%
Visitation	1-2%
Sunday School	4-5%
Evangelistic crusade/TV	1/2%
Church program	2-3%
Friend or relative	75-90%!!

--Church Growth, Inc. Monrovia, CA

Elements of an Oikos • Web and Circle of Relationships

Common Kinship Relationships
Immediate, extended, and adopted family members

Acquaintances & Friendships
Significant others, neighbors in proximity, "friends of friends"

Associates & Connections
Work mates, special interests, ethnic, national, cultural ties

Least Threatening

Entirely Natural

Biblically Based

Relationally Receptive

Historically Effective

No "Cold Calling"

Strategically Powerful

Oikos (household) in the OT
"A household usually contained four generations, including men, married women, unmarried daughters, slaves of both sexes, persons without citizenship, and "sojourners," or resident foreign workers." – *Hans Walter Wolff, Anthology of the Old Testament.*

Oikos (household) in the NT
Evangelism and disciple making in our NT narratives are often described as following the flow of the relational networks of various people within their *oikoi* (households), that is, those natural lines of connection in which they resided and lived (c.f., Mark 5.19; Luke 19.9; John 4.53; 1.41-45, etc.). Andrew to Simon (John 1.41-45), and both Cornelius (Acts 10-11) and the Philippian jailer (Acts 16) are notable cases of evangelism and discipling through *oikoi*.

Oikos (household) among the urban poor
While great differences exist between cultures, kinship relationships, special interest groups, and family structures among urban populations, it is clear that urbanites connect with others far more on the basis of connections through relationships, friendships, and family than through proximity and neighborhood alone. Often times the closest friends of urban poor dwellers are not immediately close-by in terms of neighborhood; family and friends may dwell blocks, even miles away. Taking the time to study the precise linkages of relationships among the dwellers in a certain area can prove extremely helpful in determining the most effective strategies for evangelism and disciple making in inner city contexts.

Old Testament Names, Titles, and Epithets for the Messiah

*Adapted from Norman L. Geisler, **A Popular Survey of the Old Testament***

1. Advocate, Job 16.19
2. Angel (messenger), Job 33.23
3. Anointed, 1 Sam. 2.19; Ps. 2.2
4. Battle-bow, Zech. 10.4
5. Bethlehem's Ruler, Mic. 5.2
6. Breaker, Mic. 2.13
7. Commander, Isa. 55.4
8. Cornerstone (Capstone), Ps. 118.22; Isa. 28.16
9. Covenant of the People, Isa. 42.6
10. Crusher, Gen. 3.15
11. David, Hos. 3.5; Jer. 30.9
12. Desire of all Nations, Hag. 2.7
13. Eternal One, Ps. 102.25-27
14. Eternal Priest, Ps. 110.4
15. Everlasting Father, Isa. 9.6
16. Faithful Priest, 1 Sam. 2.35
17. Firstborn, Ps. 89.27
18. Forsaken Sufferer, Ps. 22
19. Foundation, Isa. 28.16; Zech. 10.4
20. God, Ps. 45.6-7
21. Head, Hos. 1.11; Mic. 2.13
22. Healer, Isa. 42.7
23. He who Comes, Ps. 118.26
24. Horn of David, Ps. 132.17
25. Immanuel, Isa. 7.14
26. Interpreter, Job 33.23
27. Israel, Hos. 11.1; Isa. 49.3
28. King, Ps. 2.5; Hos. 3.5
29. Lamp for David, Ps. 132.17
30. Last, Job 19.25
31. Launderer, Mal. 3.2
32. Leader, Isa. 55.4
33. Liberator, Isa. 42.7
34. Light, Isa. 9.2
35. Light of the Gentiles, Isa. 42.6; 49.6
36. Lord, Mal. 3.1
37. Man, Zech. 6.12; 13.7
38. Man of Sorrows, Isa. 53.3
39. Mediator, Job 33.23
40. Messenger of the Covenant, Mal. 3.1
41. Messiah-Prince, Dan. 9.25
42. Mighty God, Isa. 9.6
43. Mighty Hero, Ps. 45.3
44. My Equal, Zech. 13.7
45. Nail (peg), Zech. 10.4
46. Our Peace, Mic. 5.5
47. Parable Teller, Ps. 78.1-2
48. Pierced One, Zech. 12.10

Old Testament Names, Titles, and Epithets for the Messiah (continued)

49. Poor and Afflicted, Ps. 69.29

50. Priestly Ruler, Jer. 30.21; Zech. 6.13

51. Prince, Ezek. 37.25; 44-48

52. Prince of Peace, Isa. 9.6

53. Proclaimer of Good Tidings to the Poor, Isa. 61.2

54. Prophet like Moses, Deut. 18.15,18

55. Redeemer, Job 19.25; Isa. 59.20

56. Refiner, Mal. 3.2

57. Refuge, Isa. 32.1

58. Rejected Shepherd, Zech. 11

59. Rejected Stone, Ps. 118.22

60. Righteous Shoot, Jer. 23.5; 33.15

61. Root out of Dry Ground, Isa. 53.2

62. Ruler of all Nature, Ps. 8.5-8

63. Ruler of the Earth, Isa. 16.5

64. Scepter, Num. 24.17

65. Second Moses, Hos. 11.1

66. Seed of Abraham, Gen. 12.3; 18.18

67. Seed of David, 2 Sam. 2.12

68. Seed of the Woman, Gen. 3.15

69. Servant, Isa. 42.1; 49.3, 6

70. Shade, Isa. 32.2

71. Shelter, Isa. 32.1

72. Shepherd, Ezek. 34.23; 37.24

73. Shiloh, Gen. 49.10

74. Shoot, Zech. 3.8; 6.12

75. Shoot from the Stump of Jesse, Isa. 11.1

76. Shoot of Yahweh, Isa. 4.2

77. Sign and Wonder, Isa. 8.18

78. Signet Ring, Hag. 2.23

79. Son of God, 2 Sam. 7.14; Ps. 2.7

80. Son of Man, Ps. 8.4; Dan. 7.13

81. Star, Num. 24.17

82. Stone, Zech. 3.9

83. Substitutionary Sufferer, Isa. 53

84. Sun of Righteousness, Mal. 4.5

85. Teacher, Isa. 30.20

86. Teacher for Righteousness, Joel 2.23

87. Tender Shoot, Isa. 53.2

88. Tender Twig, Ezek. 17.22

89. Temple Builder, Zech. 6.12

90. Tent Dweller, Gen. 9.26-27

91. Tested Stone, Isa. 28.16

92. Trailblazer, Ps. 16.11

93. Victor, Ps. 68.18

94. Volunteer, Ps. 40.7

95. Water of Life, Isa. 32.2

96. Witness, Job 16.19

97. Witness to the Peoples, Isa. 55.4

98. Wonderful Counselor, Isa. 9.6

99. Yahweh, Our Righteousness, Jer. 23.6

100. Zerubbabel, Hag. 2.23

Old Testament Witness to Christ and His Kingdom

Rev. Dr. Don L. Davis

Christ Is Seen in the OT's:	Covenant Promise and Fulfillment	Moral Law	Christophanies	Typology	Tabernacle, Festival, and Levitical Priesthood	Messianic Prophecy	Salvation Promises
Passage	Gen. 12.1-3	Matt. 5.17-18	John 1.18	1 Cor. 15.45	Heb. 8.1-6	Mic. 5.2	Isa. 9.6-7
Example	The Promised Seed of the Abrahamic covenant	The Law given on Mount Sinai	Commander of the Lord's army	Jonah and the great fish	Melchizedek, as both High Priest and King	The Lord's Suffering Servant	Righteous Branch of David
Christ As	Seed of the woman	The Prophet of God	God's present Revelation	Antitype of God's drama	Our eternal High Priest	The coming Son of Man	Israel's Redeemer and King
Where Illustrated	Galatians	Matthew	John	Matthew	Hebrews	Luke and Acts	John and Revelation
Exegetical Goal	To see Christ as heart of God's sacred drama	To see Christ as fulfillment of the Law	To see Christ as God's revealer	To see Christ as antitype of divine typos	To see Christ in the Temple cultus	To see Christ as true Messiah	To see Christ as coming King
How Seen in the NT	As fulfillment of God's sacred oath	As telos of the Law	As full, final, and superior revelation	As substance behind the historical shadows	As reality behind the rules and roles	As the Kingdom made present	As the One who will rule on David's throne
Our Response in Worship	God's veracity and faithfulness	God's perfect righteousness	God's presence among us	God's inspired Scripture	God's ontology: his realm as primary and determinative	God's anointed servant and mediator	God's resolve to restore his kingdom authority
How God Is Vindicated	God does not lie: he's true to his word	Jesus fulfills all righteousness	God's fullness is revealed to us in Jesus of Nazareth	The Spirit spoke by the prophets	The Lord has provided a mediator for humankind	Every jot and tittle written of him will occur	Evil will be put down, creation restored, under his reign

Once Upon a Time
The Cosmic Drama through a Biblical Narration of the World
Rev. Dr. Don L. Davis

From everlasting to everlasting, our Lord is God

From everlasting, in that matchless mystery of existence before time began, our Triune God dwelt in perfect splendor in eternal community as Father, Son, and Holy Spirit, the I AM, displaying his perfect attributes in eternal relationship, needing nothing, in boundless holiness, joy, and beauty. According to his sovereign will, our God purposed out of love to create a universe where his splendor would be revealed, and a world where his glory would be displayed and where a people made in his own image would dwell, sharing in fellowship with him and enjoying union with himself in relationship, all for his glory.

Who, as the Sovereign God, created a world
that would ultimately rebel against his rule

Inflamed by lust, greed, and pride, the first human pair rebelled against his will, deceived by the great prince, Satan, whose diabolical plot to supplant God as ruler of all resulted in countless angelic beings resisting God's divine will in the heavenlies. Through Adam and Eve's disobedience, they exposed themselves and their heirs to misery and death, and through their rebellion ushered creation into chaos, suffering, and evil. Through sin and rebellion, the union between God and creation was lost, and now all things are subject to the effects of this great fall– alienation, separation, and condemnation become the underlying reality for all things. No angel, human being, or creature can solve this dilemma, and without God's direct intervention, all the universe, the world, and all its creatures would be lost.

Yet, in mercy and loving-kindness, the Lord God promised
to send a Savior to redeem his creation

In sovereign covenantal love, God determined to remedy the effects of the universe's rebellion by sending a Champion, his only Son, who would take on the form of the fallen pair, embrace and overthrow their separation from God, and suffer in the place of all humankind for its sin and disobedience. So, through his covenant faithfulness, God became directly involved in human history for the sake of their salvation. The Lord God stoops to engage his creation for the sake of restoring it, to put down evil once and for all, and to establish a people out of which his Champion would come to establish his reign in this world once more.

So, he raised up a people from which the Governor would come

And so, through Noah, he saves the world from its own evil, through Abraham, he selects the clan through which the seed would come. Through Isaac, he continues the promise to Abraham, and through Jacob (Israel) he establishes his nation, identifying the tribe out of which he will come (Judah). Through Moses, he delivers his own from oppression and gives them his covenantal law, and through Joshua, he brings his people into the land of promise. Through judges and leaders he superintends his people, and through David, he covenants to bring a King from his clan who will reign forever. Despite his promise, though, his people fall short of his covenant time after time. Their stubborn and persistent rejection of the Lord finally leads to the nation's judgment, invasion, overthrow, and captivity. Mercifully, he remembers his covenant and allows a remnant to return – for the promise and the story were not done.

Who, as Champion, came down from heaven, in the fullness of time, and won through the Cross

Some four hundred years of silence occurred. Yet, in the fullness of time, God fulfilled his covenant promise by entering into this realm of evil, suffering, and alienation through the incarnation. In the person of Jesus of Nazareth, God came down from heaven and lived among us, displaying the Father's glory, fulfilling the requirements of God's moral law, and demonstrating the power of the Kingdom of God in his words, works, and exorcisms. On the Cross he took on our rebellion, destroyed death, overcame the devil, and rose on the third day to restore creation from the Fall, to make an end of sin, disease, and war, and to grant never-ending life to all people who embrace his salvation.

And, soon and very soon, he will return to this world and make all things new

Ascended to the Father's right hand, the Lord Jesus Christ has sent the Holy Spirit into the world, forming a new people made up of both Jew and Gentile, the Church. Commissioned under his headship, they testify in word and deed the gospel of reconciliation to the whole creation, and when they have completed their task, he will return in glory and complete his work for creation and all creatures. Soon, he will put down sin, evil, death, and the effects of the Curse forever, and restore all creation under its true rule, refreshing all things in a new heavens and new earth, where all beings and all creation will enjoy the shalom of the triune God forever, to his glory and honor alone.

And the redeemed shall live happily ever after . . .

The End

Our Declaration of Dependence: Freedom in Christ

Rev. Dr. Don L. Davis, January 11, 2003

It is important to teach morality within the realm of freedom (i.e., Gal. 5.1, "It is for freedom Christ has set you free"), and always in the context of using your freedom in the framework of bringing God glory and advancing Christ's Kingdom. I emphasize the "6-8-10" principles of 1 Corinthians, and apply them to all moral issues.

1. 1 Cor. 6.9-11, Christianity is about transformation in Christ; no amount of excuses will get a person into the Kingdom.

2. 1 Cor. 6.12a, We are free in Christ, but not everything one does is edifying or helpful.

3. 1 Cor. 6.12b, We are free in Christ, but anything that is addictive and exercising control over you is counter to Christ and his Kingdom.

4. 1 Cor. 8.7-13, We are free in Christ, but we ought never to flaunt our freedom, especially in the face of Christians whose conscience would be marred and who would stumble if they saw us doing something they found offensive.

5. 1 Cor. 10.23, We are free in Christ; all things are lawful for us, but neither is everything helpful, nor does doing everything build oneself up.

6. 1 Cor. 10.24, We are free in Christ, and ought to use our freedom to love our brothers and sisters in Christ, and nurture them for other's well being (cf. Gal. 5.13).

7. 1 Cor. 10.31, We are free in Christ, and are given that freedom in order that we might glorify God in all that we do, whether we eat or drink, or anything else.

8. 1 Cor. 10.32-33, We are free in Christ, and ought to use our freedom in order to do what we can to give no offense to people in the world or the Church, but do what we do in order to influence them to know and love Christ, i.e., that they might be saved.

This focus on freedom, in my mind, places all things that we say to adults or teens in context. Often, the way in which many new Christians are discipled is through a rigorous taxonomy (listing) of different vices and moral ills, and this can at times give them the sense that Christianity is an anti-act religion (a religion of simply not doing things), and/or a faith overly concerned with not sinning. Actually, the moral focus in Christianity is on freedom, a freedom won at a high price, a freedom to love God and advance the Kingdom, a freedom to live a surrendered life before the Lord. The moral responsibility of urban Christians is to live free in Jesus Christ, to live free unto God's glory, and to not use their freedom from the law as a license for sin.

The core of the teaching, then, is to focus on the freedom won for us through Christ's death and resurrection, and our union with him. We are now set free from the law, the principle of sin and death, the condemnation and guilt of our own sin, and the conviction of the law on us. We serve God now out of gratitude and thankfulness, and the moral impulse is living free in Christ. Yet, we do not use our freedom to be wiseguys or knuckle-heads, but to glorify God and love others. This is the context in which we address the thorny issues of homosexuality, abortion, and other social ills. Those who engage in such acts feign freedom, but, lacking a knowledge of God in Christ, they are merely following their own internal predispositions, which are not informed either by God's moral will or his love.

Freedom in Christ is a banner call to live holy and joyously as urban disciples. This freedom will enable them to see how creative they can be as Christians in the midst of so-called "free" living which only leads to bondage, shame, and remorse.

Overview of Church Plant Planning Phases

Rev. Dr. Don L. Davis

	Prepare	Launch	Assemble	Nurture	Transition
Definition	Forming a team of called members who ready themselves to plant a church under the Holy Spirit's direction	Penetrating the selected community by conducting evangelistic events among the target population	Gathering the cells of converts together to form a local assembly of believers, announcing the new church to the neighbors in the community	Nurturing member and leadership discipleship, enabling members to function in their spiritual gifts, and establishing solid infrastructure within the Christian assembly	Empowering the church for independence by equipping leaders for autonomy, transferring authority, and creating structures for financial independence
Purpose	Seek God regarding the target population and community, the formation of your church plant team, organizing strategic intercession for the community, and doing research on its needs and opportunities	Mobilize team and recruit volunteers to conduct ongoing evangelistic events and holistic outreach to win associates and neighbors to Christ	Form cell groups, Bible studies, or home fellowships for follow-up, continued evangelism, and ongoing growth toward public birth of the church	Develop individual and group discipleship by filling key roles in the body based on burden and gifting of members	Commission members and elders, install pastor, and foster church associations
Parent-Child Metaphor	Decision and Conception	Pre-natal Care	Childbirth	Growth and Parenting	Maturity to Adulthood
Question Focus During Dialogue	Questions about: • Preparing your team • The target community • Strategic prayer initiatives • Demographic studies	Questions about: • Character and number of evangelistic events • Communication and advertisement of events • Recruiting and coordinating volunteers • Identity and name of the outreach	Questions about: • Follow-up and incorporation of new believers • Make-up of small group life • The character of public worship • Initial church structures and procedures • Initial body life and growth • Cultural friendliness of church	Questions about: • Discipling individuals and leaders • Helping members identify gifts and burdens (teams) • Credentials for leadership • Church order, government and discipline	Questions about: • Incorporation • Affiliations and associations • Transferring leadership • Missionary transition • Ongoing reproduction
Cardinal Virtue	Openness to the Lord	Courage to engage the community	Wisdom to discern God's timing	Focus upon the faithful core	Dependence on the Spirit's ability
Cardinal Vices	Presumption and "paralysis of analysis"	Intimidation and haughtiness	Impatience and cowardice	Neglect and micromanagement	Paternalism and quick release
Bottom Line	Cultivate a period of listening and reflecting	Initiate your engagement with boldness and confidence	Celebrate the announcement of your body with joy	Concentrate on investing in the faithful	Pass the baton with confidence in the Spirit's continued working

Overview Plant to Birth Models

Rev. Dr. Don L. Davis

World Impact Model	Phases of Church Planting Compared to Childbirth	Emphasis During Particular Phase of Childbearing
Prepare	Commitment to Parent	Commitment to give birth and to parent secured from qualified parents
	Conception	Core team, volunteers gathered/prepared, parenting church engaged, target population and community selected, studied, canvassed
Launch	Prenatal Care	Ongoing outreach, small group community, structured in-reach of nucleus
Assemble	Birth	Announcement of public gathering and worship, celebration of gathered groups
Nurture	Growth Toward Maturity	Building foundations, developing vital ministries, forming systems, achieving leadership autonomy
Transition	Reproduction	Congregational "adulthood," new church as kingdom outpost: spiritual DNA planting new congregations

The Parables of Jesus

adapted from The Bible Made Easy. Peabody: Hendrickson Publishers, 1997.

1	The Good Samaritan	Luke 10.30-37		21	The Fruitless Fig Tree	Luke 13.6-9
2	The Lost Sheep	Luke 15.4-6		22	The Leafless Fig Tree	Luke 21.29-31
3	The Lost Coin	Luke 15.8-10		23	The Mustard Seed	Luke 13.18-19
4	The Prodigal Son	Luke 15.11-32		24	The Leaven	Luke 13.20-21
5	The Dishonest Manager	Luke 16.1-8		25	The Wedding Guests	Luke 14.7-14
6	The Rich Man and Lazarus	Luke 16.1-8		26	The Great Banquet	Luke 14.16-24
7	The Servants	Luke 17.7-10		27	Tower Building and Warfare	Luke 14.28-33
8	The Persistent Widow	Luke 18.2-5		28	The Pharisee and the Publican	Luke 18.10-14
9	The Talents	Luke 19.12-27		29	The Returning House Owner	Mark 12.1-9
10	The Wicked Tenants	Luke 20.9-16		30	The Growing Seed	Mark 4.26-29
11	New Cloth	Luke 5.36		31	The Weeds	Matt. 13.24-30
12	New Wine	Luke 5.37-38		32	The Hidden Treasure	Matt. 13.44
13	The House on the Rock	Luke 6.47-49		33	The Pearl of Great Price	Matt. 13.45-46
14	Two Debtors	Luke 7.41-43		34	The Net	Matt. 13.47-48
15	The Sower	Luke 8.5-8		35	The Unforgiving Servant	Matt. 18.23-24
16	The Lamp	Luke 16.1-12		36	The Workers in the Vineyard	Matt. 20.1-16
17	The Watching Servants	Luke 12.35-40		37	The Two Sons	Matt. 21.28-31
18	The Persistent Friend	Luke 11.5-8		38	The Ten Virgins	Matt. 25.1-13
19	The Rich Fool	Luke 12.16-21		39	The Sheep and the Goats	Matt. 25.31-36
20	The Faithful Steward	Luke 12.42-48		40	The Wedding Banquet	Matt. 22.2-14

Paul's Partnership Theology
Our Union with Christ and Partnership in Kingdom Ministry
Adapted from Brian J. Dodd. **Empowered Church Leadership**. *Downers Grove: InterVarsity Press, 2003.*

The apostolic fondness for Greek terms compounded with the prefix syn (with or co-)

English Translation of the Greek Term	Scripture References
Co-worker (*Synergos*)	Rom 16.3, 7, 9, 21; 2 Cor. 8.23; Phil. 2.25; 4.3; Col. 4.7, 10, 11, 14; Philem. 1, 24
Co-prisoner (*Synaichmalotos*)	Col. 4.10; Philem. 23
Co-slave (*Syndoulous*)	Col. 1.7; 4.7
Co-soldier (*Systratiotes*)	Phil. 2.25; Philem. 2
Co-laborer (*Synathleo*)	Phil. 4.2-3

Paul's Team Members

Don L. Davis

Achaicus, A Corinthian who visited Paul at Philippi, 1 Cor. 16.17.

Archippus, Colossian disciple whom Paul exhorted to fulfill his ministry, Col. 4.17; Philem. 2.

Aquila, Jewish disciple Paul found at Corinth, Acts 18.2, 18, 26; Rom. 16.3; 1 Cor. 16.19; 2 Tim. 4.19.

Aristarchus, With Paul on 3rd journey, Acts 19.29; 20.4; 27.2; Col. 4.10; Philem. 24.

Artemas, Companion of Paul at Nicopolis, Titus 3.12.

Barnabas, A Levite, cousin of John Mark, and companion with Paul in several of his journeys, cf. Acts 4.36, 9.27; 11.22, 25, 30; 12.25; chs. 13, 14, and 15; 1 Cor. 9.6; Gal. 2.1, 9, 13; Col. 4.13.

Carpus, Disciple of Troas, 2 Tim. 4.13.

Claudia, Female disciple of Rome, 2 Tim. 4.21.

Clement, Fellow-laborer at Phillipi, Phil. 4.3.

Crescens, A disciple at Rome, 2 Tim. 4.10.

Demas, A laborer of Paul at Rome, Col. 4.14; Philem. 24; 2 Tim. 4.10.

Epaphras, Fellow laborer and prisoner, Col. 1.7, 4.12; Philem. 23.

Epaphroditus, Messenger between Paul and the churches, Phil. 2.25, 4.18.

Eubulus, Disciple of Rome, 2 Tim. 4.21.

Euodia, Christian woman of Philippi, Phil. 4.2

Fortunatus, Part of the Corinthian team, 1 Cor. 16.17.

Gaius, 1) A Macedonian companion, Acts 19.29; 2) A disciple/companion in Derbe, Acts 20.4.

Jesus (Justus), A Jewish disciple at Colossae, Col. 4.11.

John Mark, Companion of Paul and cousin of Barnabas, Acts 12.12, 15; 15.37, 39; Col. 4.10; 2 Tim. 4.11; Philem. 24.

Linus, A Roman Companion of Paul, 2 Tim. 4.21.

Luke, Physician and fellow-traveler with Paul, Col. 4.14; 2 Tim. 4.11; Philem. 24.

Onesimus, Native of Colossae and slave of Philemon who served Paul, Col. 4.9; Philem. 10.

Hermogenes, A team member who abandoned Paul in prison, 2 Tim. 1.15.

Phygellus, One with Hermogenes turned from Paul in Asia, 2 Tim. 1.15.

Priscilla (Prisca), Wife of Aquila of Pontus and fellow-worker in the Gospel, Acts 18.2, 18, 26; Rom. 16.3; 1 Cor. 16.19.

Pudens, A Roman companion of Paul, 2 Tim. 4.21.

Secundus, Companion of Paul on his way from Greece to Syria, Acts 20.4.

Silas, Disciple, fellow laborer, and prisoner with Paul, Acts 15.22, 27, 32, 34, 40; 16.19, 25, 29; 17.4, 10, etc.

Sopater, Accompanied Paul to Syria, Acts 20.4.

Sosipater, Kinsman of Paul, Rom. 16.21.

Silvanus, Probably same as Silas, 2 Cor. 1.19; 1 Thess. 1.1; 2 Thess. 1.1.

Sosthenes, Chief Ruler of the Synagogue of Corinth, laborer with Paul there, Acts 18.17.

Stephanus, One of the first believers of Achaia and visitor to Paul, 1 Cor. 1.16; 16.15; 16.17.

Syntyche, One of Paul's female "fellow workers" in Philippi, Phil. 4.2.

Tertius, Slave and person who wrote the Epistle to the Romans, Rom. 16.22.

Timothy, A young man of Lystra with a Jewish mother and Greek father who labored on with Paul in his ministry, Acts 16.1;17.14, 15; 18.5; 19.22; 20.4; Rom. 16.21; 1 Cor. 4.17; 16.10; 2 Cor. 1.1, 19; Phil. 1.1; 2.19; Col. 1.1; 1 Thess. 1.1; 3.2, 6; 2 Thess. 1.1; 1 Tim. 1.2, 18; 6.20; 2 Tim. 1.2; Philem. 1; Heb. 13.23.

Titus, Greek disciple and co-laborer of Paul, 2 Cor. 2.13; 7.6, 13, 14; 8.6, 16, 23; 12.18; Gal. 2.1, 3; 2 Tim. 4.10; Titus 1.4.

Trophimus, A Ephesian disciple who accompanied Paul to Jerusalem from Greece, Acts 20.4; 21.29; 2 Tim. 4.20.

Tryphena and Tryphosa, Female disciples of Rome, probably twins, who Paul calls laborers in the Lord, Rom. 16.12.

Tychicus, A disciple of Asia Minor who accompanied Paul in various trips, Acts 20.4; Eph. 6.21; Col. 4.7; 2 Tim. 4.12; Titus 3.12.

Urbanus, Roman disciple and aid to Paul, Rom. 16.9.

A People Reborn

Foundational Insights on People Movements

Donald McGavran

This article was taken from Mission Frontiers: The Bulletin of the US Center for World Mission,
Vol. 27, No. 5; September-October 2005; ISSN 0889-9436.

Editor's note: What follows are excerpts from the late Donald McGavran's foreword to the English edition of Christian Keysser's classic book, A People Reborn (William Carey Library, 1980). McGavran's pen portraits and autobiographical notes reveal the extent to which, consciously or not, today's proponents of either insider movements or church-planting movements are building on foundations laid by pioneers such as Keysser, McGavran, and others in the first half of the 20th century. Note, in the final paragraph, McGavran's prescient observations about mission in the 21st century.

[Christian Keysser] was born in Bavaria in 1877, went to Kaiser Wilhelm Land (East New Guinea) in 1899, and remained in or near Sattelberg as a missionary till 1921, when he returned to Germany.... A literal translation of [Keysser's book] is *A New Guinean Congregation*. A truer, better title is: *A People Reborn: Caring Communities, Their Birth and Development.* . . .

People Movements to Christ

. . . Around 1900 Keysser found himself evangelizing the Kate (pronounced Kawtai or kotte) tribe in the mountains near the sea.... Keysser's genius recognized that Christianization ought to preserve this people consciousness, and transform it into Tribal Christianity or Folk Christianity. . . .

In 1935, largely through [Waskom] Pickett's writings and lectures, I woke to a discipling of ethnic units. I accompanied him while he studied missions in Mid-India and contributed several chapters to his *Christian Missions in Mid-India*, 1938. I, too, saw that the goal was not one-by-one conversion out of the castes and tribes, but rather the conversion of social units which remained part of the caste or tribe, and continued living in their ancestral homes. For the next two decades I worked at encouraging a Satnami people movement to develop – and failed. In 1955, my *Bridges of God* called castewise or tribal movements to Christian

Faith "people movements".… What Keysser, Pickett and [Bruno] Gutmann had described in New Guinea, India and Tanganyika – *Bridges of God* – indebted only to Pickett, described in universal terms.

The discovery of all of us was that group decisions, which preserved the corporate life of the society and enabled men and women to become Christians without social dislocation, was the route by which most humans have moved to Christian Faith from non-Christian Faith, and was a good route. For all four of us, the discovery was difficult because missionaries came out of the most dedicated parts of the Western Church. They had learned that real Christians are those who individually and at great cost believe in Jesus Christ, love Him, obey His word, and venture out alone across the seven seas to do His bidding. They believed that "one-by-one-against-the-tide" was the right, the best, and often the only way for men and women to become Christians. . . .

Keysser's discovery in 1903 should be seen against his common erroneous conviction. He broke through that mindset to see that for a people to come to Christ "with social structure intact" was the best possible way. He, of course, went on immediately to describe the way in which such a people movement should be nurtured, guarded against formalism, fed on the Word, and made strong through constant exercise of its Christian options. This is his great contribution. His book is essential reading for any who wish to understand a) that discipling ethnic units is a splendid way for multitudes to become Christian, and b) how discipling and perfecting can be done so they result in genuine Christians in a truly Christian Congregation – a true Homogeneous Unit Church.

The Objective Thinker

. . . The people movement really began to roll. The outlying clans and villages clamored to become Christian, precisely because they saw that the Christians had become *greatly changed for the better*. This is the fundamental reason why people movements occur. Human beings are highly intelligent. After all, man is homo sapiens. When he sees that the new order, the Church, is actually different from and *superior* to the old order, then homo sapiens in corporate decisions moves to Christian Faith. A chain reaction runs through the tribal fabric. Congregations multiply. In general, it may be said that the higher the standard of Christianity achieved by the first groups to become Christian, the more influential is their example. Keysser, the objective thinker, saw this. . . .

Forming a True Congregation

[Another reason] why missiologists will profit from this book is Keysser's determined emphasis on the privilege and duty of the missionary *to form a Christian congregation out of various villages and clans.* By this he does not mean taking individuals, as separate pebbles, and forming them into a new organization called the church. Rather, he means taking the social organism, which the clan or village had been from time immemorial, and by exposing it to God's will and God's Word, and by leading it to act in a Christian fashion *transforming it into a Christian tribe.* This is not done simply by baptizing it. Hearing the Gospel, seeing the Gospel, receiving ample instruction, some of it in dramatic form, being baptized with clanal approval, and then for years led by the missionary and the Word, thinking through what in specific circumstances Christ requires the village, clan or tribe (the Christian Congregation) to do – all these steps are required to transform non-Christian social units into a Christian congregation. . . .

Dr. Keysser's adverse judgments concerning the churches in Germany must be seen as part of his convictions concerning the True Church. Throughout this volume he criticizes congregations in Germany for not being true communities, i.e. true *congregations.* . . . When in 1922 Keysser went back to Germany, he experienced culture shock in reverse. He found "churches" which as churches exercised little if any pastoral care of their members. . . . The congregations were not real communities. . . .

Today, when the establishment of caring communities in western churches has become one of the main purposes of contemporary Christianity, Keysser's comments about the German Church are particularly pertinent. They can be affirmed about the Church in most developed nations. When society becomes fragmented, individualism rages out of control and loneliness afflicts millions. The Church must provide loving, caring, powerful *communities.* Life is richest when lived in such. In the ancient world New Testament churches were such communities. Churches can again become such in New Guinea and New York, in Tokyo and Berlin, and in short, in every land. *True Churches are functioning communities.*

. . . Professor Keysser has given the world of mission many insights which will be of great use in the coming century. In his day, animistic tribes were turning to Christ by people movements and forming genuine communities (congregations) in the Christian fold. In the twenty-first century, we shall see great segments of developing *and developed* nations turn to Christian Faith without social dislocation. They will remain real communities in becoming real congregations. Modern missiology is indebted to Christian Keysser.

Perception and Truth

Rev. Dr. Don L. Davis

Levels of Perception

What is really happening
What is apparent
What you see
What others see
What the enemy sees
What the enemy wants you to think about what you see
What God sees
What God wants you to know about what you see

The Present Situation

What's going on here?
What does this mean?

State of unawareness
Distraction and preoccupation
Proneness to doubt

Keen spiritual awareness
Spiritually alert
Sober and Ready to fight

4 Your Current Spiritual, Experiential, and Psychological Predisposition ("Habits of the Heart")

3 Opinions of Key People

Significant Others
Leaders
Experts
Friends and Family

2 The Common Prognosis

What usually happens
What we can expect
What it feels like

1 The So-Called "Facts" of the Matter

What is apparent to all of us
What we're going through
Our initial reactions and categories

5 The Lying Persuasion of the Enemy ("Dirty Fighter")

Awareness of deep inadequacy
Fear of vulnerability
Impossibility of change
Certainty of chronic bondage
Prospect of failure

6 The Testimony of the Divine Promise

Certainty of God's supply
Assurance of safety
Possibility of radical transformation
Power of Divine deliverance
Affirmation of victory

Picking Up on Different Wavelengths
Integrated vs. Fragmented Mindsets and Lifestyles
Dr. Don L. Davis

A Fragmented Mindset and Lifestyle	An Integrated Lifestyle and Mindset
Sees things primarily in relation to one's own needs	Sees all things as one and whole
Sees something other than God as a substitute point of reference and coordination for meaning and truth	Sees God in Christ as the ultimate point of reference and coordination for all meaning and truth
Seeks God's blessing upon one's own personal enhancement	Aligns personal goals with God's ultimate plan and purposes
Understands the purpose of life to experience the greatest level of personal fulfillment and enhancement possible	Understands the purpose of life to make the maximum contribution possible to God's purpose in the world
Only relates to others in connection to their effect upon and place within one's individual personal space	Deeply identifies with all people and things as an integral part of God's great plan for his own glory
Defines theology as seeking to express someone's perspective on some religious idea or concept	Defines theology as seeking to comprehend God's ultimate designs and plans for himself in Jesus Christ
Applications are rooted in seeking right responses to particular issues and situations	Applications are byproducts of understanding what God is doing for himself in the world
Focuses on the style of analysis (to discern the processes and make-up of things)	Focuses on the style of synthesis (to discern the connection and unity of all things)
Seeks to understand biblical revelation primarily from the standpoint of one's private life ("God's plan for my life")	Seeks to understand biblical revelation primarily from the standpoint of God's plan for whole ("God's plan for the ages")
Governed by pressing concerns to ensure one's own security and significance in one's chosen endeavors ("My personal life plan")	Decision making is governed by commitment to participate as co-workers with God in the overall vision ("God's working in the world")
Coordinates itself around personal need as a working paradigm and project	Connects and correlates itself around God's vision and plan as a working paradigm
Sees mission and ministry as the expression of one's personal giftedness and burden, bringing personal satisfaction and security	Sees mission and ministry as the present, practical expression of one's identity vis-a-vis the panoramic vision of God
Relates knowledge, opportunity, and activity to the goals of personal enhancement and fulfillment	Relates knowledge, opportunity, and activity to a single, integrated vision and purpose
All of life is perceived to revolve around the personal identity and needs of the individual	All of life is perceived to revolve around a single theme: the revelation of God in Jesus of Nazareth

Picking Up on Different Wavelengths (continued)

Scriptures on the Validity of Seeing All Things as Unified and Whole

Ps. 27.4 (ESV) - One thing have I asked of the Lord, that will I seek after: that I may dwell in the house of the Lord all the days of my life, to gaze upon the beauty of the Lord and to inquire in his temple.

Luke 10.39-42 (ESV) - And she had a sister called Mary, who sat at the Lord's feet and listened to his teaching. [40] But Martha was distracted with much serving. And she went up to him and said, "Lord, do you not care that my sister has left me to serve alone? Tell her then to help me." [41] But the Lord answered her, "Martha, Martha, you are anxious and troubled about many things, [42] but one thing is necessary. Mary has chosen the good portion, which will not be taken away from her."

Phil. 3.13-14 (ESV) - Brothers, I do not consider that I have made it my own. But one thing I do: forgetting what lies behind and straining forward to what lies ahead [14] I press on toward the goal for the prize of the upward call of God in Christ Jesus.

Ps. 73.25 (ESV) - Whom have I in heaven but you? And there is nothing on earth that I desire besides you.

Mark 8.36 (ESV) - For what does it profit a man to gain the whole world and forfeit his life?

Luke 18.22 (ESV) - When Jesus heard this, he said to him, "One thing you still lack. Sell all that you have and distribute to the poor, and you will have treasure in heaven; and come, follow me."

John 17.3 (ESV) - And this is eternal life, that they know you the only true God, and Jesus Christ whom you have sent.

1 Cor. 13.3 (ESV) - If I give away all I have, and if I deliver up my body to be burned, but have not love, I gain nothing.

Gal. 5.6 (ESV) - For in Christ Jesus neither circumcision nor uncircumcision counts for anything, but only faith working through love.

Col. 2.8-10 (ESV) - See to it that no one takes you captive by philosophy and empty deceit, according to human tradition, according to the elemental spirits of the world, and not according to Christ. [9] For in him the whole fullness of deity dwells bodily, [10] and you have been filled in him, who is the head of all rule and authority.

1 John 5.11-12 (ESV) - And this is the testimony, that God gave us eternal life, and this life is in his Son. [12] Whoever has the Son has life; whoever does not have the Son of God does not have life.

Ps. 16.5 (ESV) - The Lord is my chosen portion and my cup; you hold my lot.

Ps. 16.11 (ESV) - You make known to me the path of life; in your presence there is fullness of joy; at your right hand are pleasures forevermore.

Ps. 17.15 (ESV) - As for me, I shall behold your face in righteousness; when I awake, I shall be satisfied with your likeness.

Eph. 1.9-10 (ESV) - making known to us the mystery of his will, according to his purpose, which he set forth in Christ [10] as a plan for the fullness of time, to unite all things in him, things in heaven and things on earth.

John 15.5 (ESV) - I am the vine; you are the branches. Whoever abides in me and I in him, he it is that bears much fruit, for apart from me you can do nothing.

Ps. 42.1 (ESV) - As a deer pants for flowing streams, so pants my soul for you, O God.

Hab. 3.17-18 (ESV) - Though the fig tree should not blossom, nor fruit be on the vines, the produce of the olive fail and the fields yield no food, the flock be cut off from the fold and there be no herd in the stalls, [18] yet I will rejoice in the Lord; I will take joy in the God of my salvation.

Matt. 10.37 (ESV) - Whoever loves father or mother more than me is not worthy of me, and whoever loves son or daughter more than me is not worthy of me.

Ps. 37.4 (ESV) - Delight yourself in the Lord, and he will give you the desires of your heart.

Ps. 63.3 (ESV) - Because your steadfast love is better than life, my lips will praise you.

Picking Up on Different Wavelengths (continued)

Ps. 89.6 (ESV) - For who in the skies can be compared to the Lord? Who among the heavenly beings is like the Lord

Phil. 3.8 (ESV) - Indeed, I count everything as loss because of the surpassing worth of knowing Christ Jesus my Lord. For his sake I have suffered the loss of all things and count them as rubbish, in order that I may gain Christ

1 John 3.2 (ESV) - Beloved, we are God's children now, and what we will be has not yet appeared; but we know that when he appears we shall be like him, because we shall see him as he is.

Rev. 21.3 (ESV) - And I heard a loud voice from the throne saying, "Behold, the dwelling place of God is with man. He will dwell with them, and they will be his people, and God himself will be with them as their God.

Rev. 21.22-23 (ESV) - And I saw no temple in the city, for its temple is the Lord God the Almighty and the Lamb. [23] And the city has no need of sun or moon to shine on it, for the glory of God gives it light, and its lamp is the Lamb.

Ps. 115.3 (ESV) - Our God is in the heavens; he does all that he pleases.

Jer. 32.17 (ESV) - Ah, Lord God! It is you who has made the heavens and the earth by your great power and by your outstretched arm! Nothing is too hard for you.

Dan. 4.35 (ESV) - all the inhabitants of the earth are accounted as nothing, and he does according to his will among the host of heaven and among the inhabitants of the earth; and none can stay his hand or say to him, "What have you done?"

Eph. 3.20-21 (ESV) - Now to him who is able to do far more abundantly than all that we ask or think, according to the power at work within us, [21] to him be glory in the Church and in Christ Jesus throughout all generations, forever and ever. Amen.

The Picture and the Drama

Image and Story in the Recovery of Biblical Myth

Don L. Davis

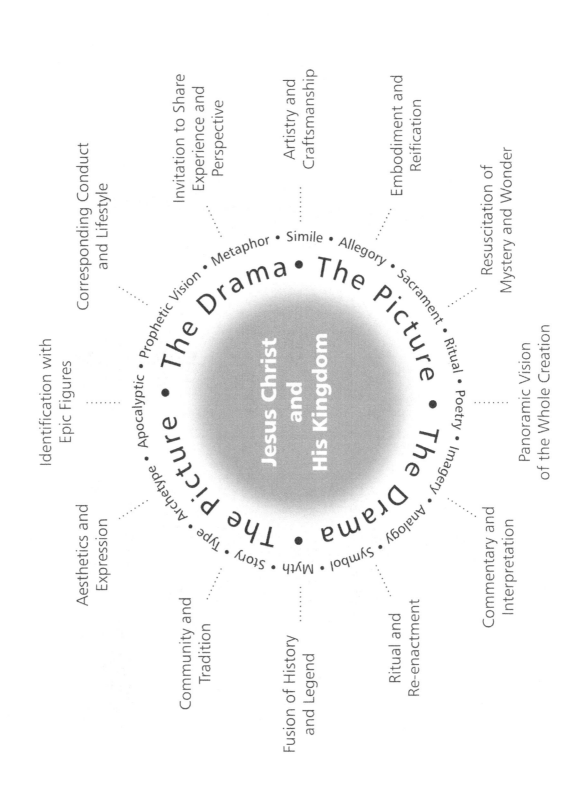

Jesus Christ and His Kingdom

The Drama • The Picture • The Drama • The Picture

Prophetic Vision • Metaphor • Simile • Allegory • Sacrament • Ritual • Poetry • Imagery • Analogy • Symbol • Myth • Story • Type • Archetype • Apocalyptic •

- Invitation to Share Experience and Perspective
- Artistry and Craftsmanship
- Embodiment and Reification
- Resuscitation of Mystery and Wonder
- Panoramic Vision of the Whole Creation
- Commentary and Interpretation
- Ritual and Re-enactment
- Fusion of History and Legend
- Community and Tradition
- Aesthetics and Expression
- Identification with Epic Figures
- Corresponding Conduct and Lifestyle

Plot Line of the Church Year
Rev. Ryan Carter

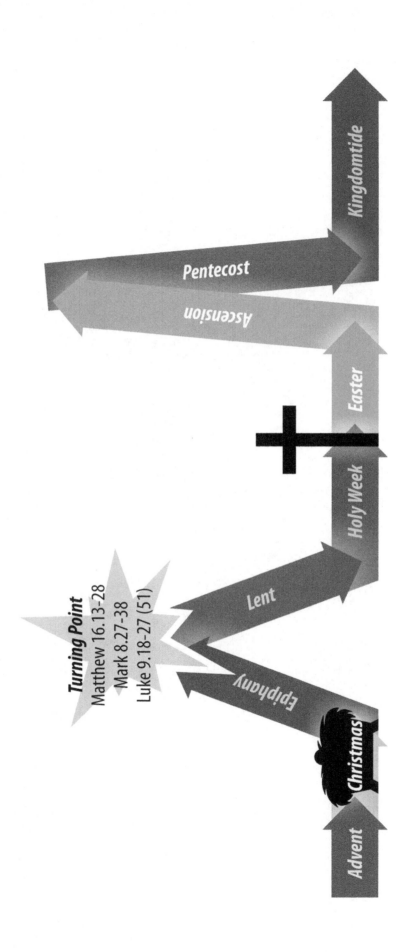

Portrayals of Jesus in the New Testament Books

Adapted from John Stott, The Incomparable Christ

The Thirteen Letters of Paul				
Approximate Date of Writing	Period	Group	Letters	How Messiah is Presented
48-49	End of 1st missionary journey	A polemical letter	Galatians	Christ the Liberator
50-52	During 2nd missionary journey	The early letters	1 and 2 Thessalonians	Christ the Coming Judge
53-57	During 3rd missionary journey	The major letters	Romans, 1 and 2 Corinthians	Christ the Savior
60-62	During 1st imprisonment in Rome	The prison letters	Colossians, Philemon, Ephesians, and Philippians	Christ the Supreme Lord
62-67	During release and 2nd imprisonment	The pastoral letters	1 and 2 Timothy and Titus	Christ the Head of the Church
General Epistles and Revelation				
Before 70	During the Pauline and Petrine ministry	Epistle to believing Jews	Hebrews	Christ our Great High Priest
45-50	First book of the NT to be written	General epistles	James	Christ our Teacher
64-67	Early period of persecution	General epistles	1 and 2 Peter	Christ our Exemplary Sufferer
90-100	Toward end of Apostle's ministry	General epistles	1, 2, and 3 John	Christ our Life
66-69	Threat and rise of early apostasy	General epistles	Jude	Christ our Advocate
95	Written while in exile	Prophecy	Revelation	King of kings and Lord of lords

Preaching and Teaching
Jesus of Nazareth as Messiah and Lord
Is the Heart of All Biblical Ministry

Don L. Davis

Phil. 3.8 (ESV) - Indeed, I count everything as loss because of the surpassing worth of *knowing Christ [Messiah] Jesus my Lord*. For his sake I have suffered the loss of all things and count them as rubbish, in order *that I may gain Christ [Messiah]*.

Acts 5.42 (ESV) - And every day, in the temple and from house to house, they *did not cease teaching and preaching Jesus as the Christ [Messiah]*.

1 Cor. 1.23 (ESV) - but we preach *Christ [Messiah] crucified*, a stumbling block to Jews and folly to Gentiles.

2 Cor. 4.5 (ESV) - For what we proclaim is not ourselves, but *Jesus Christ [Messiah] as Lord*, with ourselves as your servants for Jesus' sake.

1 Cor. 2.2 (ESV) - For I decided to know nothing among you except *Jesus Christ [Messiah] and him crucified*.

Eph. 3.8 (ESV) - To me, though I am the very least of all the saints, this grace was given, *to preach to the Gentiles the unsearchable riches of Christ [Messiah]*.

Phil. 1.18 (ESV) - What then? Only that in every way, whether in pretense or in truth, *Christ [Messiah] is proclaimed*, and in that I rejoice. Yes, and I will rejoice.

Col. 1.27-29 (ESV) - To them God chose to make known how great among the Gentiles are the riches of the glory of this mystery, which is *Christ [Messiah] in you, the hope of glory*. [28] Him we proclaim, warning everyone and teaching everyone with all wisdom, that we may *present everyone mature in Christ [Messiah]*. [29] *For this I toil, struggling with all his energy* that he powerfully works within me.

Principles Behind Prophecy

Dr. Don L. Davis

1. Prophecy provides divinely inspired truth about God, his universe, and his will.

   - Who is God and what is the nature of the "real"?

   - What is the truth, and how can we know it?

   - Where did we come from, why are we here, and how shall we act?

2. Prophecy originates and has its source in the Holy Spirit.

   - It is his gift (Rom. 12.6; 1 Cor. 12.10; Eph. 4.8).

   - Prophet = "person of the Spirit," *pneumatikos* (1 Cor. 14.37 and Hos. 9.7)

   - The hope of Moses (Num. 11.16, 29; cf. Luke 10.1)

3. Diverse and various forms of revelation (Jer. 18.18, Law from the priest, counsel from the wise, and word from the prophet).

   - Lived in communities and guilds, some were attached to the temple, while others were priests (cf. 2 Kings 2.3ff.; Ezek. 1.3; Jer. 1.1).

   - Sages and wisdom teachers were "recipients and mediators" of the divine gift (cf. Gen. 41.38; 2 Sam. 14.20; 16.23; 1 Kings 3.9, etc.).

   - Wisdom teacher and prophet both: Daniel.

4. Prophecy not self-authenticating: it must be judged valid.

   - Conflict existed between prophets within both the Old Testament and New Testament (cf. 1 Kings 22; Jer. 23; 28 and 2 Cor. 11.4, 13; 1 John 4.1-3).

   - Prophetic claims must agree with Moses (Deut. 13.1-5) and Jesus (Matt. 7.15; 24.11; 2 Pet. 2.1).

   - If the word comes to pass, it is from the Lord (Deut. 18.15-22).

   - All prophecy is to be examined for its truth value (1 Thess. 5.19-21).

5. The testimony of Jesus is the spirit of prophecy (Rev. 19.10).

   - Prophecy speaks to Messiah's suffering and glory (Luke 24.25-27; 44).

   - The prophetic Scriptures focus on his person and work (John 5.39-40).

   - Apostolic preaching connected him to their message (Acts 3.12-18; 10.43; 13.27; Rom. 3.21-22; 1 Pet. 1.10-12; 2 Pet. 1.19-21).

The Profile of a 21st-Century Disciple

Rev. Dr. Don L. Davis

1. **He/she enjoys an intimate communion with the Lord (John 10.1-6; 15.12-14).**

   a. Is unconditionally available to Christ as Lord (filled with the Holy Spirit)

   b. Hungers to become more and more like Christ in vision, character, and service

   c. Solid devotional life of personal worship, meditation, and prayer

   d. Lifestyle of praise, worship, and celebration

   e. Abiding trust in the leading and provision of God in Christ

   f. Glorifies God in the temple of his/her body, mind, and spirit

2. **He/she upholds a believing stance grounded upon a biblical vision of Christ and his Kingdom (John 8.31-32).**

   a. Thorough understanding of the Holy Scriptures (i.e. its themes, history, and key principles)

   b. Maintains a Christ-centered world view, seeing life from God's vantage point

   c. Grounded in the fundamentals of the faith, able to share and reproduce them

   d. Growing ability to rightly divide the Word of truth (i.e. hear, read, study, memorize, and meditate)

   e. Increasing competence to contend for the faith against all opposition

3. **He/she displays a godly walk through conduct and lifestyle at home, on the job and in the community (John 17.14-23).**

   a. Walks worthy of the Lord in speech, purity, conduct, faith, and character

   b. Fulfills sacrificially various roles as a godly member of his/her own household and family

   c. Represents Christ in excellence, service, respect, and single-mindedness on the job

   d. Maintains godly reputation with friends, neighbors, and community

4. **He/she maintains a faithful membership in the body, expressed in active participation in a local congregation of believers (John 13.34-35).**

   a. Has been baptized into the faith based on their confession of faith in Jesus Christ

   b. Participates actively in corporate worship and celebration of the body in praise, worship, and the Lord's Supper

   c. Gathers regularly with other members of the body to build up the church through fellowship, prayer, service, and celebration

   d. Uses his/her gifts in ministry by serving with other members of the body

   e. Communicates regularly in a building and edifying way with the body

5. **He/she implements a compelling strategy to make disciples of Jesus at home and abroad (John 20.21).**

   a. Prays consistently and fervently that the Lord would raise up laborers in his harvest wherever Christ is not yet known, worshiped, and glorified

   b. Gives generously of his/her time and resources toward evangelism and missions as God leads

   c. Looks for opportunities to share his/her personal testimony with others in order to win others to Christ

   d. Spends time establishing new converts in the faith by incorporating them in the body

   e. Asks the Spirit for opportunity to disciple faithful Christians who can become laborers together with him/her in fulfilling the Great Commission

Promise vs. Prediction

The Apostolic Hermeneutic of the Old Testament

Adapted from Christopher J. H. Wright

And So It Was Fulfilled: Five Scenes of Jesus' Early Life				
Incident in Jesus' Life	Matthew Citation	The Old Testament Reference	Commentary on the Actual Historical Context of the Old Testament Text	Hermeneutic Significance
Assurance to Joseph concerning the child conceived in Mary	Matt. 1.18-25	Isa. 7.14, the Immanuel sign given to King Ahaz by Isaiah	Immanuel prophecy was given as a sign to King Ahaz in his own historical context, and does not immediately provide any sense of a long range prediction of Messianic relevance	The Holy Spirit provided the Apostles with divine wisdom in making connections with not only the plain Messianic predictions, but also those aspects of the history of Israel which represent in a direct way some aspect of the life and ministry of Jesus.
Jesus' birth in Bethlehem, the city of David	Matt. 2.1-12	Mic. 5.2, prophecy of the Governor and Ruler of Israel to come from Bethlehem	A direct Messianic prediction about the birthplace of the future Governor of Israel and the nations	
The escape to Egypt, and the return from there	Matt. 2.13-15	Hos. 11.1, God's deliverance of his people Israel, his "son," out of Egypt at the Exodus	No prediction present; Hosea reference is a prophetic allusion to the Exodus of the people of God from Egypt	The ability to correlate particular events of Israel to the life and ministry of Messiah Jesus is precisely the nature of the apostolic Spirit-illumined hermeneutic which coincides with divine and Spirit-inspired Scripture.
Herod's murder of the boys in Bethlehem	Matt. 2.16-18	Jer. 31.15, Jeremiah's lament for the Israelite nation who were going into exile, into Babylonian captivity	The OT text is a figurative picture of the mourning of Rachel (Israel) at the time of the Exile in 587 BC after the fall of Jerusalem to the Babylonians. No explicit Messianic prediction is contained in the text.	We are invited to exegete the Scriptures and make correlations in the same way as the Lord and the Apostles, although our connections should never be considered normative in the same way as theirs.
Jesus' family settlement in Nazareth of Galilee	Matt. 2.19-23	Several possible allusions in the OT, Judg. 13.5; 1 Sam. 1.11; Amos 2.10-11	Texts have relevance within their setting, but not in an explicit way to fulfill Messianic predictions	

The Prophetic Vision as Source of Biblical Faith Commitment

Rev. Dr. Don L. Davis

Faith is an essential part of human life. Humans are confessing, believing and trusting creatures. *And where we place our faith determines the world view which we will adopt. Put another way, our ultimate faith commitment sets the contours of our world view.* It shapes our vision for a way of life. People who doubt their world view are restless and feel they have no ground to stand on. They are often in the throes of a psychological crisis. *But the emotional crisis is fundamentally religious because our world view rests on a faith commitment.*

What is a faith commitment? It is the way we answer four basic questions facing everyone:

1) *Who am I?* Or, what is the nature, task, and purpose of human beings?

2) *Where am I?* Or, what is the nature of the world and universe I live in?

3) *What's wrong?* Or, what is the basic problem or obstacle that keeps me from attaining fulfillment? In other words, how do I understand evil?

4) *What is the remedy?* Or, how is it possible to overcome this hindrance to my fulfillment? In other words, how do I find salvation?

When we've answered these questions, that is, when our faith is settled, then we begin to see reality in some sensible pattern. *Out of our faith proceeds a world view, without which human life simply cannot go on.*

~ Brian J. Walsh and J. Richard Middleton. **The Transforming Vision**.
Downers Grove: InterVarsity Press, 1984. p. 35.

Pursuing Faith, Not Religion
The Liberating Quest for Contextualization
Charles Kraft

This article was taken from Mission Frontiers: The Bulletin of the US Center for World Mission, Vol. 27, No. 5; September-October 2005; ISSN 0889-9436.

*The following is excerpted from chapters 5 and 6 of **Appropriate Christianity** (William Carey Library Publishers, 2005).*

It is not widely understood either outside of or even inside of Christianity that our faith is intended to be different from the religions in its relationship to the culture of the people who practice it. Whereas religions such as Islam, Buddhism and Hinduism require a sizeable chunk of the culture in which they were developed, Christianity rightly understood does not. Jesus came to bring life (Jn. 10:10), not a religion. It is people who have reduced our faith to a religion and exported it as if it is simply a competitor with the religions. And so, those receiving our message tend to interpret Christianity as if it was simply another religion—a culturally-encapsulated religion—rather than a faith that can be expressed in terms of any culture.

But Christianity correctly understood is commitment- and meaning-based, not form-based. A commitment to Jesus Christ and the meanings associated with that commitment can, therefore, be practiced in a wide variety of cultural forms. This is what contextualization is all about. And this is an important feature of Christianity that is often misunderstood by advocates as well as potential receptors.

Still another part of the reputation of Christianity worldwide is that it is more a matter of thinking than of practicality. For many, our faith has little to do with the issues of real life such as how to gain protection from evil spirits, how to gain and keep physical health and how to maintain good family relationships. Instead, Christianity is often seen as a breaker-up of families. And when the issue is a need for spiritual power and protection, even Christians need to keep on good terms with a shaman, priest or medicine man/woman since, in spite of biblical promises, Christian pastors can only recommend secular approaches to healing and protection.

A Christianity that is appropriate both to the Bible and to the receiving culture will confront these misperceptions and, hopefully, get them changed.

Dr. Charles H. Kraft has served as a missionary in Nigeria, taught African languages and linguistics at Michigan State University and UCLA for ten years, and taught Anthropology and Intercultural Communication in the School of Intercultural Studies, Fuller Seminary for the past 35 years. He travels widely, has pioneered in the field of Contextualization, and is widely used in a ministry of inner healing. He is the author or editor of many books, including Appropriate Christianity (William Carey Library Publishers, 2005).

Traditions Die Hard

Any discussion of this topic needs to take into account the fact that the situations most cross-cultural workers are working in nowadays are seldom pioneer situations. Thus, we who teach contextualization are dealing primarily with those whose major concern will have to be on how to bring about change in already existing situations rather than on how to plant culturally appropriate churches.

Typically, then, those who learn what contextualization is all about find themselves working with churches that are quite committed to their Western approach to Christianity. This has become their tradition and they are not open to changing it.

The leaders of many such churches may never have seen culturally appropriate Christianity and probably lack the ability to imagine it. And if they can imagine such an approach, they are unlikely to want to risk what they are familiar with in hopes of gaining greater cultural appropriateness. For many, the risk of losing their position may be very real since their colleagues, committed to preserving the "sacred" tradition, may turn against them and oust them from their parishes.

We need to learn, then, not only the principles of cultural appropriateness, but the principles of effective communication. And this needs to be coupled with patience and prayer plus a readiness to make the right kind of suggestions if asked to.

Fear of Syncretism

A major hindrance to many, especially those who have received theological instruction, is the fear that they might open the door to an aberrant form of Christianity. They see Latin American "christo-paganism" and shy away from what is called Christian but is not really. Fearing that if they deviate from the Western Christianity that they have received they are in danger of people carrying things too far, they fall back on the familiar and do nothing to change it, no matter how much misunderstanding there might be in the community of unbelievers concerning the real meanings of Christianity.

There are, however, at least two roads to syncretism: an approach that is too nativistic and an approach that is too dominated by foreignness. With respect to the latter, it is easy to miss the fact that Western Christianity is quite syncretistic when it is very intellectualized, organized according to foreign patterns, weak on the Holy Spirit and spiritual power, strong on Western forms of communication

Pursuing Faith, Not Religion (continued)

(e.g., preaching) and Western worship patterns and imposed on non-Western peoples as if it were scriptural. It is often easier to conclude that a form of Christian expression is syncretistic when it looks too much like the receiving culture than when it looks "normal," that is, Western.

But Western patterns are often farther from the Bible than non-Western patterns. And the amount of miscommunication of what the gospel really is can be great when people get the impression that ours is a religion rather than a faith and that, therefore, foreign forms are a requirement. To give that impression is surely syncretistic and heretical. I call this "communicational heresy."

But, what about the concept of syncretism? Is this something that can be avoided or is it a factor of human limitations and sinfulness? I vote for the latter and suggest that there is no way to avoid it. Wherever there are imperfect understandings made by imperfect people, there will be syncretism. That syncretism exists in all churches is not the problem. Helping people to move from where they are to more ideal expressions of Christian faith is what we need to address.

As long as we fear something that is inevitable, however, we are in bondage. I remember the words of one field missionary who was studying with us, "Until I stopped worrying about syncretism, I could not properly think about contextualization." Our advice to national leaders (and to missionaries), then, is to stop fearing syncretism. Deal with it in its various forms as a starting point, whether it has come from the receiving society or from the source society and help people to move toward more ideal expressions of their faith ....

Domestication and "Cultural Christianity"

[Down] through the centuries, those who have come to Christ have tended to "domesticate" their Christianity. Just as the early Jewish Christians who disagreed with Paul required Gentiles to accept Christ in a Jewish cultural package, so Romans and Germans and Americans have pressured those who convert to Christ to also convert to the culture of those who bring the message.

Thus, our faith has come to be known as primarily a cultural thing, a religion wrapped in the cultural forms of the group in power. And from about the fourth century on it has been seen largely as a European cultural thing—captured by our European ancestors and domesticated in cultures very different from that in which the faith was originally planted. Converts to Christianity, then, are seen as those who have abandoned their own cultural religion and chosen to adopt the religion and, usually, many of the forms of European culture. Often such converts are regarded as traitors to their own people and their ways.

If ours is simply a "form religion," … it can be *adapted but not contextualized*, it can be in *competition with other forms of religion* but not flow through those forms because by definition it seeks to replace those forms. But biblical Christianity is not simply a set of cultural forms. Cultural Christianity, however, is. And we get tangled up in our discussions because it is often not clear whether we are speaking of essential, biblical Christianity or of the traditional religion of Western societies that is also called Christianity. In one of my books (1979a) I have attempted to make this distinction by spelling biblical Christianity with a capital C and cultural christianity with a small c.…

I would … call religion a form thing, the expression through cultural forms of deep-level (worldview) assumptions and meanings. Religious forms are culture-specific and, if the religion has been borrowed from another cultural context, it requires certain of the forms of that other culture to be borrowed. Islam, for example, requires certain forms of prayer, a specific pilgrimage, an untranslatable Arabic book, even clothing styles. Likewise Judaism, Hinduism, Buddhism and cultural christianity. These are religions.

Essential biblical Christianity, however, requires none of the original cultural forms. That's how it can be "captured" by the West and be considered Western even though its origin is not Western. *Essential Christianity is an allegiance, a relationship, from which flow a series of meanings that are intended to be expressed through the cultural forms of any culture.* These forms are intended, then, to be chosen for their appropriateness to convey proper biblical meanings in the receptors' contexts.

I believe Christianity is intended to be "a faith," not a set of cultural forms and therefore different in essence from the religions. Religions, because they are cultural things, can be *adapted* to new cultures. Adaptation is an external thing resulting in smaller or larger changes in the forms of the religion. Christianity, however, can be *contextualized*, a process in which appropriate meanings may be carried by quite different forms in various cultures. Unfortunately, due to the interference of cultural christianity, we have not seen all the variety that is possible . . . .

Readings on Christ

Rev. Dr. Don L. Davis

What Is Christianity without Christ?

Christianity without Christ is a chest without its treasure, a frame without a portrait, a corpse without breath.

~ John Stott. **Focus on Christ.**
Cleveland: William Collins Publishers, Inc., 1979.

What Is the Bible all About?

What is the Bible all about? How can I understand its meaning? Why are there sixty-six books in the Bible? How do I know it is the Word of God?

All of these questions can be answered in one word - Christ.

Jesus Christ is the key to both the inspiration and the interpretation of the Bible. Further, it is Christ who confirmed the collection of books as both complete and authoritative.

~ Norman Geisler. **A Popular Survey of the Old Testament.**
Grand Rapids: Baker Book House, 1977. p. 11.

The End of the Line

[Matthew] is being deliberately schematic [i.e., providing us with a big picture], with a theological intention. He is pointing out that Old Testament history falls into three approximately equal spans of time between the critical events:

- from the foundational covenant with Abraham to the establishing of the monarchy under David;

- from David to the destruction and loss of the monarchy in the Babylonian exile;

- and from the exile to the coming of the Messiah himself who alone could occupy the throne of David.

Jesus is thus 'the end of the line,' as far as the Old Testament story goes. It has run its completed course in preparation for him, and now its goal and climax has been reached.

~ Christopher J. H. Wright. **Knowing Jesus through the Old Testament.**
Downers Grove: InterVarsity Press, 1992. pp. 6-7.

The Cosmic and All-Sufficient Center

Jesus of Nazareth continues to enjoy an extraordinary boom. People are fascinated by him, even in spite of themselves. Many who never reach the point of confessing him as God and Savior yet regard him with profound admiration. True, there are others who resent and reject him. But the one thing people seem unable to do is to ignore him and leave him alone.

Even in other religions and ideologies Jesus is held in high honor. . . . As T.R. Glover wrote in *The Jesus of History*: "Jesus remains the very heart and soul of the Christian movement, still controlling men, still capturing men. . . . In fine, there is no figure in human history that signifies more. Men may love him or hate him, but they do it intensely."

. . Jesus Christ is the center of Christianity, and therefore both the Christian faith and the Christian life, if they are to be authentic, must be focused on Christ. In his work *Christian Faith and Other Faiths*, the late Bishop Stephen Neill wrote: "The old saying 'Christianity is Christ' is almost exactly true. The historical figure of Jesus of Nazareth is the criterion by which every Christian affirmation has to be judged, and in the light of which it stands or falls."

~ John Stott. **Life in Christ**.
Grand Rapids: Baker Books, 1991. p. 7.

The Magnetism of Jesus' Teaching: Where Did it Come From?

Why was Jesus such a fascinating teacher? What caused these large crowds to follow him? In reply one might say that it was what Jesus said that drew the crowds. With Jesus the voice of prophecy had once again returned to Israel after 400 years. In the ministry of Jesus, the Spirit of God was once again active in Israel (cf. Matt. 12.28; Luke 4.16-21). God was once again visiting his people and proclaiming his will. One reason people came to hear Jesus was that many were convinced that God was speaking through Jesus of Nazareth and that what he was saying was indeed the Word of God (Luke 5.1; 11.28; Mark 4.14-20). . . .

No doubt an additional factor that enters the picture involves the personality of Jesus, for the personality of Jesus gave life and vitality to his message. It was the Word made flesh (John 1.14) which was the medium through which and by which the Word of God came. People loved to listen to Jesus because of the kind of

Readings on Christ (continued)

person he was. Publicans, sinners, children, the crowds—all found in Jesus one whom they enjoyed being near. It was therefore not only *what* he taught but also *who* he was that attracted people to hear him. . . . The *what* of his message and the *who*, i.e., the "personality" and "authority" of the messenger, all played a part in making Jesus an exciting teacher.

~ Robert H. Stein. **The Method and Message of Jesus' Teachings**.
Philadelphia: The Westminster Press, 1978. pp.7-8.

The Challenge of the Biblical Stories

John Dominic Crossan

The Gospels are normative, I think for us as Christians not just in their production, in what they have created, but in the way they are written. A Gospel goes back, as it were, to the twenties. It writes Jesus from the 20s into the 70s, the 80s, the 90s. A Gospel always takes the historical Jesus and laminates him together with the Christ we believe in—the two of them together. John rewrites the 20s as Mark had done before him. The historical Jesus remains crucial for Christianity because we must in each generation of the Church redo our historical work and redo our theological work. We can't skip it. . . .

When I look a Buddhist friend in the face, I cannot say with integrity: "Our story about Jesus' virginal birth is true and factual. Your story that when the Buddha came out of his mother's womb, he was walking, talking, teaching, and preaching (which I must admit is even better than our story)—that's a myth. We have the truth; you have a lie."

I don't think that can be said any longer, for our insistence that our faith is fact and that others' faith is a lie is, I think, a cancer that eats at the heart of Christianity.

~ William F. Buckley, Jr. **Will the Real Jesus Please Stand Up?** Paul Copan, ed.
Grand Rapids: Baker Books, 1998. p. 39.

John Dominic Crossan is an original member and former co-chair of the Jesus Seminar as well as chairman of the Historical Jesus Section of the Society of Biblical Literature. He earned a doctorate in divinity from Maynooth College, Ireland. His postdoctoral studies have been in biblical research at the Pontifical Biblical Institute, Rome, and in archeological research at the Ecole Biblique, Jerusalem. Crossan has taught at several seminaries in the Chicago area and was professor of religious studies at DePaul University for twenty-six years. He has written over a dozen books on the historical Jesus.

Christus Victor: The Warrior Who Is Messiah

> Ps. 68.10 - You ascended on high, leading a host of captives in your train and receiving gifts among men, even among the rebellious, that the Lord God may dwell there.

> Ps. 110.1-2 - The Lord says to my Lord: "Sit at my right hand, until I make your enemies your footstool." The Lord sends forth from Zion your mighty scepter. Rule in the midst of your enemies!

[*Christus Victor's*] central theme is the idea of the Atonement as a Divine conflict and victory; Christ–*Christus Victor*–fights against and triumphs over the evil powers of the world, the 'tyrant' under which mankind is in bondage and suffering, and in him God reconciles the world to himself . . . . The background of the idea is dualistic; God is pictured as in Christ carrying through a victorious conflict against powers of evil which are hostile to his will. This constitutes Atonement, because the drama is a cosmic drama, and the victory over the powers bring to pass a new relation, a relation of reconciliation, between God and the world; and, still more, because in a measure the hostile powers are regarded as in the service of the will of God the Judge of all, and the executants of his judgment. Seen from this side, the triumph over the opposing powers is regarded as a reconciling of God himself; he is reconciled by the very act in which he reconciles the world to himself.

~ Gustaf Aulen, **Christus Victor**.
New York: MacMillan Publishers, 1969. pp. 20-21.

The Risen Messiah Himself Is Our Life

> Col. 3.1-4 - If then you have been raised with Christ, seek the things that are above, where Christ is, seated at the right hand of God. Set your minds on things that are above, not on things that are on earth. For you have died, and your life is hidden with Christ in God. When Christ who is your life appears, then you also will appear with him in glory.

Let us keep in mind that instead of giving us one object after another, God gives his Son to us. Because of this, we can always lift up our hearts and look to the Lord, saying, "Lord, You are my way; Lord, You are my truth; Lord, You are my life. It is you, Lord, who is related to me, not your things." May we ask God to give us grace that we may see Christ in all spiritual things. Day by day we are

Readings on Christ (continued)

convinced that aside from Christ there is no way, nor truth, nor life. How easily we make things as way, truth, and life. Or, we call hot atmosphere as life, we label clear thought as life. We consider strong emotion or outward conduct as life. In reality, though, these are not life. We ought to realize that only the Lord is life, Christ is our life. And it is the Lord who lives out this life in us. Let us ask him to deliver us from the many external and fragmentary affairs that we may touch only him. May we see the Lord in all things —way, truth, and life are all found in knowing him. May we really meet the Son of God and let him live in us. Amen.

~ Watchman Nee. **Christ, the Sum of All Spiritual Things**.
New York: Christian Fellowship Publishers, 1973. p. 20.

Readings on Messianic Prophecy

Rev. Dr. Don L. Davis

Rudolph Bultmann and the Predictions of Passion and Resurrection

> *Rudolph Bultmann,*
> *Theology of the New*
> *Testament. Vol. 1.*
> *Trans. Kendrick Grobel.*
> *New York: Charles*
> *Scribner's Sons, 1951.*
> *pp. 29-30*

And how would Jesus have conceived *the relation of his return as Son of Man to his present historical activity*? He would have had to count upon being removed from the earth and raised to heaven before the final End, the irruption of God's Reign, in order to come from there on the clouds of heaven to perform his real office. But how would he have conceived his removal from the earth?

As a *miraculous translation*? Among his sayings there is no trace of any such fantastic idea. As *departure by natural death*, then? Of that, too, his words say nothing.

By *a violent death, then?* But if so, could he count on that as an absolute certainty–as the consciousness of being raised to the dignity of the coming Son of Man would presuppose?

To be sure, *the predictions of the passion* (Mark 8.31; 9.31; 10.33-34; cf. 10.45; 14.21, 41) foretell his execution as divinely foreordained. *But can there be any doubt that they are all vaticinia ex eventu?* Besides, they do not speak of his parousia! And the predictions of the parousia (Mark 8.38; 13.26-27; 14.62; Matt. 24.27, 37, 44) on their part, do not speak of the death and resurrection of the Son of Man.

Clearly the predictions of the parousia originally had nothing to do with the predictions of death and resurrection; i.e., in the sayings that speak of the coming of the Son of Man there is no idea that this Son of Man is already here in person and must be removed by death before he can return from heaven.

Modern Biblical Interpretation: *Not What Happened* but What Did the Church Preach?

> *Rudolph Bultmann,*
> *Theology of the New*
> *Testament. Vol. 1. p. 31*

Now it is true that in the predictions of the passion the Jewish concept Messiah-Son-of-Man is re-interpreted–or better, singularly enriched–insofar as the idea of a suffering, dying, rising Messiah or Son of Man was unknown to Judaism. But this reinterpretation of the concept was done not by Jesus himself but by the Church ex eventu. Of course, the attempt is made to carry the idea of the suffering Son of Man back into Jesus' own outlook by assuming that Jesus regarded himself as Deutero-Isaiah's Servant of God who suffers and dies for the sinner, and fused together the two ideas Son of Man and Servant of God into the single figure of the suffering, dying and rising Son of Man. At the very outset, the misgivings which must be raised as to the historicity of the predictions of the passion speak against this attempt. In addition, the tradition of Jesus' sayings reveals no trace of a consciousness on his part of being the Servant of God of Isaiah 53.

[To the early Church] it was all the more significant and impressive that the risen Lord was he who had previously died on the cross. Here too, formula-like expressions promptly form, as the tradition of 1 Corinthians 15.3-4 again indicates, and also the description at Romans 4.25: "who was put to death for our trespasses and raised for our justification."–a statement that had evidently existed before Paul and had been handed down to him . . .. This same thing is shown by the predictions put into Jesus mouth in Mark (and also in Matthew and Luke) carrying back the Hellenistic kerygma into the preaching of Jesus.

◄ *Rudolph Bultmann,*
Theology of the New
Testament. Vol. 1.
pp. 82-83

Messianic Prophecy: Something More Sure

2 Peter 1.19-21 (ESV) - And we have something more sure, the prophetic word, to which *you will do well to pay attention as to a lamp shining in a dark place, until the day dawns and the morning star rises in your hearts*, [20] knowing this first of all, that no prophecy of Scripture comes from someone's own interpretation. [21] For no prophecy was ever produced by the will of man, but men spoke from God as they were carried along by the Holy Spirit.

Questions about Messianic prophecy

1.   What does the prophecy *say exactly*?

2.   How does Jesus' life and ministry *make it plain*?

3.   How does it shine on my understanding of . . .

What *God's master plan* for reestablishing his kingdom rule?

What *the enemy's schemes* are to undermine it?

What we can expect as God fulfills his Word?

Readings on Pastoral Care

Rev. Dr. Don L. Davis

Pastoral Care Demands Spiritual Discernment

The pastor was becoming greatly concerned that things were not "happening" in the church as he believed the Lord wanted at this critical time of the church's growth. Seeking the counsel of one of his leading deacons, the pastor asked, "What is wrong with our church? Is it *ignorance* or *apathy*?

The deacon responded, *"I don't know*, and *I don't care!"*

Pastoral Care Focuses on Growth to Maturity

Paul's vision of the church and its ministry *works against the trends of the past century*. Because his ecclesial vision is *apostolic*, it stands in judgment of our pastoral methods and offers to any generation a foundation for church and ministry appropriate to any person, church, or era.

While our pastoral work involves an incredibly wide variety of tasks and responsibilities, and while our role in the church and community offers us many opportunities to use our gifts and abilities, all our labors are merely *means to a divine end*. We ourselves are a means God uses to accomplish a *divine purpose. God calls pastors to grow or to build the church.*

When I came to my current pastorate, I joined a long line of pastors who serve the same end. *We are all different, and we have different emphases, opportunities, gifts, and results; but our goal is singular: We exist to build the temple of the Holy Spirit. We are called to grow Christ's church.* It is easy to confuse means and ends. Every individual and church does it. Yet the result can be tragic.

~ David Fisher. **The 21st Century Pastor.**
Grand Rapids: Zondervan, 1996. p. 192.

Discerning and Addressing the Root Issues Is Key to All Pastoral Care

1 Thess. 5.14-15 (ESV) - And we urge you, brothers, admonish the idle, encourage the fainthearted, help the weak, be patient with them all. [15] See that no one repays anyone evil for evil, but always seek to do good to one another and to everyone.

Admonish the idle

Encourage the Fainthearted

Help the weak

Be patient with all

Repay evil to none

Do good to one another and to everyone

Readings on Servanthood

Jesus' Concept of Servanthood

When Jesus speaks to his disciples of servanthood, he has two aspects in mind. First is the service rendered *to God as the supreme authority to whom they owe their allegiance*, and the second is the service which they render *to people as an expression of humility and love*.

~ David Bennett. **Metaphors of Ministry.** p. 25

Taking Our Cues from the Master Himself: Jesus as Servant

It is with an issue like [servanthood] that I see one distinguishing characteristic that sets Christians apart from the world: we serve because Christ was a servant and clearly told us to do this in memory of him.

We are not to serve because it makes us feel good or serves as some kind of therapy. We are not to serve because it is a good example for our children. We are not to serve because it will make the wheels of society turn more smoothly.

We serve because Christ was a servant.

~ Kenneth H. Carter, Jr. **The Gifted Pastor.** p. 495

Readings on the Church

The People of God: Living the Adventure of the *Ekklesia*

1 Pet. 2.9-12 (ESV) - But you are a chosen race, a royal priesthood, a holy nation, a people for his own possession, that you may proclaim the excellencies of him who called you out of darkness into his marvelous light. [10] Once you were not a people, but now you are God's people; once you had not received mercy, but now you have received mercy. [11] Beloved, I urge you as sojourners and exiles to abstain from the passions of the flesh, which wage war against your soul. [12] Keep your conduct among the Gentiles honorable, so that when they speak against you as evildoers, they may see your good deeds and glorify God on the day of visitation.

The identification of Christians as "the people of God" appears a number of times in the New Testament (e.g. Luke 1.17; Acts 15.14; Titus 2.14; Heb. 4.9; 8.10; 1 Pet. 2.9-10; Rev. 18.4; 21.3). But it is used by Paul with special significance in Romans 9.25-26; 11.1-2; 15.10, and 2 Corinthians 6.16 to set the Christian church in the context of the long story of God's dealing with his chosen people Israel. "People of God," a covenant expression, speaks of God's choosing and calling a particular people into covenantal relationship (Exod. 19.5; Deut. 7.6; 14.2; Ps. 135.4; Heb. 8.10; 1 Pet. 2.9-10; Rev. 21.3). They are God's gracious initiative and magnanimous action in creating, calling, saving, judging, and sustaining them. And as God's people, they experience God's presence among them.

~ Richard Longenecker, ed.
Community Formation in the Early Church and in the Church Today.
Peabody, MA: Hendrickson Publishers, 2002. p. 75.

Where Biblical Study of Leadership Begins: The Church as Context for World Change

[A] biblical study on leadership must begin with the story of the church that came into existence on the Day of Pentecost. The term *ekklesia* is used more than one hundred times in the New Testament. In fact, it's virtually impossible to understand God's will for our lives as believers without comprehending this wonderful "mystery of Christ" that has "been revealed by the Spirit to God's holy apostles and prophets" (Eph. 3.4-5).

Beyond the Gospels, most of the NT is the story of "local churches" and how God intended them to function. True, Jesus Christ came to lay the foundation and to build his *ekklesia* (Matt. 16.18) and when he said to Peter, "I will build my *church*," He was certainly thinking more broadly than establishing a "local church" in Caesarea Philippi where this conversation took place (Matt. 16.13-20). . . .

On the other hand, Jesus was also anticipating the multitude of *local churches* that would be established in Judea and Samaria and throughout the Roman Empire-- and eventually all over the world as we know it today. This story begins in the book of Acts and spans a significant period during the first century (approximately from A.D. 33 to A.D. 63). Furthermore, during this time frame, most of the New Testament letters were written to these local churches--or to men like Timothy and Titus who were helping to establish these churches.

~ Gene Getz. **Elders and Leaders.**
Chicago: Moody, 2003. pp. 47-48.

A World to Change, a World to Win

If anyone is going to change the world for the better, it may be argued, it ought to be the Christians, not the Communists. For myself, I would say that if we started applying our Christianity to the society in which we live, then it would be we, indeed, who would change the world. Christians, too, have a world to change and a world to win. Had the early Christians gone in for slogans these might well have been theirs. They might be ours too. There is no reason at all why they should be the monopoly of the Communists *[and the Muslims, and the atheists, and the hedonists, and the secular humanists, and the . . .]*

~ Douglas Hyde, **Dedication and Leadership**, pp. 32-33

Those Who Turn the World Upside Down Have Themselves Been Turned Inside Out

The bitterest foe became the greatest friend. The Blasphemer became the preacher of Christ's love. The hand that wrote the indictment of the disciples of Christ when he brought them before magistrates and into prison now penned epistles of God's redeeming love. The heart that once beat with joy when Stephen sank beneath the bloody stones now rejoiced in scourgings and stonings for the sake of Christ.

Readings on the Church (continued)

From this erstwhile enemy, persecutor, blasphemer came the greater part of the New Testament, the noblest statements of theology, the sweetest lyrics of Christian love.

~ C. E. Macartney in **Dynamic Spiritual Leadership** by J. Oswald Sanders. pp. 33-34

Readings on the New Testament's Historical Credibility

The Historical Accounts of Yeshua: Truth or Fiction?

➢ *Verses taken from David H. Stern, **The Complete Jewish Bible***

Luke 1.1-4 - Dear Theophilos: concerning the matters that have taken place among us, many people have undertaken to draw up accounts based on what was handed down to us by those who from the start were eyewitnesses and proclaimers of the message. Therefore, Your Excellency, since *I have carefully investigated all these things from the beginning, it seemed good to me that I too should write you an accurate and ordered narrative*, so that you might know how well-founded are the things about which you have been taught.

John 20.30-31 - In the presence of the talmidim, Yeshua performed many other miracles which have not been recorded in this book. *But these which have been recorded are here so that you may trust that Yeshua is the Messiah*, the Son of God, and that by this trust you have life because of who he is.

John 21.24-25 - This one is the talmid who is testifying about these things and who has recorded them. And *we know that his testimony is true*. But there are also many other things Yeshua did; and if they were all to be recorded, I don't think the whole world could contain the books that would have to be written!

The Modern Critical View I: What Is the Historical Credibility of the New Testament?

➢ *Howard Clark Kee. Understanding the New Testament.* Englewood Cliffs, NJ: Prentice-Hall, 1983. p. 9.

Once it is acknowledged that there are differences of outlook within the New Testament and that there are discrepancies within the narrative accounts, *many feel that the credibility of the New Testament as a historical document is compromised or even denied.* Candor requires us to acknowledge, no matter what our point of view, that the New Testament writings record events that occurred at least a generation before they were written down.

When we add to this the New Testament's own description of the disciples as illiterate (Acts 4.13), we must acknowledge that *there was a crucial stage of oral transmission of the Jesus tradition before the Gospels were produced as we have them.* The differences that are evident among them are in some cases not matters of great consequence–such as whether the family of Jesus lived originally in Bethlehem (Matt. 2) or whether they were only temporarily there, but resided in Nazareth (Luke 2). Nevertheless, a serious effort to understand the NT must come to terms with these differences and seek to account for them.

Readings on the Historical Credibility of the New Testament (continued)

The Modern Critical View II: Are the Accounts of Jesus' Passion Propaganda?

We must also call into question whether it is appropriate for us to impose our supposed standards of historical objectivity on documents like the NT. As John 20.31 puts it, he has reported the story of Jesus' spectacular acts ("signs") in order "that you may believe that Jesus is the Christ, the Son of the Living God." Clearly not all his readers are going to share his conclusions, but he is forthright in telling his readers his aims. And those aims are not objective reporting. *Using the term in its root sense, of a means of propagating a point of view or belief, the New Testament is not objective history, but propaganda.* But then history in any time and culture is always event plus interpretation; it is never merely objective, in the sense of lacking a framework of interpretation or point of view. *What is required is to be aware of the writer's assumptions, the aims of the writings, what its vocabulary, style, and conceptual language presuppose.*

≺ *Howard Clark Kee.*
Understanding the
New Testament.
Englewood Cliffs, NJ:
Prentice-Hall, 1983. p. 9.

The Modern Critical View III: Did Community Needs Dictate the Message?

Jesus of Nazareth is the historical base for the Christian claim to be the community of the new covenant. Yet, as we have observed, our documentary evidence about him was written long after his death, probably in the last half of the first century. *Our records are a series of responses to Jesus by those who saw in him the agent of God, not the reports of detached observers.* In the process of analyzing these documents of faith we learn about Jesus, but we also learn about *the communities in which the tradition about him was treasured and transmitted.*

≺ *Howard Clark Kee.*
Understanding the
New Testament.
Englewood Cliffs, NJ:
Prentice-Hall, 1983.
p. 78, 121.

The death of Christ was itself identified with the Passover in *the Pauline churches* (1 Cor. 5.7); and *in Johannine circles* [that is, in the churches of John], Jesus was regarded as the Lamb of God (John 1.29; Rev. 5) . . .. But just Mark was content to affirm only that the death of Jesus was necessary, without explaining why or how, so he simply states that Jesus' death is in behalf of others. This is what *the community of Mark* celebrates in the communion, while looking forward to the completion of the number of the elect in the new age.

Receptivity Scale

The Holmes-Rahe Social Readjustment Scale indicates different events, in approximate order of their importance, that have an effect in producing periods of personal or family transition. The numbers on the right indicate the importance of the event relative to other transition-producing events. Various events may compound each other when an individual experiences more than one incident over a relatively short period of time. The higher the number, the more receptive the person is to the Gospel. For example, someone who was just married and is also having trouble with his or her boss will be more receptive than if either event had occurred separately. Also, the larger the number or accumulation of numbers, the longer the period of transition will last and the more intense it will be.

~ Win Arn and Charles Arn.
The Master's Plan for Making Disciples. 2nd ed.
Grand Rapids: Baker Books, 1998.
pp. 88-89

The Holmes-Rahe Social Readjustment Scale

Death of Spouse	100
Divorce	73
Marital Separation	65
Jail Term	63
Death of Close Family Member	63
Personal Injury or Illness	53
Marriage	50
Fired from Work	47
Marital Reconciliation	45
Retirement	45
Change in Family Member's Health	44
Pregnancy	40
Sex Difficulties	39
Addition to Family	39
Business Readjustment	39
Change in Financial Status	38
Death of Close Friend	37
Change in Number of Marital Arguments	35
Mortgage or Loan over $75,000	31
Foreclosure of Mortgage or Loan	30
Change in Work Responsibilities	29
Son or Daughter Leaving Home	29
Trouble with In-Laws	29
Outstanding Personal Achievement	28
Spouse Starts Work	26
Starting or Finishing School	26
Change in Living Conditions	25
Revision of Personal Habits	24
Trouble with Boss	23
Change in Work Hours or Conditions	20
Change in Residence	20
Change in Schools	20
Change in Recreational Habits	19
Change in Social Activities	18
Mortgage or Loan under $75,000	18
Easter Season	17
Change in Sleeping Habits	16
Change in Number of Family Gatherings	15
Vacation	13
Christmas Season	12
Minor Violation of the Law	11

Relationship of Cost and Effectiveness in Disciple-Making Endeavors

Taken from Win Arn and Charles Arn, The Master's Plan for Making Disciples. 2nd ed. Grand Rapids: Baker Books, 1998. pp. 166

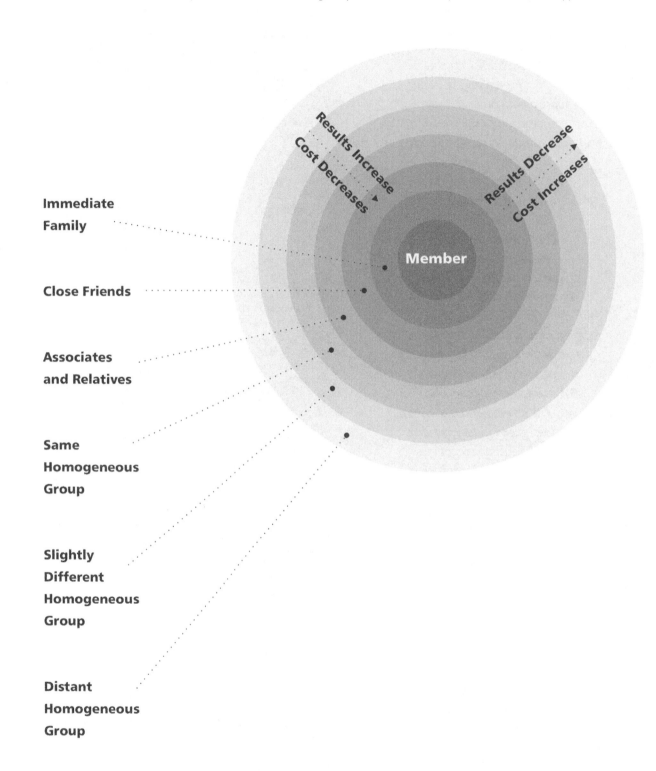

Representin'
Jesus as God's Chosen Representative
Rev. Dr. Don L. Davis

To represent another

Is to be selected to stand in the place of another, and thereby fulfill the assigned duties, exercise the rights and serve as deputy for, as well as to speak and act with another's authority on behalf of their interests and reputation.

The Public Preaching Ministry of Jesus Christ
Communication and Conveyance by God's Rep

Mark 1.14-15 (ESV) Now after John was arrested, Jesus came into Galilee, proclaiming the gospel of God, **[15]** and saying, "The time is fulfilled, and the kingdom of God is at hand; repent and believe in the gospel."

The Temptation of Jesus Christ
Challenge to and Contention with God's Rep

Mark 1.12-13 (ESV)
The Spirit immediately drove him out into the wilderness. **[13]** *And he was in the wilderness forty days, being tempted by Satan.* And he was with the wild animals, and the angels were ministering to him.

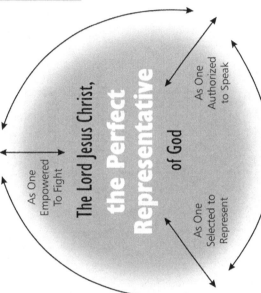

The Lord Jesus Christ, **the Perfect Representative** of God

As One Authorized to Speak

As One Empowered To Fight

As One Selected to Represent

Jesus Fulfills The Duties Of Being an Emissary

1. Receiving an *Assignment,*
   John 10.17-18
2. Resourced with an *Entrustment,*
   John 3.34; Luke. 4.18
3. Launched into *Engagement,*
   John 5.30
4. Answered with an *Assessment,*
   Matthew 3.16-17
5. New assignment after *Assessment,*
   Philippians 2.9-11

The Baptism of Jesus Christ
Commissioning and Confirmation of God's Rep

Mark 1.9-11 (ESV) *In those days Jesus came from Nazareth of Galilee and was baptized by John in the Jordan.* **[10]** And when he came up out of the water, immediately he saw the heavens opening and the Spirit descending on him like a dove. **[11]** And a voice came from heaven, "You are my beloved Son; with you I am well pleased."

Re-presenting Messiah

Don L. Davis

"Gentilization" of modern Christian faith expressions

Contextualization: freedom in Christ to enculturate the gospel
Common modern portrayal of Messianic hope as Gentile faith
Tendency of tradition/culture to usurp biblical authority
Present day eclipse of biblical framework by "captivities"

Strange fires on the altar: examples of socio-cultural captivities

Nationalism
Capitalism
Scientific rationalism
Denominationalism

Personal existentialism
Asceticism/moralism
Ethnocentrism
Nuclear family life

Jesus' critique of socio-cultural captivity

Bondage to religious tradition, Matt. 15.3-9
Ignorance of Scripture and God's power, Matt. 22.29
Zealous effort without knowledge, Romans 10.1-3

Hermeneutic habits that lead toward a syncretistic faith

Selective choice of texts
Tradition viewed as canon
Cultural readings of texts
Preaching and teaching based on eisegesis and audience
Uncritical approaches to one's own doctrine and practice
Apologetics for socio-cultural identity

"Paradigm paralysis" & biblical faith

Blind to one's own historical conditionedness
Limited vantage point and perspective
Privilege and power: political manipulation
Inability to receive criticism
Persecution of opposite viewpoints and new interpretations of faith

---

Rediscover the Hebraic roots of the biblical Messianic hope (return)

Recognize the socio-cultural captivity of Christian profession (exile)

Re-present Messiah Yeshua with passion and clarity

with fidelity to Scripture
in sync with historic orthodoxy
without cultural distortion
without theological bias

Rediscovery of the Jewish origins of biblical faith, John 4.22

YHWH as God of lovingkindness in covenant faithfulness

Messianic fulfillment in OT: prophecy, type, story, ceremony, and symbol

Hebraic roots of the Promise: YHWH as a Warrior God

People of Israel as community of Messianic hope

Psalms and Prophets emphasize divine rulership of Messiah

Tracing the Seed
Seed of the Woman, Gen. 3.15
Seed of Shem, Gen. 9.26-27
Seed of Abraham, Gen. 12.3
Seed of Isaac and Jacob, Gen. 26.2-5; 28.10-15
Seed of Judah, Gen. 49.10
Seed of David, 2 Sam. 7

Suffering Servant of YHWH: humiliation and lowliness of God's Davidic king

Glimmers of Gentile salvation and global transformation

Live the adventure of NT apocalyptic myth (possession)

Apocalyptic as the "mother tongue and native language" of the apostles and early Church as eschatological community

Yeshua Messiah as the Cosmic Warrior:
YHWH as God who wins ultimate victory over his enemies

Messiah Yeshua as Anointed One and Binder of the Strong Man: the Messianic Age to come inaugurated in Jesus of Nazareth

"Already/Not Yet" Kingdom orientation:
The Reign of God as both manifest but not consummated

The Evidence and Guarantee of the Age to Come:
The Spirit as down payment, first fruits, and seal of God

The Role of the Holy Spirit in Spiritual Guidance

Terry G. Cornett

Through the Holy Spirit, God has made himself available to believers so that they can be in constant, friendship relationship with him, receiving ongoing guidance and direction as to what he wants from them.

I.   Key Texts

A.   Rom. 8.14 (ESV) - For all who are led by the Spirit of God are sons of God.

B.   Isa. 63.10-14 (ESV) - But they rebelled and grieved his Holy Spirit; therefore he turned to be their enemy, and himself fought against them. [11] Then he remembered the days of old, of Moses and his people. Where is he who brought them up out of the sea with the shepherds of his flock? Where is he who put in the midst of them his Holy Spirit, [12] who caused his glorious arm to go at the right hand of Moses, who divided the waters before them to make for himself an everlasting name, [13] who led them through the depths? Like a horse in the desert, they did not stumble. [14] Like livestock that go down into the valley, the Spirit of the Lord gave them rest. So you led your people, to make for yourself a glorious name.

C.   John 10.1-5 (ESV) - Truly, truly, I say to you, he who does not enter the sheepfold by the door but climbs in by another way, that man is a thief and a robber. [2] But he who enters by the door is the shepherd of the sheep. [3] To him the gatekeeper opens. The sheep hear his voice, and he calls his own sheep by name and leads them out. [4] When he has brought out all his own, he goes before them, and the sheep follow him, for they know his voice. [5] A stranger they will not follow, but they will flee from him, for they do not know the voice of strangers.

The Role of the Holy Spirit in Spiritual Guidance (continued)

D. John 14.25-26 (ESV) - These things I have spoken to you while I am still with you. [26] But the Helper, the Holy Spirit, whom the Father will send in my name, he will teach you all things and bring to your remembrance all that I have said to you.

E. John 16.13 (ESV) - When the Spirit of truth comes, he will guide you into all the truth, for he will not speak on his own authority, but whatever he hears he will speak, and he will declare to you the things that are to come.

F. Acts 16.7-8 (ESV) - And when they had come up to Mysia, they attempted to go into Bithynia, but the Spirit of Jesus did not allow them. [8] So, passing by Mysia, they went down to Troas (cf. Acts 20.22-23).

II. Why is the Guidance of the Holy Spirit so important?

Christian, then, recognizes that when faced with the alternatives of good and evil, there is no choice; one must do good. But the greater challenge comes when we are faced with multiple alternatives that are all morally good. The question then becomes, which is the good to which God is calling me? And the good then becomes the enemy of the best, since it is quite possible for us to fill our days doing good things but neglecting the one thing that we must do and to which we are called. . . .Every choice is then both a yes and a no. . .If I take on this assignment or this job, it means saying no to other opportunities. If I choose to spend my day in this way, it means I am saying no to other activities that might have filled my day. And surely this is what makes decisions making a challenge: we cannot be everywhere and we cannot do everything. There are many good things that we might do, and we cannot do them all. Again, this would be a terrifying and impossible burden were it not for the providential care of God. He is a God who is present and alive in all that is—the land, the sea, and the sky—but also a God who is personally present in each one of us. We are not alone! This is exceedingly good news. . . .When we make a choice, the Spirit is with us. Indeed we speak of God as Shepherd, that is, as one who guides (Ps. 23). And we experience this guidance most keenly in our times of choosing. Still, our decision making is our responsibility; it is our act of choosing in response to the options, problems, and opportunities that are placed before us. God does not choose for us, and we cannot expect others to make our choices for us, not if we want to accept adult responsibility for our lives. Indeed the capacity to discern well and make wise decisions is a critical sign of spiritual maturity. And further, it is something that we learn as we mature in faith and grow in wisdom.

~ Gordon T. Smith.
The Voice of Jesus: Discernment, Prayer, and the Witness of the Spirit. pp 130-132.

III. How Do We Hear God's Voice?

A. Know what God the Spirit has already spoken: God's Written Word

    1. The Scriptures are the record of the Spirit's guidance. The Scriptures are not only the infallible judge of guidance or prophecy, they are also our training in the recognition of God's voice.

    2. John 5.46-47 (ESV) - If you believed Moses, you would believe me; for he wrote of me. [47] But if you do not believe his writings, how will you believe my words?

B. Set your heart to obey

    1. Usually, the problem is NOT with our hearing!

        a. Ps. 119.10 (ESV) - With my whole heart I seek you; let me not wander from your commandments!

        b. The fundamental question relating to guidance is not whether I will be able to hear God speak but whether I intend to obey what he says.

The Role of the Holy Spirit in Spiritual Guidance (continued)

2. God is a competent, clear-speaking guide.

   a. John 10.2-5, 27 (ESV) - But he who enters by the door is the shepherd of the sheep. [3] To him the gatekeeper opens. The sheep hear his voice, and he calls his own sheep by name and leads them out. [4] When he has brought out all his own, he goes before them, and the sheep follow him, for they know his voice. [5] A stranger they will not follow, but they will flee from him, for they do not know the voice of strangers. . . . [27] My sheep hear my voice, and I know them, and they follow me.

   b. The metaphors of Scripture describe a God who will be heard!

      (1) The images given by God to describe his leadership are very helpful. God is a king, a parent, a shepherd. The biblical question is seldom, "How do we hear?" Jesus says quite confidently that his sheep know his voice. Like all kings or parents or shepherds, God has no difficulty communicating to us in ways that we will understand.

      (2) How many of us, for example, find that the IRS has difficulty communicating with us that we need to pay taxes? How many of us just forget about April 15th and never think about it again once it is passed?

      (3) How many of you as kids sat around and agonized whether you were going to be able to recognize your parent's voice. What initiative did you take as a child to make sure you could hear and understand your parents?

      (4) In the same manner, God takes the initiative to communicate his will to his people.

c. If God is silent it usually means that we are either free to choose among the good choices he has placed at our disposal, or alternatively, that we are operating under a preexisting command.

(1) If God wants us to do something, he will make it clear to the listening heart.

(2) When God has a already communicated his will through the Scriptures, the question will not be hearing but obeying.

d. The importance of a listening heart.

The foundational ground rule: We cannot be ignoring God or running away from obedience and then claim that God is not saying anything.

(1) God's Church as the natural environment for listening.

(a) The family analogy holds true. My children came home after school everyday, ate at my table, lived in my house, and participated in our family life. Because that was true, they could be confident that they were hearing what I wanted from them. We must do the same in our spiritual walk.

(b) If we ignore our relationship with the family of God and do not spend time in his presence, and hearing his Word, he will speak, but we will likely not attend to his voice. On the other hand, active participation in family life is an important part of listening

(c) In my own experience God often speaks to me at church. Sometimes through the sermon and sometimes along a line completely different from the sermon or worship emphasis. The point is that I am at his family table. He can speak through the preacher or he can simply capture my attention and speak directly to my heart but I must participate in the family to have a reasonable expectation of receiving direction. If we run away from time with

The Role of the Holy Spirit in Spiritual Guidance (continued)

God's family (like the prodigal son) we cannot, then, claim the excuse that we do not hear him saying anything.

(d) Hearing the voice of God is not a private function. It takes place in community. We hear the voice of God best when we listen along with others.

(e) Our pastors and spiritual leaders have a unique role to play in this process.

(f) Heb. 13.17 (ESV) - Obey your leaders and submit to them, for they are keeping watch over your souls, as those who will have to give an account. Let them do this with joy and not with groaning, for that would be of no advantage to you.

(g) Consulting our pastoral leadership for their insights and counsel is a natural starting point for decisions where God's will is not clear.

(h) Our brothers and sisters in Christ are also a rich resource for speaking the mind of Christ to us.

(i) 1 Cor. 12.7 (ESV) - To each is given the manifestation of the Spirit for the common good.

(j) 1 Cor. 14.26 (ESV) - What then, brothers? When you come together, each one has a hymn, a lesson, a revelation, a tongue, or an interpretation. Let all things be done for building up.

(k) Prov. 27.17 (ESV) - Iron sharpens iron, and one man sharpens another.

(l) Prov. 11.14 (ESV) - Where there is no guidance, a people falls, but in an abundance of counselors there is safety.

(m) Listening to the voice of the Spirit necessarily means that we must listen to the counsel of the church community and its leaders.

The Role of the Holy Spirit in Spiritual Guidance (continued)

(2) The role of attention.

I make it my business to persevere in his Holy presence, wherein I keep myself by a simple attention and a general fond regard to God, which I may call an ACTUAL PRESENCE of God; or, to speak better, an habitual, silent, and secret conversation of the soul with God, which often causes me joys and raptures inwardly, and sometimes also outwardly, so great that I am forced to use means to moderate them and prevent their appearance to others.

~ Brother Lawrence quoted in Dallas Willard. **Hearing God**.

(3) A Prayer from Saint Anselm of Canterbury (1033-1109).

Teach me to seek you
And as I seek you, show yourself to me,
For I cannot seek you unless you show me how,
And I will never find you unless you show yourself to me.
Let me seek you by desiring you,
And desire you by seeking you;
Let me find you by loving you,
And love you in finding you.
Amen.

IV. **For further reading:**

Richard J. Foster. Chapter 12. "Guidance." *Celebration of Discipline: The Path to Spiritual Growth.* San Francisco: HarperSanFrancisco, 1998.

Gordon T. Smith. *The Voice of Jesus: Discernment, Prayer and the Witness of the Spirit.* Downers Grove, IL: InterVarsity Press, 2003

Charles Stanley. *How to Listen to God.* Nashville: Thomas Nelson, 1985.

Mark Water. *Knowing God's Will Made Easier.* Peabody, MA: Hendrickson, 1998.

The Role of Women in Ministry
Dr. Don L. Davis

While it is plain that God has established a clearly designed order of responsibility within the home, it is equally clear that women are called and gifted by God, led by his own Spirit to bear fruit worthy of their calling in Christ. Throughout the NT, commands are directed specifically to women to submit, with the particular Greek verb *hupotasso*, occurring frequently which means "to place under" or "to submit" (cf. 1 Tim. 2.11). The word also translated into our English word "subjection" is from the same root. In such contexts these Greek renderings ought not to be understood in any way except as positive admonitions towards God's designed framework for the home, where women are charged to learn quietly and submissively, trusting and working within the Lord's own plan.

This ordering of the woman's submission in the home, however, must not be misinterpreted to mean that women are disallowed from ministering their gifts under the Spirit's direction. Indeed, it is the Holy Spirit through Christ's gracious endowment who assigns the gifts as he wills, for the edification of the Church (1 Cor. 12.1-27; Eph. 4.1-16). The gifts are not given to believers on the criteria of gender; in other words, there is no indication from the Scriptures that some gifts are for men only, and the others reserved for women. On the contrary, Paul affirms that Christ provided gifts as a direct result of his own personal victory over the devil and his minions (cf. Eph. 4.6ff.). This was his own personal choice, given by his Spirit to whomever he wills (cf. 1 Cor. 12.1-11). In affirming the ministry of women we affirm the right of the Spirit to be creative in all saints for the well-being of all and the expansion of his Kingdom, as he sees fit, and not necessarily as we determine (Rom. 12.4-8; 1 Pet. 4.10-11).

Furthermore, a careful study of the Scriptures as a whole indicates that God's ordering of the home in no way undermines his intention for men and women to serve Christ as disciples and laborers together, under Christ's leading. The clear NT teaching of Christ as head of the man, and the man of the woman (see 1 Cor. 11.4) shows God's esteem for godly spiritual representation within the home. The apparent forbidding of women to hold teaching/ruling positions appears to be an admonition to protect God's assigned lines of responsibility and authority within the home. For instance, the particular Greek term in the highly debated passage in 1 Timothy 2.12, *andros*, which has often times been translated "man," may also be translated "husband." With such a translation, then, the teaching would be that a wife ought not to rule over her husband.

This doctrine of a woman who, in choosing to marry, makes herself voluntarily submissive to "line up under" her husband is entirely consistent with the gist of the NT teaching on the role of authority in the Christian home. The Greek word *hupotasso*, which means to "line up under" refers to a wife's voluntary submission to her own husband (cf. Eph. 5.22, 23; Col. 3.18; Titus 2.5; 1 Pet. 3.1). This has nothing to do with any supposed superior status or capacity of the husband; rather, this refers to God's design of godly headship, authority which is given for comfort, protection, and care, not for destruction or domination (cf. Gen. 2.15-17; 3.16; 1 Cor. 11.3). Indeed, that this headship is interpreted in light of Christ's headship over the Church signifies the kind of godly headship that must be given, that sense of tireless care, service, and protection required from godly leadership.

Of course, such an admonition for a wife to submit to a husband would not in any way rule out that women be involved in a teaching ministry (e.g., Titus 2.4), but, rather, that in the particular case of married women, that their own ministries would come under the protection and direction of their respective husbands (Acts 18.26). This would assert that a married woman's ministry in the Church would be given serving, protective oversight by her husband, not due to any notion of inferior capacity or defective spirituality, but for the sake of, as one commentator has put it, "avoiding confusion and maintaining orderliness" (cf. 1 Cor. 14.40).

In both Corinth and Ephesus (which represent the contested Corinthian and Timothy epistolary comments), it appears that Paul's restriction upon women's participation was prompted by occasional happenings, issues which grew particularly out of these contexts, and therefore are meant to be understood in those lights. For instance, the hotly-contested test of a women's "silence" in the church (see both 1 Cor. 14 and 1 Tim. 2) does not appear in any way to undermine the prominent role women played in the expansion of the Kingdom and development of the Church in the first century. Women were involved in the ministries of prophecy and prayer (1 Cor. 11.5), personal instruction (Acts 18.26), teaching (Titus 2.4,5), giving testimony (John 4.28, 29), offering hospitality (Acts 12.12), and serving as co-laborers with the apostles in the cause of the Gospel (Phil. 4.2-3). Paul did not relegate women to an inferior role or hidden status but served side-by-side with women for the sake of Christ "I urge Euodia and I urge Syntyche to live in harmony in the Lord. Indeed, true companion, I ask you also to help these women who have shared my struggle

The Role of Women in Ministry (continued)

in *the cause* of the Gospel, together with Clement also and the rest of my fellow workers, whose names are in the book of life" (Phil. 4.2-3).

Furthermore, we must be careful in subordinating the personage of women *per se* (that is, their nature as women) versus their subordinated role in the marriage relationship. Notwithstanding the clear description of the role of women as heirs together of the grace of life in the marriage relationship (1 Pet. 3.7), it is equally plain that the Kingdom of God has created a dramatic shift in how women are to be viewed, understood, and embraced in the kingdom community. It is plain that in Christ there is now no difference between rich and poor, Jew and Gentile, barbarian, Scythian, bondman and freemen, as well as man and woman (cf. Gal. 3.28; Col. 3.11). Women were allowed to be disciples of a Rabbi (which was foreign and disallowed at the time of Jesus), and played prominent roles in the NT church, including being fellow laborers side by side with the apostles in ministry (e.g., see Euodia and Syntyche in Phil. 4.1ff.), as well as hosting a church in their houses (cf. Phoebe in Rom. 16.1-2, and Apphia in Philem. 1).

In regards to the issue of pastoral authority, I am convinced that Paul's understanding of the role of equippers (of which the pastor-teacher is one such role, cf. Eph. 4.9-15) is not gender specific. In other words, the decisive and seminal text for me on the operation of gifts and the status and function of offices are those NT texts which deal with the gifts (1 Cor. 12.1-27; Rom. 12.4-8; 1 Pet. 4.10-11, and Eph. 4.9-15). There is no indication in any of these formative texts that gifts are gender-specific. In other words, for the argument to hold decisively that women were never to be in roles that were pastoral or equipping in nature, the simplest and most effective argument would be to show that the Spirit simply would never even consider giving a woman a gift which was not suited to the range of callings which she felt a calling towards. Women would be forbidden from leadership because the Holy Spirit would never grant to a woman a calling and its requisite gifts because she was a woman. Some gifts would be reserved for men, and women would never receive those gifts.

A careful reading of these and other related texts show no such prohibition. It appears that it is up to the Holy Spirit to give any person, man or woman, any gift that suits him for any ministry he wishes them to do, as he wills (1 Cor. 12.11 "But one and the same Spirit works all these things, distributing to each one individually as he wills"). Building upon this point, Terry Cornett has even written a fine theological essay showing how the NT Greek for the word "apostle" is unequivocally applied to women, most clearly shown in the rendering of the female noun, "Junia" applied to "apostle" in Romans 16.7, as well as allusions to co-laboring, for instance, with the twins, Tryphena and Tryphosa, who "labored" with Paul in the Lord (16.12).

Believing that every God-called, Christ-endowed, and Spirit-gifted and led Christian ought to fulfill their role in the body, we affirm the role of women to lead and instruct under godly authority that submits to the Holy Spirit, the Word of God, and is informed by the tradition of the Church and spiritual reasoning. We ought to expect God to give women supernatural endowments of grace to carry out his bidding on behalf of his Church, and his reign in the Kingdom of God. Since men and women both reflect the *Imago Dei* (i.e., image of God), and both stand as heirs together of God's grace (cf. Gen. 1.27; 5.2; Matt. 19.4; Gal. 3.28; 1 Pet. 3.7), they are given the high privilege of representing Christ together as his ambassadors (2 Cor. 5.20), and through their partnership to bring to completion our obedience to Christ's Great Commission of making disciples of all nations (Matt. 28.18-20).

Roles of Representational Leadership

Rev. Dr. Don L. Davis

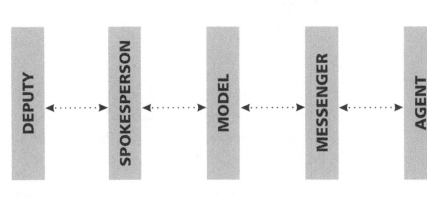

Roles of Representational Leadership

DEPUTY ◄┄┄► SPOKESPERSON ◄┄┄► MODEL ◄┄┄► MESSENGER ◄┄┄► AGENT

Things that may or may not have any bearing on the personal representation of another:

Background

Experience

Competence

Confidence

Opinion of Others

Education

Majority Acceptance

Officials

Traditional Ways of Promotion and Demotion

Seniority

Voting Habits

Has someone granted to you the right and responsibility to stand for them in this situation?

What precisely have you been authorized to do and entrusted to steward or accomplish on behalf of the person who granted these rights to you?

What is at stake in my faithful accomplishment of my entrusted status--what will I gain or what will I forfeit with this charge?

Salvation as Joining the People of God

Terry Cornett

I. The Most Significant Way to Define Salvation in the Biblical Context Is to Describe it as Being Joined to the People of God.

A. Old Testament

1. The prototype Old Testament image of salvation is the Exodus where God "saved" his people from bondage and slavery in Egypt.

   a. To be saved meant to be joined to the people of God who were being delivered together out of bondage and placed directly under God's lordship, laws, protection, provision, and presence.

   b. Exod. 6.7 (ESV) - *I will take you as my own people*, and I will be your God. Then you will know that I am the LORD your God, who brought you out from under the yoke of the Egyptians (cf. Lev. 26.12; Deut. 4.20, Hos. 13.4).

2. God's selection of Israel as "his people" gave them a unique position among all the peoples of the earth.

   a. Deut. 7.6 (ESV) - For you are a people holy to the LORD your God. *The LORD your God has chosen you out of all the peoples on the face of the earth to be his people, his treasured possession* (cf. Deut. 14.2, 26.18, 33.29).

   b. Deut. 27.9 (ESV) - Then Moses and the priests, who are Levites, said to all Israel, "Be silent, O Israel, and listen! *You have now become the people of the LORD your God.*"

3. The means of salvation for anyone outside of Israel was to join themselves to the people of God.

   a. Exod. 12.37-38, 48a (ESV) - The Israelites journeyed from Rameses to Succoth. There were about six hundred thousand men on foot, besides women and children. *Many other people went up with them*, as well as large droves of livestock, both flocks and

Salvation as Joining the People of God (continued)

herds. . . . *"An alien living among you who wants to celebrate the LORD'S Passover must have all the males in his household circumcised; then he may take part like one born in the land."*

b. Isa. 56.3-8 (ESV) - *Let no foreigner who has bound himself to the LORD say, "The LORD will surely exclude me from his people."* And let not any eunuch complain, "I am only a dry tree." For this is what the LORD says: "To the eunuchs who keep my Sabbaths, who choose what pleases me and hold fast to my covenant-to them I will give within my temple and its walls a memorial and a name better than sons and daughters; I will give them an everlasting name that will not be cut off. And foreigners who bind themselves to the LORD to serve him, to love the name of the LORD, and to worship him, *all who keep the Sabbath without desecrating it and who hold fast to my covenant-these I will bring to my holy mountain and give them joy in my house of prayer. Their burnt offerings and sacrifices will be accepted on my altar;* for my house will be called a house of prayer for all nations." *The Sovereign LORD declares-he who gathers the exiles of Israel: "I will gather still others to them besides those already gathered."*

4. The New Testament suggests that even Moses (an ethnic Hebrew but raised culturally as an Egyptian and therefore a foreigner) had to make a conscious choice to join himself to the people of God in faith so that he could experience salvation.

Heb. 11.25 (ESV) - *He* [Moses] *chose to be mistreated along with the people of God* rather than to enjoy the pleasures of sin for a short time.

5. Summary: [In the Old Testament] salvation came, not by the man's mere merit, but because the man belonged to a nation peculiarly chosen by God ("Salvation," *International Standard Bible Encyclopedia* [Electronic ed.]. Cedar Rapids: Parsons Technology, 1998.).

B. New Testament

"... who gave himself for us to redeem us from all wickedness *and to purify for himself a people that are his very own, eager to do what is good*" (Titus 2.14).

1. Both Peter and Paul suggest that the New Testament view of salvation is equally concerned as the Old Testament with God calling out a people but that the people "called out" are bound to Christ and his Church rather than to a political or ethnic "nation."

    a. 1 Pet. 2.9-10 (ESV) - *But you are a chosen people, a royal priesthood, a holy nation, a people belonging to God*, that you may declare the praises of him who called you out of darkness into his wonderful light. *Once you were not a people, but now you are the people of God; once you had not received mercy, but now you have received mercy.*

    b. Acts 15.14 (ESV) - Simon has described to us how God at first showed his concern *by taking from the Gentiles a people for himself.*

    c. Eph. 2.13, 19 (ESV) - But now in Christ Jesus you who once were far away have been brought near through the blood of Christ. . . . Consequently, you are no longer foreigners and aliens, *but fellow citizens with God's people* and members of God's household.

    d. Rom. 9.24-26 (ESV) - Even us, whom he also called, *not only from the Jews but also from the Gentiles?* As he says in Hosea: *"I will call them 'my people' who are not my people*; and I will call her 'my loved one' who is not my loved one," and, *"It will happen that in the very place where it was said to them, 'You are not my people,' they will be called 'sons of the living God.'"*

2. "On the other hand, while the [Gospel] message involved in every case is strict individual choice, yet the individual who accepted it entered into social relations with the others who had so chosen. *So salvation involved admission to a community of service* (Mark 9.35, etc.)" (International Standard Bible Encyclopedia [Electronic Edition]).

II. The Metaphors of Salvation: Joined to a People.

In human society, belonging to a "people" (family, clan, nation) happens through either:

* birth,

* adoption, or

* marrying into a family group

Thus, the New Testament language of salvation draws from these three primary metaphors to describe what happens at salvation.

A. Birth

1. John 1.12-13 (ESV) - Yet to all who received him, to those who believed in his name, he gave the right to become children of God - *children born not of natural descent*, nor of human decision or a husband's will, *but born of God.*

2. John 3.3 (ESV) - In reply Jesus declared, "I tell you the truth, *no one can see the Kingdom of God unless he is born again.*"

3. 1 Pet. 1.23 (ESV) - *For you have been born again*, not of perishable seed, but of imperishable, through the living and enduring word of God.

4. 1 Pet. 1.3 (ESV) - Praise be to the God and Father of our Lord Jesus Christ! *In his great mercy he has given us new birth* into a living hope through the resurrection of Jesus Christ from the dead.2B

B. Adoption

1. Rom. 8.23 (ESV) - Not only so, but we ourselves, who have the firstfruits of the Spirit, groan inwardly *as we wait eagerly for our adoption as sons*, the redemption of our bodies.

2. Eph. 1.4-6 (ESV) - For he chose us in him before the creation of the world to be holy and blameless in his sight. *In love he predestined us to be adopted as his sons through Jesus Christ*, in accordance with his pleasure and will - to the praise of his glorious grace, which he has freely given us in the One he loves.

3. Gal. 4.4-7 (ESV) - But when the time had fully come, God sent his Son, born of a woman, born under law, to redeem those under law, *that we might receive the full rights of sons.* Because you are sons, God sent the Spirit of his Son into our hearts, the Spirit who calls out, "Abba, Father." *So you are no longer a slave, but a son; and since you are a son, God has made you also an heir.*

C. Marriage

1. John 3.29 (ESV) - *The bride belongs to the bridegroom.* The friend who attends the bridegroom waits and listens for him, and is full of joy when he hears the bridegroom's voice. That joy is mine, and it is now complete. *[Spoken by John the Baptist in reference to Christ.]*

2. 2. Eph. 5.31-32 (ESV) - "For this reason *a man will leave his father and mother and be united to his wife, and the two will become one flesh.*" This is a profound mystery - *but I am talking about Christ and the Church.*

3. Rev. 19.7 (ESV) - Let us rejoice and be glad and give him glory! *For the wedding of the Lamb has come, and his bride has made herself ready.*

A Schematic for a Theology of the Kingdom and the Church

The Urban Ministry Institute

The Reign of the One, True, Sovereign, and Triune God, the LORD God, Yahweh, God the Father, Son, and Holy Spirit

The Father	The Son	The Spirit
Love - 1 John 4.8 Maker of heaven and earth and of all things visible and invisible	Faith - Heb. 12.2 Prophet, Priest, and King	Hope - Rom. 15.13 Lord of the Church
Creation All that exists through the creative action of God.	**Kingdom** The Reign of God expressed in the rule of his Son Jesus the Messiah.	**Church** The one, holy, apostolic community which functions as a witness to (Acts 28.31) and a foretaste of (Col. 1.12; James 1.18; 1 Pet. 2.9; Rev. 1.6) the Kingdom of God.

Rev. 8.18-31 →

Freedom (Slavery)

The eternal God, sovereign in power, infinite in wisdom, perfect in holiness, and steadfast in love, is the source and goal of all things.

Jesus replied, "I tell you the truth, everyone who sins is a slave to sin. Now a slave has no permanent place in the family but a son belongs to it forever. So if the Son sets you free, you will be free indeed." - John 8.34-36 (NIV)

The Church is an Apostolic Community Where the Word is Rightly Preached, Therefore it is a Community of:

Calling - It is for freedom that Christ has set us free. Stand firm, then, and do not let yourselves be burdened again by a yoke of slavery. - Gal. 5.1 (NIV) (cf. Rom. 8.28-30; 1 Cor. 1.26-31; Eph. 1.18; 2 Thess. 2.13-14; Jude 1.1)

Faith - "If you do not believe that I am the one I claim to be, you will indeed die in your sins." . . . To the Jews who had believed him Jesus said, "If you hold to my teaching you are really my disciples. Then you will know the truth and the truth will set you free." - John 8.24b, 31-32 (NIV) (cf. Ps. 119.45; Rom. 1.17; 5.1-2; Eph. 2.8-9; 2 Tim. 1.13-14; Heb. 2.14-15; James 1.25)

Witness - The Spirit of the Lord is upon me because he has anointed me to preach good news to the poor. He has sent me to proclaim freedom for the prisoners and recovery of sight for the blind, to release the oppressed, to proclaim the year of the Lord's favor. - Luke 4.18-19 (NIV) (cf. Lev. 25.10; Prov. 31.8; Matt. 4.17; 28.18-20; Mark 13.10; Acts 1.8; 8.4, 12; 13.1-3; 25.20; 28.30-31)

Rev. 21.1-5 →

Wholeness (Sickness)

O, the depth of the riches of the wisdom and knowledge of God! How unsearchable his judgments, and his paths beyond tracing out! Who has known the mind of the Lord? Or who has been his counselor? Who has ever given to God, that God should repay him? For from him and through him and to him are all things. To him be glory forever! Amen. - Rom. 11.33-36 (NIV) (cf. 1 Cor. 15.23-28; Rev.)

But he was pierced for our transgressions, he was crushed for our iniquities; the punishment that brought us peace was upon him and by his wounds we are healed. - Isa. 53.5 (NIV)

The Church is One Community Where the Sacraments are Rightly Administered, Therefore it is a Community of:

Worship - Worship the Lord your God, and his blessing will be on your food and water. I will take away sickness from among you. - Exod. 23.25 (NIV) (cf. Ps. 147.1-3; Heb. 12.28; Col. 3.16; Rev. 15.3-4; 19.5)

Covenant - The Holy Spirit also testifies to us about this. First he says: "This is the covenant I will make with them after that time, says the Lord. I will put My laws in their hearts, and I will write them on their minds." Then he adds: "Their sins and lawless acts I will remember no more." - Heb. 10.15-17 (NIV) (cf. Isa. 54.10-17; Ezek. 34.25-31; 37.26-27; Mal. 2.4-5; Luke 22.20; 2 Cor. 3.6; Col. 3.15; Heb. 8.7-13; 12.22-24; 13.20-21)

Presence - And in him you too are being built together to become a dwelling in which God lives by his Spirit. - Eph. 2.22 (NIV) (cf. Exod. 40.34-38; Ezek. 48.35; Matt. 18.18-20)

Isa. 11.6-9 →

Justice (Selfishness)

Here is my servant whom I have chosen, the one I love, in whom I delight; I will put my spirit on him and he will proclaim justice to the nations. He will not quarrel or cry out; no one will hear his voice in the streets. A bruised reed he will not break and a smoldering wick he will not put out till he leads justice to victory. - Matt. 12.18-20 (NIV)

The Church is a Holy Community Where Discipline is Rightly Ordered, Therefore it is a Community of:

Reconciliation - For he himself is our peace, who has made the two one and has destroyed the barrier, the dividing wall of hostility by abolishing in his flesh the law with its commandments and regulations. His purpose was to create one new man out of two, thus making peace and in this one body to reconcile both of them to God through the cross, by which he put to death their hostility. He came and preached peace to those who were far off and peace to those who were near. For through him we have access to the Father by one Spirit. - Eph. 2.14-18 (NIV) (cf. Exod. 23.4-9; Lev. 19.34; Deut. 10.18-19; Ezek. 22.29; Mic. 6.8; 2 Cor. 5.16-21)

Suffering - Therefore, since Christ suffered in his body, arm yourselves also with the same attitude, because he who has suffered in his body is done with sin. As a result, he does not live the rest of his earthly life for evil human desires, but rather for the will of God. - 1 Pet. 4.1-2 (NIV) (cf. Luke 6.22; 10.3; Rom. 8.17; 2 Tim. 2.3; 3.12; 1 Pet. 2.20-24; Heb. 5.8; 13.11-14)

Service - Jesus called them together and said, "You know that the rulers of the Gentiles lord it over them, and their high officials exercise authority over them. Not so with you. Instead, whoever wants to become great among you must be your servant, and whoever wants to be first must be your slave - just as the Son of Man did not come to be served, but to serve and to give his life as a ransom for many." - Matt. 20.25-27 (NIV) (cf. 1 John 4.16-18; Gal. 2.10)

Selecting a Credible Criteria for Independence
Navigating Toward a Healthy Transition
Don L. Davis

In order to establish a smooth transition from a missionary-led community to an indigenous, independent church community, we must identify and agree upon a clear criteria which would help us know when the transition is complete. In other words, everything depends on all of the key players' ability (i.e., missionaries, elders, and church community) to be crystal clear regarding our assumptions about what the transition involves and what we are seeking to accomplish. If, for any reason, we are unclear as to our expectations and directions together, we can easily misunderstand one another, and prolong the process, or even make the transition period unnecessarily painful.

The following categories are given as a guide, a criteria which may help you as leaders critically assess whether you have covered all necessary areas of transition. The list is suggestive, not exhaustive, and is not meant to be a final summary, but a tickler to help you think carefully through all of the issues necessary to make your period of transition an open and supportive one.

1. **A Faithful Group of Converted, Gathered, Maturing Disciples of Jesus**

   a. Solid conversions to Jesus Christ as Lord and Savior

   b. Self-identity as a separate Christian assembly with its own passionate spirituality, inspiring worship, and presence in the community

   c. Possess a clear sense of membership, ownership, belonging; able to bring new members in easily through strong orientation and loving relationships

   d. Clear sense of entering membership, disciplining members, restoring them

   e. Incorporating people smoothly into the life of the body (i.e., small group life, friendships, large group fellowship, etc.)

2. **Identified, Commissioned, and Released Indigenous Leaders**

   a. Selected by and for the body publicly and prayerfully

   b. Determiners of the church's direction and operation

   c. Accountable to the church's membership for their life and ministry

Selecting a Credible Criteria for Independence (continued)

    d. The body exercising wisdom as it determines which leaders to fund (i.e., how many it can afford to fund fully or partially), while at the same time relying on lay leaders and members to meet its needs as God leads

    e. Acknowledged separately from missionary leadership as authority of the body

3. **Selection of its Own Pastor and Pastoral Staff**

    a. Creation of a charter/by-laws/constitution/covenant delineating role of pastor(s) and relationship to body

    b. Installation of a pastor duly ratified by membership and endorsed by leadership

    c. Formal recognition of pastor's authority and responsibility

    d. Affirmation of community's support and submission to pastoral leadership

4. **Limited and Decreasing Oversight, Participation, and Direction**

    a. Missionaries have surrendered all significant positions and authority

    b. Clear understanding of the role of the missionaries presently serving our body

    c. Distinct lines between missionaries and indigenous leaders in decision-making and direction setting of the church

    d. Encouragement for missionaries to seek God's leading regarding new communities to target for new outreaches of the Gospel

5. **Distinctive and Unique Burden-Driven, Gift-Oriented Ministries of the Church**

    a. Clear mission and vision of the church's purpose and goals to mature and grow in number as God leads

    b. Reproducing new assemblies built into the DNA of our church (i.e., to fund and support other efforts of church planting around our city and beyond)

    c. Open doorways for members to explore ministry opportunities that coincide with the body's vision to mobilize its members to minister in their community.

    d. Ongoing equipping of the body members by the pastoral staff to enable members to do the work of the ministry

    e. Regular programming for worship, teaching, fellowship, and mission funded and directed by the church's personnel and members

6. Generating Non-Missionary Ministry Resources and Operating Income

    a. Deep conviction within the congregation that they will look to God alone as the source of supply to implement their vision

    b. Development of a plan to make the congregation financially free and independent of outside missionary support

    c. Clear guidelines under which support and aid can be given to the body

    d. Identifying independent sources for ongoing access to cash resources that would help support the effort

7. Acquisition and Stewardship of the Church's Equipment, Resources, and Facilities

    a. Functional, user-friendly structures created to administer the church's business and stewardship

    b. Careful, ongoing inventory of the church's resources

    c. Clear record keeping of the church's funds and finances, purchases, and allocations

    d. Responsible purchase and upkeep of the church's equipment and facilities

8. Development of its Own New Friends, Siblings, Volunteers, and Partners

    a. Recognition from other Christian communities, inside and outside community

    b. New relationships with outside churches or other organizations who would continue to support the effort with work groups and short term help

    c. New affiliation with church denominations or groups whose vision resonates with the church

    d. Associations to increase the effectiveness of the church's outreach and mission

The Self-Consciousness of Jesus Christ

Rev. Dr. Don L. Davis

The Self-Consciousness of Jesus Christ

God-Consciousness

Prophetic Orientation

Divine Representation

Apocalyptic Imagination

John 17.25-26 (ESV) - O righteous Father, even though the world does not know you, I know you, and these know that you have sent me. [26] I made known to them your name, and I will continue to make it known, that the love with which you have loved me may be in them, and I in them.

John 5.17 (ESV) - But Jesus answered them, "My Father is working until now, and I am working."

John 5.19-20 (ESV) - So Jesus said to them, "Truly, truly, I say to you, the Son can do nothing of his own accord, but only what he sees the Father doing. For whatever the Father does, that the Son does likewise. [20] For the Father loves the Son and shows him all that he himself is doing. And greater works than these will he show him, so that you may marvel."

John 8.26 (ESV) - I have much to say about you and much to judge, but he who sent me is true, and I declare to the world what I have heard from him.

John 8.42 (ESV) - Jesus said to them, "If God were your Father, you would love me, for I came from God and I am here. I came not of my own accord, but he sent me."

John 14.10 (ESV) - Do you not believe that I am in the Father and the Father is in me? The words that I say to you I do not speak on my own authority, but the Father who dwells in me does his works.

John 5.21-22 (ESV) - For as the Father raises the dead and gives them life, so also the Son gives life to whom he will. [22] The Father judges no one, but has given all judgment to the Son.

John 11.23-26 (ESV) - Jesus said to her, "Your brother will rise again." [24] Martha said to him, "I know that he will rise again in the resurrection on the last day." [25] Jesus said to her, "I am the resurrection and the life. Whoever believes in me, though he die, yet shall he live, [26] and everyone who lives and believes in me shall never die. Do you believe this?"

John 4.25-26 (ESV) - The woman said to him, "I know that Messiah is coming (he who is called Christ). When he comes, he will tell us all things." [26] Jesus said to her, "I who speak to you am he."

Mark 14.61-62 (ESV) - But he remained silent and made no answer. Again the high priest asked him, "Are you the Christ, the Son of the Blessed?" [62] And Jesus said, "I am, and you will see the Son of Man seated at the right hand of Power, and coming with the clouds of heaven."

John 5.34 (ESV) - Not that the testimony that I receive is from man, but I say these things so that you may be saved.

John 3.11 (ESV) - Truly, truly, I say to you, we speak of what we know, and bear witness to what we have seen, but you do not receive our testimony.

John 5.30 (ESV) - I can do nothing on my own. As I hear, I judge, and my judgment is just, because I seek not my own will but the will of him who sent me.

John 8.26 (ESV) - I have much to say about you and much to judge, but he who sent me is true, and I declare to the world what I have heard from him.

John 12.47-49 (ESV) - If anyone hears my words and does not keep them, I do not judge him; for I did not come to judge the world but to save the world. [48] The one who rejects me and does not receive my words has a judge; the word that I have spoken will judge him on the last day. [49] For I have not spoken on my own authority, but the Father who sent me has himself given me a commandment—what to say and what to speak.

John 5.30 (ESV) - "I can do nothing on my own. As I hear, I judge, and my judgment is just, because I seek not my own will but the will of him who sent me.

John 6.38 (ESV) - For I have come down from heaven, not to do my own will but the will of him who sent me.

John 14.10 (ESV) - Do you not believe that I am in the Father and the Father is in me? The words that I say to you I do not speak on my own authority, but the Father who dwells in me does his works.

John 17.8 (ESV) - For I have given them the words that you gave me, and they have received them and have come to know in truth that I came from you; and they have believed that you sent me.

The Shadow and the Substance
Understanding the Old Testament as God's Witness to Jesus Christ

Rev. Dr. Don L. Davis

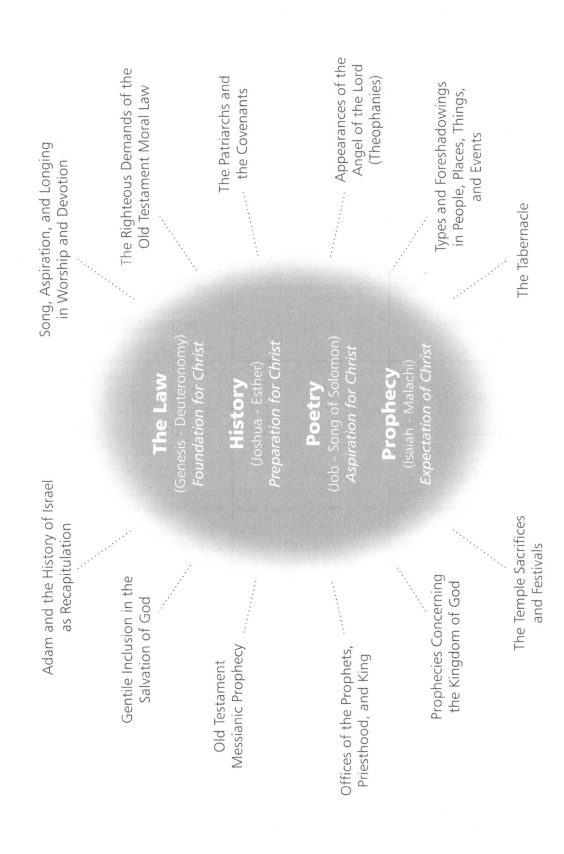

Song, Aspiration, and Longing in Worship and Devotion

The Righteous Demands of the Old Testament Moral Law

The Patriarchs and the Covenants

Appearances of the Angel of the Lord (Theophanies)

Types and Foreshadowings in People, Places, Things, and Events

The Tabernacle

Adam and the History of Israel as Recapitulation

The Law
(Genesis - Deuteronomy)
Foundation for Christ

History
(Joshua - Esther)
Preparation for Christ

Poetry
(Job - Song of Solomon)
Aspiration for Christ

Prophecy
(Isaiah - Malachi)
Expectation of Christ

Gentile Inclusion in the Salvation of God

Old Testament Messianic Prophecy

Offices of the Prophets, Priesthood, and King

Prophecies Concerning the Kingdom of God

The Temple Sacrifices and Festivals

Six Kinds of New Testament Ministry for Community

Rev. Dr. Don L. Davis

Type	Greek	Text	Task
Proclamation	*evanggelion*	Rom. 1.15-17	Preaching the Good News
Teaching	*idasko*	Matt. 28.19	To make disciples of Jesus
Worship	*latreuo*	John 4.20-24	Ushering into God's presence
Fellowship	*agape*	Rom. 13.8-10	The communion of saints
Witness	*martyria*	Acts 1.8	Compelling testimony to the lost
Service	*diakonia*	Matt. 10.43-45	Caring for the needs of others

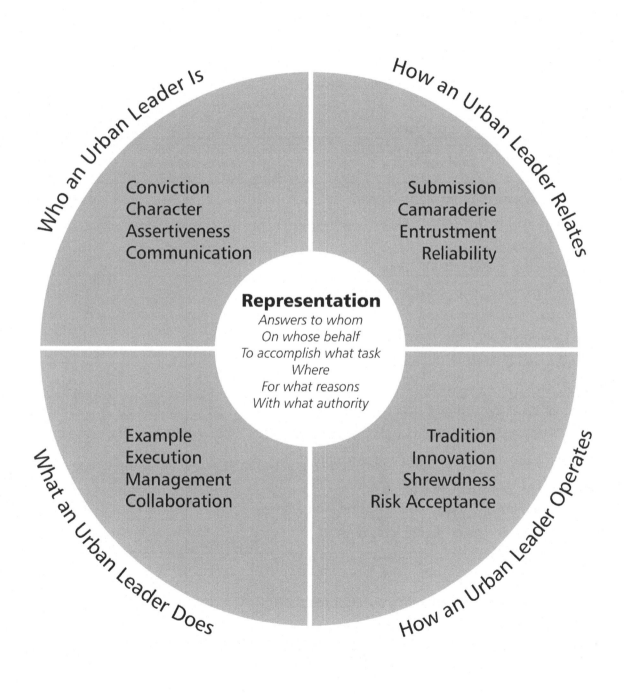

A Sociology of Urban Leadership Development
A Tool for Assessment and Training
Rev. Dr. Don L. Davis

Who an Urban Leader Is

How an Urban Leader Relates

Conviction
Character
Assertiveness
Communication

Submission
Camaraderie
Entrustment
Reliability

Representation
Answers to whom
On whose behalf
To accomplish what task
Where
For what reasons
With what authority

Example
Execution
Management
Collaboration

Tradition
Innovation
Shrewdness
Risk Acceptance

What an Urban Leader Does

How an Urban Leader Operates

The Sojourner's Quest

Don L. Davis

Sojourning as pilgrims on a quest to see the Great King
To share the same core, the same hope, the same dream

Walking should-to-shoulder, every burden we bear
With patient conviction, with warmth and great care

In friendship with Christ, our Glory and Crown
That in him alone our real joy would be found

To see with new eyes ev'ry single soul's worth
To cherish the least of these above all else on earth

To burn with deep longing that his praises might flow
And through our sweet unity his beauty might show

Yes, this is our goal, our glory, our aim
That Christ might be seen on this earth once again
That his Kingdom and glory would be powerfully known
That more of his likeness through us might be shown
That for the sake of our friends we would lay down our lives
That his fruit might be borne, and his grace multiplied
That by sharing in common our lights would so shine
That the world might be drawn to him, one heart at a time
And every broken vessel, however humble or meek
Might taste our Lord's mercies, be healed, and set free.

We count now as dung all this world's sweetest pleasures
We press toward the goal for the Kingdom's true treasures
We invite you to join us in our glorious quest
To sojourn with us gladly to his coronation, as guest
We give all that we are and we have to one thing-
To dine soon at his banquet before Christ the Great King.

Some of the Ways in Which Christians Disagree about Sanctification

Rev. Terry G. Cornett

I. Two Key Questions

A. The First Question: *Can a person be entirely sanctified (completely free from sin), in this present life?*

   1. Reformed/Baptistic and some Pentecostal theologies say NO.

   2. Holiness and some Pentecostal theologies say YES.

B. The Second Question: *Does the experience of sanctification include a second distinct experience with God, received by grace through faith?*

   What you believe about the first question, tends to influence what you believe about the second.

   1. If you believe that complete holiness must wait for the transforming event of death or Christ's return, you hope to grow in holiness but there is no distinct point in this life where it can be achieved.

   2. If you believe that complete holiness is attainable, you know it must come through a transforming event (you can't work your way into holiness). So holiness and Pentecostal-holiness groups say there is a distinct second experience.

Some of the Ways in Which Christians Disagree about Sanctification (continued)

II. Traditional Reformation Teaching

A. Sanctification is begun at salvation and continues progressively until glorification. God completely sanctifies us positionally at the moment of salvation, but practical sanctification is worked out in our experience gradually and daily.

B. Sin is primarily defined as "falling short of God's glory."

C. Arguments in favor:

1. Jesus taught us to pray daily, "Forgive us our trespasses" (Matt. 6.12) and added "But if you do not forgive others their trespasses, neither will your Father forgive your trespasses" (Matt. 6.15).

2. The Corinthian church was identified by Paul as "sanctified by Christ Jesus and called to be holy" but in practice was anything but. Paul had to say in 1 Corinthians 3.3, "For you are still of the flesh. For while there is jealousy and strife among you, are you not of the flesh and behaving only in a human way?" Paul understood the difference between being sanctified in God's sight but not yet sanctified in practice.

   a. Experience teaches us that:

      (1) We sin.

      (2) People who claim perfection tend to become legalistic, condemning, boastful, and tend to deny sin when it occurs.

Some of the Ways in Which Christians Disagree about Sanctification (continued)

    b. Romans 7 – This passage is understood as describing Paul's experience following conversion.

    c. Complete sinless perfection is not attainable in this life. When the word "Perfect" occurs in Scripture it is understood as "complete" or "mature." *Glorification is when sinlessness is achieved.* Sanctification is the movement toward holiness that draws on the resources given at salvation.

    d. Most important historical proponent: Martin Luther

    Luther spoke about Christians as "*simul justus et peccator*"- at one and the same time a righteous man and a sinner. He believed that this paradox will not find resolution until faith become sight. Lutheranism in no way condones sin. Rather it recognizes "that where sin abounded, grace did much more abound."

III. Holiness Movements

A. Sanctification is a second and distinct experience from salvation. Like salvation it is received by grace through faith and is frequently spoken of as "the Baptism in the Holy Spirit."

Entire Sanctification more commonly designated as "sanctification," "holiness," "Christian perfection," or "perfect love," represents that second definite stage in Christian experience wherein, by the baptism with the Holy Spirit, administered by Jesus Christ, and received instantaneously by faith, the justified believer is delivered from inbred sin, and consequently is saved from all unholy tempers, cleansed from all moral defilement, made perfect in love and introduced into full and abiding fellowship with God.

~ Doctrinal Statement of The First General Holiness Assembly held in Chicago, May, 1885
[Robert M. Anderson, **Vision of the Disinherited**]

B. Sin is primarily defined as "knowing, willful disobedience."

1. The concept of Christian Perfection [entire sanctification] is carefully defined.

    Perfection is not: perfect knowledge (ignorance remains), not freedom from mistakes, not free from weakness or character flaws, not free from temptation, not free from the need to grow, [See John Wesley, *On Christian Perfection*] It is not, a loss of the ability to sin. There is no point, short of glorification, where people could not fall.

    Perfection is: Walking in love by faith so that one does not sin willfully and habitually.

2. There is still a process of sanctification that follows the event of sanctification.

    I believe this perfection is always wrought in the soul by a simple act of faith; consequently in an instant. But I believe [in] a gradual work, both preceding and following that instant. As to the time, I believe this instant generally is the instant of death, the moment before the soul leaves the body. But I believe it may be ten, twenty, or forty years before. I believe it is usually many years after justification.

    > ~ Brief Thoughts on Christian Perfection.
    > **The Works of John Wesley.** Vol. 11, p. 466.

    Some holiness groups disagree with Wesley about timing. They believe entire sanctification can, and should, come more quickly.

C. Arguments for:

1. It is commanded by Jesus and the Apostles

    Matt. 5.48 - "Therefore you are to be perfect, as your heavenly Father is perfect." Compare with Apostle's injunction (1 John 5.3 - This is love for God: to obey his commands. And his commands are not burdensome).

2. It is the logical implication of what happens when an all-powerful God sets his Spirit to work against sin in our lives.

3. It seems to be frequently assumed by Scripture to be what happens in the life of the believer.

4. Romans 7 – This passage is understood as describing Paul's experience before conversion.

D. Most important historical proponent: John Wesley (who learned from the Puritan writer William Law)

E. Key Document: "A Plain Account of Christian Perfection."

    Wesley's key concern was to avoid conceding the possibility of perfection because he felt it impugned God's nature and power. (Don't say that God cannot or will not do what he clearly desires). It is an issue of faith for Wesley. Even if he had never seen this happen he would still believe in God's ability to accomplish his desire for our holiness.

Some of the Ways in Which Christians Disagree about Sanctification (continued)

IV. Putting it Together: Theological Common Ground and Key Implications

What Reformed and Holiness Christians agree on:

A. Sanctification is becoming like Christ and is the aim of the Christian life. [Scripture teaches us that this [holiness] is the goal of our calling- John Calvin, "Institutes of the Christian Religion].

B. Sanctification begins at the moment of salvation and faith is its sole condition (Doctrinal Minutes of the Methodist Conferences 1744-47).

C. Sanctification is both imputed and imparted and comes only by the grace of God.

D. Sanctification involves both a unique point of decision[1] and an on-going process of living out that decision.

[1] *For Reformed theology this point is conversion, for Holiness theologies it is conversion and a second experience of grace with the Holy Spirit.*

Spiritual Gifts Specifically Mentioned in the New Testament

Rev. Terry G. Cornett

Administration	1 Cor. 12.28	The ability to bring order to Church life.
Apostleship	1 Cor. 12.28; Eph. 4.11	The ability to establish new churches among the unreached, nurture them to maturity, and exercise the authority and wisdom necessary to see them permanently established and able to reproduce; and/or A gift unique to the founding of the Church age which included the reception of special revelation and uniquely binding leadership authority
Discernment	1 Cor. 12.10	The ability to serve the Church through a Spirit-given ability to distinguish between God's truth (his presence, working, and doctrine) and fleshly error or satanic counterfeits
Evangelism	Eph. 4.11	The passion and the ability to effectively proclaim the Gospel so that people understand it
Exhortation	Rom. 12.8	The ability to give encouragement or rebuke that helps others obey Christ
Faith	1 Cor. 12.9	The ability to build up the Church through a unique ability to see the unrealized purposes of God and unwaveringly trust God to accomplish them
Giving	Rom. 12.8	The ability to build up a church through taking delight in the consistent, generous sharing of spiritual and physical resources
Healing	1 Cor. 12.9; 12.28	The ability to exercise faith that results in restoring people to physical, emotional, and spiritual health
Interpretation	1 Cor. 12.10	The ability to explain the meaning of an ecstatic utterance so that the Church is edified
Knowledge	1 Cor. 12.8	The ability to understand scriptural truth, through the illumination of the Holy Spirit, and speak it out to edify the body; and/or The supernatural revelation of the existence, or nature, of a person or thing which would not be known through natural means

Spiritual Gifts Specifically Mentioned in the New Testament (continued)

Leadership	Rom. 12.8	Spiritually inspired courage, wisdom, zeal, and hard work which motivate and guide others so that they can effectively participate in building the Church
Mercy	Rom. 12.8	Sympathy of heart which enables a person to empathize with and cheerfully serve those who are sick, hurting, or discouraged
Ministering (or Service, or Helping, or Hospitality)	Rom. 12.7; 1 Pet. 4.9	The ability to joyfully perform any task which benefits others and meets their practical and material needs (especially on behalf of the poor or afflicted)
Miracles	1 Cor. 12.10; 12.28	The ability to confront evil and do good in ways that make visible the awesome power and presence of God
Pastoring	Eph. 4.11	The desire and ability to guide, protect, and equip the members of a congregation for ministry
Prophecy	1 Cor. 12.28; Rom. 12.6	The ability to receive and proclaim openly a revealed message from God which prepares the Church for obedience to him and to the Scriptures
Teaching	1 Cor. 12.28; Rom. 12.7; Eph. 4.11	The ability to explain the meaning of the Word of God and its application through careful instruction
Tongues	1 Cor. 12.10; 12.28	Ecstatic utterance by which a person speaks to God (or others) under the direction of the Holy Spirit
Wisdom	1 Cor. 12.8	Spirit-revealed insight that allows a person to speak godly instruction for solving problems; and/or Spirit-revealed insight that allows a person to explain the central mysteries of the Christian faith

Spiritual Growth Diagrams

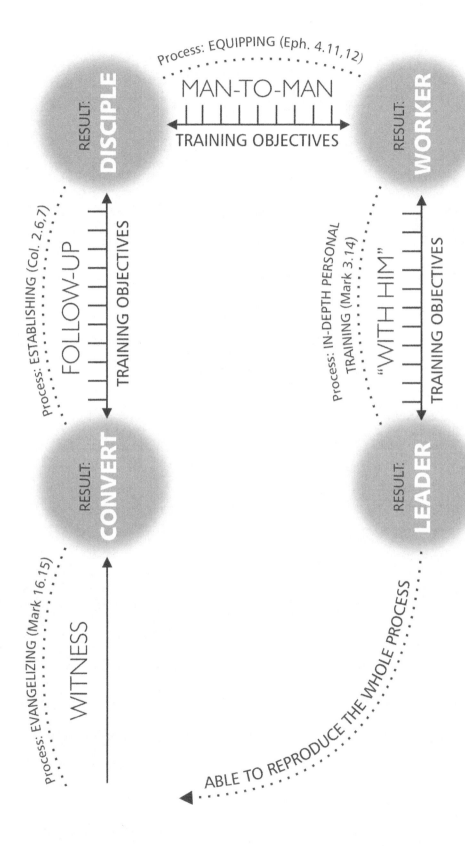

Process: EQUIPPING (Eph. 4.11,12)

MAN-TO-MAN
TRAINING OBJECTIVES

RESULT: **DISCIPLE**

RESULT: **WORKER**

Process: ESTABLISHING (Col. 2.6,7)

FOLLOW-UP
TRAINING OBJECTIVES

Process: IN-DEPTH PERSONAL TRAINING (Mark 3.14)

"WITH HIM"
TRAINING OBJECTIVES

RESULT: **CONVERT**

RESULT: **LEADER**

Process: EVANGELIZING (Mark 16.15)

WITNESS

ABLE TO REPRODUCE THE WHOLE PROCESS

Leroy Eims, The Lost Art of Discipling, Grand Rapids: Zondervan, 1978, p. 124

Spiritual Growth Diagrams (continued)

*Adapted from Rick Warren, **The Purpose-Driven Church**, p. 144*

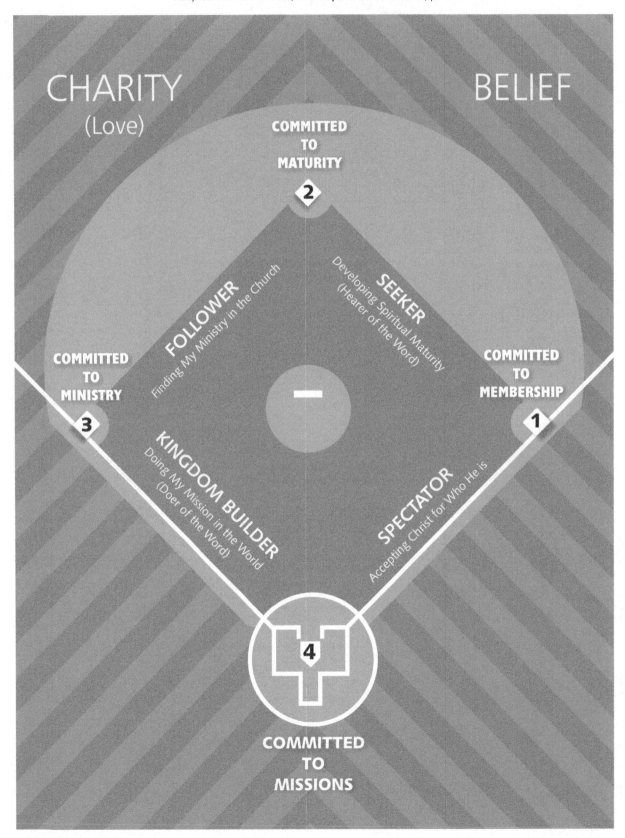

CHARITY
(Love)

BELIEF

COMMITTED
TO
MATURITY
2

FOLLOWER
Finding My Ministry in the Church

SEEKER
Developing Spiritual Maturity
(Hearer of the Word)

COMMITTED
TO
MINISTRY
3

COMMITTED
TO
MEMBERSHIP
1

KINGDOM BUILDER
Doing My Mission in the World
(Doer of the Word)

SPECTATOR
Accepting Christ for Who He is

4

COMMITTED
TO
MISSIONS

Spiritual Service Checklist

Rev. Dr. Don L. Davis

1. *Salvation*: Has this person believed the Gospel, confessed Jesus as Lord and Savior, been baptized, and formally joined our church as a member?

2. *Personal integrity*: Are they walking with God, growing in their personal life, and demonstrating love and faithfulness in their family, work, and in the community?

3. *Equipped in the Word*: How equipped is this person in the Word of God to share and teach with others?

4. *Support of our church*: Do they support the church through their presence, pray for the leaders and members, and give financially to its support?

5. *Submission to authority*: Does this person joyfully submit to spiritual authority?

6. *Identification of spiritual gifts*: What gifts, talents, abilities, or special resources does this person have for service, and what is their particular burden for ministry now?

7. *Present availability*: Are they open to be assigned to a task or project where we could use their service to build up the body?

8. *Reputation amongst leaders*: How do the other leaders feel about this person's readiness for a new role of leadership?

9. *Resources needed to accomplish*: If appointed to this role, what particular training, monies, resources, and/or input will they need to accomplish the task?

10. *Formal commissioning*: When and how will we make known to others that we have appointed this person to their task or project?

11. *Timing and reporting*: Also, if we dedicate this person to this role/task, when will they be able to start, and how long ought they serve before we evaluate them.

12. *Evaluate and re-commission*: When will we evaluate the performance of the person, and determine what next steps we ought to take in their leadership role at the church?

St. Basil, the Nicene Creed, and the Doctrine of the Holy Spirit

Rev. Terry G. Cornett

The original Nicene Creed came out the first worldwide gathering of Christian leaders at Nicea in Bithynia (what is now Isnik, Turkey) in the year 325. It was called to deal with a heresy called Arianism which denied that Jesus was God and taught that he was instead the greatest created being. The council at Nicaea, condemned Arianism, and hammered out language that the bishops could use to teach their churches who Jesus truly was.

A little over 50 years later, however, additional challenges were being faced by the Church. A modified form of the Arian heresy was making a comeback; Macedonius, an Arian theologian, had been elected as Bishop of Constantinople in 341. A new problem had also emerged: some Christian bishops had begun teaching that the Holy Spirit was not God. Macedonius eventually became the leader of the sect of Pneumatomachi, whose distinctive tenet was that the Holy Spirit is not God but rather a created being similar to the angels. They taught that the Holy Spirit is subordinate to the Father and the Son and functions as their servant.

Basil[1] is one of the key ancient theologians who communicated and defended the biblical doctrine of the Holy Spirit against these heresies. Basil was a bishop of Caesarea who lived in the 4th century A.D. He wrote *De Spiritu Sancto* ("On the Holy Spirit") in 374 just a few years before his death in 379. This book defended the belief that the Holy Spirit is God. Basil worked tirelessly to see that a new Church council would be called to affirm this doctrine and see that it was taught in the churches.

In 381, shortly after Basil's death, a council of 150 bishops of the Eastern Church were gathered in Constantinople (modern day Istanbul, Turkey). This council reaffirmed the fact that Jesus was fully God and then turned their attention to the question of the Holy Spirit which the Nicene council had left untouched. (The original Nicene Creed read simply, "We believe in the Holy Spirit"). Building on Basil's writings, the council turned this simple statement into a paragraph which explained more fully the person and work of the Holy Spirit.

[1] *Basil was born in 329, in the region of Pontus (now modern day Turkey), to a wealthy and rather remarkable family. His grandfather, his father, his mother, his sister and his two younger brothers were all eventually named as saints by the Church. He received an outstanding education at schools in Caesarea, Constantinople, and Athens. Following his education Basil became first a monk in Pontus, then a presbyter (a pastoral position) at Caesarea (where he eventually became a bishop) and developed into a vigorous theologian as well. In these roles, he developed a reputation for personal integrity and great compassion. Even as a bishop he owned only one undergarment and one outer garment and did not eat meat at his table. He lived simply, treated his body harshly, and was personally involved with the distribution to the poor. Because of his personal integrity his many theological opponents through the years had difficulty finding anything wrong to charge him with.*

St. Basil, the Nicene Creed, and the Doctrine of the Holy Spirit (continued)

This amended version of the original Nicene Creed (technically the Nicene-Constantinopolitan Creed) is commonly referred to simply as the "Nicene Creed" since it is the final version of the statement started at Nicea. It is accepted by Catholics, Orthodox[2], and Protestant Christians alike as the summary of scriptural teaching which separates orthodoxy from heresy.

Steps to Equipping Others

Rev. Dr. Don L. Davis

Step One

*You **become a Master** at it, striving toward mastery by practicing it with regularity, excellence, and enjoyment.* You must learn to do it, and do it excellently. While you need not be perfect, you should be able to do it, be doing it regularly, and growing in your practice of it. This is the most fundamental principle of all mentoring and discipling. You cannot teach what you do not know or cannot do, and when your Apprentice is fully trained, they will become like you (Luke 6.40).

Step Two

*You **select an Apprentice** who also desires to develop mastery of the thing, one who is teachable, faithful, and available.* Jesus called the Twelve to be with him, and to send them out to preach (Mark 3.14). His relationship was clear, neither vague nor coerced. The roles and responsibilities of the relationship must be carefully outlined, clearly discussed, and openly agreed upon.

Step Three

*You instruct and model the task **in the presence of and accompanied by** your Apprentice.* He/she comes alongside you to listen, observe, and watch. You do it with regularity and excellence, and your Apprentice comes along "for the ride," who is brought along to see how it is done. A picture is worth a thousand words. This sort of non-pressure participant observation is critical to in-depth training (2 Timothy 2.2; Philippians 4.9).

Step Four

*You do the task and **practice the thing together**.* Having modeled the act for your Apprentice in many ways and at many times, you now invite them to cooperate with you by becoming a partner-in-training, working together on the task. The goal is to do the task together, taking mutual responsibility. You coordinate your efforts, working together in harmony to accomplish the thing.

Step Five

Your Apprentice does the task on their own, **in the presence of and accompanied by you.** You provide opportunity to your Apprentice to practice the thing in your presence while you watch and listen. You make yourself available to help, but offer it in the background; you provide counsel, input, and guidance as they request it, but they do the task. Afterwards, you evaluate and clarify anything you may have observed as you accompanied your Apprentice (2 Corinthians 11.1).

Step Six

Your Apprentice does the thing solo, practicing it regularly, automatically, and excellently **until mastery of the thing is gained.** After your Apprentice has done the task under your supervision excellently, he/she is ready to be released to make the thing his/her own by habituating the act in his/her own life. You are a co-doer with your Apprentice; both of you are doing the task without coercion or aid from the other. The goal is familiarity and skillfulness in the task (Hebrews 5.11-15).

Step Seven

Your Apprentice **becomes a Mentor of others,** *selecting other faithful Apprentices to equip and train.* The training process bears fruit when the Apprentice, having mastered the thing you have equipped him/her to do, becomes a trainer of others. This is the heart of the discipling and training process (Hebrews 5.11-14; 2 Timothy 2.2)

The Story God Is Telling

Rev. Don Allsman

Chapter Title	Chapter Summary	Theme Verse
An Attempted Coup (Before Time) Genesis 1.1a	God exists in Perfect Fellowship before creation. The devil and his followers rebel and bring evil into existence.	In the beginning was the Word, and the Word was with God and the Word was God. He was in the beginning with God. All things were made through him, and without him was not any thing made that was made (John 1.1-3).
Insurrection (Creation and the Fall) Genesis 1.1b – 3.13	God creates man in his image, who joins Satan in rebellion	Therefore, just as sin came into the world through one man, and death through sin, and so death spread to all men because all sinned (Rom. 5.12).
Preparing for Invasion (The Patriarchs, Kings, and Prophets) Genesis 3.14 – Malachi	God contends to set apart a people for his own, out of which will come a King to deliver mankind, including Gentiles. Clues to his battle plans are hinted at along the way.	They are Israelites, and to them belong the adoption, the glory, the covenants, the giving of the law, the worship, and the promises. To them belong the patriarchs, and from their race, according to the flesh, is the Christ who is God over all, blessed forever. Amen (Rom. 9.4-5).
Victory and Rescue (Incarnation, Temptation, Miracles, Resurrection) Matthew – Acts 1.11	The Savior comes to deal a disarming blow to his enemy.	The reason the Son of God appeared was to destroy the works of the devil (1 John 3.8b).
The Army Advances (The Church) Acts 1.12 – Revelation 3	The Savior reveals his plan of a people assigned to take progressive ownership from the enemy as they enjoy a foretaste of the Kingdom to come.	So that through the church the manifold wisdom of God might now be made known to the rulers and authorities in the heavenly places. This was according to the eternal purpose that he has realized in Christ Jesus our Lord (Eph. 3.10-11).
The Final Conflict (The Second Coming) Revelation 4 – 22	The Savior returns to destroy his enemy, marry his bride, and resume his rightful place on the throne.	Then comes the end, when he delivers the Kingdom to God the Father after destroying every rule and authority and power. For he must reign until he has put all his enemies under his feet. The last enemy to be destroyed is death (1 Cor. 15.24-26).
The War between the Kingdoms	The common thread of the Bible narrative is warfare.	The kingdom of the world has become the kingdom of our Lord and of his Christ. And he shall reign forever and ever (Rev. 11.15b).

It is a world where terrible things happen and wonderful things too. It is a world where goodness is pitted against evil, love against hate, order against chaos, in a great struggle where often it is hard to be sure who belongs to which side because appearances can be deceptive. Yet for all its confusion and wildness, it is a world where the battle goes ultimately to the good, who live happily ever after, and where in the long run everybody, good and evil alike, becomes known by his true name.

~ Frederick Buechner. *Telling the Truth.*

The Story of God: Our Sacred Roots

Rev. Dr. Don L. Davis

The LORD God is the source, sustainer, and end of all things in the heavens and earth. All things were formed and exist by his will and for his eternal glory. the triune God, Father, Son, and Holy Spirit, Rom. 11.36.

The Alpha and the Omega	Christus Victor	Come, Holy Spirit	Your Word Is Truth	The Great Confession	His Life in Us	Living in the Way	Reborn to Serve
THE TRIUNE GOD'S UNFOLDING DRAMA — God's Self-Revelation in Creation, Israel, and Christ				THE CHURCH'S PARTICIPATION IN GOD'S UNFOLDING DRAMA — Fidelity to the Apostolic Witness to Christ and His Kingdom			
The Objective Foundation: The Sovereign Love of God — God's Narration of His Saving Work in Christ				The Subjective Practice: Salvation by Grace through Faith — The Redeemed's Joyous Response to God's Saving Work in Christ			
The Author of the Story	*The Champion of the Story*	*The Interpreter of the Story*	*The Testimony of the Story*	*The People of the Story*	*Re-enactment of the Story*	*Embodiment of the Story*	*Continuation of the Story*
The Father as Director	Jesus as Lead Actor	The Spirit as Narrator	Scripture as Script	As Saints, Confessors	As Worshipers, Ministers	As Followers, Sojourners	As Servants, Ambassadors
Christian Worldview	Communal Identity	Spiritual Experience	Biblical Authority	Orthodox Theology	Priestly Worship	Congregational Discipleship	Kingdom Witness
Theistic and Trinitatian Vision	Christ-centered Foundation	Spirit-Indwelt and -Filled Community	Canonical and Apostolic Witness	Ancient Creedal Affirmation of Faith	Weekly Gathering in Christian Assembly	Corporate, Ongoing Spiritual Formation	Active Agents of the Reign of God
Sovereign Willing	Messianic Representing	Divine Comforting	Inspired Testifying	Truthful Retelling	Joyful Excelling	Faithful Indwelling	Hopeful Compelling
Creator — True Maker of the Cosmos	Recapitulation — Typos and Fulfillment of the Covenant	Life-Giver — Regeneration and Adoption	Divine Inspiration — God-breathed Word	The Confession of Faith — Union with Christ	Song and Celebration — Historical Recitation	Pastoral Oversight — Shepherding the Flock	Explicit Unity — Love for the Saints
Owner — Sovereign Disposer of Creation	Revealer — Incarnation of the Word	Teacher — Illuminator of the Truth	Sacred History — Historical Record	Baptism into Christ — Communion of Saints	Homilies and Teachings — Prophetic Proclamation	Shared Spirituality — Common Journey through the Spiritual Disciplines	Radical Hospitality — Evidence of God's Kingdom Reign
Ruler — Blessed Controller of All Things	Redeemer — Reconciler of All Things	Helper — Endowment and the Power	Biblical Theology — Divine Commentary	The Rule of Faith — Apostles' Creed and Nicene Creed	The Lord's Supper — Dramatic Re-enactment	Embodiment — Anamnesis and Prolepsis through the Church Year	Extravagant Generosity — Good Works
Covenant Keeper — Faithful Promisor	Restorer — Christ, the Victor over the powers of evil	Guide — Divine Presence and Shekinah	Spiritual Food — Sustenance for the Journey	The Vincentian Canon — Ubiquity, antiquity, universality	Eschatological Foreshadowing — The Already/Not Yet	Effective Discipling — Spiritual Formation in the Believing Assembly	Evangelical Witness — Making Disciples of All People Groups

Story: The Crux of Revelation
Rev. Ryan Carter

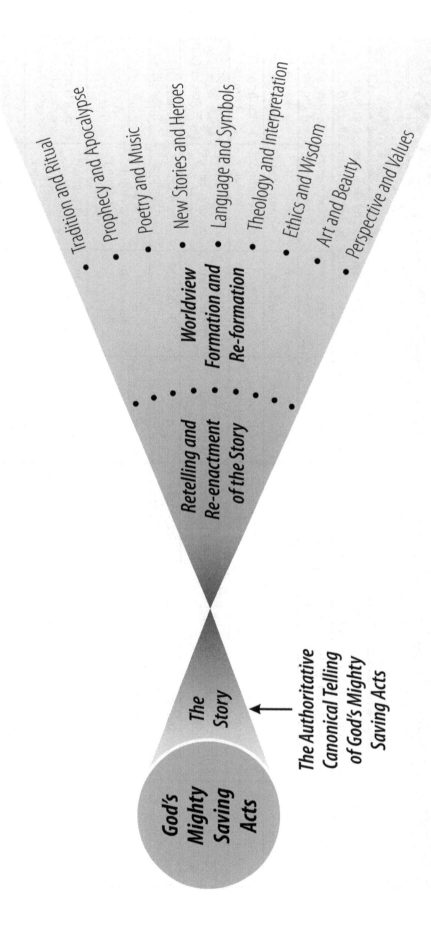

Tradition and Ritual

Prophecy and Apocalypse

Poetry and Music

New Stories and Heroes

Language and Symbols

Theology and Interpretation

Ethics and Wisdom

Art and Beauty

Perspective and Values

Worldview Formation and Re-formation

Retelling and Re-enactment of the Story

The Authoritative Canonical Telling of God's Mighty Saving Acts

The Story

God's Mighty Saving Acts

Story, Theology, and Church

*William J. Bausch. **Storytelling: Imagination and Faith**. Mystic, CT: 23rd Publications, 1984. pp. 195-199.*

At this point in our book, drawing to a close as it is, it might be well to put aside for the moment the direct story and illustration (to be resumed, however, in the final two chapters) and briefly list ten propositions of a theological nature. This exercise will, I hope, not be heavy or obtuse. It will serve as a means of extracting, for the sake of clarity and reflection, the theological implications of what has been stated here and there in the past chapters. So this is a very brief chapter-an interlude really-and is intended as a kind of theological summary, an overall view of how stories relate to theology and the structures of the church.

First Proposition: Stories introduce us to sacramental presences.

Stories are designed to force us to consider possibilities. To that extent they are grounded in hope. Even the most outlandish fairy tales, for example, raise possibilities and tease our hopes. The biblical stories do the same, only more overtly. Their whole point is to coax us to look beyond our limits and experiences of limitation and to suggest, through the wonderful, Wonder itself. Stories hint that our taken-for-granted daily realities may, in fact, be fraught with surprise. There are "rumors of angels" and grace abounding in our world. If a frog might be a prince, a lost sailor an angel, a pilgrim the Christ, then all of creation may be a sacramental presence pointing to "Something More." Stories declare that this just might be the case.

Second Proposition: Stories are always more important than facts.

Facts, in relation to story, are inert. It is the genius of story to arrange the facts and proclaim the good news about them. For example, the pivotal "fact" of the resurrection is fundamentally less important in its description and verification as a statement of Jesus of Nazareth rising from the dead than as a central proposition of hope. What counts are the implications the resurrection story has for us in our living and in sustaining our outlook on life and death. Otherwise you have reportage, not gospel.

Third Proposition: Stories remain normative.

We have seen in the first chapter of this book that all of theology is but a reflection on the original story. To test a theology, we must always go back to the pristine material (and its subsequent unfolding). To this extent the biblical stories will always remain normative. There is a serious caution, however. Some may go back to the original story and make an idol of it; that is, they will take it as a rigid and finished document, detach it from its history, contemporary and subsequent, and force it to remain compressed and restricted. This is the fault of literalists or fundamentalists.

Fourth Proposition: Traditions evolve through stories.

Traditions evolve through stories: that's the nature of important and critical stories. People "caught" by the story, its hero or heroine and its message, want not only to share an experience but to share an experience faithful to the original story. Hence tradition arises that has two functions: preserving and protecting. Preserving is "handing on," which is what the word tradition means literally. Protecting may need more explanation.

Because stories are really extended metaphors, they are open-ended. They are freely adaptable and can easily be recast and retold. Details, names, and locales are easily accommodated to different audiences and places. We detect this even in the short span of the writing of the four gospels. Still, a boundary is implicitly set beyond which flexibility may not go and still be true to the founding story. To take a secular example: Santa Claus may be metamorphosed throughout the centuries easily enough. He can be tall or short, smooth faced or bearded, clothed in purple or green, rotund or as slim as Ichabod Crane. But Santa can never be a child abuser. After all, he derives from St. Nicholas, who derives from the Christ Child, who derives from the Father of all gifts. The core tradition would not permit a connection between Santa and harm when his whole point is benevolence and kindness. Along the way somewhere, tradition would protect the image from intrinsic contradiction. The biblical stories about Jesus evoke the same process of protection. This is where church tradition fits in. And since the stories of Jesus are varied, varied traditions will not only arise but will be quite legitimate.

Fifth Proposition: Stories precede and produce the church.

This we noted early on. The story exists first, then people are caught by it, savor it, reflect on it, retell it, preserve it, and pass it on (tradition). When many people are caught by, believe in, and celebrate the same story, you have a church.

Sixth Proposition: Stories imply censure.

This proposition is a logical outcome of the preceding two. If you have a tradition dedicated to preserving and passing on the core story, and if you have a church to live by and celebrate the core story, then those of the group who at any time might radically contradict the essential story must be dealt with. This is quite commonplace in all walks of life. Here is where we get-in any religion, government, or university-the censure, the reprimand, the excommunication. Wide latitude may be allowed, but not beyond contradicting what the story stands for. A civil liberties group could not, for example, tolerate an overt bigot. Of course, as history has shown, people tend to be far more restrictive of what they perceive to be the "true" tradition than may be accurate. One person's orthodoxy may be another's heresy, depending on who wields the power. But that is beside the point here. The point is that when story gives rise to tradition, and tradition to a church, then censure is implied sooner or later. (Quite soon, in fact, as we learn from Paul's epistles.) In our Catholic tradition this is the origin of penalties and excommunications.

Seventh Proposition: Stories produce theology.

Reflection on and conclusions from the Jesus stories began early in the church. We see this in the church's earliest writings, the epistles of Paul. When you reflect on the story, make associations, and draw conclusions, you have a theology. We can see this easily, for example, in the faith trajectory concerning the nature of Jesus. In a very special way the story tells us that he is God's man. If he is God's man, then maybe he is his spokesman. If he is his spokesman, then maybe he is his very word. If he is his word, then maybe he has a special relationship with the Father. If he has a special relationship with the Father, maybe he is his son -and in a unique way. If God's son, then maybe he is his equal. If equal, maybe he is God in the flesh. Theology is a putting of pieces together and discovering richer conclusions than might first be grasped.

Story, Theology, and Church (continued)

Or we might put it this way. Theology arises because there is always more to the story than even the tellers either realize or intend. We have a classic example in John's gospel (11:49-52): "But one of them, Caiaphas, who was high priest that year, said to them, 'You know nothing at all; you do not understand that it is expedient that one man should die for the people and that the whole nation should not perish.'" John then goes on to give his reflection and expansion concerning these words (theology): "He did not say this of his own accord, but being high priest that year, he prophesied that Jesus should die for the nation, and not for the nation only, but to gather into one the children of God who are scattered abroad." Time and hindsight often reveal deeper and richer motifs to stories. Theology grabs onto this and draws it out. Theology is rooted in and flows from the story.

Eighth Proposition: Stories produce many theologies.

The Jesus stories themselves are varied and obviously reflect different traditions. Even a casual reading of the four gospels demonstrates this. Since this is so, we expect that such varied story traditions will give rise to varied theologies. No one system is made absolute-nor should it be. The normative stories themselves, after all, are not only open-ended but conditioned by the assumptions and frame of references of their times. There have been and will continue to be many systems of theology in the church. Although there has been a drive in modern times to reduce all systems to one, in the history of the church there has been a wide tolerance of diversity.

Ninth Proposition: Stories produce ritual and sacrament.

We must remember that the experience of Jesus came before reflections about him. This is a way of saying that life came before thought, and that story came before theology. The experience of Jesus was indeed, as we have seen, enshrined in stories, but it must also be noted that it was simultaneously enshrined in ritual and in celebration. Signs, actions, gesture, and symbol also became part of the overall story. Ritual itself is a story line in action. So right away there arose rituals reenacting the death, burial, and resurrection of Jesus. Paul calls this baptism. Then there was a ritual meal breaking bread and sharing a cup, signs of the very givingness of Jesus. In short, there were also lived and shared stories we have come to describe as celebrating the mysteries of God or have come to call simply the sacraments. Story (word), celebration (festivity), and ritual (sacrament) all go together.

Of course, it can happen and has happened that a ritual can lose its story connection through routine, boredom, and repetition. When this happens, people often continue the ritual out of rote, but no longer remember the story it was attached to or expressed. To revitalize or recast the ritual we must go back and remember the story. Church renewals are basically an exercise in this.

Tenth Proposition: Stories are history.

Since stories are open-ended, they cannot be or must not be literalized. Stories have a life of their own and each age extracts from and adds to the story in a kind of symbiotic relationship. The result is a profound enrichment. History is the bridge from which we view the story in all its forms and in all its aspects of truth. Ideally, history saves the story from the twin dangers of idolatry and irrelevance.

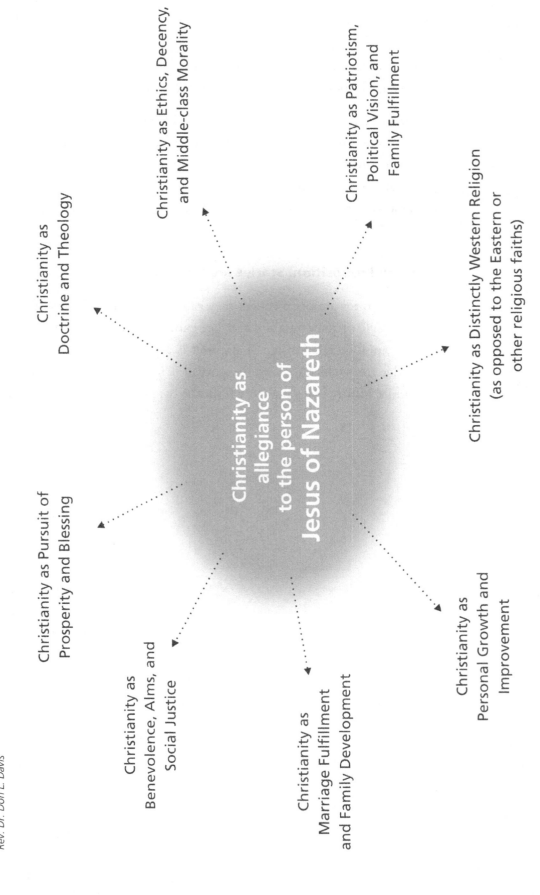

Substitute Centers to a Christ-Centered Vision

Goods and Effects Which Our Culture Substitutes as the Ultimate Concern

Rev. Dr. Don L. Davis

Christianity as
Doctrine and Theology

Christianity as Ethics, Decency,
and Middle-class Morality

Christianity as Patriotism,
Political Vision, and
Family Fulfillment

Christianity as
allegiance
to the person of
Jesus of Nazareth

Christianity as Pursuit of
Prosperity and Blessing

Christianity as Distinctly Western Religion
(as opposed to the Eastern or
other religious faiths)

Christianity as
Benevolence, Alms, and
Social Justice

Christianity as
Marriage Fulfillment
and Family Development

Christianity as
Personal Growth and
Improvement

Substitution
Don L. Davis

The Principle of
Substitution

Myth
Story
Narrative
Parable
Allegory
Re-enactment
Ritual
Liturgy
Remembrance
Festival

**Resemblance
Analogy
Comparison**

Metaphor
Personification
Imagery
Symbol
Representation
Type
Archetype
Simile

$$\frac{A}{B} :: \frac{C}{D}$$

"As a *shepherd* is to *sheep*
so *the Lord* is to *his people*."

*The Lord is my Shepherd,
I shall not want for anything.* ~ Psalm 23.1

The Lord   A Shepherd

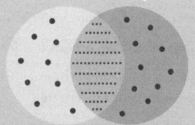

Analysis of Imagistic and Narratival Substitution

1. Main subject of discourse or religious idea

2. A concrete image or narrative derived from a cultural fund or reservoir of images and stories

3. Analogy-resemblance-comparison of selected elements or characteristics of (2) to illumine the nature of (1)

4. Implicit or explicit association, comparison, and identification of the two together

5. New understanding and experience of (1) through its association and identification with (2) representing new knowledge

Levels of Association

1. The Holy Spirit's inspiration of associations

2. The cultural fund of associations for societal meaning

3. The missiological association to communicate truth

Rules of Association

1. No analogy is perfect

2. Selection of elements to compare is critical

3. Theology explores connections and possible connections

4. Creative connection demands mastery of core images and stories

Suffering: The Cost of Discipleship and Servant-Leadership

Don L. Davis

To be a disciple is to bear the stigma and reproach of the One who called you into service (2 Tim. 3.12). Practically, this may mean the loss of comfort, convenience, and even life itself (John 12.24-25).

All of Christ's Apostles endured insults, rebukes, lashes, and rejections by the enemies of their Master. Each of them sealed their doctrines with their blood in exile, torture, and martyrdom. Listed below are the fates of the Apostles according to traditional accounts.

- Matthew suffered martyrdom by being slain with a sword at a distant city of Ethiopia.

- Mark expired at Alexandria, after being cruelly dragged through the streets of that city.

- Luke was hanged upon an olive tree in the classic land of Greece.

- John was put in a caldron of boiling oil, but escaped death in a miraculous manner, and was afterward branded at Patmos.

- Peter was crucified at Rome with his head downward.

- James, the Greater, was beheaded at Jerusalem.

- James, the Less, was thrown from a lofty pinnacle of the temple, and then beaten to death with a fuller's club.

- Bartholomew was flayed alive.

- Andrew was bound to a cross, whence he preached to his persecutors until he died.

- Thomas was run through the body with a lance at Coromandel in the East Indies.

- Jude was shot to death with arrows.

- Matthias was first stoned and then beheaded.

- Barnabas of the Gentiles was stoned to death at Salonica.

- Paul, after various tortures and persecutions, was at length beheaded at Rome by the Emperor Nero.

Summary of Messianic Interpretations in the Old Testament

Rev. Dr. Don L. Davis, adapted from James Smith, The Promised Messiah

Legend

EJ - Early Jewish Interpretation   NTA - New Testament Allusion

NTE - New Testament Exegesis   CF - Church Fathers

	Bible Reference	Summary of the Messianic Prophecy	EJ	NTA	NTE	CF
1	Gen. 3.15	One from the ranks of the seed of the woman will crush the head of the serpent	X	X		X
2	Gen. 9.25-27	God will come and dwell in the tents of Shem	X	X		X
3	Gen. 12.3; 18.18; 22.18; 26.4; 28.14	All nations of the earth will be blessed through the seed of Abraham, Isaac, and Jacob	X	X	X	X
4	Gen. 49.10-11	The scepter won't depart from Judah until Shiloh comes, and all the nations will be obedient to him	X	X		X
5	Num. 24.16-24	A powerful ruler from Israel will come and crush the enemies of God's people	X	X		X
6	Deut. 18.15-18	A prophet like Moses will come and all the righteous will listen to him		X	X	X
7	Deut. 32.43	The angels of God commanded to rejoice as the Firstborn of God comes into the world		X		
8	1 Sam. 2.10	God will judge the ends of the earth but will give strength to his anointed	X			X
9	1 Sam. 2.35-36	A faithful Priest will come and dispense blessing upon the people				
10	2 Sam. 7.12-16	The Seed of David will sit upon an eternal throne and will build the house of God		X		X
11	Ps. 89	God's covenant to send Messiah through David cannot be revoked	X			
12	Ps. 132	God has chosen David and Zion		X		
13	Ps. 8	The Son of Man is made a little lower than the angels, and is exalted as ruler over all creation		X	X	X
14	Ps. 40	Messiah volunteers to enter the world, to suffer, and is delivered			X	X

Summary of Messianic Interpretations in the Old Testament (continued)

	Bible Reference	Summary of the Messianic Prophecy	EJ	NTA	NTE	CF
15	Ps. 118	Messiah survives the power of death to become the chief Cornerstone, the Capstone of God's building			X	X
16	Ps. 78.1-2	Messiah will speak to the people in parables			X	
17	Ps. 69	Messiah's zeal for the house of God will bring hatred and abuse, but his enemies will receive their just dues			X	X
18	Ps. 109	The one who betrays Messiah will suffer a terrible fate			X	X
19	Ps. 22	After unparalleled suffering, Messiah conquers death and rejoices with his brethren			X	X
20	Ps. 2	Messiah is enthroned in Zion, defeats his opposition, and rules over creation	X		X	X
21	Ps. 16	Yahweh will not allow Messiah to see corruption in Sheol			X	X
22	Ps. 102	Messiah the Creator is eternal, though suffering severe persecution				X
23	Ps. 45	Messiah is God, and has been anointed by God to sit upon an eternal throne; his people are his lovely bride	X			X
24	Ps. 110	Messiah is a priest-king after the order of Melchizedek, and he sits at the right hand of God, ruling over all humankind	X		X	X
25	Ps. 72	Messiah reigns over a universal and righteous kingdom of blessing	X			X
26	Ps. 68	Messiah wins a great victory, then ascends back on high	X		X	X
27	Job 9.33; 16.19-21; 17.3; 33.23-28	A Mediator, Interpreter, Advocate, and Witness will walk in the latter days upon the earth				
28	Job 19.23-27	A Redeemer will stand upon the earth in the latter days and the righteous will see him				X
29	Joel 2.23	A Wonderful Teacher will arise and usher in an age of great abundance	X			X
30	Hos. 1.10-2.1	A Second Moses will lead God's people out of bondage into a glorious new era			X	
31	Hos. 3.5	After the exile, God's people will serve Yahweh their God, and David their king	X			
32	Hos. 11.1	God calls his Son, the Second Israel, out of Egypt			X	

Summary of Messianic Interpretations in the Old Testament (continued)

	Bible Reference	Summary of the Messianic Prophecy	EJ	NTA	NTE	CF
33	Isa. 4.2-6	The beautiful and glorious Shoot of Yahweh will be the pride of the remnant of Israel	X			
34	Isa. 7.14-15	A virgin will conceive and bear a son whose name will be called Immanuel			X	X
35	Isa. 8.17-18	Messiah waits for the time of his coming, and he and his children are signs and wonders in Israel		X	X	
36	Isa. 9.1-7	Messiah will bring light to Galilee and one will sit on the throne of David to usher in the reign of God in righteousness and justice	X	X		X
37	Isa. 11.1-16	A Shoot from the stem of Jesse will be filled with the Spirit of Yahweh, and will usher into the earth a Kingdom of righteousness and peace	X	X	X	X
38	Isa. 16.5	Downtrodden peoples will look to the house of David for justice and lovingkindness				
39	Isa. 28.16	God is going to lay in Zion a tried and tested Stone, a precious Cornerstone	X	X	X	X
40	Isa. 30.19-26	The people of God will see their divine Teacher and will enjoy his abundant blessing as a result of listening to him	X			
41	Isa. 32.1-2	A Leader of the future will be a shelter from the storm, like water in a dry place				
42	Isa. 33.17	The eyes of the people of God will see the King in his beauty				
43	Isa. 42.17	Yahweh's Servant will bring forth justice to the nations, and will be a Covenant to the people, a Light to the nations	X		X	X
44	Isa. 49.1-13	Yahweh's Servant is divinely appointed to teach, to raise up the tribes of Jacob, and to be a Light to the Gentiles	X			X
45	Isa. 50.4-11	Yahweh's Servant is an obedient disciple who endures suffering and indignity				X
46	Isa. 52.13-53.12	God's Servant is rejected, suffers horribly for the sins of others, dies, but then sees his seed and is satisfied	X	X	X	X
47	Isa. 55.3-5	A son of David will be made a Witness, Leader, and Commander for the peoples				X
48	Isa. 59.20-21	A Redeemer will come to penitent Zion	X		X	

Summary of Messianic Interpretations in the Old Testament (continued)

	Bible Reference	Summary of the Messianic Prophecy	EJ	NTA	NTE	CF
49	Isa. 61.1-11	Messiah has been anointed by the Spirit of Yahweh to proclaim the Good News to the poor, and liberty and deliverance to the captives	X		X	X
50	Mic. 2.12-13	The divine Breaker will lead the people of God out of bondage	X			
51	Mic. 5.1-5	A glorious Ruler will arise from Bethlehem to shepherd the people of God and give them victory over their enemies	X	X	X	X
52	Hab. 3.12-15	Yahweh comes forth from the salvation of his Anointed, and will strike through the head of the house of evil				
53	Jer. 23.5-6	God will raise up a Righteous Branch who will act wisely and execute justice and righteousness in the land	X			
54	Jer. 30.9, 21	Upon return from exile, God's people will serve David their King who will serve as Mediator and draw near to God for them	X			
55	Jer. 31.21-22	God will create a new thing in the land	X			X
56	Jer. 33.14-26	Yahweh will raise up his righteous Servant in the land, and will not fail to fulfill his promise to David and to Levi	X			
57	Ezek. 17.22-24	A tender Twig from the house of David will become a stately Cedar with birds of every kind nesting under it	X			X
58	Ezek. 21.25-27	The crown is removed from the last king of Judah until he comes whose right it is				
59	Ezek. 34.23-31	God will set over those who return from Babylon one Shepherd, his servant, David		X		
60	Ezek. 37.21-28	God's people will be united and will have one King, "My Servant David"		X		
61	Ezek. 44.48	A Prince in the future age will be accorded honor, and through him sacrifices will be offered to God	X			
62	Dan. 7.13-14	One like a Son of Man will come before the Ancient of Days to receive an everlasting Kingdom and Dominion	X	X	X	X
63	Dan. 9.24-27	After 69 "weeks" of years, Messiah will appear, he will be cut off, and will cause sacrifice and oblation to cease	X			X
64	Hag. 2.6-9	After the shaking of the nations, the Desire of all Nations will come and fill the Temple of God with glory	X		X	

Summary of Messianic Interpretations in the Old Testament (continued)

	Bible Reference	Summary of the Messianic Prophecy	EJ	NTA	NTE	CF
65	Hag. 2.21-23	Zerubbabel will be made God's signet Ring in the day when the thrones of kingdoms and the Gentiles are overthrown by Yahweh				
66	Zech. 3.8-10	The Servant of Yahweh, his Shoot, is symbolized by Joshua the High Priest and by an engraved stone	X			X
67	Zech. 6.12-13	A man whose name is Shoot shall build the Temple of the Lord, and he will be a Priest and a King	X			X
68	Zech. 9.9-11	The King of Zion comes riding upon the foal of a donkey	X		X	X
69	Zech. 10.3-4	God will send one who is the Cornerstone, the Tent Peg, the Battle Bow, the one who possesses all sovereignty	X			
70	Zech. 11.4-14	Thirty pieces of silver thrown to the potter in the house of God			X	X
71	Zech. 13.7	The sword of divine justice smites the Shepherd and the sheep are scattered			X	X
72	Mal. 3.1	The Lord's messenger will clear the way before him, and the Lord will suddenly come to his Temple	X	X	X	X
73	Mal. 4.2	The Sun of Righteousness will arise with healing in his wings	X	X		

Summary Outline of the Scriptures

Rev. Dr. Don L. Davis

The Old Testament

1. **Genesis** – *Beginnings*
   a. Adam   d. Isaac
   b. Noah   e. Jacob
   c. Abraham   f. Joseph

2. **Exodus** – *Redemption (out of)*
   a. Slavery   c. Law
   b. Deliverance   d. Tabernacle

3. **Leviticus** – *Worship and Fellowship*
   a. Offerings and sacrifices
   b. Priests
   c. Feasts and festivals

4. **Numbers** – *Service and Walk*
   a. Organized
   b. Wanderings

5. **Deuteronomy** – *Obedience*
   a. Moses reviews history and law
   b. Civil and social laws
   c. Palestinian Covenant
   d. Moses' blessing and death

6. **Joshua** – *Redemption (into)*
   a. Conquer the land
   b. Divide up the land
   c. Joshua's farewell

7. **Judges** – *God's Deliverance*
   a. Disobedience and judgment
   b. Israel's twelve judges
   c. Lawless conditions

8. **Ruth** – *Love*
   a. Ruth chooses
   b. Ruth works
   c. Ruth waits
   d. Ruth rewarded

9. **1 Samuel** – *Kings, Priestly Perspective*
   a. Eli   c. Saul
   b. Samuel   d. David

10. **2 Samuel** – *David*
    a. King of Judah (9 years - Hebron)
    b. King of all Israel (33 years - Jerusalem)

11. **1 Kings** – *Solomon's Glory, Kingdom's Decline*
    a. Solomon's glory
    b. Kingdom's decline
    c. Elijah the prophet

12. **2 Kings** – *Divided Kingdom*
    a. Elisha
    b. Israel (Northern Kingdom falls)
    c. Judah (Southern Kingdom falls)

13. **1 Chronicles** – *David's Temple Arrangements*
    a. Genealogies
    b. End of Saul's reign
    c. Reign of David
    d. Temple preparations

14. **2 Chronicles** – *Temple and Worship Abandoned*
    a. Solomon
    b. Kings of Judah

15. **Ezra** – *The Minority (Remnant)*
    a. First return from exile - Zerubbabel
    b. Second return from exile - Ezra (priest)

16. **Nehemiah** – *Rebuilding by Faith*
    a. Rebuild walls
    b. Revival
    c. Religious reform

17. **Esther** – *Female Savior*
    a. Esther
    b. Haman
    c. Mordecai
    d. Deliverance: Feast of Purim

18. **Job** – *Why the Righteous Suffer*
    a. Godly Job
    b. Satan's attack
    c. Four philosophical friends
    d. God lives

19. **Psalms** – *Prayer and Praise*
    a. Prayers of David
    b. Godly suffer; deliverance
    c. God deals with Israel
    d. Suffering of God's people - end with the Lord's reign
    e. The Word of God (Messiah's suffering and glorious return)

20. **Proverbs** – *Wisdom*
    a. Wisdom vs. folly
    b. Solomon
    c. Solomon - Hezekiah
    d. Agur
    e. Lemuel

21. **Ecclesiastes** – *Vanity*
    a. Experimentation
    b. Observation
    c. Consideration

22. **Song of Solomon** – *Love Story*

23. **Isaiah** – *The Justice (Judgment) and Grace (Comfort) of God*
    a. Prophecies of punishment
    b. History
    c. Prophecies of blessing

24. **Jeremiah** – *Judah's Sin Leads to Babylonian Captivity*
    a. Jeremiah's call; empowered
    b. Judah condemned; predicted Babylonian captivity
    c. Restoration promised
    d. Prophesied judgment inflicted
    e. Prophecies against Gentiles
    f. Summary of Judah's captivity

25. **Lamentations** – *Lament over Jerusalem*
    a. Affliction of Jerusalem
    b. Destroyed because of sin
    c. The prophet's suffering
    d. Present desolation vs. past splendor
    e. Appeal to God for mercy

26. **Ezekiel** – *Israel's Captivity and Restoration*
    a. Judgment on Judah and Jerusalem
    b. Judgment on Gentile nations
    c. Israel restored; Jerusalem's future glory

27. **Daniel** – *The Time of the Gentiles*
    a. History; Nebuchadnezzar, Belshazzar, Daniel
    b. Prophecy

28. **Hosea** – *Unfaithfulness*
    a. Unfaithfulness
    b. Punishment
    c. Restoration

29. **Joel** – *The Day of the Lord*
    a. Locust plague
    b. Events of the future Day of the Lord
    c. Order of the future Day of the Lord

30. **Amos** – *God Judges Sin*
    a. Neighbors judged
    b. Israel judged
    c. Visions of future judgment
    d. Israel's past judgment blessings

31. **Obadiah** – *Edom's Destruction*
    a. Destruction prophesied
    b. Reasons for destruction
    c. Israel's future blessing

32. **Jonah** – *Gentile Salvation*
    a. Jonah disobeys
    b. Others suffer
    c. Jonah punished
    d. Jonah obeys; thousands saved
    e. Jonah displeased, no love for souls

33. **Micah** – *Israel's Sins, Judgment, and Restoration*
    a. Sin and judgment
    b. Grace and future restoration
    c. Appeal and petition

34. **Nahum** – *Nineveh Condemned*
    a. God hates sin
    b. Nineveh's doom prophesied
    c. Reasons for doom

35. **Habakkuk** – *The Just Shall Live by Faith*
    a. Complaint of Judah's unjudged sin
    b. Chaldeans will punish
    c. Complaint of Chaldeans' wickedness
    d. Punishment promised
    e. Prayer for revival; faith in God

36. **Zephaniah** – *Babylonian Invasion Prefigures the Day of the Lord*
    a. Judgment on Judah foreshadows the Great Day of the Lord
    b. Judgment on Jerusalem and neighbors foreshadows final judgment of all nations
    c. Israel restored after judgments

37. **Haggai** – *Rebuild the Temple*
    a. Negligence
    b. Courage
    c. Separation
    d. Judgment

38. **Zechariah** – *Two Comings of Christ*
    a. Zechariah's vision
    b. Bethel's question; Jehovah's answer
    c. Nation's downfall and salvation

39. **Malachi** – *Neglect*
    a. The priest's sins
    b. The people's sins
    c. The faithful few

The New Testament

1. **Matthew** – *Jesus the King*
   a. The Person of the King
   b. The Preparation of the King
   c. The Propaganda of the King
   d. The Program of the King
   e. The Passion of the King
   f. The Power of the King

2. **Mark** – *Jesus the Servant*
   a. John introduces the Servant
   b. God the Father identifies the Servant
   c. The temptation initiates the Servant
   d. Work and word of the Servant
   e. Death burial, resurrection

3. **Luke** – *Jesus Christ the Perfect Man*
   a. Birth and family of the Perfect Man
   b. Testing of the Perfect Man; hometown
   c. Ministry of the Perfect Man
   d. Betrayal, trial, and death of the Perfect Man
   e. Resurrection of the Perfect Man

4. **John** – *Jesus Christ is God*
   a. Prologue - the Incarnation
   b. Introduction
   c. Witness of works and words
   d. Witness of Jesus to his apostles
   e. Passion - witness to the world
   f. Epilogue

5. **Acts** – *The Holy Spirit Working in the Church*
   a. The Lord Jesus at work by the Holy Spirit through the apostles at Jerusalem
   b. In Judea and Samaria
   c. To the uttermost parts of the Earth

6. **Romans** – *The Righteousness of God*
   a. Salutation
   b. Sin and salvation
   c. Sanctification
   d. Struggle
   e. Spirit-filled living
   f. Security of salvation
   g. Segregation
   h. Sacrifice and service
   i. Separation and salutation

7. **1 Corinthians** – *The Lordship of Christ*
   a. Salutation and thanksgiving
   b. Conditions in the Corinthian body
   c. Concerning the Gospel
   d. Concerning collections

8. **2 Corinthians** – *The Ministry of the Church*
   a. The comfort of God
   b. Collection for the poor
   c. Calling of the Apostle Paul

9. **Galatians** – *Justification by Faith*
   a. Introduction
   b. Personal - Authority of the apostle and glory of the Gospel
   c. Doctrinal - Justification by faith
   d. Practical - Sanctification by the Holy Spirit
   e. Autographed conclusion and exhortation

10. **Ephesians** – *The Church of Jesus Christ*
    a. Doctrinal - the heavenly calling of the Church
    - A Body
    - A Temple
    - A Mystery
    b. Practical - the earthly conduct of the Church
    - A New Man
    - A Bride
    - An Army

11. **Philippians** – *Joy in the Christian Life*
    a. Philosophy for Christian living
    b. Pattern for Christian living
    c. Prize for Christian living
    d. Power for Christian living

12. **Colossians** – *Christ the Fullness of God*
    a. Doctrinal - Christ, the fullness of God; in Christ believers are made full
    b. Practical - Christ, the fullness of God; Christ's life poured out in believers, and through them

13. **1 Thessalonians** – *The Second Coming of Christ:*
    a. Is an inspiring hope
    b. Is a working hope
    c. Is a purifying hope
    d. Is a comforting hope
    e. Is a rousing, stimulating hope

14. **2 Thessalonians** – *The Second Coming of Christ*
    a. Persecution of believers now; judgment of unbelievers hereafter (at coming of Christ)
    b. Program of the world in connection with the coming of Christ
    c. Practical issues associated with the coming of Christ

15. **1 Timothy** – *Government and Order in the Local Church*
    a. The faith of the Church
    b. Public prayer and women's place in the Church
    c. Officers in the Church
    d. Apostasy in the Church
    e. Duties of the officer of the Church

16. **2 Timothy** – *Loyalty in the Days of Apostasy*
    a. Afflictions of the Gospel
    b. Active in service
    c. Apostasy coming; authority of the Scriptures
    d. Allegiance to the Lord

17. **Titus** – *The Ideal New Testament Church*
    a. The Church is an organization
    b. The Church is to teach and preach the Word of God
    c. The Church is to perform good works

18. **Philemon** – *Reveal Christ's Love and Teach Brotherly Love*
    a. Genial greeting to Philemon and family
    b. Good reputation of Philemon
    c. Gracious plea for Onesimus
    d. Guiltless substitutes for guilty
    e. Glorious illustration of imputation
    f. General and personal requests

19. **Hebrews** – *The Superiority of Christ*
    a. Doctrinal - Christ is better than the Old Testament economy
    b. Practical - Christ brings better benefits and duties

20. **James** – *Ethics of Christianity*
    a. Faith tested
    b. Difficulty of controlling the tongue
    c. Warning against worldliness
    d. Admonitions in view of the Lord's coming

21. **1 Peter** – *Christian Hope in the Time of Persecution and Trial*
    a. Suffering and security of believers
    b. Suffering and the Scriptures
    c. Suffering and the sufferings of Christ
    d. Suffering and the Second Coming of Christ

22. **2 Peter** – *Warning against False Teachers*
    a. Addition of Christian graces gives assurance
    b. Authority of the Scriptures
    c. Apostasy brought in by false testimony
    d. Attitude toward return of Christ: test for apostasy
    e. Agenda of God in the world
    f. Admonition to believers

23. **1 John** – *The Family of God*
    a. God is light
    b. God is love
    c. God is life

24. **2 John** – *Warning against Receiving Deceivers*
    a. Walk in truth
    b. Love one another
    c. Receive not deceivers
    d. Find joy in fellowship

25. **3 John** – *Admonition to Receive True Believers*
    a. Gaius, brother in the Church
    b. Diotrephes
    c. Demetrius

26. **Jude** – *Contending for the Faith*
    a. Occasion of the epistle
    b. Occurrences of apostasy
    c. Occupation of believers in the days of apostasy

27. **Revelation** – *The Unveiling of Christ Glorified*
    a. The person of Christ in glory
    b. The possession of Jesus Christ - the Church in the World
    c. The program of Jesus Christ - the scene in Heaven
    d. The seven seals
    e. The seven trumpets
    f. Important persons in the last days
    g. The seven vials
    h. The fall of Babylon
    i. The eternal state

Symbols of Christian Leadership

The Christian Leader as Deacon (Servant)

Illustrated by Tim Ladwig

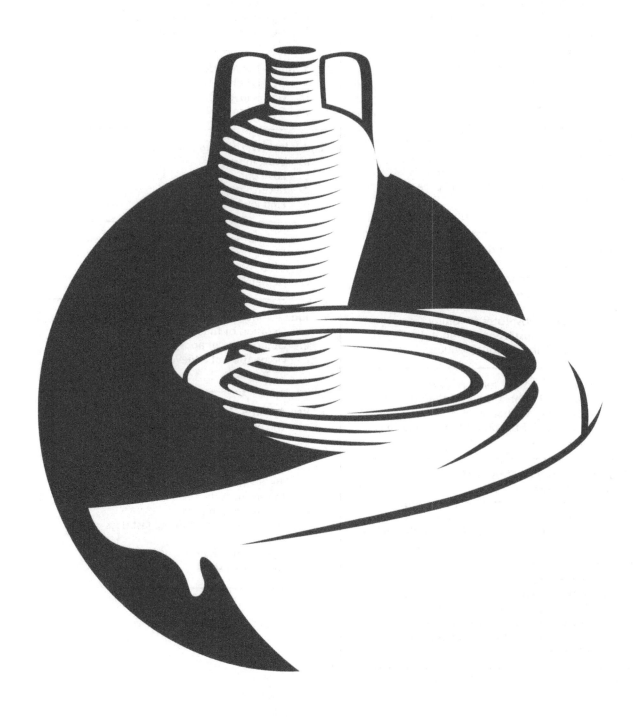

Symbols of Christian Leadership (continued)

The Christian Leader as Elder

Illustrated by Tim Ladwig

Symbols of Christian Leadership (continued)

The Christian Leader as Pastor

Illustrated by Tim Ladwig

The Christian Leader as Bishop

Illustrated by Tim Ladwig

The Tabernacle of Moses

Vern Poythress, The Shadow of Christ in the Law of Moses, p. 17.

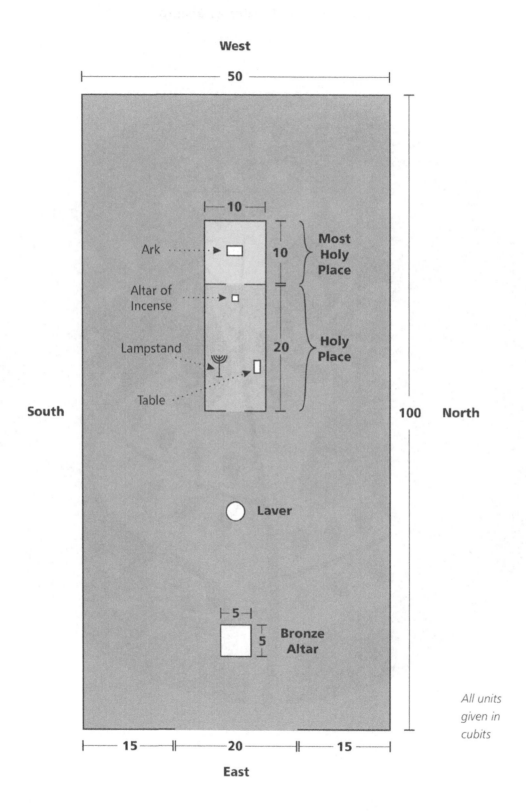

Targeting Unreached Groups in Churched Neighborhoods
Mission Frontiers

Many Different Peoples!

Many Homogenous Congregations

**The Extent of Normal "Outreach":
Incorporating and Gathering
According to Culture**

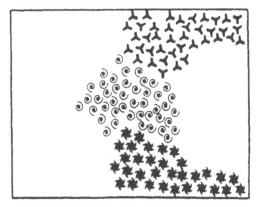

**"So Close and Yet so Far Away":
The Unreached, Unaffected
Neighbors**

That We May Be One
Elements of an Integrated Church Planting Movement Among the Urban Poor
Rev. Dr. Don L. Davis

Church Planting Movements among the Urban Poor = an integrated and aggressive advance of the Kingdom of God among the urban poor resulting in a significant increase of indigenous churches which fundamentally share in common a constellation of elements which provides them with a distinct and unique identity, purpose, and practice.

Ministry among the urban poor must be grounded in a vision and understanding of the liberty we have in Christ to conceive of coherent, integrated movements of followers of Jesus who because of shared experience, proximity, culture, and history *determine to reflect their unique faith and practice in a way consistent with the historic faith but distinct to their life and times.* This is not an arbitrary act; movements cannot ignore the nature of the one (unity), holy (sanctity), catholic (universality), and apostolic (apostolicity) Church, the one true people of God.

Nevertheless, as was affirmed by the emerging leaders of the then American Episcopal Church, the freedom that we have in Christ allows for different forms and usages of worship in the body of Christ without any offense whatsoever, as long as we are faithful to the historic orthodox beliefs of the Church as taught to us by the prophets and apostles of our Lord. Doctrine must remain anchored and complete; discipline, however, can be based on the contingencies and exigencies of the people who embrace them, as long as all that is shaped and conceived builds up the body of Christ, and glorifies God our Father through our Lord Jesus Christ.

"The congregations in an Integrated Church Planting Movement Among the Urban Poor *will exhibit together.*"

1. *A shared history and identity* (i.e., *a common name and heritage*). CPMs among the urban poor will seek to link themselves to and identify themselves by a well defined and joyfully shared history and persona that all members and congregations share.

It is a most invaluable part of that blessed "liberty wherewith Christ hath made us free," that in his worship different forms and usages may without offence be allowed, provided the substance of the Faith be kept entire; and that, in every Church, what cannot be clearly determined to belong to Doctrine must be referred to Discipline; and therefore, by common consent and authority, may be altered, abridged, enlarged, amended, or otherwise disposed of, as may seem most convenient for the edification of the people, "according to the various exigency of times and occasions."
~ 1789 Preface to the Book of Common Prayer. 1928 Episcopal edition.

2. *A shared liturgy and celebration* (i.e., *a common worship*). CPMs among the urban poor should reflect a shared hymnody, practice of the sacraments, theological focus and imagery, aesthetic vision, vestments, liturgical order, symbology, and spiritual formation that enables us to worship and glorify God in a way that lifts up the Lord and attracts urbanites to vital worship.

3. *A shared membership, well-being, welfare, and support* (i.e., *a common order and discipline*). CPMs among the urban poor must be anchored in evangelical and historically orthodox presentations of the Gospel that result in conversions to Jesus Christ and incorporation into local churches.

4. *A shared catechism and doctrine* (i.e., *a common faith*). CPMs among the urban poor must embrace a common biblical theology and express it practically in a Christian education that reflects their commonly held faith.

5. *A shared church government and authority* (i.e., *a common polity*). CPMs among the urban poor must be organized around a common polity, ecclesial management, and submit to flexible governing policies that allow for effective and efficient management of their resources and congregations.

6. *A shared leadership development structure* (i.e., *a common pastoral strategy*). CPMs among the urban poor are committed with supplying each congregation with godly undershepherds, and seek to identify, equip, and support its pastors and missionaries in order that their members may grow to maturity in Christ.

7. *A shared financial philosophy and procedure* (i.e., *a common stewardship*). CPMs among the urban poor strive to handle all of their financial affairs and resources with wise, streamlined, and reproducible policies that allow for the good management of their monies and goods, locally, regionally, and nationally.

8. *A shared care and support ministry* (i.e., *a common service*). CPMs among the urban poor seek to practically demonstrate the love and justice of the Kingdom among its members and towards others in the city in ways that allow individuals and congregations to love their neighbors as they love themselves.

9. *A shared evangelism and outreach* (i.e., *a common mission*): CPMs among the urban poor network and collaborate among their members in order to clearly present Jesus and his Kingdom to the lost in the city in order to multiply new congregations in unreached urban areas as quickly as possible.

That We May Be One (continued)

10. ***A shared vision for connection and association*** (i.e., *a common partnership*). CPMs among the urban poor must seek to make fresh connections, links, and relationships with other movements for the sake of regular communication, fellowship, and mission.

These principles of belonging, camaraderie, and identity lay the foundation for a new paradigm of authentic ecumenical unity, the kind that can lead to partnerships and collaboration of grand scope and deep substance. Below is a short overview of the TUMI biblical basis for the kind of partnerships which can fuel and sustain credible church planting movements among the urban poor.

God's Partners and Fellow Workers

1 Cor. 3.1-9 (ESV) - But I, brothers, could not address you as spiritual people, but as people of the flesh, as infants in Christ. [2] I fed you with milk, not solid food, for you were not ready for it. And even now you are not yet ready, [3] for you are still of the flesh. For while there is jealousy and strife among you, are you not of the flesh and behaving only in a human way? [4] For when one says, "I follow Paul," and another, "I follow Apollos," are you not being merely human? [5] What then is Apollos? What is Paul? Servants through whom you believed, as the Lord assigned to each. [6] I planted, Apollos watered, but God gave the growth. [7] So neither he who plants nor he who waters is anything, but only God who gives the growth. [8] He who plants and he who waters are one, and each will receive his wages according to his labor. [9] For we are God's fellow workers. You are God's field, God's building.

To Facilitate Pioneer Church Planting Movements Among America's Unreached C$_1$ Communities

As a ministry of World Impact, TUMI is dedicated to generating and strategically facilitating dynamic, indigenous C1 church planting movements targeted to reach the 80% Window of America's inner cities. In order to attain this purpose, we will help form strategic alliances between and among urban missionaries and pastors, theologians and missiologists, churches and denominations, and other kingdom-minded individuals and organizations in order to trigger robust pioneer church planting movements that multiply thousands of culturally conducive evangelical C1 churches among America's urban poor. We will offer our expertise to assure that these churches in every way glorify God the Father in their Christ-centered identity, Spirit-formed worship and community life, historically orthodox doctrine, and kingdom-oriented practice and mission.

I. Partnership, Involves Recognizing our Fundamental Unity in Christ: We Share the Same Spiritual DNA.

A. *Our faith in Jesus has made us one together.*

1. 1 John 1.3 (ESV) - that which we have seen and heard we proclaim also to you, so that you too may have fellowship with us; and indeed our fellowship is with the Father and with his Son Jesus Christ.

2. John 17.11 (ESV) - And I am no longer in the world, but they are in the world, and I am coming to you. Holy Father, keep them in your name, which you have given me, that they may be one, even as we are one.

B. *The organic unity between the Father and Son, and the people of God,* John 17.21-22 (ESV) - that they may all be one, just as you, Father, are in me, and I in you, that they also may be in us, so that the world may believe that you have sent me. [22] The glory that you have given me I have given to them, that they may be one even as we are one.

C. *Our unity leads to a common effort in glorifying God the Father of our Lord,* Rom. 15.5-6 (ESV) - May the God of endurance and encouragement grant you to live in such harmony with one another, in accord with Christ Jesus, [6] that together you may with one voice glorify the God and Father of our Lord Jesus Christ.

D. *God's will for the body is unity in mind and judgment,* 1 Cor. 1.10 (ESV) - I appeal to you, brothers, by the name of our Lord Jesus Christ, that all of you agree and that there be no divisions among you, but that you be united in the same mind and the same judgment.

E. *The Holy Spirit's baptism has made us of one spiritual body and spirit,* 1 Cor. 12.12-13 (ESV) - For just as the body is one and has many members, and all the members of the body, though many, are one body, so it is with

That We May Be One (continued)

Christ. [13] For in one Spirit we were all baptized into one body— Jews or Greeks, slaves or free—and all were made to drink of one Spirit.

F.   *The very essence of biblical faith is unity*, Eph. 4.4-6 (ESV) - There is one body and one Spirit—just as you were called to the one hope that belongs to your call [5] one Lord, one faith, one baptism, [6] one God and Father of all, who is over all and through all and in all.

G.   *Our bond of partnership precludes unity with those not united to Christ*, 2 Cor. 6.14-16 (ESV) - Do not be unequally yoked with unbelievers. For what partnership has righteousness with lawlessness? Or what fellowship has light with darkness? [15] What accord has Christ with Belial? Or what portion does a believer share with an unbeliever? [16] What agreement has the temple of God with idols? For we are the temple of the living God; as God said, "I will make my dwelling among them and walk among them, and I will be their God, and they shall be my people.

II.   Partnership₂ Involves the Sharing of Monies, Persons, and Resources to Fund a Common Cause: We Share a Common Source, Table, and Pot.

A.   *The partnership between those who share the Word and receive it involves concrete blessing and giving.*

1.   *The taught share with the teacher*, Gal. 6.6 (ESV) - One who is taught the word must share all good things with the one who teaches.

2.   *Illustrated in the relationship of the Jew to the Gentile in the body*, Rom. 15.27 (ESV) - They were pleased to do it, and indeed they owe it to them. For if the Gentiles have come to share in their spiritual blessings, they ought also to be of service to them in material blessings.

B.   *The power of unity extends to those who are appointed by God to serve his people*, Deut. 12.19 (ESV) - Take care that you do not neglect the Levite as long as you live in your land.

C.   *Those who labor deserve the generous supply of those who benefit from that labor.*

1.   *Christ's exhortation to the disciples*, Matt. 10.10 (ESV) - No bag for your journey, nor two tunics nor sandals nor a staff, for the laborer deserves his food.

2. *Illustrated from OT Scripture and analogy*, 1 Cor. 9.9-14 (ESV) - For it is written in the Law of Moses, "You shall not muzzle an ox when it treads out the grain." Is it for oxen that God is concerned? [10] Does he not speak entirely for our sake? It was written for our sake, because the plowman should plow in hope and the thresher thresh in hope of sharing in the crop. [11] If we have sown spiritual things among you, is it too much if we reap material things from you? [12] If others share this rightful claim on you, do not we even more? Nevertheless, we have not made use of this right, but we endure anything rather than put an obstacle in the way of the gospel of Christ. [13] Do you not know that those who are employed in the temple service get their food from the temple, and those who serve at the altar share in the sacrificial offerings? [14] In the same way, the Lord commanded that those who proclaim the gospel should get their living by the gospel.

3. *Double honor: respect and sharing of resources*, 1 Tim. 5.17-18 (ESV) - Let the elders who rule well be considered worthy of double honor, especially those who labor in preaching and teaching. [18] For the Scripture says, "You shall not muzzle an ox when it treads out the grain," and, "The laborer deserves his wages."

D. *The Philippian relationship with Paul is a prototype of this kind of essential partnership.*

1. *From the beginning they shared tangibly with Paul*, Phil. 1.3-5 (ESV) - I thank my God in all my remembrance of you, [4] always in every prayer of mine for you all making my prayer with joy, [5] because of your partnership in the gospel from the first day until now.

2. *Epaphroditus was their messenger to transport their aid to Paul*, Phil. 2.25 (ESV) - I have thought it necessary to send to you Epaphroditus my brother and fellow worker and fellow soldier, and your messenger and minister to my need

3. *The Philippians were completely engaged in the support of Paul's ministry from the first*, Phil. 4.15-18 (ESV) - And you Philippians yourselves know that in the beginning of the gospel, when I left Macedonia, no church entered into partnership with me in giving and receiving, except you only. [16] Even in Thessalonica you sent me help for my needs once

and again. [17] Not that I seek the gift, but I seek the fruit that increases to your credit. [18] I have received full payment, and more. I am well supplied, having received from Epaphroditus the gifts you sent, a fragrant offering, a sacrifice acceptable and pleasing to God.

III. Partnership₃ Involves Collaborating Together as Co-workers and Co-laborers in the Work of Advancing the Kingdom: We Share a Common Cause and Task.

A. *Partnership assumes that each person and congregation brings their unique experience, perspective, and gifting to the table for use*, Gal. 2.6-8 (ESV) - And from those who seemed to be influential (what they were makes no difference to me; God shows no partiality)—those, I say, who seemed influential added nothing to me. [7] On the contrary, when they saw that I had been entrusted with the gospel to the uncircumcised, just as Peter had been entrusted with the gospel to the circumcised [8] (for he who worked through Peter for his apostolic ministry to the circumcised worked also through me for mine to the Gentiles).

B. *Authentic partnerships involve discerning the Lord's leading, opportunity, and blessing on those who are called to represent his interests in the places where he has led them,* Gal. 2.9-10 (ESV) - and when James and Cephas and John, who seemed to be pillars, perceived the grace that was given to me, they gave the right hand of fellowship to Barnabas and me, that we should go to the Gentiles and they to the circumcised. [10] Only, they asked us to remember the poor, the very thing I was eager to do.

C. *Partnership in terms of co-working and co-laboring involves a shared vision and commitment to a common cause*, e.g., Timothy, Phil. 2.19-24 (ESV) - I hope in the Lord Jesus to send Timothy to you soon, so that I too may be cheered by news of you. [20] For I have no one like him, who will be genuinely concerned for your welfare. [21] They all seek their own interests, not those of Jesus Christ. [22] But you know Timothy's proven worth, how as a son with a father he has served with me in the gospel. [23] I hope therefore to send him just as soon as I see how it will go with me, [24] and I trust in the Lord that shortly I myself will come also.

That We May Be One (continued)

D. *Paul's unique words for his partners in the Gospel*

1. Co-worker (*synergos*), Rom. 16.3, 7, 9, 21; 2 Cor. 8.23; Phil. 2.25; 4.3; Col. 4.7, 10, 11, 14; Philem. 1, 24.

2. Co-prisoner (*synaichmalotos*), Col. 4.10; Philem. 23

3. Co-slave (*syndoulos*), Col. 1.7, 4.7

4. Co-soldier (*systratiotes*) Phil. 2.25; Philem. 2

5. Co-laborer (*synatheleo*), Phil. 4.2-3

E. A brief listing of Paul's partners in ministry (these accompanied him at every phase and effort of the work, with diverse backgrounds, giftings, tasks, and responsibilities along the way of his ministry)

1. John Mark (Col. 4.10; Philem. 24)

2. Artistarchus (Col. 4.10; Philem. 24)

3. Andronicus and Junia (Rom. 16.7)

4. Philemon (Philem. 1)

5. Epaphroditus (same as Epaphras) (Col. 1.7; Philem. 23; Phil. 2.25)

6. Clement (Phil. 4.3)

7. Urbanus (Rom. 16.9)

8. Jesus (Justus) (Col. 4.11)

9. Demas (who later apostocized in the world), (Col. 4.14; Philem. 24; 2 Tim. 4.20)

10. Tychicus (Col. 4.7; Phil. 4.3)

11. Archippus (Philem. 2)

12. Euodia (Phil. 4.2-3)

13. Syntyche (Phil. 4.2-3)

14. Tertius (Rom. 16.22)

434 / CapstoneCurriculum   Picturing Theology

That We May Be One (continued)

15. Phoebe (Rom. 16.1)

16. Erastus (Rom. 16.23)

17. Quartus (Rom. 16.23)

18. Tryphaena (Rom. 16.12)

19. Tryphosa (Rom. 16.12)

20. Persis (Rom. 16.12)

21. Mary (Rom. 16.6)

22. Onesiphorus (2 Tim. 1.16-18)

IV. Implications of Partnership Principles in Light of TUMI's Visions

To Facilitate Pioneer Church Planting Movements Among America's Unreached C_1 Communities

As a ministry of World Impact, TUMI is dedicated to generating and strategically facilitating dynamic, indigenous C1 church planting movements targeted to reach the 80% Window of America's inner cities. In order to attain this purpose, we will help form strategic alliances between and among urban missionaries and pastors, theologians and missiologists, churches and denominations, and other kingdom-minded individuals and organizations in order to trigger robust pioneer church planting movements that multiply thousands of culturally conducive evangelical C1 churches among America's urban poor. We will offer our expertise to assure that these churches in every way glorify God the Father in their Christ-centered identity, Spirit-formed worship and community life, historically orthodox doctrine, and kingdom-oriented practice and mission.

A. *TUMI will help form strategic alliances to trigger urban church plant movements.*

B. *TUMI seeks to support dynamic movements which produce and sustain healthy C_1 churches.*

C. Clear implications of this for us

1. We don't recruit people to ourselves, but to participate in Christ's kingdom advance.

2. We don't own the vision, it is God's desire to impact the world, and we contribute alongside others.

3. Our contribution is no better or worse than others: we are co-laborers with others.

4. The work that others do will probably be more critical and fruitful than our own.

Bottom Line

There is virtually no limit to what we can accomplish if we as a team are willing to give our all for the sake of our common cause, if we do not care what role we have to play in order to win, nor care who gets the credit after the victory.

A Theological Overview of the Equipping Gifts Described in Ephesians 4.11

Rev. Terry Cornett, M.A., M.A.R.

I. Evangelists

A. Linguistic Considerations

Euaggelistes

"A preacher of the gospel" (*Strong's Greek Dictionary of New Testament Words*)

"The word translated in the NT 'evangelist' is a noun from the verb *euangelizomai* 'to announce news' and usually rendered . . . as 'preach the gospel'" (D.B. Knox, "Evangelist," *New Bible Dictionary*, 2nd Edition, J. D. Douglas and others, eds. Leicester, England-Downers Grove, IL: InterVarsity Press, 1982, p. 356).

"The Greek word for evangelist (Eph. 4.11) is a compound of two words. The first Greek word means "well, good, kind, right, and proper," eu. The second word means "messenger, envoy, one sent, an angel of God," *aggelos*. Evangelist conveys one who is a good messenger, a messenger who comes to bring good news–news that will fill a listeners heart with joy and thanksgiving" (Harley H. Schmitt, *Many Gifts, One Lord*, Fairfax, VA: Xulon Press, 2002, p. 76).

B. Relevant Theological Quotes

1. "An evangelist knew the gospel narrative thoroughly and was capable of explaining it, as Philip the evangelist did to the eunuch. . . . Originally, *euaggelistes* denoted a function rather than an office. There could have been little difference between an apostle and an evangelist, all the apostles being evangelists, but not all evangelists being apostles" (Spiros Zodhiates, *The Complete Word Study Dictionary*: New Testament, Chattanooga, TN: AMG Publishers, 1992, pp. 670-671).

2. "All Christians are called to play their part in fulfilling Jesus' Great Commission, but some believers have a special call to, and a spiritual gift for, communicating Christ and leading others to him. These

A Theological Overview of the Equipping Gifts Described in Ephesians 4.11 (continued)

we call evangelists, as does the New Testament" (The Amsterdam Declaration, published in *Christianity Today*, August 7, 2000, [Amsterdam 2000 was a world-wide gathering of evangelicals in mission called by the Billy Graham Evangelistic Association with a special focus on itinerant evangelists and their role in world mission]).

3. "It will be seen then that though the apostles were evangelists, not all evangelists were apostles. This distinction is confirmed in Ephesians 4.11, where the office of 'evangelist' is mentioned after 'apostle' and 'prophet,' and before 'pastor' and teacher.' From this passage it is plain that the gift of evangelism was a distinct gift within the Christian church; and although all Christians doubtless performed this sacred task, as opportunity was given to them, there were some who were pre-eminently called and endowed by the Holy Spirit for this work (D.B. Knox, "Evangelist," *New Bible Dictionary*, 2nd Edition, J. D. Douglas and others, eds. Leicester, England-Downers Grove, IL: InterVarsity Press, 1982, pp. 356-57).

4. "Such individuals were not specifically called to serve a specific congregation, but moved about from place to place, proclaiming the gospel to people wherever they had opportunity. . . .Evangelists share the gospel of Jesus Christ in such a manner that it becomes good news to the hearers. The hearers respond and become faithful and committed followers of Jesus Christ. The evangelist also has a specific anointing "to equip the saints, for the work of ministry for building up the body of Christ" (Eph. 4.12). The official recognition of such individuals within the congregation and in the church at large enables the process of bringing people to faith in Christ" (Harley H. Schmitt, *Many Gifts, One Lord*, Fairfax, VA: Xulon Press, 2002, p. 77).

5. "The evangelist of the Scriptures is, without question, the messenger to the unevangelized, preparing the way for the pastor and teacher in his more constant ministry in the church" (Lewis Sperry Chafer, *True Evangelism*, Grand Rapids: Zondervan, 1967, p. 6).

6. "It will be seen that as an order in the ministry, the evangelist precedes that of the pastor and teacher, a fact which harmonizes with the character of the work each is still recognized as doing. The evangelist has no fixed place of residence, but moves about

in different localities, preaching the gospel to those ignorant of it before. As these are converted and united to Jesus Christ by faith, the work of the pastor and teacher begins, to instruct them further in the things of Christ and build them up in the faith" (J. M. Gray, *The International Standard Bible Encyclopedia*, Vol. 2, Geoffrey W. Bromily, Gen. ed. Grand Rapids: Eerdmans, 1982, p. 204).

C. Summary

1. Like the apostolic and prophetic ministries, the primary function of the evangelistic office is itinerant and missionary in nature. The evangelistic office recognizes that while Christianity spreads naturally through the *oikos* (family and friends) of converted individuals, it often comes across barriers (culture, geography, resistant religions, etc.) that the ordinary spread of the Gospel will not quickly overcome. It is the unique function of the evangelist to break open ground that the Gospel can then spread in through more ordinary means.

2. The gift of evangelism ensures that a special endowment of the Spirit's wisdom and power is present so that the evangelist is unusually effective at receiving a hearing for the Gospel, even in hostile environments. The office of evangelist both frees the gifted person for itinerant ministry in a way that can be underwritten by the larger church, and mandates for this person a special responsibility to stimulate and train evangelists in the local congregations created by missionary outreach, since like all the offices of Ephesians 4.11, it exists to "equip the saints for the work of ministry."

3. Although the evangelist plays a distinct function in mission, the task of the evangelist is not to be separated from the task of church planting. This is seen clearly in Acts 8, where Philip's evangelistic success in Samaria culminates in a visit from the apostles who confirm the conversions, baptize the new believers, ensure that the presence of the Holy Spirit is understood and experienced by the new community of Christians, use the laying on of hands as a formal recognition of the new converts legitimacy, exercise teaching and church discipline (correcting Simon the former sorcerer), and extend the outreach of the mission by preaching in other Samaritan towns. In other words, evangelists are the first stage in a process of church

A Theological Overview of the Equipping Gifts Described in Ephesians 4.11 (continued)

planting and discipleship, not an independent office which exists for an isolated exercise of its own ministry gifts.

II. Pastors[1]

A. Linguistic Considerations

Poimen

"A shepherd" (literally or figuratively) (*Strong's Greek Dictionary of New Testament Words*).

"Herdsman, shepherd, is an Indo-European word which is frequently used in metaphorical senses: leader, ruler, commander. . . .Plato reminds us of the religious use of the word when he compares the rulers of the city-state to shepherds who care for their flock" (E. Beyreuther, *The New International Dictionary of New Testament Theology*, Vol. 3, Colin Brown, Gen. ed., Grand Rapids: Zondervan, 1986, p. 564).

"[Shepherd is] a word naturally of frequent occurrence in Scripture. Sometimes the word "pastor" is used instead (Jer. 2.8; 3.15; 10.21; 12.10; 17.16). This word is used figuratively to represent the relation of rulers to their subjects and of God to his people (Ps. 23.1; 80.1; Isa. 40.11; 44.28; Jer. 25.34, 35; Nahum 3.18; John 10.11, 14; Heb. 13.20; 1 Pet. 2.25; 5.4). The duties of a shepherd in an unenclosed country like Palestine were very onerous. "In early morning he led forth the flock from the fold, marching at its head to the spot where they were to be pastured. Here he watched them all day, taking care that none of the sheep strayed, and if any for a time eluded his watch and wandered away from the rest, seeking diligently till he found and brought it back. In those lands sheep require to be supplied regularly with water, and the shepherd for this purpose has to guide them either to some running stream or to wells dug in the wilderness and furnished with troughs. At night he brought the flock home to the fold, counting them as they passed under the rod at the door to assure himself that none were missing. Nor did his labours always end with sunset. Often he had to guard the fold through the dark hours from the attack of wild beasts, or the wily attempts of the prowling thief" (see 1 Sam. 17.34) ("Shepherd," *Easton's Bible Dictionary*).

[1] Because Paul in Ephesians 4.11 omits the definite article before the word "teachers," it has long been debated in the Church whether he intended to describe only one office, "pastor-teacher" or two "pastors" and "teachers." John Calvin outlines the debate when he says, "Pastors and Teachers are supposed by some to denote one office. . . . Chrysostom and Augustine are of this opinion. . . . I partly agree with them, that Paul speaks indiscriminately of pastors and teachers as belonging to one and the same class, and that the name teacher does, to some extent apply to all pastors. But this does not appear to me a sufficient reason why two offices, which I find to differ from each other, should be confounded. Teaching is, no doubt, the duty of all pastors; but to maintain sound doctrine requires a talent for interpreting Scripture, a man may be a teacher who is not qualified to preach" ("Epistle to the Ephesians," Calvin's Commentaries, vol. XXI, Grand Rapids: Baker, 1981, pp. 279-280). This paper follows Calvin in supporting the possibility of two separate offices, while understanding practically that both offices are often combined in the same individual.

A Theological Overview of the Equipping Gifts Described in Ephesians 4.11 (continued)

    B.   Relevant Theological Quotes

       1.   "Apostles and evangelists had a particular task in planting the church in every place; prophets, for bringing a particular word of God to a situation. Pastors and teachers were gifted to be responsible for the day-to-day building up of the church" (Francis Foulkes *The Epistle of St. Paul to the Ephesians, Tyndale New Testament Commentaries*, Grand Rapids: Eerdmans, 1956, p. 119).

       2.   "'Pastors' may readily be identified with the ministers who are elsewhere called 'elders' (*presbyteroi*) or 'bishops' (*episkopoi* rendered 'guardians' in our preceding citation of Acts 20.28: 'shepherd the flock of God that is in your charge' is the injunction given to elders by a 'fellow elder' in 1 Pet. 5.2). (It is fitting that this injunction should be ascribed to the apostle whose final commission from the Lord, according to John 21.15-17, was 'Feed my sheep.'") (F. F. Bruce, "Epistle to the Colossians, to Philemon, and to the Ephesians," *The New International Commentary on the New Testament*, Vol. 10., Grand Rapids: Eerdmans, 1984, pp. 348).

       3.   "The ministry of a pastor is a ministry of love. No man can perform this ministry without a shepherd's heart as a gift from God. . . .Jesus pointed out that the disposition of a true shepherd is to lay down his life for his sheep. . .When a man has been given the heart of a true shepherd, he is there for the best interest of the flock regardless of personal cost. . . .The duties of the pastor are varied but most can be grouped under three general headings. In the first place, the pastor must oversee and feed the flock of God. . . .Secondly, he has the responsibility of guarding and instructing the people. . . .Thirdly, the pastor must be a teacher of the Word by precept and example" (Joe H. Cothen, *Equipped for Good Work*, Gretna, LA: Pelican Publishing, 1996, pp. 13-15).

       4.   "In addition to whatever else it may be, the gift of pastoring is a catalyst geared to release the gift potential of those in the flock" (Kenneth O. Gangel, *Unwrap Your Spiritual Gifts*, Wheaton, IL: Victor Books, 1983, p. 72).

       5.   "The apostles preached the gospel before they planted churches and gave their converts further teaching; they were in effect evangelists

A Theological Overview of the Equipping Gifts Described in Ephesians 4.11 (continued)

(as well as pastors and teachers) though they are not specifically called so" (F. F. Bruce, "Epistle to the Colossians, to Philemon, and to the Ephesians," *The New International Commentary on the New Testament*, Vol. 10., Grand Rapids: Eerdmans, 1984, p. 347).

C. Summary

Pastors organize, nurture, train, and protect Christian communities and their members. The ultimate goal of the pastoral task is to present everyone "complete in Christ" so that the community of believers acts and speaks in the world just as Christ would. The core task of the pastor is not "doing ministry" but "equipping members to do ministry" by training them in the Word of God and by recognizing their spiritual gifts and helping them to put these gifts into action for ministry and mission. Missionaries with pastoral gifts have a special responsibility to train indigenous leaders to take over the work from their charge.

III. Teachers

A inguistic Considerations

didaskalos

"An instructor" (*Strong's Greek Dictionary of New Testament Words*).

"Acts 13.1 refers to *didáskaloi*, teachers with *prophetai*, prophets. From this it is concluded that in the Christian church the *didáskaloi*, teachers appear as having a special function (Acts 13.1; 1 Cor. 12.23,29; Eph. 4.11; James 3.1). These *didáskaloi* answer to the Jewish *grammateís* (pl.), scribes, and are to be viewed as in a special sense acquainted with and interpreters of God's salvation (Matt. 13.52; Luke 2.46). To them fell the duty of giving progressive instruction of God's redeeming purpose, a function which, according to Eph. 4.11, may have been united with *poimen*, pastor, in one person. Notwithstanding, linguists have debated the precise relationship between teachers and pastors in that text. There is a growing consensus that pastors are a sub-group within the larger body of teachers" (Spiros Zodhiates, *The Complete Word Study Dictionary: New Testament*, Chattanooga, TN: AMG Publishers, 1992).

B. Relevant Theological Quotes

1. "The words *pastor* and *teacher* are grouped as though this were one single office, and in many ways it is. However, there may be teachers who are not called to be pastors. The teacher is one who instructs, especially in doctrine" (Joe H. Cothen, *Equipped for Good Work*, Gretna, LA: Pelican Publishing, 1996, p. 301).

2. "The content of the teaching was wide-ranging: it included the teaching of Jesus with its implications for Christian belief and conduct. In Acts 2.42 it is called 'the apostles' teaching,' to which the primitive church of Jerusalem is said to have devoted itself. . . . Paul assumes, in writing to Rome, that the 'form of teaching' which the Christians of that city had received was sufficiently clear and comprehensive to enable them to detect and reject propaganda which was incompatible with it (Rom. 6. 17; 16.17)" (F. F. Bruce, "Epistle to the Colossians, to Philemon, and to the Ephesians," *The New International Commentary on the New Testament*, Vol. 10., Grand Rapids: Eerdmans, 1984, pp. 348-349).

3. "Let us remember that Jesus was not only *the* pastor or shepherd, but He was *the* teacher (even as He was *the* apostle, *the* prophet, and *the* evangelist). . . . His teaching was the life-giving word of God. Early in His ministry, in response to a temptation by Satan, Jesus declared, "Man shall not live by bread alone, but by every word that proceeds from the mouth of God" (Matt. 4.4). . . . Thus the primary purpose of all Christian teaching is to feed people with the same life-giving word. . . .Recall that Peter was commanded by Jesus not only to tend His sheep–referring essentially to overseeing and guarding–but also to feed His lambs and feed His sheep. This feeding can occur only through "every word that proceed from the mouth of God"–and it is the teacher's responsibility to enable people to understand and receive this word" (J. Rodman Williams, *Renewal Theology: Systematic Theology from a Charismatic Perspective, Vol. 3: The Church, the Kingdom and Last Things*, Grand Rapids: Zondervan, 1996, pp. 180-81).

4. "In 1 Cor. 12.28 *didaskalos* is mentioned as the third charismatic office of a triad (alongside apostles and prophets). Men holding this office had the task of explaining the Christian faith to others and of providing a Christian exposition of the OT. . . . Jas. 3.1, warning

[2] *While it is useful to understand the linguistic and social context of the Greek world which informs the word Paul uses here, it is probably that there is relatively little overlap between the prophecy common to the Hellenistic world and Paul's much more Judeo-Christian use of the term. Christopher Forbes makes a strong case for these differences in his book **Prophecy and Inspired Speech in Early Christianity and its Hellenistic Environment** (Peabody: Hendrickson, 1997). Among other things, Forbes points out that the social forms that defined Christian prophecy differed dramatically from Greek prophecy. "The early Christian groups . . . had no priestly hierarchies, no consciously formalized prophetic ritual beyond a few simple rules of procedure . . . no oracular places, and no procedure for securing an oracle should one be required. . . prophecy in early Christianity took a very different overall form from that which it took in the wider Hellenistic world" (p. 319). As opposed to the divination prophecy of Greek culture, "Early Christian prophecy was characteristically spontaneous in at least this sense: one did not approach the prophet with an inquiry. The prophet addressed the congregation, without prior inquiry, in the confidence that his revelation as God's word for their need, whether or not that need had yet been perceived" (p. 289).*

A Theological Overview of the Equipping Gifts Described in Ephesians 4.11 (continued)

against too strong an influx into the teaching office (an office which the writer himself appears to hold) points out that the failures of teachers will incur severe penalties in the judgment" (K. Wegenast, *The New International Dictionary of New Testament Theology*, Vol. 3, Colin Brown, Gen. ed., Grand Rapids: Zondervan, 1986, p. 768).

C. Summary

The core of the teaching office is the ability to explain the Scriptures in such a way that "the deposit of faith" is passed on to congregations and the individuals in them, and to oppose false doctrine with scriptural truth. Because they guard sound doctrine, it is important that those who hold the teaching "office" be formally recognized and authorized to speak on behalf of the congregation. Missionaries with teaching gifts must constantly work to entrust sound doctrine to "faithful men who will be able to teach others also" (2 Tim. 2.2 ESV).

IV. Prophets

A. Linguistic Considerations

Prophetes

"A foreteller" ("prophet"); by analogy, an inspired speaker; by extension, a poet (*Strong's Greek Dictionary of New Testament Words*)

"'One who speaks forth openly,' 'a proclaimer of the divine message'. . . . In general, 'the prophet' was one upon whom the Spirit of God rested . . . one, to whom and through whom, God speaks" (W. E. Vine, *Vine's Complete Expository Dictionary of Old and New Testament Words*, Nashville: Thomas Nelson, 1996, p. 493).

In ancient Greek[2] culture, the term *prophet* could describe an oracle prophet such as the one at Delphi, where it was clearly used to describe an official position (office). "The oracle prophet enjoys such social esteem that he may be invited to fulfill representative functions like leading delegations and serving as a spokesman for them. The official character of his position is plain from the fact that it was common to name the year after his period of office" (*Theological Dictionary of the New Testament*, Vol.6, Gerhard Kittel,

A Theological Overview of the Equipping Gifts Described in Ephesians 4.11 (continued)

ed., Grand Rapids: Wm. B. Eerdmans, 1964, p. 792). However, it could also be used to describe much more informal prophets such as those engaging in prophetic manticism, and poets who created under the influence of their Muse. The majority of prophecy in the Greek world was in the form of divination in which a person approached the prophet with an inquiry which the prophet answered. In Greek thought, "The prophet occupies a mediatorial role. He is the mouthpiece of the god and he is also man's spokesman to the god." (*Theological Dictionary of the New Testament*, Vol.6, Gerhard Kittel, ed., Grand Rapids: Wm. B. Eerdmans, 1964, p. 794).

B. Relevant Theological Quotes

1. "All may agree that there appears no new revelation to be expected concerning God in Christ. But there appears to be no good reason why the living God, who both speaks and acts (in contrast to dead idols), cannot use the gift of prophecy to give particular local guidance to a church, nation or individual, or to warn or encourage by way of prediction as well as by reminders, in full accord with the written word of Scripture, by which all such utterances must be tested. Certainly the NT does not see it as the job of the prophet to be a doctrinal innovator, but to deliver the word the Spirit gives him in line with the truth once for all delivered to the saints (Jude 3), to challenge and encourage our faith" (J. P. Baker, "Prophecy," *New Bible Dictionary*, 2nd Edition, J. D. Douglas and others, eds., Leicester, England-Downers Grove, IL: InterVarsity Press, 1982, p. 985).

2. "The prophet knows something of the divine mysteries. . . . Nevertheless, primitive Christian prophecy does not consist only of the disclosure of future events. . . .The prophet speaks out on contemporary issues. He does not say only what God intends to do; he also proclaims what God would have done by men. . . .The prophet admonishes the indolent and weary and consoles and encourages those under assault, 1 Co. 14.3; Ac. 15.32. Through his preaching he brings to light the secret wickedness of men, 1 Co. 14.25. Since he speaks with a sense of God-given authority, he gives authoritative instruction, though he is not above criticism" (Gerhard Kittel, ed., *Theological Dictionary of the New Testament*, Vol.6, Grand Rapids: Wm. B. Eerdmans, 1964, p. 848).

A Theological Overview of the Equipping Gifts Described in Ephesians 4.11 (continued)

3. "At all times [*in the history of the church*] there have not been lacking persons having the spirit of prophecy, not indeed for the declaration of any new doctrine of faith, but for the direction of human acts" (Thomas Aquinas, *Summa Theologica*, Vol. IV., Westminster, MD: Christian Classics, © Benziger Brothers, 1948, p. 1906).

4. "[Prophecy] was given unquestioned authority only after it was vetted (cf. 1 Thes. 5.19-21). Even when it was recognized to be a divine word, it did not necessarily become a canonical word. Prophecy had (and has) important uses for its immediate recipients but it was given canonical status only when it was recognized also to be normative revelation for future generations and a touchstone by which future prophecies might be tested" (E. E. Ellis, "Prophecy, Theology of," *New Dictionary of Theology*, Sinclair Ferguson, David F. Wright, and J. I. Packer, eds., Downers Grove, IL/Leicester, England: InterVarsity Press, 1988, p. 538).

5. Wayne Gruden argues in his book *The Gift of Prophecy in the New Testament and Today*, (Wheaton, IL: Crossway Books, 2000) that Old Testament prophets and New Testament Apostles (in the narrow sense of the Twelve plus Paul) are functionally equivalent in that they are the *only* people authorized to give immediate revelation from God that cannot be broken. What is true of Old Testament prophets is also true of New Testament apostles in that both of these speak with an authority that surpasses that of New Testament prophets. In other words, a New Testament prophet is not speaking for God in the same way as an Old Testament prophet or a New Testament apostle (narrowly defined). This view is shared by D.A. Carson who writes that,

   "it can be argued rather compellingly that the true NT analogue of the OT prophet is not the NT prophet but the NT apostle (in the narrow sense). . . . It is virtually impossible to conceive of 1 Cor. 14.29 being applied to OT prophets (once their credentials were accepted) or to NT apostles." (See "Church, Authority in," *The Evangelical Dictionary of Theology*, Walter A. Elwell, ed, Grand Rapids: Baker Book House, 1984, pp. 228-229.)

Graham Houston nuances this view further by arguing that even in the Old Testament there was a distinction between types of prophecy. There was the authoritative word from the Lord which had a uniquely binding character (like the NT Apostles) but there were also many instances *"where a type of prophecy is described which seems to have been regarded differently, not so much as a revelation of God's secrets but as a powerful sign of his presence with his people at crucial times in the unfolding of God's purposes"* (*Prophecy: A Gift for Today?* Downers Grove, IL: InterVarsity Press, 1989, p. 35). Among instances of this less authoritative, secondary-type prophecy could be named King Saul's sudden bout of prophecy that changed his mind about pursing David and the prophecy of the seventy elders in Numbers 11 which did not result in a specific recorded message but was a confirming sign of God's presence with them. Likewise, Moses' desire that all of God's people become prophets (Num. 11.29) seems to suggest by necessity this second-order prophecy focused on God's presence and leading rather than authoritative pronouncements of the Divine will and corresponds closely to Joel's prophetic vision of a time when the Spirit would be poured out in such a way that all of God's people both young and old, male and female, would receive prophetic words and visions (Joel 2.28).

C. Summary

Prophecy is the open proclamation of a revealed message from God which prepares the Church for obedience to him and to the Scriptures. In New Testament practice the prophetic message is received spontaneously and declared immediately (i.e. it is not something prepared in advance). New Testament prophecy is associated with a variety of spiritual functions including guidance, comfort, exhortation, and prediction. It is not itself a proclamation of the Gospel but rather a means by which the principles of Scripture can be more clearly understood in regard to a particular situation. Its purpose is always to strengthen the Church.

All Christian traditions have some means by which people can affirm, "I believe that God is saying to us that . . . ." Whenever God's voice is discerned to be speaking among us, a prophetic word has been given. Prophecy encourages, guides, and motivates obedience to God among a particular people facing particular situations. It is always judged

A Theological Overview of the Equipping Gifts Described in Ephesians 4.11 (continued)

by it conformity to the written Word of God (and in some traditions preaching and prophecy are held to be synonymous). This prophetic leadership and its development may employ a number of different forms in regard to how the voice of the Holy Spirit that guides into all truth is discerned, evaluated, and obeyed. Baptists, Pentecostals, Mennonites, and Presbyterians have very different traditions as to the language and means that are employed in this process but all of them take seriously that the Church must hear specifically what God is saying to them in the present.

V. Apostles

A. Linguistic Considerations

Apostolos

A *delegate*; specially, an *ambassador* of the Gospel; officially a commissioner of Christ (*Strong's Greek Dictionary of New Testament Words*).

"*A delegate, messenger, one sent forth with orders.* . . . specifically applied to the twelve disciples whom Christ selected, out of the multitude of his adherents, to be his constant companions and the heralds to proclaim to men the kingdom of God. . . . In a broader sense the name is transferred to other eminent Christian teachers; as Barnabas, Acts xiv. 14., and perhaps also Timothy and Silvanus," (1 Th. ii. 7, cf. too Ro. xvi. 7). (Joseph Henry Thayer, *A Greek-English Lexicon of the New Testament*, Grand Rapids: Baker, 1977, p. 68).

Linguistic authorities generally agree that there is relatively little in common between the way that classical Greek or intertestamental Judaism used the term *apostle* and the significance that it came to have in the ministry of Jesus or the post-Pentecost Church.[3]

B. Relevant Theological Quotes

1. [Paul] then, in a general way, calls those in this place [Rom. 16.7][4] Apostles, who planted Churches by carrying here and there the doctrine of salvation . . ." (John Calvin, "Romans," *Calvin's Commentaries*, Vol. XIX, Grand Rapids: Baker Book House, 1981, p. 546).

[3] *See, for example, the article on "Apostolos" in Theological Dictionary of the New Testament, vol. 1, Gerhard Kittel, ed. Grand Rapids: Wm. B. Eerdmans, 1964, pp. 398-420.*

[4] *Romans 16.7 refers to Andronicus and Junias, who were not part of the twelve, but were spoken of as apostles by Paul.*

A Theological Overview of the Equipping Gifts Described in Ephesians 4.11 (continued)

2. "The titles 'apostle' and 'prophet' occur in the NT with both wide and narrow meanings. Sometimes the term 'apostle' is filled with connotations of special election and authority; in these cases it is restricted to the twelve disciples of Jesus and Paul. On other occasions it is used in a wider sense: every witness of the resurrected Christ and anyone delegated by a church for mission work can bear the same title (Matt. 10.1-5; Gal. 1.1,17, 19; 1 Cor. 9.1-2; 2 Cor. 8.23)" (Karl Barth, *Ephesians 4-6*, Garden City, N.Y.: Doubleday & Co., 1974, p. 314 quoted in Harley H. Schmitt, *Many Gifts, One Lord*, Fairfax, VA: Xulon Press, 2002).

3. "[Apostle] is a comprehensive term for "bearers of the NT message." The name is first borne by the circle of the twelve, i.e., the original apostles. . . . Yet the name is also applied to the first Christian missionaries or their most prominent representatives, including some who did not belong even to the wider groups of disciples" (Gerhard Kittel, ed., *Theological Dictionary of the New Testament*, Vol. 1, Grand Rapids: Wm. B. Eerdmans, 1964, p. 422).

4. "The term *apostles* designates three different groups of people. Initially, only the original disciples (meaning "students, learners") of Jesus were called apostles (meaning "those sent forth with a mission"). Later, the name was given to missionaries involved in church planting who were also eyewitnesses of Christ's resurrection, such as Paul himself (1 Cor. 9.1-1) and a group of Jesus' followers other than the Twelve (1 Cor. 15.5,7). Finally, the designation was extended to people who had never seen Christ but who were involved with apostles in pioneer missionary efforts—Apollos (1 Cor. 4.6,9); Epaphroditus (Phil. 2.25); Silvanus and Timothy (1 Thess. 1.1, cf. 2.6). The definition of "apostles" as one of the higher gifts to be desired bears evidence to the continued accessibility to this ministry for qualified individuals (1 Cor. 12.28, cf. 31). Corinthian Christians could aspire to become apostles, prophets, or teachers. The term *apostle* was still used in this broad sense in the post-apostolic writings of the Didache" (Gilbert Bilezikian, *Beyond Sex Roles: What the Bible says about a Woman's Place in Church and Family*, Grand Rapids, MI: Baker Book House, 1986).

A Theological Overview of the Equipping Gifts Described in Ephesians 4.11 (continued)

5. "Most evangelicals feel very uncomfortable using the term *apostle* to describe any office or leader in the church today. Is it possible, however, for us to conceive of a separation of gift and office after the first century? Rather than assigning this gift to the history of the early church, can we not recognize the broad sense of the verb form *apostello*? Could it not be that in the time between the 1st and 20th centuries the Holy Spirit has given this gift to God's people in what we have come to call *missionary service*? . . . Many have chosen the option of locking several of the spiritual gifts into the first century, lest some explanation be required for their presence in the church today. I would prefer to allow the Holy Spirit the broadest latitude to produce in Christ's body any gift in any age as He sees fit. It seems quite safe to say that the *office* of the apostles was restricted to the establishing of the New Testament church. But . . .we may be justified in seeing evidence of "apostleship" not only as a gift, but as a gift which has operated in the church throughout all the years of its history" (Kenneth O. Gangel, *Unwrap Your Spiritual Gifts*, Wheaton, IL: Victor Books, 1983, pp. 26-27).

6. "A distinction may be made between the foundational ministry of apostle, that is, the apostleship, and the ongoing ministry of others who are called apostles. In this broader sense an apostle is one *sent, commissioned*, and therefore is not affixed to a particular location or church. He does not have the authority of a foundational apostle nor are his words equally inspired. Such an apostle operates in translocal manner, but he does not operate independently. He is church-based, representing a particular church, but ministering largely in a field beyond. *Such apostles are always essential to the life of a church that realizes its call to reach out beyond itself in the mission of the gospel*" (J. Rodman Williams, *Renewal Theology: Systematic Theology from a Charismatic Perspective, Vol. 3: The Church, the Kingdom and Last Things*, Grand Rapids: Zondervan, 1996, pp. 169-70).

7. "The word is occasionally applied in a less restrictive sense in the N.T. to men of apostolic gifts, graces, labors, and successes. It is so notably of Barnabas, who was sent forth with Paul (Acts 13.3; 14.4, 14). Similarly one still meets with such expressions, as Judson, the apostle of Burma" ("Apostle," *The Westminster Dictionary of the Bible*, John D. Davis, ed. Philadelphia: The Westminster Press, 1944, p. 36).

A Theological Overview of the Equipping Gifts Described in Ephesians 4.11 (continued)

8. "One of the principal functions—indeed, the primary function–of an apostle (in the special Christian use of the word) was the preaching of the gospel. The apostles, as an order of ministry in the church, were not perpetuated beyond the apostolic age, but the various functions which they discharged did not lapse with their departure, but continued to be performed by others-notably by the evangelists and the pastors and teachers listed here [in Ephesians 4.11] . . . The apostles preached the gospel before they planted churches and gave their converts further teaching; they were in effect evangelists (as well as pastors and teachers) though they are not specifically called so" (F. F. Bruce, "Epistle to the Colossians, to Philemon, and to the Ephesians," *The New International Commentary on the New Testament*, Vol. 10., Grand Rapids: Eerdmans, 1984, pp. 346-347).

9. "The word *apostle* means *one who is sent*, and is used for others in addition to the original twelve. Today, he is the missionary to new areas" (Avery Willis, Jr. *Biblical Basis of Missions*, Baptist Doctrine Series, Nashville: Convention Press, 1979, p. 108).

10. "In light of [Ephesians] 2.20 and 3.5 and the fact that Paul himself functioned as both apostle and prophet, the first three designations [apostles, prophets and evangelists] refer primarily though in the case of prophets and evangelists not exclusively, to itinerant ministries among the early churches. Itinerant workers founded churches by evangelizing and built them up through prophetic utterances. There can be little question that this is the understanding of the term "apostle" in Paul's letters" (Gordon D. Fee, *God's Empowering Presence*, Peabody, MA: Hendrickson, 1994, p. 707).

C. Summary

The idea that the broad sense of apostleship used in the Pauline letters and the modern term missionary are functionally equivalent has widespread support in current biblical and theological scholarship and this understanding is commonly (although not universally) found both in the Reformed and the Arminian sectors of evangelical theology.[5] In this wide sense the apostolic gifting is strongly associated with those called to a ministry of *itinerant* church-planting mission.

[5] *Likewise, Roman Catholicism which promotes an active office of apostle in a way that Protestants do not (i.e. the bishops of the church are successors of the Apostles narrowly defined and exercise their office authoritatively through a direct line of apostolic succession), nevertheless, also retain a distinction between the narrow and wide sense of the term "apostle." Thus, the Catholic Church can teach the existence of a wider kind of apostolic ministry in the broad sense of missionary and ministry outreach saying, "Indeed, we call an apostolate 'every activity of the Mystical Body' that aims 'to spread the Kingdom of Christ over all the earth'" (Catechism of the Catholic Church, Liguori, MO: Liguori Publications, 1994, p. 229).*

A Theological Overview of the Equipping Gifts Described in Ephesians 4.11 (continued)

[6] *All legitimate Christian authority is based on its ability to edify (cf. 2 Cor. 10.8). Blessing, not control, is the point of authority. Even the direct "submission to leaders" language of Hebrews 13.17 is predicated on the fact that it brings "advantage" to the follower. Christians submit to leaders because they are God's gift to provide edification and protection. Any Christian leader who claims an authority that is separated from obedience to Christ, submission to the Scripture, the growth of Christ's Church, or the edification of its members is no longer exercising biblical authority. Paul will make this idea plain in the upcoming portions of the text when he writes that the "equipping of the saints for ministry" is intended to result in "building up (edifying) the body of Christ" (Eph. 4.13).*

In spite of this, however, it is probably best to restrict the idea of an "Apostolic office" to the more narrow sense of the Twelve (substituting Matthias for Judas) plus Paul. Hence, missionary is a better term than apostle for the modern cross-cultural church planter because it retains the linguistic sense of one sent out in mission without detracting from the *special authority* retained by the original Apostles who were directly commissioned by the Risen Lord. Nonetheless, it should be recognized that the nature of the missionary task is to be "little apostles" bearing witness to Christ and exercising authority over the formation of their congregations within the bounds of Scripture. The original Apostles could speak authoritatively to the whole church, missionaries can speak authoritatively to the churches they have planted within the bounds of Scripture. Ultimately, for both Apostles and missionaries, the issue of authority is not one of control but of developing congregations and leaders that can themselves hear and obey Christ.[6]

The missionary (apostolic) gifting, defined in this way, indicates that:

- a person feel an urgent call to the unreached,

- they will constantly press on to new unreached groups,

- they will aggressively adapt themselves to new cultures in order to win as many as possible,

- and, they will raise up leadership for the new churches they establish so that they functionally serve as a "pastor to pastors."

Theological Visions and Approaches
The Urban Ministry Institute

The following outline provides a bare bones overview of some of the philosophical approaches and understandings related to God and his relationship to the universe. Individuals pose different arguments for the existence of God and the relationship between God and his universe based on their 1) understanding of Scripture, 2) under-lying assumptions about the existence of God, 3) view of the material universe and world, and 4) the human capacity to know God (if he exists), and what that knowledge involves. Many modern approaches think of God's existence and all speech about God as the possibility of religion *within the bounds of knowledge.*

I. Principles of Natural Theology

    A. *Ontological argument* - Anselm *Proslogion*

        1. Logical necessity of God's existence by reason alone

        2. God = that than which no greater can be thought

        3. To exist in reality is greater than to exist merely in thought.

        4. "That than which no greater can be thought" must exist both in reality and in thought.

        5. Tautology – (argument in a circle) merely to define an entity as existing does not provide grounds for inferring its existence.

        6. Kant – a merchant cannot increase his wealth by adding zeroes to the figures in his accounts.

    B. *Cosmological argument* – existence of a first cause of the cosmos

        1. The things we observe in the world all have antecedent causes. Nothing is totally self-caused, and there must be a first cause.

        2. God is the Prime Mover and the First Cause.

C. *Teleological argument* – (physico-teleological)

    1. Telos = end

    2. Things in our experience appear to serve ends beyond their devising or control. Purpose observed in nature, implying a cosmic mind.

    3. Key warrant: purpose does not occur without a Purposer.

D. *Moral argument* – People of different cultures and beliefs recognize certain basic moral values and obligations.

    1. These universal values cannot be reduced to mere conventions.

    2. These do not emerge from the material universe.

    3. We can, therefore, posit a personal, moral being as the source of all moral values and as the One to whom all moral beings are ultimately responsible.

II. Facts about Natural Theology

A. Most prevalent in *Catholic theology*

B. *Calvinistic theology*: believes in a general revelation of God in nature and providence

    1. Spoke of 'divinity' or 'sense of God' which was 'the seed of religion'

    2. For sure and certain knowledge of God we must turn to the Word of God in Scripture

C. *Karl Barth*: rejected all natural theology on the grounds that God reveals himself in his Word, and is pointless to look elsewhere

Theological Visions and Approaches (continued)

D. *Emil Brunner:* argued for a natural theology based on such ideas as the image of God, general revelation, preserving grace, divine ordinances, point of contact, and the contention that race does not abolish nature but perfects it.

III. Dualism

A. A *dualism* exists when there are two substances, or powers, or modes, neither of which is reducible to the other.

1. Monism – there is only one substance, power, or mode.

2. Twins of all things

B. Four different contexts (God and creation)

1. Identifying God with his creation

   a. Metaphysical pantheism

   b. Mystical connection

2. God is distinct from his creation in the sense of its GROUND.

3. Unlike deism, God is its SUSTAINING CAUSE (both transcendently and imminently).

4. Difficulties: what is precisely the relationship between the divine and human action in creation

IV. Materialism

"The doctrine that whatever exists is either physical matter, or depends upon physical matter."

A. A philosophical position with definite ontological explanations (the denial of the existence of minds or spirits)

B. Research program and methodology with no such implications

C. Opposed by mind-body dualism

D. What of humanity as part of the creation, and life after death?

V. Deism

"Belief in a remote creator, uninvolved in the world whose mechanism he devised"

A. Stands for the abolition of dogma founded on alleged revelation

B. Promotes a natural religion with blessings bestowed on all by a beneficent God

C. Religion of moral law: "rationalists with a heart hunger for religion"

D. Non-christocentric worship of God

E. Ecclesiastical power as a hindrance of free thinking people

F. Fall and redemption is dismissed, its literary form regarded as crude, corrupt, and flawed

VI. Determinism

A. *Scientific determinism* – the form of every physical event is determined uniquely by the conjunction of events preceding it; discovering the interdependence and expressing it in laws.

Theological Visions and Approaches (continued)

B. *Theological determinism* – the form of all events is determined according to the "determinate counsel and foreknowledge of God" (Acts 2.23).

C. What of the *theodicy* questions? (Theodicy as the problem of evil happening to good or innocent persons)

D. Limited freedom or no freedom at all: what of the relationship between the material world, causative events, and the sovereignty of God?

The Theology of Christus Victor
A Christ-Centered Biblical Motif for Integrating and Renewing the Urban Church

Rev. Dr. Don L. Davis

	The Promised Messiah	The Word Made Flesh	The Son of Man	The Suffering Servant	The Lamb of God	The Victorious Conqueror	The Reigning Lord in Heaven	The Bridegroom and Coming King
Biblical Framework	Israel's hope of Yahweh's anointed who would redeem his people	In the person of Jesus of Nazareth, the Lord has come to the world	As the promised king and divine Son of Man, Jesus reveals the Father's glory and salvation to the world	As Inaugurator of the Kingdom of God, Jesus demonstrates God's reign present through his words, wonders, and works	As both High Priest and Paschal Lamb, Jesus offers himself to God on our behalf as a sacrifice for sin	In his resurrection from the dead and ascension to God's right hand, Jesus is proclaimed as Victor over the power of sin and death	Now reigning at God's right hand till his enemies are made his footstool, Jesus pours out his benefits on his body	Soon the risen and ascended Lord will return to gather his Bride, the Church, and consummate his work
Scripture References	Isa. 9.6-7 / Jer. 23.5-6 / Isa. 11.1-10	John 1.14-18 / Matt. 1.20-23 / Phil. 2.6-8	Matt. 2.1-11 / Num. 24.17 / Luke 1.78-79	Mark 1.14-15 / Matt. 12.25-30 / Luke 17.20-21	2 Cor. 5.18-21 / Isa. 52-53 / John 1.29	Eph. 1.16-23 / Phil. 2.5-11 / Col. 1.15-20	1 Cor. 15.25 / Eph. 4.15-16 / Acts 2.32-36	Rom. 14.7-9 / Rev. 5.9-13 / 1 Thess. 4.13-18
Jesus' History	The pre-incarnate, only begotten Son of God in glory	His conception by the Spirit, and birth to Mary	His manifestation to the Magi and to the world	His teaching, exorcisms, miracles, and mighty works among the people	His suffering, crucifixion, death, and burial	His resurrection, with appearances to his witnesses, and his ascension to the Father	The sending of the Holy Spirit and his gifts, and Christ's session in heaven at the Father's right hand	His soon return from heaven to earth as Lord and Christ: the Second Coming
Description	The biblical promise for the seed of Abraham, the prophet like Moses, the son of David	In the Incarnation, God has come to us; Jesus reveals to humankind the Father's glory in fullness	In Jesus, God has shown his salvation to the entire world, including the Gentiles	In Jesus, the promised Kingdom of God has come visibly to earth, demonstrating his binding of Satan and rescinding the Curse	As God's perfect Lamb, Jesus offers himself up to God as a sin offering on behalf of the entire world	In his resurrection and ascension, Jesus destroyed death, disarmed Satan, and rescinded the Curse	Jesus is installed at the Father's right hand as Head of the Church, Firstborn from the dead, and supreme Lord in heaven	As we labor in his harvest field in the world, so we await Christ's return, the fulfillment of his promise
Church Year	Advent	Christmas	Season after Epiphany — Baptism and Transfiguration	Lent	Holy Week — Passion	Eastertide — Easter, Ascension Day, Pentecost	Season after Pentecost — Trinity Sunday	Season after Pentecost — All Saints Day, Reign of Christ the King
	The Coming of Christ	*The Birth of Christ*	*The Manifestation of Christ*	*The Ministry of Christ*	*The Suffering and Death of Christ*	*The Resurrection and Ascension of Christ*	*The Heavenly Session of Christ*	*Reign of Christ*
Spiritual Formation	As we await his Coming, let us proclaim and affirm the hope of Christ	O Word made flesh, let us every *heart prepare him room* to dwell	Divine Son of Man, show the nations your salvation and glory	In the person of Christ, the power of the reign of God has come to earth and to the Church	May those who share the Lord's death be resurrection with him	Let us participate by faith in the victory of Christ over the power of sin, Satan, and death	Come, indwell us, Holy Spirit, and empower us to advance Christ's Kingdom in the world	We live and work in expectation of his soon return, seeking to please him in all things

A Theology of the Church

Don L. Davis and Terry Cornett ©1996 World Impact Press

The Church Is an Apostolic Community
Where the Word Is Rightly Preached

I.   A Community of Calling

A.   The essential meaning of Church is *Ekklesia*: those who have been *"called out"* in order to be *"called to"* a New Community.

1.   Like the Thessalonians, the Church is called out from idolatry to serve the living God and *called to* wait for his Son from heaven.

2.   The Church is *called out* in order that it may belong to Christ (Rom. 1.6). Jesus speaks of the Church as "my *ekklesia*" that is the "called out ones" who are his unique possession (Matt. 16.18; Gal. 5.24; James 2.7).

3.   The components of God's call:

a.   The foundation is God's desire to save (John 3.16, 1 Tim. 2.4).

b.   The message is the good news of the Kingdom (Matt. 24.14).

c.   The recipients are "whosoever will" (John 3.15).

d.   The method is through faith in the shed blood of Christ and acknowledgment of his lordship (Rom. 3.25; 10.9-10; Eph. 2.8).

e.   The result is regeneration and placement into the body of Christ (2 Cor. 5.17; Rom. 12.4-5; Eph. 3.6; 5.30).

B.   The Church is *called out*.

1.   Called out of the world:

a.   The world is under Satan's dominion and stands in opposition to God.

b.   Conversion and incorporation in Christ's Church involves repentance (*metanoia*) and a transfer of kingdom allegiances.

A Theology of the Church (continued)

    c. The Church exists as strangers and aliens who are "in" but not "of" this world system.

  2. Called out from sin:

    a. Those in the Church are being sanctified, set apart for holy action, so that they may live out their calling as saints of God (1 Cor. 1.2; 2 Tim. 1.9, 1 Pet. 1.15).

    b. The Church must be available for God's purpose and use (Rom. 8.28-29; Eph. 1.11; Rom. 6.13).

    c. The Church must bring glory to God alone (Isa. 42.8; John 13.31-32; 17.1; Rom. 15.6; 1 Pet. 2.12).

    d. The Church must now be characterized by obedience to God (2 Thess. 1.8; Heb. 5.8-9; 1 John 2.3).

C. The Church is ***called to***:

  1. Salvation and new life

    a. Forgiveness and cleansing from sin (Eph. 1.7; 5.26; 1 John 1.9).

    b. Justification (Rom. 3.24; 8.30; Titus 3.7) in which God pronounces us guiltless as to the penalty of his divine law.

    c. Regeneration (John 3.5-8; Col. 3.9-10) by which a "new self" is birthed in us through the Spirit.

    d. Sanctification (John 17.19; 1 Cor. 1.2) in which we are "set apart" by God for holiness of life.

    e. Glorification and Life Eternal (Rom. 8.30, 1 Tim. 6.12; 2 Thess. 2.14) in which we are changed to be like Christ and prepared to live forever in the presence of God (Rom. 8.23; 1 Cor. 15.51-53; 1 John 3.2).

A Theology of the Church (continued)

    2.   Participation in a new community of God's chosen people (1 Pet. 2.9-10)

        a.   Members of Christ's body (1 Cor. 10.16-17; 12.27).

        b.   Sheep of God's flock under one Shepherd (John 10; Heb. 13.20; 1 Pet. 5.2-4).

        c.   Members of God's family and household (Gal. 6.10; 1 Tim. 3.15).

        d.   Children of Abraham and recipients of covenant promise (Rom. 4.16; Gal. 3.29; Eph. 2.12).

        e.   Citizens of the New Jerusalem (Phil. 3.20; Rev. 3.12).

        f.   The firstfruits of the Kingdom of God (Luke 12.32; James 1.18).

    3.   Freedom (Gal. 5.1, 13)

        a.   Called out of the dominion of darkness which suppresses freedom (Col. 1.13-14).

        b.   Called away from sin which enslaves (John 8.34-36).

        c.   Called to God the Father who is the Liberator of his people (Exod. 6.6).

        d.   Called to God the Son who gives the truth which sets free (John 8.31-36).

        e.   Called to God the Spirit whose presence creates liberty (2 Cor. 3.17).

II. A Community of Faith

A. The Church is a community of faith, which has, by faith, confessed Jesus as Lord and Savior.

Faith refers both to ***the content of our belief*** and to ***the act of believing*** itself. Jesus is the object (content) of our faith and his life is received through faith (our belief) in him and his word. In both of these senses, the Church is a community of faith.

1. The Church places its faith:

    a. in the Living Word (Jesus the Messiah),

    b. who is revealed in the written Word (Sacred Scripture),

    c. and who is now present, teaching and applying his Word to the Church (through the ministry of the Holy Spirit).

2. The Church guards the deposit of faith, given by Christ and the apostles, through sound teaching and the help of the Holy Spirit who indwells its members (2 Tim. 1.13-14).

B. Because it is a community of faith, the Church is also a community of grace.

1. The Church exists by grace-through faith rather than through human merit or works (Gal. 2.21; Eph. 2.8).

2. The Church announces, in faith, the grace of God to all humanity (Titus 2.11-15).

3. The Church lives by grace in all actions and relationships (Eph. 4.1-7).

C. The Church is a community where the Scriptures are preached, studied, meditated upon, memorized, believed, and obeyed (Ezek. 7.10; Jos. 1.8; Ps. 119; Col. 3.16; 1 Tim. 4.13; James 1.22-25).

1. The Church preaches the Gospel of the Kingdom, as revealed in Scripture, and calls people to repentance and faith which leads to obedience (Matt. 4.17; 28.19-20; Acts 2.38-40).

2. The Church studies and applies the Scriptures through teaching, rebuking, correcting, and training in righteousness so that all members of the community are equipped to live godly lives characterized by good works (2 Tim. 3.16-17; 4.2).

3. The Church intentionally reflects on the Scriptures in light of reason, tradition, and experience, learning and doing theology as a means of more fully understanding and acting upon truth (Ps. 119.97-99; 1 Tim. 4.16; 2 Tim. 2.15).

A Theology of the Church (continued)

4. The Church functions as a listening community which is aware of the Spirit's presence and relies upon him to interpret and apply the Scriptures to the present moment (John 14.25-26).

D. The Church contends for the faith that was once for all entrusted to the saints (Jude 3).

III. A Community of Witness

A. The Church witnesses to the fact that in the incarnation, life, teaching, death and resurrection of Jesus the Christ, God's Kingdom has begun (Mark 1.15; Luke 4.43; 6.20; 11.20; Acts 1.3; 28.23; 1 Cor. 4.20; Col. 1.12-13).

1. The Church proclaims Jesus as *Christus Victor* whose reign will:

a. Rescind the curse over creation and humankind (Rev. 22.3).

b. Defeat Satan and the powers and destroy their work (1 John 3.8).

c. Reverse the present order by defending and rewarding the meek, the humble, the despised, the lowly, the righteous, the hungry, and the rejected (Luke 1.46-55; 4.18-19; 6.20-22).

d. Propitiate God's righteous anger (Gal. 3.10-14; 1 John 2.1-2).

e. Create a new humanity (1 Cor. 15.45-49; Eph. 2.15; Rev. 5.9-10).

f. Destroy the last enemy- death (1 Cor. 15.26).

2. Ultimately, the very Kingdom itself will be turned over to God the Father, and the freedom, wholeness, and justice of the Lord will abound throughout the universe (Isa. 10.2-7; 11.1-9; 53.5; Mic. 4.1-3; 6.8; Matt. 6.33; 23.23; Luke 4.18-19; John 8.34-36; 1 Cor. 15.28; Rev. 21).

A Theology of the Church (continued)

B.   The Church witnesses by:

1.   Functioning as a sign and foretaste of the Kingdom of God; the Church is a visible community where people see that:

   a.   Jesus is acknowledged as Lord (Rom. 10.9-10).

   b.   The truth and power of the Gospel is growing and producing fruit among every kindred, tribe, and nation (Acts 2.47; Rom. 1.16; Col. 1.6; Rev. 7.9-10).

   c.   The values of God's Kingdom are accepted and acted upon (Matt. 6.33).

   d.   God's commands are obeyed on earth as they are in heaven (Matt. 6.10; John 14.23-24).

   e.   The presence of God is experienced (Matt. 18.20; John 14.16-21).

   f.   The power of God is demonstrated (1 Cor. 4.20).

   g.   The love of God is freely received and given (Eph. 5.1-2; 1 John 3.18; 4.7-8).

   h.   The compassion of God is expressed in bearing each other's burdens, first within the Church, and then, in sacrificial service to the whole world (Matt. 5.44-45; Gal. 6.2, 10; Heb. 13.16).

   i.   The redemptiveness of God transcends human frailty and sin so that the treasure of the Kingdom is evident in spite of being contained in earthen vessels (2 Cor. 4.7).

2.   Performing signs and wonders which confirm the Gospel (Mark 16.20; Acts 4.30; 8.6,13; 14.3; 15.12; Rom. 15.18-19; Heb. 2.4)

3.   Accepting the call to mission

   a.   Going into all the world to preach the Gospel (Matt. 24.14; 28.18-20; Acts 1.8, Col. 1.6).

   b.   Evangelizing and making disciples of Christ and his Kingdom (Matt. 28.18-20; 2 Tim. 2.2).

A Theology of the Church (continued)

      c.   Establishing churches among those unreached by the Gospel (Matt. 16.18; 28.19; Acts 2.41-42; 16.5; 2 Cor. 11.28; Heb. 12.22-23).

      d.   Displaying the excellencies of Christ's Kingdom by engendering freedom, wholeness, and justice in his Name (Isa. 53.5; Mic. 6.8; Matt. 5.16; 12.18-20; Luke 4.18-19; John 8.34-36; 1 Pet. 3.11).

   4.   Acting as a prophetic community

      a.   Speaking the Word of God into situations of error, confusion, and sin (2 Cor. 4.2; Heb. 4.12; James 5.20; Titus 2.15).

      b.   Speaking up for those who cannot speak up for themselves so that justice is defended (Prov. 31.8-9).

      c.   Announcing judgment against sin in all its forms (Rom. 2.5; Gal. 6.7-8; 1 Pet. 4.17).

      d.   Announcing hope in situations where sin has produced despair (Jer. 32.17; 2 Thess. 2.16; Heb. 10.22-23; 1 Pet. 1.3-5).

      e.   Proclaiming the return of Jesus, the urgency of the hour, and the reality that soon every knee will bow and every tongue confess that Jesus is Lord to the glory of God the Father (Matt. 25.1-13; Phil. 2.10-11; 2 Tim. 4.1, Titus 2.12-13).

The Church Is One Community
Where the Sacraments Are Rightly Administered

IV. A Community of Worship

   A. The Church recognizes that worship is the primary end of all creation.

     1.   The worshiper adores, praises, and gives thanks to God for his character and actions, ascribing to him the worth and glory due his Person. This worship is directed to:

      a.   The Father Almighty who is the Maker of all things visible and invisible.

A Theology of the Church (continued)

      b. The Son who by his incarnation, death, and resurrection accomplished salvation and who is now glorified at the Father's right hand.

      c. The Spirit who is the Lord and Giver of Life.

  2. Worship is the primary purpose of the material heavens and earth, and all life therein (Pss. 148-150; Luke 19.37-40; Rom. 11.36; Rev. 4.11; 15.3-4).

  3. Worship is the central activity of the angelic hosts who honor God in his presence (Isa. 6; Rev. 5).

  4. Worship is the chief vocation of the "community of saints," all true Christians, living and dead, who seek to glorify God in all things (Ps. 29.2; Rom. 12.1-2; 1 Cor. 10.31; Col. 3.17).

B. The Church offers acceptable worship to God. This means:

  1. The worshipers have renounced all false gods or belief systems that lay claim to their allegiance and have covenanted to serve and worship the one true God (Exod. 34.14; 1 Thess. 1.9-10).

  2. The worshipers worship:

      a. In Spirit - as regenerated people who, through saving faith in Jesus Christ, are filled with the Holy Spirit and under his direction.

      b. In Truth - understanding God as he is revealed in Scripture and worshiping in accordance with the teaching of the Word.

      c. In Holiness - Living lives that demonstrate their genuine commitment to serve the Living God.

C. The Church worships as a royal priesthood, wholeheartedly offering up sacrifices of praise to God and employing all its creative resources to worship him with excellence.

  1. The Christian Church is a people who worship, not a place of worship.

A Theology of the Church (continued)

2. The entire congregation ministers to the Lord, each one contributing a song, a word, a testimony, a prayer, etc. according to their gifts and capacities (1 Cor. 14.26).

3. The Church worships with the full range of human emotion, intellect, and creativity:

    a. Physical expression- raising of hands, dancing, kneeling, bowing, etc.

    b. Intellectual engagement- striving to understand God's nature and works.

    c. Artistic expression- through music and the other creative arts.

    d. Celebratory expression- the Church plays in the presence of God (Prov. 8.30-31) experiencing "Sabbath rest" through festivals, celebrations, and praise.

4. The Church worships liturgically by together reenacting the story of God and his people.

    a. The Church proclaims and embodies the drama of God's redemptive action in its ritual, tradition, and order of worship.

    b. The Church, like the covenant people Israel, orders its life around the celebration of the Lord's Supper and Baptism which reenact the story of God's salvation (Deut. 16.3; Matt. 28.19; Rom. 6.4; 1 Cor. 11.23-26).

    c. The Church remembers the worship and service of saints through the ages, learning from their experiences with the Spirit of God (Deut. 32.7; Pss. 77.10-12; 143.5; Isa. 46.9; Heb. 11).

5. The Church worships in freedom:

    a. Constantly experiencing new forms and expressions of worship which honor God and allow his people to delight in him afresh (Pss. 33.3; 40.3; 96.1; 149.1; Isa. 42.9-10; Luke 5.38; Rev. 5.9).

      b.   Being led by the Spirit so that its worship is responsive to God himself (2 Cor. 3.6; Gal. 5.25; Phil. 3.3).

      c.   Expressing the unchanging nature of God in forms that are conducive to the particular cultures and personalities of the worshipers (Acts 15).

  6.   The Church worships in right order, making sure that each act of worship edifies the body, and stands in accordance with the Word of God (1 Cor. 14.12, 33, 40; Gal. 5.13-15, 22-25; Eph. 4.29; Phil. 4.8).

D.   The Church's worship leads to wholeness:

  1.   Health and blessing attend the worshiping community (Exod. 23.25; Ps. 147.1-3).

  2.   The community takes on the character of the One who is worshiped (Exod. 29.37; Ps. 27.4; Jer. 2.5; 10.8; Matt. 6.21; Col. 3.1-4; 1 John 3.2).

V.   A Community of Covenant

A.   The Church is the gathering of those who participate in the New Covenant. This New Covenant:

  1.   Is mediated by Jesus Christ, the Great High Priest, and is purchased and sealed by his blood (Matt. 26.28; 1 Tim. 2.5; Heb. 8.6; 4.14-16).

  2.   Is initiated and participated in only through the electing grace of God (Rom. 8.29-30; 2 Tim. 1.9; Titus 1.1; 1 Pet. 1.1).

  3.   Is a covenant of peace (*Shalom*) which gives access to God (Ezek. 34.23-31; Rom. 5.1-2; Eph. 2.17-18; Heb. 7.2-3).

  4.   Is uniquely celebrated and experienced in the Lord's Supper and Baptism (Mark 14.22-25; 1 Cor. 10.16; Col. 2.12; 1 Pet. 3.21).

A Theology of the Church (continued)

    5.   By faith, both imputes and imparts righteousness to the participants so that God's laws are put in the hearts and written on their minds (Jer. 31.33; Rom. 1.17; 2 Cor. 5.21; Gal. 3.21-22; Phil. 1.11; 3.9; Heb. 10.15-17; 12.10-11; 1 Pet. 2.24).

B. The Covenant enables us to understand and experience Christian sanctification:

    1.   Righteousness: right relationships with God and others (Exod. 20.1-17; Mic. 6.8; Mark 12.29-31; James 2.8).

    2.   Truth: right beliefs about God and others (Ps. 86.11; Isa. 45.19; John 8.31-32, 17.17; 1 Pet. 1.22).

    3.   Holiness: right actions toward God and others (Lev. 11.45; 20.8; Eccles. 12.13; Matt. 7.12; 2 Cor. 7.1; Col. 3.12; 2 Pet. 3.11).

C. The purpose of the New Covenant is to enable the Church to be like Christ Jesus:

    1.   Jesus is the new pattern for humanity:

        a.   The second Adam (Rom. 5.12-17; 1 Cor. 15.45-49).

        b.   The likeness into which the Church is fashioned (Rom. 8.29; 1 John 3.2).

        c.   His life, character, and teaching are the standard for faith and practice (John 13.17; 20.21; 2 John 6, 9, 1 Cor. 11.1).

    2.   This covenant is made possible by the sacrifice of Christ himself (Matt. 26.27-29; Heb. 8-10).

    3.   The apostolic ministry of the new covenant is meant to conform believers to the image of Christ (2 Cor. 3; Eph. 4.12-13).

A Theology of the Church (continued)

D. The Covenant binds us to those who have gone before.

1. It recognizes that the Church is one (Eph. 4.4-5).

2. It reminds us that we are surrounded by a cloud of witnesses who have participated in the same covenant (Heb. 12.1).

3. It reminds us that we are part of a sacred chain:

God-Christ-Apostles-Church.

4. It reminds us that we share the same:

a. Spiritual parentage (John 1.13; 3.5-6; 2 Cor. 1.2; Gal. 4.6; 1 John 3.9).

b. Family likeness (Eph. 3.15; Heb. 2.11).

c. Lord, faith and baptism (Eph. 4.5).

d. Indwelling Spirit (John 14.17; Rom. 8.9; 2 Cor. 1.22).

e. Calling and mission (Eph. 4.1; Heb. 3.1; 2 Pet. 1.10).

f. Hope and destiny (Gal. 5.5; Eph. 1.18; Eph. 4.4; Col. 1.5).

5. Causes us to understand that since we share the same covenant, administered by the same Lord, under the leadership of the same Spirit with those Christians who have come before us, we must necessarily reflect upon the creeds, the councils, and the actions of the Church throughout history in order to understand the apostolic tradition and the ongoing work of the Holy Spirit (1 Cor. 11.16).

VI. A Community of Presence

A. "Where Jesus Christ is, there is the Church" - Ignatius of Antioch (Matt. 18.20).

A Theology of the Church (continued)

B. The Church is the dwelling place of God (Eph. 2.19-21):

1. His nation

2. His household

3. His temple

C. The Church congregates in eager anticipation of God's presence (Eph. 2.22).

1. The Church now comes into the presence of God at every gathering:

a. Like the covenant people in the Old Testament, the Church gathers in the presence of God (Exod. 18.12; 34.34; Deut. 14.23; 15.20; Ps. 132.7; Heb. 12.18-24).

b. The gathered Church makes manifest the reality of the Kingdom of God by being in the presence of the King (1 Cor. 14.25).

2. The Church anticipates the future gathering of the people of God when the fullness of God's presence will be with them all (Ezek. 48.35; 2 Cor. 4.14; 1 Thess. 3.13; Rev. 21.13).

D. The Church is absolutely dependent on the presence of the Spirit of Christ.

1. Without the presence of the Holy Spirit there is no Church (Acts 2.38; Rom. 8.9; 1 Cor. 12.13; Gal. 3.3; Eph. 2.22; 4.4; Phil. 3.3).

2. The Holy Spirit creates, directs, empowers, and teaches congregations of believers (John 14.16-17, 26; Acts 1.8; 2.17; 13.1; Rom. 15.13, 19; 2 Cor. 3.18).

3. The Holy Spirit gives gifts to the Church so that it can accomplish its mission, bringing honor and glory to God (Rom. 12.4-8; 1 Cor. 12.1-31; Heb. 2.4).

4. The Holy Spirit binds the Church together as the family of God and the body of Christ (2 Cor. 13.14; Eph. 4.3).

A Theology of the Church (continued)

E. The Church is a Kingdom of priests which stands in God's presence (1 Pet. 2.5, 9):

1. Ministering before the Lord (Ps. 43.4; Ps. 134.1-2).

2. Placing God's blessing on his people (Num. 6.22-27; 2 Cor. 13.14).

3. Bringing people before the attention of God (1 Thess. 1.3; 2 Tim. 1.3).

4. Offering themselves and the fruit of their ministry to God (Isa. 66.20, Rom. 12.1; 15.16).

F. The Church lives in God's presence through prayer.

1. Prayer as access to the Holy of Holies (Rev. 5.8).

2. Prayer as communion with God (Ps. 5.3; Rom. 8.26-27).

3. Prayer as intercession.

a. For the world (1 Tim. 2.1-2).

b. For the saints (Eph. 6.18-20, 1 Thess. 5.25).

4. Prayer as thanksgiving (Phil. 4.6; Col. 1.3).

5. Prayer as the warfare of the Kingdom.

a. Binding and loosing (Matt. 16.19).

b. Engaging the principalities and powers (Eph. 6.12,18).

The Church Is a Holy Community
Where Discipline Is Rightly Ordered

VII. A Community of Reconciliation

A. The Church is a community that is reconciled to God: all reconciliation is ultimately dependent on God's reconciling actions toward humanity.

A Theology of the Church (continued)

   1.   God's desire to reconcile is evidenced by sending his prophets and in the last days by his Son (Heb. 1.1-2).

   2.   The incarnation, the life, the death, and the resurrection of Jesus are the ultimate acts of reconciliation from God toward humanity (Rom. 5.8).

   3.   The Gospel is now a message of reconciliation, made possible by Christ's death, that God offers to humanity (2 Cor. 5.16-20).

B. The Church is a community of individuals and peoples that are reconciled to each other by their common identity as one body.

   1.   By his death Christ united his people who are born of the same seed (1 John 3.9), reconciled as fellow citizens and members of a new humanity (Eph. 2.11-22).

   2.   The Church community treats all members of God's household with love and justice in spite of differences in race, class, gender, and culture because they are organically united by their participation in the body of Christ (Gal. 3.26-29; Col. 3.11).

C. The Church is a community that is concerned for reconciliation among all peoples.

   1.   The Church functions an ambassador that invites all people to be reconciled to God (2 Cor. 5.19-20). This task of mission lays the foundation for all the reconciling activities of the Church.

   2.   The Church promotes reconciliation with and between all people.

      a. Because the Church is commanded to love its enemies (Matt. 5.44-48).

      b. Because the Church is an incarnational community which seeks, like Christ, to identify with those alienated from itself.

    c. Because the Church embodies and works for the vision of the Kingdom of God in which peoples, nations, and nature itself will be completely reconciled and at peace (Isa. 11.1-9; Mic. 4.2-4; Matt. 4.17; Acts 28.31).

    d. Because the Church recognizes the eternal plan of God to reconcile all things in heaven and on earth under one head, the Lord Jesus Christ, in order that the Kingdom may be handed over to God the Father who will be all in all (Eph. 1.10; Rom. 11.36; 1 Cor. 15.27-28; Rev. 11.15, 21.1-17).

D. The Church is a community of friendship: friendship is a key part of reconciliation and spiritual development.

    1. Spiritual maturity results in friendship with God (Exod. 33.11; James 2.23).

    2. Spiritual discipleship results in friendship with Christ (John 15.13-15).

    3. Spiritual unity is expressed in friendship with the saints (Rom. 16.5, 9, 12; 2 Cor. 7.1; Phil. 2.12; Col. 4.14; 1 Pet. 2.11; 1 John 2.7; 3 John 1.14).

VIII. A Community of Suffering

A. The Church community suffers because it exists in the world as "sheep among wolves" (Luke 10.3).

    1. Hated by those who reject Christ (John 15.18-20).

    2. Persecuted by the world system (Matt. 5.10; 2 Cor. 4.9; 2 Tim. 3.12).

    3. It is uniquely the community of the poor, the hungry, the weeping, the hated, the excluded, the insulted, and the rejected (Matt. 5.20-22).

    4. It is founded on the example and experience of Christ and the apostles (Isa. 53.3; Luke 9.22; Luke 24.46; Acts 5.41; 2 Tim. 1.8; 1 Thess. 2.2).

A Theology of the Church (continued)

    B.   The Church community imitates Christ in his suffering.

        1.   Because it purifies from sin (1 Pet. 4.1-2).

        2.   Because it teaches obedience (Heb. 5.8).

        3.   Because it allows them to know Christ more fully (Phil. 3.10).

        4.   Because those who share in Christ's suffering will also share in his comfort and glory (Rom. 8.17-18; 2 Cor. 1.5; 1 Pet. 5.1).

    C.   The Church community suffers because it identifies with those who suffer.

        1.   The body of Christ suffers whenever one of its members suffers (1 Cor. 12.26).

        2.   The body of Christ suffers because it voluntarily identifies itself with the despised, the rejected, the oppressed, and the unlovely (Prov. 29.7; Luke 7.34; Luke 15.1-2).

    D.   The cross of Christ is both the instrument of salvation and the pattern for Christian life. The cross embodies the values of the Church community.

        1.   The cross of Christ is the most fundamental Christian symbol. It serves as a constant reminder that the Church is a community of suffering.

        2.   The basic requirement of discipleship is a willingness to take up the cross daily and follow Jesus (Mark 8.34; Luke 9.23; Luke 14.27).

IX. A Community of Works

    A.   "Works of Service" are the hallmark of Christian congregations as they do justice, love mercy, and walk humbly with God.

        1.   The leadership of the Church is charged with preparing God's people for "works of service" (Eph. 4.12).

        2.   These good works are central to the new purpose and identity which is given us during the new birth. "For we are his workmanship, created

in Christ Jesus for good works, which God prepared beforehand, that we should walk in them." (Eph. 2.10).

3. These works of service reveal God's character to the world and lead people to give him praise (Matt. 5.16; 2 Cor. 9.13).

B. Servanthood characterizes the Christian's approach to relationships, resources, and ministry.

1. The Church community serves based on the example of Christ who came "not to be served but to serve" (Matt. 20.25-28; Luke 22.27; Phil. 2.7).

2. The Church community serves based on the command of Christ and the apostles (Mark 10.42-45; Gal. 5.13; 1 Pet. 4.10).

3. The Church community serves, first of all, "the least of these" according to the mandates of Christ's teaching (Matt. 18.2-5; Matt. 25. 34-46; Luke 4.18-19).

C. Generosity and hospitality are the twin signs of kingdom service.

1. Generosity results in the giving of one's self and one's good for the sake of announcing and obeying Christ and his kingdom reign.

2. Hospitality results in treating the stranger, the foreigner, the prisoner, and the enemy as one of your very own people (Heb. 13.2).

3. These signs are the true fruit of repentance (Luke 3.7-14; Luke 19.8-10; James 1.27)

D. Stewardship is the foundational truth which governs the way the Church uses resources in order to do "Works of Service."

1. Our resources (time, money, authority, health, position, etc.) belong not to ourselves but to God.

A Theology of the Church (continued)

    a.   We answer to God for our management of the things entrusted to us personally and corporately (Matt. 25.14-30).

    b.   Money should be managed in such as way that treasures are laid up in heaven (Matt. 6.19-21; Luke 12.32-34; Luke 16.1-15; 1 Tim. 6.17-19).

    c.   Seeking first the Kingdom of God is the standard by which our stewardship is measured and the basis upon which more will be entrusted (Matt. 6.33).

  2.   Proper stewardship should contribute to equality and mutual sharing (2 Cor. 8.13-15).

  3.   Greed is indicative of dishonest stewardship and a repudiation of God as the owner and giver of all things (Luke 12.15; Luke 16.13; Eph. 5.5; Col. 3.5; 1 Pet. 5.2).

E. Justice is a key goal of the Church as it serves God and others.

  1.   Doing justice is an essential part of fulfilling our service to God (Deut. 16.20; 27.19; Pss. 33.5; 106.3; Prov. 28.5; Mic. 6.8; Matt. 23.23).

  2.   Justice characterizes the righteous servant but is absent from the hypocrite and the unrighteous (Prov. 29.7; Isa. 1.17; 58.1-14; Matt. 12.18-20; Luke 11.42).

A Theology of the Church in Kingdom Perspective

Don Davis and Terry Cornett

Theories of Inspiration

Rev. Terry G. Cornett

Theory of Inspiration	Explanation	Possible Objection(s)
Mechanical or Dictation	The human author is a passive instrument in God's hands. The author simply writes down each word as God speaks it. This direct dictation is what protects the text from human error.	The books of Scripture show diverse writing styles, vocabularies, and manners of expression which vary with each human author. This theory doesn't seem to explain why God would use human authors rather than giving us a direct written word from himself.
Intuition or Natural	Gifted people with exceptional spiritual insight were chosen by God to write the Bible	The Bible indicates that Scripture came from God, through human authors (2 Pet. 1.20-21).
Illumination	The Holy Spirit heightened the normal capacities of human authors so that they had special insight into spiritual truth.	The Scriptures indicate that the human authors expressed the very words of God ("Thus saith the Lord" passages; Rom. 3.2.)
Degrees of Inspiration	Certain parts of the Bible are more inspired than others. Sometimes this position is used to argue that portions dealing with key doctrines or ethical truths are inspired while portions dealing with history, economics, culture, etc. are less inspired or not inspired.	The biblical authors never indicate that some of Scripture is more inspired or treat only one kind of biblical material as inspired in their use of it. Jesus speaks about the entire scriptural revelation up to his day as an unchanging word from God (Matt. 5.17-18; John 3.34-35).
Verbal-Plenary	Both divine and human elements are present in the production of Scripture. The entire text of Scripture, including the words, are a product of the mind of God expressed in human terms and conditions, through human authors that he foreknew (Jer. 1.5) and chose for the task.	It seems unlikely that the human elements which are finite and culture-bound could be described as the unchanging words of God.

"There Is a River"

Identifying the Streams of a Revitalized Authentic Christian Community in the City[1]

Rev. Dr. Don L. Davis • Psalm 46.4 (ESV) - There is a river whose streams make glad the city of God, the holy habitation of the Most High.

Tributaries of Authentic Historic Biblical Faith			
Recognized Biblical Identity	Revived Urban Spirituality	Reaffirmed Historical Connectivity	Refocused Kingdom Authority
The Church Is **One**	The Church Is **Holy**	The Church Is **Catholic**	The Church Is **Apostolic**
A Call to Biblical Fidelity *Recognizing the Scriptures as the anchor and foundation of the Christian faith and practice*	A Call to the Freedom, Power, and Fullness of the Holy Spirit *Walking in the holiness, power, gifting, and liberty of the Holy Spirit in the body of Christ*	A Call to Historic Roots and Continuity *Confessing the common historical identity and continuity of authentic Christian faith*	A Call to the Apostolic Faith *Affirming the apostolic tradition as the authoritative ground of the Christian hope*
A Call to Messianic Kingdom Identity *Rediscovering the story of the promised Messiah and his Kingdom in Jesus of Nazareth*	A Call to Live as Sojourners and Aliens as the People of God *Defining authentic Christian discipleship as faithful membership among God's people*	A Call to Affirm and Express the Global Communion of Saints *Expressing cooperation and collaboration with all other believers, both local and global*	A Call to Representative Authority *Submitting joyfully to God's gifted servants in the Church as undershepherds of true faith*
A Call to Creedal Affinity *Embracing the Nicene Creed as the shared rule of faith of historic orthodoxy*	A Call to Liturgical, Sacramental, and Catechetical Vitality *Experiencing God's presence in the context of the Word, sacrament, and instruction*	A Call to Radical Hospitality and Good Works *Expressing kingdom love to all, and especially to those of the household of faith*	A Call to Prophetic and Holistic Witness *Proclaiming Christ and his Kingdom in word and deed to our neighbors and all peoples*

---

[1] *This schema is an adaptation and is based on the insights of the* **Chicago Call** *statement of May 1977, where various leading evangelical scholars and practitioners met to discuss the relationship of modern evangelicalism to the historic Christian faith.*

33 Blessings in Christ

Rev. Dr. Don L. Davis

Did you know that 33 things happened to you at the moment you became a believer in Jesus Christ? Lewis Sperry Chafer, the first president of Dallas Theological Seminary, listed these benefits of salvation in his *Systematic Theology, Volume III* (pp. 234-266). These points, along with brief explanations, give the born-again Christian a better understanding of the work of grace accomplished in his/her life as well as a greater appreciation of his/her new life.

1. In the eternal plan of God, the believer is:

    a. *Foreknown* - Acts 2.23; 1 Pet. 1.2, 20. God knew from all eternity every step in the entire program of the universe.

    b. *Predestined* - Rom. 8.29-30. A believer's destiny has been appointed through foreknowledge to the unending realization of all God's riches of grace.

    c. *Elected* - Rom. 8.38; Col. 3.12. He/she is chosen of God in the present age and will manifest the grace of God in future ages.

    d. *Chosen* - Eph. 1.4. God has separated unto himself his elect who are both foreknown and predestined.

    e. *Called* - 1 Thess. 6.24. God invites man to enjoy the benefits of his redemptive purposes. This term may include those whom God has selected for salvation, but who are still in their unregenerate state.

2. A believer has been *redeemed* - Rom. 3.24. The price required to set him/her free from sin has been paid.

3. A believer has been *reconciled* - 2 Cor. 6.18, 19; Rom. 5.10. He/she is both restored to fellowship by God and restored to fellowship with God.

4. A believer is related to God through *propitiation* - Rom. 3.24-26. He/she has been set free from judgment by God's satisfaction with his Son's death for sinners.

5. A believer has been *forgiven* all trespasses - Eph. 1.7. All his/her sins are taken care of - past, present, and future.

6. A believer is vitally *conjoined to Christ* for the judgment of the old man "unto a new walk" - Rom. 6.1-10. He/she is brought into a union with Christ.

7. A believer is *"free from the law"* - Rom. 7.2-6. He/she is both dead to its condemnation, and delivered from its jurisdiction.

8. A believer has been made a *child of God* - Gal. 3.26. He/she is born anew by the regenerating power of the Holy Spirit into a relationship in which God the First Person becomes a legitimate Father and the saved one becomes a legitimate child with every right and title - an heir of God and a joint heir with Jesus Christ.

9. A believer has been *adopted as an adult child* into the Father's household - Rom. 8.15, 23.

10. A believer has been *made acceptable to God* by Jesus Christ - Eph. 1.6. He/she is made *righteous* (Rom. 3.22), *sanctified* (set apart) positionally (1 Cor. 1.30, 6.11); *perfected forever in his/her standing and position* (Heb. 10.14), and *made acceptable* in the Beloved (Col. 1.12).

11. A believer has been *justified* - Rom. 5.1. He/she has been declared righteous by God's decree.

12. A believer is *"made right"* - Eph. 2.13. A close relation is set up and exists between God and the believer.

13. A believer has been *delivered from the power of darkness* - Col. 1.13; 2.13. A Christian has been delivered from Satan and his evil spirits. Yet the disciple must continue to wage warfare against these powers.

14. A believer has been *translated into the Kingdom of God* - Col. 1.13. The Christian has been transferred from Satan's kingdom to Christ's Kingdom.

15. A believer is *planted* on the Rock, Jesus Christ - 1 Cor. 3.9-15. Christ is the foundation on which the believer stands and on which he/she builds his/her Christian life.

16. A believer is a *gift from God to Jesus Christ* - John 17.6, 11, 12, 20. He/she is the Father's love gift to Jesus Christ.

17. A believer is *circumcised in Christ* - Col. 2.11. He/she has been delivered from the power of the old sin nature.

18. A believer has been made a *partaker of the Holy and Royal Priesthood* - 1 Pet. 2.5, 9. He/she is a priest because of his/her relation to Christ, the High Priest, and will reign on earth with Christ.

33 Blessings in Christ (continued)

19. A believer is part of a ***chosen generation, a holy nation and a peculiar people*** - 1 Pet. 2.9. This is the company of believers in this age.

20. A believer is a ***heavenly citizen*** - Phil. 3.20. Therefore he/she is called a stranger as far as his/her life on earth is concerned (1 Pet. 2.13), and will enjoy his/her true home in heaven forever.

21. A believer is in ***the family and household of God*** - Eph. 2.1, 9. He/she is part of God's "family" which is composed only of true believers.

22. A believer is in ***the fellowship of the saints*** - John 17.11, 21-23. He/she can be a part of the fellowship of believers with one another.

23. A believer is in ***a heavenly association*** - Col. 1.27; 3.1; 2 Cor. 6.1; Col. 1.24; John 14.12-14; Eph. 5.25-27; Titus 2.13. He/she is ***a partner with Christ*** now in life, position, service, suffering, prayer, betrothal as a bride to Christ, and expectation of the coming again of Christ.

24. A believer has ***access to God*** - Eph. 2.18. He/she has access to God's grace which enables him/her to grow spiritually, and he/she has unhindered approach to the Father (Heb. 4.16).

25. A believer is within ***the "much more" care of God*** - Rom. 5.8-10. He/she is an object of God's love (John 3.16), God's grace (Eph. 2.7-9), God's power (Eph. 1.19), God's faithfulness (Phil. 1.6), God's peace (Rom. 5.1), God's consolation (2 Thess. 2.16-17), and God's intercession (Rom. 8.26).

26. A believer is ***God's inheritance*** - Eph. 1.18. He/she is given to Christ as a gift from the Father.

27. A believer ***has the inheritance of God himself*** and all that God bestows - 1 Pet. 1.4.

28. A believer has ***light in the Lord*** - 2 Cor. 4.6. He/she not only has this light, but is commanded to walk in the light.

29. A believer is ***vitally united to the Father, the Son and the Holy Spirit*** - 1 Thess. 1.1; Eph. 4.6; Rom. 8.1; John 14.20; Rom. 8.9; 1 Cor. 2.12.

30. A believer is blessed with ***the earnest or firstfruits of the Spirit*** - Eph. 1.14; 8.23. He/she is born of the Spirit (John 3.6), and baptized by the Spirit (1 Cor. 12.13), which is a work of the Holy Spirit by which the believer is joined to Christ's body and comes to be "in Christ," and therefore is a partaker of

all that Christ is. The disciple is also indwelt by the Spirit (Rom. 8.9), sealed by the Spirit (2 Cor. 1.22), making him/her eternally secure, and filled with the Spirit (Eph. 5.18) whose ministry releases his power and effectiveness in the heart in which he dwells.

31. A believer is ***glorified*** - Rom. 8.18. He/she will be a partaker of the infinite story of the Godhead.

32. A believer is ***complete in God*** - Col. 2.9, 10. He/she partakes of all that Christ is.

33. A believer ***possesses every spiritual blessing*** - Eph. 1.3. All the riches tabulated in the other 32 points made before are to be included in this sweeping term, "all spiritual blessings."

. . . .

Come, Thou Fount of Every Blessing,
Robert Robinson, 1757

Come Thou Fount of every blessing
Time my heart to sing Thy grace;
Streams of mercy, never ceasing,
Call for songs of loudest praise
Teach me some melodious sonnet,
Sung be flaming tongues above.
Praise the mount! I'm fixed upon it,
Mount o God's unchanging love.

Here I raise my Ebenezer;
Hither by Thy help I'm come;
And I hop, by Thy good pleasure,
Safely to arrive at home.
Jesus sought me when a stranger,
Wandering from the field of God;
He, to rescue me from danger,
Interposed His precious blood.

O to grace how great a debtor
Daily I'm constrained to be!
Let that grace now like a fetter,
Bing my wandering heart to Thee.
Prone to wander, Lord, I feel it,
Prone to leave the God I love;
Here's my heart, O take and seal it,
Seal it for Thy courts above.

Three Contexts of Urban Christian Leadership Development

Rev. Dr. Don L. Davis

Ephesians 4.11 (ESV) - And he himself gave some to be apostles, some prophets, some evangelists, and some pastors and teachers,

12. for the equipping of the saints for the work of ministry, for the edifying of the body of Christ

Three Contexts of Leadership Function

I. Forming, Leading, and Reproducing Dynamic Small Group Life and Ministry

- Inreach (discipling, fellowship, care giving, etc.)
- Outreach (evangelism, service, witness)

II. Facilitating and Reproducing Vital Congregational Life and Ministry

III. Nurturing and Cultivating Inter-congregational Support, Cooperation, and Collaboration

God has appointed leaders in the Church to equip Christians for "the work of the ministry," that they might walk worthy of the Lord in all things, bear abundant fruit in Christ, to win, follow-up, and disciple members within their *oikos* (their family, friends, and associates), and to be zealous in good works to reveal the Kingdom's life

---

Less than all of us

"Us" (My church)

More than all of us

Small Group

Congregational Form

"The Church Assembled"

The Locale Church

Any recognized part of a larger assembly, e.g., Cell group, Women's study, Prayer group, BibleStudy, Sunday School class, Street Ministry team, Prison outreach team, etc.

The church together as one, from house church to mega-church (i.e., Any distinct gathering of believers who identify with one another, give and serve together, under one pastoral head, where their presence and allegiance are shown and known)

According to some biblical linguists, the phrase in the NT for the church in assembly, *en ekklesia*, applies to the local expressions of the people of God when they "come together as a *church*," cf. 1 Cor. 11.18. The people of God can thus be called the "church/assembly," that is, those who by faith in Jesus Christ and his Holy Spirit now represent his called ones in a particular place and locale.

Clusters of churches which band together in partnership for mutual support, refreshment, service, and mission (e.g., Associations, denominations, conferences, etc.)

God has given to the Church leaders of unique gifting - apostles, prophets, evangelists, pastors and teachers in order that the "Church Assembled" might be edified and equipped to fulfill its mission and ministry as it scatters, as individuals, into the world. **Luke 10.2-3 (ESV)**. And he said to them, "The harvest is plentiful but the laborers are few. Therefore pray earnestly to the Lord of the harvest to send out laborers into his harvest. **[3]** Go your way; behold, I am sending you out as lambs in the midst of wolves").

Three Levels of Ministry Investment

Rev. Dr. Don L. Davis

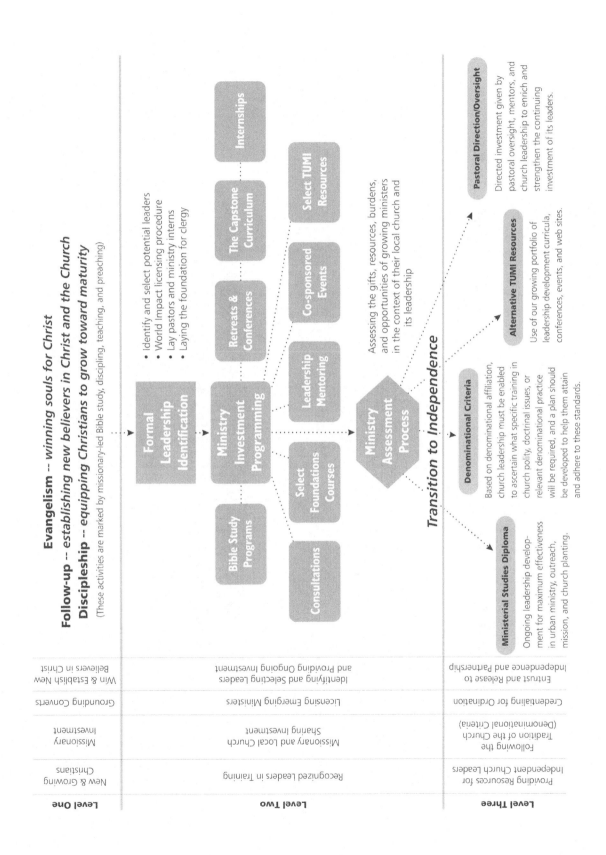

Evangelism -- winning souls for Christ
Follow-up -- establishing new believers in Christ and the Church
Discipleship -- equipping Christians to grow toward maturity
(These activities are marked by missionary-led Bible study, discipling, teaching, and preaching.)

Formal Leadership Identification

- Identify and select potential leaders
- World Impact licensing procedure
- Lay pastors and ministry interns
- Laying the foundation for clergy

Ministry Investment Programming

- Bible Study Programs
- Retreats & Conferences
- Internships
- The Capstone Curriculum
- Select Foundations Courses
- Leadership Mentoring
- Co-sponsored Events
- Select TUMI Resources
- Consultations

Ministry Assessment Process

Assessing the gifts, resources, burdens, and opportunities of growing ministers in the context of their local church and its leadership

Transition to Independence

Ministerial Studies Diploma

Ongoing leadership development for maximum effectiveness in urban ministry, outreach, mission, and church planting.

Denominational Criteria

Based on denominational affiliation, church leadership must be enabled to ascertain what specific training in church polity, doctrinal issues, or relevant denominational practice will be required, and a plan should be developed to help them attain and adhere to these standards.

Alternative TUMI Resources

Use of our growing portfolio of leadership development curricula, conferences, events, and web sites.

Pastoral Direction/Oversight

Directed investment given by pastoral oversight, mentors, and church leadership to enrich and strengthen the continuing investment of its leaders.

	Level One	Level Two	Level Three
	Win & Establish New Believers in Christ	Identifying and Selecting Leaders and Providing Ongoing Investment	Entrust and Release to Independence and Partnership
	Grounding Converts	Licensing Emerging Ministers	Credentialing for Ordination
	Missionary Investment	Missionary and Local Church Sharing Investment	Following the Tradition of the Church (Denominational Criteria)
	New & Growing Christians	Recognized leaders in Training	Providing Resources for Independent Church Leaders

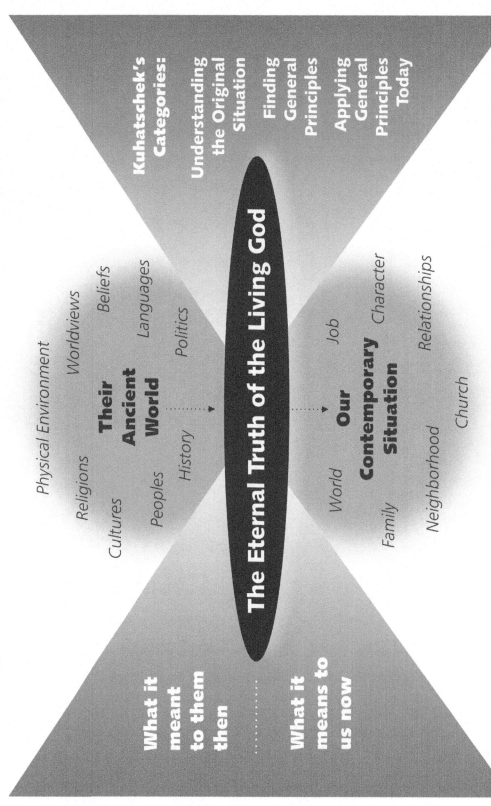

The Three-Step Model

Don L. Davis and Terry G. Cornett

Discovering the Word and Works of God in the Lives of the People of Scripture

Kuhatschek's Categories:

Understanding the Original Situation

Finding General Principles

Applying General Principles Today

Beliefs

Worldviews

Languages

Physical Environment

Politics

Their **Ancient** **World**

Religions

History

Cultures

Peoples

The Eternal Truth of the Living God

Job

Character

Relationships

Our **Contemporary** **Situation**

World

Church

Family

Neighborhood

What it meant to them then

What it means to us now

Applying Principles of God's Word to our Lives in the Church and in the World

Thy Kingdom Come!
Readings on the Kingdom of God
Edited by Terry G. Cornett and Don L. Davis

Taken from "The Agony and The Ecstasy" in Why We Haven't Changed the World, by Peter E. Gillquist. Old Tappan, New Jersey: Fleming H. Revell Company, 1982. pp. 47-48.

A Tale of Two Kingdoms

Hear the parable of a kingdom, a usurper-prince of the realm of this world. By means of a masterful program of clever deception, he has managed to bring millions of subjects under his powerful rule. Granted, he has enticed them from the realm of another Monarch, but he considers them his. After all, they have been under his dominion for some considerable time now, and the Enemy hasn't yet taken them back. Yes, in the mind of this prince, these people are legally his people and this land *his* land. Possession is, after all, he says, nine-tenths of the law.

Suddenly, without much warning, the rival Government takes action. The Son of the Enemy Monarch is dispatched to the prince's very own turf (well, yes, he did steal it, but. . .) to take back those who would resubmit to his reign. The Monarch's plan is to draw these people out from under the prince's authority, philosophy, and life-style.

Most outrageous of all, the Monarch sets up his Government on the prince's own real estate. And instead of immediately removing his restored subjects from the country, he is keeping them there until a disease called *death* (a consequence of the prince's regime which eventually claims everyone) brings about a change in their state of existence. To make the matter even more aggravating, the Son even promises people that he will save them from death, and become the firstfruits by dying and coming back to life again himself.

Unsettled, but undefeated (he thinks), the prince launches an all fronts counterattack. Plainly, he is no match for the other King one on One. So he launches a renewed program of deception, simply lying to his citizens about the other Government. That doesn't always work, for the Monarch's Son keeps taking subjects back. Since they are such weak creatures, however, the prince sees no reason to give up hope for their eventual return. Consequently, even after they become citizens of that other kingdom, he keeps the pressure on.

Falsehood is the prince's most common weapon. He uses it at the most strategic points. Since the most committed people are the most dangerous, he attacks the zealots among his former subjects by spreading rumors about them and

Thy Kingdom Come! Readings on the Kingdom of God (continued)

intimidating them by hints of his power. By and large his successes are few, however, for these people demonstrate an almost supernatural attachment to the Enemy Monarch.

Still, the prince in encouraged by one relatively small, though nonetheless significant, source of help he had not counted on.

There are some servants of the Monarch's Son, mostly honest and well intentioned, who mis-state his promises. These servants are so intent upon winning people back from the realm of the evil prince, that they leave out of their messages some very important facts concerning responsible citizenship in that Domain. They rarely, if ever, mention warfare, or the prince's subversive devices, or the residual effects of the dread diseases caught under his reign. Frankly, they portray the Son's Government as sort of a spiritual welfare state, where there are free goodies for all, with little work or responsibility. One gets the picture of a sort of laid-back paradise, with the Monarch running a giant handout program.

Gleefully, the wicked prince capitalizes on this unexplained chink in their armor. All he has to do is let them preach these omissions, and then cash in on the contradictions the people experience in their daily lives. After all, his best source of returnees just might turn out to be the disappointed hearers who listen to these enthusiastic servants.

Excerpted from "Introduction and Chapter One" in A Kingdom Manifesto, by Howard A. Snyder. Downers Grove: InterVarsity Press, 1985. pp. 11-25

The Kingdom as a Key to All of Scripture

Jesus was always full of surprises, even with his disciples. Perhaps the biggest surprise was his news about the Kingdom of God.

Jesus came announcing the Kingdom, creating a stir. Through a brief span of public ministry he kept showing his disciples what the Kingdom was really like. They understood only in part.

Later, risen from the dead, Jesus spent six weeks teaching his disciples more about the Kingdom (Acts 1.3). He explained that his own suffering, death and resurrection were all part of the kingdom plan foretold by Old Testament prophets (Luke 24.44-47).

Now, after the resurrection, his disciples ask, "Are *you finally* going to set up your Kingdom?" (paraphrasing Acts 1.6). How does Jesus respond? He says, in effect,

"The time for the full flowering of the new order still remains a mystery to you; it's in God's hands. But. . . . the Holy Spirit will give you the power to live the kingdom life now. So you are to be witnesses of the Kingdom and its power from here to the very ends of the earth" (Acts 1.7-8).

And so it was, and so it has been. Today we are finally nearing the fulfillment of Jesus' prophecy that "this gospel of the Kingdom will be preached in the whole world as a testimony to all nations" (Matt. 24.14 [NIV]).

And so, as never before, it is time to speak of God's Kingdom now!

This is no attempt to outguess God or pre-empt the sovereign mystery of the Kingdom. The Kingdom still and always remains in God's hands. So this book is not about "times or dates" (Acts 1.7) - a tempting but disastrous detour - but about the plain kingdom teachings which run throughout Scripture. My point is simply this: The Bible is full of teaching on the Kingdom of God, and the Church has largely missed it. But in the providence of God we may now have reached a time when the good news of the Kingdom can be heard and understood as never before. This is due not to any one person, not to any human wisdom or insight, but to God's own working in our day, bringing a new kingdom consciousness.

Thus the theme of this book: The Kingdom of God in Scripture and its meaning for us today.

The Kingdom of God is a key thread in Scripture, tying the whole Bible together. It is not the only unifying theme, nor should it replace other themes which are clearly biblical. Yet it is a critically important theme, especially today. And its recent resurgence in the Church is, I believe, one of the most significant developments of this century!

Once you begin to look in Scripture for the theme of God's reign or Kingdom, it turns up everywhere! Take an example I recently encountered in my own devotional study:

> All you have made will praise you, O LORD; your saints will extol you. They will tell of the glory of your kingdom and speak of your might, so that all men may know of your mighty acts and the glorious splendor of your kingdom. Your kingdom is an everlasting kingdom, and your dominion endures through all generations.

> ~ Psalm 145.10-13 (NIV)

Thy Kingdom Come! Readings on the Kingdom of God (continued)

This one psalm in fact contains a substantial theology of the Kingdom, stressing God's sovereign reign, his mighty acts, his compassion and nearness to those who seek him, his righteousness and justice.

The Kingdom is such a key theme of Scripture that Richard Lovelace can say, "The Messianic Kingdom is not only the main theme of Jesus' preaching; it is the central category unifying biblical revelation." And John Bright comments, "The concept of the Kingdom of God involves, in a real sense, the total message of the Bible. . . . To grasp what is meant by the Kingdom of God is to come very close to the heart of the Bible's gospel of salvation." As E. Stanley Jones wrote over four decades ago, Jesus' message "was the Kingdom of God. It was the center and circumference of all he taught and did. . . . The Kingdom of God is the master-conception, the master-plan, the master-purpose, the master-will that gathers everything up into itself and gives it redemption, coherence, purpose, goal."

True, seeing the Kingdom of God as the only unifying theme of Scripture could be misleading. Personally, I believe the overarching truth is the revelation of the nature and character of God (not merely his existence, which is clear from the created order - Romans 1.20). Here God's love, justice and holiness are central - the character of God's *person* in his tri-unity. Still the reign/rule of God is a key theme of Scripture, for the loving, just, holy God rules consistent with his character and in a way that produces the reflection of his character in all who willingly serve him.

So the Kingdom is indeed a key strand running through the Bible. If it seems less evident in Paul's writings, that is because Paul often speaks of the Kingdom in terms of the sovereign *plan* of God realized through Jesus Christ (as, for example, in Ephesians 1.10), and, for very good reasons, uses less kingdom language. But it is incorrect to say, as some have, that the kingdom theme "disappears" in Paul. . . .

The Bible is full of God's Kingdom. . . . We learn more about the Kingdom when we view all of Scripture as the history of God's "economy" or plan to restore a fallen creation, bringing all God has made - woman, man and their total environment - to the fulfillment of his purposes under his sovereign reign.

One evening my seven-year-old son and I walked through a little patch of woods and came out on an open field. The sun was westering; the sky was serenely laced with blue and gold. Birds flitted in the trees. We talked about peace, the future and the Kingdom of God. Somehow we both sensed, despite our differences in age and understanding, that God desires peace and that what he desires he will bring. Someday, we said and knew, all the world will be like this magic moment. But not without cost and struggle.

Jesus urges: "Enter through the narrow gate." For "small is the gate and narrow the road that leads to life, and only a few find it" (Matthew 7.13-14). The Kingdom of God is life in abundance (John 10.10), but the way to life is through the narrow gate of faith and obedience to Jesus Christ. If Christians today want to experience the peaceable order of the Kingdom, they must learn and live God's way of peace.

The Preaching and Teaching of Jesus
Summary of Teaching, Vic Gordon

1. The most important thing in life is to be a disciple of Jesus Christ. To do that we must learn from him and then obey what we hear. He must be our Teacher and Lord (Matthew 7.24-27; 11.29; 28.18-20; John 13.13).

2. Obviously, we cannot follow Jesus if we do not know what he taught. The main theme of his preaching and teaching was the Kingdom of God. Most Christians do not know this, yet they call him Lord and Master Teacher!

3. But we are then faced with an immediate problem. As soon as we know the main theme of his teaching, we automatically misunderstand it. Kingdom means something different in the biblical idiom (Hebrew, Aramaic, Greek) than in contemporary English. To us "Kingdom" means "realm" (a place over which a king rules) or "a group of people who live in a king's realm" (the people over whom a king rules). In the Bible, however, the primary meaning of "Kingdom" is "reign" or "rule." The Kingdom of God thus means the reign of God or the rule of God. The Kingdom of God is not a place nor a people, but God's active, dynamic rule. The Kingdom is an act of God, i.e. something he does.

4. The burden and purpose of Jesus' three year public ministry leading up to his death and resurrection was to preach, proclaim and teach about the Kingdom of God (Mark 1.14ff; Matthew 4.17, 23; 9.35; Luke 4.42ff; 8.1; 9.2, 6, 11; 10.1, 9; Acts 1.3; 28.31).

5. Jesus was the original proclaimer of the Gospel, and he proclaimed it originally in terms of the Kingdom of God (Mark 1.14ff; Matthew 4.23; 9.35; 24.14; Luke 20.1). The good news is about God's reign. Of course this is a metaphor, a word picture describing a profound reality.

Thy Kingdom Come! Readings on the Kingdom of God (continued)

6. Jesus' teaching on the Kingdom of God as we will see, determines the basic structure of all his teaching, and indeed the structure of the teaching of the entire New Testament.

7. Why did Jesus choose the word picture "Kingdom of God" to proclaim the good news of God to the world? Two basic reasons:

   a. **It was biblical.** While the exact phrase "Kingdom of God" never occurs in the Old Testament (maybe once in 1 Chronicles 28.5), the idea is everywhere present in the Old Testament. God is always and everywhere King in the Old Testament, especially in the prophets. His kingship is not always realized in this sinful world. In fact the major emphasis in the Old Testament, stated in hundreds of ways and different word pictures, is on God's future, coming reign. The hope of the Old Testament is that God himself will come and bring salvation to his people and judgment/ destruction to his enemies. (See e.g. 1 Chronicles 29.11; Psalms 22.28; 96.10-13; 103.19; 145.11-13; Isaiah 25ff; 65ff; Daniel 2.44; 4.3, 34; 6.26; 7.13ff, 27.)

   b. **It was understood and meaningful to the first century Palestinian Jews to whom he proclaimed the Good News.** In fact, the phrase "Kingdom of God" had developed a great deal in the 400 years between the Old Testament and the coming of Jesus. Kingdom of God now summarized the entire Old Testament hope! The first century Jews were expecting God to come as king and reign over the entire world, destroying his enemies and giving all his blessings to his people, Israel. This concept was especially meaningful to the Jews who, on the one hand, strongly believed that their God Yahweh was the one and only true God who ruled over all the universe, and who, on the other, experienced over 700 years of foreign domination at the hands of pagan rulers from Assyria, then Babylon, then Persia, then Greece and finally Rome. Jesus never defines the Kingdom of God for them, because they all knew what it meant. This is a great example for us in our ministries. Jesus went to the people where they were (the incarnation!), was faithful to the biblical message, and spoke it to them in terms they could understand. (See e.g. Luke 1.32ff; 19.11; 23.51; Mark 11.10; 15.43; Acts 1.6.) The phrase Kingdom of God summarized all of the Old Testament hope and promise. "All that God has said and done in Israel's history is brought to completion in the Kingdom of God" (Dale Patrick).

8. But Jesus offers a new understanding of an already understood concept. He pours his own authoritative meaning into the Kingdom of God and offers a definitive new interpretation of the Old Testament promise and teaching. He makes it certain that the "Kingdom of God" is the interpretive key for the Old Testament. He agrees with the Jews that the Kingdom is God coming into history and reigning by giving salvation to his people and judgment to his enemies. But Jesus goes far beyond this in providing a grand new interpretation of God's reign.

9. Jesus startles and stuns his hearers by saying the Kingdom of God which they have all been waiting for is now present (Mark 1.15). The time of the fulfillment of the Old Testament promises has now arrived. He goes even further than this by teaching that the Kingdom is present in his own person and ministry. (Matthew 11.1-15; 12.28; Luke 10.23ff; 17.20ff.) This teaching that the Kingdom of God has arrived or is here is radically new. No Jewish rabbi had ever taught such a thing (Luke 10.23ff).

10. But Jesus, like most of the Jews of his day, also taught that the Kingdom of God was still future, i.e. it was yet to come (e.g. Matthew 6.10; 8.11ff; 25.31-34; Luke 21.31; 22.17ff. Cf. Matthew 5.3-12; Mark 9.47).

11. The solution to this strange teaching is to realize that Jesus' new perspective on the Kingdom of God contains both elements: the Kingdom is present and future. Jesus taught two comings of the Kingdom. First, the Kingdom came partially in his own person and ministry in history. Second, Jesus taught that there will be a future complete coming of his Kingdom when he returns at the end of human history.

12. Now we can understand what Jesus meant by the "mystery of the Kingdom" (Mark 4.10ff). This strange, new perspective on the Kingdom of God taught that the Old Testament promises could be fulfilled without being consummated. Thus, the mystery of the Kingdom is fulfillment without consummation. **The Kingdom of God has come into history in the person and ministry of Jesus Christ without consummation.** This mystery has been hidden until now revealed in Christ.

Thy Kingdom Come! Readings on the Kingdom of God (continued)

13. In one way or another, all of Jesus' kingdom parables ("The Kingdom of God is like. . .") proclaim and/or explain this mystery. This understanding of the Kingdom is radically new. The first century Palestinian Jews needed to hear this message, understand it and believe it. This is the major concern of Jesus' preaching and teaching.

14. Thus, we can understand Jesus' teaching on the coming of God's Kingdom as being both present and future. The Kingdom is now and it is not yet. Jesus announces the presence of the future.

15. This chart of the Kingdom of God in the teaching of Jesus can help us see more clearly what he is saying. The chart is a time line from Creation into an eternal future (eternal in the Bible means unending time).

    a. The age of the Kingdom is the age to come. We now live in both this age and the age to come.

    b. The Kingdom of God has two moments, each one characterized by a coming of Jesus as the Messianic King to bring God's reign.

16. The Kingdom of God brings the blessings of God. As the people of the Kingdom live now in the tension of both the presence and the future of the Kingdom, some of the blessings have already arrived for us and some await the consummation of the Kingdom in the future.

Present Blessings of the Kingdom

    a. The Gospel is proclaimed.

    b. The forgiveness of sin.

    c. The Holy Spirit indwells God's people.

    d. Sanctification has begun.

Thy Kingdom Come! Readings on the Kingdom of God (continued)

Future Blessings of the Kingdom

a.   The Presence of God

b.   Resurrection bodies

c.   Full sanctification

d.   Shalom: peace, righteousness, joy, health, wholeness

e.   A new heaven and a new earth

f.   Judgment and destruction of all God's enemies including sin, death, the devil and his demons, all evil

17.   Let us not overlook the obvious fact that for Jesus his preaching about the Kingdom is fundamentally a proclamation about God. God brings his Kingdom as a seeking, inviting, gracious Abba Father. He also comes as judge to those who refuse his Kingdom.

18.   The Kingdom of God is altogether God's work. He graciously comes into human history in the person of his Son Jesus Christ to bring his rule to the earth. The Kingdom is therefore completely supernatural and gracious. Humans cannot bring, build or accomplish the Kingdom. It is wholly God's act.

19.   Jesus' miracles and exorcisms are signs that the Kingdom of God is present in him and his ministry (Matthew 11.1-6; 4.23; 9.35; 10.7ff; Luke 9.1, 2, 6, 11).

20.   The Kingdom of God invades the kingdom of Satan when Jesus comes bringing the Kingdom (Matthew 12.22-29; 25.41; Mark 1.24, 34; Luke 10.17ff; 11.17-22).

21.   The Kingdom of God is of great value, indeed the greatest thing by far in the whole world (Matthew 13.44-46). Therefore, we must ask, "How should we then respond to this Kingdom?" or "How do we receive this gift of the Kingdom of God?"

Toward a Hermeneutic of Critical Engagement

Rev. Dr. Don L. Davis

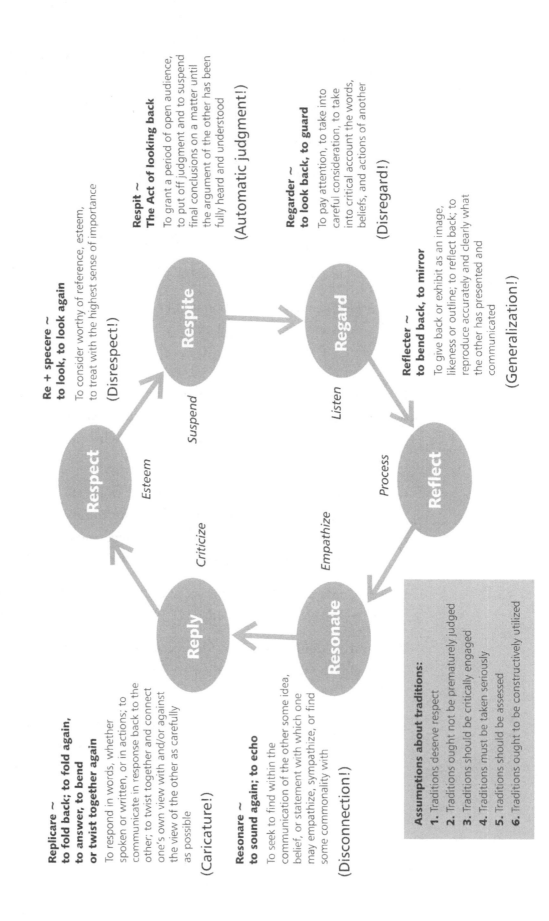

Respit ~
The Act of looking back

To grant a period of open audience, to put off judgment and to suspend final conclusions on a matter until the argument of the other has been fully heard and understood

(Automatic judgment!)

Regarder ~
to look back, to guard

To pay attention, to take into careful consideration, to take into critical account the words, beliefs, and actions of another

(Disregard!)

Reflecter ~
to bend back, to mirror

To give back or exhibit as an image, likeness or outline; to reflect back; to reproduce accurately and clearly what the other has presented and communicated

(Generalization!)

Re + specere ~
to look, to look again

To consider worthy of reference, esteem, to treat with the highest sense of importance

(Disrespect!)

Replicare ~
to fold back; to fold again, to answer, to bend or twist together again

To respond in words, whether spoken or written, or in actions; to communicate in response back to the other; to twist together and connect one's own view with and/or against the view of the other as carefully as possible

(Caricature!)

Resonare ~
to sound again; to echo

To seek to find within the communication of the other some idea, belief, or statement with which one may empathize, sympathize, or find some commonality with

(Disconnection!)

Respite

Regard

Reflect

Resonate

Reply

Respect

Suspend

Listen

Process

Empathize

Criticize

Esteem

Assumptions about traditions:

1. Traditions deserve respect
2. Traditions ought not be prematurely judged
3. Traditions should be critically engaged
4. Traditions must be taken seriously
5. Traditions should be assessed
6. Traditions ought to be constructively utilized

Traditions
(Paradosis)
Dr. Don L. Davis and Rev. Terry G. Cornett

Strong's Definition

Paradosis. Transmission, i.e. (concretely) a precept; specifically, the Jewish traditionary law

Vine's Explanation

denotes "a tradition," and hence, by metonymy, (a) "the teachings of the rabbis," . . . (b) "apostolic teaching," . . . of instructions concerning the gatherings of believers, of Christian doctrine in general . . . of instructions concerning everyday conduct.

1.   The concept of tradition in Scripture is essentially positive.

Jer. 6.16 (ESV) – Thus says the Lord: "Stand by the roads, and look, and ask for the ancient paths, where the good way is; and walk in it, and find rest for your souls. But they said, 'We will not walk in it'" (cf. Exod. 3.15; Judg. 2.17; 1 Kings 8.57-58; Ps. 78.1-6).

2 Chron. 35.25 (ESV) – Jeremiah also uttered a lament for Josiah; and all the singing men and singing women have spoken of Josiah in their laments to this day. They made these a rule in Israel; behold, they are written in the Laments (cf. Gen. 32.32; Judg. 11.38-40).

Jer. 35.14-19 (ESV) – "The command that Jonadab the son of Rechab gave to his sons, to drink no wine, has been kept, and they drink none to this day, for they have obeyed their father's command. I have spoken to you persistently, but you have not listened to me. I have sent to you all my servants the prophets, sending them persistently, saying, 'Turn now every one of you from his evil way, and amend your deeds, and do not go after other gods to serve them, and then you shall dwell in the land that I gave to you and your fathers.' But you did not incline your ear or listen to me. The sons of Jonadab the son of Rechab have kept the command that their father gave them, but this people has not obeyed me. Therefore, thus says the Lord, the God of hosts, the God of Israel: Behold, I am bringing upon Judah and all the inhabitants of Jerusalem all the disaster that I have pronounced against them, because I have spoken to them and they have not listened, I have called to them and they have not answered." But to the house of the Rechabites Jeremiah said, "Thus says the Lord of hosts, the God of Israel: Because you have obeyed the command of Jonadab your father and kept all his precepts and done all that he commanded you, therefore thus says the Lord of hosts, the God of Israel: Jonadab the son of Rechab shall never lack a man to stand before me."

2. Godly tradition is a wonderful thing, but not all tradition is godly.

Any individual tradition must be judged by its faithfulness to the Word of God and its usefulness in helping people maintain obedience to Christ's example and teaching.[1] In the Gospels, Jesus frequently rebukes the Pharisees for establishing traditions that nullify rather than uphold God's commands.

Mark 7.8 (ESV) – You leave the commandment of God and hold to the tradition of men (cf. Matt. 15.2-6; Mark 7.13).

Col. 2.8 (ESV) – See to it that no one takes you captive by philosophy and empty deceit, according to human tradition, according to the elemental spirits of the world, and not according to Christ.

3. Without the fullness of the Holy Spirit, and the constant edification provided to us by the Word of God, tradition will inevitably lead to dead formalism.

Those who are spiritual are filled with the Holy Spirit, whose power and leading alone provides individuals and congregations a sense of freedom and vitality in all they practice and believe. However, when the practices and teachings of any given tradition are no longer infused by the power of the Holy Spirit and the Word of God, tradition loses its effectiveness, and may actually become counterproductive to our discipleship in Jesus Christ.

Eph. 5.18 (ESV) – And do not get drunk with wine, for that is debauchery, but be filled with the Spirit.

[1] *"All Protestants insist that these traditions must ever be tested against Scripture and can never possess an independent apostolic authority over or alongside of Scripture." (J. Van Engen, "Tradition,"* **Evangelical Dictionary of Theology,** *Walter Elwell, Gen. ed.) We would add that Scripture is itself the "authoritative tradition" by which all other traditions are judged. See "Appendix A, The Founders of Tradition: Three Levels of Christian Authority," p. 4.*

Gal. 5.22-25 (ESV) – But the fruit of the Spirit is love, joy, peace, patience, kindness, goodness, faithfulness, gentleness, self-control; against such things there is no law. And those who belong to Christ Jesus have crucified the flesh with its passions and desires. If we live by the Spirit, let us also walk by the Spirit.

2 Cor. 3.5-6 (ESV) – Not that we are sufficient in ourselves to claim anything as coming from us, but our sufficiency is from God, who has made us competent to be ministers of a new covenant, not of the letter but of the Spirit. For the letter kills, but the Spirit gives life.

4. **Fidelity to the Apostolic Tradition (teaching and modeling) is the essence of Christian maturity.**

2 Tim. 2.2 (ESV) – and what you have heard from me in the presence of many witnesses entrust to faithful men who will be able to teach others also.

1 Cor. 11.1-2 (ESV) – Be imitators of me, as I am of Christ. Now I commend you because you remember me in everything and maintain the traditions even as I delivered them to you (cf. 1 Cor. 4.16-17, 2 Tim. 1.13-14, 2 Thess. 3.7-9, Phil. 4.9).

1 Cor. 15.3-8 (ESV) – For I delivered to you as of first importance what I also received: that Christ died for our sins in accordance with the Scriptures, that he was buried, that he was raised on the third day in accordance with the Scriptures, and that he appeared to Cephas, then to the twelve. Then he appeared to more than five hundred brothers at one time, most of whom are still alive, though some have fallen asleep. Then he appeared to James, then to all the apostles. Last of all, as to one untimely born, he appeared also to me.

5. **The Apostle Paul often includes an appeal to the tradition for support in doctrinal practices.**

1 Cor. 11.16 (ESV) – If anyone is inclined to be contentious, we have no such practice, nor do the churches of God (cf. 1 Cor. 1.2, 7.17, 15.3).

Traditions (continued)

1 Cor. 14.33-34 (ESV) – For God is not a God of confusion but of peace. As in all the churches of the saints, the women should keep silent in the churches. For they are not permitted to speak, but should be in submission, as the Law also says.

6. **When a congregation uses received tradition to remain faithful to the "Word of God," they are commended by the apostles.**

1 Cor. 11.2 (ESV) – Now I commend you because you remember me in everything and maintain the traditions even as I delivered them to you.

2 Thess. 2.15 (ESV) – So then, brothers, stand firm and hold to the traditions that you were taught by us, either by our spoken word or by our letter.

2 Thess. 3.6 (ESV) – Now we command you, brothers, in the name of our Lord Jesus Christ, that you keep away from any brother who is walking in idleness and not in accord with the tradition that you received from us.

Appendix A

The Founders of Tradition: Three Levels of Christian Authority

Exod. 3.15 (ESV) – God also said to Moses, "Say this to the people of Israel, 'The Lord, the God of your fathers, the God of Abraham, the God of Isaac, and the God of Jacob, has sent me to you.' This is my name forever, and thus I am to be remembered throughout all generations."

1. **The Authoritative Tradition: The Apostles and the Prophets (The Holy Scriptures)**

Eph. 2.19-21 (ESV) – So then you are no longer strangers and aliens, but you are fellow citizens with the saints and members of the household of God, built on the foundation of the apostles and prophets, Christ Jesus himself being the cornerstone, in whom the whole structure, being joined together, grows into a holy temple in the Lord.

~ The Apostle Paul

Traditions (continued)

Those who gave eyewitness testimony to the revelation and saving acts of Yahweh, first in Israel, and ultimately in Jesus Christ the Messiah. This testimony is binding for all people, at all times, and in all places. It is the authoritative tradition by which all subsequent tradition is judged.

2. The Great Tradition: the Ecumenical Councils and their Creeds[2]

See Appendix B, "Defining the Great Tradition,"

What has been believed everywhere, always, and by all.

~ Vincent of Lerins

The Great Tradition is the core dogma (doctrine) of the Church. It represents the teaching of the Church as it has understood the Authoritative Tradition (the Holy Scriptures), and summarizes those essential truths that Christians of all ages have confessed and believed. To these doctrinal statements the whole Church (Catholic, Orthodox, and Protestant)[3] gives its assent. The worship and theology of the Church reflects this core dogma, which finds its summation and fulfillment in the person and work of Jesus Christ. From earliest times, Christians have expressed their devotion to God in its Church calendar, a yearly pattern of worship which summarizes and reenacts the events of Christ's life.

[3] Even the more radical wing of the Protestant reformation (Anabaptists) who were the most reluctant to embrace the creeds as dogmatic instruments of faith, did not disagree with the essential content found in them. "They assumed the Apostolic Creed – they called it 'The Faith,' Der Glaube, as did most people." See John Howard Yoder, Preface to Theology: Christology and Theological Method. Grand Rapids: Brazos Press, 2002. pp. 222-223.

3. Specific Church Traditions: the Founders of Denominations and Orders

The Presbyterian Church (U.S.A.) has approximately 2.5 million members, 11,200 congregations and 21,000 ordained ministers. Presbyterians trace their history to the 16th century and the Protestant Reformation. Our heritage, and much of what we believe, began with the French lawyer John Calvin (1509-1564), whose writings crystallized much of the Reformed thinking that came before him.

~ The Presbyterian Church, U.S.A.

Christians have expressed their faith in Jesus Christ in various ways through specific movements and traditions which embrace and express the Authoritative Tradition and the Great Tradition in unique ways. For instance,

Catholic movements have arisen around people like Benedict, Francis, or Dominic, and among Protestants people like Martin Luther, John Calvin, Ulrich Zwingli, and John Wesley. Women have founded vital movements of Christian faith (e.g., Aimee Semple McPherson of the Foursquare Church), as well as minorities (e.g., Richard Allen of the African Methodist Episcopal Church or Charles H. Mason of the Church of God in Christ, who also helped to spawn the Assemblies of God), all which attempted to express the Authoritative Tradition and the Great Tradition in a specific way consistent with their time and expression.

The emergence of vital, dynamic movements of the faith at different times and among different peoples reveal the fresh working of the Holy Spirit throughout history. Thus, inside Catholicism, new communities have arisen such as the Benedictines, Franciscans, and Dominicans; and outside Catholicism, new denominations have emerged (Lutherans, Presbyterians, Methodists, Church of God in Christ, etc.). Each of these specific traditions have "founders," key leaders whose energy and vision helped to establish a unique expression of Christian faith and practice. Of course, to be legitimate, these movements must adhere to and faithfully express both the Authoritative Tradition and the Great Tradition. Members of these specific traditions embrace their own practices and patterns of spirituality, but these particular features are not necessarily binding on the Church at large. They represent the unique expressions of that community's understanding of and faithfulness to the Authoritative and Great Traditions.

Specific traditions seek to express and live out this faithfulness to the Authoritative and Great Traditions through their worship, teaching, and service. They seek to make the Gospel clear within new cultures or sub-cultures, speaking and modeling the hope of Christ into new situations shaped by their own set of questions posed in light of their own unique circumstances. These movements, therefore, seek to contextualize the Authoritative tradition in a way that faithfully and effectively leads new groups of people to faith in Jesus Christ, and incorporates those who believe into the community of faith that obeys his teachings and gives witness of him to others.

Appendix B

Defining the "Great Tradition"

The Great Tradition (sometimes called the "classical Christian tradition") is defined by Robert E. Webber as follows:

> *[It is] the broad outline of Christian belief and practice developed from the Scriptures between the time of Christ and the middle of the fifth century.*
>
> ~ Webber. **The Majestic Tapestry.**
> Nashville: Thomas Nelson Publishers, 1986. p. 10.

This tradition is widely affirmed by Protestant theologians both ancient and modern.

> *Thus those ancient Councils of Nicea, Constantinople, the first of Ephesus, Chalcedon, and the like, which were held for refuting errors, we willingly embrace, and reverence as sacred, in so far as relates to doctrines of faith, for they contain nothing but the pure and genuine interpretation of Scripture, which the holy Fathers with spiritual prudence adopted to crush the enemies of religion who had then arisen.*
>
> ~ John Calvin. **Institutes.** IV, ix. 8.

> *. . . most of what is enduringly valuable in contemporary biblical exegesis was discovered by the fifth century.*
>
> ~ Thomas C. Oden. **The Word of Life.**
> San Francisco: HarperSanFrancisco, 1989. p. xi

> *The first four Councils are by far the most important, as they settled the orthodox faith on the Trinity and the Incarnation.*
>
> ~ Philip Schaff. **The Creeds of Christendom.** Vol. 1.
> Grand Rapids: Baker Book House, 1996. p. 44.

Our reference to the Ecumenical Councils and Creeds is, therefore, focused on those Councils which retain a widespread agreement in the Church among Catholics, Orthodox, and Protestants. While Catholic and Orthodox share common agreement on the first seven councils, Protestants tend to affirm and use primarily the first four. Therefore, those councils which continue to be shared by the whole Church are completed with the Council of Chalcedon in 451.

Traditions (continued)

It is worth noting that each of these four Ecumenical Councils took place in a pre-European cultural context and that none of them were held in Europe. They were councils of the whole Church and they reflected a time in which Christianity was primarily an eastern religion in it's geographic core. By modern reckoning, their par- ticipants were African, Asian, and European. The councils reflected a church that ". . . has roots in cultures far distant from Europe and preceded the development of modern European identity, and [of which] some of its greatest minds have been African" (Oden, *The Living God*, San Francisco: HarperSanFrancisco, 1987, p. 9).

Perhaps the most important achievement of the Councils was the creation of what is now commonly called the Nicene Creed. It serves as a summary statement of the Christian faith that can be agreed on by Catholic, Orthodox, and Protestant Christians.

The first four Ecumenical Councils are summarized in the following chart:

Name/Date/Location	Purpose	
First Ecumenical Council 325 A.D. Nicea, Asia Minor	Defending against:	*Arianism*
	Question answered:	*Was Jesus God?*
	Action:	*Developed the initial form of the Nicene Creed to serve as a summary of the Christian faith*
Second Ecumenical Council 381 A.D. Constantinople, Asia Minor	Defending against:	*Macedonianism*
	Question answered:	*Is the Holy Spirit a personal and equal part of the Godhead?*
	Action:	*Completed the Nicene Creed by expanding the article dealing with the Holy Spirit*
Third Ecumenical Council 431 A.D. Ephesus, Asia Minor	Defending against:	*Nestorianism*
	Question answered:	*Is Jesus Christ both God and man in one person?*
	Action:	*Defined Christ as the Incarnate Word of God and affirmed his mother Mary as theotokos (God-bearer)*
Fourth Ecumenical Council 451 A.D. Chalcedon, Asia Minor	Defending against:	*Monophysitism*
	Question answered:	*How can Jesus be both God and man?*
	Action:	*Explained the relationship between Jesus' two natures (human and Divine)*

Translating the Story of God

Rev. Dr. Don L. Davis

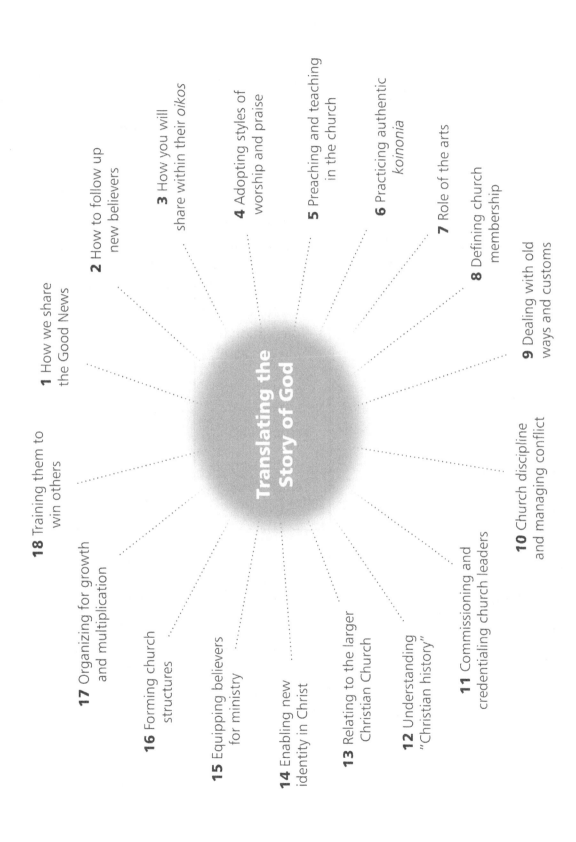

Translating the Story of God

1 How we share the Good News

2 How to follow up new believers

3 How you will share within their *oikos*

4 Adopting styles of worship and praise

5 Preaching and teaching in the church

6 Practicing authentic *koinonia*

7 Role of the arts

8 Defining church membership

9 Dealing with old ways and customs

10 Church discipline and managing conflict

11 Commissioning and credentialing church leaders

12 Understanding "Christian history"

13 Relating to the larger Christian Church

14 Enabling new identity in Christ

15 Equipping believers for ministry

16 Forming church structures

17 Organizing for growth and multiplication

18 Training them to win others

Translation Methodology

Rev. Terry G. Cornett

	Grade Level	Formal Equivalence	Dynamic Equivalence	Paraphrase
Hard to Read	12th 11th 10th 9th	King James Version (KJV) New American Standard Bible (NASB)		
Average Adult Level	8th 7th 6th	New International Version (NIV) New Revised Standard Version (NRSV) New King James Version (NKJV)	New Living Translation (NLT)	The Living Bible (TLB) The Message
Children's Bibles	5th 4th 3rd	New International Reader's Version (NIrV)	Contemporary English Version (CEV) International Children's Bible (ICB)	

Typology Readings

Rev. Dr. Don L. Davis

The Study of Types Critical to New Testament Mastery

➤ *Ada R. Habershon,* **Study of the Types***. Grand Rapids: Kregel Publishing, (1957) 1974. pp. 19, 21*

There are many passages in the New Testament which we cannot understand without having become in some measure familiar with the types. The epistle to the Hebrews is almost entirely made up of references to the Old Testament: as the substance, Christ, is proved to be better than the shadows–better than Moses, than Joshua, than Abraham, than Aaron, than the first Tabernacle, than the Levitical sacrifices, than the whole cloud of witnesses in the picture gallery of faith; and lastly, his blood is proved to be better than the blood of Abel.

We sometimes forget that the writers of the New Testament were *students of the Old Testament*; that it was *their Bible,* and that they would naturally allude again and again to the types and shadows, expecting their readers also to be familiar with them. *If we fail to see these allusions, we lose much of the beauty of the passage, and cannot rightly understand it. . . .*

[The study of types] gives us a sure antidote for the poison of the so-called "higher criticism." If we acknowledge the Divine intention of every detail of the types, even though we may not understand all their teaching, and if we believe there is a lesson in every incident recorded, the attacks of modern criticism will not harm us. We may not be clear enough to understand what the critics say, or to answer their criticisms; but *if our eyes have been opened to see the beauty of the types, the doubts which such writers suggest will not trouble us, and we shall have a more profitable occupation than reading their works.* When so much of this destructive criticism is about, we cannot do better than urge all–even the youngest Christians–to take up the typical study of God's Word; for though *he has hid these things from the wise and prudent, he reveals them unto babes.*

Do We Presently Study the Bible in the Same Way and with the Same Methods as the Lord and the Apostles?

➤ *James DeYoung and Sarah Hurty,* **Beyond the Obvious***. Gresham, OR: Vision House Publishing, 1995. p. 24*

After more than twenty years of teaching the grammatical-historical hermeneutic, I can see only one problem with it: it doesn't appear to be the way the biblical writers always did it! When we examine how the biblical writers used previously written Scripture, we see that they seemed to "discover" meaning there that, judged by its original context, can hardly be imagined to have been in the mind

Typology Readings (continued)

of the original author. This problem is especially evident in the way the New Testament authors used Old Testament passages to prove that Jesus Christ fulfilled prophecy (or to make some theological point.)

Can or Should We Reproduce the Exegesis of the New Testament?

To the question whether we can reproduce the exegesis of the New Testament, S. L. Johnson answers: "Unhesitatingly the reply is yes, although we are not allowed to claim for our results the infallibility of the Lord and his Apostles. They are reliable teachers of biblical doctrine and they are reliable teachers of hermeneutics and exegesis. We not only can reproduce their exegetical methodology, we must if we are to be taught their understanding of the Scriptures."

◄ *James DeYoung and Sarah Hurty,* **Beyond the Obvious***. p. 265*

What of Typology as a Valid, Important Method of Bible Interpretation?

[Typology] is a genuine approach widely practiced in the New Testament. For example, the furniture of the tabernacle and other matters associated with it and the temple (the altar and sacrifices, the veil, the golden cover of the ark of the covenant) are all types of Christ and of the heavenly realm (see Heb. 9). When we come to typology, we must avoid being too broad or too narrow in our interpretation. We can be too broad if we find typology everywhere. We can be too narrow if we reject typology as an exegetical method on the basis of the claim that it is not consistent with a literal meaning which embraces on meaning, found by means of grammatical-historical study. . . .

◄ *James DeYoung and Sarah Hurty,* **Beyond the Obvious***. p. 74*

Yet we believe that typology is not to be divorced from exegesis, even though it cannot be fully "regulated hermeneutically, but takes place in the freedom of the Holy Spirit." It very much involves a deeper meaning and was readily practiced by the Bible in its exegetical method (see 1 Cor. 10; Rom. 5).

Diverse Usages of the Term *Typos* in the New Testament

➤ *Patrick Fairbairn,*
Typology of Scripture.
Grand Rapids: Kregel
Publishing. p. 42

The language of Scripture being essentially popular, its use of particular terms naturally partakes of the freedom and variety which are wont to appear in the current speech of a people; and it rarely if ever happens that words are employed, in respect to topics requiring theological treatment, with such precision and uniformity as to enable us, from this source alone, to attain to proper accuracy and fullness.

The word type (*typos*) forms no exception to this usage.

- Occurring once, at least, in the natural sense of *mark* or *impress* made by a hard substance on one of softer material (John 20.25)

- It commonly bears the general import of *model, pattern,* or *exemplar,* but with such a wide diversity of application as to comprehend a material object of worship, or idol (Acts 7.43)

- An *external framework* constructed for the service of God (Acts 7.44; Heb. 8.5)

- The *form* or *copy* of an epistle (Acts 23.25)

- A *method of doctrinal instruction* delivered by the first heralds and teachers of the Gospel (Rom. 7.17)

- A *representative character,* or, in certain respects, normal example (Rom. 5.14; 1 Cor. 10.11; Phil. 3.17; 1 Thess. 1.7; 1 Pet. 5.3)

Such in the New Testament Scriptures is the diversified use of the word *type* (disguised, however, under other terms in the authorized version).

Extreme Misuse of Typology is Very Possible

➤ *J. Sidlow Baxter,*
The Strategic Grasp
of the Bible.

We marvel with peculiar awe at the ability and agility which some well-meaning brethren display in seeing what is not there; as also we marvel, with a sense of our denseness, at the super-spirituality which they evince in aerifying the most unsuspicious details of Scripture into rare spiritual significances.

The "three white baskets" which Pharaoh's ill-fated baker dreamed were on his head are to ourselves part of a true story; but to see in those same three basket

Typology Readings (continued)

recondite bearings upon the doctrine of the Trinity makes one part of our mind laugh and another part groan. We feel the same sort of reaction when we are assured that the bride's hair in the Song of Solomon is the mass of the nations converted to Christianity.

It is an eye-opener to learn that the "two pence" which the Good Samaritan gave to the innkeeper were covertly Baptism and the Lord's Supper. We cannot but feel sorry for Matthew, Mark, Luke and John, when another ministerial victim of typomania tells us the "four barrels" of water which Elijah commanded to be poured over the altar on Mount Carmel were the four Gospel writers.

As for the clergyman who would persuade us the boat in which our Lord crossed Galilee is the Church of England, while the "other little ships" which accompanied it were the other denominations, we cannot shake off a sly idea that the novel expositor himself, like the boats, must have been all "at sea." We feel just the same about Pope Gregory the Great's exposition of Job, in which Job's verbose "friends" typify heretics; and his seven sons the twelve Apostles; his seven thousand sheep God's faithful people and his three thousand hump-backed camels the depraved Gentiles!"

The Three Errors of Typology to Avoid

There are three dangers, however, which must be avoided:

- Limiting the type, and therefore not using it

- Exaggerating the type, and therefore overusing it

- Imagining the type, and therefore misusing it

◄ J. Boyd Nicholson from the foreword to **Harvest Festivals***.*

The Case Against the "Older View" of Typology

The case against typology:

- Concerned only with finding "prefigurations" of Christ all over the Old Testament

- God ordained Old Testament events, institutions, and/or persons for the primary purpose of foreshadowing Christ.

◄ Christopher J. H. Wright, **Knowing Jesus through the Old Testament***.. Downers Grove: InterVarsity Press, 1992. pp. 115-116*

Two bad results of this old hermeneutic:

- No need to find much reality and meaning in the events and persons themselves (Old Testament becomes nothing more than a collection of shadows)

- Interpreted every obscure detail of Old Testament "type" as a foreshadowing of Jesus (hermeneutics becomes magic, like pulling a rabbit out of a hat)

Conclusion: typology is not *the* way of interpreting the Old Testament for itself. "But when we go back and read the whole of Psalm 2, Isaiah 42 and Genesis 22, it is equally true that they have enormous depths of truth and meaning for us to explore which are not *directly* related to Jesus himself. Typology is a way of helping us understand Jesus in the light of the Old Testament. It is not the exclusive way to understand the full meaning of the Old Testament itself" (Wright, 116).

Rebutting Wright's Claims

- Jesus used typology (e.g., the brazen serpent, manna in the wilderness, the Temple of his body, the Good Shepherd, etc.)

- The Apostles and early Christian interpreters used typology as their normal way of reading the Old Testament (e.g., Moses' striking the Rock, the wilderness journey of the nation of Israel, Jesus as the second Israel, etc.)

- The Bible refers to itself in this way (e.g., the Book of Hebrews, the Tabernacle, the priesthood, etc.)

The question: Should we use the Old Testament as Jesus and the Apostles did, with some reference to *typology*?

The Christological Hermeneutic: Messiah Jesus Connects the Testaments

> Norman Geisler, *To Understand the Bible Look for Jesus*. (1979) 2002. p. 68

Christ at once sums up in himself the *perfection of the Old Testament precepts*, the *substance of Old Testament shadows and types*, and the *fulfillment of Old Testament forecasts*. Those truths about him which bud forth in the Old Testament come

Typology Readings (continued)

into full bloom in the New Testament; the flashlight of prophetic truth turns into the floodlight of divine revelation.

The Old Testament foreshadows find their fulfillment in the New Testament in several ways: (1) The *moral precepts* of the Old Testament become fulfilled or perfected in the life and teachings of Christ. (2) The *ceremonial* and *typical* truths were only shadows of the true substance to be found in Christ. (3) The *Messianic prophecies* foretold in the Old Testament were finally fulfilled in the history of the New Testament. In each of these relationships it can be seen that the Testaments are inseparably connected. The New is not only supplementary to the Old but it is the necessary complement to it.

As the book of Hebrews puts it, "God had foreseen something better for us, that apart from us they [Old Testament believers] should not be made perfect" (Heb. 11.40). For what was contained in the Old Testament is fully explained only in the New Testament.

The Way Paul and the Apostles Read Scripture

As can be clearly seen, the hermeneutical procedure which Paul and the other New Testament authors use to interpret the Law in a spiritual sense is allegorical, in that a meaning other than the literal or immediate sense is perceived from the given text. The usual term which Paul employs to define the relationship between the two levels of meaning is *typos* = form, figure, symbol, or prefiguration (Rom. 5.14; 1 Cor. 10.6, etc.); but in Galatians 4.24, where he presents the sons of Hagar and Sarah as prefigurations of the Jews and Christians, he says 'Now this is an allegory (*allegoroumena*), showing that he regarded 'typos' as synonymous with 'allegory.'

In deference to Paul's terminology, modern scholars call this kind of interpretation - which, as we shall see, enjoyed immense success and became the authentic Christian way of reading the Old Testament - 'typology' or 'typological interpretation.' In antiquity [i.e., in olden times] it was called 'spiritual' or 'mystical.'

It was rooted in the firm conviction that the old Law was consistently directed towards the great Christ-event, and that, as a result, it would give up its true significance only to those who interpreted it in Christological terms.

≺ *Manlo Simonetti, Biblical Interpretation in the Early Church. p. 11-12*

Understanding Leadership as Representation
The Six Stages of Formal Proxy
Don L. Davis

Luke 10.1 (ESV) After this the Lord appointed seventy-two others and sent them on ahead of him, two by two, into every town and place where he himself was about to go . . .

Luke 10.16 (ESV) "The one who hears you hears me, and the one who rejects you rejects me, and the one who rejects me rejects him who sent me."

John 20.21 (ESV) Jesus said to them again, "Peace be with you. As the Father has sent me, even so I am sending you."

Commissioning (1)

Formal Selection and Call to Represent
- Chosen to be an emissary, envoy, or proxy
- Confirmed by appropriate other who recognize the call
- Is recognized to be a member of a faithful community
- Calling out of a group to a particular role of representation
  - Calling to a particular task or mission
  - Delegation of position or responsibility

Equipping (2)

Appropriate Resourcing and Training to Fulfill the Call
- Assignment to a supervisor, superior, mentor, or instructor
- Disciplined instruction of principles underlying the call
- Constant drill, practice, and exposure to appropriate skills
  - Recognition of gifts and strengths
  - Expert coaching and ongoing feedback

Entrustment (3)

Corresponding Authorization and Empowerment to Act
- Delegation of authority to act and speak on commissioner's behalf
- Scope and limits of representative power provided
- Formal deputization (right to enforce and represent)
- Permission given to be an emissary (to stand in stead of)
- Release to fulfill the commission and task received

CONVICTION
The Revealed Will of God

Leadership As Representation

The Fulfillment of the Task and Mission

CHARACTER

CONSCIENCE
Consent of Your Leaders

Mission (4)

Faithful and Disciplined Engagement of the Task
- Subordination of one's will to accomplish the assignment
- Obedience: carrying out the orders of those who sent you
  - Fulfilling the task that was given to you
- Freely acting within one's delegated authority to fulfill the task
  - Maintaining loyalty to those who sent you
- Using all means available to do one's duty, whatever the cost
- Full recognition of one's answerability to the one(s) who commissioned

Reckoning (5)

Official Evaluation and Review of One's Execution
- Reporting back to sending authority for critical review
- Formal comprehensive assessment of one's execution and results
- Judgment of one's loyalties and faithfulness
- Sensitive analysis of what we accomplished
- Readiness to ensure that our activities and efforts produce results

Reward (6)

Public Recognition and Continuing Response
- Formal publishing of assessment's results
- Acknowledgment and recognition of behavior and conduct
- Corresponding reward or rebuke for execution
  - Review made basis for possible reassignment or recommissioning
- Assigning new projects with greater authority

Understanding the Bible in Parts and Whole
Rev. Don Allsman

The Bible is the authoritative account of God's plan to exalt Jesus as Lord of all, redeem all creation, and put down God's enemies forever. The subject of the Bible is Jesus Christ (John 5.39-40):

- The Old Testament is the anticipation and promise of Christ
- The New Testament is the climax and fulfillment in Christ

"In the OT the NT lies hidden; in the NT the OT stands revealed."

Elements of plot development: beginning, rising action, climax, falling action, resolution

1. **Beginning**: Creation and fall of man (the problem and need for resolution), Genesis 1.1 - 3.15

2. **Rising Action**: God's plan revealed through Israel (Genesis 3.15 - Malachi)

3. **Climax**: Jesus inaugurates his Kingdom (Matthew - Acts 1.11)

4. **Falling Action**: The Church continues Jesus' kingdom work (Acts 1.12 - Revelation 3)

5. **Resolution**: Jesus returns to consummate the Kingdom (Revelation 4 - 22)

6. **Commentary**: The people of God describe their experiences to provide wisdom (The Wisdom literature: Job, Psalms, Proverbs, Ecclesiastes, Song of Solomon)

The Bible in book order:

Genesis, Exodus, Leviticus, Numbers, Deuteronomy, Joshua, Judges, Ruth, 1-2 Samuel	History from Creation to the reign of King David
1-2 Kings	Israel's history from David to Exile
1-2 Chronicles	Various historical accounts from Creation to Exile
Ezra, Nehemiah, Esther	Accounts of Israel in Exile and return
Job (contemporary of Abraham), Psalms (primarily of David), Proverbs, Ecclesiastes, Song of Solomon (Solomon's time)	Wisdom literature
Isaiah, Jeremiah, Lamentations, Ezekiel, Daniel, Hosea, Joel, Amos, Obadiah, Jonah, Micah, Nahum, Habakkuk, Zephaniah, Haggai, Zechariah, Malachi	Writings of Israel's prophets from the time of the Kings through the return from Exile
Matthew, Mark, Luke, John	The account of Jesus of Nazareth (Gospels)
Acts, Romans, 1-2 Corinthians, Galatians, Ephesians, Philippians, Colossians, 1-2 Thessalonians, 1-2 Timothy, Titus, Philemon, Hebrews, James, 1-2 Peter, 1-3 John, Jude, Revelation	The account of the Church after Jesus' ascension, including letters of apostolic instruction to the Church (Epistles)
Revelation	The future and the end of the age (Jesus' return)

Union with Christ: The Christocentric Paradigm
Christianity as Union with, Allegiance to, and Devotion to Jesus of Nazareth
Representative Texts

Rom. 6.4-5 (ESV) - We were buried therefore with him by baptism into death, in order that, just as Christ was raised from the dead by the glory of the Father, we too might walk in newness of life. [5] For if we have been united with him in a death like his, we shall certainly be united with him in a resurrection like his.

Col. 2.6-7 (ESV) - Therefore, as you received Christ Jesus the Lord, so walk in him, [7] rooted and built up in him and established in the faith, just as you were taught, abounding in thanksgiving.

John 14.6 (ESV) - Jesus said to him, "I am the way, and the truth, and the life. No one comes to the Father except through me."

Gal. 2.20 (ESV) - It is no longer I who live, but Christ who lives in me. And the life I now live in the flesh I live by faith in the Son of God, who loved me and gave himself for me.

Eph. 2.4-7 (ESV) - But God, being rich in mercy, because of the great love with which he loved us, [5] even when we were dead in our trespasses, made us alive together with Christ - by grace you have been saved - [6] and raised us up with him and seated us with him in the heavenly places in Christ Jesus, [7] so that in the coming ages he might show the immeasurable riches of his grace in kindness toward us in Christ Jesus.

Rom. 8.16-17 (ESV) - The Spirit himself bears witness with our spirit that we are children of God, [17] and if children, then heirs - heirs of God and fellow heirs with Christ, provided we suffer with him in order that we may also be glorified with him.

Eph. 5.2 (ESV) - And walk in love, as Christ loved us and gave himself up for us, a fragrant offering and sacrifice to God.

John 15.4-5 (ESV) - Abide in me, and I in you. As the branch cannot bear fruit by itself, unless it abides in the vine, neither can you, unless you abide in me. [5] I am the vine; you are the branches. Whoever abides in me and I in him, he it is that bears much fruit, for apart from me you can do nothing.

Col. 3.17 (ESV) - And whatever you do, in word or deed, do everything in the name of the Lord Jesus, giving thanks to God the Father through him.

1 John 2.6 (ESV) - whoever says he abides in him ought to walk in the same way in which he walked.

Gal. 5.24 (ESV) - And those who belong to Christ Jesus have crucified the flesh with its passions and desires.

Rom. 8.29 (ESV) - For those whom he foreknew he also predestined to be conformed to the image of his Son, in order that he might be the firstborn among many brothers.

Rom. 13.14 (ESV) - But put on the Lord Jesus Christ, and make no provision for the flesh, to gratify its desires.

1 Cor. 15.49 (ESV) - Just as we have borne the image of the man of dust, we shall also bear the image of the man of heaven.

2 Cor. 3.18 (ESV) - And we all, with unveiled face, beholding the glory of the Lord, are being transformed into the same image from one degree of glory to another. For this comes from the Lord who is the Spirit.

Phil. 3.7-8 (ESV) - But whatever gain I had, I counted as loss for the sake of Christ. [8] Indeed, I count everything as loss because of the surpassing worth of knowing Christ Jesus my Lord. For his sake I have suffered the loss of all things and count them as rubbish, in order that I may gain Christ.

Phil. 3.20-21 (ESV) - But our citizenship is in heaven, and from it we await a Savior, the Lord Jesus Christ, [21] who will transform our lowly body to be like his glorious body, by the power that enables him even to subject all things to himself.

1 John 3.2 (ESV) - Beloved, we are God's children now, and what we will be has not yet appeared; but we know that when he appears we shall be like him, because we shall see him as he is.

John 17.16 (ESV) - They are not of the world, just as I am not of the world.

Union with Christ: The Christocentric Paradigm (continued)

Col. 1.15-18 (ESV) - He is the image of the invisible God, the firstborn of all creation. [16] For by him all things were created, in heaven and on earth, visible and invisible, whether thrones or dominions or rulers or authorities - all things were created through him and for him. [17] And he is before all things, and in him all things hold together. [18] And he is the head of the body, the church. He is the beginning, the firstborn from the dead, that in everything he might be preeminent.

Heb. 2.14-15 (ESV) - Since therefore the children share in flesh and blood, he himself likewise partook of the same things, that through death he might destroy the one who has the power of death, that is, the devil, [15] and deliver all those who through fear of death were subject to lifelong slavery.

Rev. 1.5-6 (ESV) - and from Jesus Christ the faithful witness, the firstborn of the dead, and the ruler of kings on earth. To him who loves us and has freed us from our sins by his blood [6] and made us a kingdom, priests to his God and Father, to him be glory and dominion forever and ever. Amen.

2 Tim. 2.11-13 (ESV) - The saying is trustworthy, for: If we have died with him, we will also live with him; [12] if we endure, we will also reign with him; if we deny him, he also will deny us; [13] if we are faithless, he remains faithful—for he cannot deny himself.

Rev. 3.21 (ESV) - The one who conquers, I will grant him to sit with me on my throne, as I also conquered and sat down with my Father on his throne.

Use of Reference Tools for Interpreting the Bible

Rev. Dr. Don L. Davis

	Cross-Reference Aids and Topical Concordances	Theological Workbooks, Dictionaries, and Studies	Bible Dictionaries, Bible Atlases, and Customs References
Purpose	To associate different texts together on a given subject, theme, or issue	To provide an understanding of the meanings of a word or phrase in light of its theological significance	To provide background on the history, culture, social customs, and/or life of the biblical periods
Stage Where Most Beneficial	Finding Biblical Principles	Understanding the Original Situation and Finding Biblical Principles	Understanding the Original Situation
Procedures	1. Find the reference you want to check. 2. Look up the other texts associated with passage in the reference. 3. Associate the verse with a particular theme. 4. Check the theme against those citations given.	1. Attribute the verse or passage you are studying with a particular theme. 2. Find the word or concept you would like to research. 3. Read on the background of the word in the reference or dictionary 4. Associate your text with the theme, gleaning what is helpful and discarding what is not relevant for the purpose of your study	1. Select an item, theme, issue, or custom you need help in understanding. 2. Check the item in the reference text provided. 3. Make note on the background of the issue, and factor the new information in your overall account of the passage.
Benefits	Find texts on same subject throughout the Bible Outlines provided to help digest all Scriptures on a different subject	Thorough scholarship on the various theological usages and meanings of a particular Bible word, wording, or phrase	Wealth of information given on the various sociology, anthropology, historical accounts, customs, society, geography and data on the original situation
Key Caution	Dig deeply into the text BEFORE you begin to look at other similar materials	Do not be confused by the VARIETY of usages and meanings of a theological idea	Stay focused on the meaning of the text and not merely its CONTEXT
Reliability	Good	Very Good	Excellent

Use of Reference Tools for Interpreting the Bible (continued)

	Bible Handbooks, Study Bible, and Commentaries	Topical Bibles, Textbooks, and Thematic Studies	Lexical Aids, Inter-linear Translations, and Word Studies
Purpose	To give a scholarly opinion as to the background, context, and meaning of the text	To give a sophisticated outline of passages on a given theme	To provide insight into the meaning, usage, and grammar of the biblical words and language
Stage Where Most Beneficial	Understanding the Original Situation and Finding Biblical Principles	Finding Biblical Principles	Understanding the Original Situation and Finding Biblical Principles
Procedures	1. After you have completed your own preliminary study, select a commentary or two you will check your findings against. 2. Check your findings against 2-3 other authors to see if yours harmonizes with the meanings they provide.	1. After you have done your study, and made a preliminary judgment as to what you believe the passage teaches, assign your passage a biblical or theological theme. 2. Using that theme, look in the topical reference tools to check other texts on the same subject, and incorporate their meanings into your study. 3. Do not be afraid to modify your findings if the new data illumines your study.	1. Select the words or phrases in the passage which serve as key words to define in order to understand the overall meaning of the passage. 2. Using a concordance, lexicon, or other linguistic tool, look at the various meanings of the word in the context of the book, the author, the author's contemporaries, the Bible, and finally the period. 3. Allow the richness of the biblical meanings to nuance your study's claims on what the passage meant to its original hearers and what it means today.
Benefits	Excellent scholarly opinions on both the background and meaning of the various texts of Scripture	Rich, thorough presentations on various topics, themes, and theological concepts being dealt with in a passage	Abundant expert knowledge given on every phase of the design, use, and meaning of the biblical languages in their own historical and religious setting
Key Caution	Do your own study and reflection before you RELY on the opinion of your favorite interpreter	Do not make a topical listing of texts the SUBSTITUTE for deep digging into individual texts and passages for truth	Do not pretend that a knowledge of the original meanings of the key words DISQUALIFIES a sound knowledge of the text in your own language
Reliability	Good	Good	Excellent

Watch What You Image Forth

Images are powerful. They shape what we see, by highlighting certain features and moving others into the background. They dominate our patterns of analysis and reflection. They suggest explanations of why we relate to one another the way we do, or why certain structures exist. They support particular understandings of the past, interpretations of the present, and scenarios for the future. They promote some values and discourage others. They suggest priorities, and awaken emotions.

The choice to emphasize a given metaphor and to put aside another can set the direction of a community and its leadership. Therefore, we must become aware of the images we use, and how we are using them. In particular, *we must examine the metaphors we use in the development of our future leaders.*

~ David Bennett. **Metaphors of Ministry.** p. 199.

The Way of Wisdom

Rev. Dr. Don L. Davis

The Way of Wisdom {Proverbs 2.1-9; Prov. 8.1-9; 9.1-6; Prov. 1.7; 8.13

Sowing and Reaping {Gal. 6.7-8

You will **sow**
You will **reap** what you sow
You will reap **more than** what you sow
You will reap in **proportion** to what you sow
You will reap **in kind** as you sow
You will reap in a **different season** than you sow
You determine what you sow
You can **sow differently** than you did last year
You reap more if you **cultivate and fertilize**
Your sowing can **affect what others reap** also

What you **think about**
How you **dress**
How you **speak**
Who you **hang out with**
What you **listen to and look at**
What you **read**
Where you **go**
How you **make decisions**
What your **goals** are
What's important to you

The Goal

Be like Jesus
1 Cor. 11.2
Rom. 8.29
Phil. 3.8-12

Loving God with all our heart
Deut. 6.4-6
Matt. 22.34-40

Loving our neighbors as ourselves
Lev. 19.18
Matt. 7.12

The Way of Life { Proverbs 1.7-8; 4.13; 8.10; 9.9; 10.17; 13.18; 15.32-33; 23.23

The Narrow Way {Matt. 7.13-14

Instruction in righteousness (On track)
Pss. 31.3; 48.14; Isa. 42.16; Pss. 125; 4-5; 25.5; 27.11

Correction (the way back)
Proverbs 13.1; 19.20; Heb. 5.8; Matt. 26.39; Pss. 31.3;
119.35; 143.10; Prov. 6.20-23; Jer. 42.1-3

Doctrine (The Way)
2 Timothy 3.16-17; John 8.31-32; 1 John 4.6

Rebuke (the way off)
Proverbs 9.9; 11.14; 12.1.15; 15.22; 19.20;
20.18; 24.6; 13.10; 15.10

Isa. 26.1-9

The Way That Leads to Death
Prov. 14.12; 16.25; 1.24-33; 2.10-22; 15.9; 15.19, 24, 29; 13.15;
Job 15.20; Ps. 107.17; Rom. 2.9

We Believe: Confession of the Nicene Creed (Common Meter*)

Rev. Dr. Don L. Davis, 2007. All Rights Reserved.

* This song is adapted from the Nicene Creed, and set to Common Meter (8.6.8.6.), meaning it can be sung to tunes of the same meter, such as: *O, for a Thousand Tongues to Sing; Alas, and Did My Savior Bleed?; Amazing Grace; All Hail the Power of Jesus' Name; There Is a Fountain; Joy to the World*

The Father God Almighty rules, Maker of earth and heav'n.
Yes, all things seen and those unseen, by him were made, and given!

We hold to one Lord Jesus Christ, God's one and only Son,
Begotten, not created, too, he and our Lord are one!

Begotten from the Father, same, in essence, God and Light;
Through him all things were made by God, in him were given life.

Who for us all, for salvation, came down from heav'n to earth,
Was incarnate by the Spirit's pow'r, and the Virgin Mary's birth.

Who for us too, was crucified, by Pontius Pilate's hand,
Suffered, was buried in the tomb, on third day rose again.

According to the Sacred text all this was meant to be.
Ascended to heav'n, to God's right hand, now seated high in glory.

He'll come again in glory to judge all those alive and dead.
His Kingdom rule shall never end, for he will reign as Head.

We worship God, the Holy Spirit, our Lord, Life-giver known,
With Fath'r and Son is glorified, Who by the prophets spoke.

And we believe in one true Church, God's people for all time,
Cath'lic in scope, and built upon the apostolic line.

Acknowledging one baptism, for forgiv'ness of our sin,
We look for Resurrection day–the dead shall live again.

We look for those unending days, life of the Age to come,
When Christ's great Reign shall come to earth, and God's will shall be done!

We Believe: Confession of the Nicene Creed (8.7.8.7 meter*)

Rev. Dr. Don L. Davis, 2007. All Rights Reserved.

* This song is adapted from the Nicene Creed, and set to 8.7.8.7. meter, meaning it can be sung to tunes of the same meter, such as: *Joyful, Joyful, We Adore Thee; I Will Sing of My Redeemer; What a Friend We Have in Jesus; Come, Thou Long Expected Jesus*

Father God Almighty rules, the Maker of both earth and heav'n.

All things seen and those unseen, by him were made, by him were giv'n!

We believe in Jesus Christ, the Lord, God's one and only Son,

Begotten, not created, too, he and our Father God are one!

Begotten from the Father, same, in essence, as both God and Light;

Through him by God all things were made, in him all things were giv'n life.

Who for us all, for our salvation, did come down from heav'n to earth,

Incarnate by the Spirit's pow'r, and through the Virgin Mary's birth.

Who for us too, was crucified, by Pontius Pilate's rule and hand,

Suffered, and was buried, yet on the third day, he rose again.

According to the Sacred Scriptures all that happ'ned was meant to be.

Ascended high to God's right hand, in heav'n he sits in glory.

Christ will come again in glory to judge all those alive and dead.

His Kingdom rule shall never end, for he will rule and reign as Head.

We worship God, the Holy Spirit, Lord and the Life-giver known;

With Fath'r and Son is glorified, Who by the prophets ever spoke.

And we believe in one true Church, God's holy people for all time,

Cath'lic in its scope and broadness, built on the Apostles' line!

Acknowledging that one baptism, for forgiv'ness of our sin,

And we look for Resurrection, for the dead shall live again.

Looking for unending days, the life of the bright Age to come,

When Christ's Reign shall come to earth, the will of God shall then be done!

Praise to God, and to Christ Jesus, to the Spirit–triune Lord!

We confess the ancient teachings, clinging to God's holy Word!

Wei Ji

Chua Wee Hian, **The Making of a Leader.** *Downers Grove: InterVarsity Press, 1987, p. 151.*

"Crisis"

"Opportunity"

When "Christian" Does Not Translate

Frank Decker

This article was taken from Mission Frontiers: The Bulletin of the US Center for World Mission, Vol. 27, No. 5; September-October 2005; ISSN 0889-9436.

A former missionary in Ghana, Frank Decker currently serves as Vice President for Field Operations for the Mission Society for United Methodists.

"I grew up as a Muslim, and when I gave my life to Jesus I became a Christian. Then I felt the Lord saying, 'Go back to your family and tell them what the Lord has done for you.'" Such was the beginning of the testimony of a sweet sister in Christ named Salima. As she stood before the microphone at a conference held recently in Asia, I thought about how her story would have been applauded by my Christian friends back home.

But then she said something that would have probably shocked most American Christians. She told us that in order to share Christ with her family, she now identifies herself as a Muslim rather than a Christian. "But," she added, "I could never go back to Islam without Jesus whom I love as my Lord."

Like this woman, countless people, primarily in Asia, who live in Muslim, Buddhist, and Hindu contexts are saying *yes* to Jesus, but *no* to Christianity. As Westerners, we assume that the word "Christian" *ipso facto* refers to someone who has given his or her life to Jesus, and a "non-Christian" is an unbeliever. However, in the words of one Asian attendee, "The word 'Christian' means something different here in the East."

Consider the story of Chai, a Buddhist from Thailand. "Thailand has not become a Christian country, because in the eyes of the Thai, to become a Christian means you can no longer be Thai. That's because in Thailand 'Christian' equals 'foreigner.'" So when Chai gave his life to Jesus, he began referring to himself as a "Child of God" and a "new Buddhist." He then related a subsequent incident in which he had a conversation with a Buddhist monk on a train. "After I listened to his story, I told him that he was missing one thing in life. He asked me what that was and I told him it was Jesus."

Chai continued to tell us the story in which the monk not only gave his life to Christ, but also invited Chai to come to his Buddhist temple to share about Jesus. Then Chai said, "At the beginning of our conversation the monk asked me, 'Are you a Christian?' and I said *no*. I explained that Christianity and Jesus are two different things. Salvation is in Jesus, not in Christianity. If I had said I was a

When "Christian" Does Not Translate (continued)

'Christian,' the conversation would have ended at that point." But it didn't end. And the monk now walks with Jesus.

Indeed, an American missionary that has been working in Asia for about two decades said, "For the first five or seven years of our ministry in [a Muslim country] we were frustrated because we were trying to get people to change their religion." He went on to say how in evangelical circles we talk a lot about how it is not our religion that saves us; it is *Jesus.* "If we really believe that, why do we insist that people change their religion?"

Asif is a brother in Christ with whom I have spent time in his village in a country that is 90 percent Muslim. Traditional Christian organizations in that country have only had a significant impact on the other ten percent that has never been Muslim. Make no mistake – Asif is sold out to Jesus, as are the other members of this Muslim Background Believers (MBB) movement. I will never forget seeing the tears stream down Asif's face as he told me how he and his brother, also a believer in Jesus, were beaten in an attack that his brother did not survive. These are Muslims who walk with Jesus and openly share with their Muslim friends about the Lord, who in Arabic is referred to as "Isa al-Masih" (Jesus the Messiah).

These "insider movements" are not intended to *hide* a believer's spiritual identity, but rather to enable those within the movement to *go deeper* into the cultural community – be it Islamic, Hindu, or Buddhist – and be witnesses for Jesus within the context of that culture. In some countries, such movements are just getting started. In other places, estimates of adherents are in the hundreds of thousands.

As the Body of Christ, we should be very careful that the things we uphold as sacred are not post-biblical accoutrements, but are indeed transcendent. If we are not open to "new wineskins," we may unwittingly find ourselves attached to traditions, as were the Pharisees in the day of Jesus.

The names in this story have been changed. This article is excerpted by permission from the May/June 2005 issue of Good News Magazine, a renewal ministry within the United Methodist Church (www.goodnewsmag. org).

World Impact's Vision: Toward a Biblical Strategy to Impact the Inner City

World Impact, Inc.

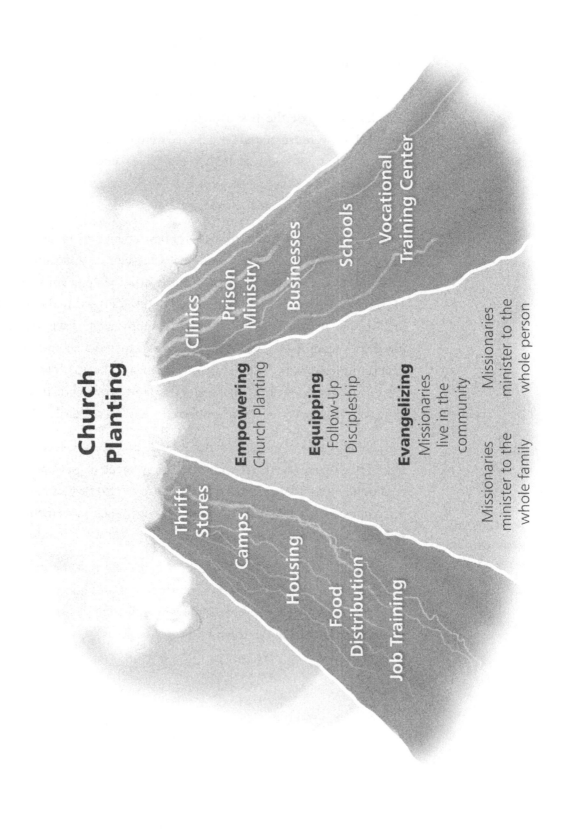

Church Planting

Empowering
Church Planting

Equipping
Follow-Up
Discipleship

Evangelizing
Missionaries
live in the
community

Missionaries
minister to the
whole family

Missionaries
minister to the
whole person

Clinics

Prison
Ministry

Businesses

Schools

Vocational
Training Center

Thrift
Stores

Camps

Housing

Food
Distribution

Job Training

"You Can Pay Me Now, Or You Can Pay Me Later"

Don L. Davis

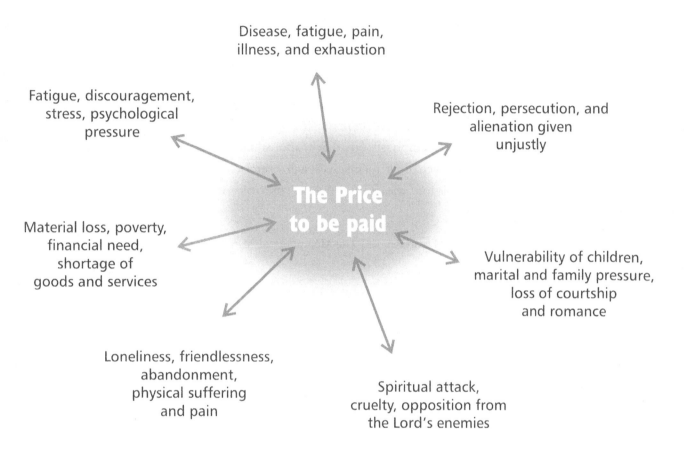

"You Got To Serve Somebody!"

Over half of the metaphors chosen by Jesus describe someone who is under the authority of another. Often the word selected is one member of a familiar role pair, such as child (of a father, *pater*), servant (of a master, *kyrios*), or disciple (of a teacher, *didaskalos*). Other images of those under authority include the shepherd (*poimen*) who tends a flock that belongs to another, the worker (*ergates*) hired by the landowner (*oikodespotes*), the apostle (*apostolos*) commissioned by his superior, and the sheep (*probaton*) obeying the voice of the shepherd. It is interesting to note that even though the disciples are being prepared for spiritual leadership in the Church, Jesus places far more emphasis on their responsibility to God's authority, than on the authority which they themselves will exercise. There is far more instruction about the role of *following* than about the role of *leading* [emphasis added].

~ David Bennett, **The Metaphors of Ministry**, p. 62.

Your Kingdom Come: "The Story of God's Glory"

Living Under His Reign and Doing Missions in an Unchurched World

Rev. Dr. Don L. Davis

I. The Significance of Story, the Importance of Myth, and the Kingdom of God

   A. Human beings operate according to their interpretive frameworks: human beings exist as "walking worldviews."

      1. Every human existence is basically a "story-ordered world."

      2. Myth-making as a primary act of human beings

      3. The role of culture: enabling us to compose our realities from scratch

   B. Integrating the details: story and the need to live purposefully

      1. Purposeful mindset: relating all details to the whole

      2. Provisional mindset: relating to details as wholes

   C. The problem of a reductionistic faith

      1. Reductionism–substituting a comprehensive religious vision of Christian faith for an alternative, smaller, usually culturally-oriented substitute notion, activity, relationship, or element

      2. Rationalism–spending the majority of time using modern scientific proofs and arguments to underwrite faith in Jesus, reducing Christian faith to holding of particular, contextualized doctrinal positions over against other contrary views

      3. Moralism–reducing the Christian vision to personal and communal decency and ethics, e.g., living well in a nuclear family context, holding certain views on selected socially controversial moral issues

   D. Elements of a comprehensive biblical worldview

      1. The recovery of "Christian myth"

      2. *The Picture and the Drama*: From Before to Beyond Time

Your Kingdom Come: "The Story of God's Glory" (continued)

3. Living in the upside-down Kingdom of God: the *Principle of Reversal*

4. Philosophical big picture: the *Presence of the Future*

E. Components of a guiding worldview (Arthur Holmes)

1. It has a *wholistic* goal. (Where did we come from and where are we going?)

2. It is a *perspectival* approach. (From what vantage point do we see things?)

3. It is an *exploratory* process. (How do we continue to understand our lives?)

4. It is *pluralistic*. (What other views are suggested by our collective vision?)

5. It has *action outcomes*. (What ought we to do in light of our mythic vision?)

F. The wonder of story

1. The centrality of human experience

2. The richness of human affections

3. The use of sanctified imagination

4. The power of concrete image, action, and symbol

5. The immediacy of heightened reality

6. The enjoyment of artistic craftsmanship

G. Key propositions of story theology

William J. Bausch lists ten propositions related to story theology that help us understand the significance and importance of the study of stories and the understanding of Bible and theology. (William J. Bausch, *Storytelling and Faith*. Mystic, Connecticut: Twenty-Third Publications, 1984.)

1. Stories introduce us to *sacramental presences*.

2. Stories are always more important than *facts*.

Your Kingdom Come: "The Story of God's Glory" (continued)

  3. Stories remain *normative (authoritative)* for the Christian community of faith.

  4. *Christian traditions* evolve and define themselves through and around stories.

  5. The stories of God precede, produce, and empower the *community of God's people.*

  6. Community story implies *censure, rebuke, and accountability.*

  7. Stories produce *theology.*

  8. Stories produce *many theologies.*

  9. Stories produce *ritual and sacrament.*

  10. Stories are *history.*

 H. The importance of the biblical framework of the Kingdom

  1. Kingdom teaching is the ultimate point of reference.

  2. Teaching on the kingdom story was the heart of Jesus' teaching.

  3. The kingdom story is the central focus of biblical theology.

  4. The kingdom story is final criterion for judging truth and value.

  5. The kingdom story provides an indispensable key to understanding human history.

  6. The kingdom story is the basic biblical concept that enables us to coordinate and fulfill our destinies under God's reign today, where we live and work.

II. *Tua Da Gloriam*: "The Story of God's Glory"

Ps. 115.1-3 - Not to us, O Lord, not to us, but to your name give glory, for the sake of your steadfast love and your faithfulness! [2] Why should the nations say, "Where is their God?" [3] Our God is in the heavens; he does all that he pleases.

Your Kingdom Come: "The Story of God's Glory" (continued)

From Before to Beyond Time (Adapted from Suzanne de Dietrich, *God's Unfolding Purpose*. Philadelphia: Westminster Press, 1976.)

A. *Before Time* (Eternity Past), Ps. 90.1-3

   1. The eternal triune God, Ps. 102.24-27

   2. God's eternal purpose, 2 Tim. 1.9; Isa. 14.26-27

      a. To glorify his name in creation, Prov. 16.4; Ps. 135.6; Isa. 48.11

      b. To display his perfections in the universe, Ps. 19.1

      c. To draw out a people for himself, Isa. 43.7, 21

   3. The mystery of iniquity: the rebellion of the Dawn of the Morning (*Lucifer*), Isa. 14.12-20; Ezek. 28.13-17

   4. The principalities and powers, Col. 2.15

B. *The Beginning of Time* (The Creation), Gen. 1-2

   1. The creative Word of the triune God, Gen. 1.3; Pss. 33.6, 9; 148.1-5

   2. The creation of humanity: the Imago Dei, Gen. 1.26-27

C. *The Tragedy of Time* (the Fall and the Curse), Gen. 3

   1. The Fall and the Curse, Gen. 3.1-9

   2. The *protoevangelium*: the promised Seed; Gen. 3.15

   3. The end of Eden and the reign of death, Gen. 3.22-24

   4. First signs of grace; Gen. 3.15, 21

D. *The Unfolding of Time* (God's plan revealed through the people Israel)

   1. The Abrahamic promise and the covenant of Yahweh (Patriarchs); Gen. 12.1-3; 15; 17; 18.18; 28.4

   2. The Exodus and the covenant at Sinai, Exodus

   3. The conquest of the inhabitants and the Promised Land, Joshua through 2 Chronicles

4. The city, the temple, and the throne, Ps. 48.1-3; 2 Chron. 7.14; 2 Sam. 7.8ff.

    a. The role of the prophet, *to declare the word of the Lord*, Deut. 18.15

    b. The role of the priest, *to represent God and the people*, Heb. 5.1

    c. The role of the king, *to rule with righteousness and justice in God's stead*, Ps. 72

5. The Captivity and the Exile, Daniel, Ezekiel, Lamentations

6. The return of the remnant, Ezra, Nehemiah

E. *The Fullness of Time* (Incarnation of the Messiah Yeshua [Christ Jesus]), Gal. 4.4-6

    1. The Word becomes flesh, John 1.14-18; 1 John 1.1-4

    2. The testimony of John the Baptist, Matt. 3.1-3

    3. The Kingdom has come in the person of Jesus of Nazareth, Mark 1.14-15; Luke 10.9-11; 10.11; 17.20-21

        a. Revealed in his person, John 1.18

        b. Exhibited in his works, John 5.36; 3.2; 9.30-33; 10.37-38; Acts 2.22; 10.38-39

        c. Interpreted in his testimony, Matt. 5-7

    4. The secret of the Kingdom revealed, Mark 1.14-15

        a. The Kingdom is already present, Matt. 12.25-29

        b. The Kingdom is not yet consummated, Matt. 25.31-46

    5. The passion and death of the crucified King, Matt. 26.36-46; Mark 14.32-42; Luke 22.39-46; John 18.1ff.

        a. To destroy the devil's work: *Christus Victor*, 1 John 3.8; Gen. 3.15; Col. 2.15; Rom. 16.20; Heb. 2.14-15

        b. To make atonement for sin: *Christus Victum*, 1 John 2.1-2; Rom. 5.8-9; 1 John 4.9-10; 1 John 3.16

Your Kingdom Come: "The Story of God's Glory" (continued)

    c. To reveal the Father's heart, John 3.16; Titus 2.11-15

  6. *Christus Victor*: the resurrection of the glorious Lord of life, Matt. 28.1-15; Mark 16.1-11; Luke 24.1-12

F. *The Last Times* (the descent and age of the Holy Spirit)

  1. The *arrabon* of God: the Spirit as Pledge and Sign of the Kingdom's presence, Eph. 1.13-14; 4.30; Acts 2.1-47

  2. "This is that:" Peter, Pentecost, and the presence of the future

    a. The Church as foretaste and agent of the Kingdom of God, Phil. 2.14-16; 2 Cor. 5.20

    b. The present reign of Messiah Jesus, 1 Cor. 15.24-28; Acts 2.34; Eph. 1.20-23; Heb. 1.13

    c. The ushering in of God's kingdom community "in-between the times"; Rom. 14.7

  3. The Church of Messiah Jesus: sojourners in the Already and the Not Yet Kingdom

    a. The Great Confession: Jesus is Lord, Phil. 2.9-11

    b. The Great Commission: go and make disciples among all nations, Matt. 28.18-20; Acts 1.8

    c. The Great Commandment: love God and people, Matt. 22.37-39

  4. The Announcement of the Mystery: Gentiles as fellow-heirs of Promise, Rom. 16.25-27; Col. 1.26-28; Eph. 3.3-11

    a. Jesus as the Last Adam, the head of a new human race, 1 Cor. 15.45-49

    b. God drawing out of the world a new humanity, Eph. 2.12-22

  5. In-between the times: tokens of *Age of Sabbath and of Jubilee*, Acts 2.17ff., cf. Joel 2; Amos 9; Ezek. 36.25-27

G. *The Fulfillment of Time* (The *Parousia* of Christ), 1 Thess. 4.13-17

1. Completion of world mission: the evangelization of the world's *ethnoi*, Matt. 24.14; Mark 16.15-16; Rom. 10.18

2. The apostasy of the Church, 1 Tim. 4.1-3; 2 Tim. 4.3; 2 Thess. 2.3-12

3. The Great Tribulation, Matt. 24.21ff; Luke 21.24

4. The *Parousia*: the Second Coming of Jesus, 1 Thess. 4.13-17; 1 Cor. 15.50-58; Luke 21.25-27; Dan. 7.13

5. The reign of Jesus Christ on earth, Rev. 20.1-4

6. The Great White Throne and Lake of Fire, Rev. 20.11-15

7. "For he must reign": the final placement of all enemies under Christ's feet, 1 Cor. 15.24-28

H. *Beyond Time* (Eternity Future)

1. The creation of the new heavens and earth, Rev. 21.1; Isa. 65.17-19; 66.22; 2 Pet. 3.13

2. The descent of the New Jerusalem: the abode of God comes to earth, Rev. 21.2-4

3. The times of refreshing: the glorious freedom of the children of God, Rom. 8.18-23

4. The Lord Christ gives over the Kingdom to God the Father, 1 Cor. 15.24-28

5. The Age to Come: the triune God as all-in-all – Zech. 14.9; 2.10; Jer. 23.6; Matt. 1.23; Ps. 72.8-11; Mic. 4.1-3

III. Implications of the *Drama of All Time*

A. God's sovereign purpose underwrites all human history.

1. Whatever he pleases, he does, Ps. 135.6.

2. God's counsels and plans stand forever, to all generations, Ps. 33.11; Ps. 115.3.

Your Kingdom Come: "The Story of God's Glory" (continued)

    3.   God declares the end of all things from the beginning, Isa. 46.10.

    4.   Nothing and no one can withstand the plan of God for salvation and redemption, Dan. 4.35.

B. God is the central character in the unfolding of the divine drama, Eph. 1.9-11.

C. Missions is the *recovery of that which was lost* at the beginning of time.

    1.   God's sovereign rule, Mark 1.14-15

    2.   Satan's infernal rebellion, Gen. 3.15 with Col. 2.15; 1 John 3.8

    3.   Humankind's tragic fall, Gen. 3.1-8 cf. Rom. 5.5-8

D. Making disciples among all nations is *fulfilling our role in the script of Almighty God!*

IV. "Thy Kingdom Come": Living Under God's Reign

A. The distinctiveness of Jesus' gospel: "The Kingdom is at hand," Mark 1.14-15.

B. Jesus and the inauguration of the Age to Come into this present age

    1.   The coming of John the Baptist, Matt. 11.2-6

    2.   The inauguration of Jesus's ministry, Luke 4.16-21

    3.   The confrontation of Jesus with demonic forces, Luke 10.18ff.; 11.20

    4.   The teaching of Jesus and his claim of absolute authority on earth, Mark 2.1-12; Matt. 21.27; 28.18

C. "The Kingdom has come and the strong man is bound": Matt. 12.28, 29

    1.   The Kingdom of God "has come" – *pleroo*

    2.   The meaning of the Greek verb: "to fulfill, to complete, to be fulfilled, as in prophecy"

    3.   The invasion, entrance, manifestation of God's kingly power

Christ's death for our sins — His payment of the penalty declared against us — was His legal victory whereby He erased Satan's legal claim to the human race. But Christ also won dynamic victory. That is, when He was justified and made alive, adjudged and declared righteous in the Supreme Court of the universe, Satan, the arch foe of God and man, was completely disarmed and dethroned. Christ burst forth triumphantly from that age-old prison of the dead. Paul says that He "spoiled principalities and powers" and "made a show of them openly, triumphing over them in it." (Colossians 2.15).
~ Paul Billheimer. *Destined for the Throne.* Minneapolis: Bethany House Publishers, 1996. p. 87.

4. Jesus as the binder of the strong man: Matt. 12.25-30 (ESV) - Knowing their thoughts, he said to them, "Every kingdom divided against itself is laid waste, and no city or house divided against itself will stand. [26] And if Satan casts out Satan, he is divided against himself. How then will his kingdom stand? [27] And if I cast out demons by Beelzebul, by whom do your sons cast them out? Therefore they will be your judges. [28] But if it is by the Spirit of God that I cast out demons, then the kingdom of God has come upon you. [29] Or how can someone enter a strong man's house and plunder his goods, unless he first binds the strong man? Then indeed he may plunder his house. [30] Whoever is not with me is against me, and whoever does not gather with me scatters."

D. Two manifestations of the Kingdom of God: The Already/Not Yet Kingdom (Oscar Cullman, *Christ and Time*; George Ladd, *The Gospel of the Kingdom*)

1. The *first advent*: the rebellious prince bound and his house looted and God's reign has come

2. The *second advent*: the rebellious prince destroyed and his rule confounded with the full manifestation of God's kingly power in a recreated heaven and earth

Jesus' message was the Kingdom of God. It was the center and circumference of all He taught and did. . . . The Kingdom of God is the master-conception, the master-plan, the master-purpose, the master-will that gathers everything up into itself and gives it redemption, coherence, purpose, goal.

~ E. Stanley Jones

V. The Christo-centric Order: Messiah Yeshua of Nazareth as Centerpiece in Both God's Revelation and Rule

A. Messiah's *mission*: to destroy the works of the devil, 1 John 3.8

B. Messiah's *birth*: the invasion of God into Satan's dominion, Luke 1.31-33

C. Messiah's *message*: the Kingdom's proclamation and inauguration, Mark 1.14-15

D. Messiah's *teaching*: kingdom ethics, Matt. 5-7

E. Messiah's *miracles*: his kingly authority and power, Mark 2.8-12

F. Messiah's *exorcisms*: his defeat of the devil and his angels, Luke 11.14-20

G. Messiah's *life and deeds*: the majesty of the Kingdom, John 1.14-18

Your Kingdom Come: "The Story of God's Glory" (continued)

H. Messiah's *resurrection*: the victory and vindication of the King, Rom.1.1-4

I. Messiah's *commission*: the call to proclaim his Kingdom worldwide, Matt 28.18-20

J. Messiah's *ascension*: his coronation, Heb. 1.2-4

K. Messiah's *Spirit*: the *arrabon* (surety, pledge) of the Kingdom, 2 Cor. 1.20

L. Messiah's *Church*: the foretaste and agent of the Kingdom, 2 Cor. 5.18-21

M. Messiah's *session in heaven*: the generalship of God's forces, 1 Cor. 15.24-28

N. Messiah's *Parousia (coming)*: the final consummation of the Kingdom, Rev. 19

VI. The Kingdom of God as Present and Offered in the Midst of the Church

A. The *Shekinah* has reappeared in our midst as his temple, Eph. 2.19-22.

B. The people (*ecclesia*) of the living God congregate here: Christ's own from every kindred, people, nation, tribe, status, and culture, 1 Pet. 2.8-9.

C. God's *Sabbath* is enjoyed and celebrated here, freedom, wholeness, and the justice of God, Heb. 4.3-10.

D. The *Year of Jubilee* has come: forgiveness, renewal, and restitution, Col. 1.13; Matt. 6.33; Eph. 1.3; 2 Pet. 1.3-4.

E. The Spirit (*arrabon*) indwells us: God lives here and walks among us here, 2 Cor. 1.20.

F. We taste the powers of the Age to Come: Satan is bound in our midst, the Curse has been broken here, deliverance is experienced in Jesus' name, Gal. 3.10-14.

G. We experience the *shalom* of God's eternal Kingdom: the freedom, wholeness, and justice of the new order are present here, Rom. 5.1; Eph. 2.13-22.

H. We herald the good news of God's reign (*evanggelion*): we invite all to join us as we journey to the full manifestation of the Age to Come, Mark 1.14-15.

I. Here we cry *Maranantha*!: our lives are structured by the living hope of God's future and the consummation, Rev. 22.17-21.

VII. The Already/Not Yet Kingdom (See *A Schematic for a Theology of the Kingdom and the Church and Living in the Already and the Not Yet Kingdom* appendices)

A. Through the Incarnation and the Passion of Christ, Satan was bound.

1. Jesus has triumphed over the devil, 1 John 3.8.

2. Jesus is crowned as Lord of all, Heb. 1.4; Phil. 2.5-11.

3. Satan is now judged, Luke 10.17-21.

4. Satan's power has been severely curtailed, James 4.8.

5. His authority has been broken, 1 Pet. 5.8.

6. His minions are being routed, Col. 2.15.

7. His system is fading away, 1 John 2.15-17.

8. Those he enslaved are being set free, Col. 13-14.

9. His eventual doom has been secured, Rom. 16.20.

B. Although Satan has been defeated, he is still lethal and awaits his own utter destruction.

1. "Bound, but with a long rope," 2 Cor. 10.3-5; Eph. 2.2

2. "A roaring lion, but sick, hungry, and mad," 1 Pet. 5.8

3. Satan continues to be God's active enemy of the Kingdom

4. Blinds the minds of those who do not believe, 2 Cor. 4.4

5. Functions through deception, lying, and accusation, John 8.44

6. Animates the affairs of nations, 1 John 5.19

7. Distracts human beings from their proper ends, cf. Gen. 3.1.ff.

When Christ took his seat in the heavens, He proved conclusively that Satan's devastation was complete, that he was utterly undone. Hell was thrown into total bankruptcy. Satan was not only stripped of his legal authority and dominion, but by an infinitely superior force he was stripped of his weapons also. But this is not all. When Jesus burst forth from that dark prison and "ascended up on high," all believers were raised and seated together with Him "But God . . . brought us to life with Christ. . . . And in union with Christ Jesus he raised us up and enthroned us with him in the heavenly realms" (Ephesians 2.4-6 NEB). ~ Paul Billheimer. *Destined for the Throne*. Minneapolis: Bethany House Publishers, 1996. p. 87.

      8.   Oppresses human beings through harassment, slander, fear, accusation, and death, Heb. 2.14-15

      9.   Resists and persecutes God's people, Eph. 6.10-18

  C. Satan's final doom is certain and future.

      1.   He has been both spoiled and utterly humiliated in the Cross, Col. 2.15.

      2.   His final demise will come by Christ at the end of the age, Rev. 20.

      3.   Missions is the announcement and demonstration of the defeat of Satan through Christ.

          a.   The ministry of reconciliation, 2 Cor. 5.18-21

          b.   The ministry of disciple-making, Matt. 28.18-20

VIII. The Call to Adventure: Embracing the Story of God as Your Story

  A. God's call to salvation and ministry involves participation by faith in the kingdom promise of God.

      1.   Salvation by grace through faith, Eph. 2.8-10

      2.   Repentance: metanoia and conversion, Acts 2.38

      3.   Regeneration by the Holy Spirit of God, John 3.3-8; Titus 3.5

      4.   Affirm our need for a biblical framework, a disciplined study of the Kingdom of God

Have I experienced the freedom, wholeness, and justice of the Kingdom that I am preaching to others?

  B. God's call to salvation and ministry involves demonstration of the life of the Kingdom in one's personal life and faith.

      1.   As a faithful servant and steward of God's mysteries, 1 Cor. 4.1-2

      2.   As a godly Christian in one's character, personal life, and family responsibilities, 1 Tim. 3; 1 Pet. 5.1-3; Titus 1

      3.   As a beloved brother or sister in the midst of the assembly, 2 Cor. 8.22

Your Kingdom Come: "The Story of God's Glory" (continued)

4. As a compelling testimony in the presence of unbelievers and outsiders, Col. 4.5; Matt. 5.14-16

Do I demonstrate in my own personal and family life, and my walk in the body and with my neighbors and associates a compelling testimony of what it means to be Christ's disciple where I live?

C. God's call to salvation and ministry involves separation of one's life and goods to testify and demonstrate the freedom, wholeness, and justice of the Kingdom of God.

1. A willingness to become all things to all men in order to save some, 1 Cor. 9.22-27

2. A readiness to suffer and even die in order for Christ's reign to be proclaimed and extended, Acts 20.24-32

3. A commitment to make oneself unconditionally available to Christ in order to be used to testify solemnly of the grace and gospel as the Spirit leads, John 12.24; Acts 1.8; Matt. 28.18-20

4. Celebrate our Father's gracious intent and action to defeat our mortal enemy, the devil

Have I made myself unconditionally available to Jesus Christ to be used as his bondservant and instrument whenever and wherever he may lead in order for the kingdom message to be proclaimed and demonstrated?

D. God's call to salvation and ministry involves preparation to steward God's mysteries of the Kingdom, the Sacred Scriptures, and the Apostolic doctrine.

1. To rightly divide the Word of truth as God's workman, 2 Tim. 2.15

2. To hear and obey the sacred Scriptures which equip for every good work, 2 Tim. 3.16

3. To defend and guard the apostolic testimony regarding Christ and his Kingdom, 2 Tim. 1.14 with Gal. 1.8-9 and 1 Cor. 15.1-4

Have I spent the requisite time in the Word and in training to be equipped even as I equip others for the work of the ministry?

Your Kingdom Come: "The Story of God's Glory" (continued)

E. God's call to salvation and ministry involves proclamation of the message of the Kingdom through preaching, teaching, and discipling in order that others may enter and make disciples of the Kingdom.

1. To preach the good news of the Kingdom with those who do not know God, its inauguration in the Son of God and its enjoyment and demonstration in the Church, Acts 2.1-18

2. To teach and disciple the faithful in the words of Jesus so that they may be his disciples and mature as members of his body, John 8.31-32; 1 Pet. 2.2; 2 Tim. 3.16-17

3. To equip those who are members of Christ's body to do the work of the ministry in order that the Church may grow numerically and spiritually, Eph. 4.9-15

4. Offer unending praise and worship to our Lord Jesus, who invaded Satan's dominion and crushed his malicious insurrection in God's universe

5. Resolve to embody, express, and proclaim Christ's present and coming reign until he comes

Am I ready and willing to preach the Word of the Kingdom in and out of season in order that the lost may be saved, the saved may mature, and the mature may multiply the fruit of the Kingdom of God?

The Bottom Line: Are you willing to suffer for the message of the Kingdom regarding Messiah Yeshua? (See *Suffering, the Cost of Discipleship and Servant-Leadership* Appendix)

Alphabetical Appendix List Cross-Referenced to Capstone Modules

Appendix Name	Appendix Number in Each Specific Module																
	FGFF	C-1	C-2	C-3	C-4	C-5	C-6	C-7	C-8	C-9	C-10	C-11	C-12	C-13	C-14	C-15	C-16
Advancing the Kingdom in the City													35				
Analytical vs. Christocentric Approach to OT Study										36							
Apostles' Creed	26																
Apostolic Band													42				
Apostolicity							17				40		41				
Appearances of the Resurrected Messiah										27	32			27			
Areas of Disagreement Concerning Spiritual Gifts															19		
Arrangement of the 12 Tribes Around Tabernacle										40							
Authentic Freedom in Jesus Christ													40				26
Bible Study Tools Worksheet						24											
Biblical Justification for Resurrection of Messiah Jesus														32			
Bibliography of Biblical Hermeneutics						28											
Capturing God's Vision for His People								43									
Center and Circumference: Christianity is Jesus											43						
Chart of Biblical Studies						16				34				34			
Checklist of Narrative Elements					18	30				42							
Christ's View of the Bible						25											
Christus Victor: An Integrated Vision	12	5	5	5	5	5	5	5	5	5	5	5	5	5	5	5	5
Chronological Table of NT	18																
Church Leadership Paradigm								49									
Church Plant Team													43				
Church Planting Models													25				
Church Year (Western Church)								40				40					
Communal Context of Authentic Christian Leadership													24				
Communicating Messiah: Relation of Gospels	19										31						
Comparison of Translation Philosophies						20											
Compass of Narrative Elements						19											
Complexity of Difference: Race, Culture, Class					32								38			27	

Appendix Number in Each Specific Module

Appendix Name	FGFF	C-1	C-2	C-3	C-4	C-5	C-6	C-7	C-8	C-9	C-10	C-11	C-12	C-13	C-14	C-15	C-16
Contextualization Among Muslims, Hindus, Buddhists					51		29						50				
Creating Coherent Urban Church Planting Movements													36				
Culture, Not Color: Interaction Class, Culture, Race					26								39			22	25
Dealing with Old Ways								30				30	29			30	19
Defining the Leaders and Members of a CPT													22				
Degrees of Authority Given to Fruit of Christocentric Use of OT										41							
Delegation and Authority in Christian Leadership								35				35					
Denominational Statements on Sanctification															22		
Developing Ears that Hear						21											
Different Traditions of African-American Response													27				
Discerning the Call: Profile of Godly Leader					22			21				21	20				
Discipleship Diagram																46	
Discipling the Faithful: Establishing Leaders			22									28				21	20
Documenting Your Work		20	42	19	54	32	38	60	18	43	45	44	53	40	23	47	29
Dynamics of Credible Spiritual Vision					48		26	48									
Editorial: Ralph Winter 2005													47				
Empowering People: Freedom, Wholeness, Justice			27		29												28
Equipping the Church Plant Team Member													23				
Ethics of the NT: Living in Upside-Down	21		26		28			28		28	23	28					
Example of the Practice of Textual Criticism						18								36			
Examps of Denom Statements on "Baptism in Holy Spirit"															16		
Faithfully Re-Presenting Jesus of Nazareth			37							15	39						
Father, Son, Holy Ghost Share Same Divine							20								15		
Figures of Speech						23											
Fit to Represent: Multiplying Disciples	20		31		46			55	14		18	43				45	
Five Views: Relationship - Christ & Culture			29		43			52					33				22
Four Contexts of Urban Christian Leadership Devel								32				32					
From Before to Beyond Time	6	8	8	8	8	8	8	8	8	8	8	8	8	8	8	8	8
From Deep Ignorance to Credible Witness	14	14	38			14	18	27		29		27	26			28	
General Facts Concerning the NT														28			

Appendix Number in Each Specific Module

Appendix Name	FGFF	C-1	C-2	C-3	C-4	C-5	C-6	C-7	C-8	C-9	C-10	C-11	C-12	C-13	C-14	C-15	C-16
Getting a Firm Grasp on Scripture		19														23	
Giving Glory to God							32										
God's Sovereignty and Universal Revelation							35										
God's Three-In-Oneness: The Trinity							34										
Going Forward by Looking Back	16																
Guide to Determining Your Worship Profile								41				41					
Harmony of the Ministry of Jesus										26	30			26			
Hindrances to Christlike Servanthood								38			19	38					
How to Interpret a Narrative (Story)						29											
How to PLANT a Church													21				
How to Start Reading the Bible	3				37												
Hump	15															40	
I Find My Lord in the Book											42						
In Christ	8		35							30	34					24	
Investment, Empowerment, and Assessment					33			33				33	32			33	
Jesus and the Poor			25		14						44						
Jesus Christ: Subject and Theme	22																
Jesus of Nazareth: Presence of the Future	4	12	12	12	12	12	12	12	12	12	12	12	12	12	12	12	12
Key Passages on Spiritual Gifts in the NT															17		
Keys to Bible Interpretation						31											
Kingdom of God Timeline			18		38												
Kingdom Texts in the NT			15														
Kingdom Texts in the OT			16														
Learning to Be a Theo-Smith										37							
Let God Arise! A Sober Call to Prevailing Prayer					47												
Let God Arise! The Seven "A's"	23																
Life of Christ According to Seasons and Years											38			35			
Living in the Already and Not Yet Kingdom	11	11		11		11	11	11	11	11	11	11	11	11	11		11
Living the Disciplines																42	
Lording Over vs. Serving Among								26				26					
Lord's Supper: Four Views				17													
Messiah Jesus: Fulfillment of the OT Types										23	28			23			
Messian Yeshua in Every Book of the Bible										20				20			
Messianic Prophecies Cited in the NT										16	22			16			
Method of the Master								46								44	
Ministry of Praise and Worship								39				39					

Appendix Name	Appendix Number in Each Specific Module																
	FGFF	C-1	C-2	C-3	C-4	C-5	C-6	C-7	C-8	C-9	C-10	C-11	C-12	C-13	C-14	C-15	C-16
Miracles of Jesus											35						
Missions in the 21st Century					53		31						52				
Models of the Kingdom			20		39		14										16
Names of Almighty God							14										
New Testament Readings														39			
Nicene Creed	24																
Nicene Creed w/ Biblical Support	25	1	1	1	1	1	1	1	1	1	1	1	1	1	1	1	1
Nurturing Authentic Christian Leadership								19				19	18			19	
Obedient Christian in Action																39	
Oikos Factor	10				34				15				37			32	24
Old Testament Names, Titles, and Epithets for Messiah										21	27			21			
Old Testament Witness to Christ & His Kingdom		6	6	6	6	6	6	6	6	6	6	6	6	6	6	6	6
Once Upon a Time: The Cosmic Drama	1																
Our Declaration of Dependence: Freedom in Christ	9		32					23				23					18
Overview of Church Plant Planning Phases													31				
Overview Plant to Birth Models													30				
Parables of Jesus											36						
Paul's Partnership Theology					15			15				15	14			15	
Paul's Team Members								18				18	17			18	
People Reborn					52		30						51				
Perception and Truth				18													
Picking Up on Different Wavelengths			34				19	57		24	15			24			
Picture and the Drama			30		45		21	54		32							
Portrayals of Jesus in the NT Books											29			29			
Preaching and Teaching Jesus as Messiah and Lord										18	24			18		25	
Principles Behind Prophecy										25				25			
Profile of a 21st-Century Disciple		16	41													34	
Promise vs. Prediction										22				22			
Prophetic Vision as Source of Biblical Faith										17				17			
Pursuing Faith, Not Religion							28						49				
Readings on Christ										14				14			
Readings on Messianic Prophecy														38			
Readings on Pastoral Care								45									
Readings on Servanthood								47									

Appendix Name	FGFF	C-1	C-2	C-3	C-4	C-5	C-6	C-7	C-8	C-9	C-10	C-11	C-12	C-13	C-14	C-15	C-16
Readings on the Church																	21
Readings on the NT's Historical Credibility								44									
Receptivity Scale														30			
Relationship of Cost & Effectiveness in Disciple-Making									16								
Representin' - Jesus as God's Chosen Rep			33					34	17		14	34					
Re-Presenting Messiah					36			36				36		15			
Role of the Holy Spirit in Spiritual Guidance															20		
Role of Women in Ministry					21			20				20	19			20	
Roles of Representational Leadership								51									
Salvation as Joining the People of God				15	24												
Schematic for Theology of the Kingdom		10	10	10	10	10	10	10	10	10	10	10	10	10	10	10	10
Selecting Credible Criteria for Independence					23								15				
Self-Consciousness of Jesus Christ							22			35	41						
Shadow and the Substance	7						23				33						
Six Kinds of NT Ministry for Community					16			16				16					
Sociology of Urban Leadership Development											21					16	
Sojourner's Quest		15															
Some Ways Christians Disagree about Sanctification															21		
Spiritual Gifts Specifically Mentioned in NT					17			17			17	17	16		18	17	
Spiritual Growth Diagrams																41	
Spiritual Service Checklist			40					25				25				26	
St. Basil, Nicene Creed, & Doctrine of Holy Spirit															14		
Steps to Equipping Others																43	
Story God Is Telling	2																
Story of God: Our Sacred Roots	5	3	3	3	3	3	3	3	3	3	3	3	3	3	3	3	3
Story, Theology, and Church						26											
Substitute Centers to a Christ-Centered Vision					30			29		31		29				29	
Substitution							36										
Suffering: Cost of Discipleship & Servant Lead	18		17				37	22			26	22		31			
Summary of Messianic Interpretations in OT										19	25			19			
Summary Outline of the Scriptures - 2 Page	7	7	7	7	7	7	7	7	7	7	7	7	7	7	7	7	7
Summary Outline of the Scriptures - 4 Page	17																
Symbols of Christian Leadership								56		39							
Tabernacle of Moses																	

Appendix Number in Each Specific Module

Appendix Number in Each Specific Module

Appendix Name	FGFF	C-1	C-2	C-3	C-4	C-5	C-6	C-7	C-8	C-9	C-10	C-11	C-12	C-13	C-14	C-15	C-16
Targeting Unreached Groups in Churched Neighborhoods					35								28				
That We May Be One					27								34				23
Theological Overview of the Equipping Gifts							15										
Theological Visions and Approaches								58									
Theology of Christus Victor	11	4	23	4	4	4	4	4	4	4	4	4	4	4	4	4	4
Theology of the Church			14	16	25		16	53									17
Theology of the Church in Kingdom Perspective				14	44												14
Theories of Inspiration		17				17	24										
There Is a River	14	9	9	9	9	9	9	9	9	9	9	9	9	9	9	9	9
Thirty-Three Blessings of Christ			19					14				14				14	
Three Contexts of Urban Christian Leader Devel					31			31				31				31	
Three Levels of Ministry Investment													45			35	
Three-Step Model																38	
Thy Kingdom Come!			21		40												
Toward a Hermeneutic of Critical Engagement							25			33	16			33		36	
Traditions		13	13	13	13	13	13	13	13	13	13	13	13	13	13	13	
Translating the Story of God			24		19								44			37	
Translation Methodology						22											
Typology Readings										38				37			
Understanding Leadership as Representation			28		41			42			20	42					
Understanding the Bible -- Parts and Whole	13																
Union with Christ: Christocentric Paradigm			36								37						
Use of Reference Tools for Interpreting the Bible						27											
Watch What You Image Forth								50									
Way of Wisdom						15											
We Believe: Nicene Creed 8.6.8.6		2	2		2		2	2	2	2	2	2	2	2	2		2
We Believe: Nicene Creed 8.7.8.7				2		2										2	
Wei Ji								59									
When "Christian" Does Not Translate					49		27						48				
World Impact's Vision: Toward Biblical Strategy					20								46				27
You Can Pay Me Now or You Can Pay Me Later								37				37					
You Got to Serve Somebody!								24				24					
Your Kingdom Come: "The Story God's Glory"			39				33										

Capstone Appendices as They Appear in Each Module

	Module 1	Page Number
1	The Nicene Creed w/ Biblical Support -- One Page	131
2	We Believe: Nicene Creed 8.7.8.7	132
3	The Story of God: Our Sacred Roots	133
4	The Theology of Christus Victor	134
5	Christus Victor: An Integrated Vision	135
6	Old Testament Witness to Christ & His Kingdom	136
7	Summary Outline of the Scriptures - 2 Page	137-138
8	From Before to Beyond Time	139-140
9	There Is a River	141
10	A Schematic for Theology of the Kingdom	142
11	Living in the Already and Not Yet Kingdom	143
12	Jesus of Nazareth: Presence of the Future	144
13	Traditions	145-152
14	From Deep Ignorance to Credible Witness	153
15	The Sojourner's Quest	154
16	The Profile of a 21st-Century Disciple	155-156
17	Theories of Inspiration	157
18	Suffering: Cost of Discipleship & Servant Lead	158
19	Getting a Firm Grasp on Scripture	159
20	Documenting Your Work	160-163

	Module 4	Page Number
1	The Nicene Creed w/ Biblical Support -- One Page	229
2	We Believe: Nicene Creed 8.6.8.6	230
3	The Story of God: Our Sacred Roots	231
4	The Theology of Christus Victor	232
5	Christus Victor: An Integrated Vision	233
6	Old Testament Witness to Christ & His Kingdom	234
7	Summary Outline of the Scriptures - 2 Page	235-236
8	From Before to Beyond Time	237-238
9	There Is a River	239
10	A Schematic for Theology of the Kingdom	240
11	Living in the Already and Not Yet Kingdom	241
12	Jesus of Nazareth: Presence of the Future	242
13	Traditions	243-250
14	Jesus and the Poor	251-256
15	Paul's Partnership Theology	257
16	Six Kinds of NT Ministry for Community	258
17	Spiritual Gifts Specifically Mentioned in NT	259-260
18	Checklist of Narrative Elements	261-263
19	Translating the Story of God	264
20	World Impact's Vision: Toward Biblical Strategy	265
21	The Role of Women in Ministry	266-269
22	Discerning the Call: Profile of Godly Leader	270
23	Selecting Credible Criteria for Independence	271-273
24	Salvation as Joining the People of God	274-278
25	A Theology of the Church	279-297
26	Culture, Not Color: Interaction Class, Culture, Race	298
27	That We May Be One	299-308
28	Ethics of the NT: Living in Upside-Down	309
29	Empowering People: Freedom, Wholeness, Justice	310-339
30	Substitute Centers to a Christ-Centered Vision	340
31	Three Contexts of Urban Christian Leader Devel	341
32	The Complexity of Difference: Race, Culture, Class	342
33	Investment, Empowerment, and Assessment	343
34	The Oikos Factor	344
35	Targeting Unreached Groups in Churched Neighborhoods	345
36	Re-Presenting Messiah	346
37	How to PLANT a Church	347-353

	Module 5	Page Number
1	The Nicene Creed w/ Biblical Support -- One Page	221
2	We Believe: Nicene Creed 8.7.8.7	222
3	The Story of God: Our Sacred Roots	223
4	The Theology of Christus Victor	224
5	Christus Victor: An Integrated Vision	225
6	Old Testament Witness to Christ & His Kingdom	226
7	Summary Outline of the Scriptures - 2 Page	227-228
8	From Before to Beyond Time	229-230
9	There Is a River	231
10	A Schematic for Theology of the Kingdom	232
11	Living in the Already and Not Yet Kingdom	233
12	Jesus of Nazareth: Presence of the Future	234
13	Traditions	235-242
14	From Deep Ignorance to Credible Witness	243
15	The Way of Wisdom	244
16	Chart of Biblical Studies	245-246
17	Theories of Inspiration	247
18	An Example of the Practice of Textual Criticism	248
19	The Compass of Narrative Elements	249
20	A Comparison of Translation Philosophies	250
21	Developing Ears that Hear	251
22	Translation Methodology	252
23	Figures of Speech	253-259
24	Bible Study Tools Worksheet	260-261
25	Christ's View of the Bible	262-264
26	Story, Theology, and Church	265-269
27	Use of Reference Tools for Interpreting the Bible	270-271
28	A Bibliography of Biblical Hermeneutics	272-275
29	How to Interpret a Narrative (Story)	276-279
30	Checklist of Narrative Elements	280-282
31	Keys to Bible Interpretation	283-291
32	Documenting Your Work	292-295

	Module 7	Page Number
1	The Nicene Creed w/ Biblical Support -- One Page	189
2	We Believe: Nicene Creed 8.7.8.7	190
3	The Story of God: Our Sacred Roots	191
4	The Theology of Christus Victor	192
5	Christus Victor: An Integrated Vision	193
6	Old Testament Witness to Christ & His Kingdom	194
7	Summary Outline of the Scriptures - 2 Page	195-196
8	From Before to Beyond Time	197-198
9	There Is a River	199
10	A Schematic for Theology of the Kingdom	200
11	Living in the Already and Not Yet Kingdom	201
12	Jesus of Nazareth: Presence of the Future	202
13	Traditions	203-210
14	Thirty-Three Blessings of Christ	211-214
15	Paul's Partnership Theology	215
16	Six Kinds of NT Ministry for Community	216
17	Spiritual Gifts Specifically Mentioned in NT	217-218
18	Paul's Team Members	219-220
19	Nurturing Authentic Christian Leadership	221
20	The Role of Women in Ministry	222-225
21	Discerning the Call: Profile of Godly Leader	226
22	Suffering: Cost of Discipleship & Servant Lead	227
23	Our Declaration of Dependence: Freedom in Christ	228-229
24	You Got to Serve Somebody!	230
25	Spiritual Service Checklist	231
26	Lording Over vs. Serving Among	232
27	From Deep Ignorance to Credible Witness	233
28	Ethics of the NT: Living in Upside-Down	234
29	Substitute Centers to a Christ-Centered Vision	235
30	Dealing with Old Ways	236
31	Three Contexts of Urban Christian Leadership Development	237
32	Four Contexts of Urban Christian Leadership Devel	238
33	Investment, Empowerment, and Assessment	239
34	Representin' - Jesus as God's Chosen Rep	240
35	Delegation and Authority in Christian Leadership	241
36	Re-Presenting Messiah	242
37	You Can Pay Me Now or You Can Pay Me Later	243

	Module 13	Page Number
1	The Nicene Creed w/ Biblical Support -- One Page	151
2	We Believe: Nicene Creed 8.7.8.7	152
3	The Story of God: Our Sacred Roots	153
4	The Theology of Christus Victor	154
5	Christus Victor: An Integrated Vision	155
6	Old Testament Witness to Christ & His Kingdom	156
7	Summary Outline of the Scriptures - 2 Page	157-158
8	From Before to Beyond Time	159-160
9	There Is a River	161
10	A Schematic for Theology of the Kingdom	162
11	Living in the Already and Not Yet Kingdom	163
12	Jesus of Nazareth: Presence of the Future	164
13	Traditions	165-172
14	Readings on Christ	173-177
15	Re-Presenting Messiah	178
16	Messianic Prophecies Cited in the NT	179-184
17	The Prophetic Vision as Source of Biblical Faith	185
18	Preaching and Teaching Jesus as Messiah and Lord	186
19	Summary of Messianic Interpretations in OT	187-191
20	Messian Yeshua in Every Book of the Bible	192-193
21	Old Testament Names, Titles, and Epithets for Messiah	194-195
22	Promise vs. Prediction	196
23	Messiah Jesus: Fulfillment of the OT Types	197-200
24	Picking Up on Different Wavelengths	201-204
25	Principles Behind Prophecy	205
26	A Harmony of the Ministry of Jesus	206
27	Appearances of the Resurrected Messiah	207
28	General Facts Concerning the NT	208-209
29	Portrayals of Jesus in the NT Books	210
30	Readings on the NT's Historical Credibility	211-212
31	Suffering: Cost of Discipleship & Servant Lead	213
32	Biblical Justification for Resurrection of Messiah Jesus	214
33	Toward a Hermeneutic of Critical Engagement	215
34	Chart of Biblical Studies	216-217
35	The Life of Christ According to Seasons and Years	218-219
36	An Example of the Practice of Textual Criticism	220
37	Typology Readings	221-226
38	Readings on Messianic Prophecy	227-228
39	New Testament Readings	228
40	Documenting Your Work	230-233

Topical Index

V

W

Y

Made in the USA
Middletown, DE
04 June 2020